FRAN
AD

Acknowledgements

This project has been carried out thanks to the support of

Jeffrey Loria

La Banque de Neuflize, Schlumberger, Mallet, Demachy

Fnac

Kodak (France)

thanks to the advice and encouragement of Alexandra de Leal, Elisabeth Nora and Marco Horvat,

thanks to the collaboration of Pictorial and Publimod,

thanks to the brain-stormings with Benoît Gillain, graphic designer of the book and of the exhibition at Musée Maillol,

thanks to the presentation of the work, by Françoise Docquiert, curator of the exhibition at Musée Maillol,

thanks to the daily participation of Véronique Aubry, in the choice of the images, the printing and the filing.

I would also like to thank all those who have allowed me to capture their image, and those whose image I caught without their knowledge.

If any of the latter recognize themselves on these pages, I wish them to understand that I did not intend to be insensitive, but that my way of working didn't allow me to ask for their prior permission, and that, in any case, it wasn't my intention to present them in an unfavourable light.

I express my gratitude to them all.

For Malte, Grégoire, Louise, Alba, Gabriel, Saskia
with the wish that they may smile, one day,
about their grandfather and his time.

First published in the UK by
Dewi Lewis Publishing
8 Broomfield Road
Heaton Moor
Stockport SK4 4ND
+44 (0)161 442 9450
www.dewilewispublishing.com

ISBN: 1-899-235-18-3

Design by Benoît Gillain
Printed by EBS, Verona, Italy

FRANK HORVAT

1999

A DAILY REPORT

"...A man sets himself the task of portraying the world. Through the years he peoples a space with images of provinces, kingdoms, mountains, bays, ships, islands, fish, rooms, instruments, stars, horses, and people. Shortly before his death, he discovers that the patient labyrinth of lines traces the image of his face."

Jorge Luis Borges, from *Epilogue*, 1960

I was born in 1928. I think that it was around the age of eight that I first began to wonder if I would see the year 2000. And when, in December 1999, I first began drafting these introductory words, I was still asking myself the same thing. One could say that time, and its inescapable deadline, has always been one of my main preoccupations.

That would both explain my vocation for photography (the illusion of stopping time); and the inner need, which led me to this undertaking: a photographic journal, conceived as a sort of composite panorama of my world.

The justification for this project wasn't just the three zeros of the millennium; it seemed to me (and no doubt I was not alone in thinking it) that at no time in human history had we had such dizzying changes in life styles and values as at the end of the twentieth century.

Even the futuristic novels of Orwell and Huxley, which I devoured in my adolescence, didn't prepare my imagination for the mix of languages and races I can now observe on the London Underground; the variety of produce, from everywhere and from every season, spread out before my eyes in any provincial supermarket; the absurd gesticulations in the streets of Rome, as passers by (and motorists) press their mobile phones to their ear with one hand, and, with the other, grandiloquently emphasise their conversation with some invisible partner; or the simple click of a mouse, allowing people at any time and place to see these same words and images on the internet.

But what perhaps astonishes me even more, is that alongside the globalisation, the new technologies, the genetic engineering, the breaking down of ideologies and taboos, certain 'islands' in our world (rather like Sleeping Beauty's castle) remain hardly touched by these changes. In East Berlin, houses still show bomb scars from the last war; on Corfu, a few miles from the international airport, peasants still lead their donkeys and their goats; in Cotignac, in the Haut Var, the cart track to my house has not been repaired since the Big Freeze of 1956, after which the farmers deserted the hillsides; and on television, night after night, I see defenceless women and children massacred in the name of some religious fanaticism or ancestral hate.

These contradictions give rise to hopes and fears for the future, all of which I feel – but which I was not seeking to express (or at least not so explicitly) in this photographic project. I would rather that this work be seen as a sort of inventory of my visual horizon; but also – and without the two aspects contradicting each other – as an expression of my gratitude to destiny, for being born (and surviving) in such an exceptional and crucial period. Rather like the votive offering that, in the past, believers would hang up in churches, to bear witness to a gift of Providence, and leave as a remembrance for their descendants: 'for grace received'.

As for the last year of the millennium (or year before last according to some – not that it matters), my objective was to take, between January 1st and December 31st, at least one significant photograph each day (though not necessarily an excellent one). I am badly qualified to say if I achieved it; but I know that in accepting this constraint I obliged myself to remain continually open to everything around me and to question the meaning of each gesture and each object. "The most difficult thing," wrote Goethe "is what is thought to be the simplest; to really see the things which are before your eyes."

As for the people, the objects, the events to photograph – the limits of 'my visual horizon' were not so easy to define. I have the good fortune to have five children and six grandchildren – and of course their images had to be part of this journal. During the year I met with people I love or admire, and I seized the opportunity to take their portraits. I photographed the house in Boulogne-Billancourt where I usually live, the 'bastide' at Cotignac where I spend my holidays, places in Paris and its suburbs which intrigue me. I went back to themes which I have been passionate about at other periods in my life and which still occupy my dreams and my imagination: faces of women, trees, animals, landscape, architecture. I undertook photo trips to the fifteen countries of the European Union; because I am quite proud to call myself a European, and because the reunification of our continent still seems to me to be one of the great events of the end of the century. And I attempted on several occasions to capture images of the seventy two year old man that I am.

Inevitably one will notice omissions. I took no photographs of war, of misery, of suffering or of madness; not because I am indifferent to these calamities, but because I have never felt that I had either the moral justification, or (in the case of war) the physical courage, to confront such situations through my lens.

I did not seek out rich, famous or powerful people in so far as they are not part of my world. I did not try to reveal my sexuality or that of others, because I've never done it in the past and at my age it would be unseemly to start. Nor did I touch on certain worlds which feature a lot in the media, but which remain to me (no doubt wrongly) totally foreign; such as sport, business, contemporary music or fashionable 'sub-cultures'.

One regret is that I did not have the time (or the means) to return to countries such as India, the United States, China or Japan, which at different times in my life have meant a lot to me; or to visit other countries in Africa, South America and the former Soviet Union which I have often dreamed about and which I still don't know.

Anyway, the panorama cannot be complete. It's not even certain that my grandchildren will recognise it as the world of their childhood. Perhaps all they will see will be the trajectory of my vision, formed by references from the nineteenth century, nourished by experiences of the twentieth and still curious as to what the small fragment of the new millennium remaining for me will bring. And so it is a sort of self-portrait. Which is to say – just one more illusion.

Frank Horvat, June 2000

JANUARY

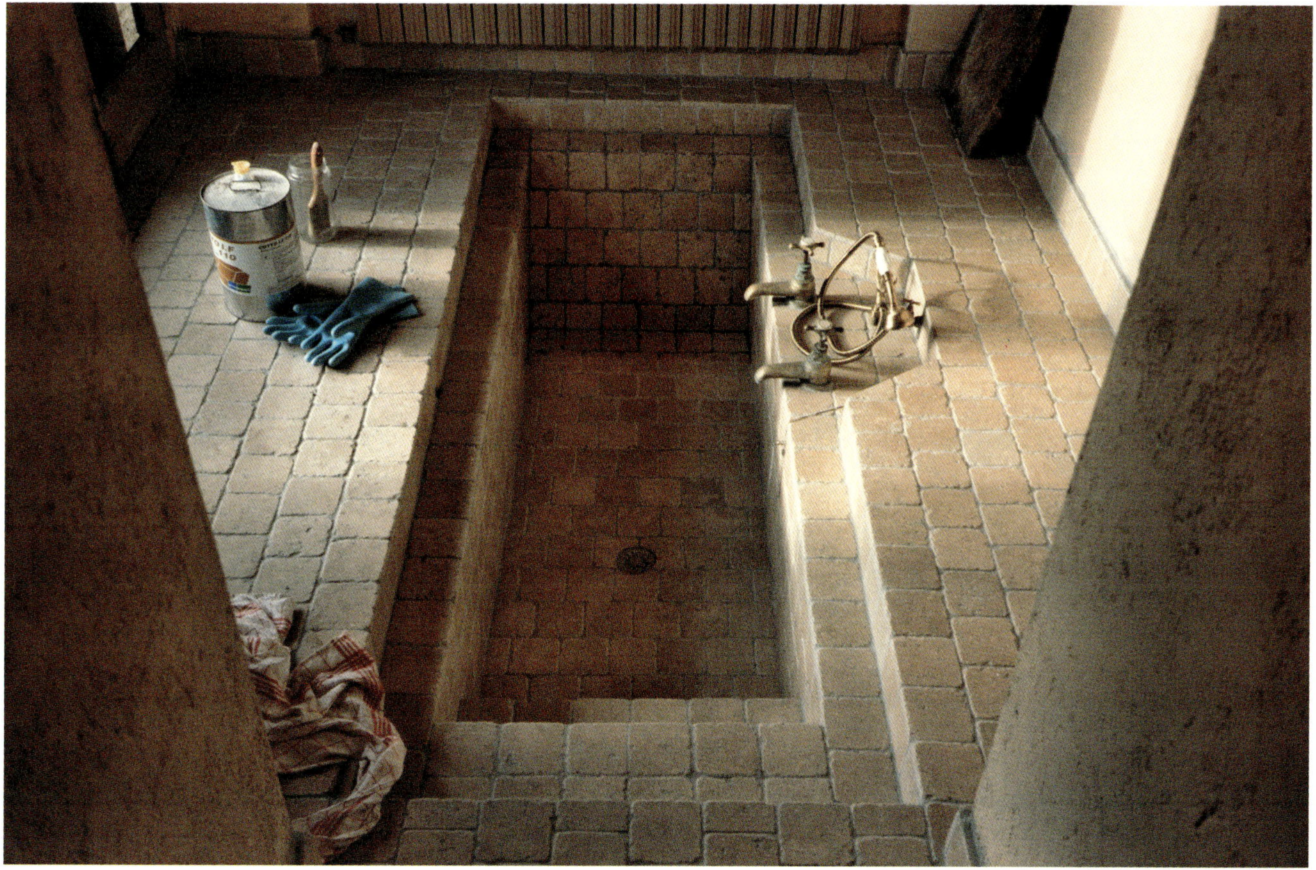

Friday, January 1. Cotignac, France. Our house in Provence, "La Véronique". The new bathroom (see note)

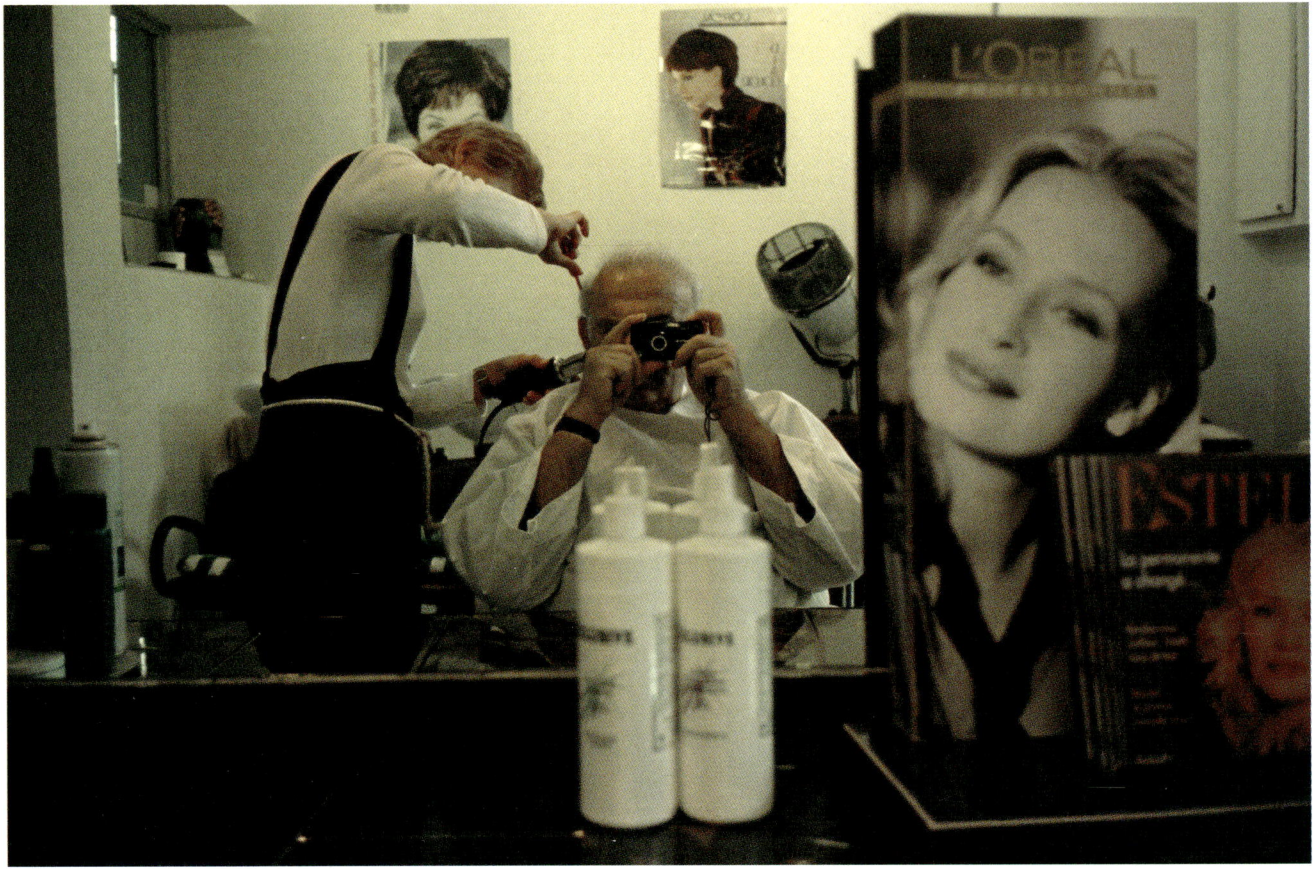

Saturday, January 2. Cotignac, France. Self-portrait during haircut

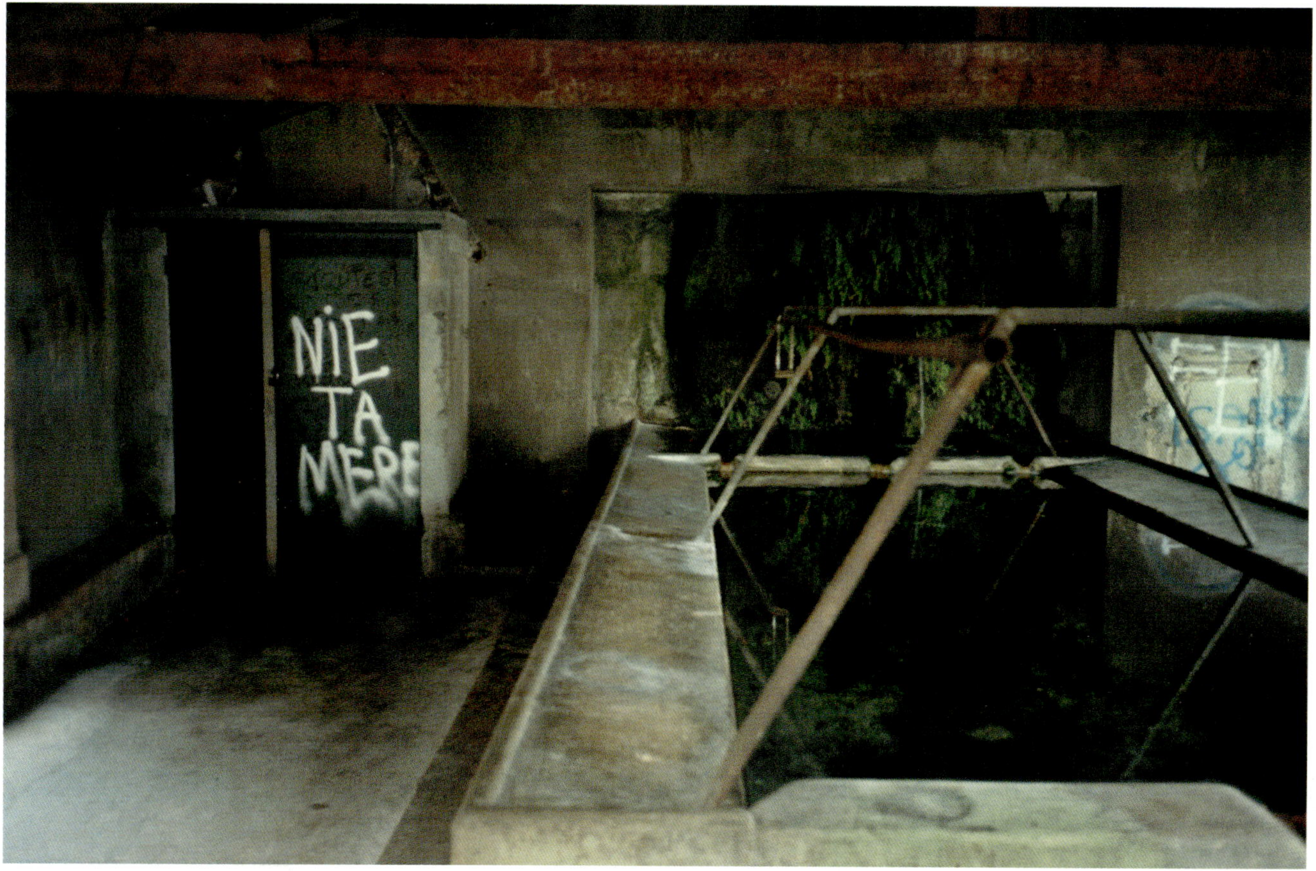

Sunday, January 3. Cotignac, France. The old public laundry *(see note)*

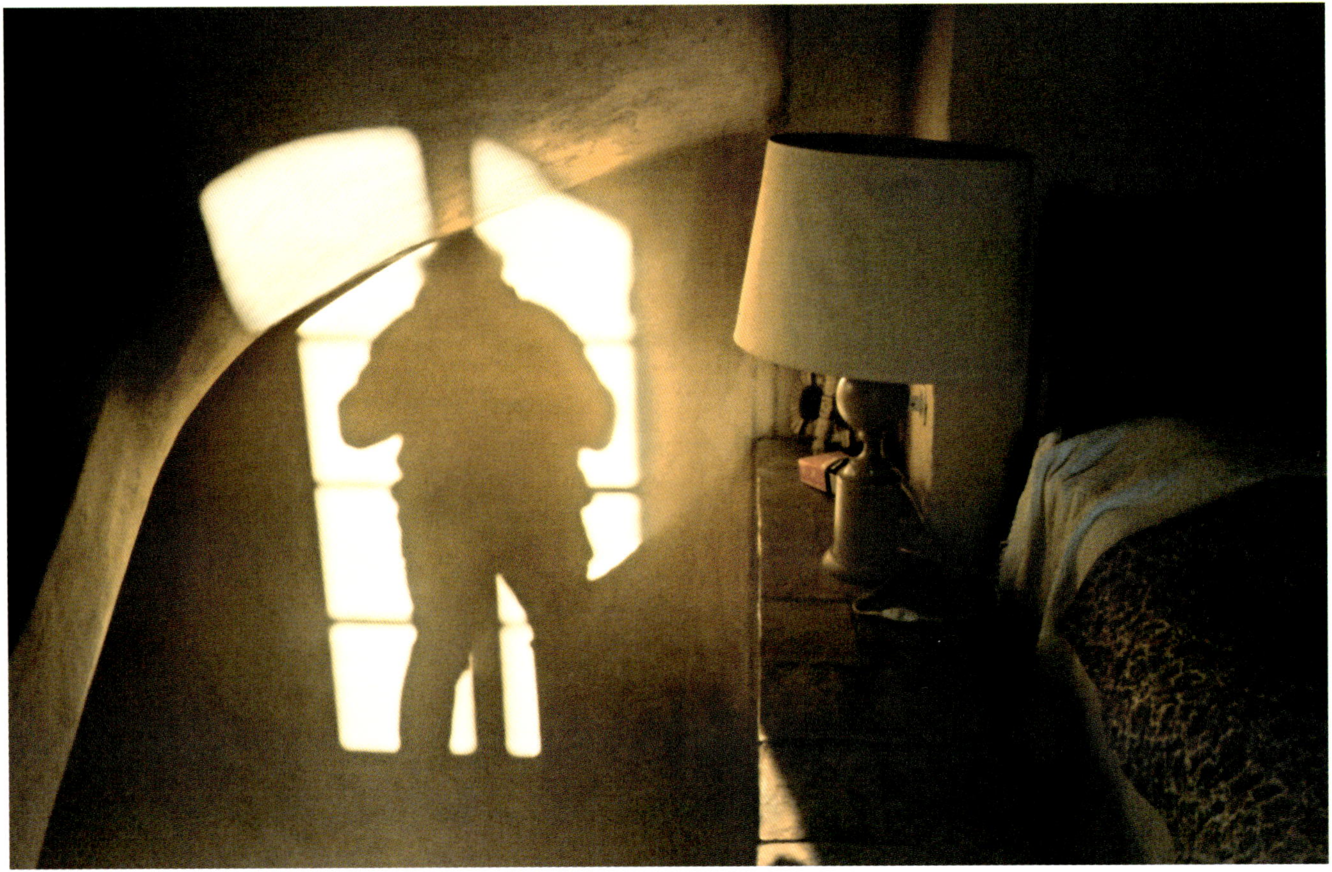

Monday, January 4. Cotignac, France. Self-portrait

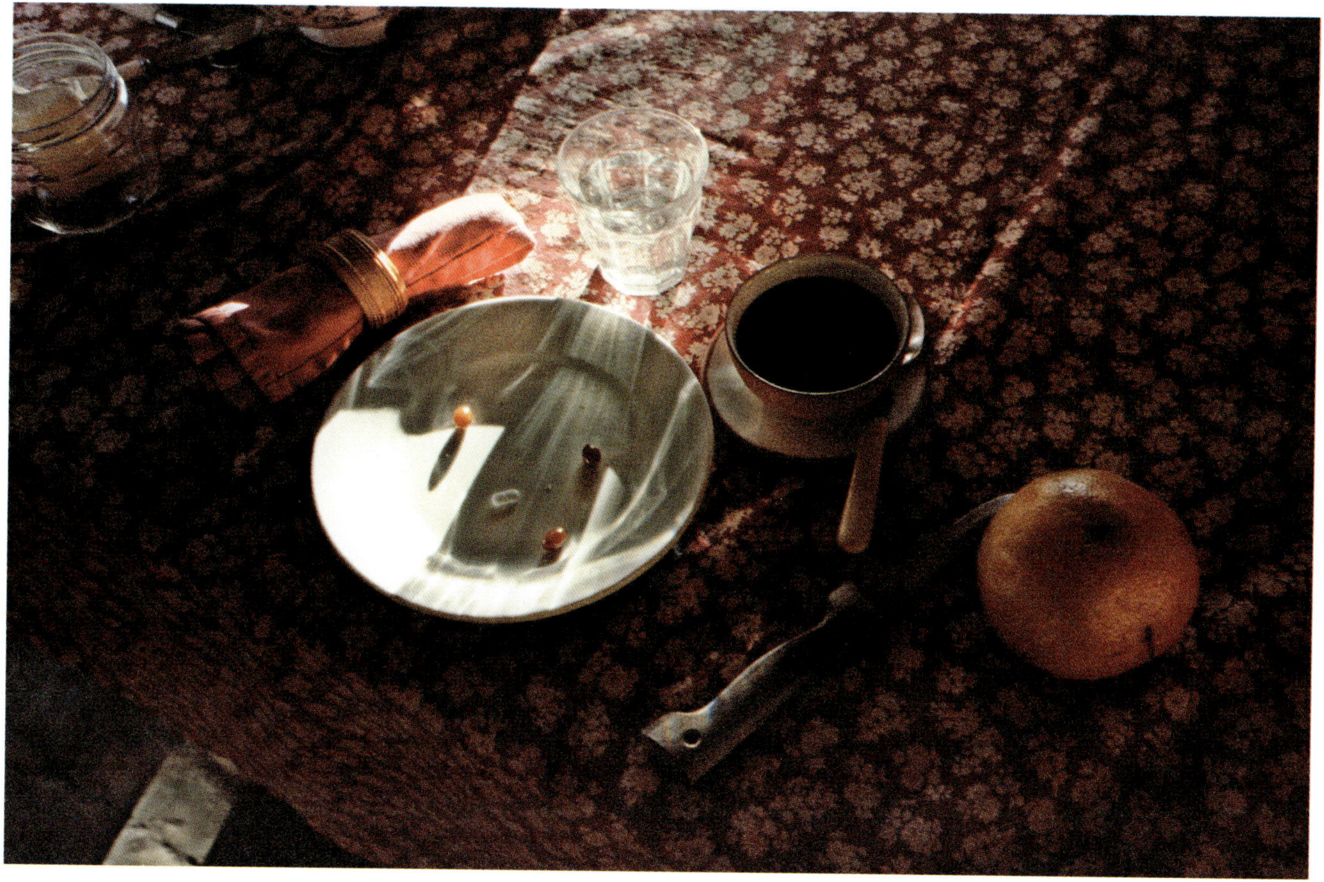

Monday, January 4. Cotignac, France. My dietary breakfast

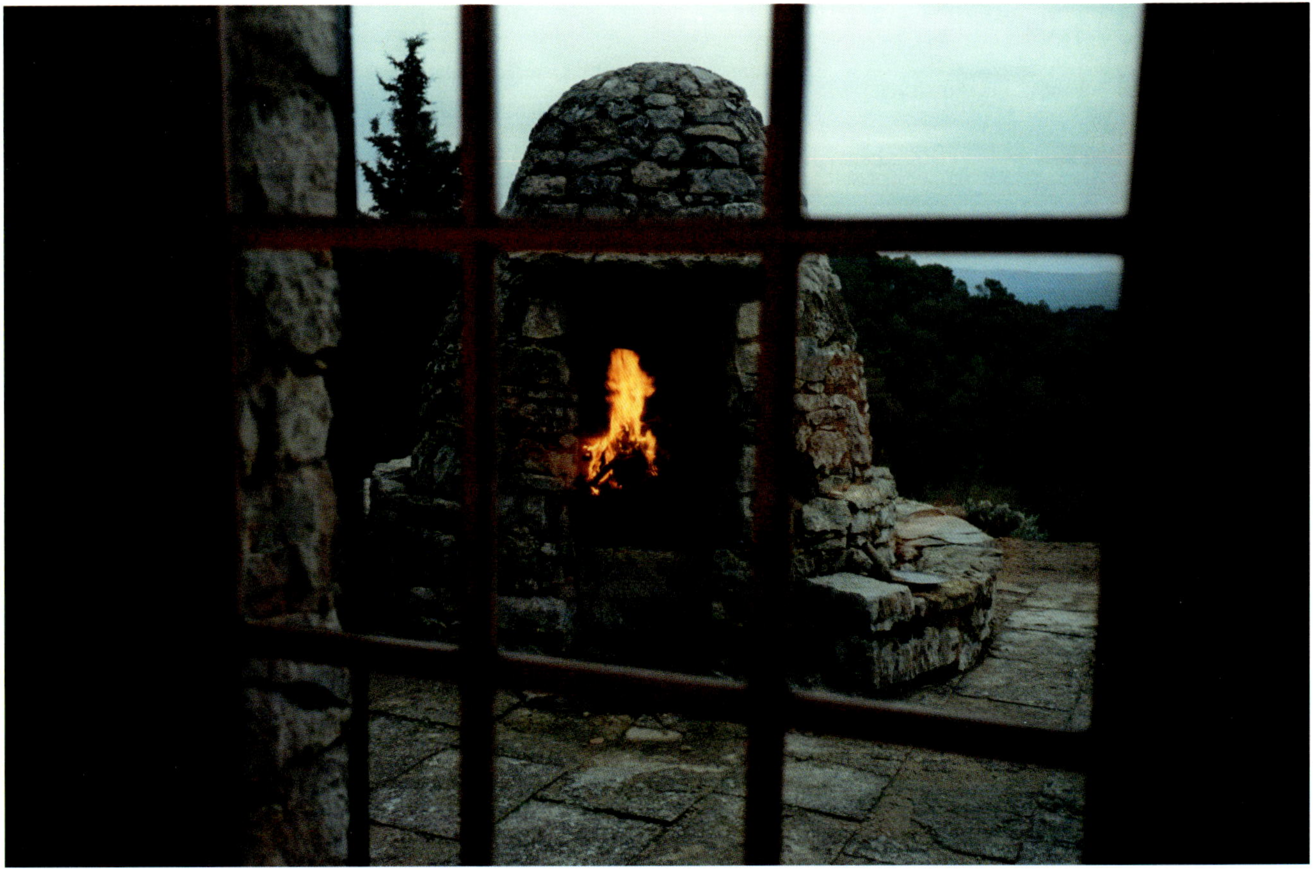

Tuesday, January 5. Cotignac, France. "La Véronique". The well, with the reflection of the fireplace

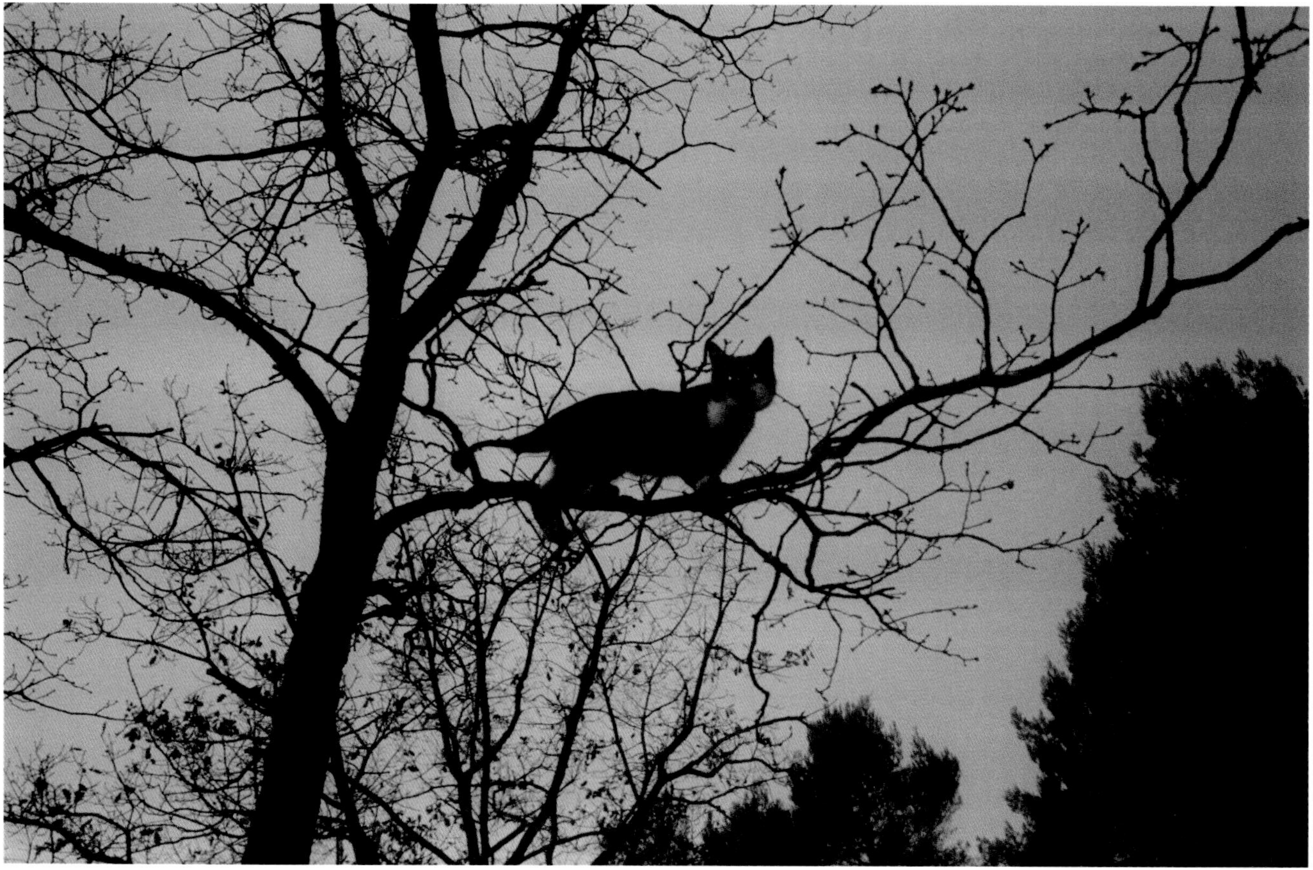

Wednesday, January 6. Cotignac, France. "Perdu", our cat

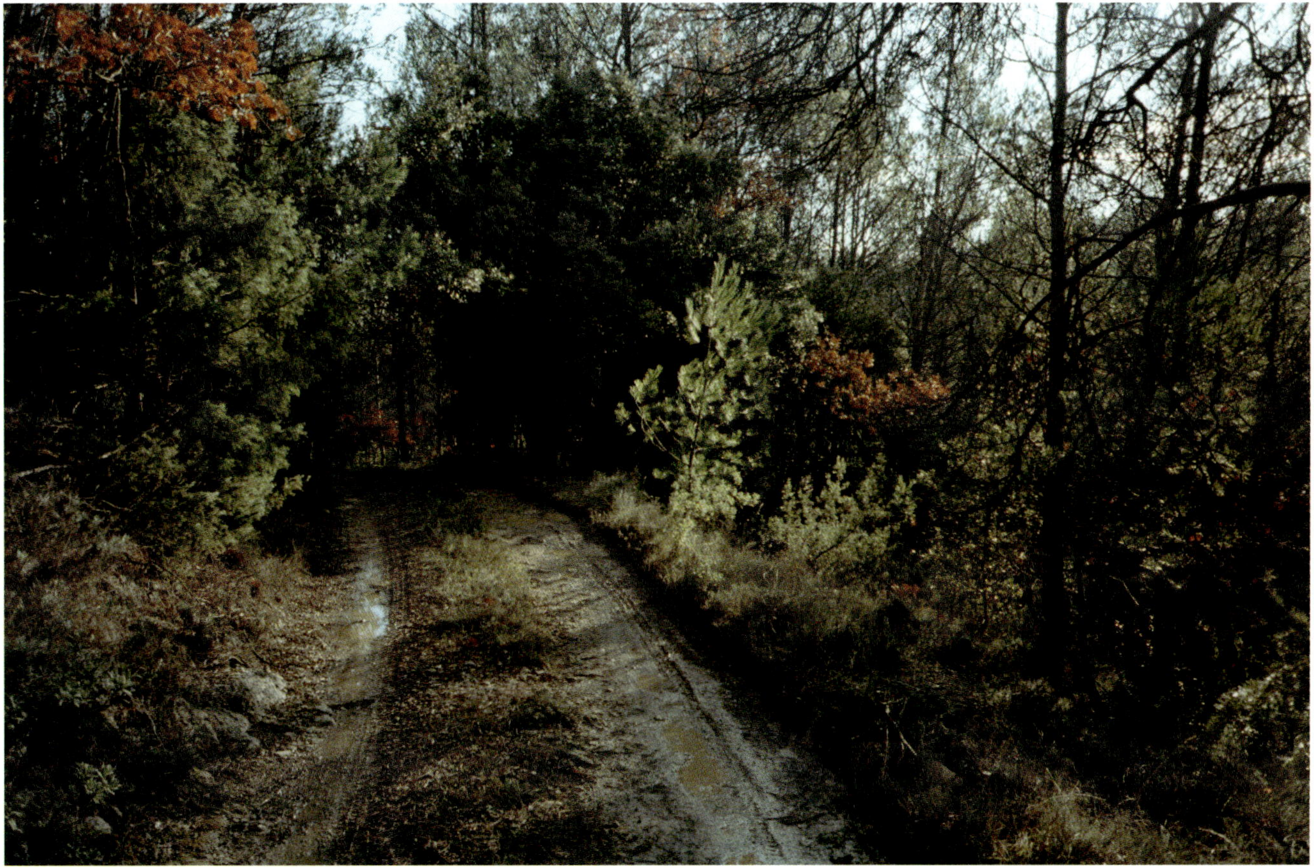

Thursday, January 7. Cotignac, France. Dirt road leading to "La Véronique"

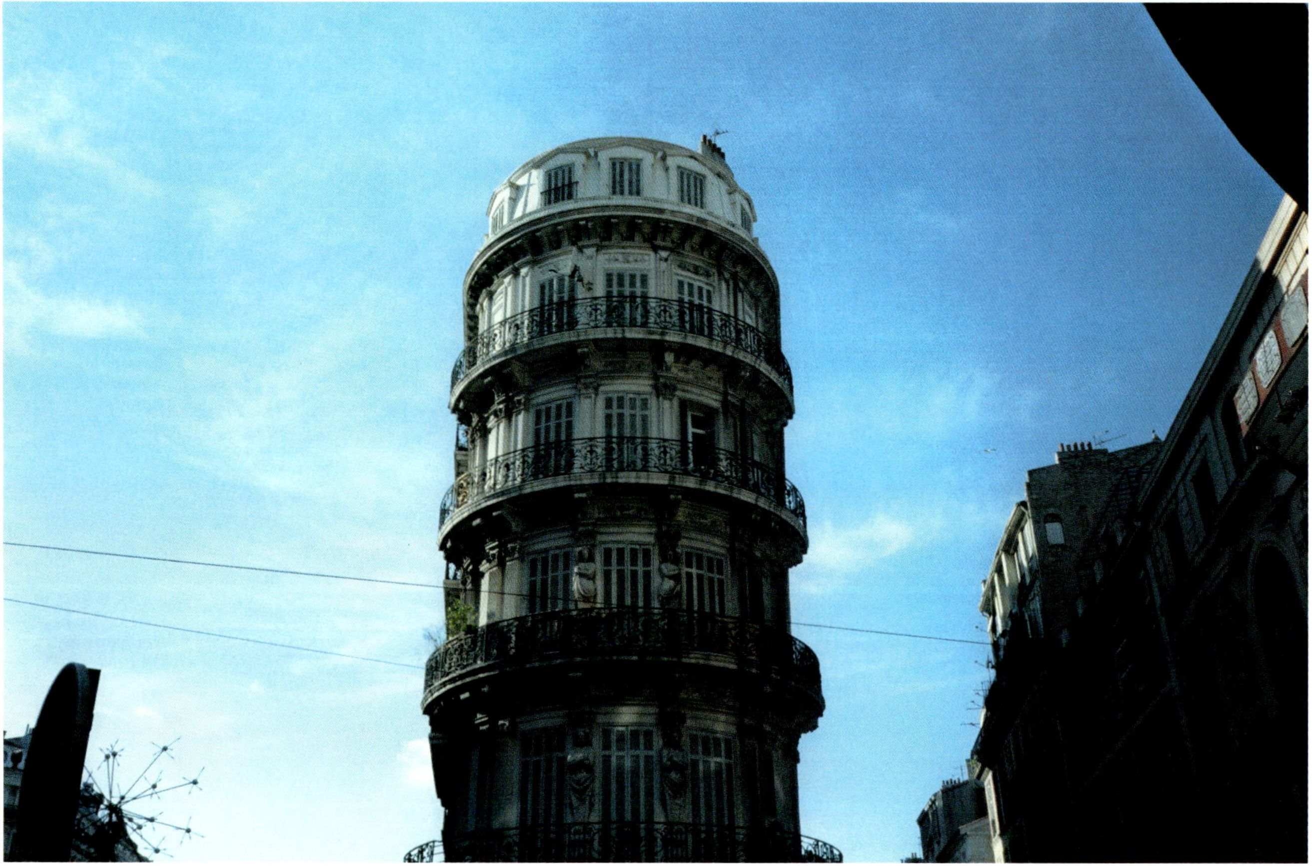

Friday, January 8. Marseilles, France. On La Canebière (the main street)

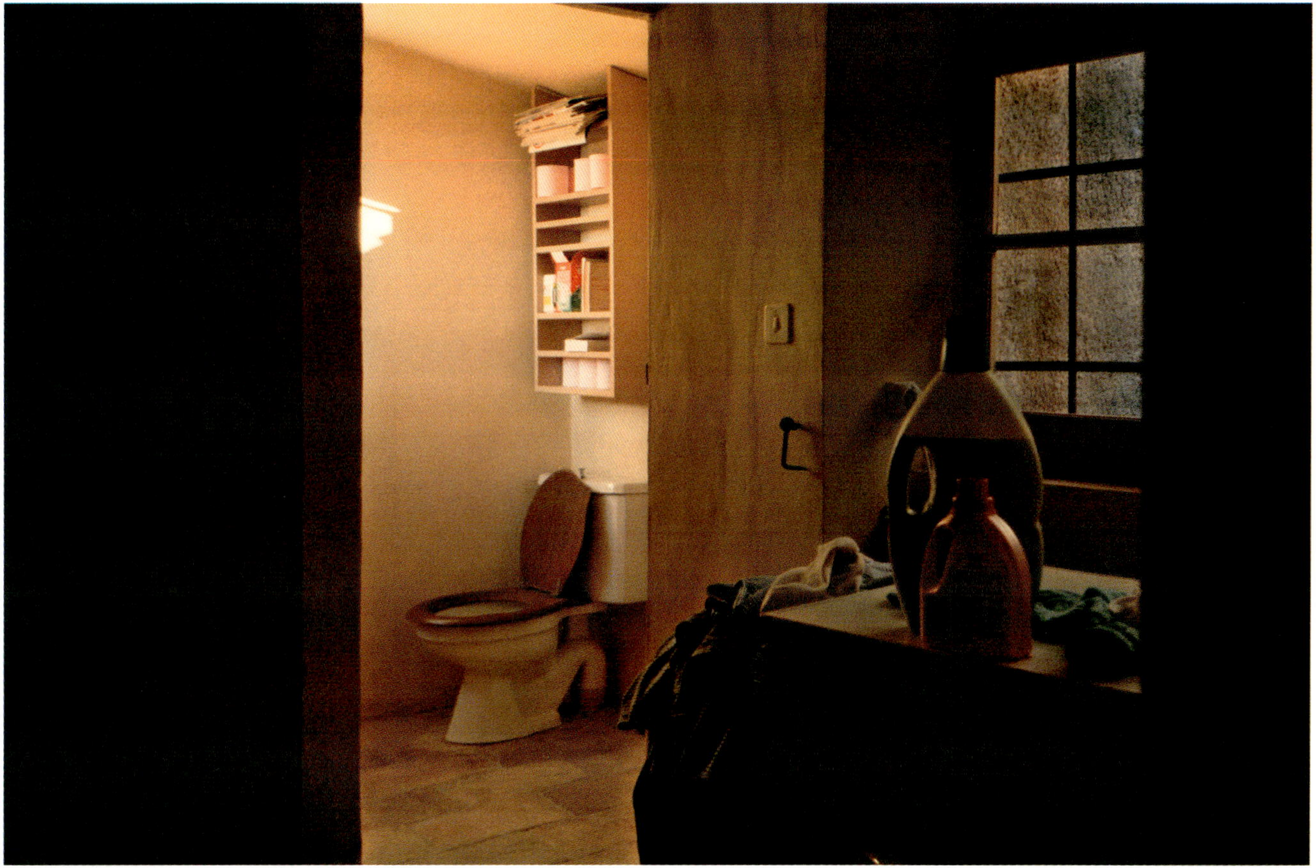

Saturday, January 9. Cotignac, France. "La Véronique", interior detail

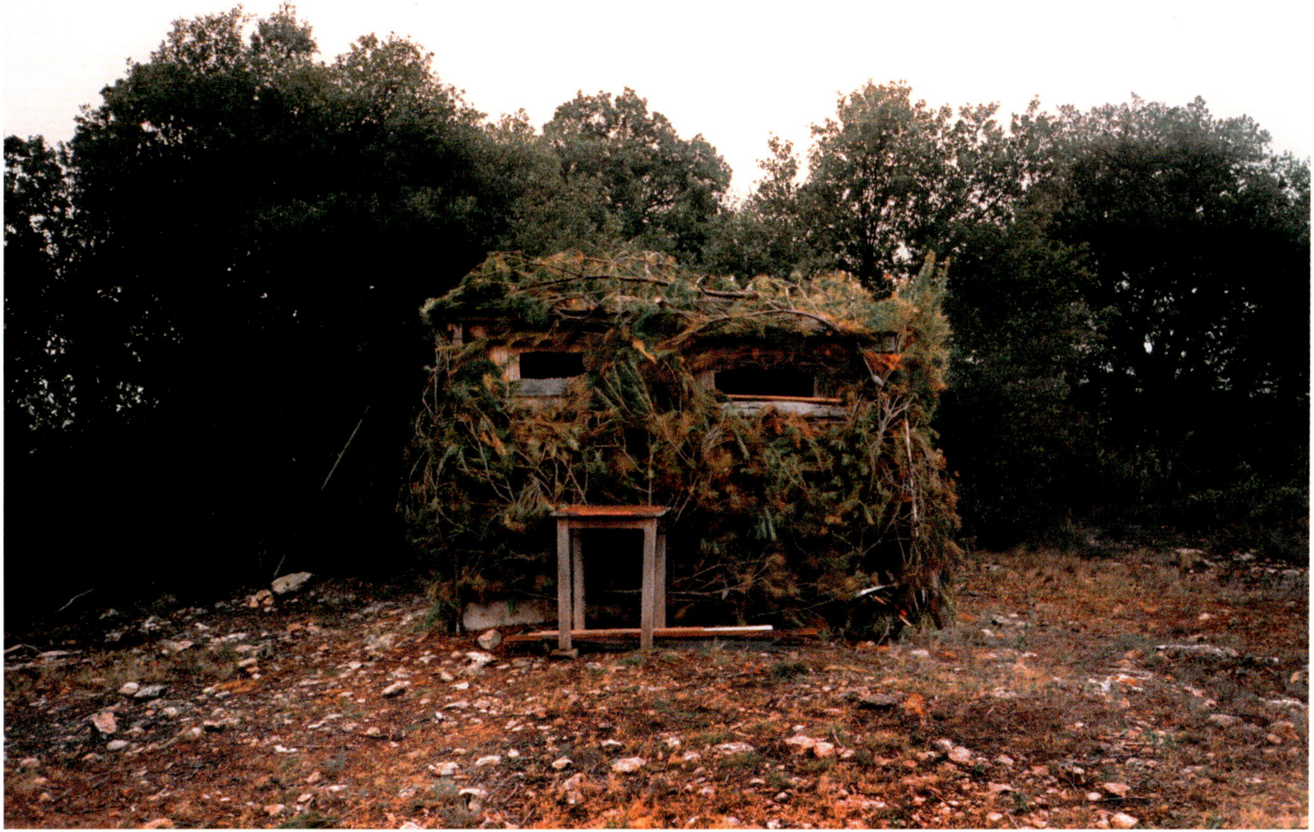

Sunday, January 10. Cotignac, France. Our neighbour Luc Marin's hunting cabin

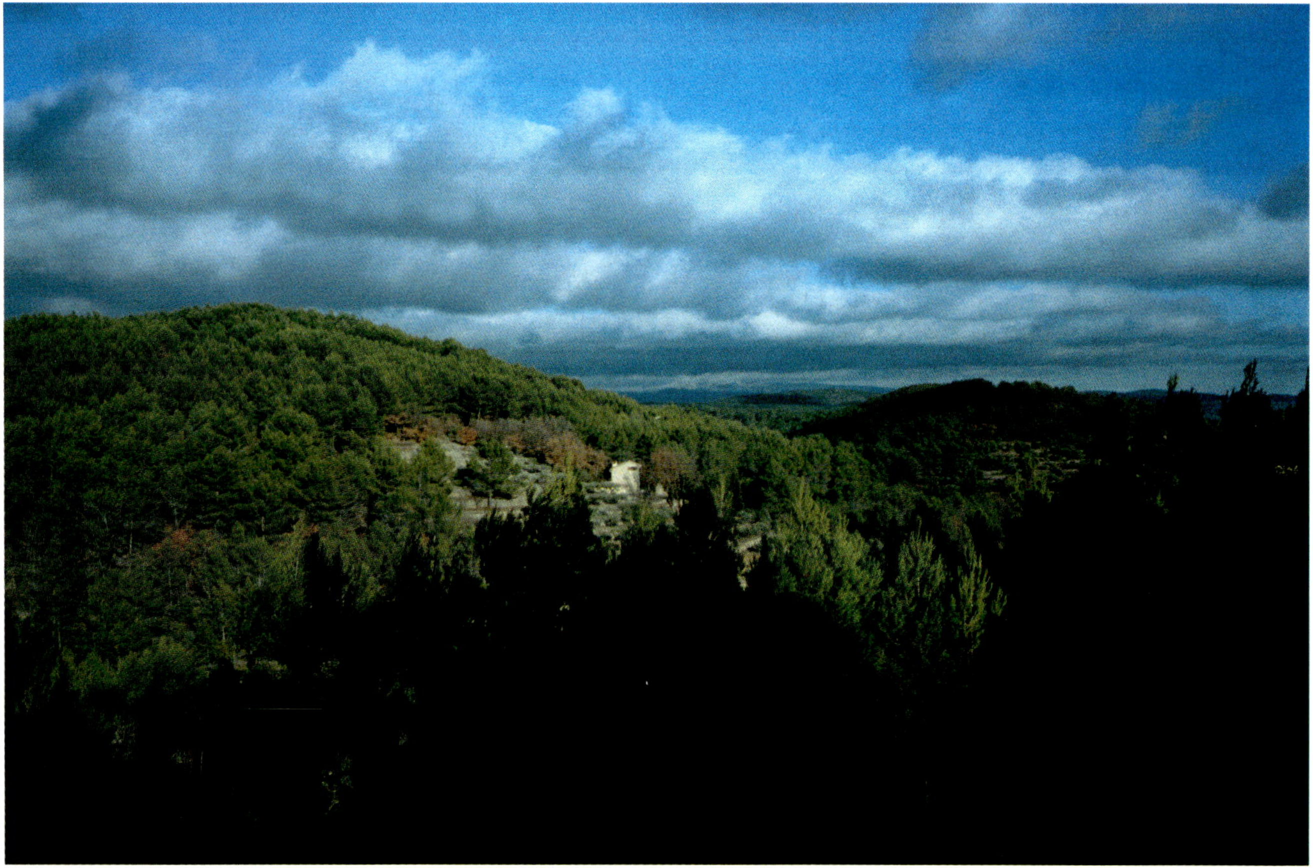

Monday, January 11. Cotignac, France. "La Véronique", seen from the opposite hill

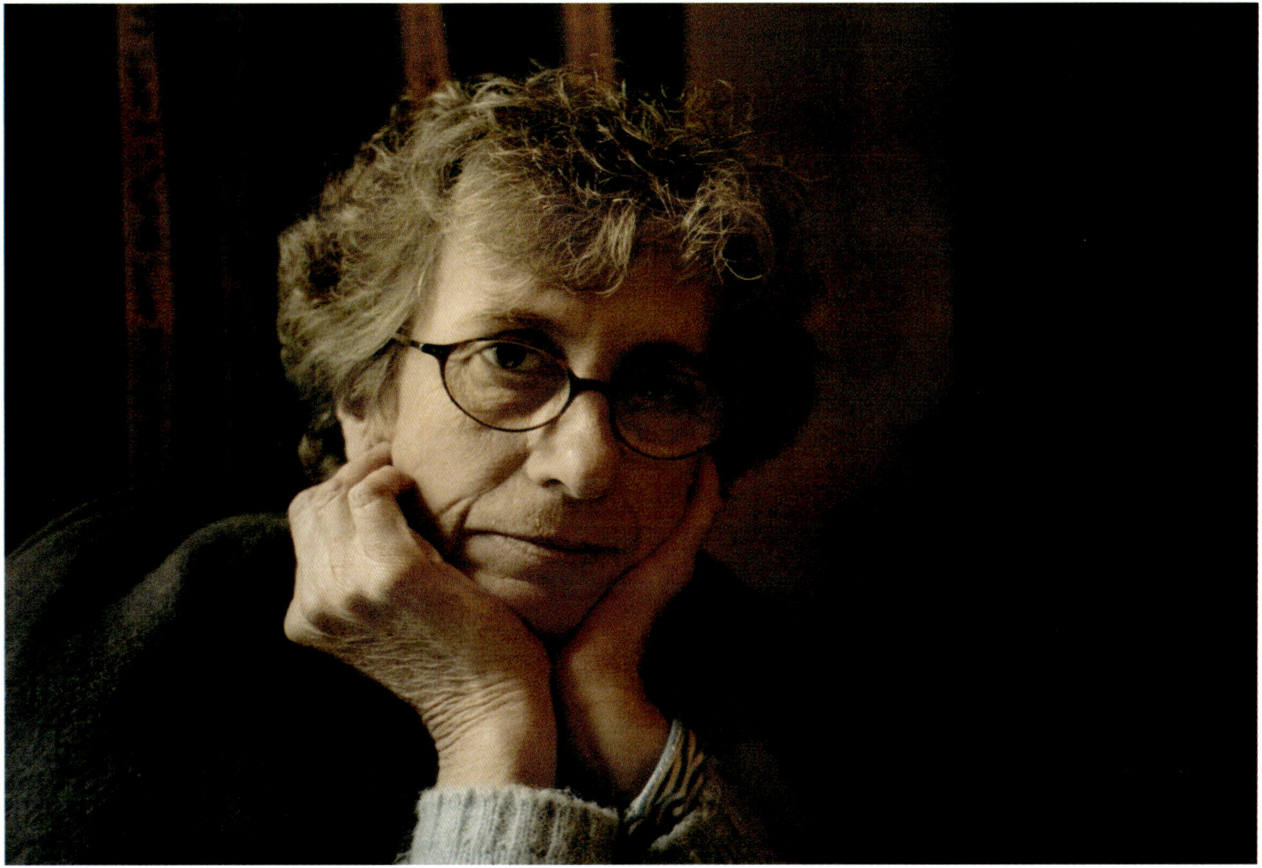

Tuesday, January 12. Villecroze, France. Véronique Aubry, my wife (see note)

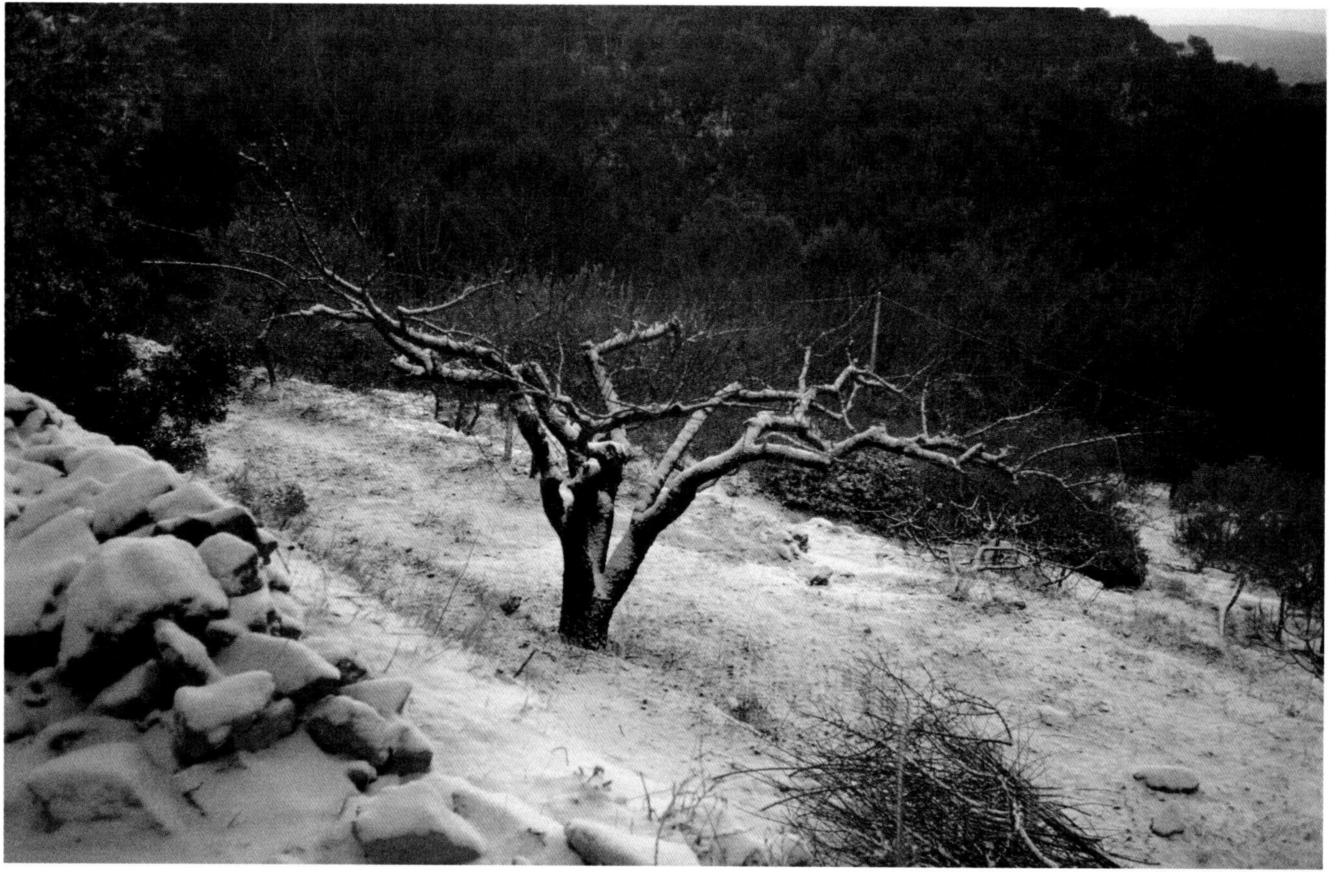

Wednesday, January 13. Cotignac, France. "La Véronique", snow on the terraces

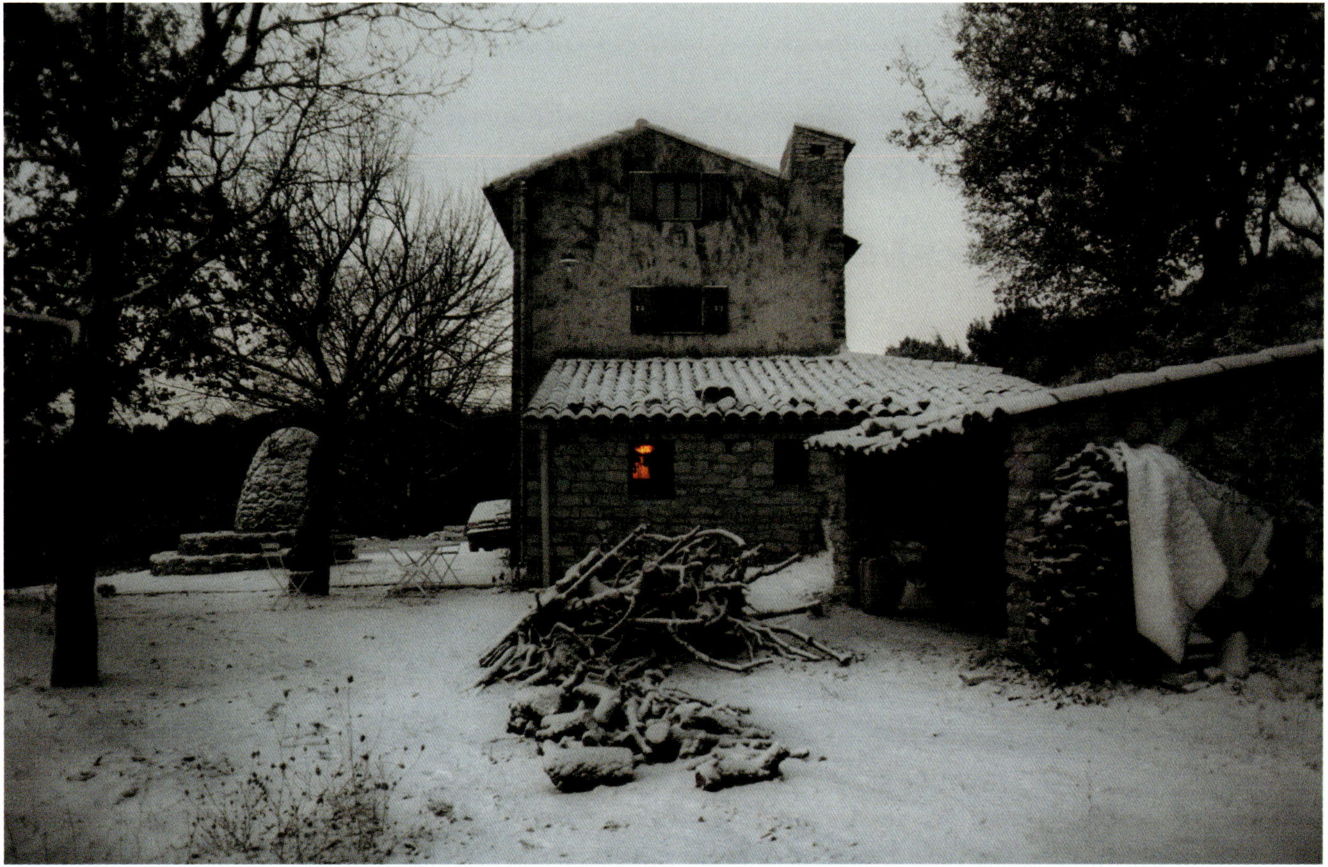

Wednesday, January 13. Cotignac, France. "La Véronique", eastern view

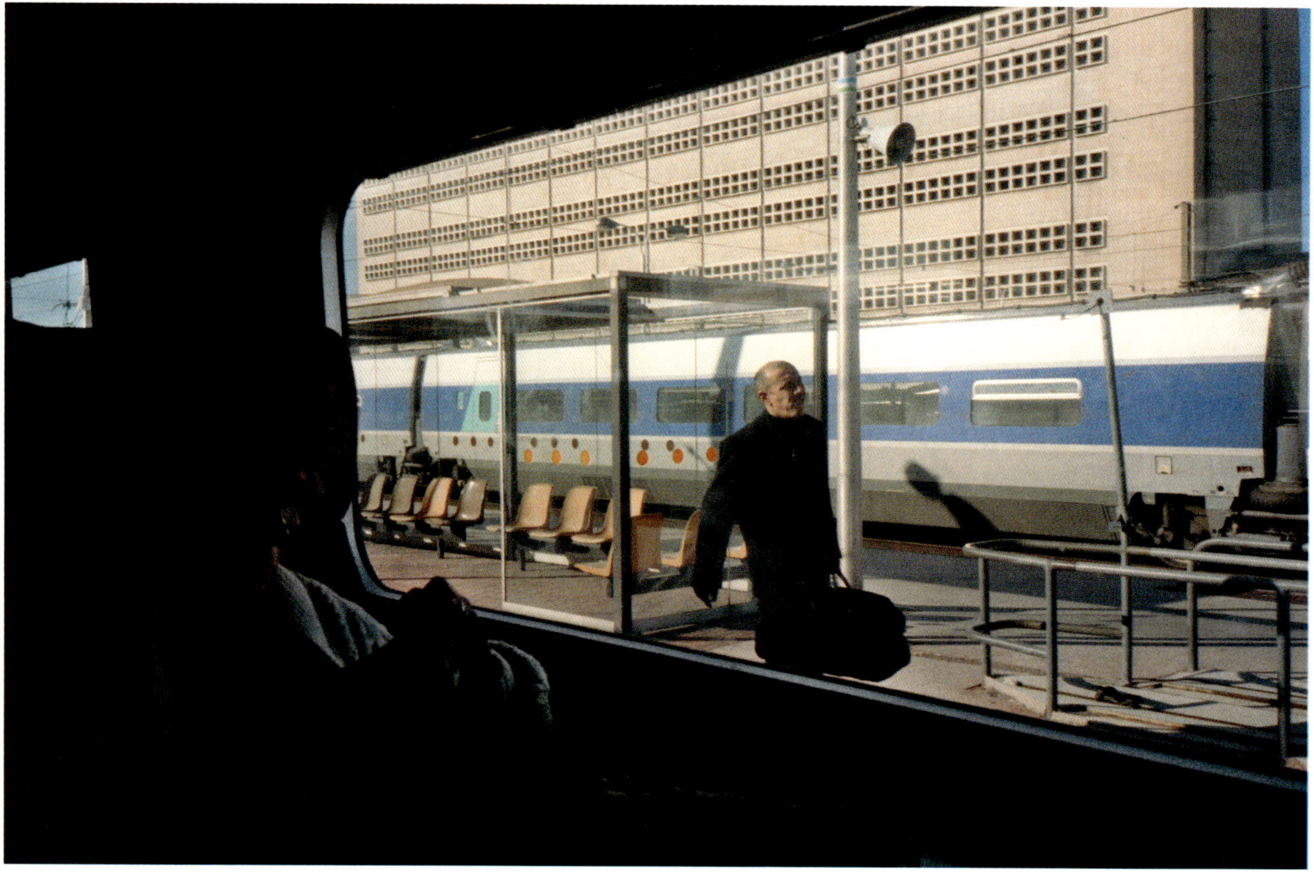

Thursday, January 14. Marseilles, France. Trainstop in Marseilles

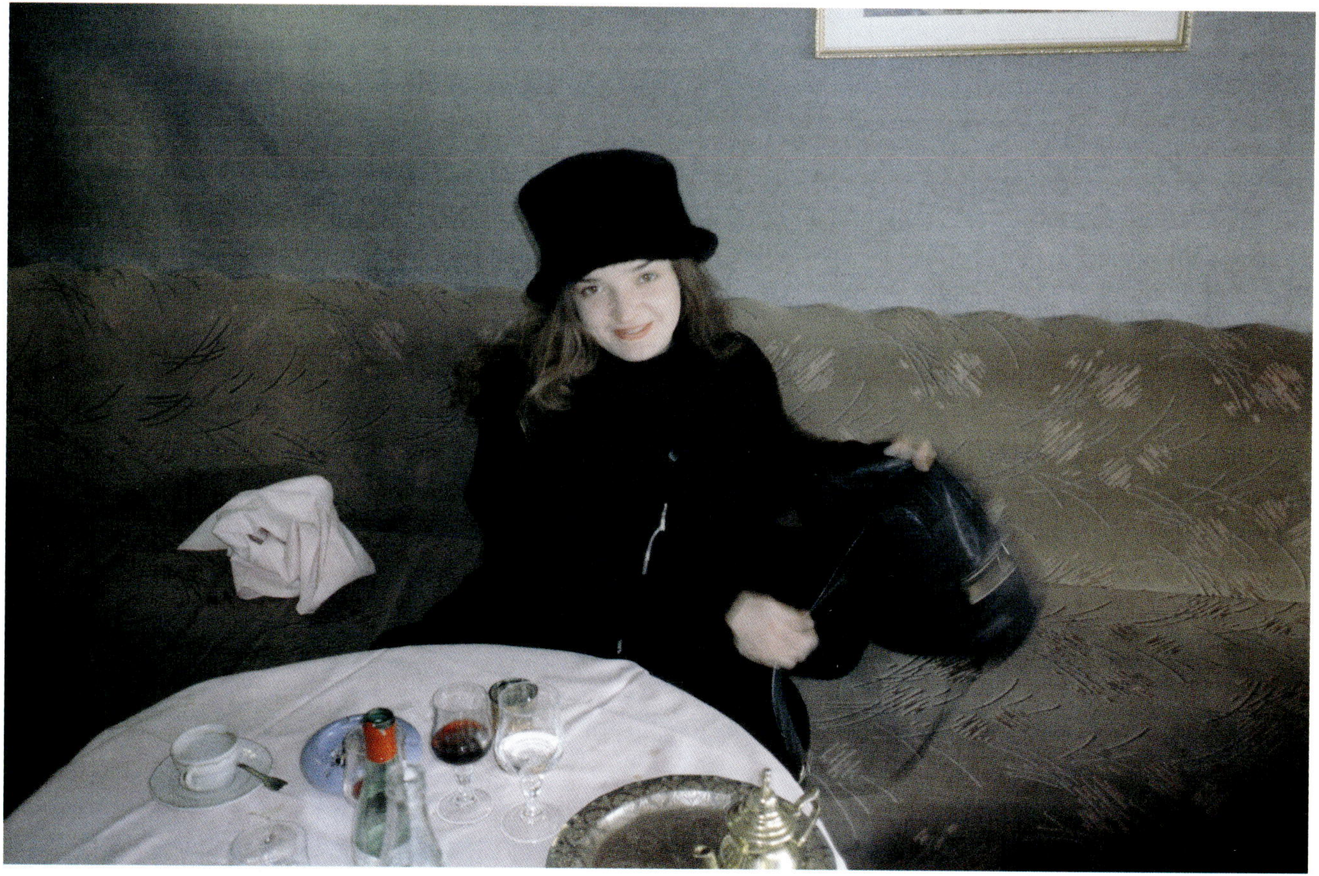

Friday, January 15. Boulogne, France. Hélène Busnel, actress and dancer

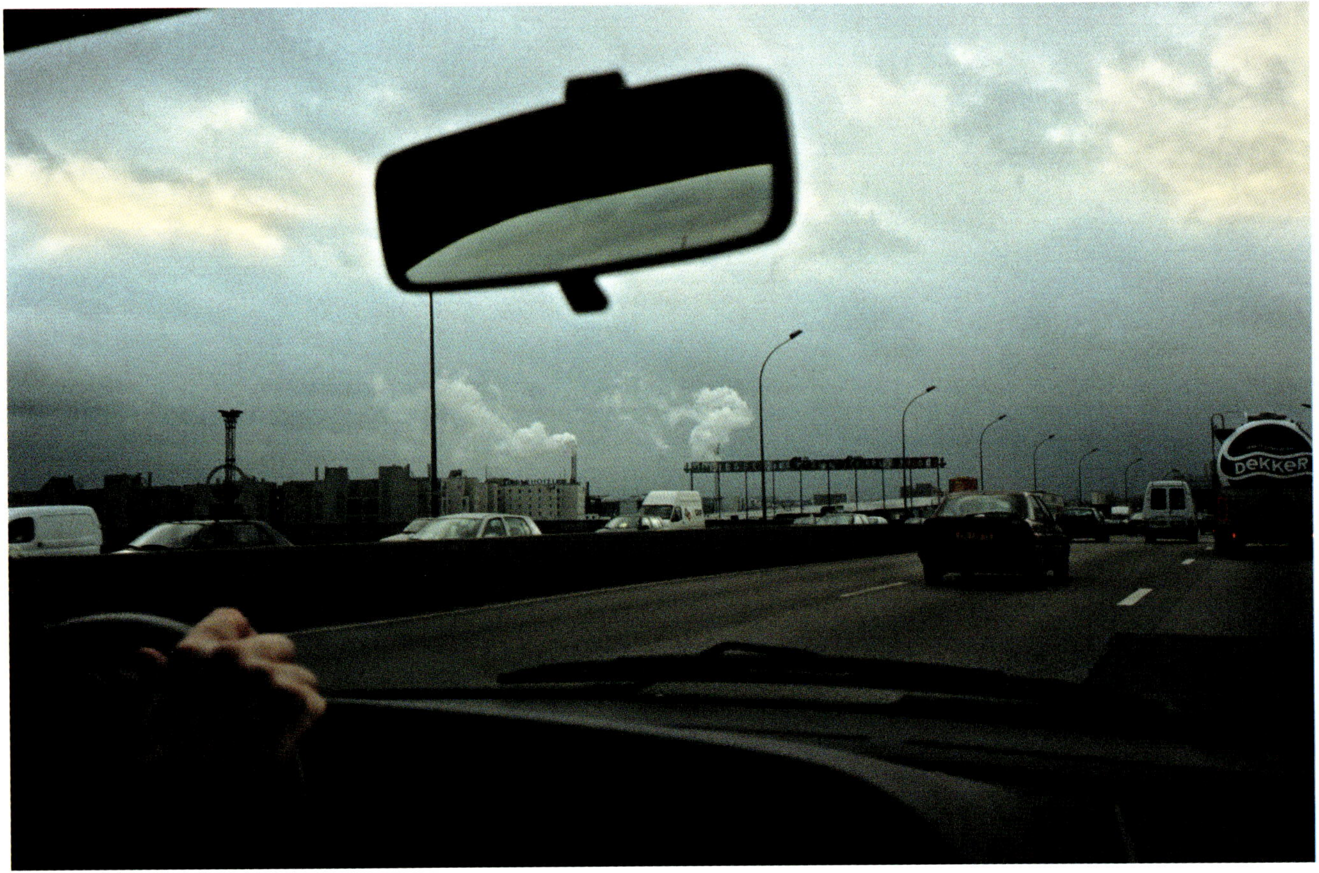

Saturday, January 16. Paris. Boulevard Périphérique

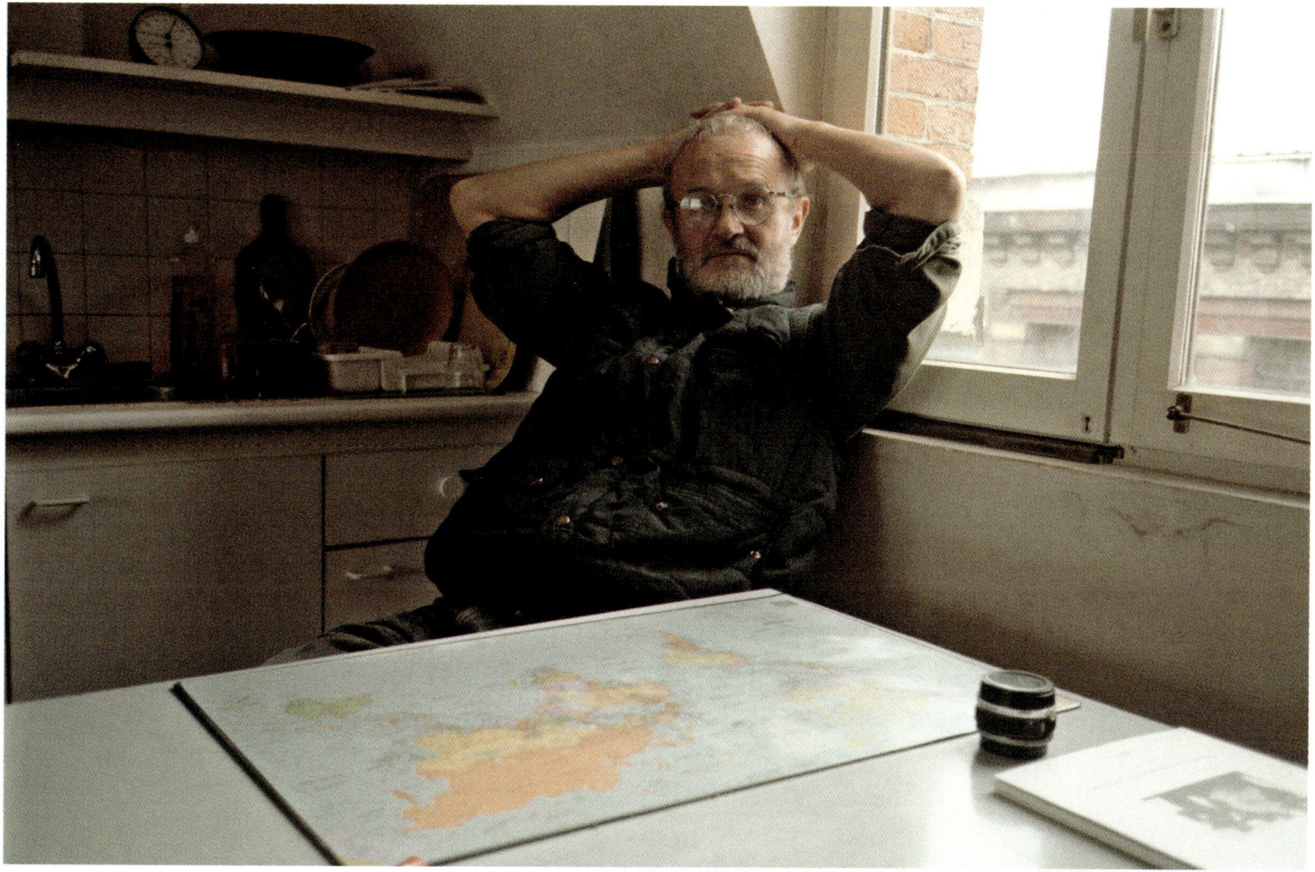

Sunday, January 17. Ivry, France. Josef Koudelka, photographer, in his kitchen

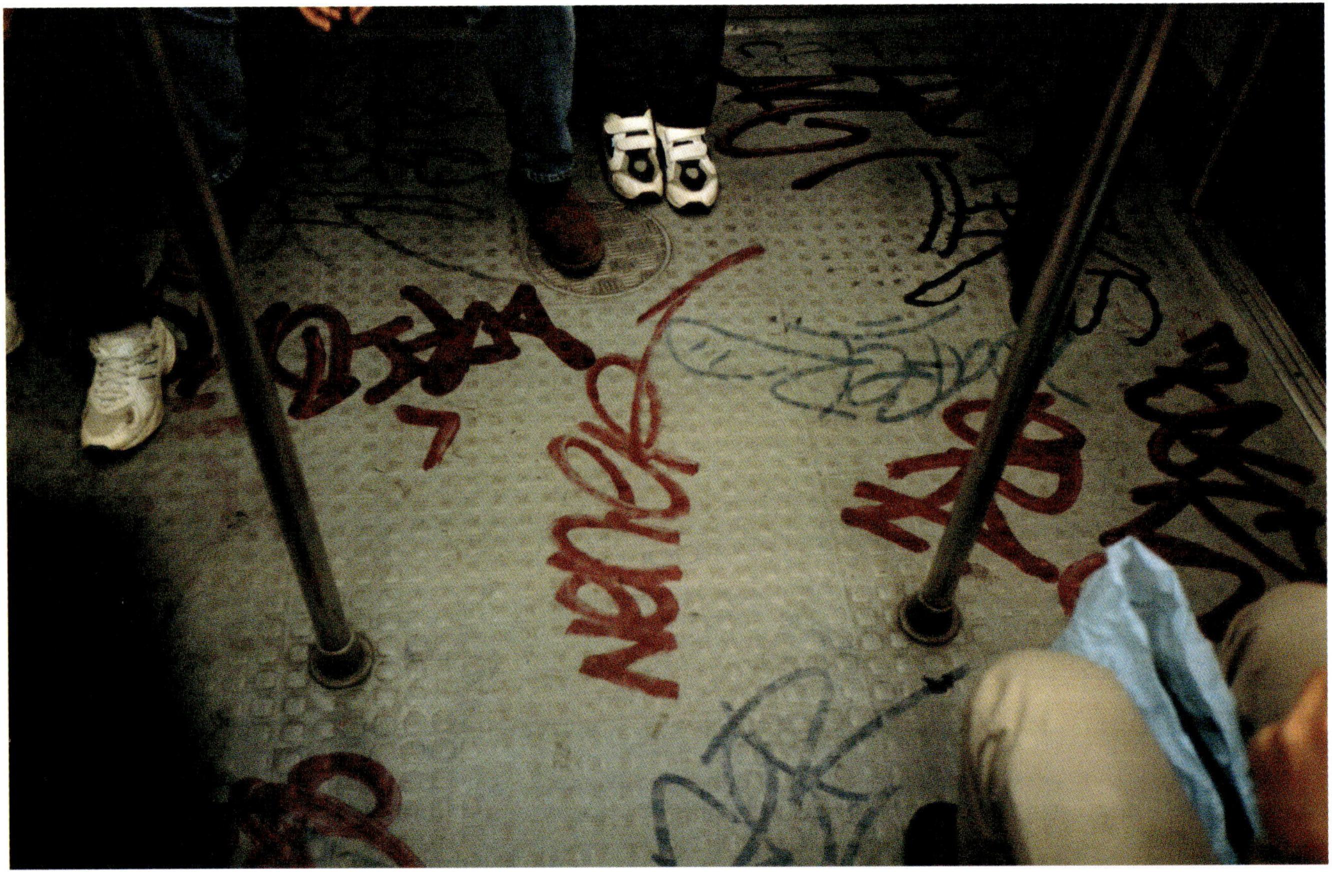

Monday, January 18. Paris. Métro, Austerlitz-Boulogne line

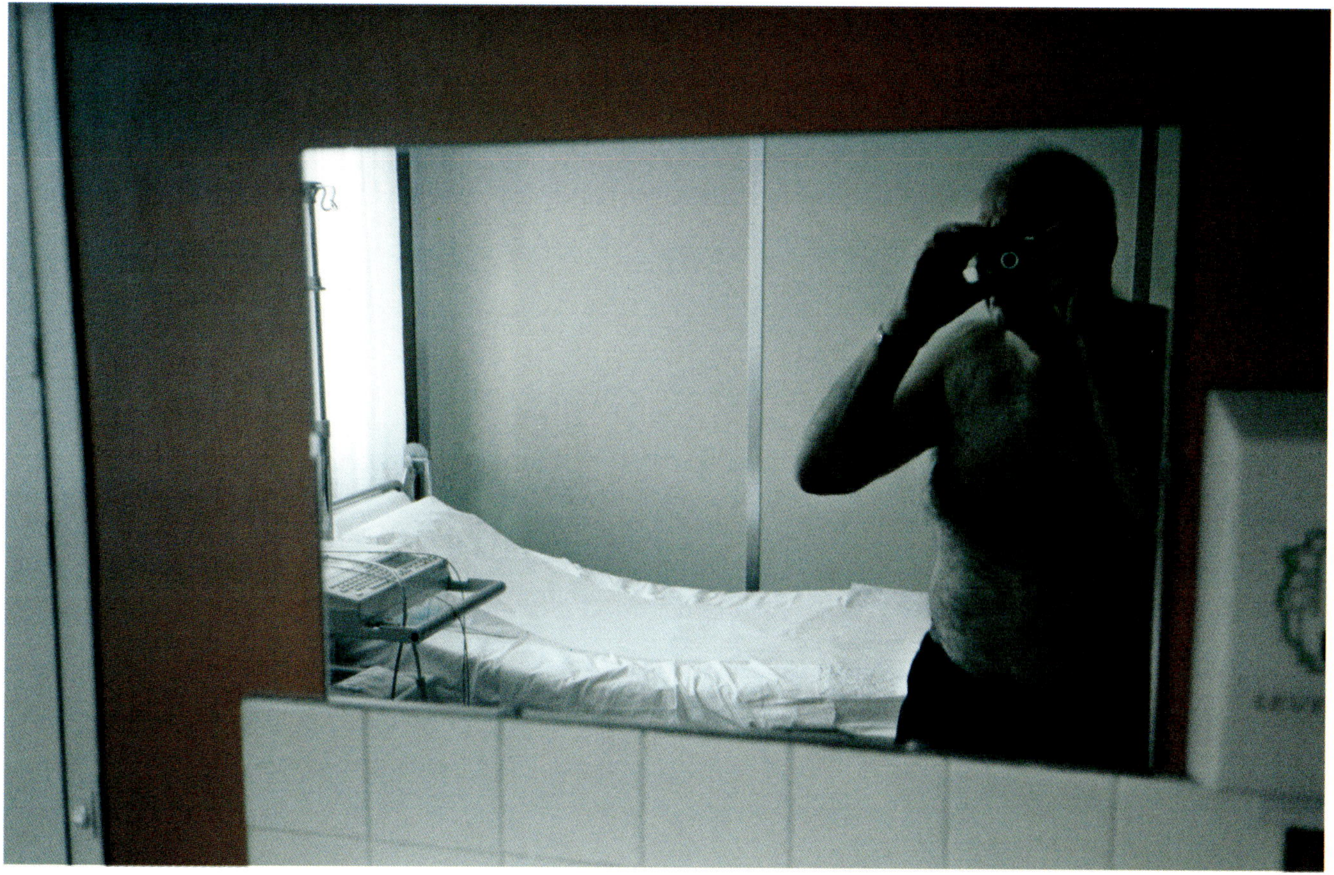

Tuesday, January 19. Boulogne, France. At the Ambroise Paré hospital, self-portrait before a check-up (see note)

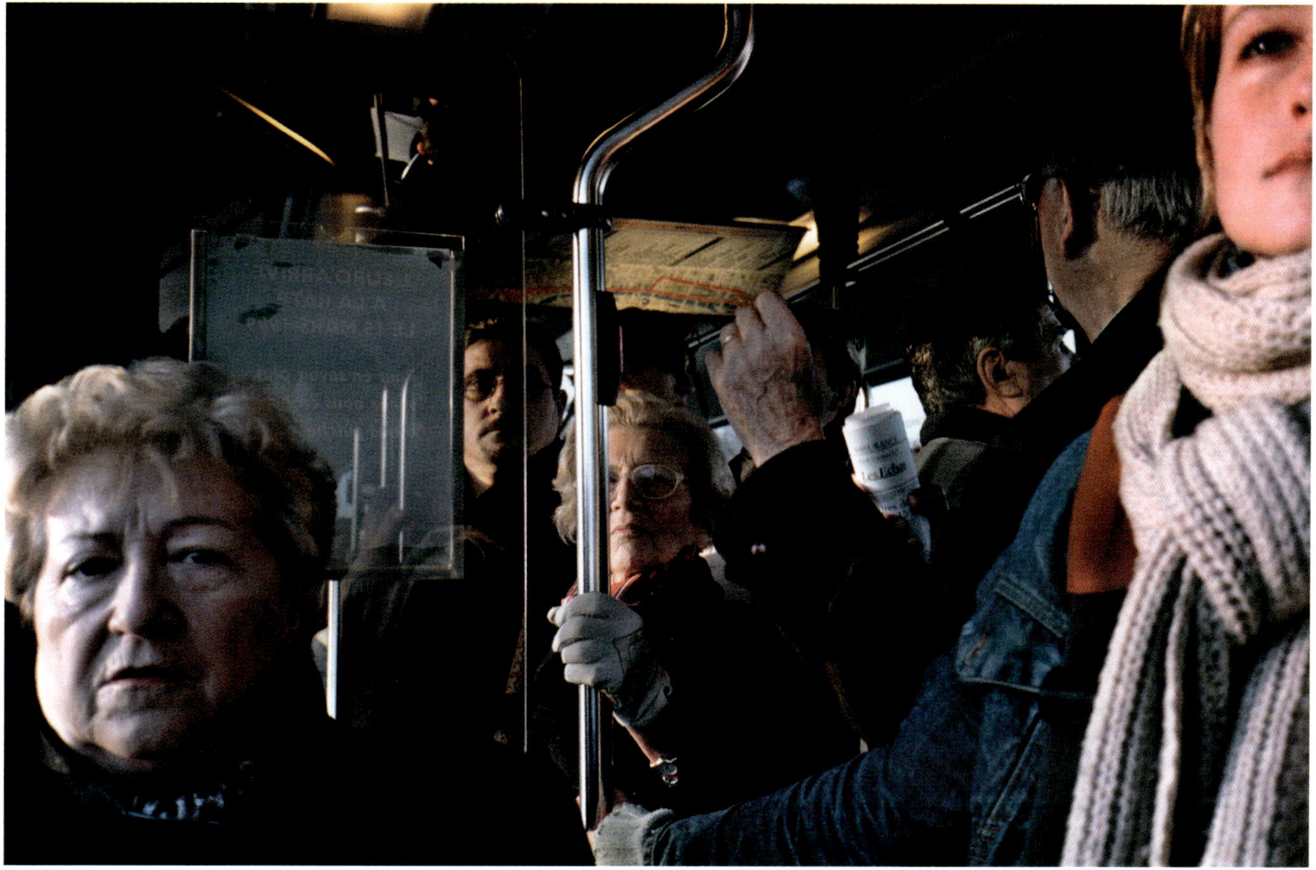

Wednesday, January 20. Paris. On the 72 bus

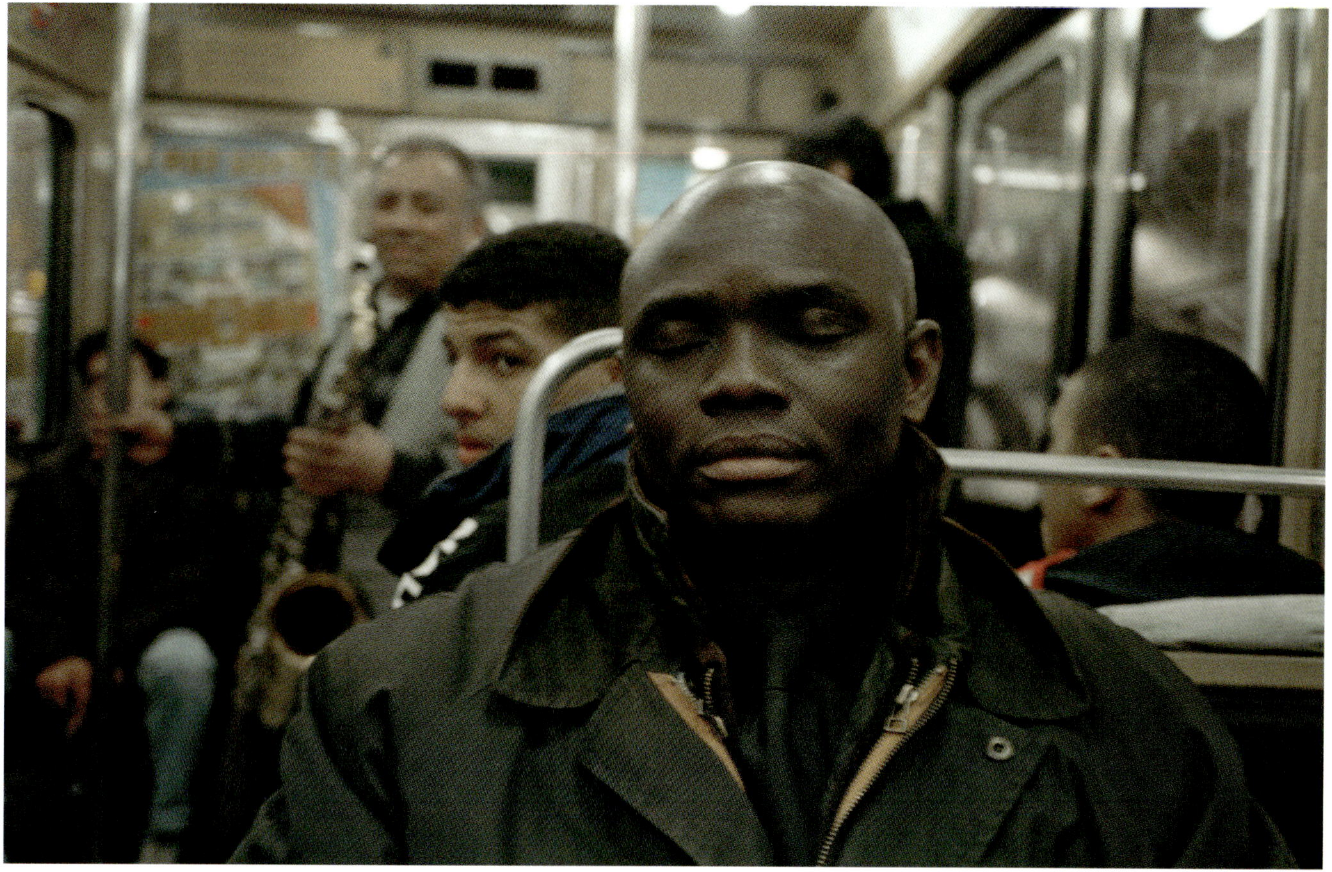

Thursday, January 21. Paris. On the Métro, Austerlitz-Boulogne line

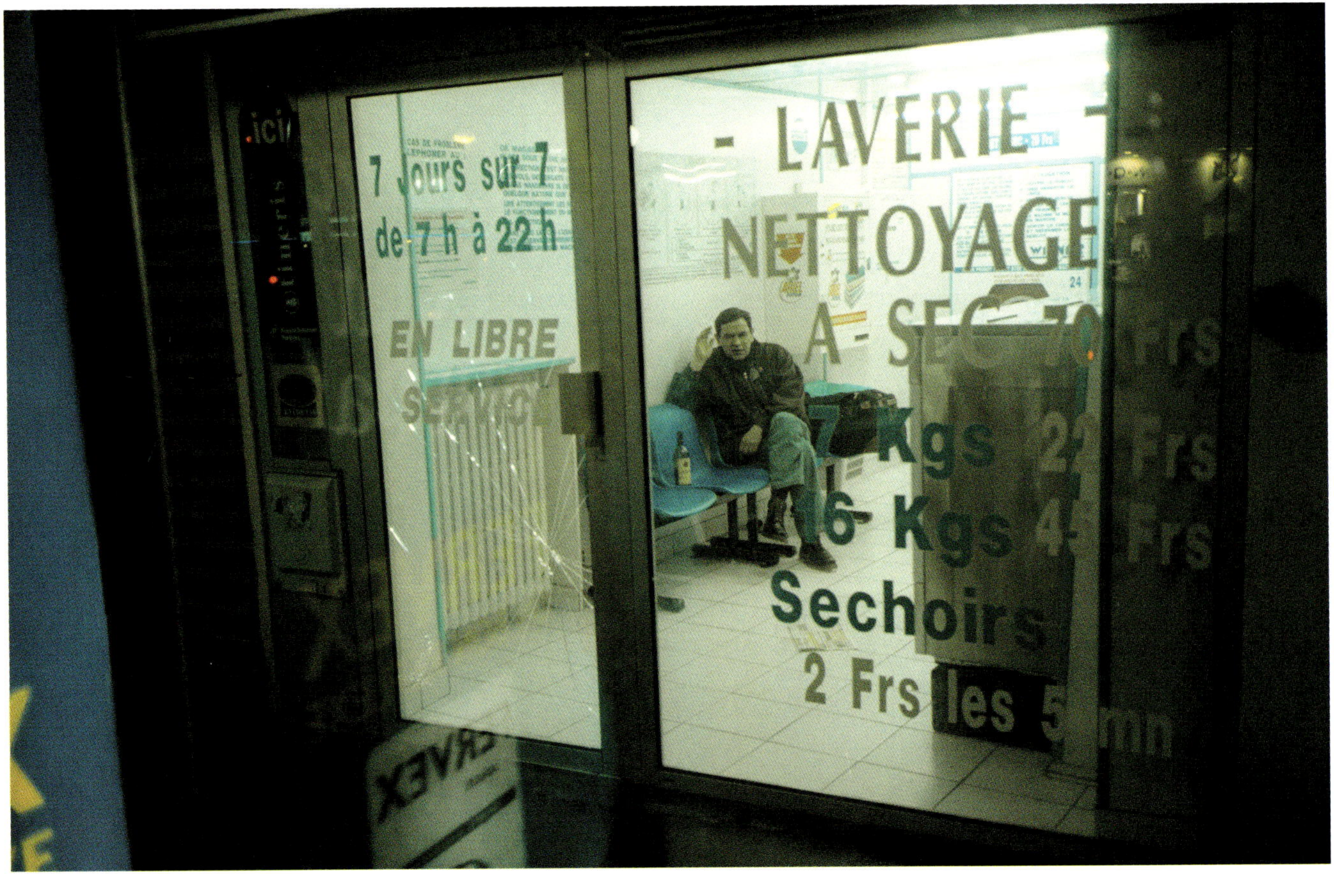

Friday, January 22. Boulogne, France. Homeless man, spending the night in a launderette

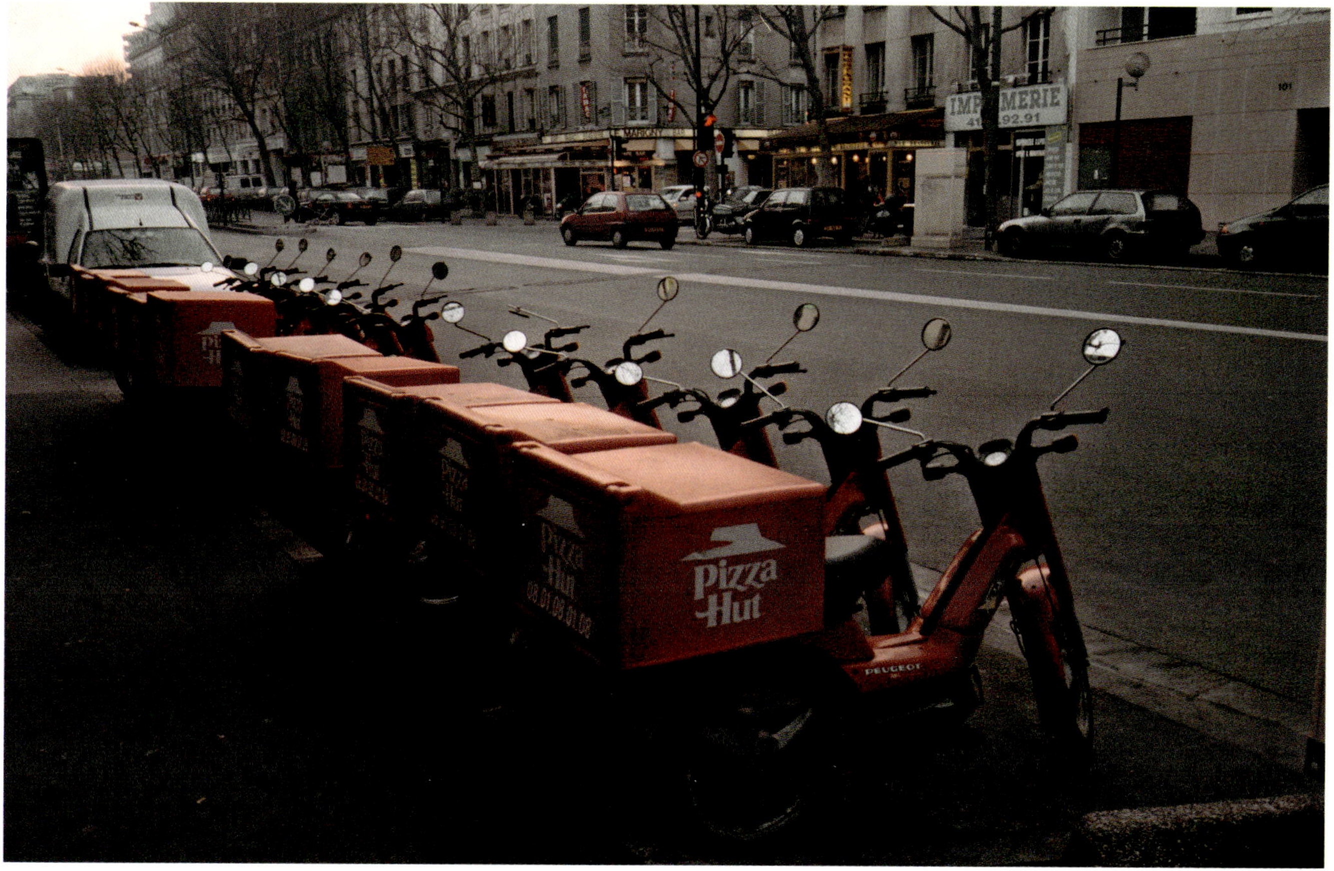

Saturday, January 23. Boulogne, France. Route de la Reine

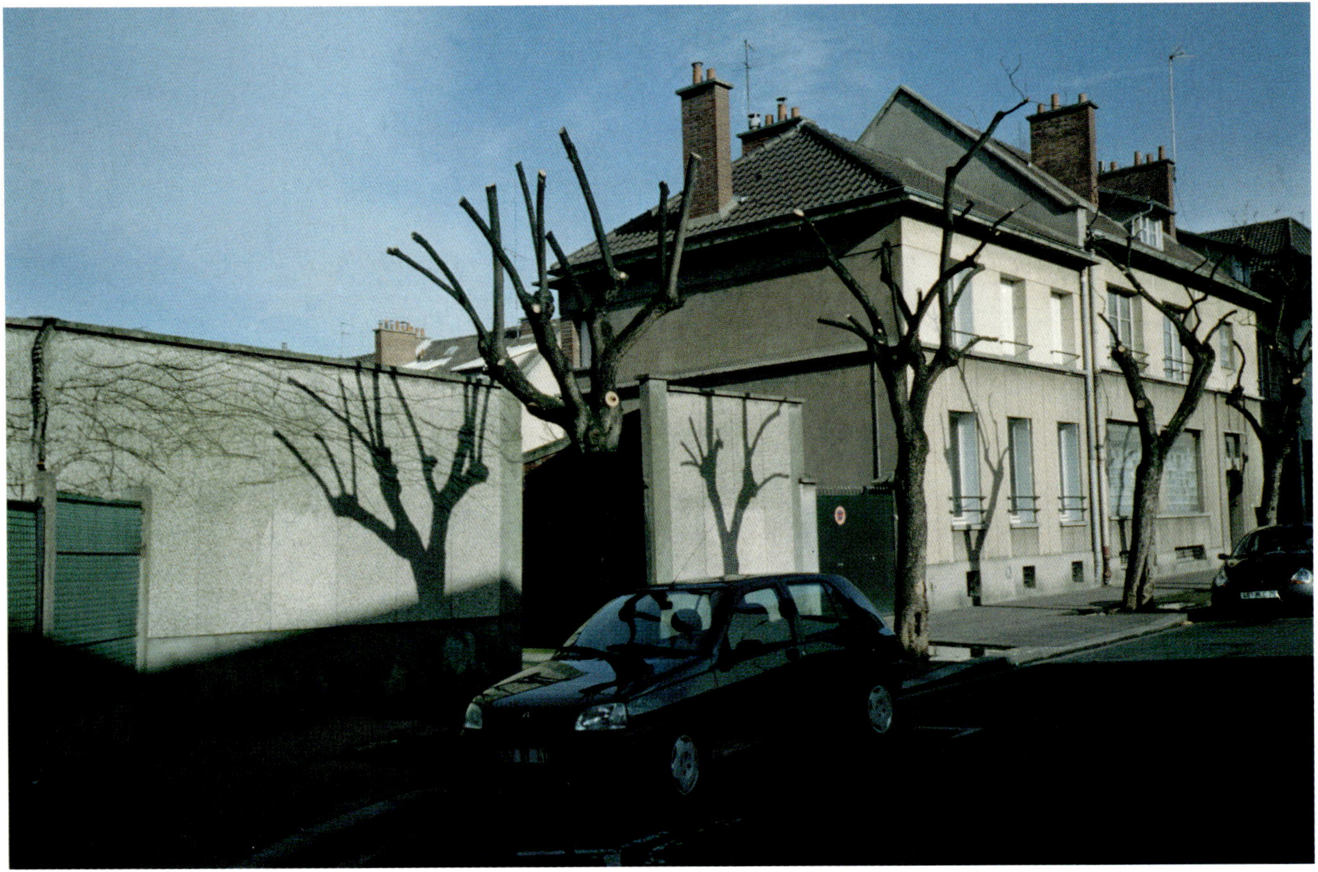

Sunday, January 24. Boulogne, France. Pruned plane trees, rue de Paris (see note)

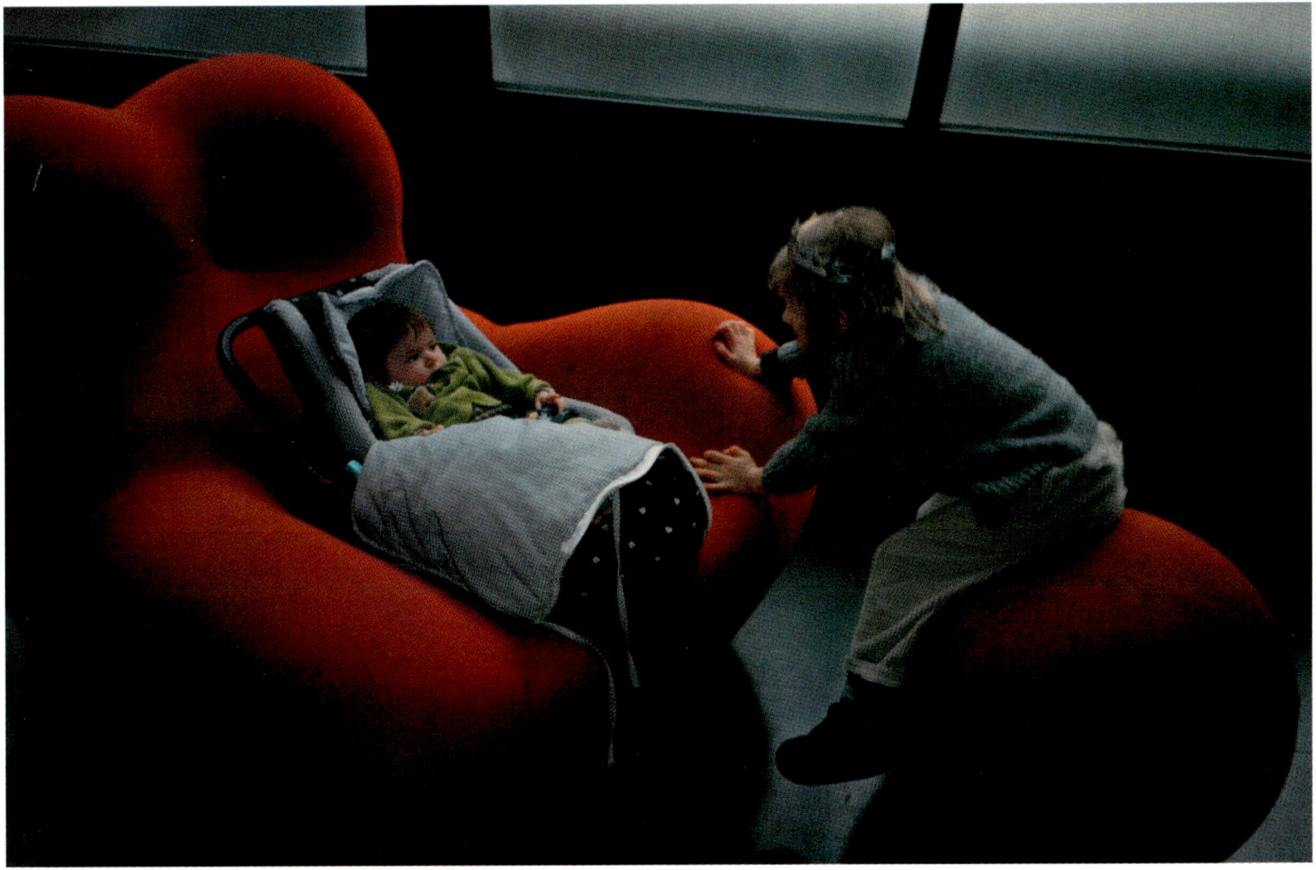

Monday, January 25. Boulogne, France. At my home. Alba and Saskia Horvat (see notes)

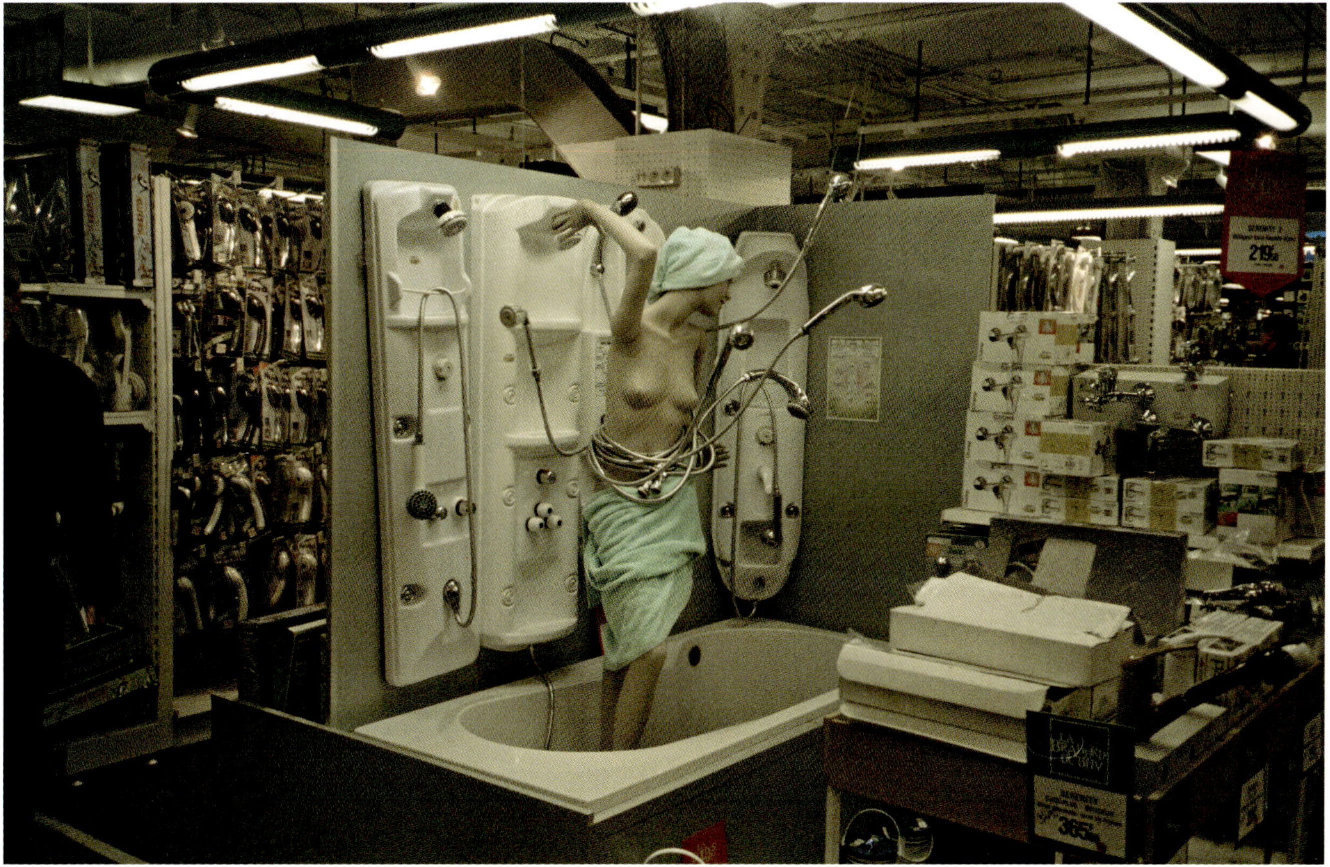

Tuesday, January 26. Paris. At Bazar de l'Hôtel de Ville department store

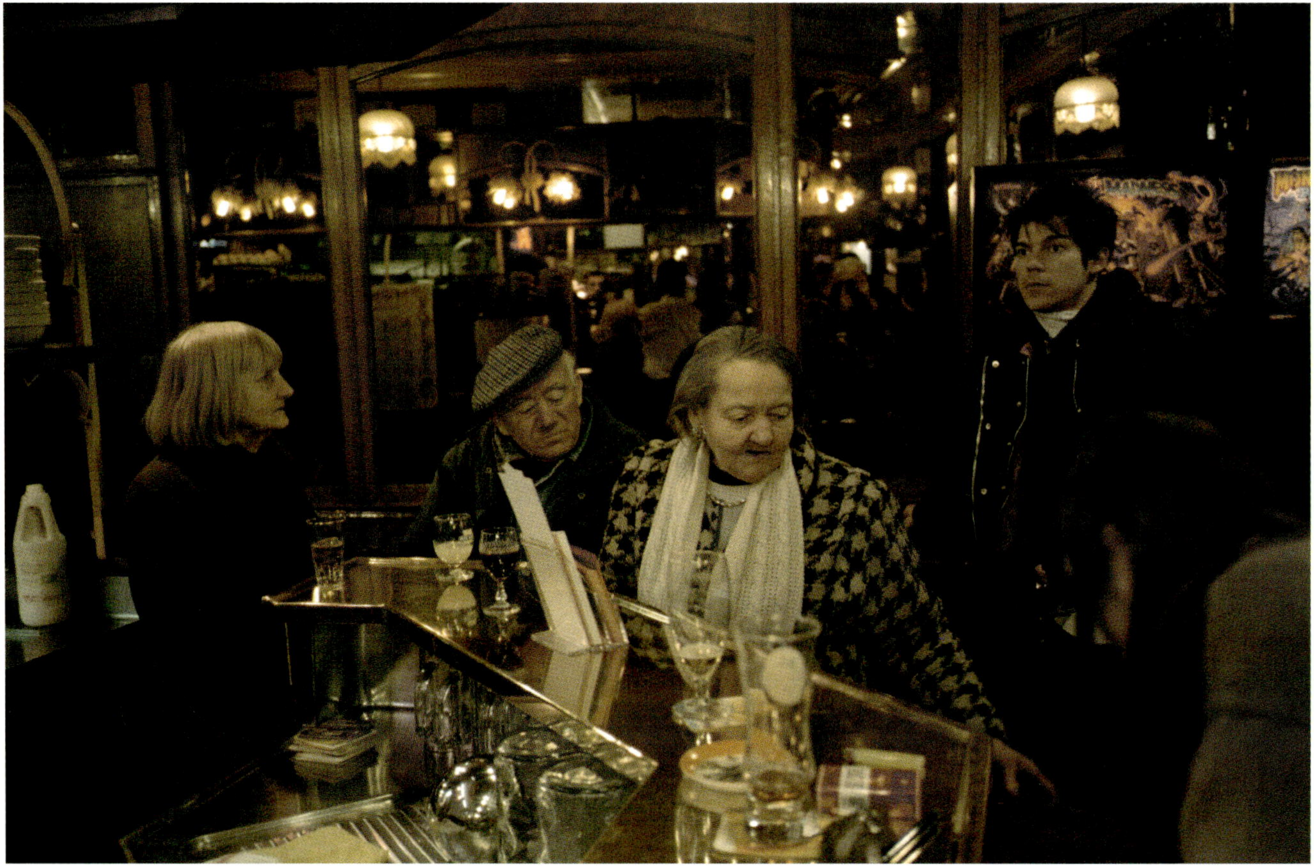

Wednesday, January 27. Paris. Café-tabac, in the Bastille area

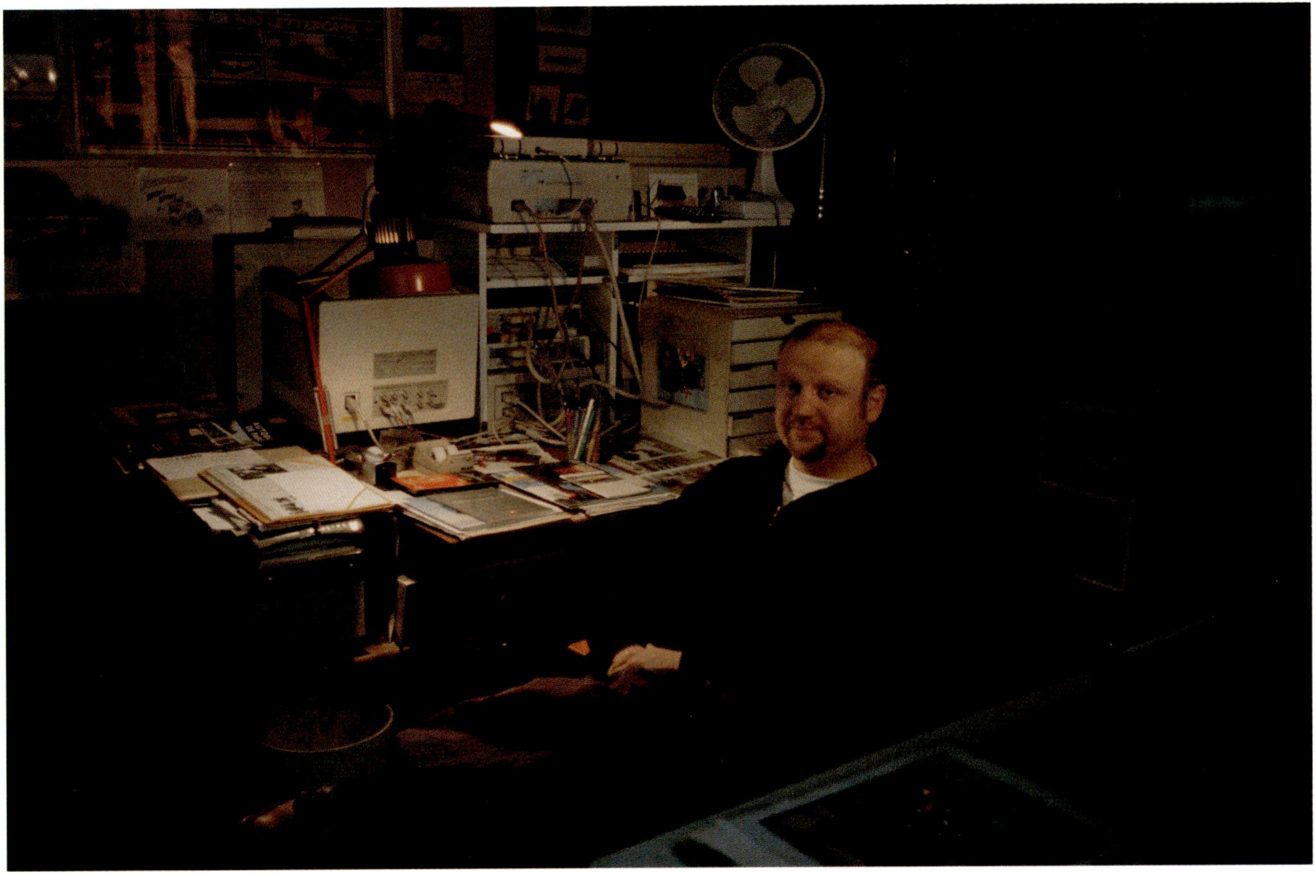

Thursday, January 28. Paris. Jean-Michel Horvat

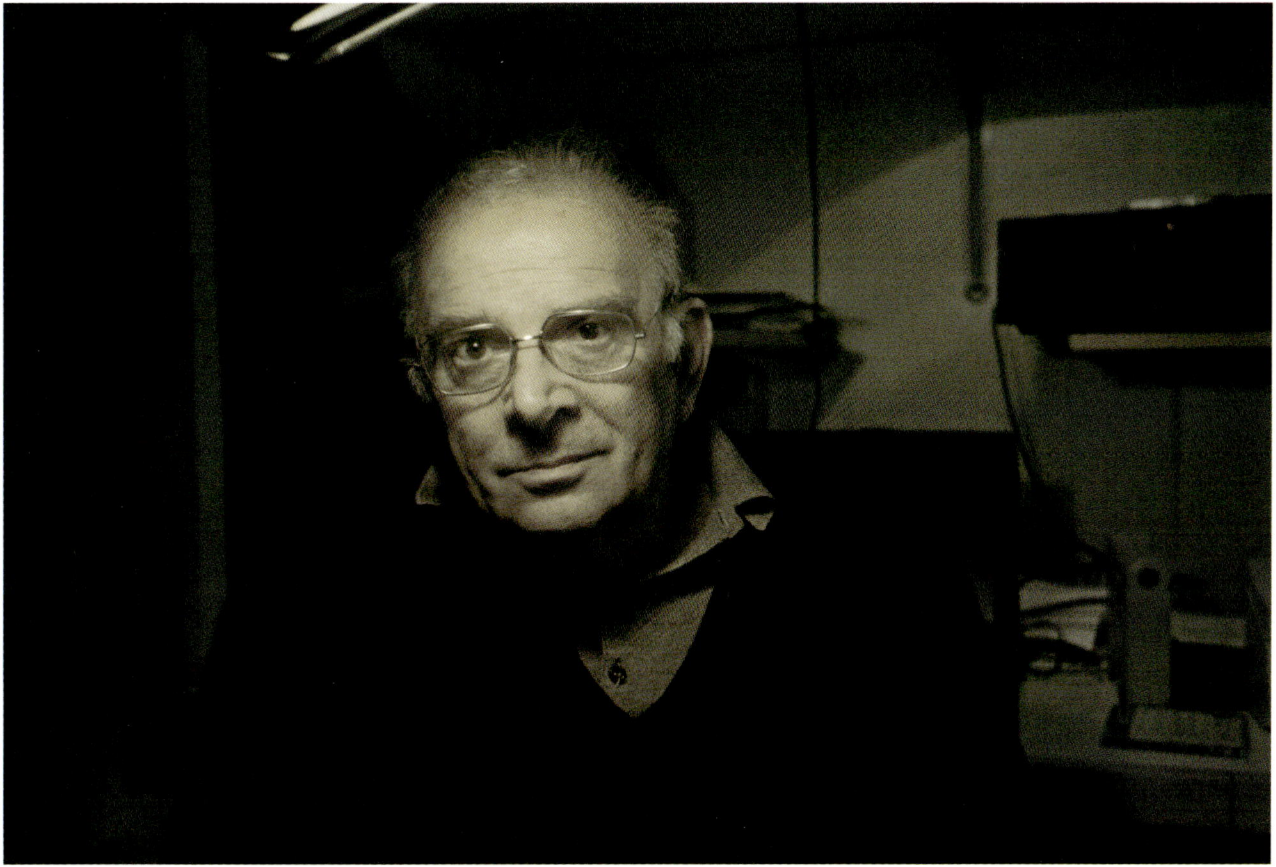

Friday, January 29. Boulogne, France. Self-portrait

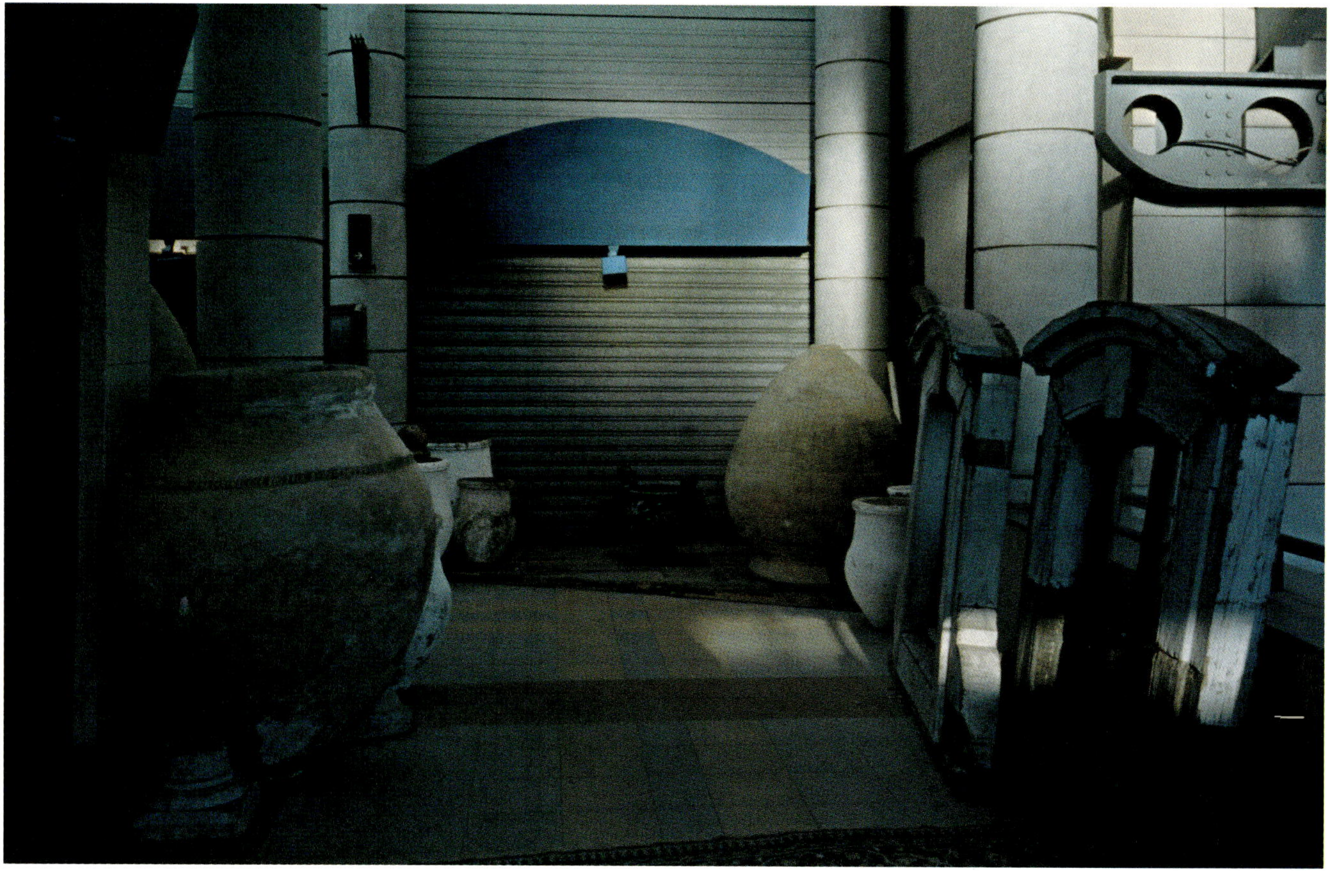

Saturday, January 30. Paris. Saint-Ouen Flea Market

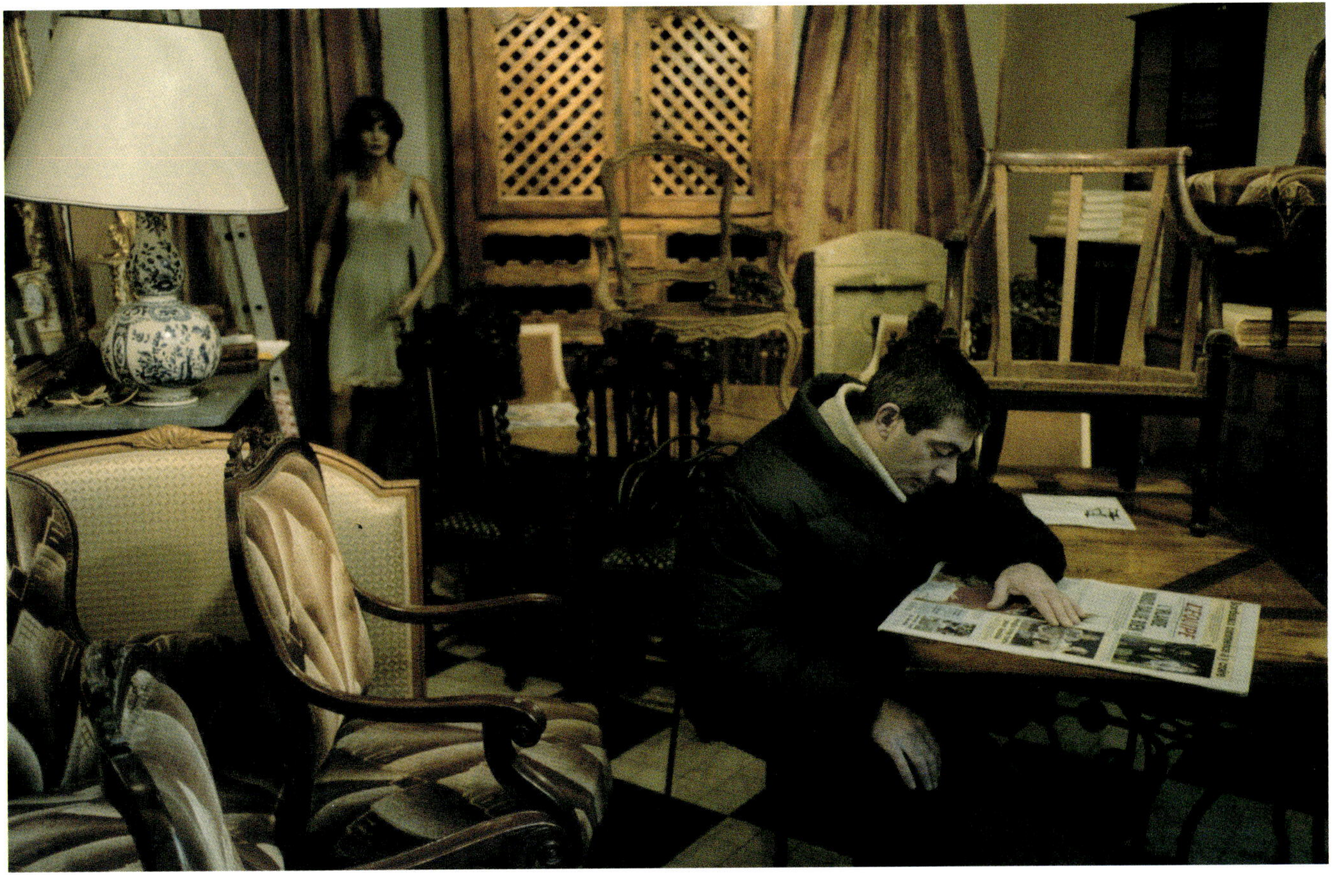

Saturday, January 30. Paris. Saint-Ouen Flea Market

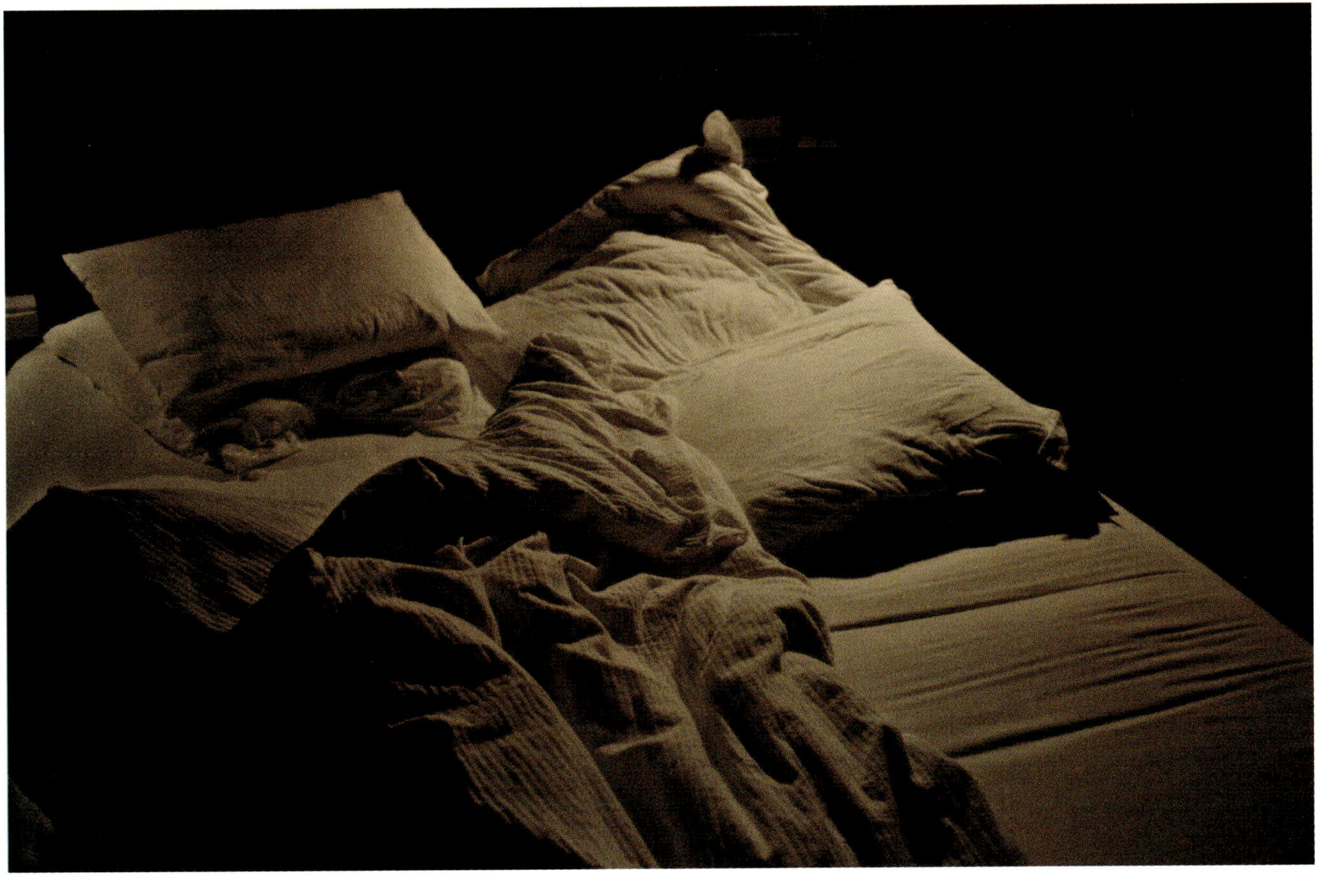

Sunday, January 31. Boulogne, France. First photograph in the morning

FEBRUARY

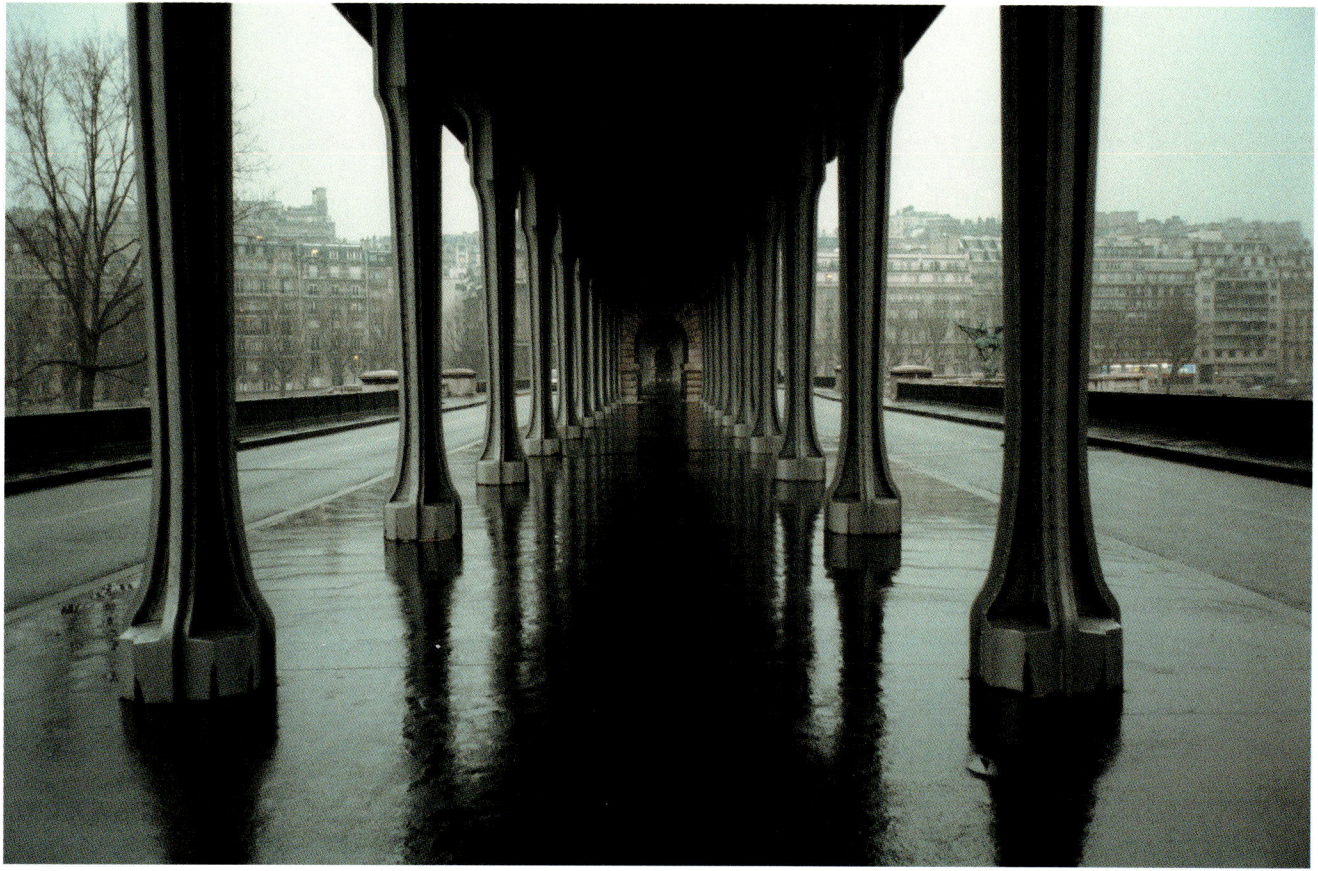

Monday, February 1. Paris. Bir Hakeim Bridge

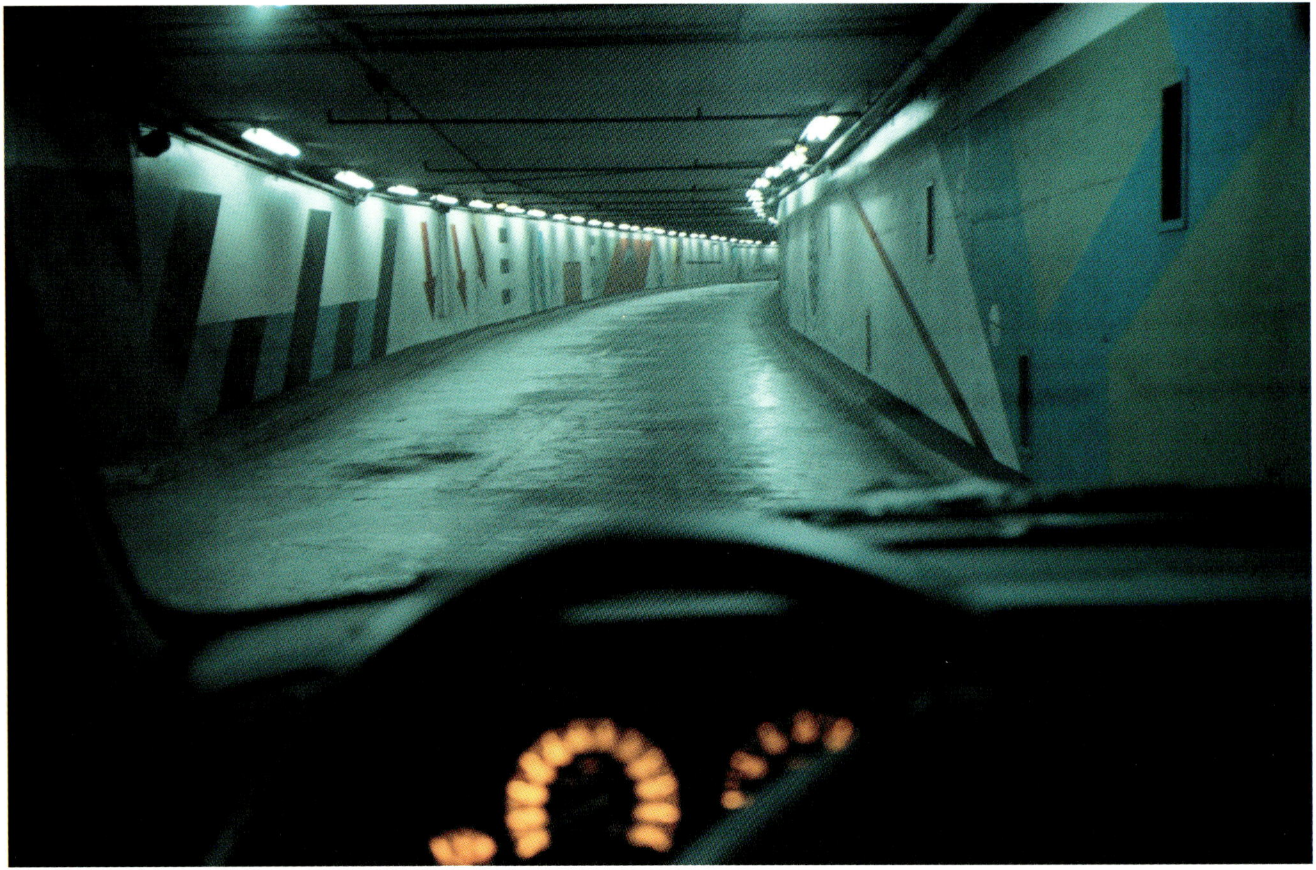

Tuesday, February 2. Paris. Entrance to underground car park, La Défense

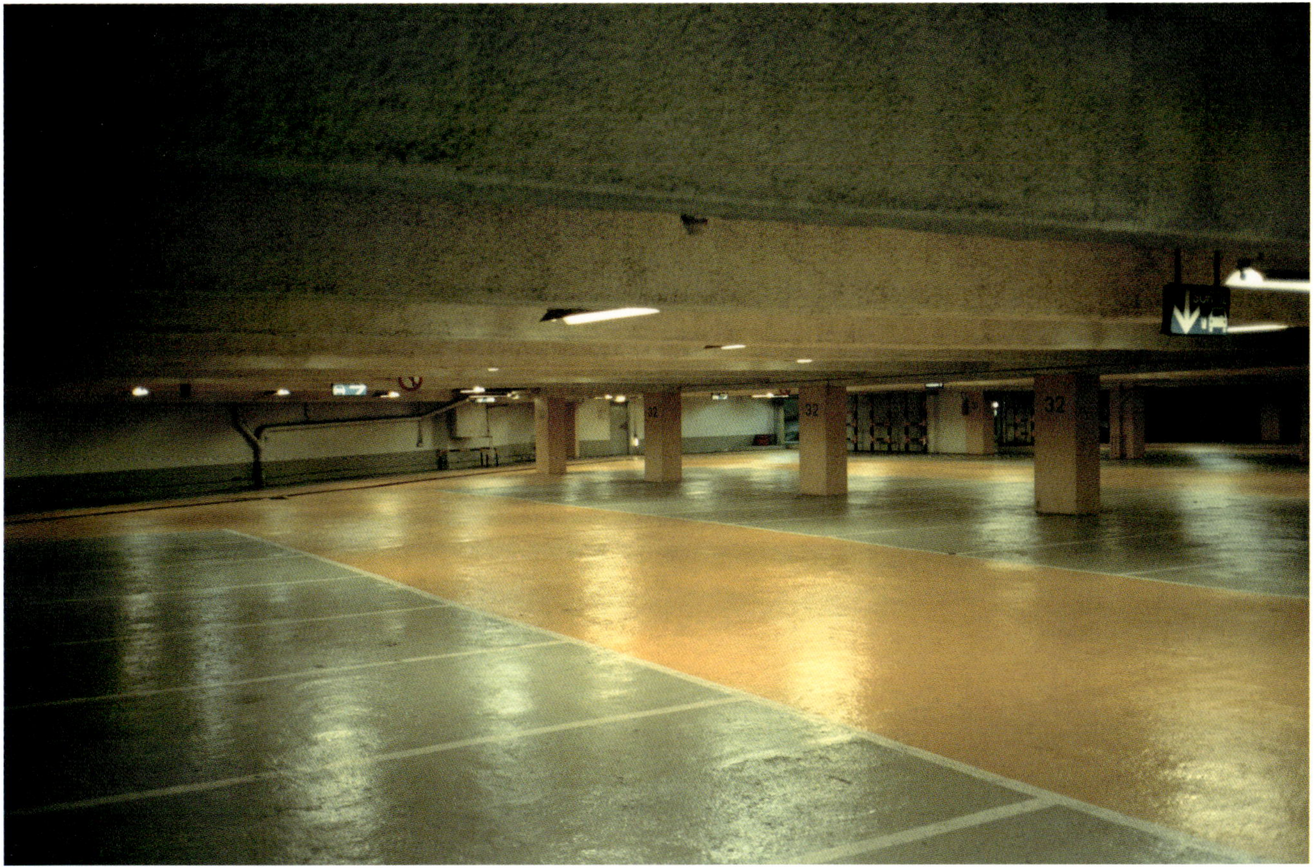

Tuesday, February 2. Paris. Underground car park, La Défense

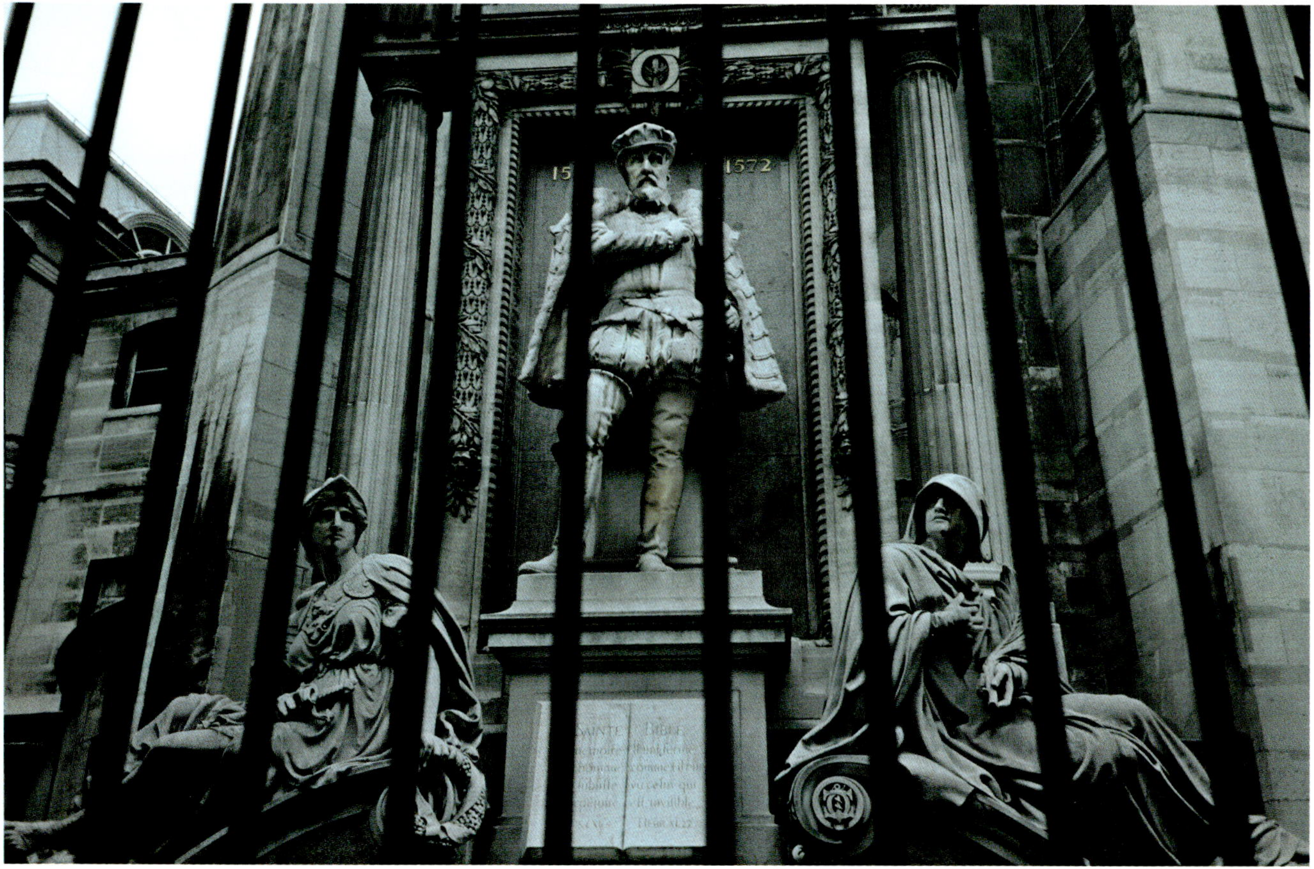

Wednesday, February 3. Paris. Rue de Rivoli, 'Amiral de Coligny' monument

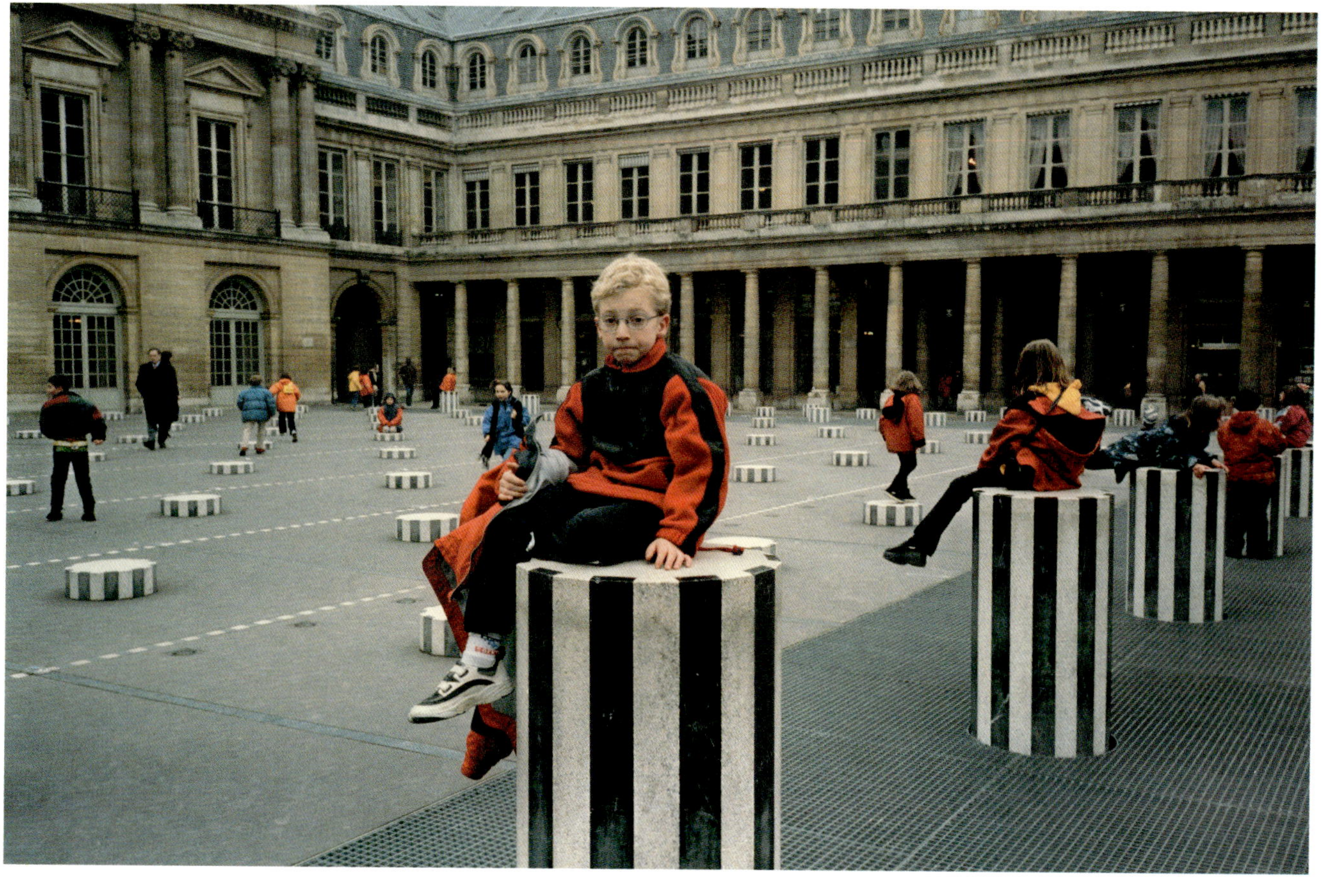

Thursday, February 4. Paris. The Buren columns at Palais Royal

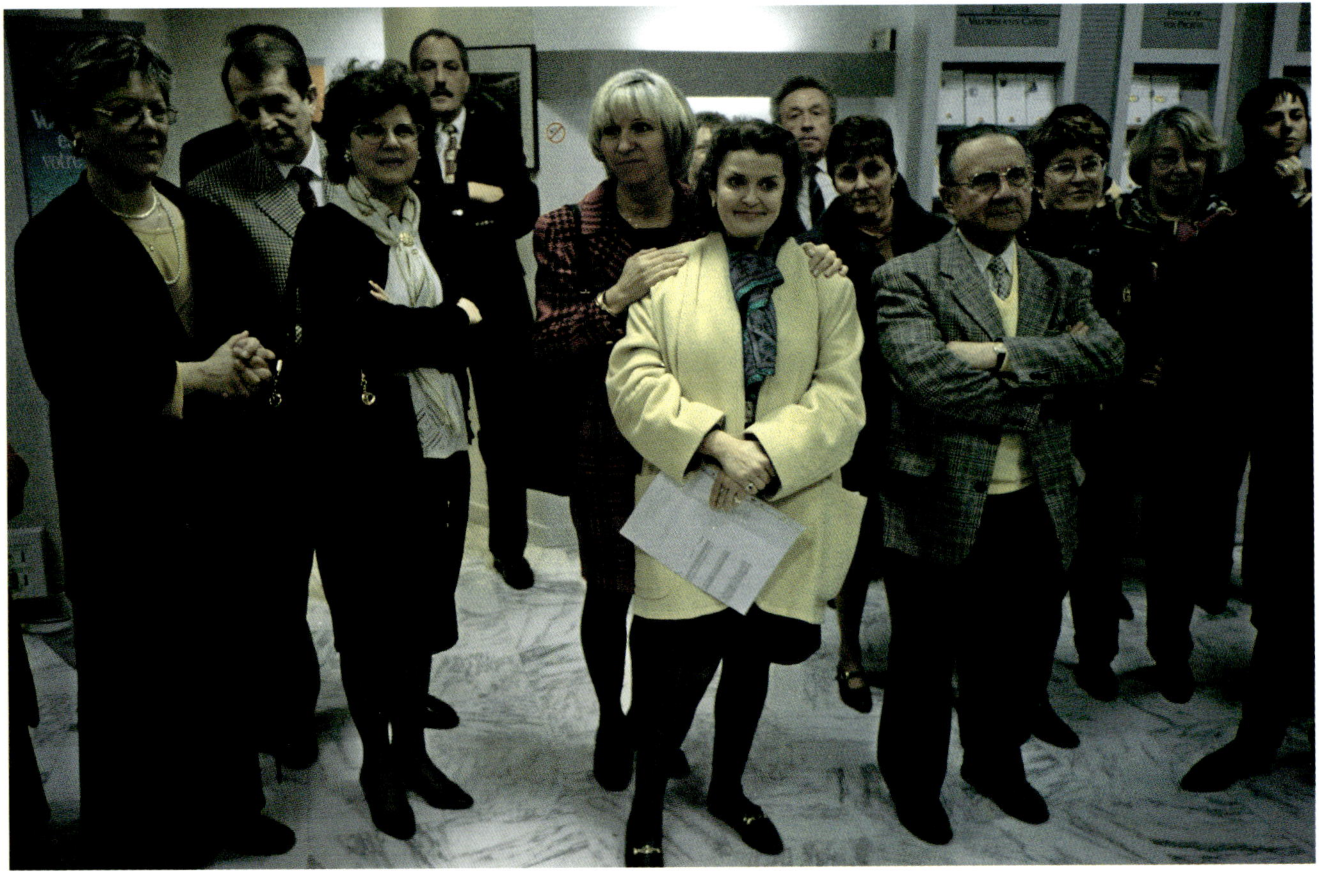

Friday, February 5. Libourne, France. Opening of my photo exhibition, on the premises of Société Générale

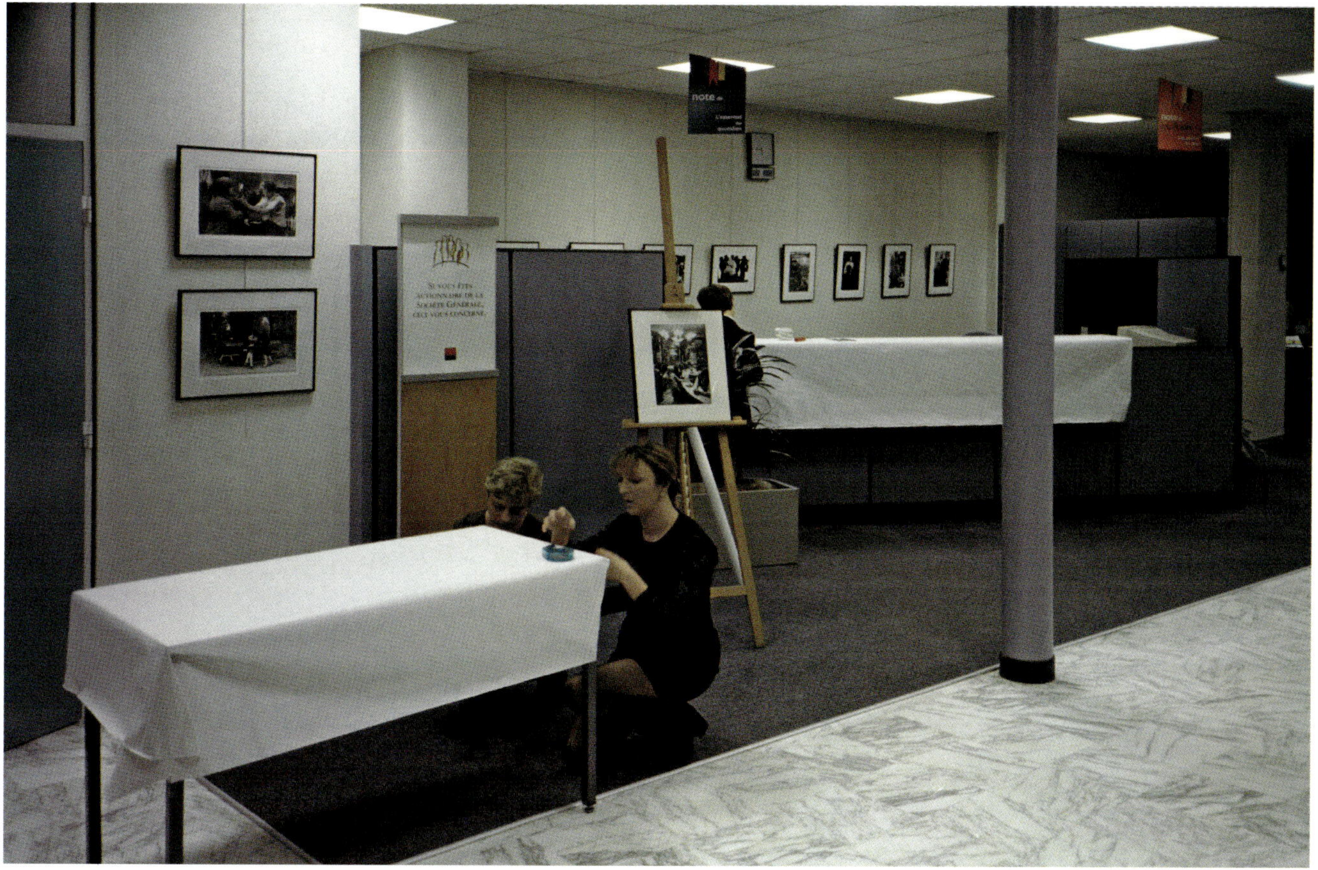

Friday, February 5. Libourne, France.

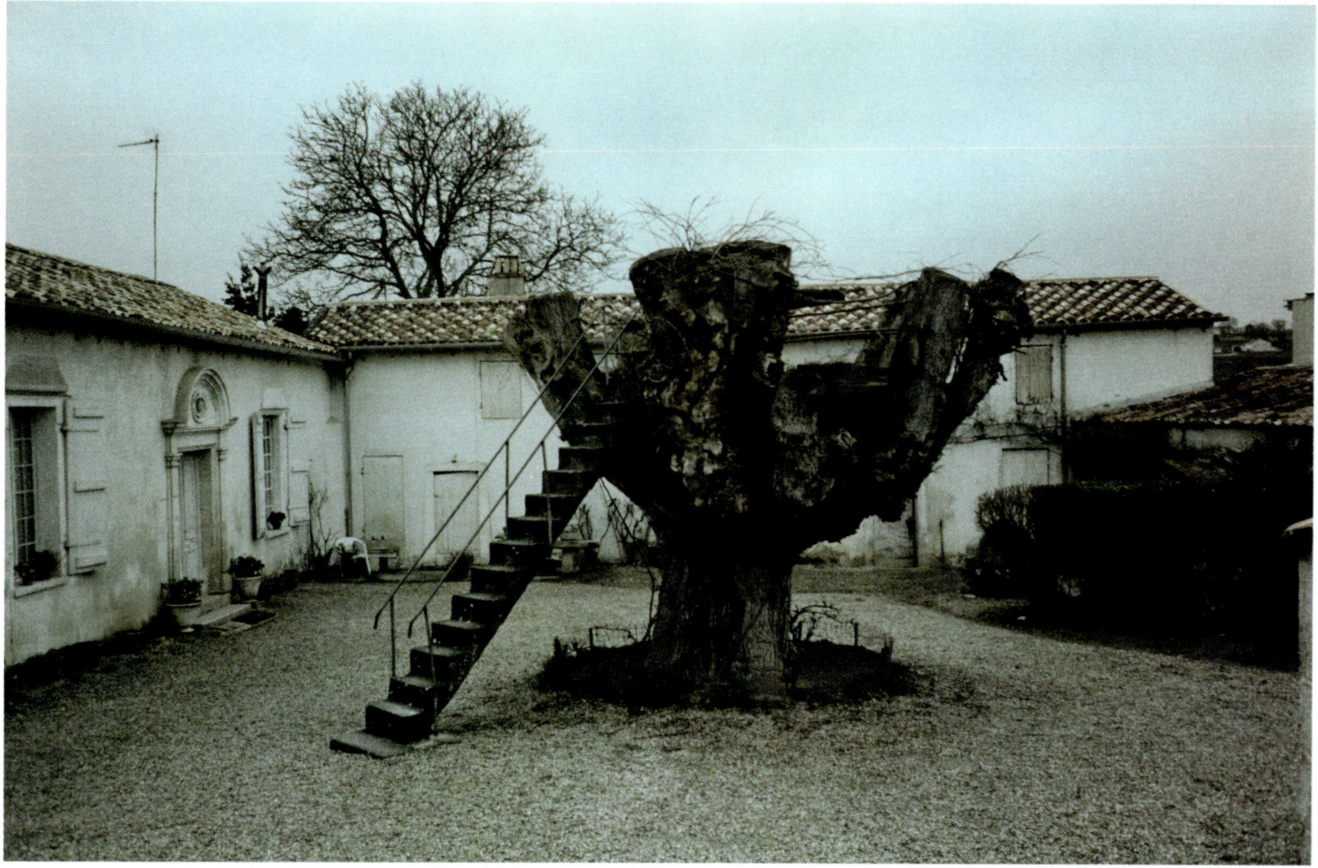

Saturday, February 6. Saint-Michel de Fronsac, France. Farmyard

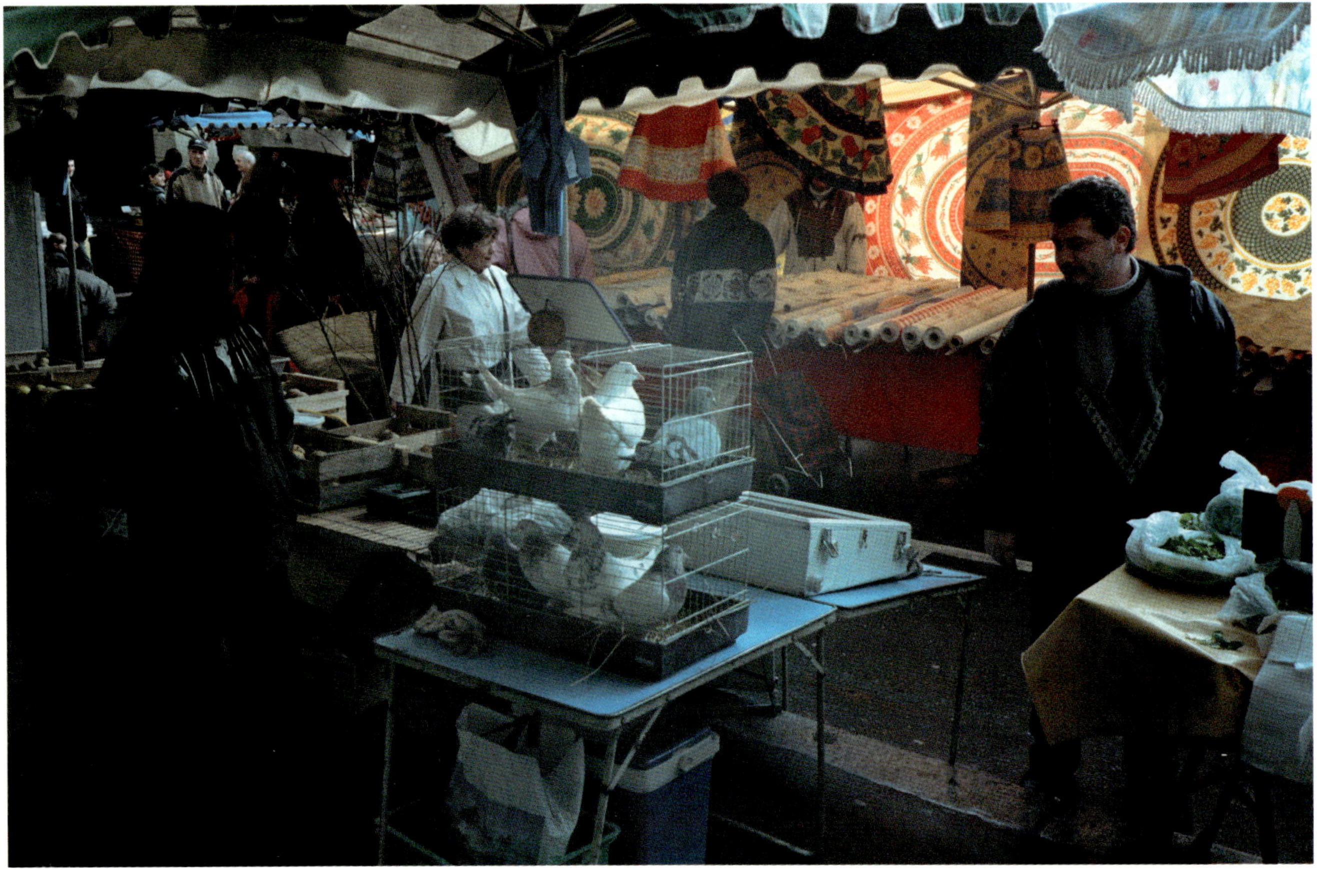

Sunday, February 7. Libourne, France. The market

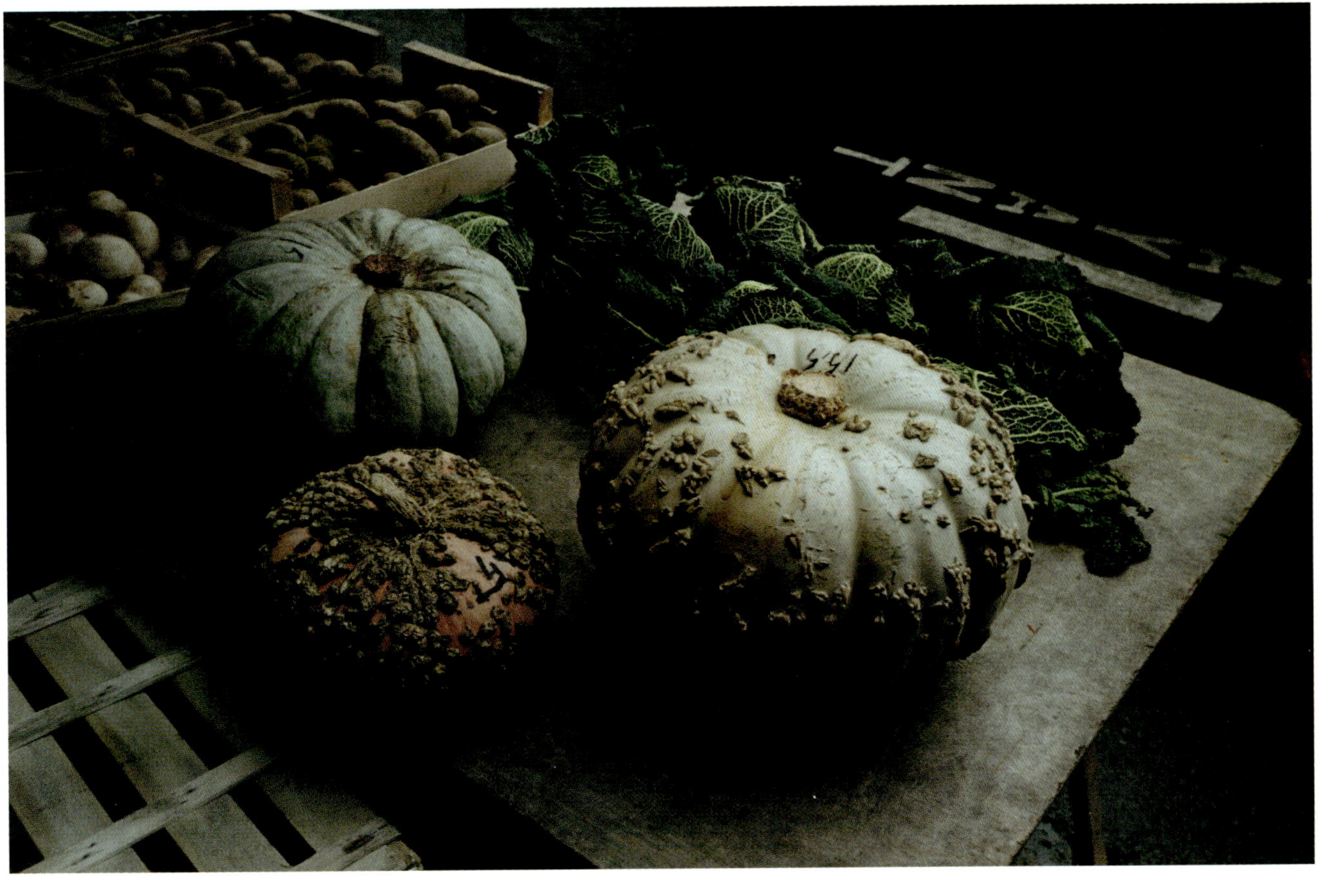

Sunday, February 7. Libourne, France. Still life at the market

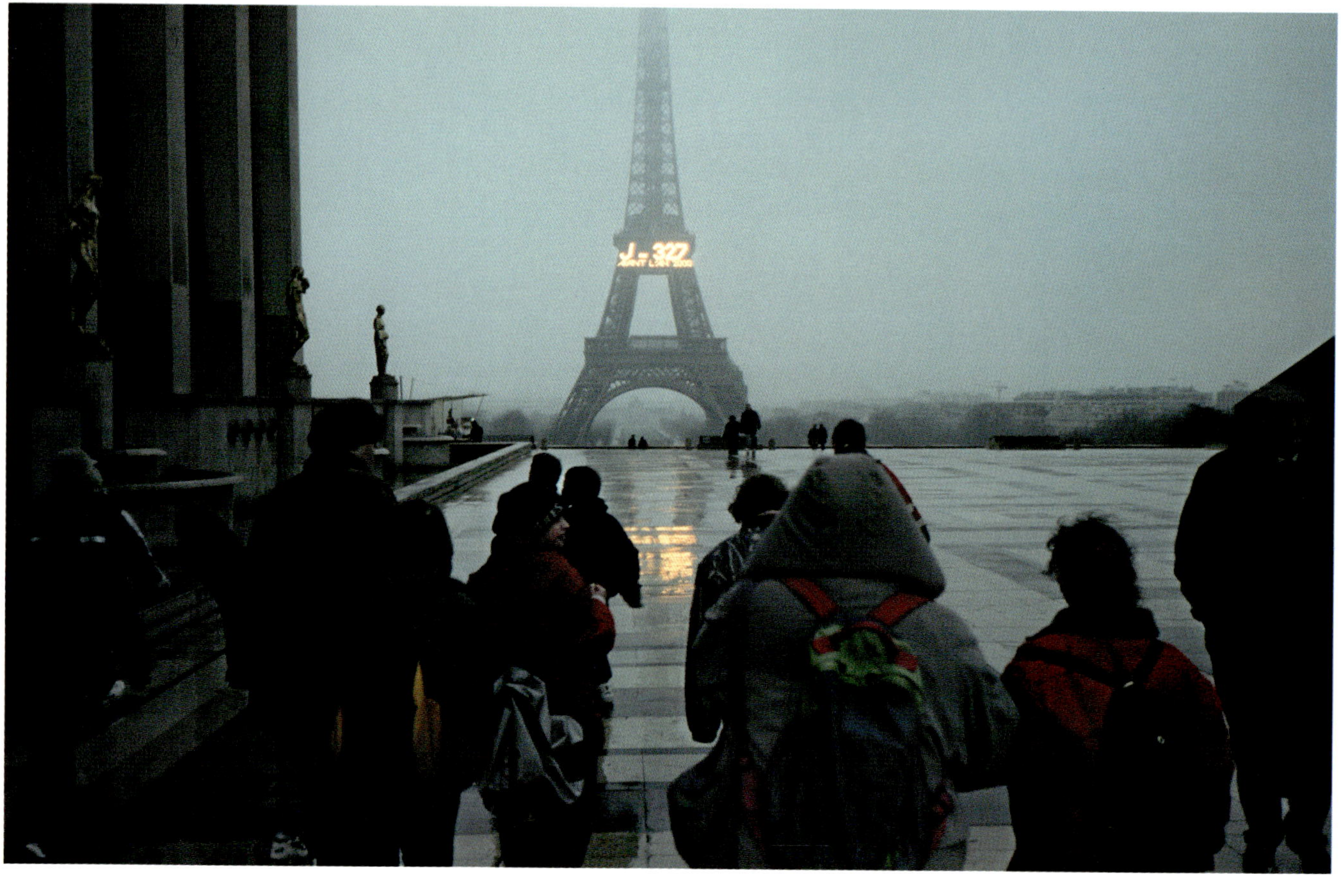

Monday, February 8. Paris. Trocadero: the sign on the Eiffel Tower says "327 more days before the year 2000"

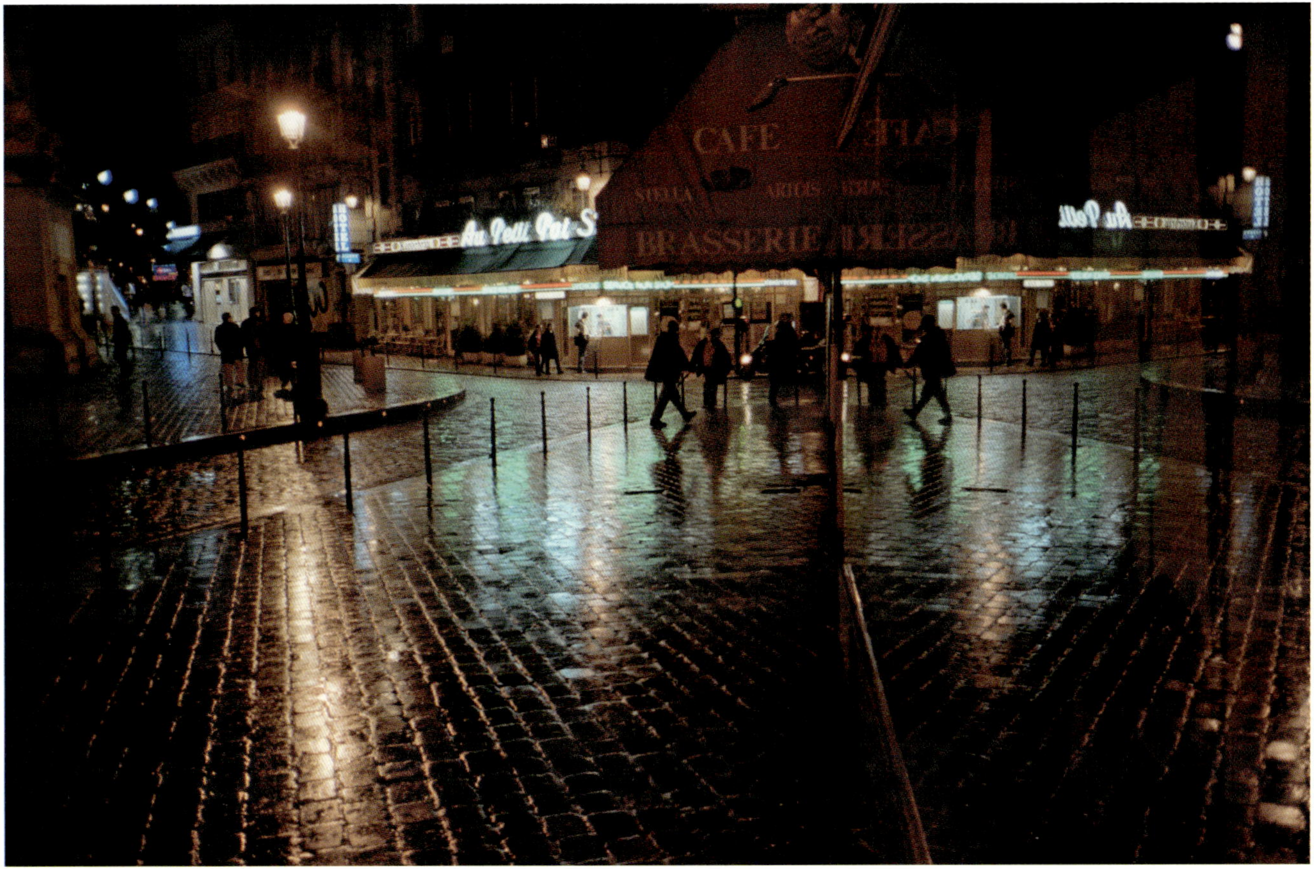

Tuesday, February 9. Paris. Porte Saint Denis

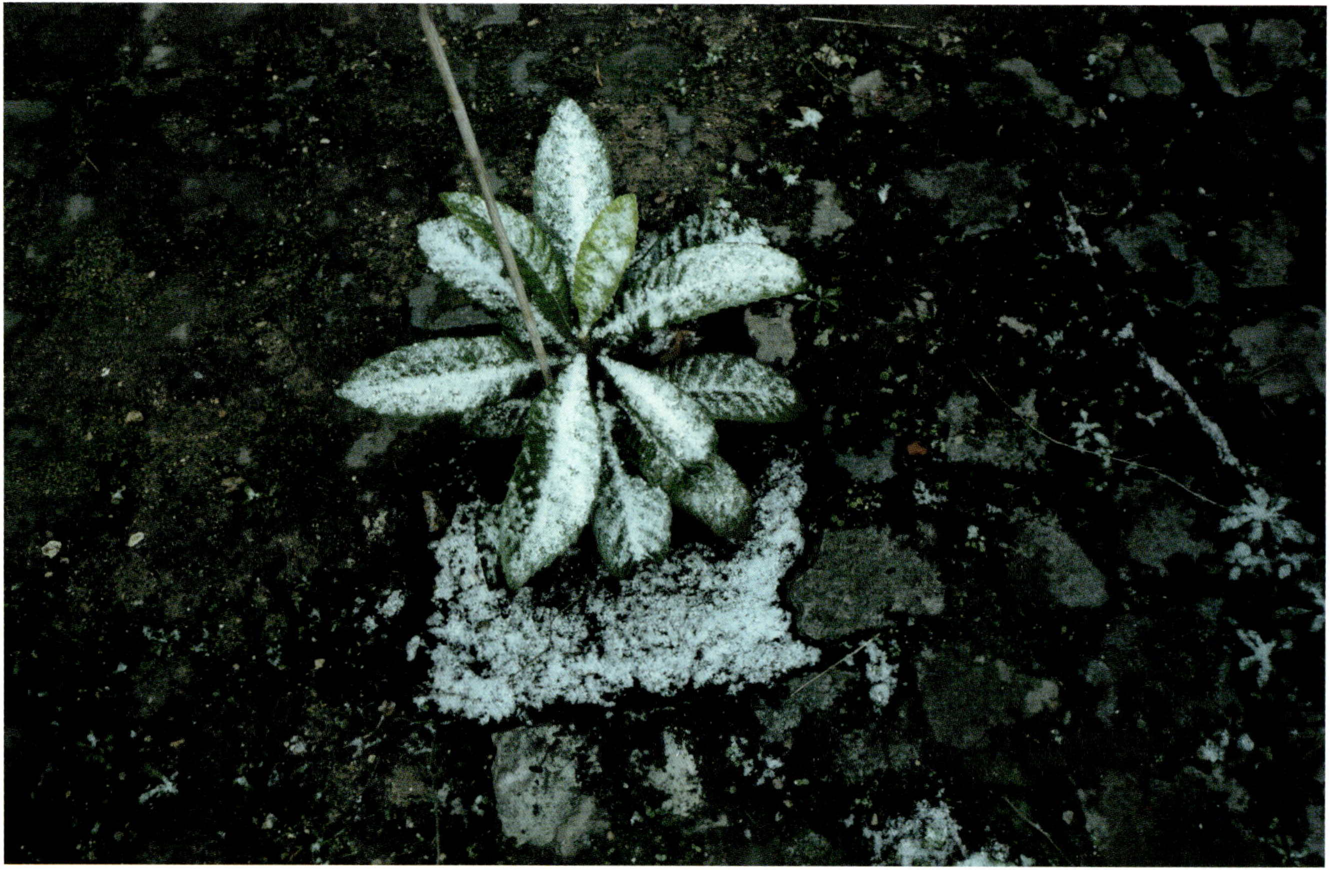

Wednesday, February 10. Boulogne, France. Young Medlar tree in my yard

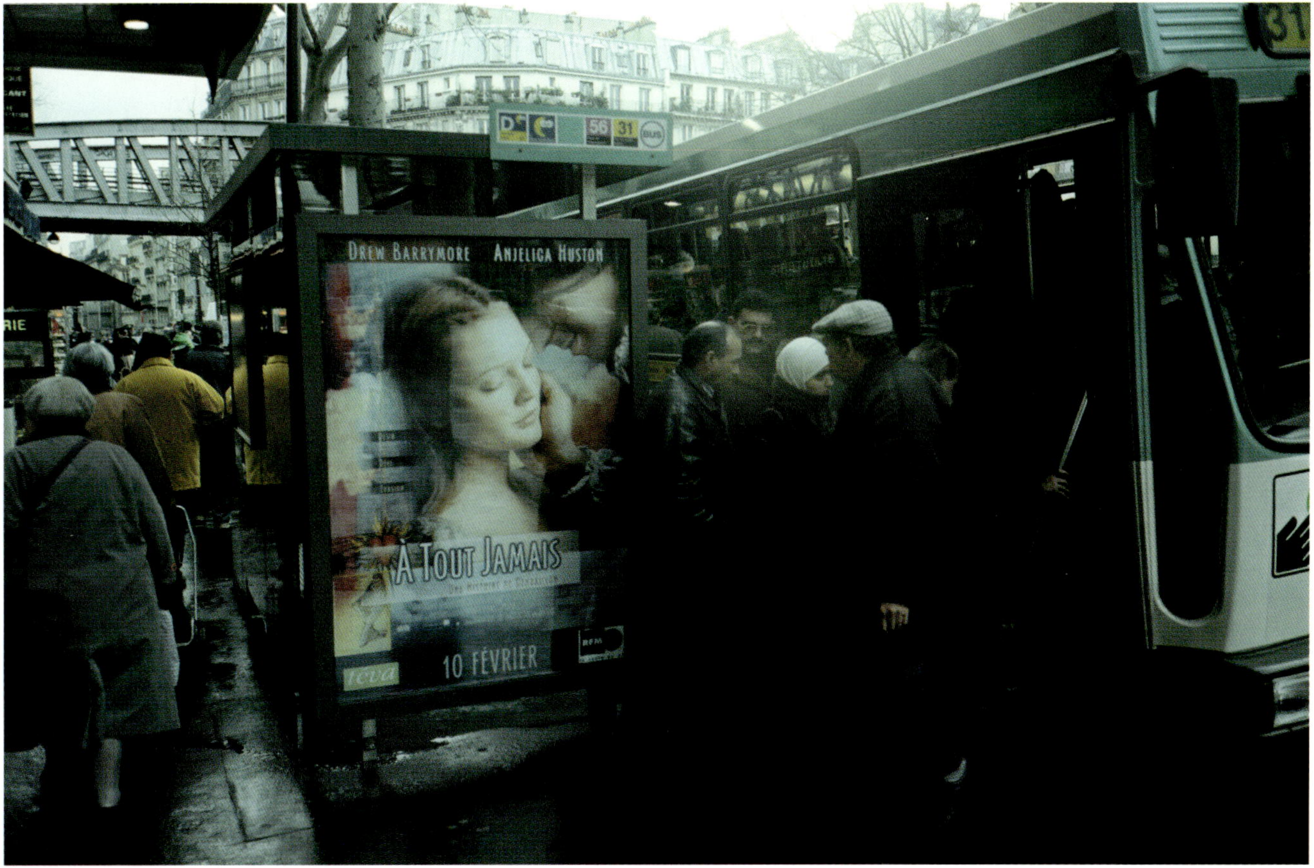

Wednesday, February 10. Paris. Boulevard Barbès (Gare du Nord area)

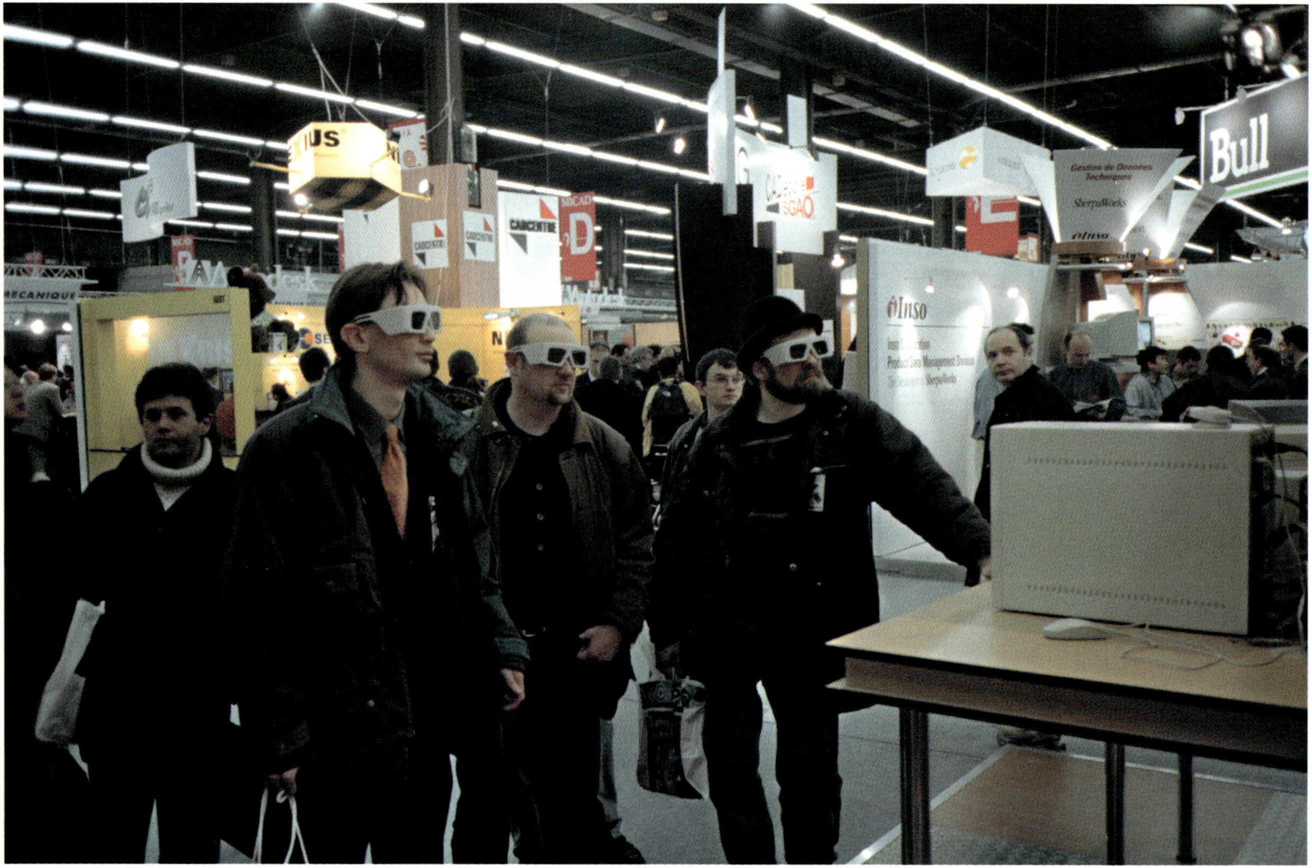

Thursday, February 11. Paris. Computer show, Porte de Versailles

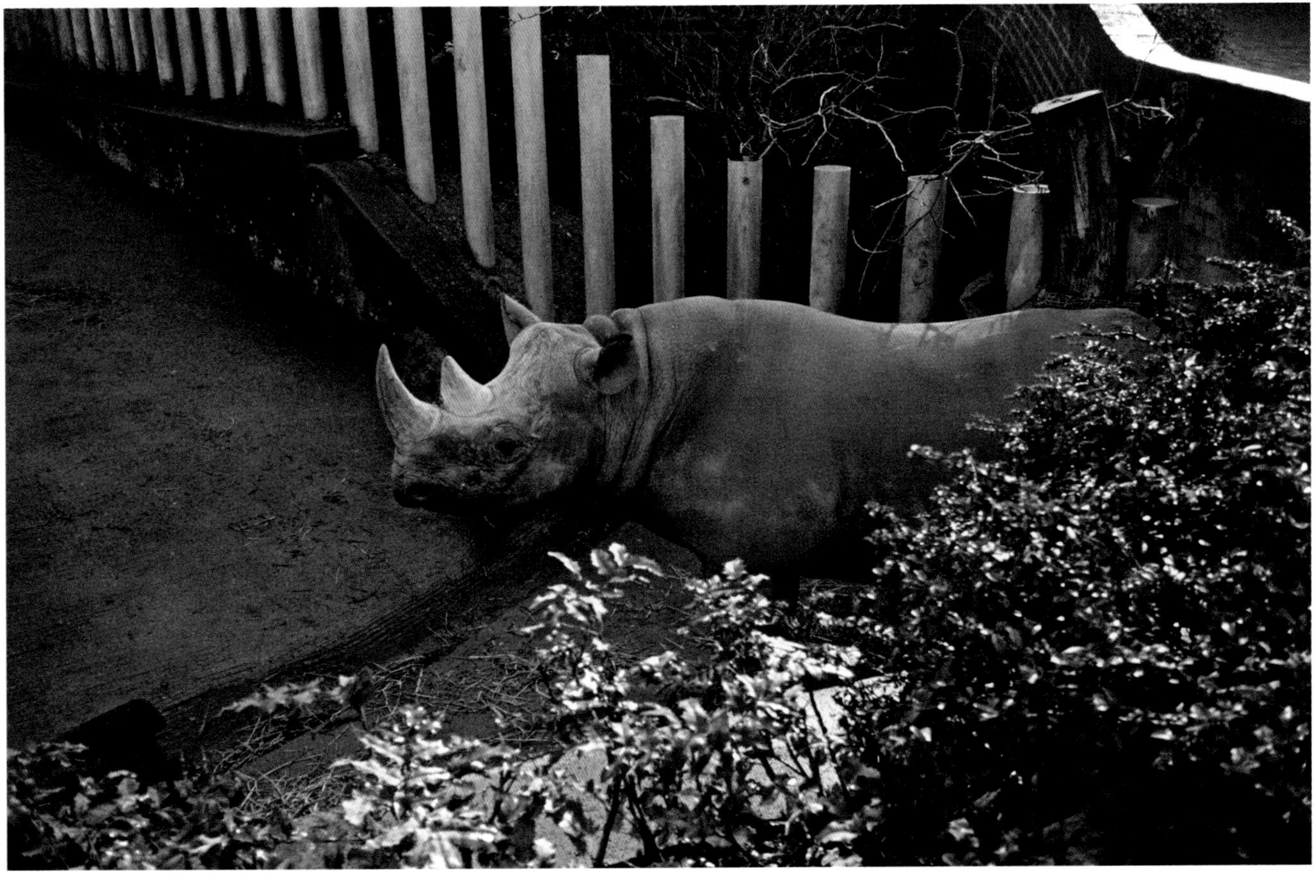

Friday, February 12. London. At the Regent's Park Zoo

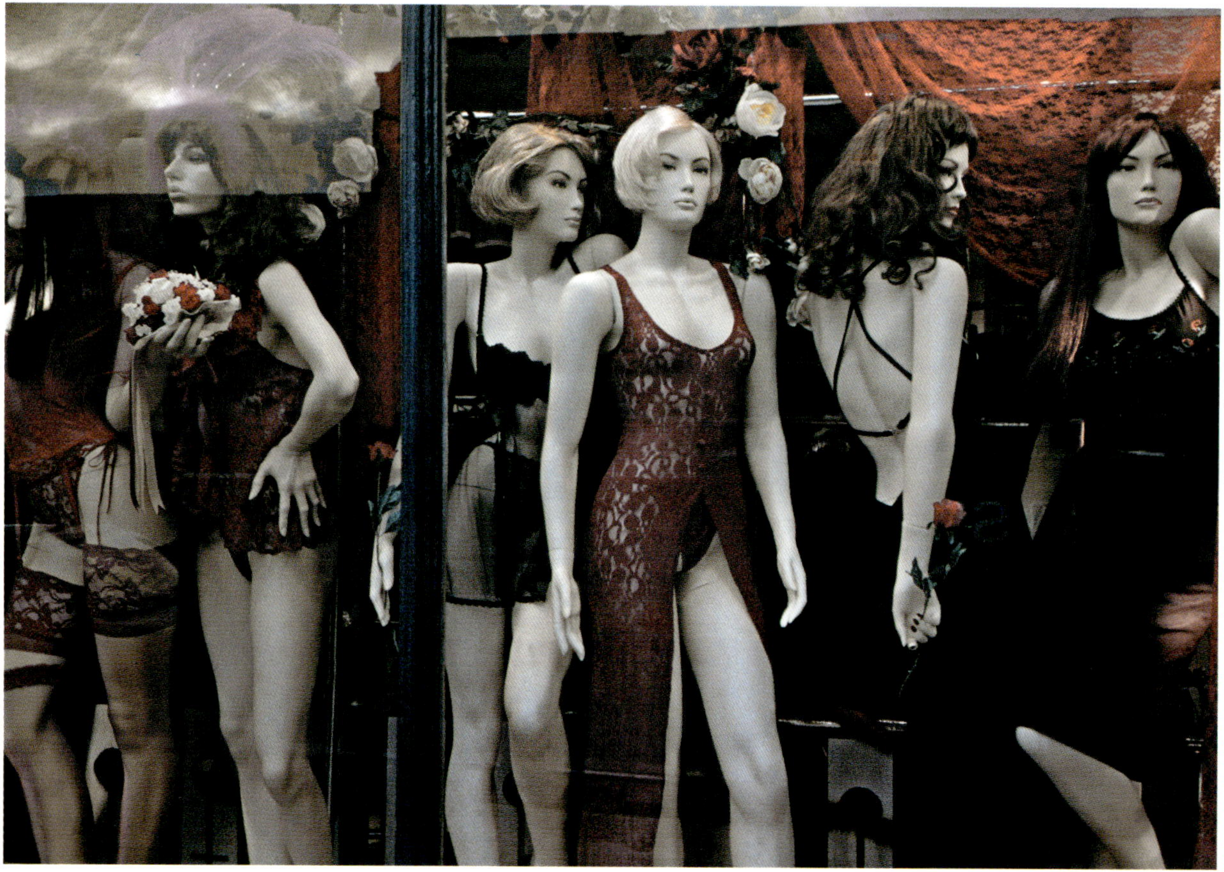

Saturday, February 13. London. Shop window in Camden Town

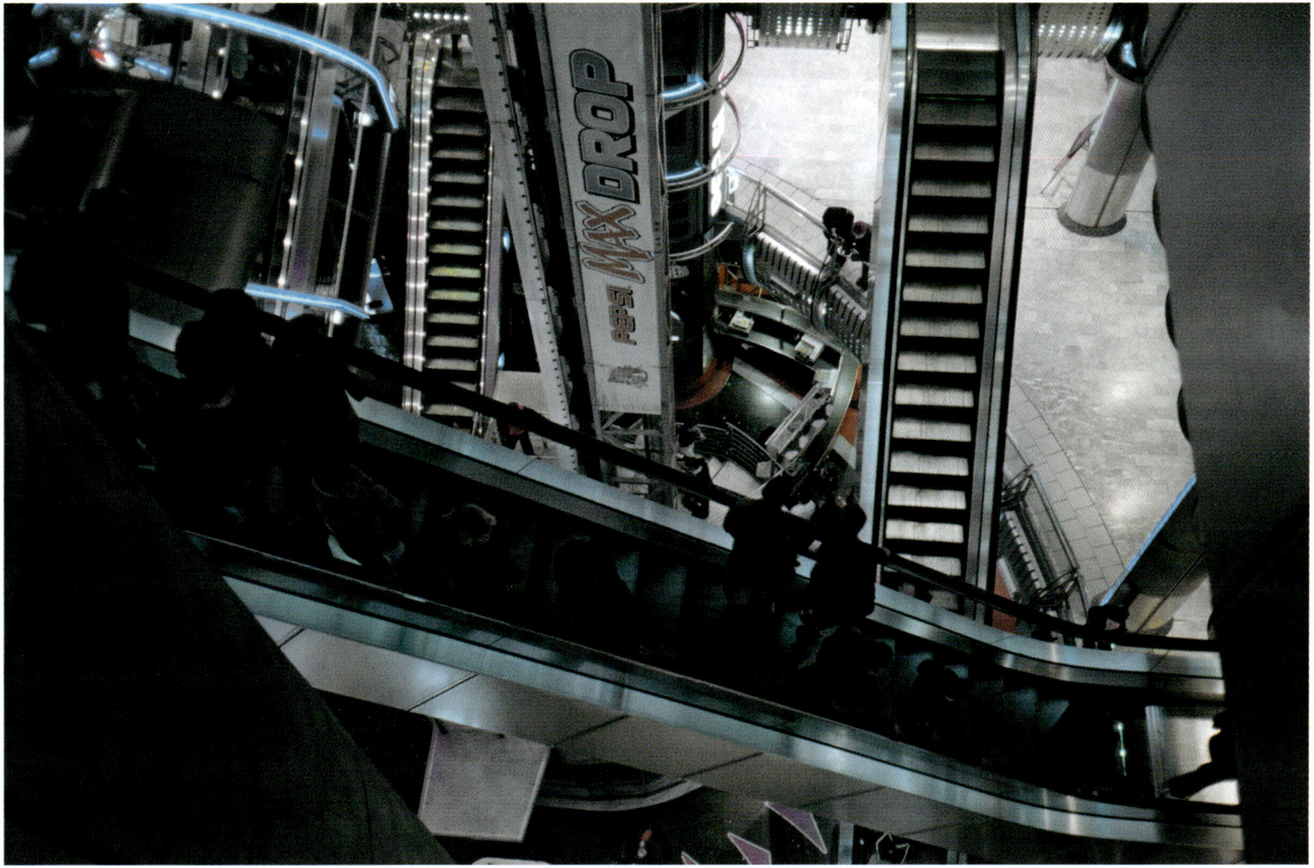

Sunday, February 14. London. Sega World, Piccadilly

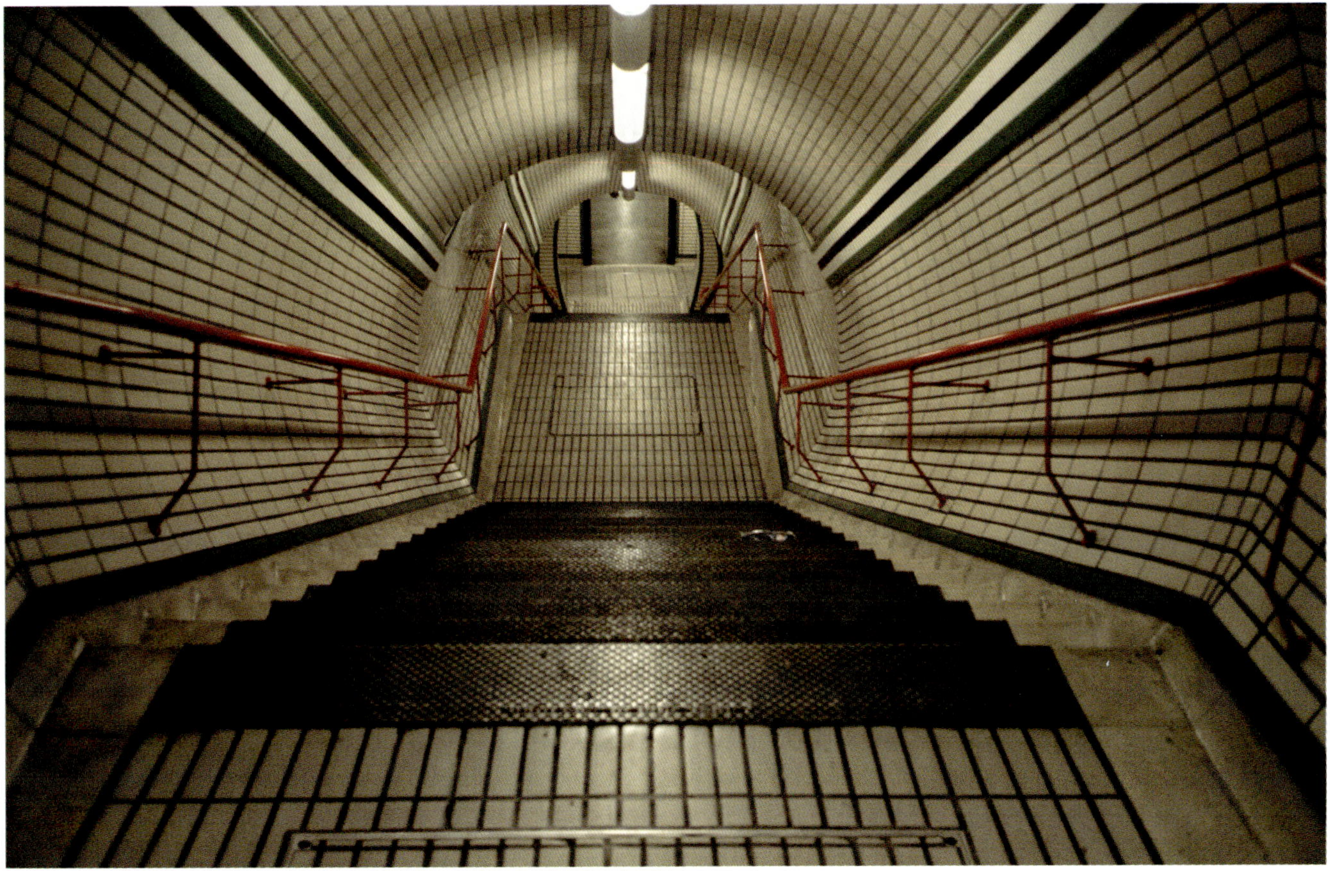

Monday, February 15. London. Stairs in an underground station

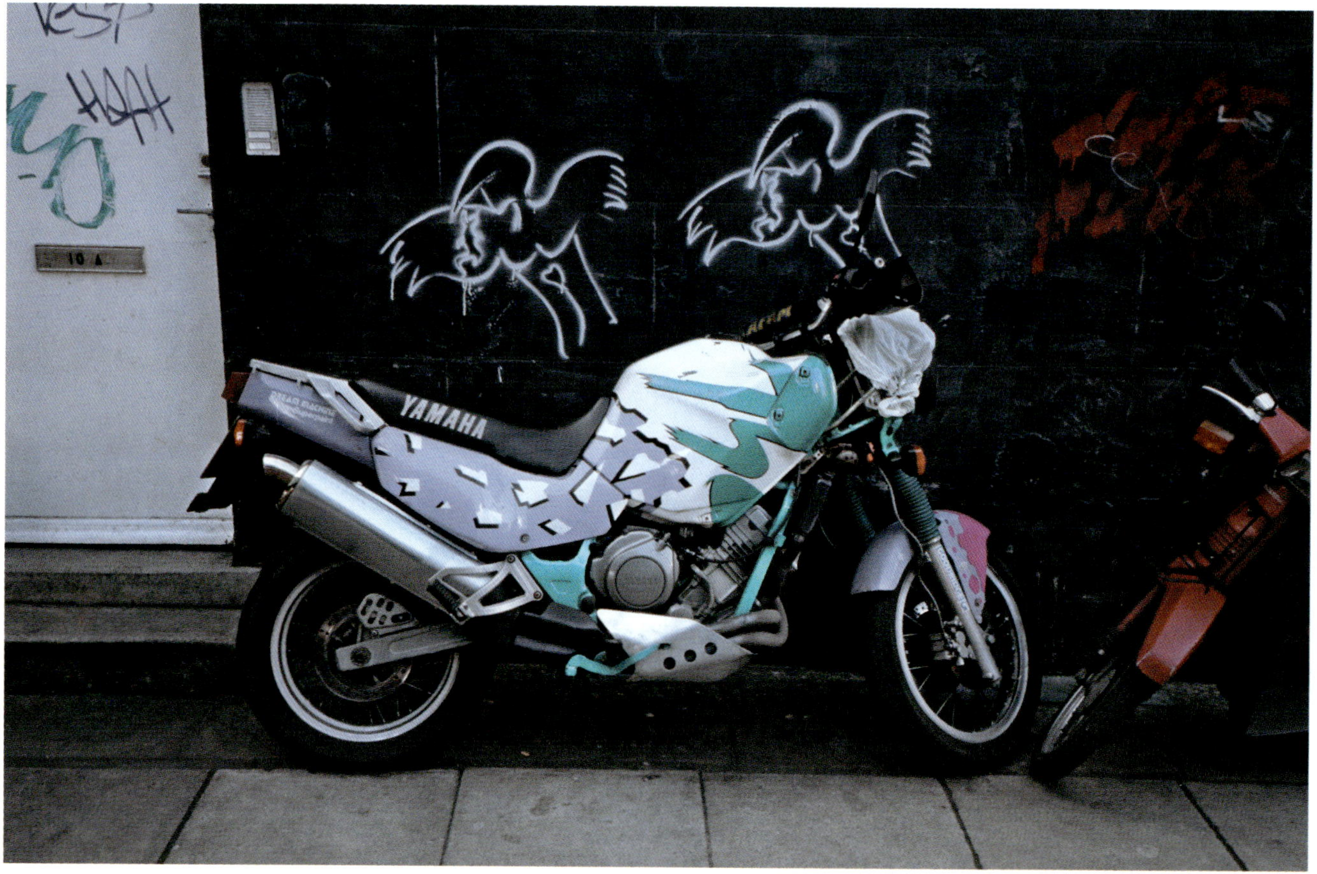

Tuesday, February 16. London. Camden Town

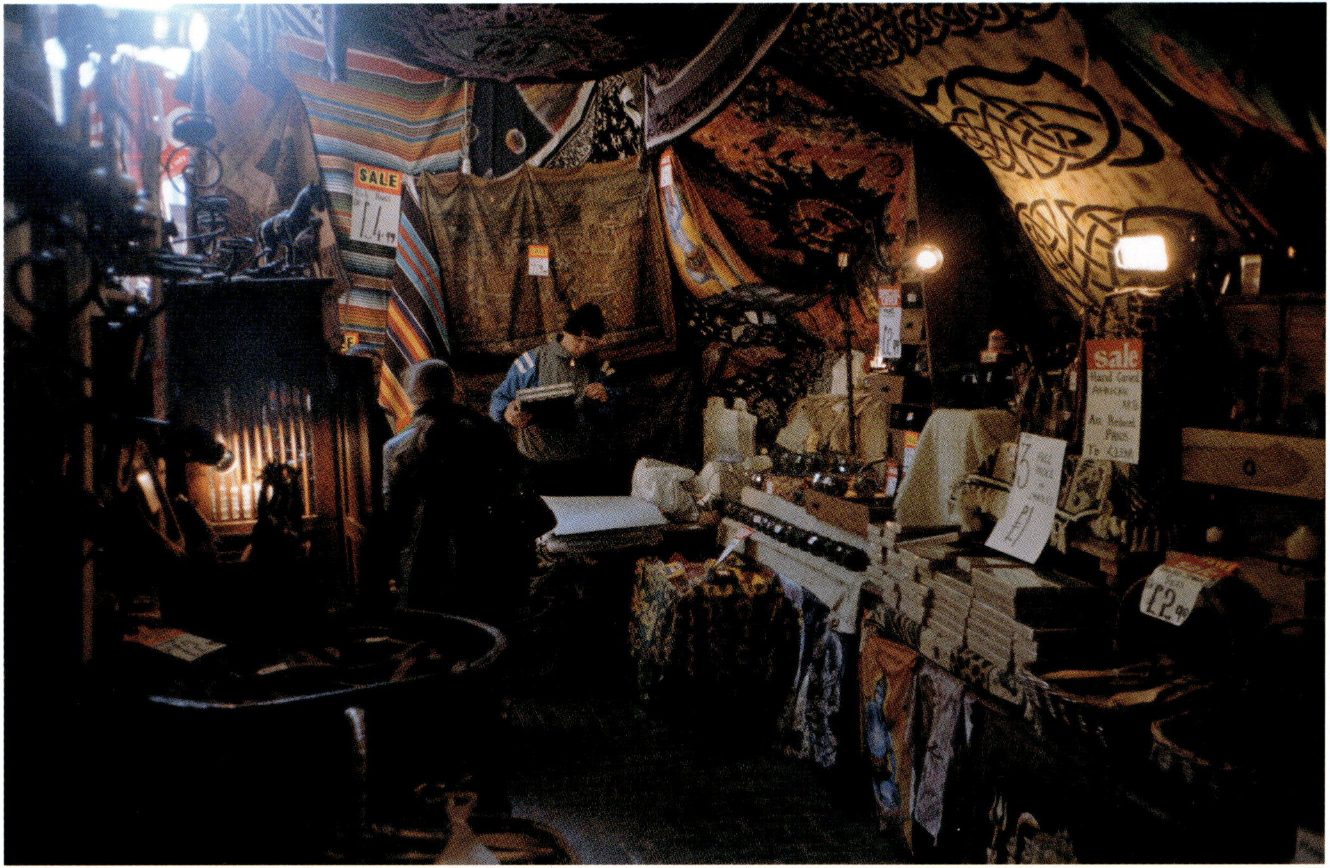

Tuesday, February 16. London. Shop in Camden Town

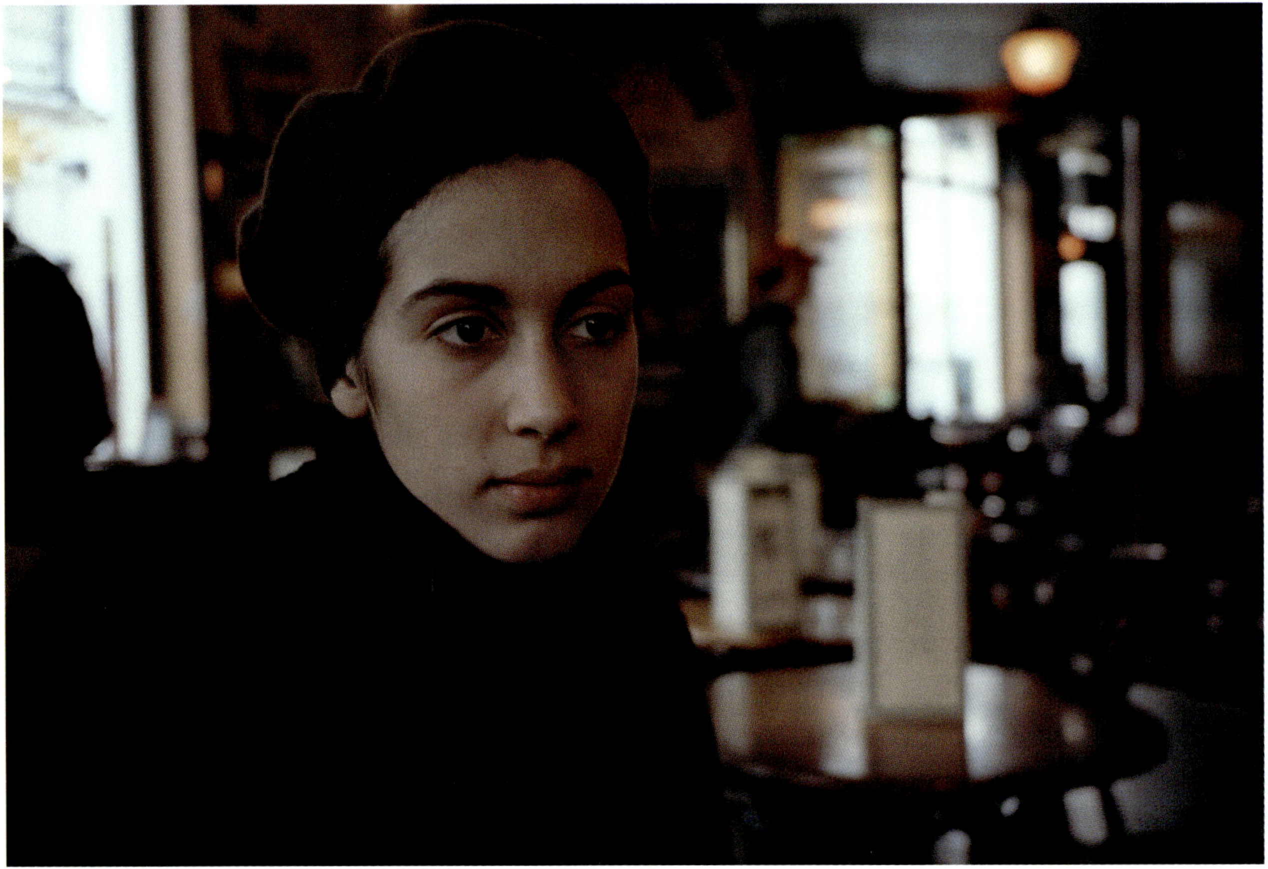

Wednesday, February 17. London. Sarah Fiammetta Horvat

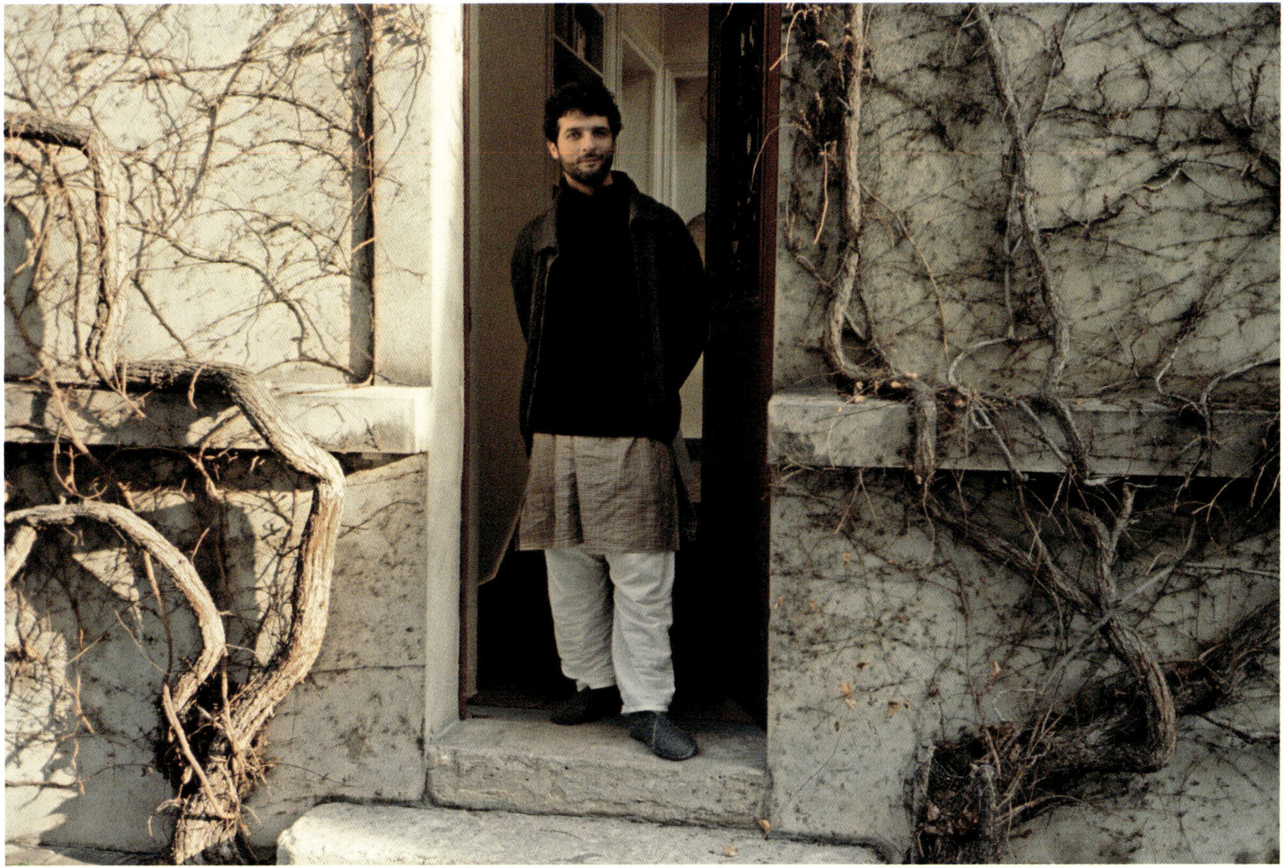

Thursday, February 18. Boulogne, France. Marco Horvat, on his return from India

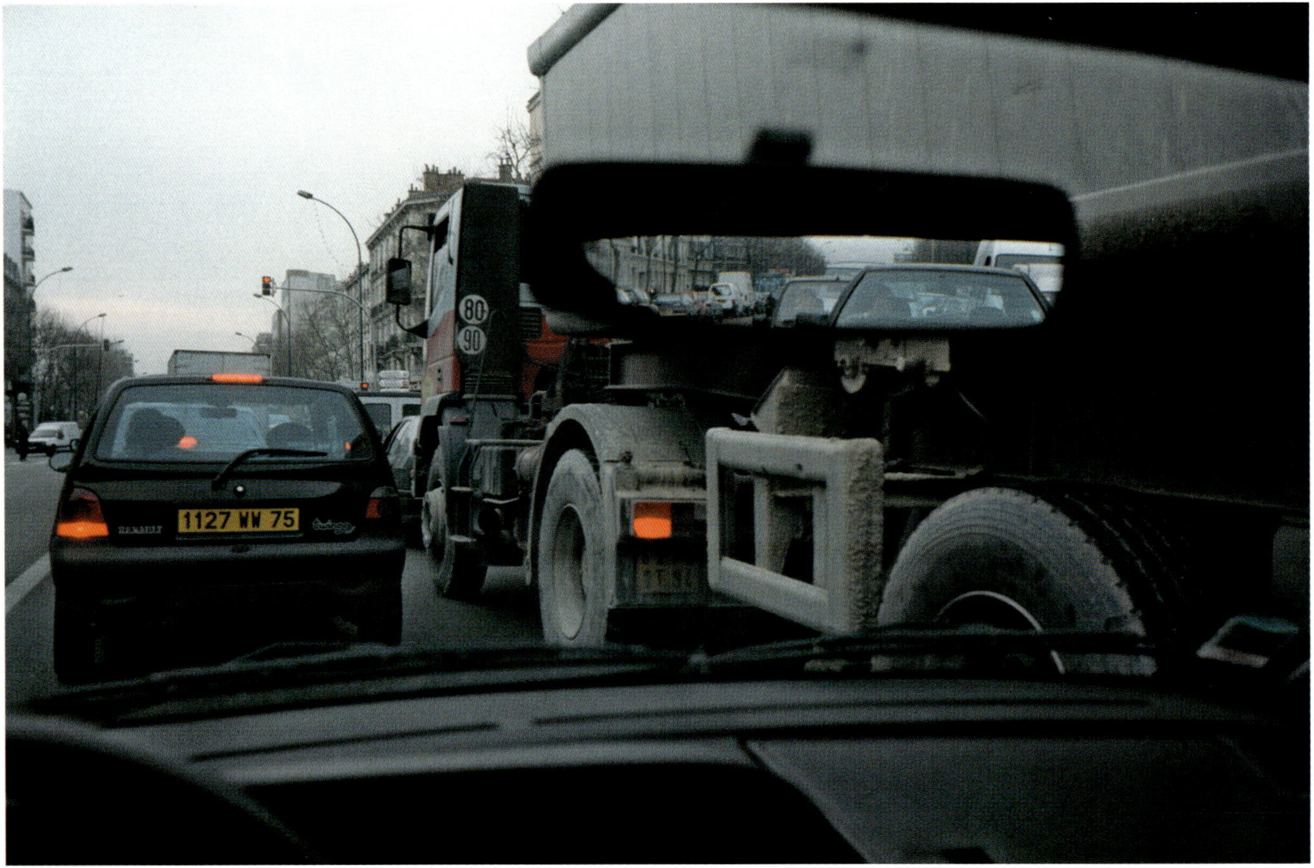

Friday, February 19. Boulogne, France. Route de la Reine

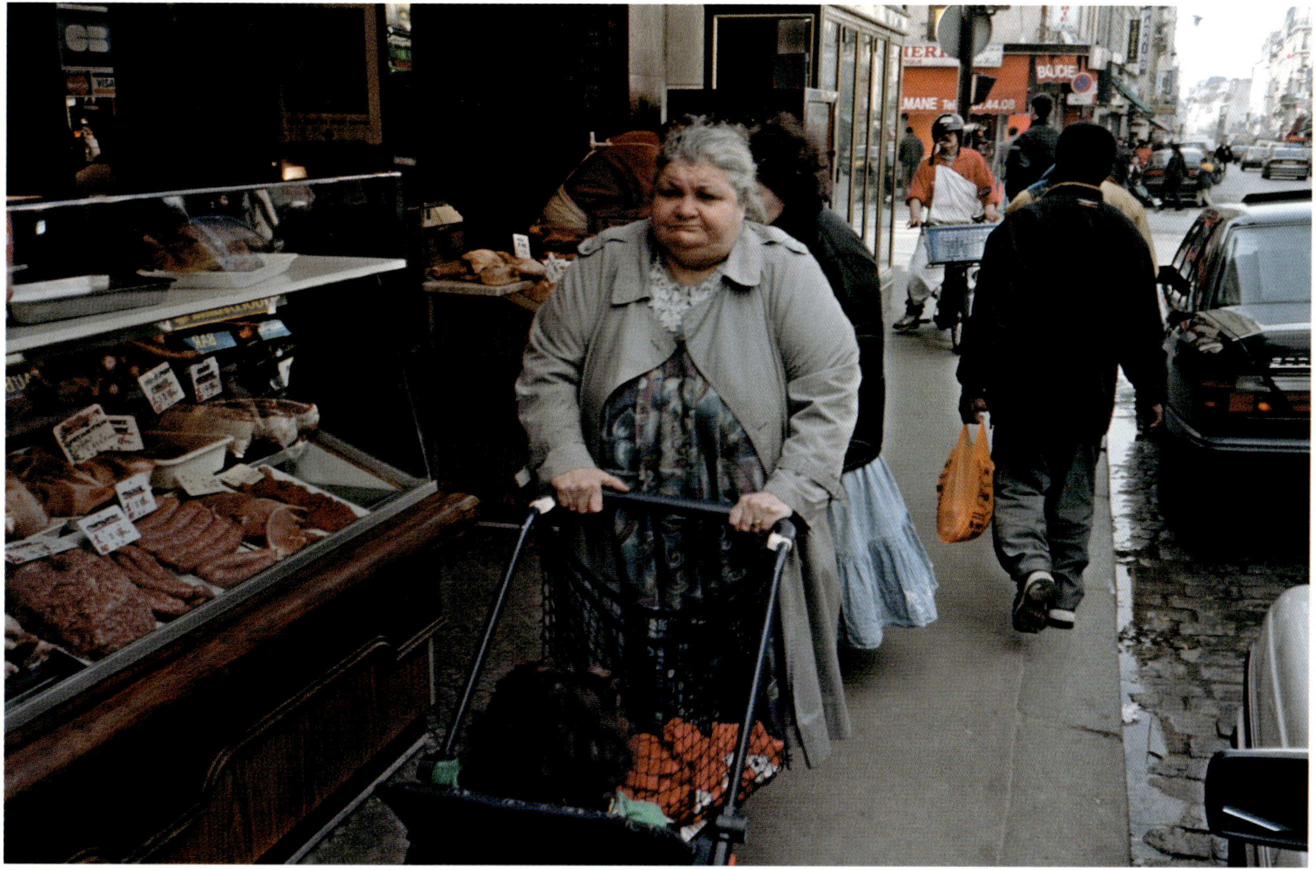

Saturday, February 20. Paris. Rue de Belleville

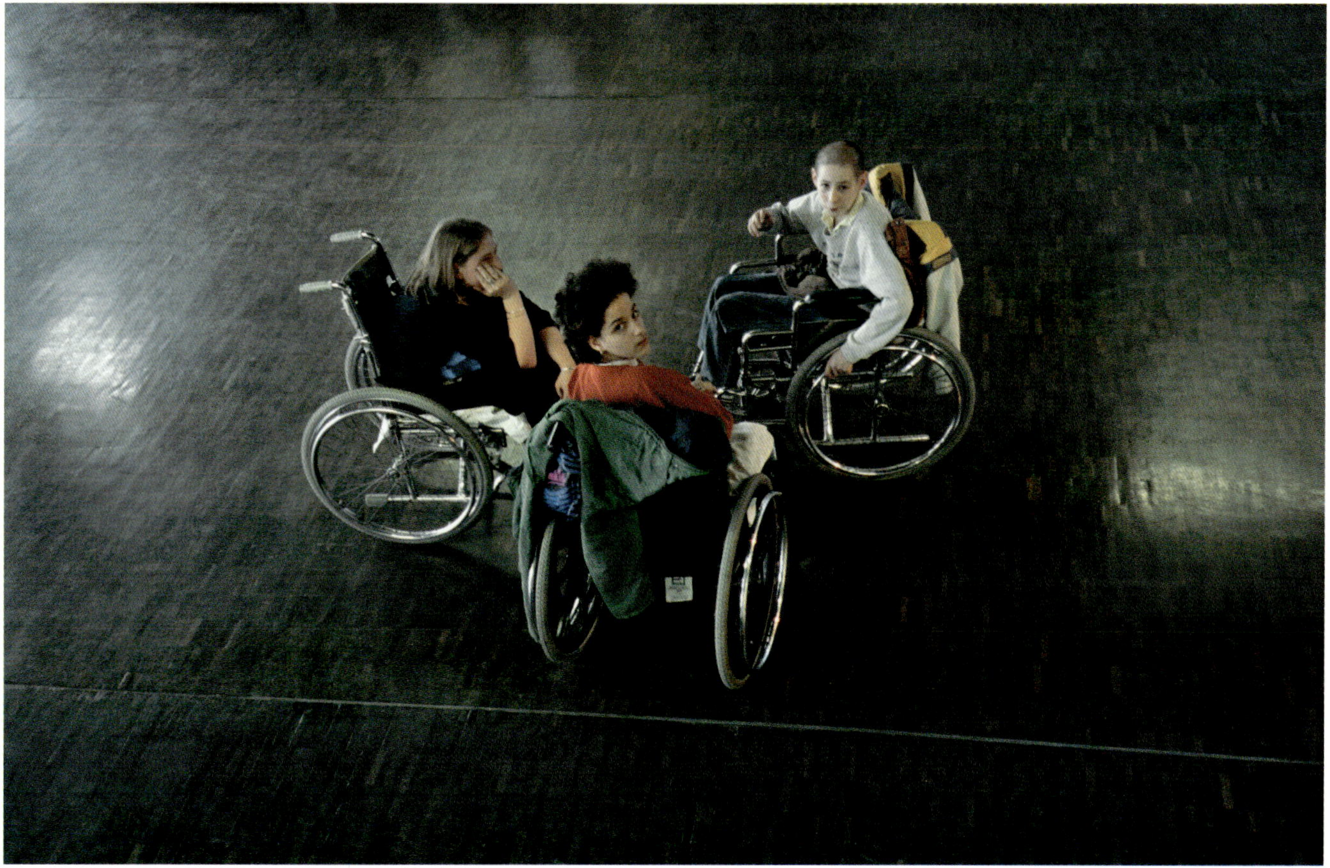

Sunday, February 21. Paris. At the Cité des Sciences museum

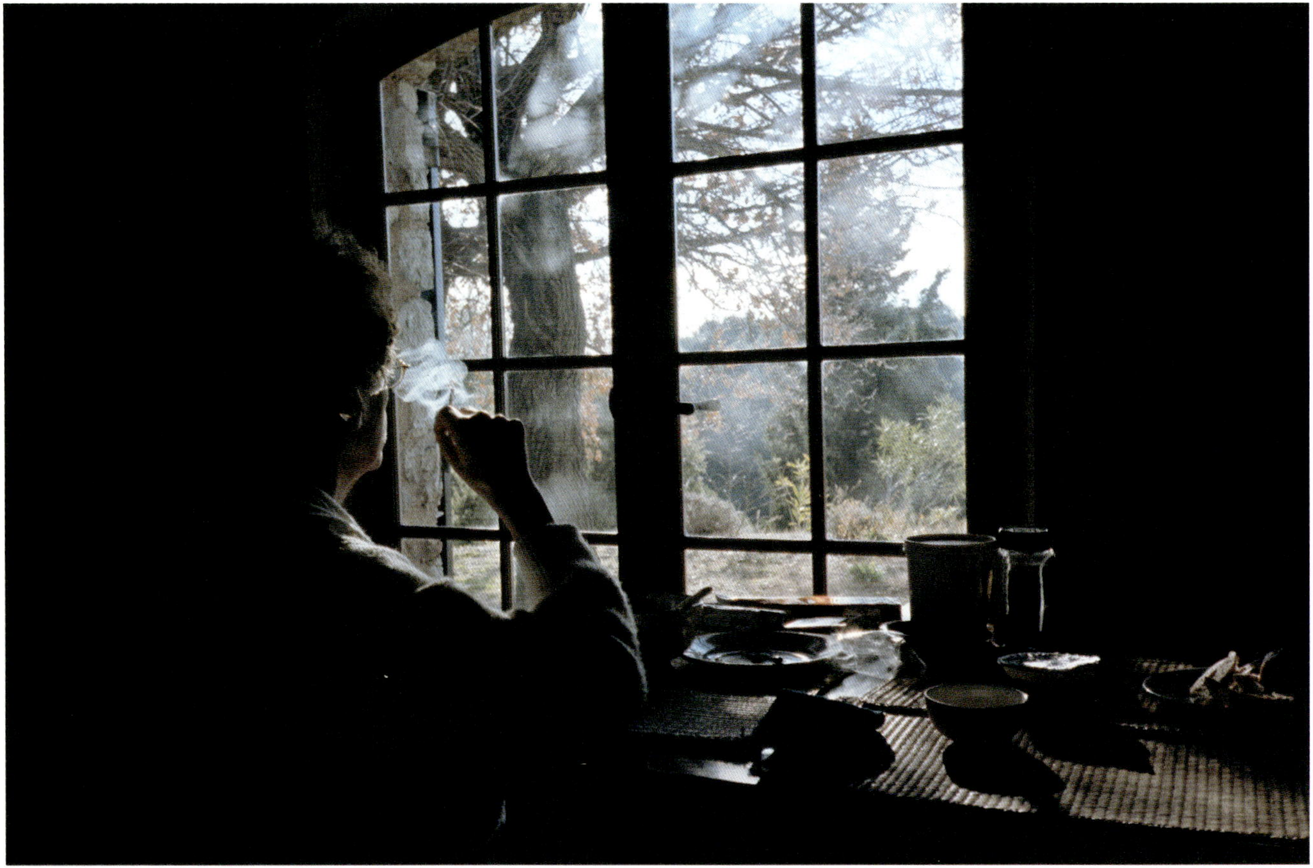

Monday, February 22. Cotignac, France. Breakfast at "La Véronique"

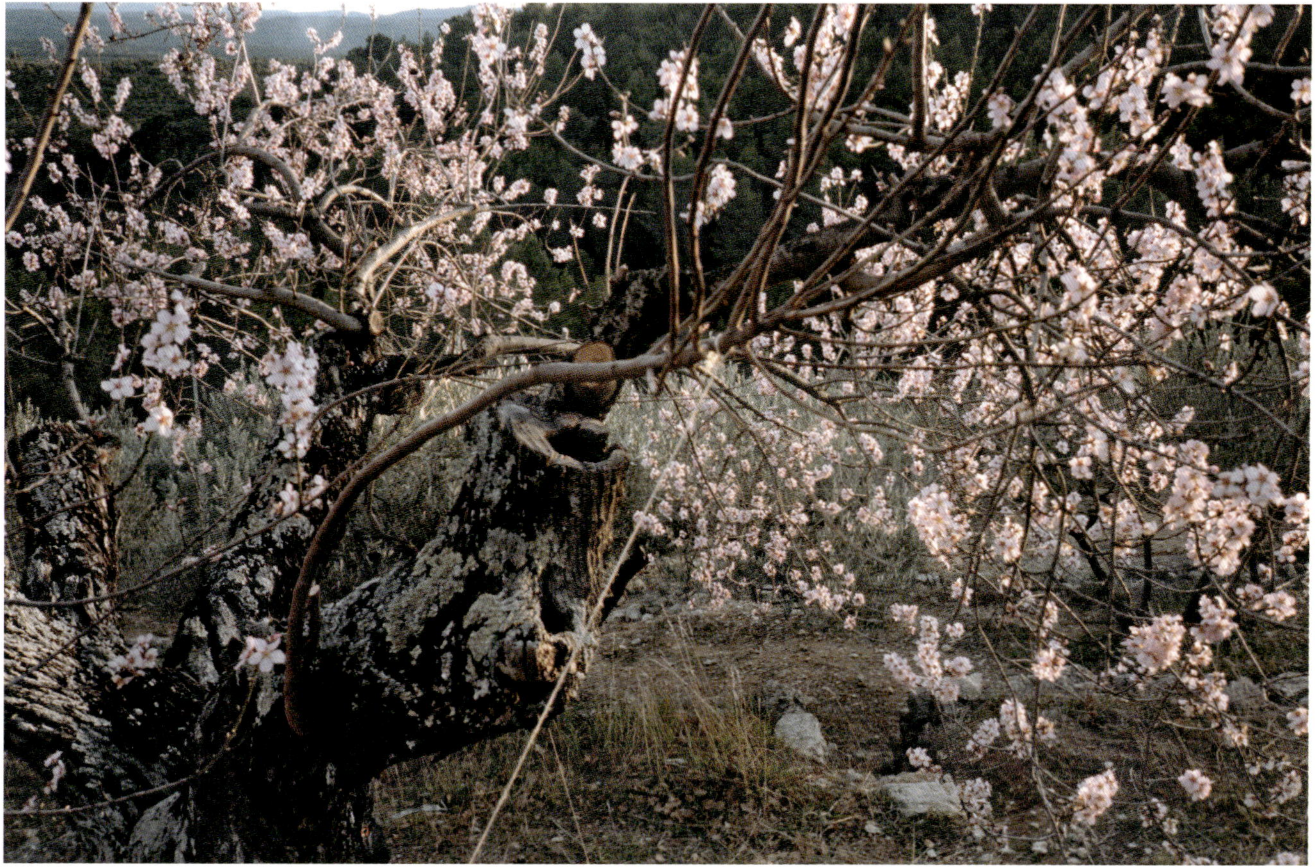

Monday, February 22. Cotignac, France. The old almond tree (see note)

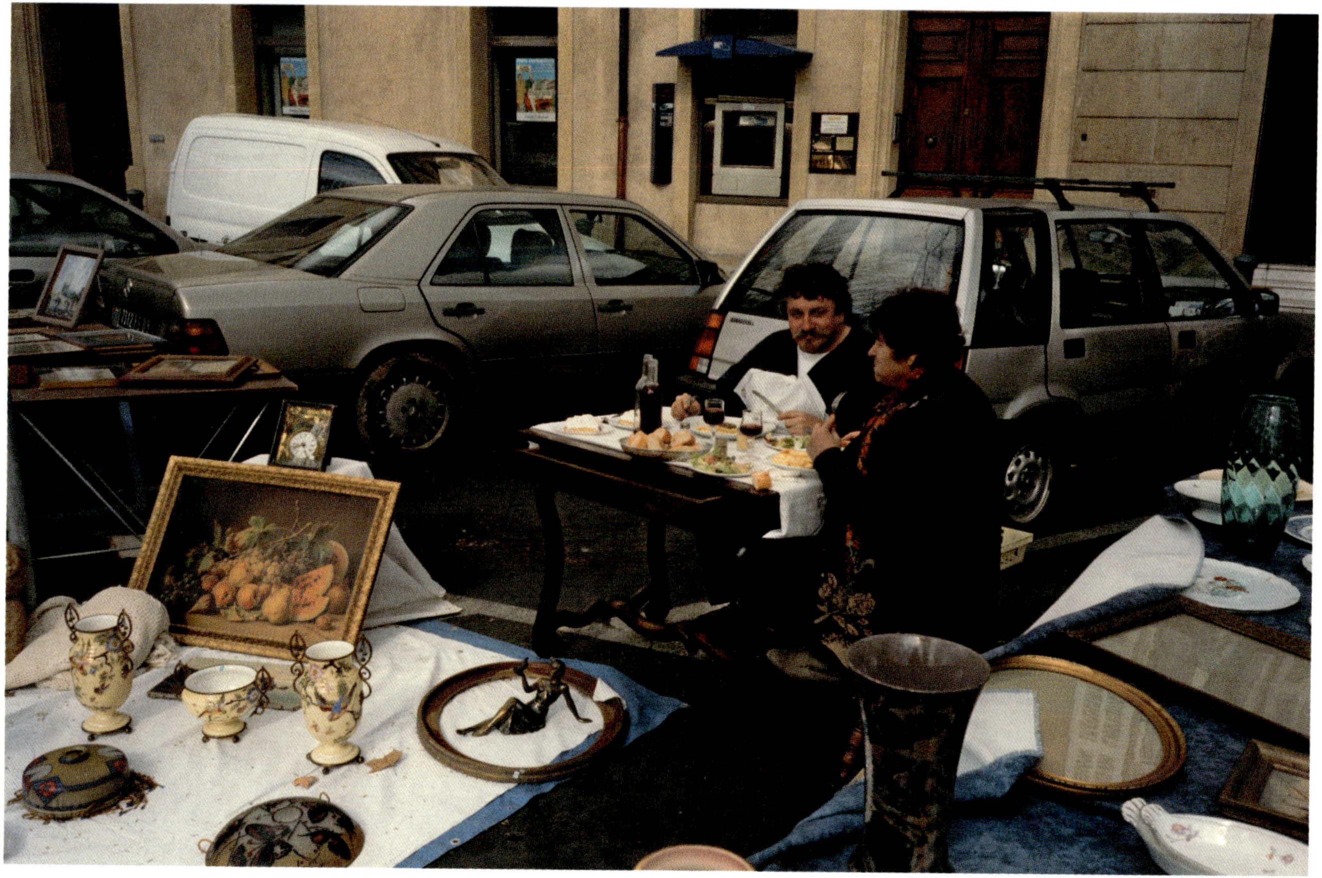

Tuesday, February 23. Aix-en-Provence, France. At the flea market

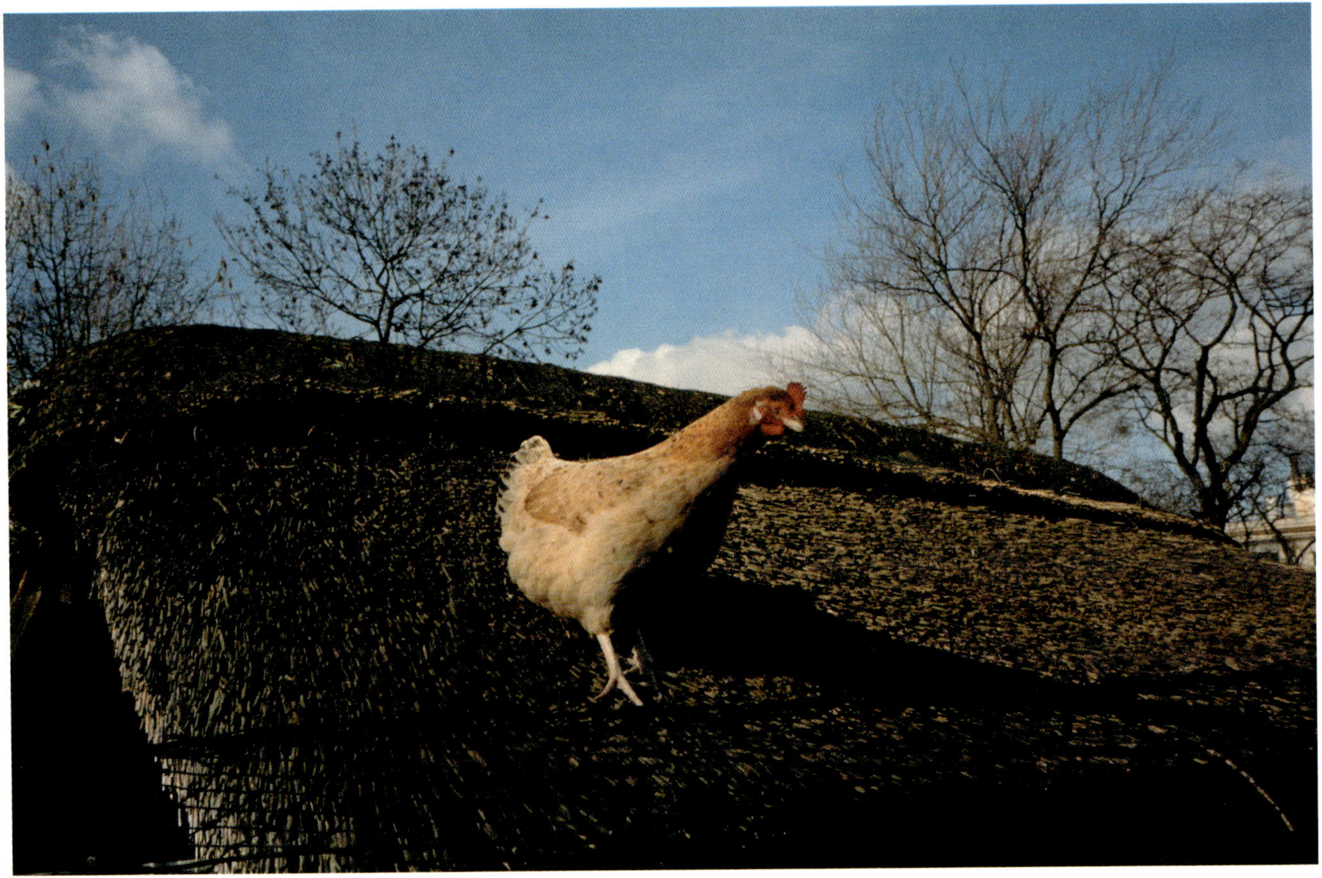

Wednesday, February 24. Paris. At the children's zoo of Jardin d'Acclimatation

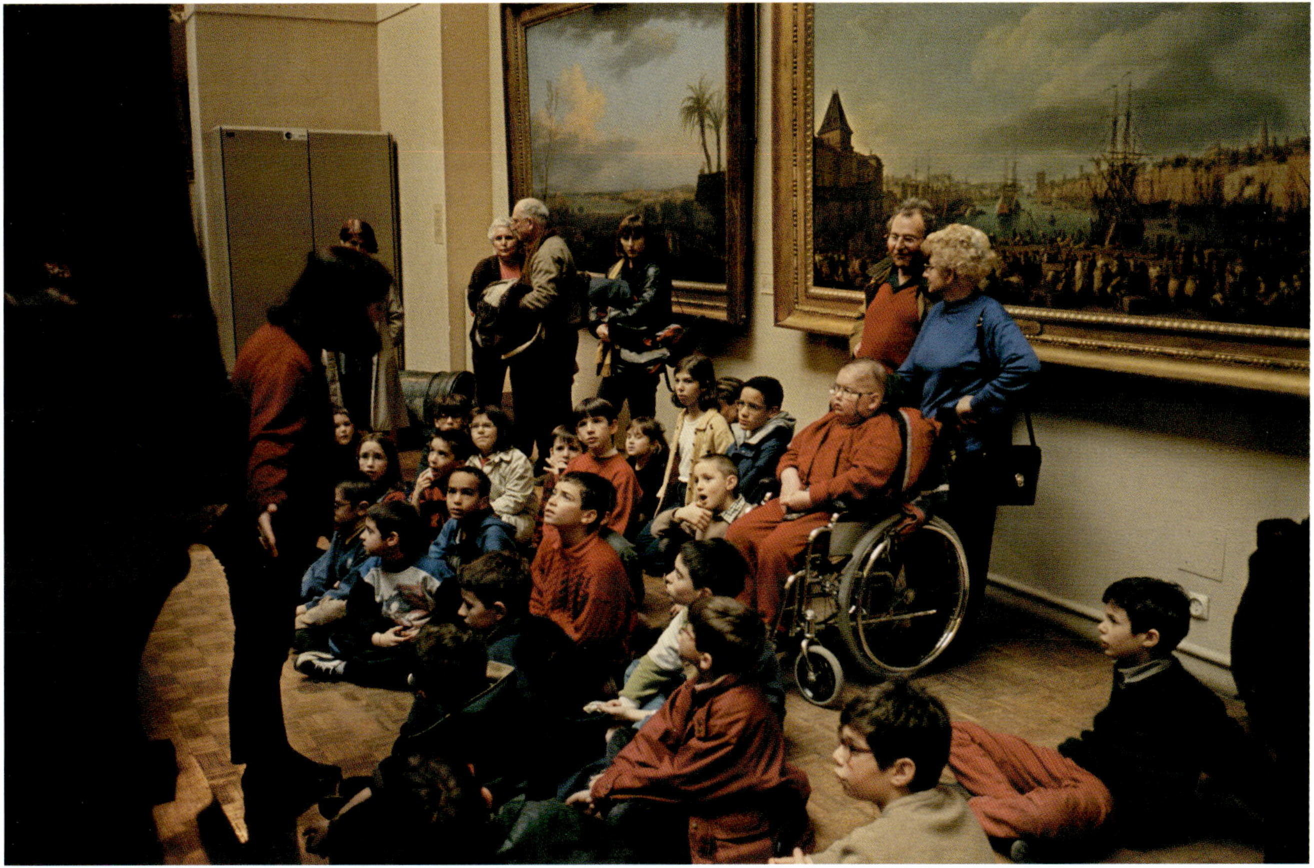

Thursday, February 25. Paris. At the Musée de la Marine, place du Trocadéro

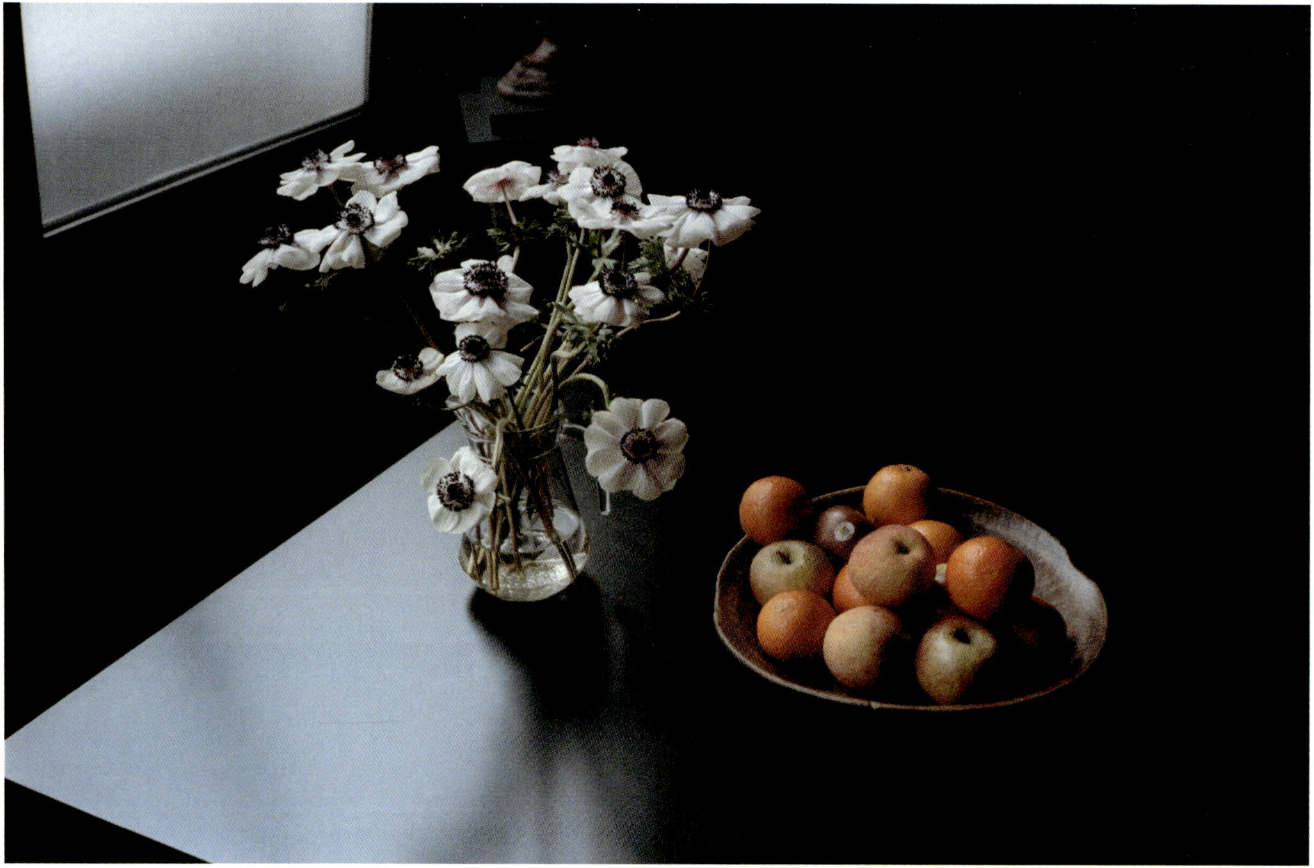

Friday, February 26. Boulogne, France. At my home

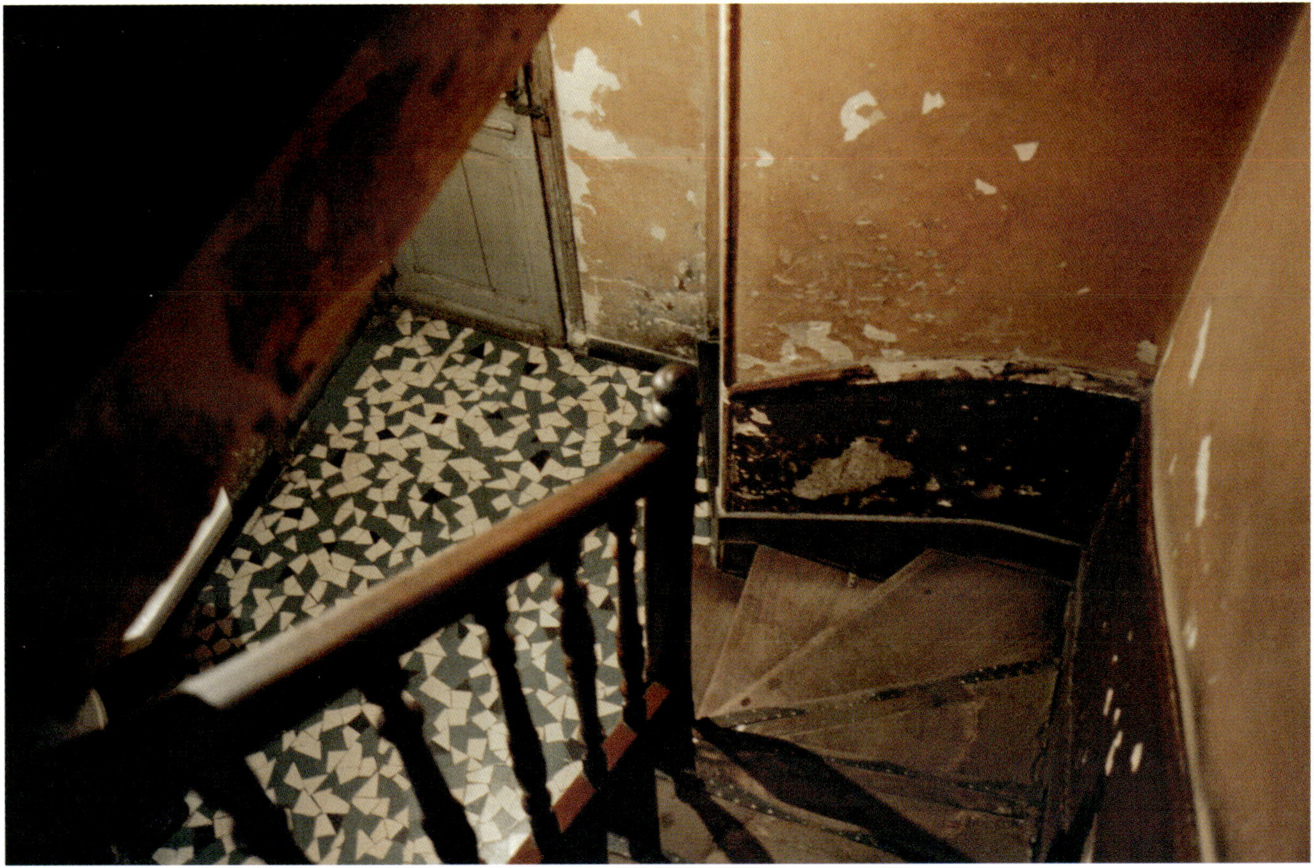

Saturday, February 27. Paris. Stairway to toilets, in a café in the Marais

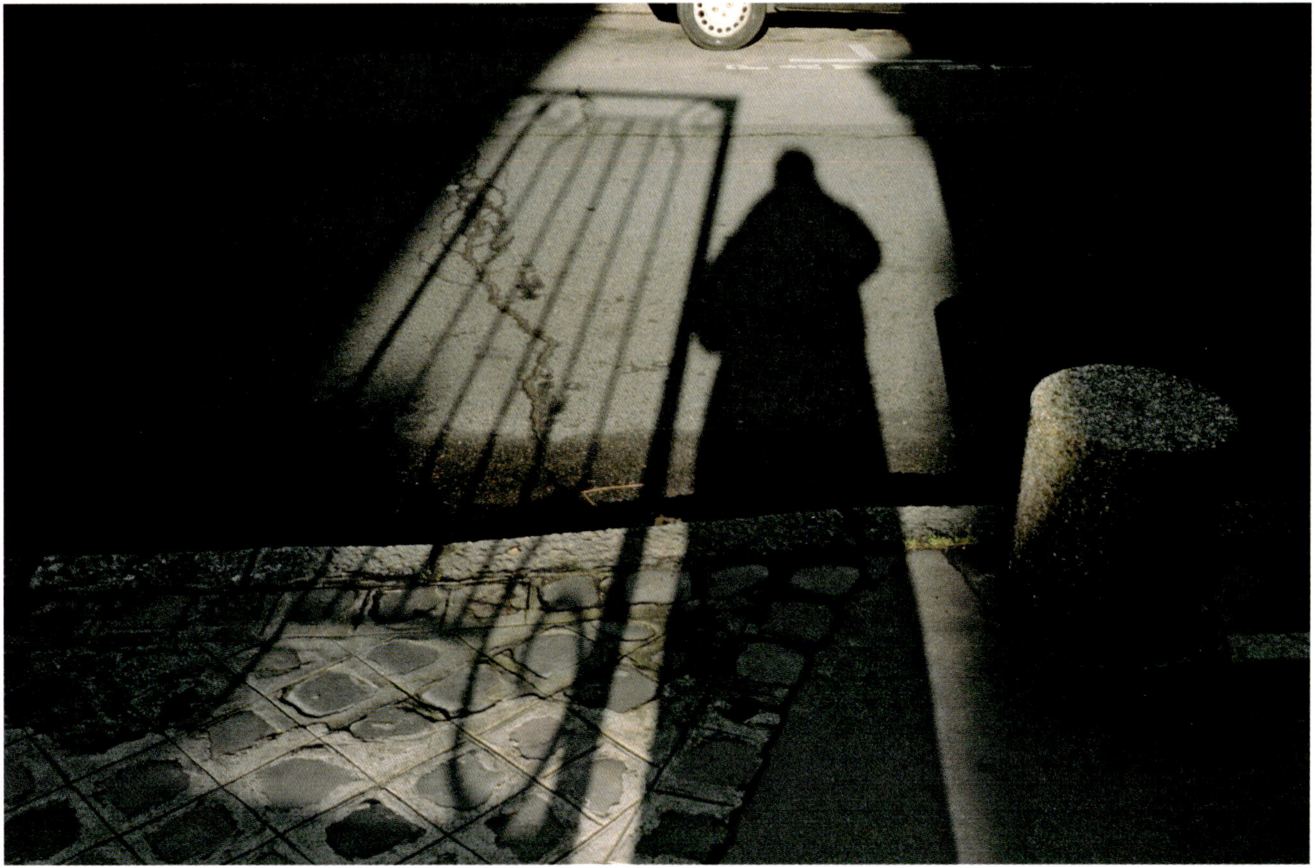

Sunday, February 28. Boulogne, France. In front of my home, self-portrait

MARCH

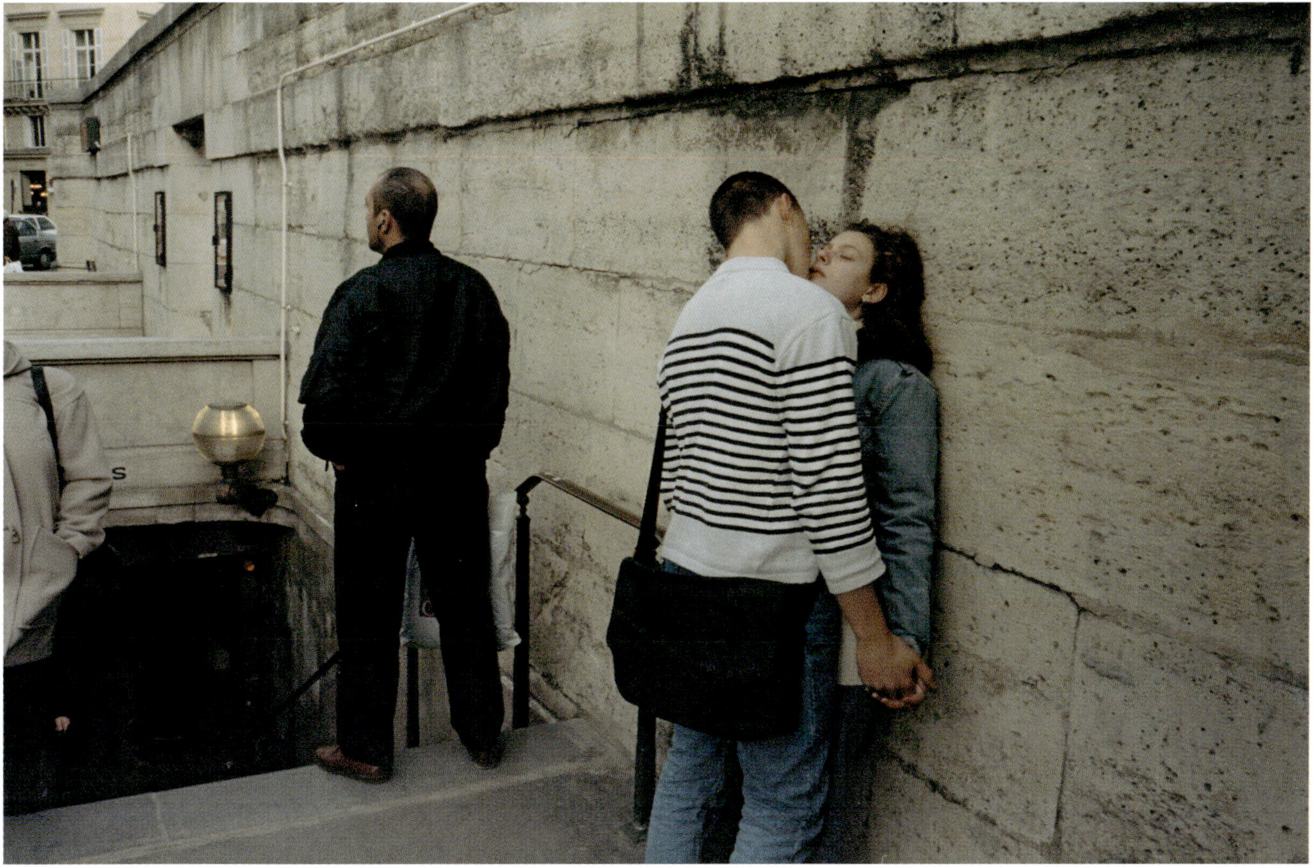

Monday, March 1. Paris. Place de la Concorde

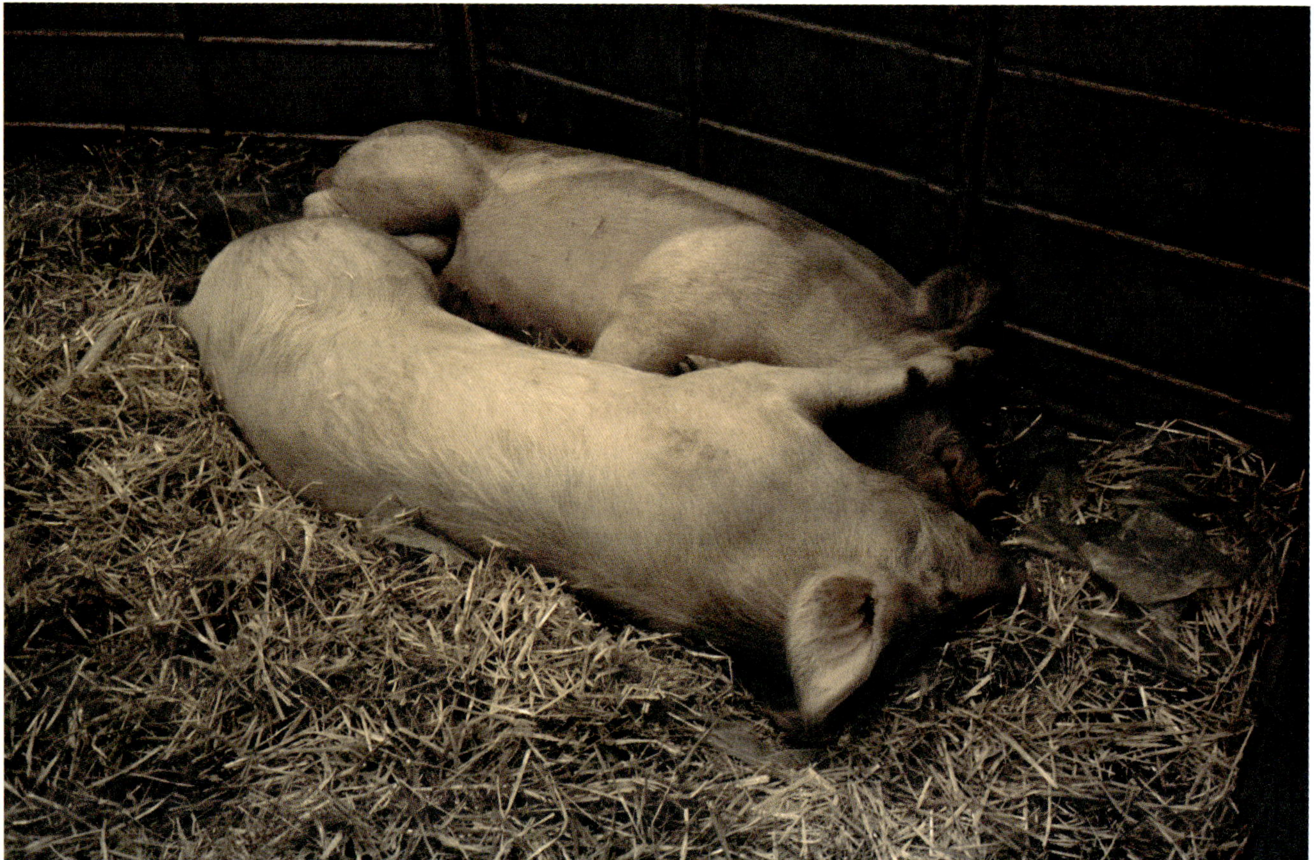

Tuesday, March 2. Paris. At the Salon de l'Agriculture (Agricultural Fair)

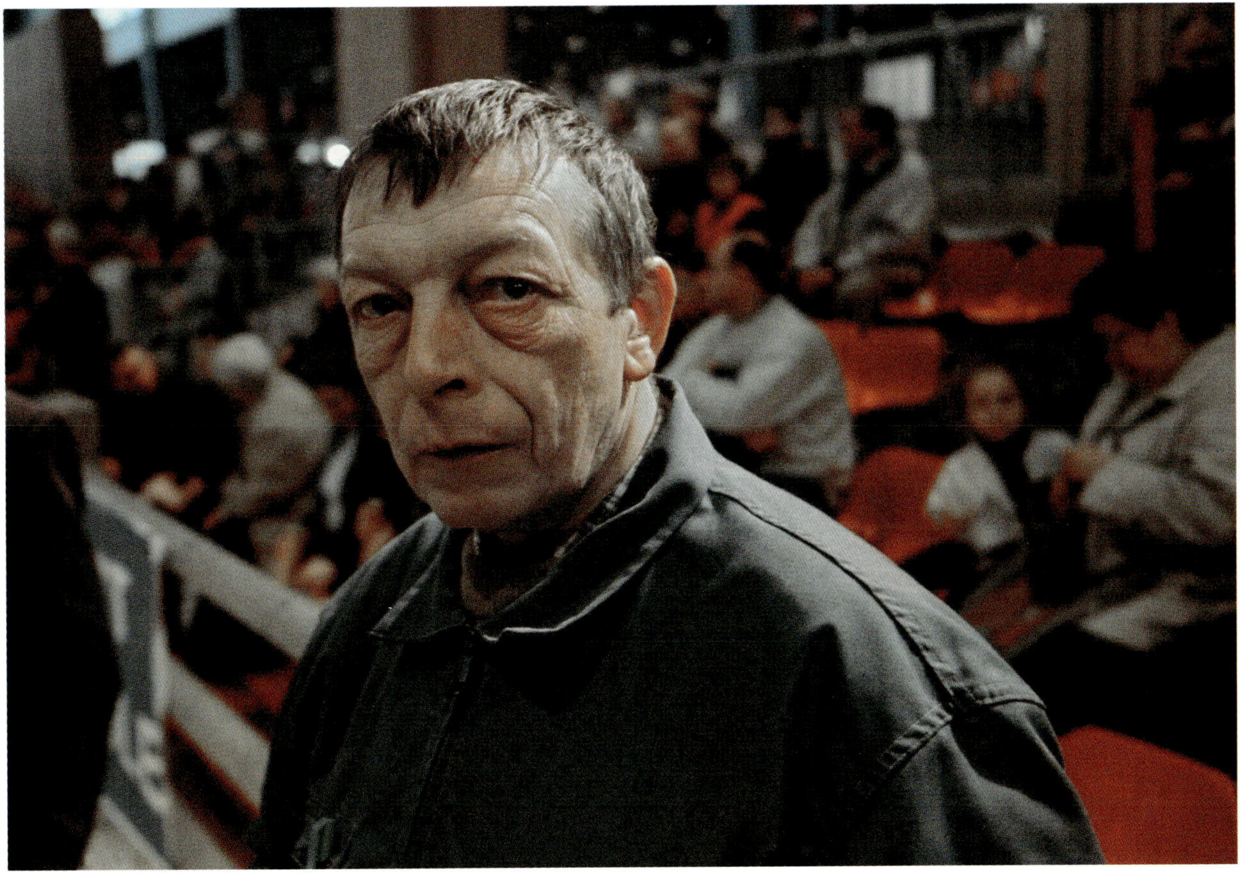

Tuesday, March 2. Paris. Farmer, at the Salon de l'Agriculture

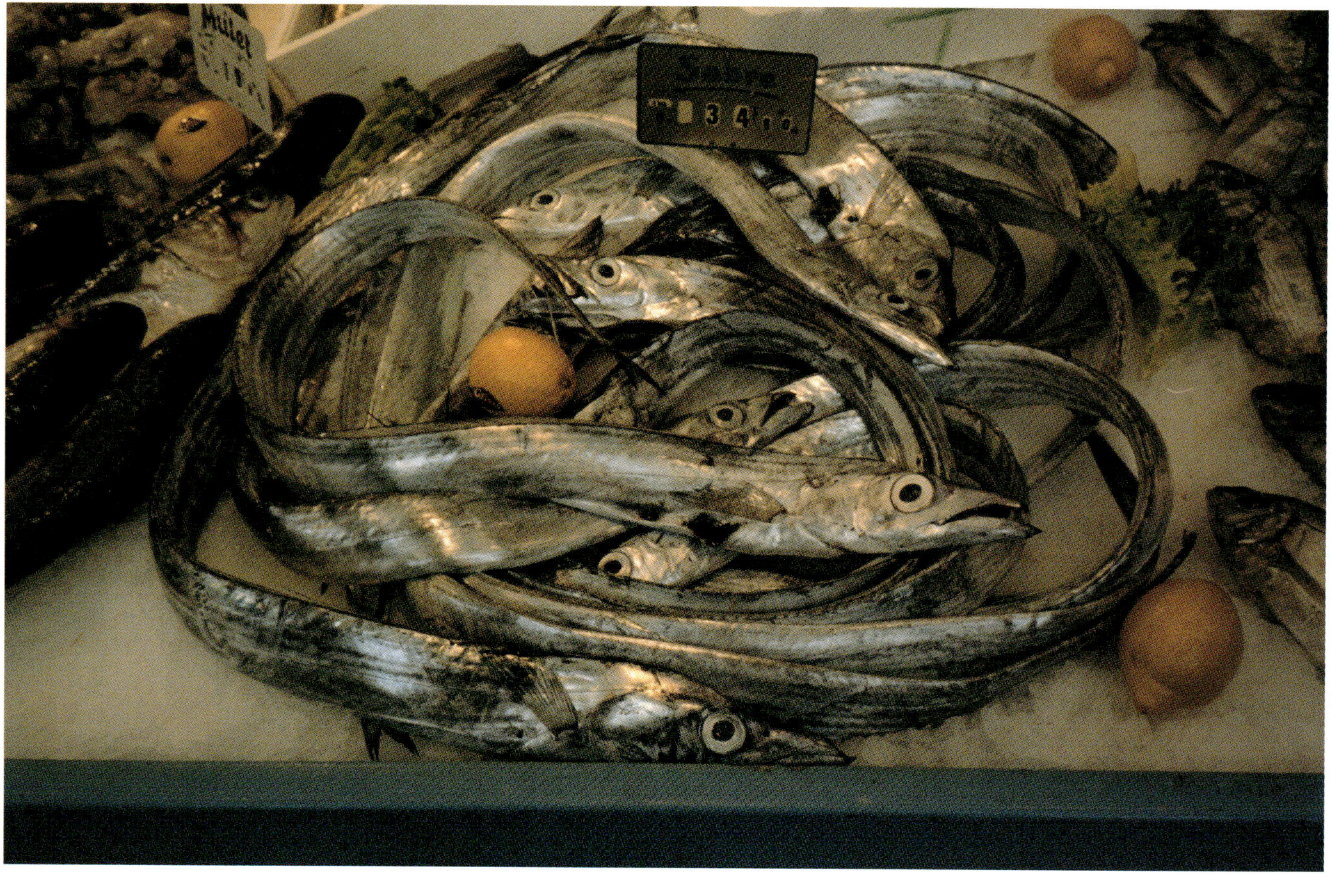

Wednesday, March 3. Paris. At the market on Boulevard Richard Lenoir

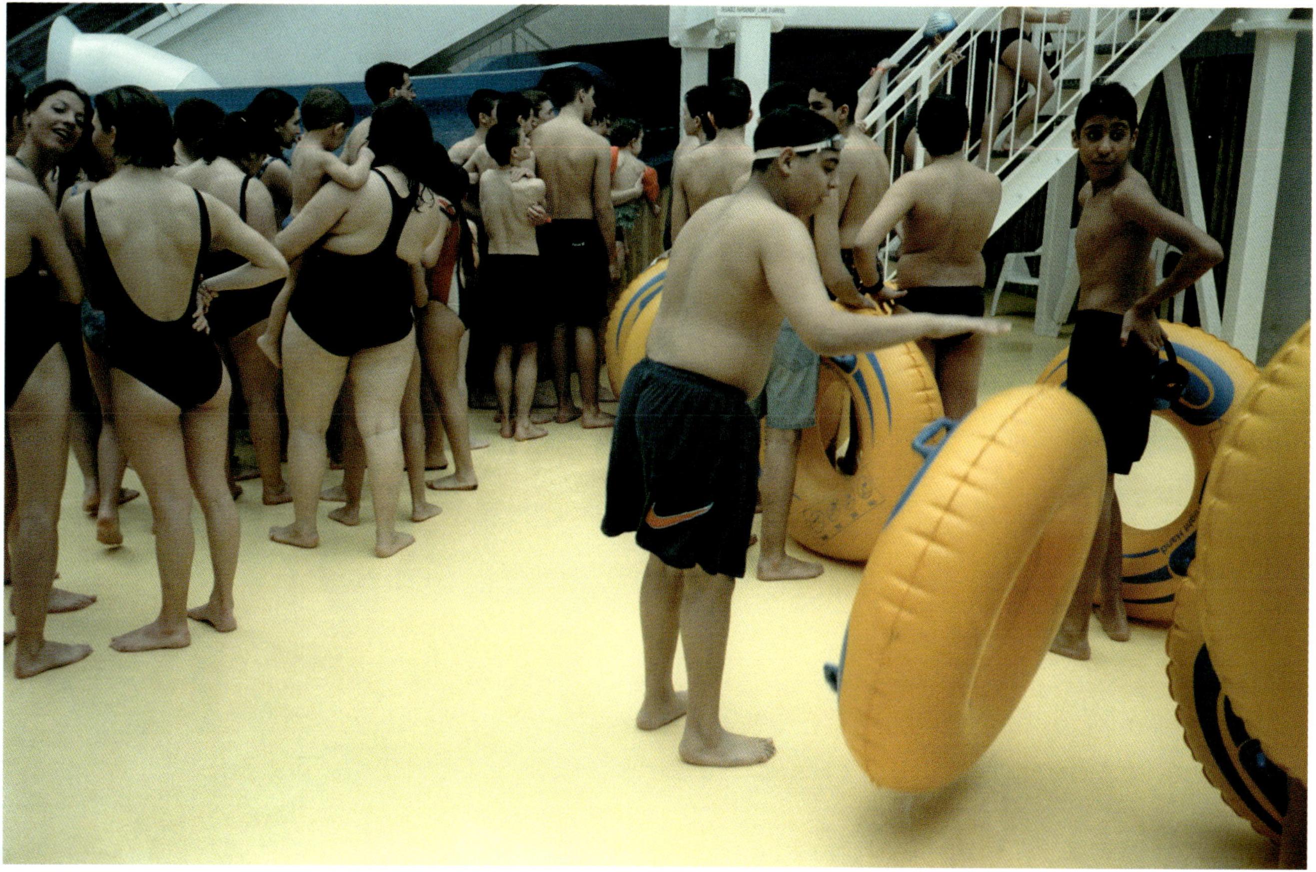

Thursday, March 4. Paris. Aquaboulevard

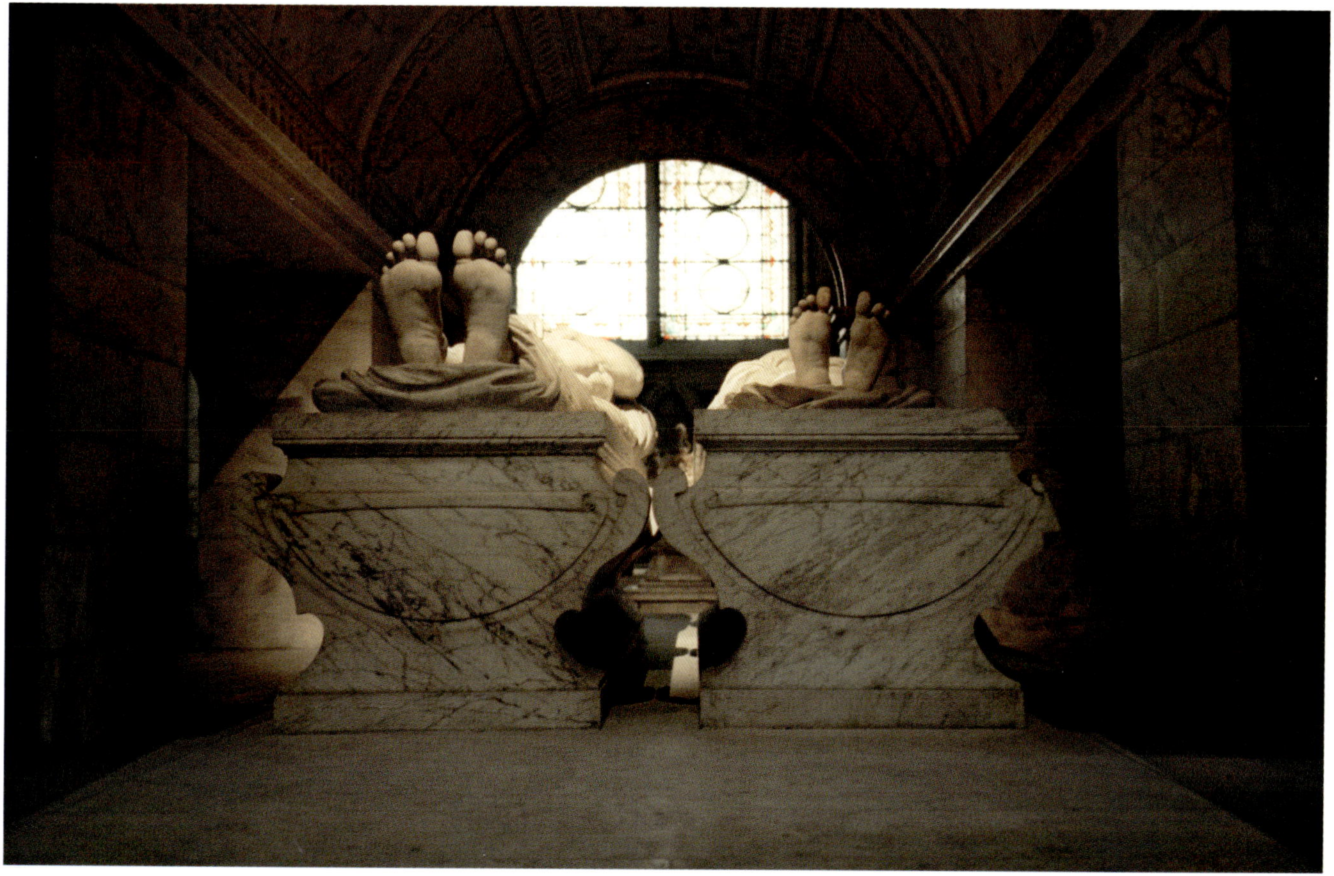

Friday, March 5. Saint-Denis, France. Les Gisants (tombs of the French kings), Basilica of Saint-Denis

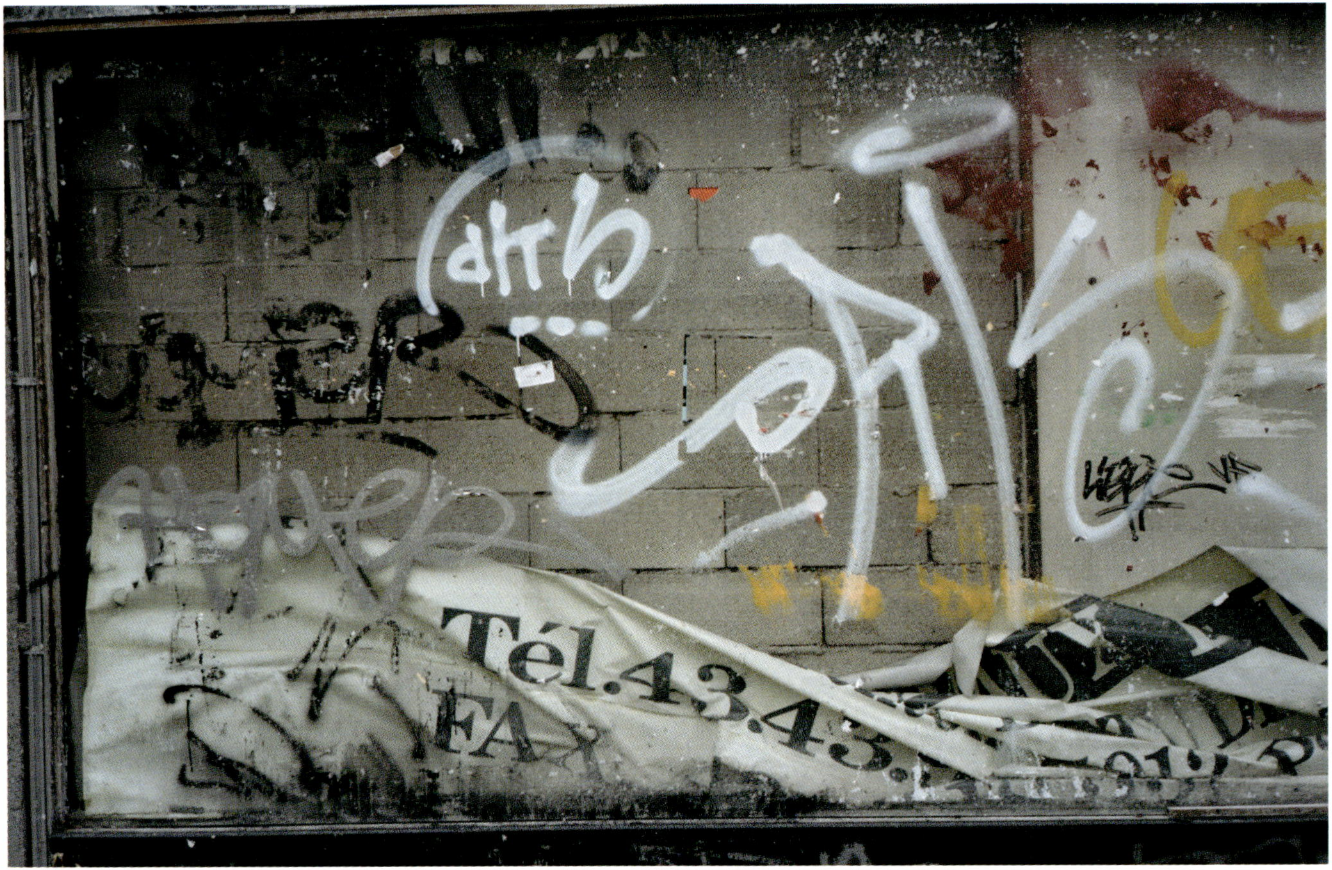

Saturday, March 6. Paris. In the Bastille area

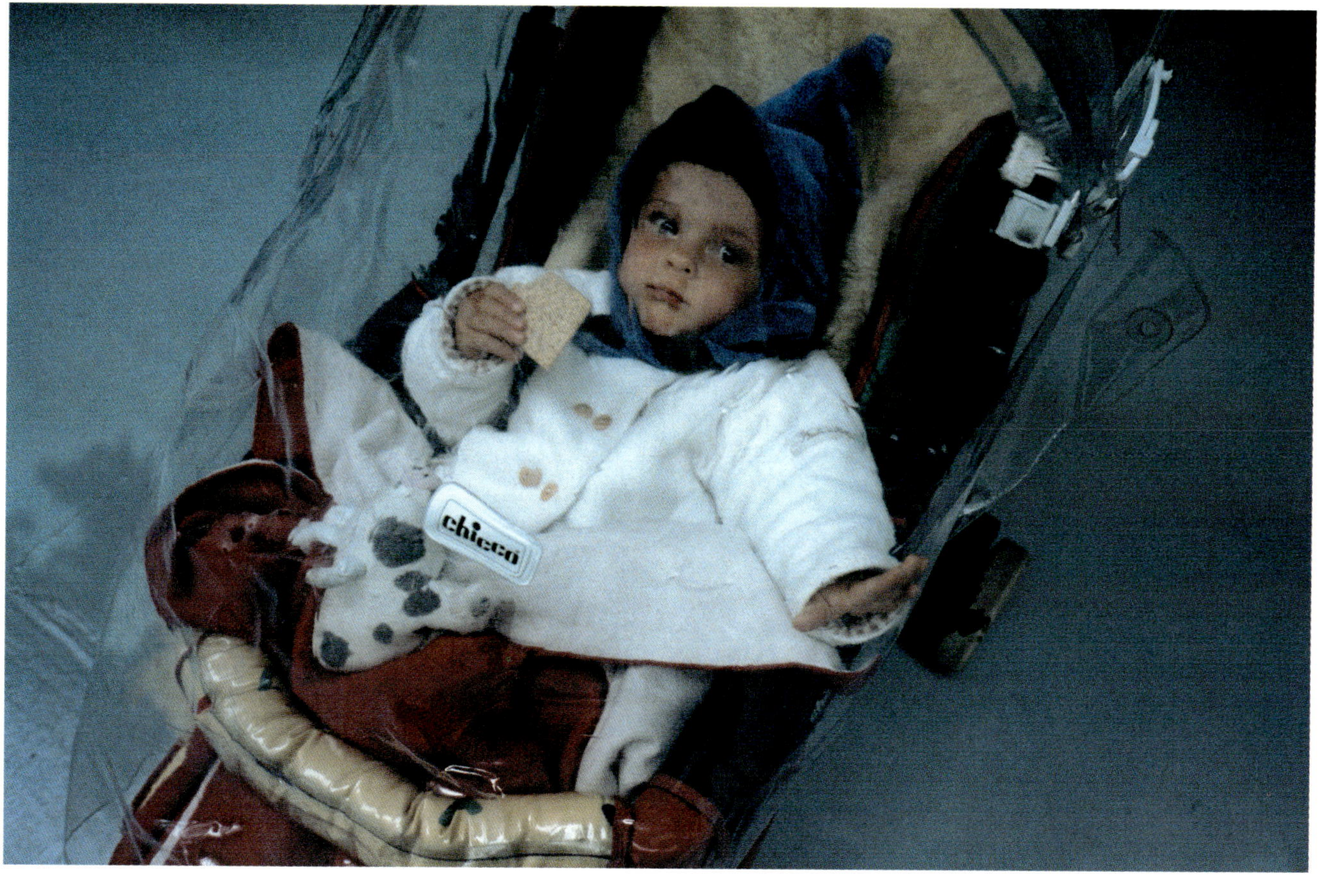

Sunday, March 7. Paris. Mereth, daughter of photographer Michael von Graffenried

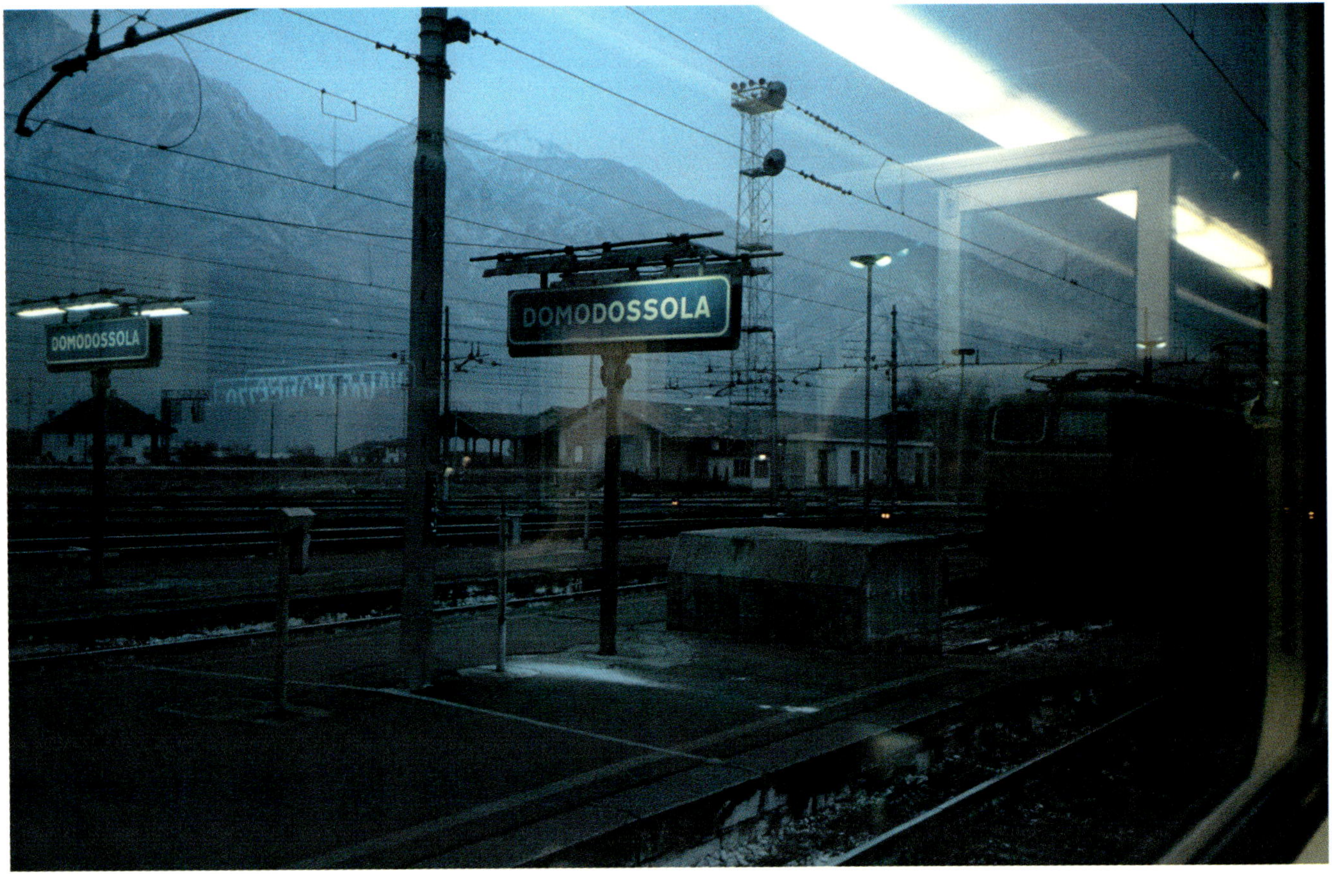

Monday, March 8. Domodossola, Italy. View from the train

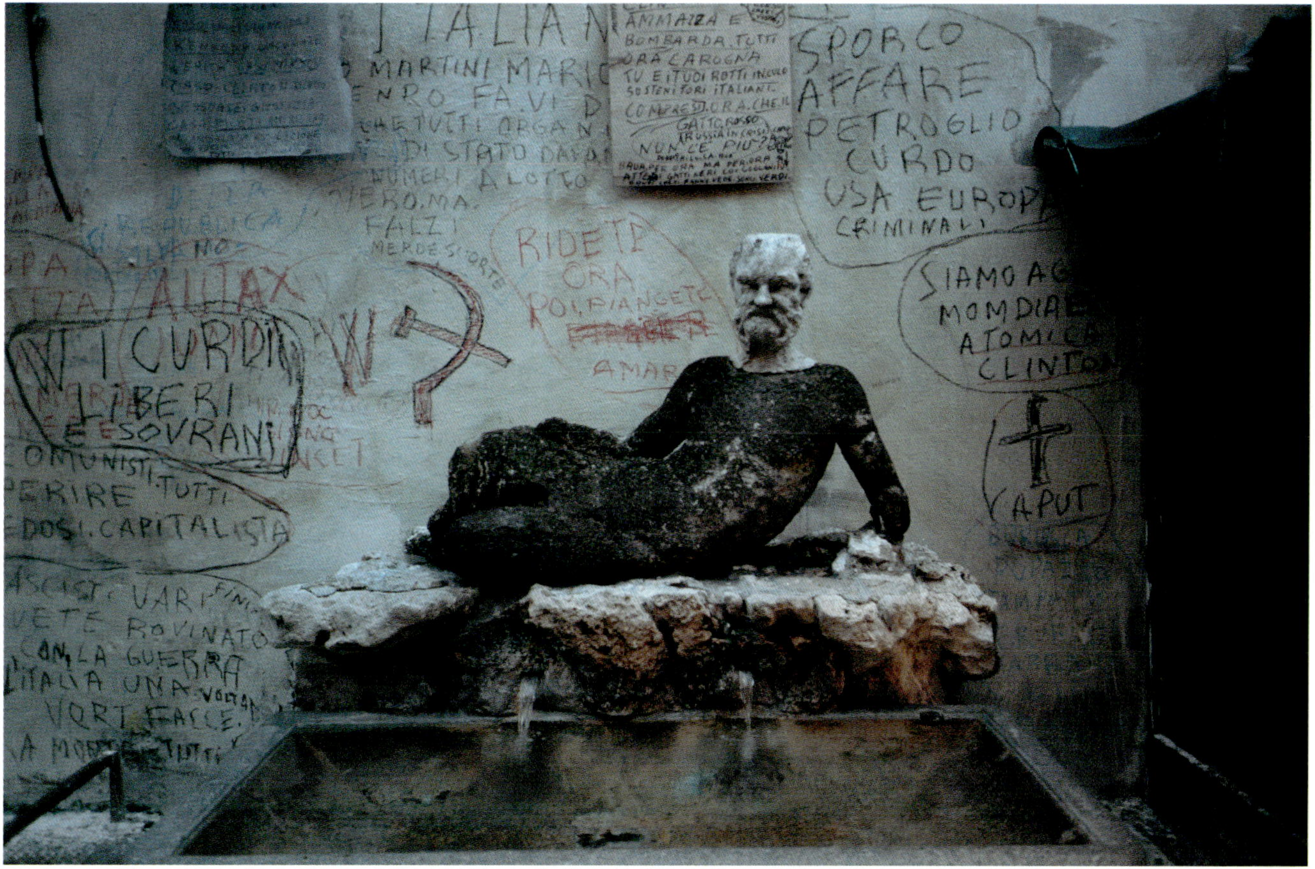

Tuesday, March 9. Rome. Monument in the Piazza di Spagna area

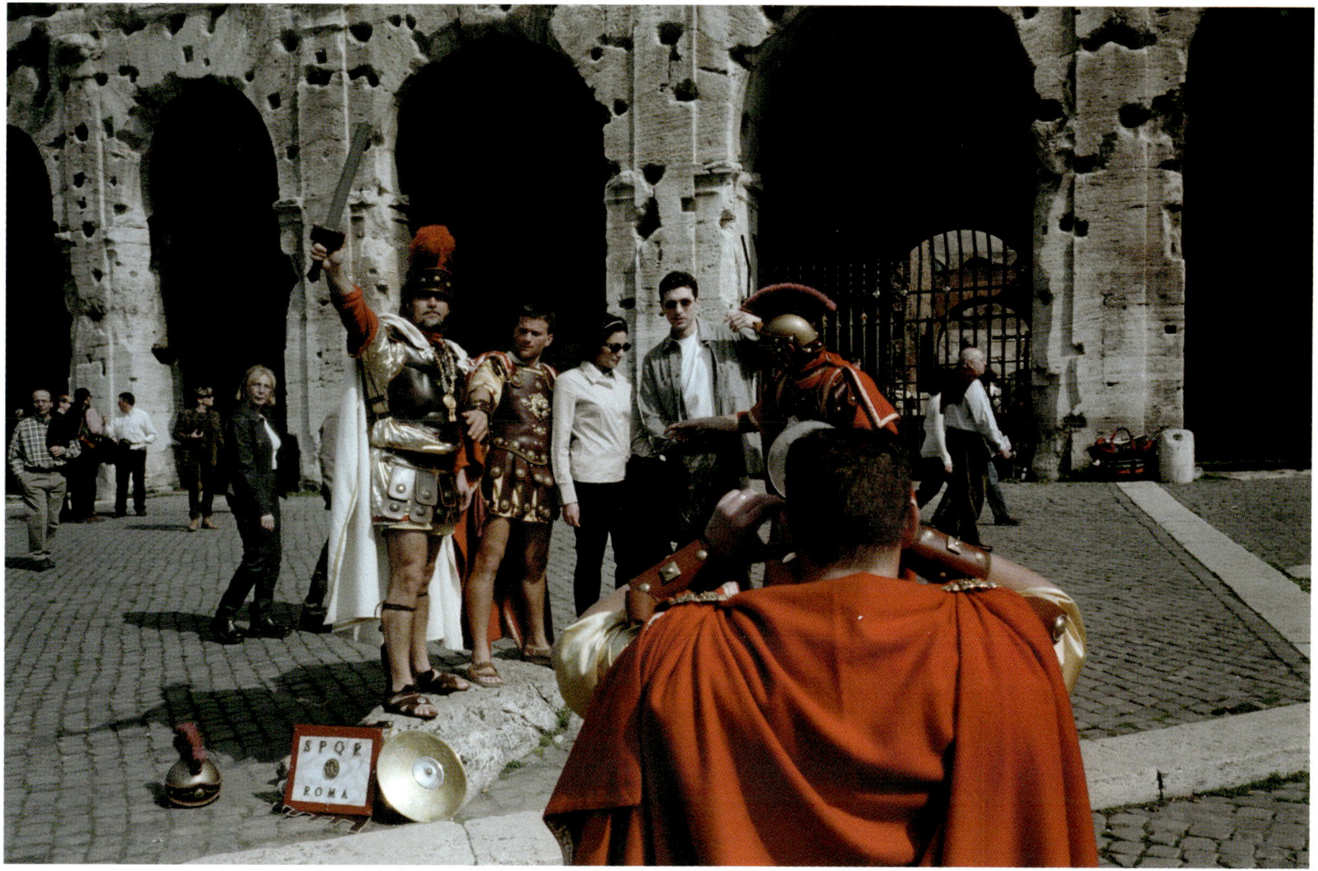

Wednesday, March 10. Rome. Tourists in front of the Colosseum

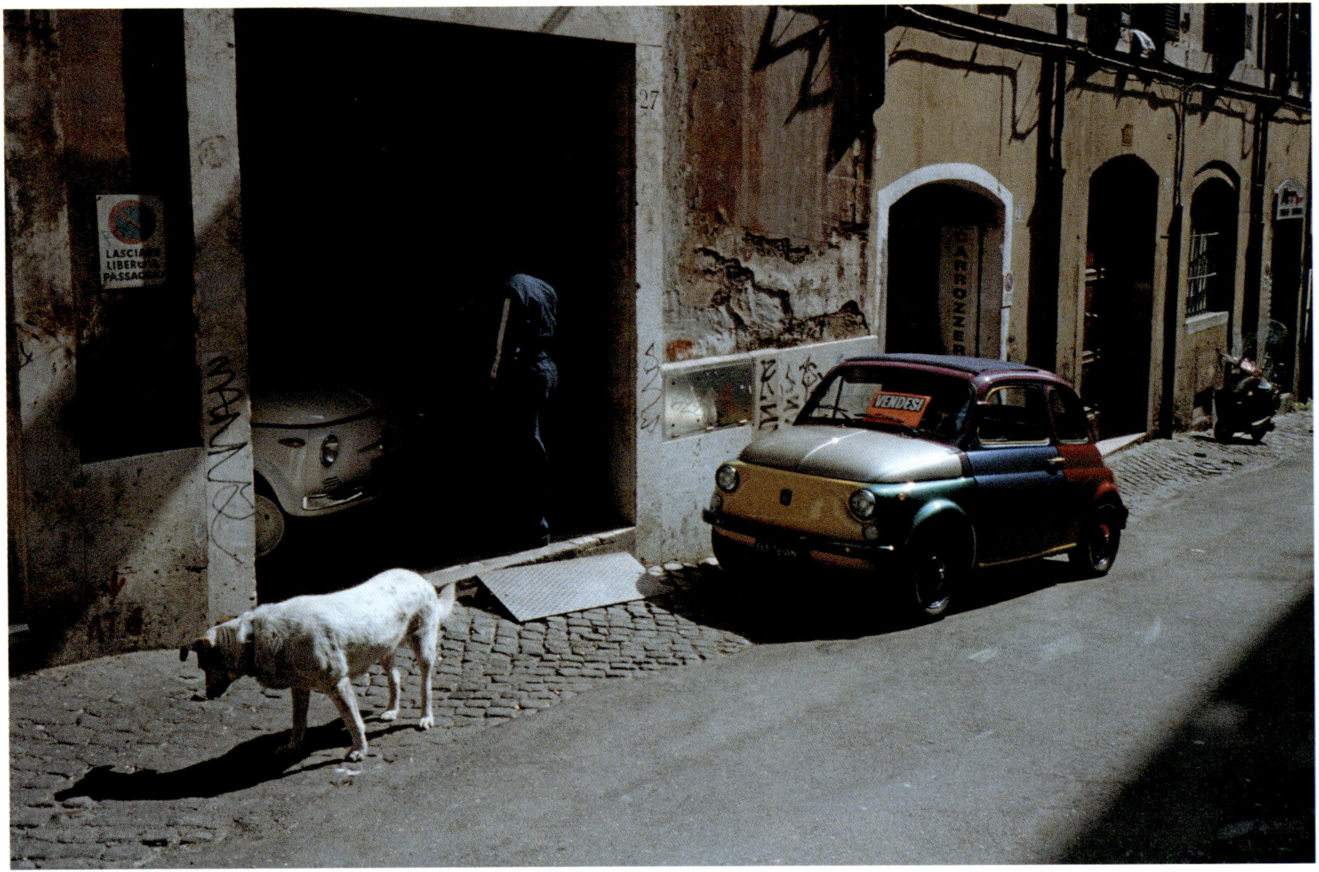

Thursday, March 11. Rome. In the Colosseum area

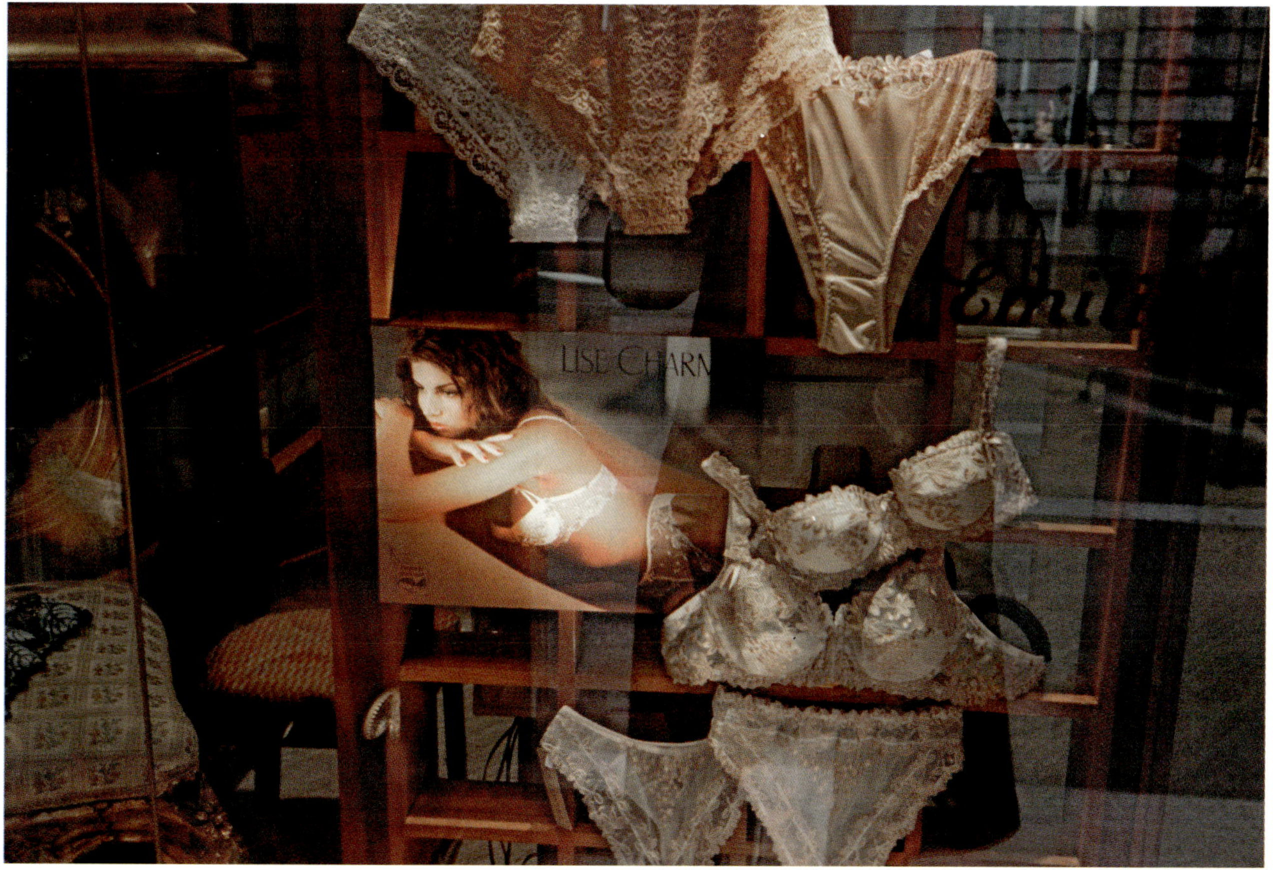

Thursday, March 11. Rome. Window display in the Corso area

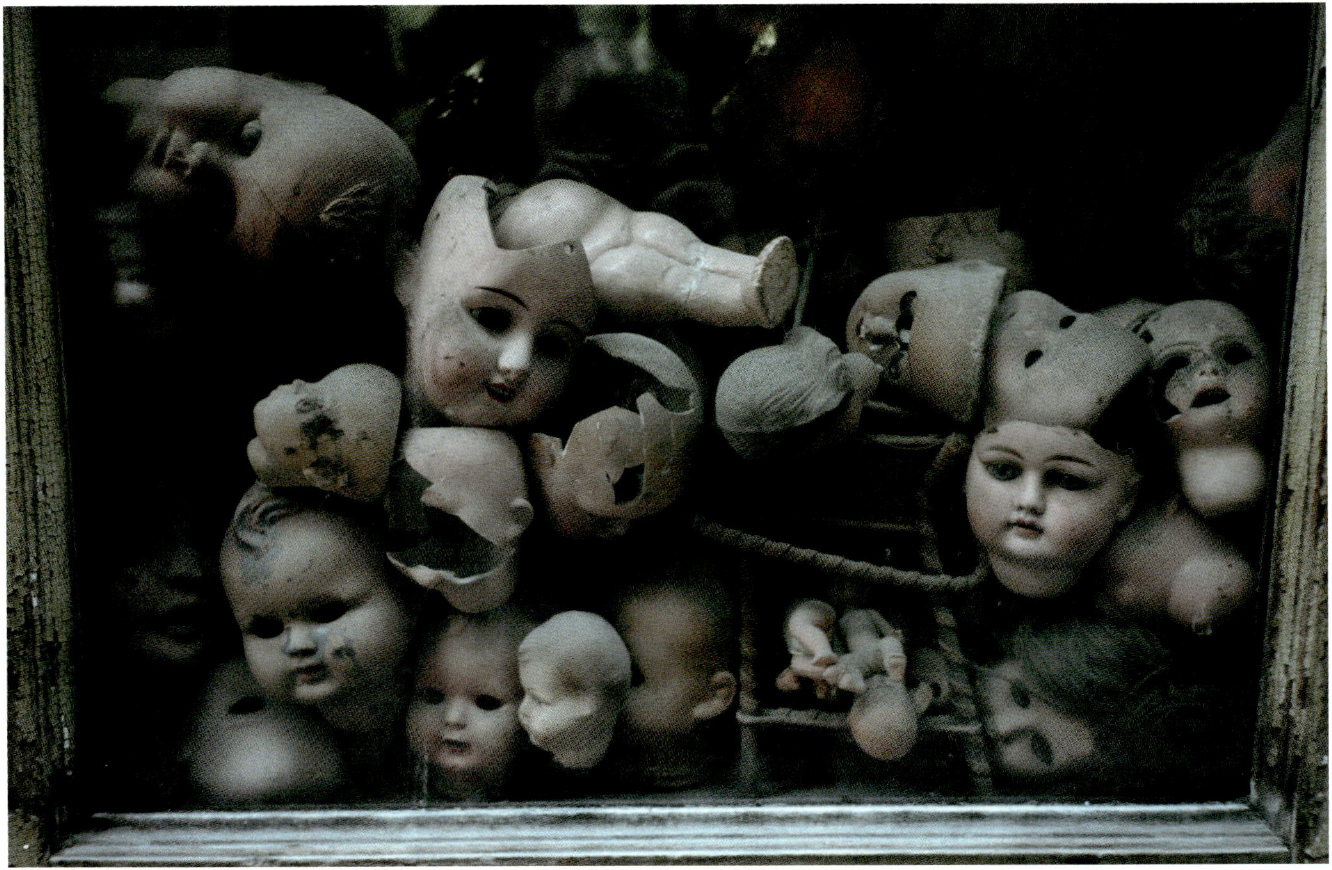

Friday, March 12. Rome. Antique dealer's shop window, Corso area

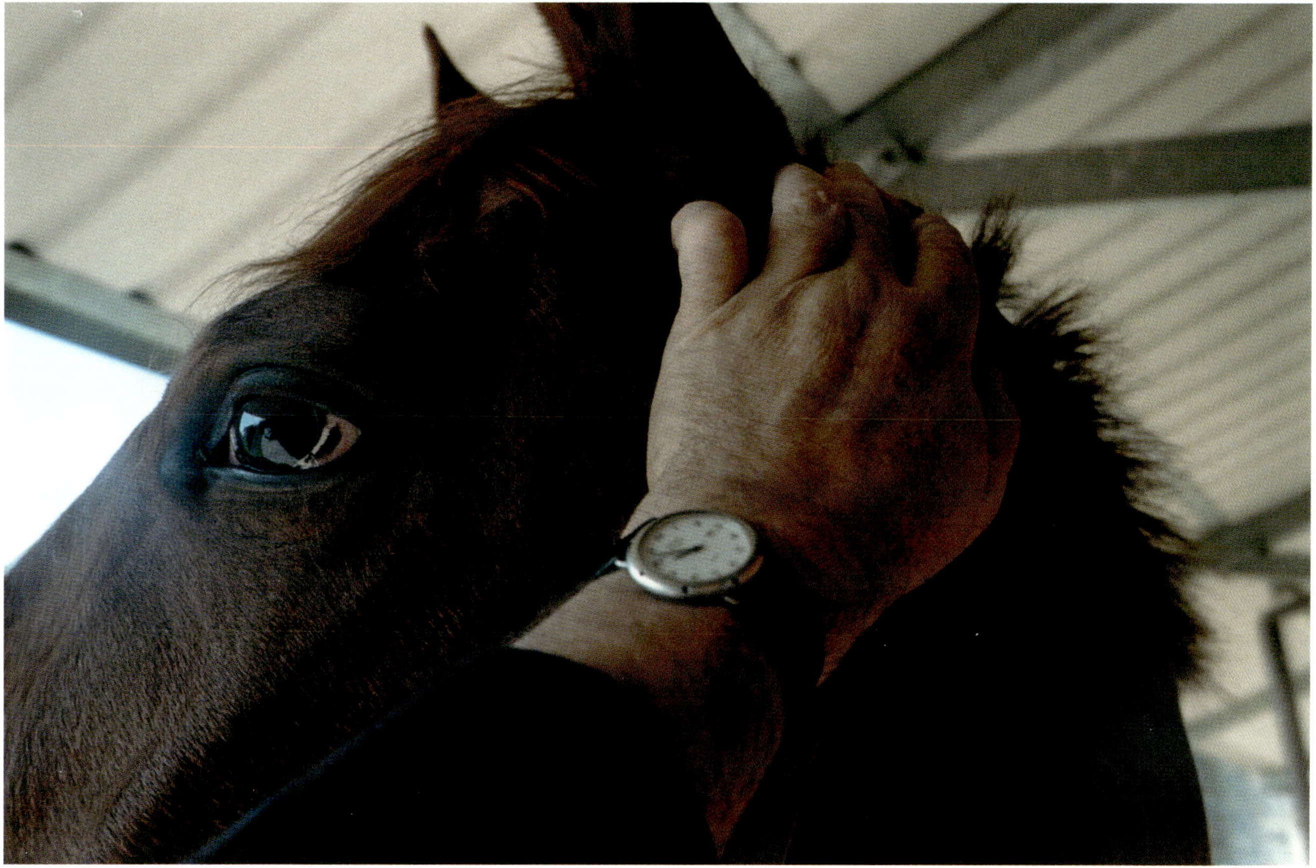

Saturday, March 13. Pantano Borghese, Italy. Self-portrait with horse

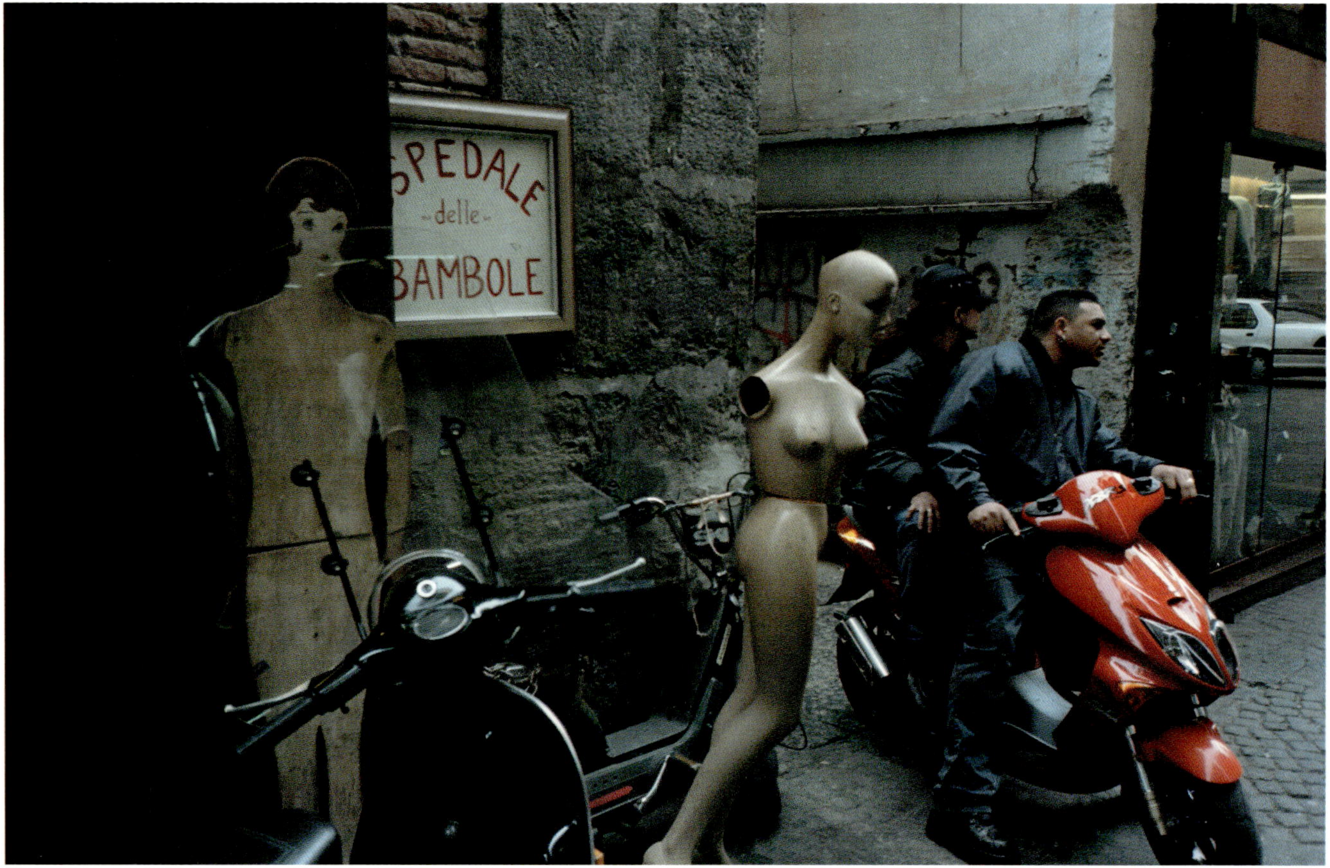

Sunday, March 14. Naples, Italy. Dolls' hospital

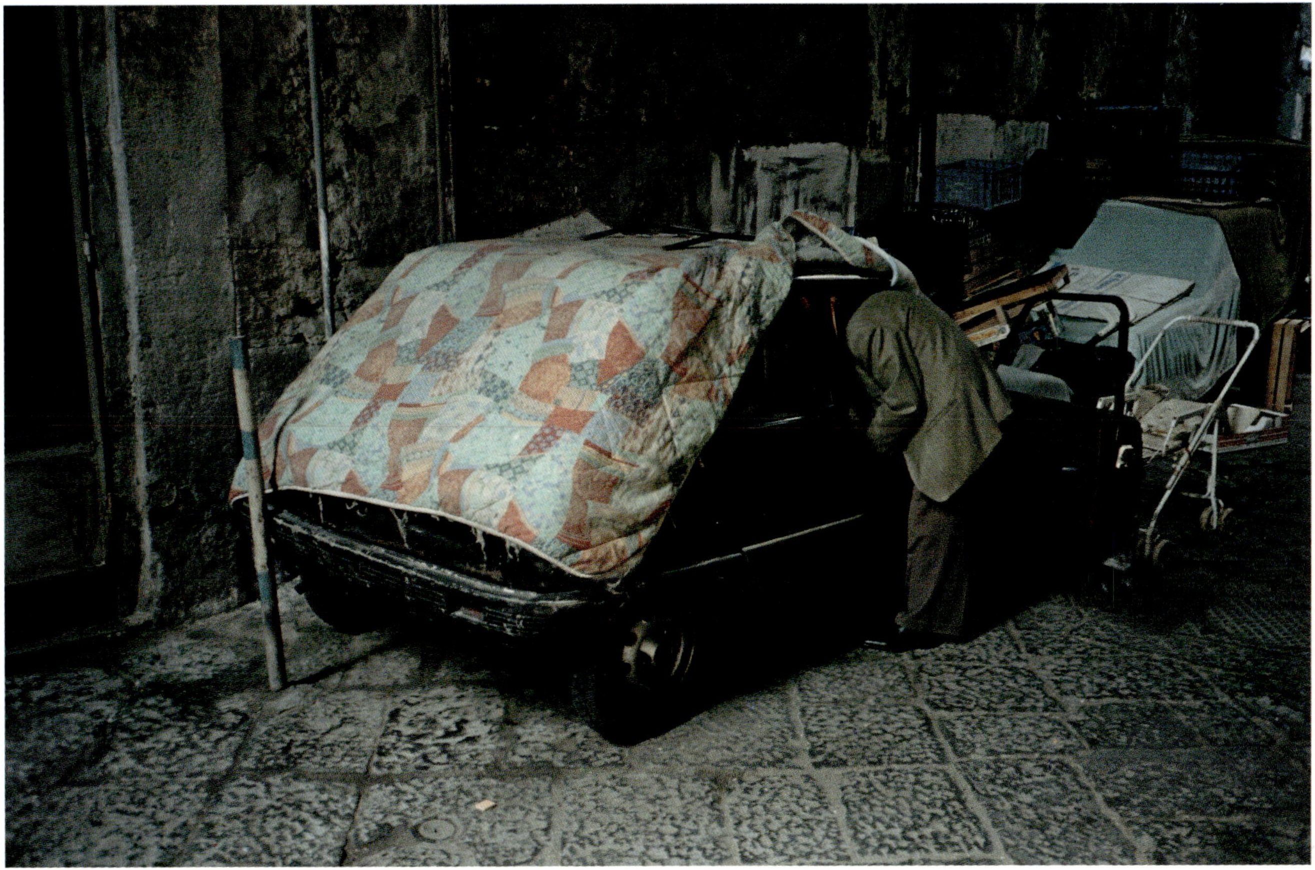

Monday, March 15. Naples, Italy. Street scene

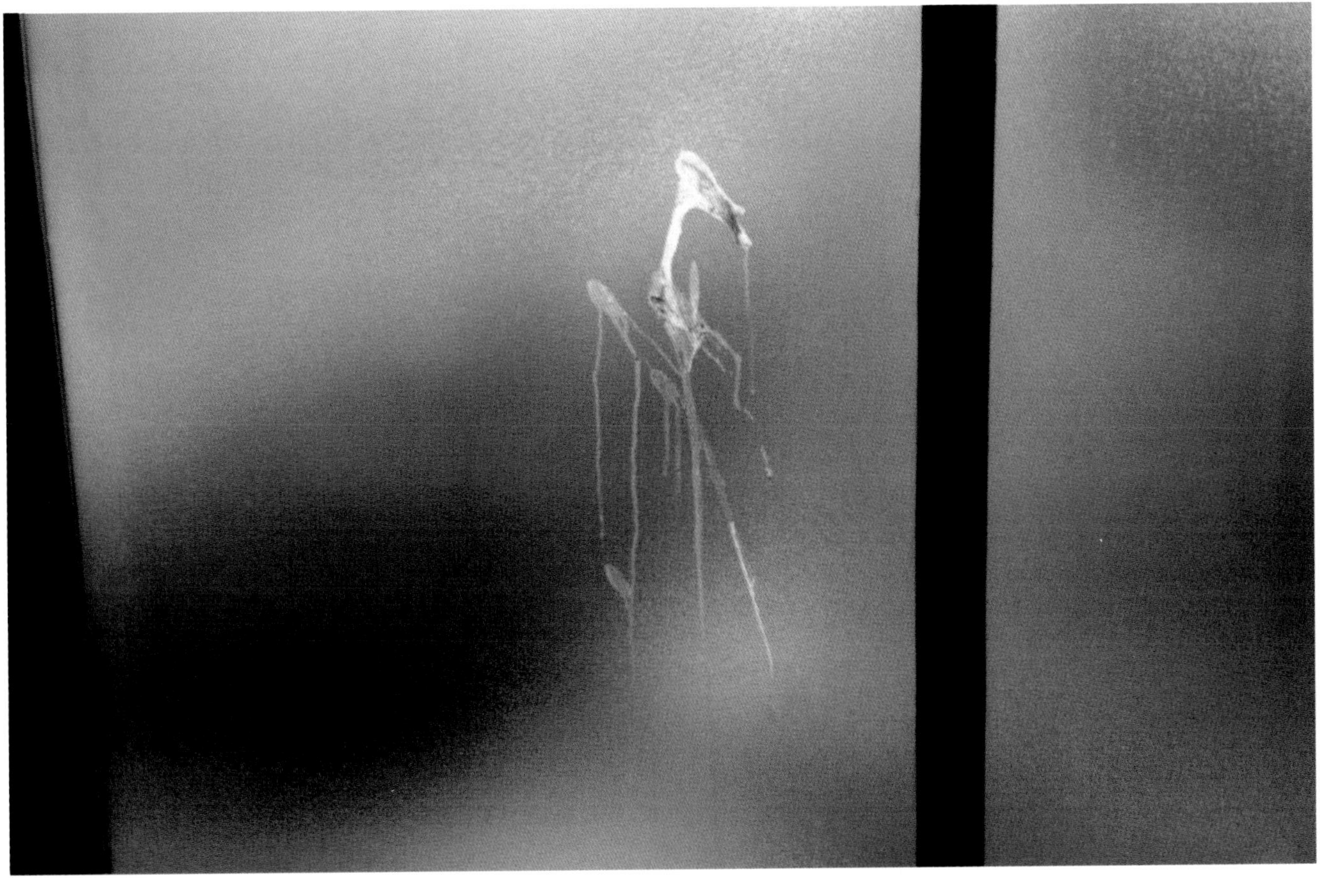

Tuesday, March 16. Boulogne, France. At home. Pigeon droppings on the window

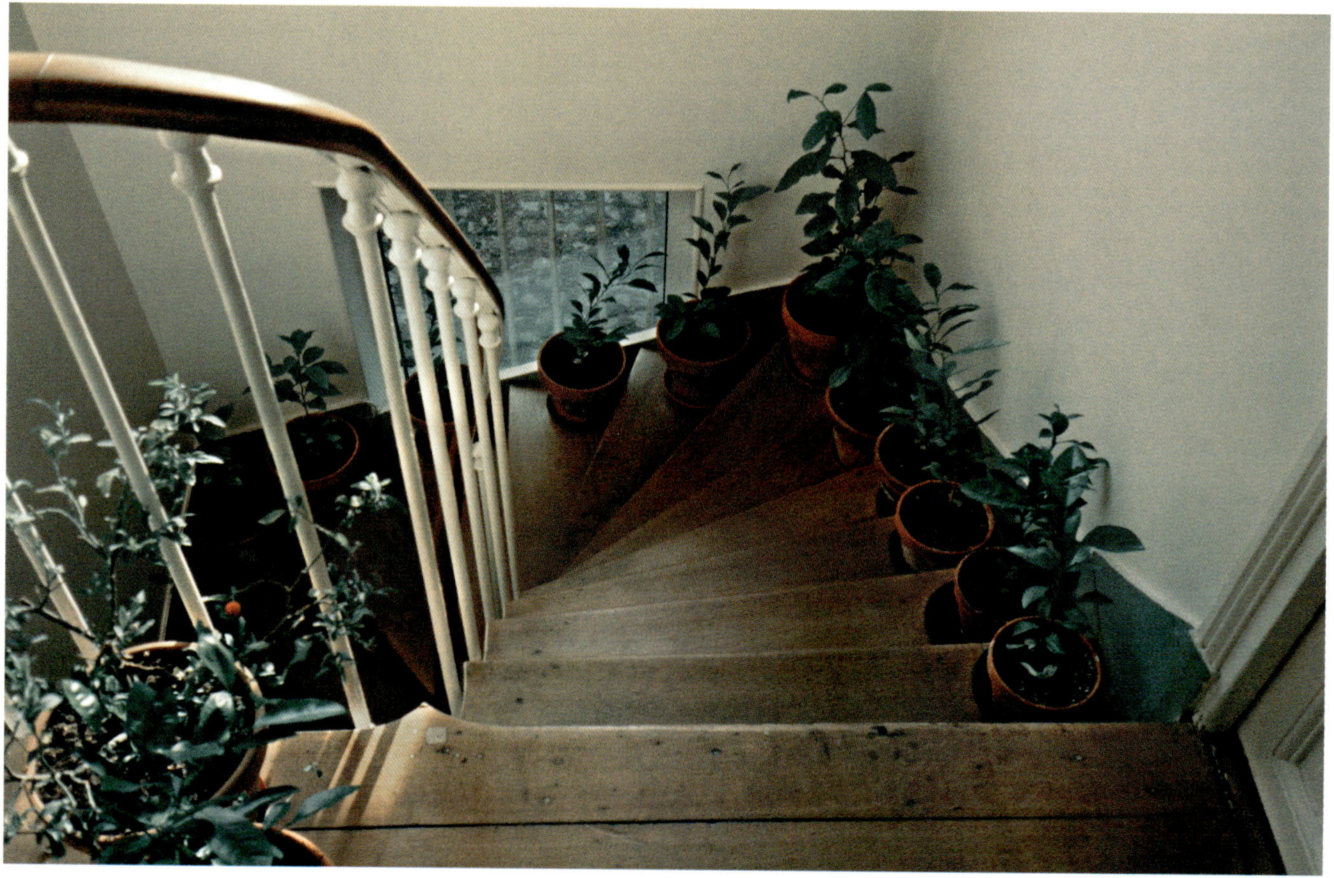

Wednesday, March 17. Boulogne, France. At my son Marco's home

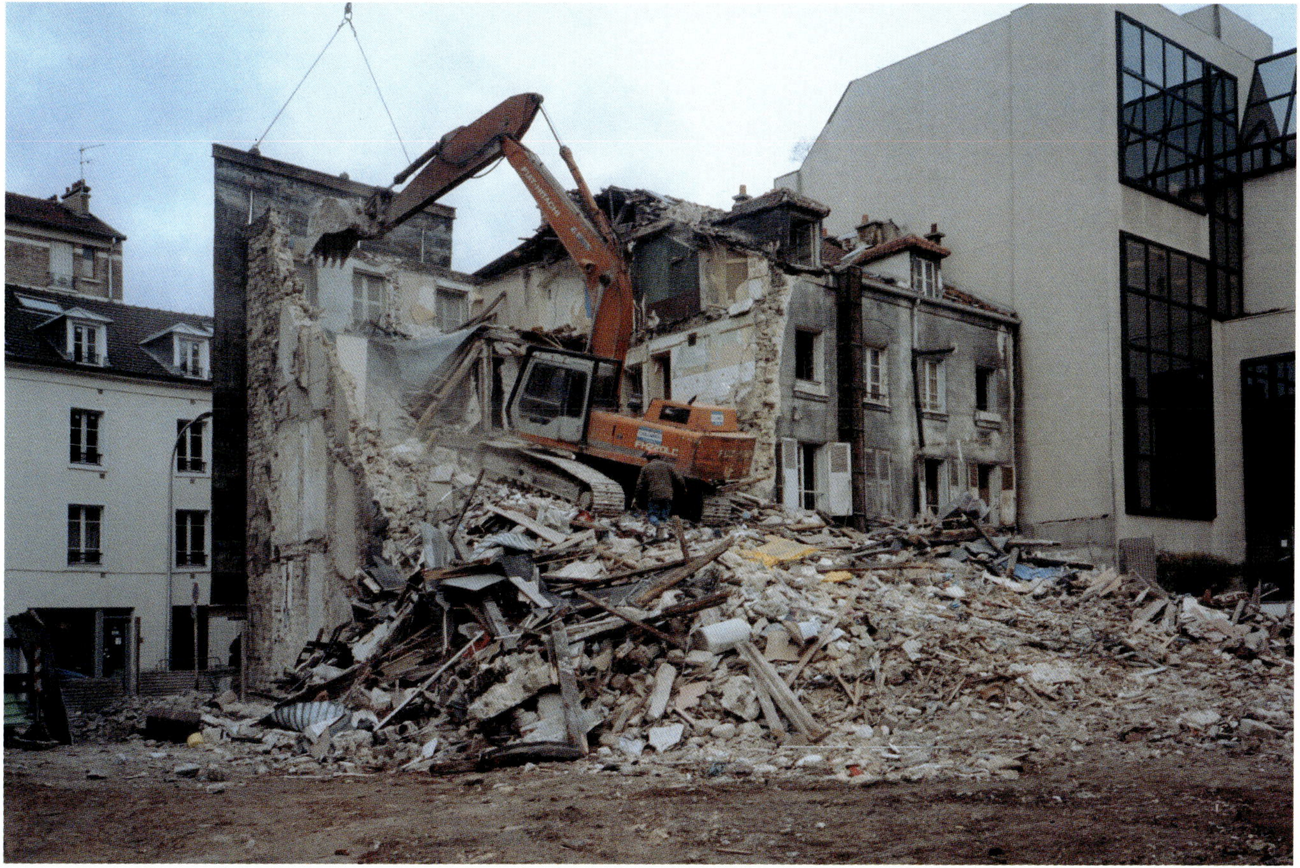

Thursday, March 18. Boulogne, France. Demolition of an old building

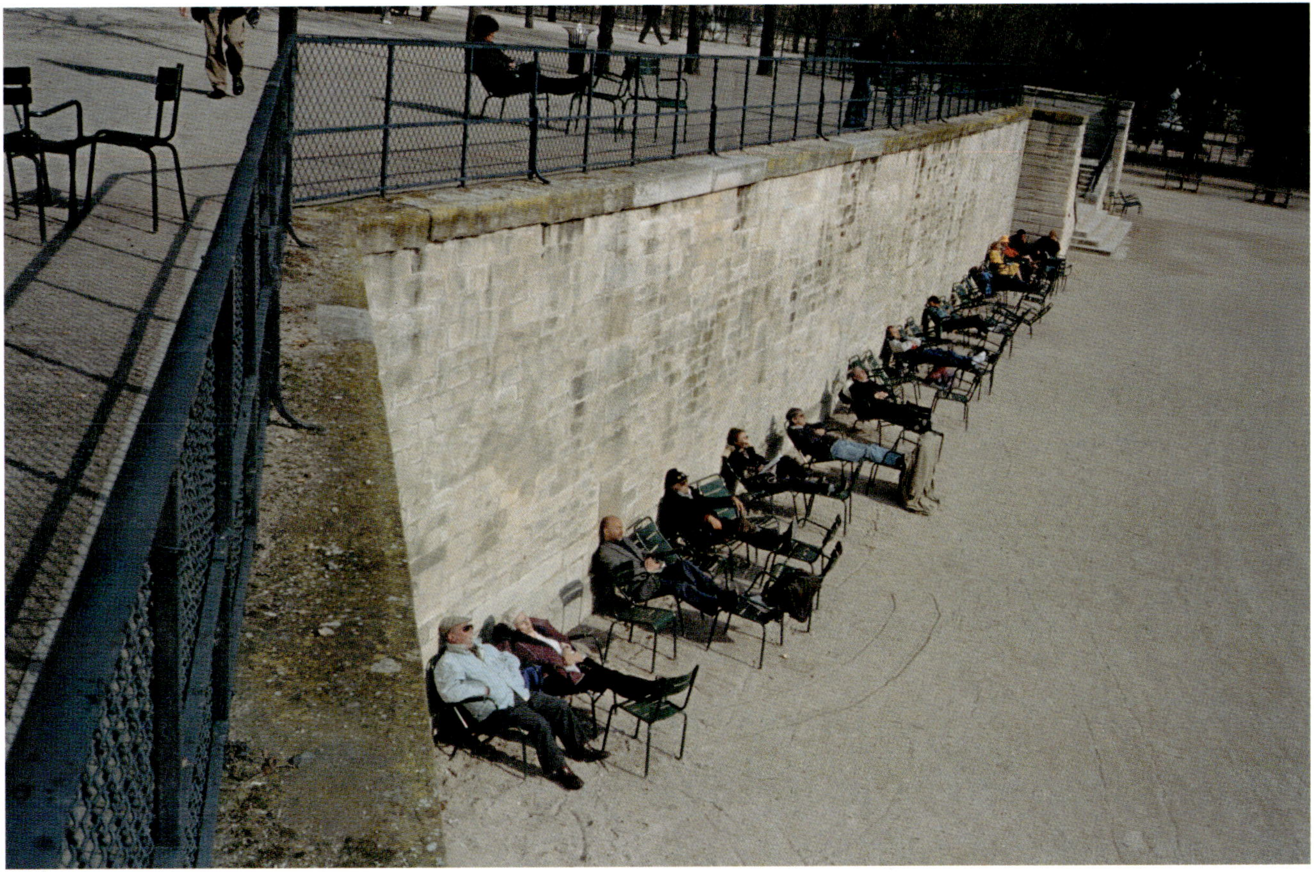

Friday, March 19. Paris. In the Tuileries garden

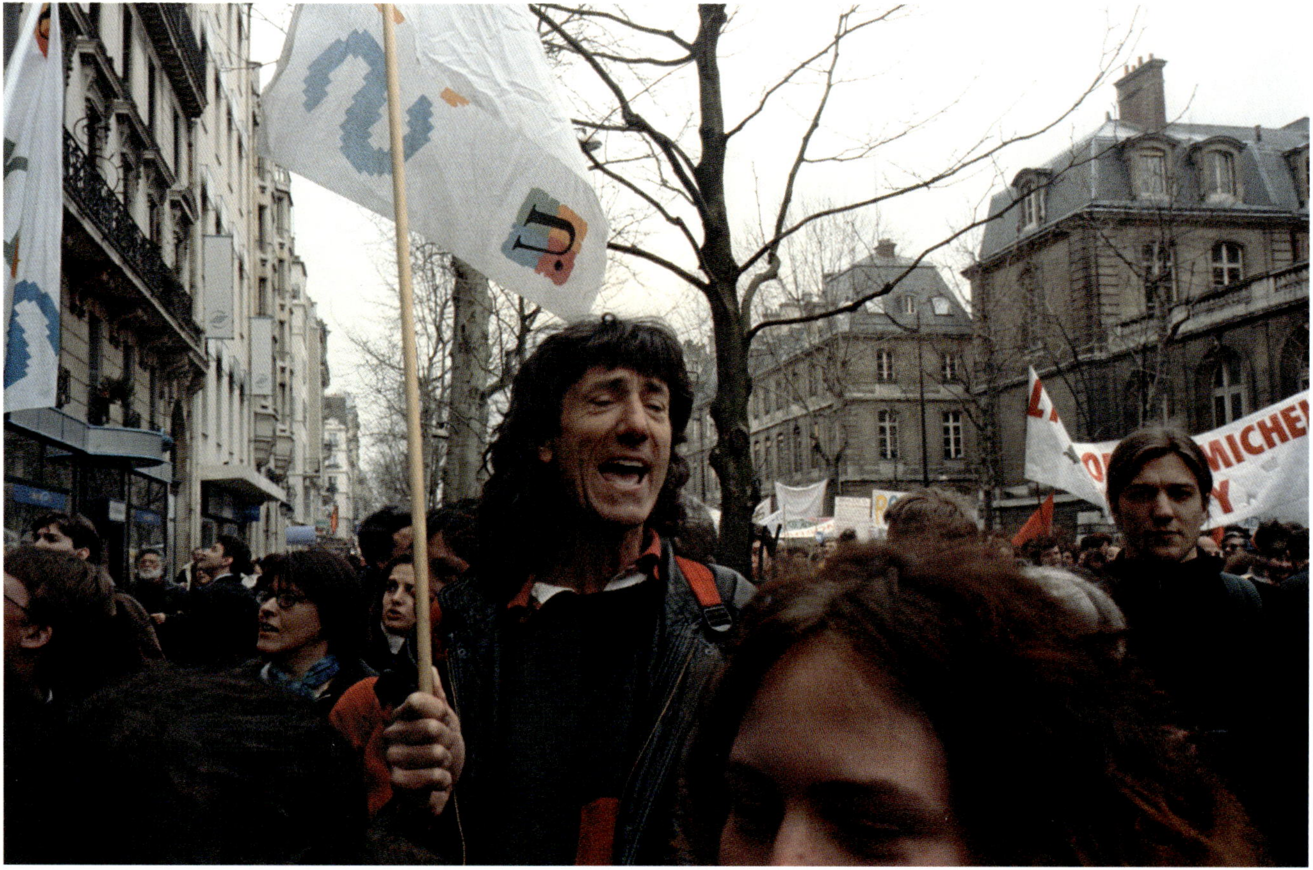

Saturday, March 20. Paris. Student demonstration, Boulevard Saint-Michel

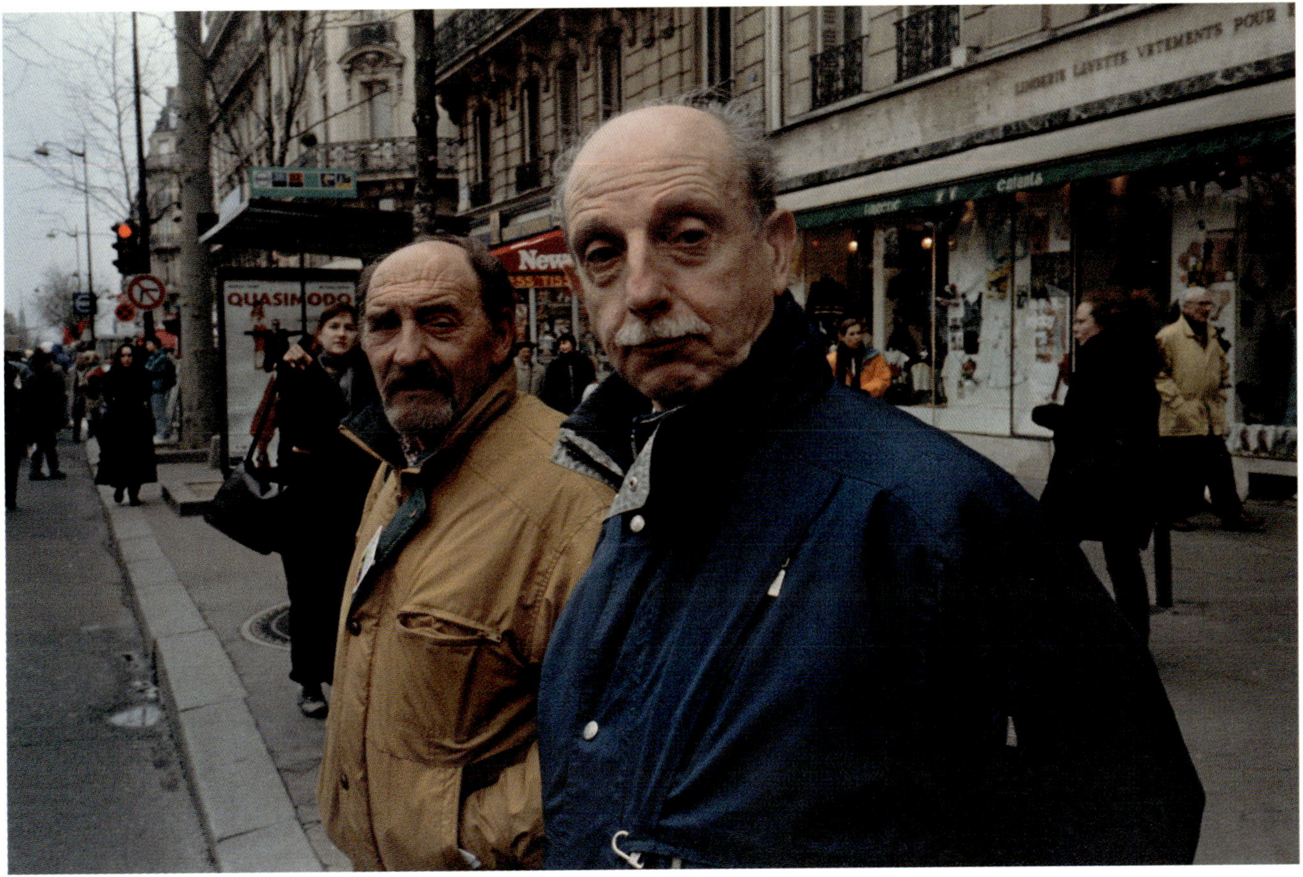

Saturday, March 20. Paris. Onlookers at a student demonstration, Boulevard Saint-Michel

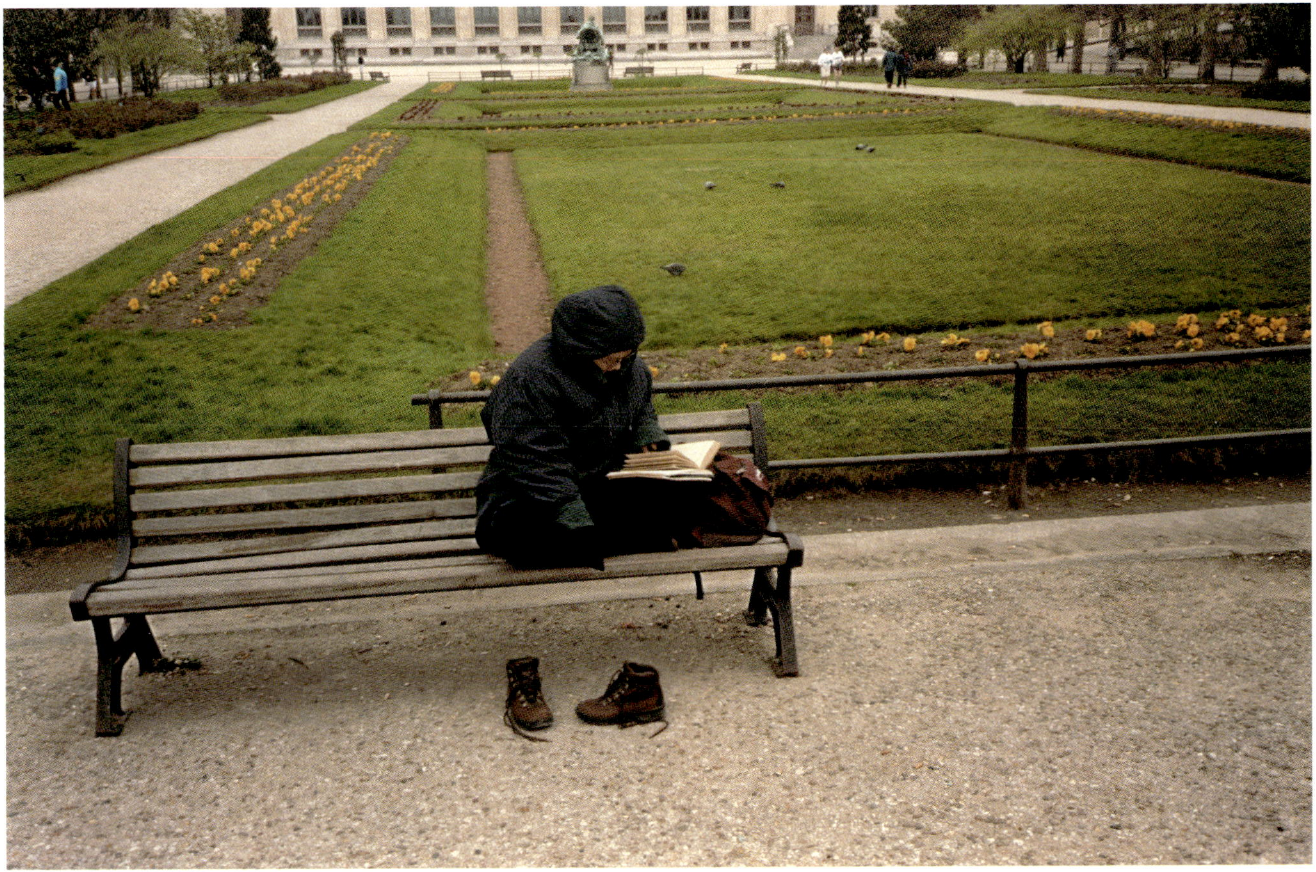

Sunday, March 21. Paris. At the Jardin des Plantes

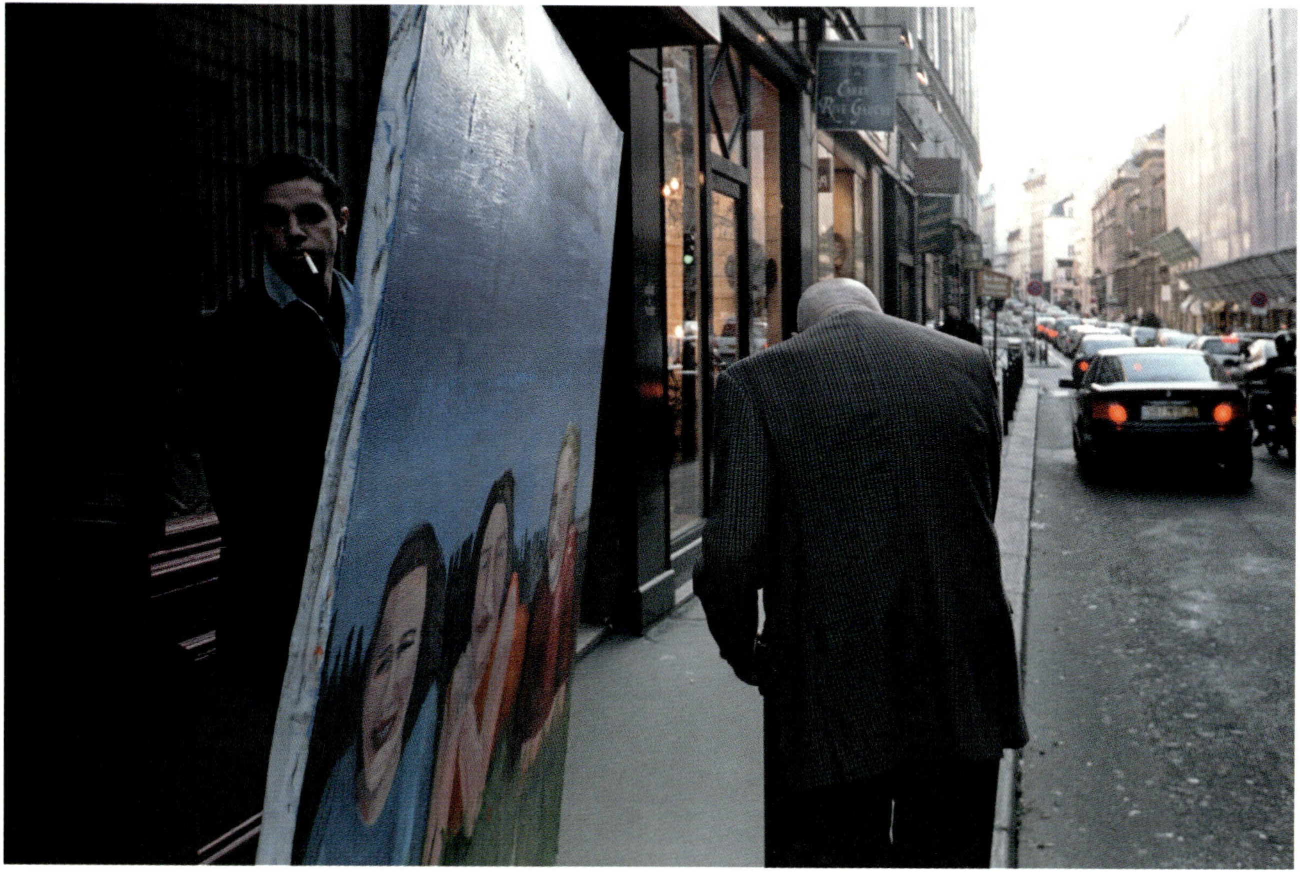

Monday, March 22. Paris. Rue du Bac, Saint-Germain

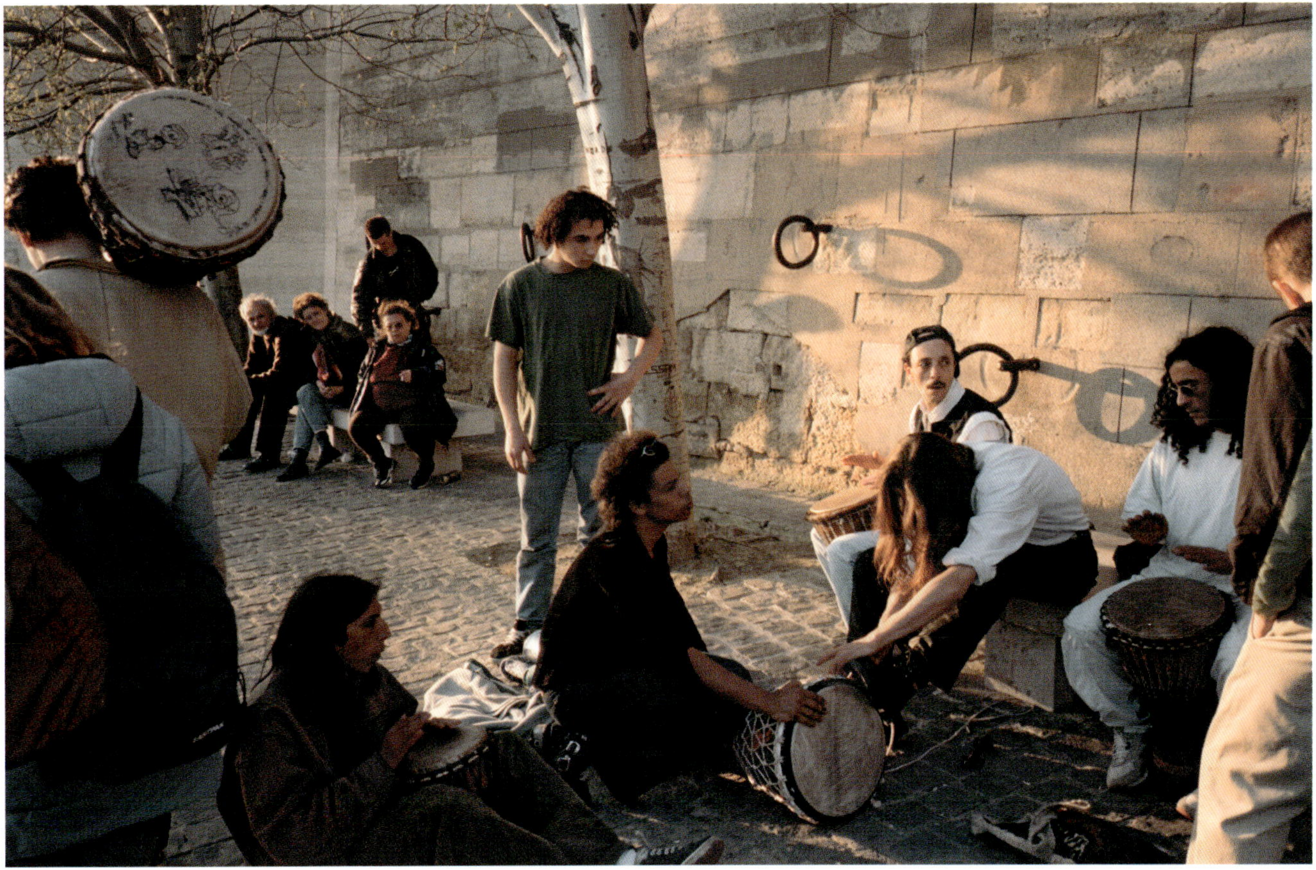

Tuesday, March 23. Paris. On the riverbank, under Pont des Arts

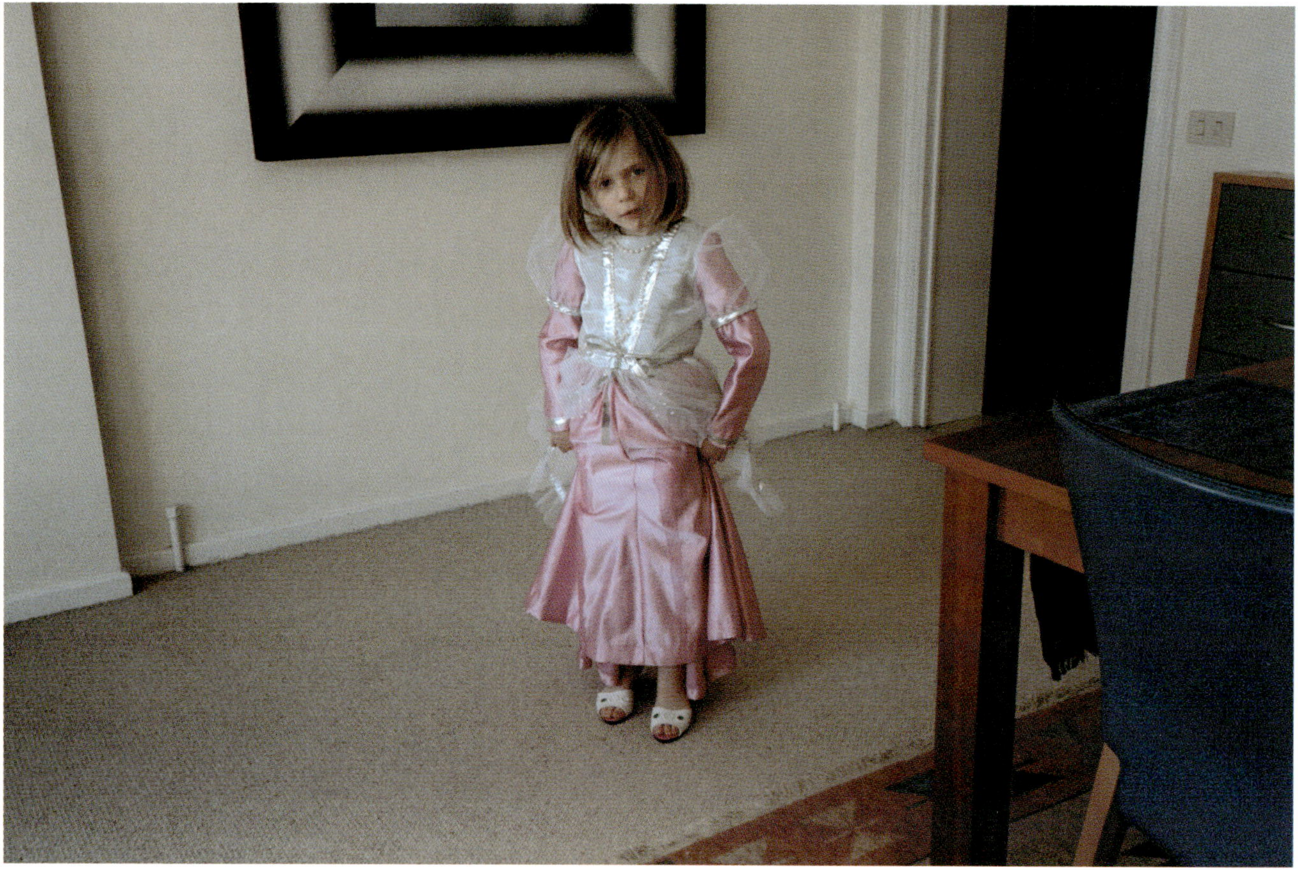

Wednesday, March 24. Brussels. Alba Horvat

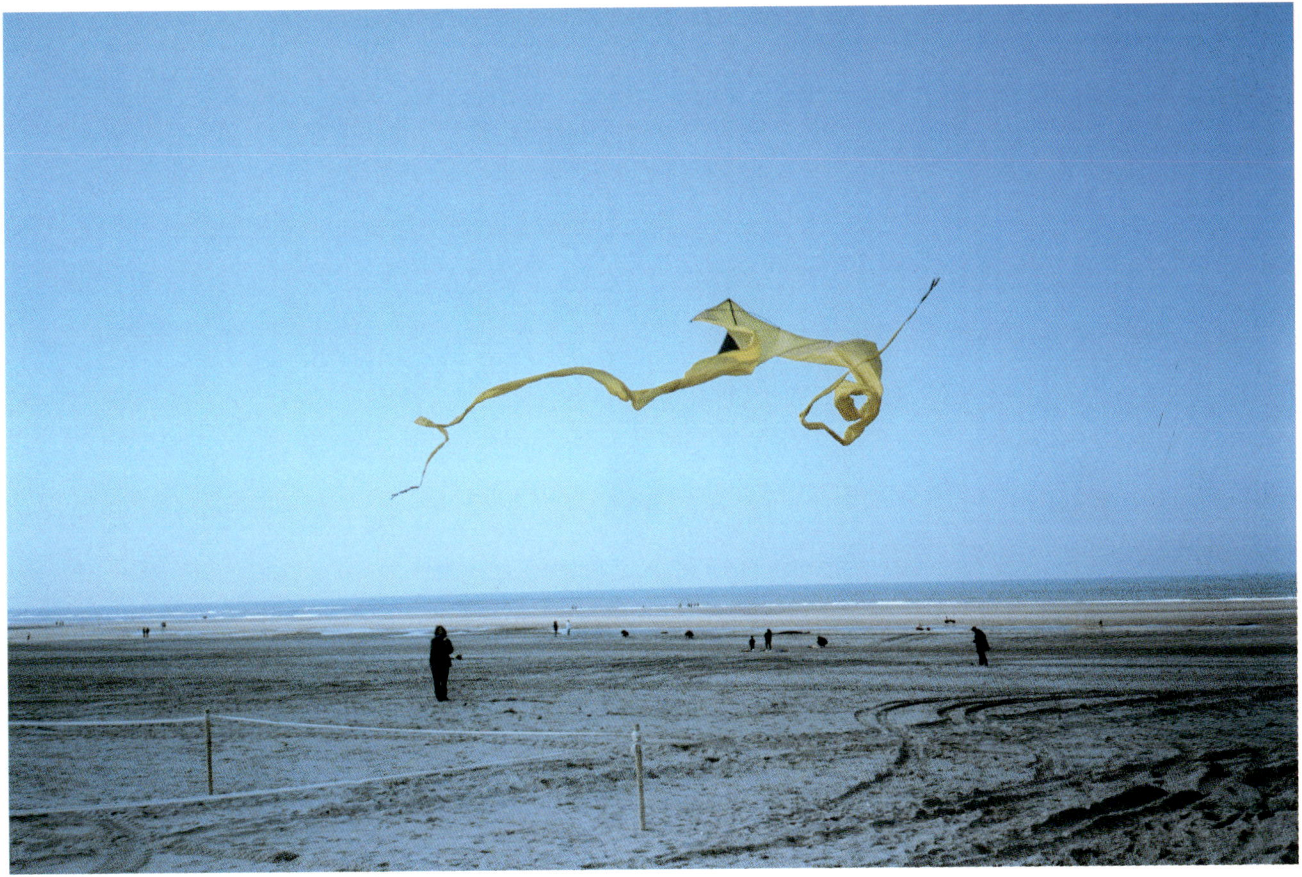

Thursday, March 25. Berck-sur-Mer, France. Kite festival

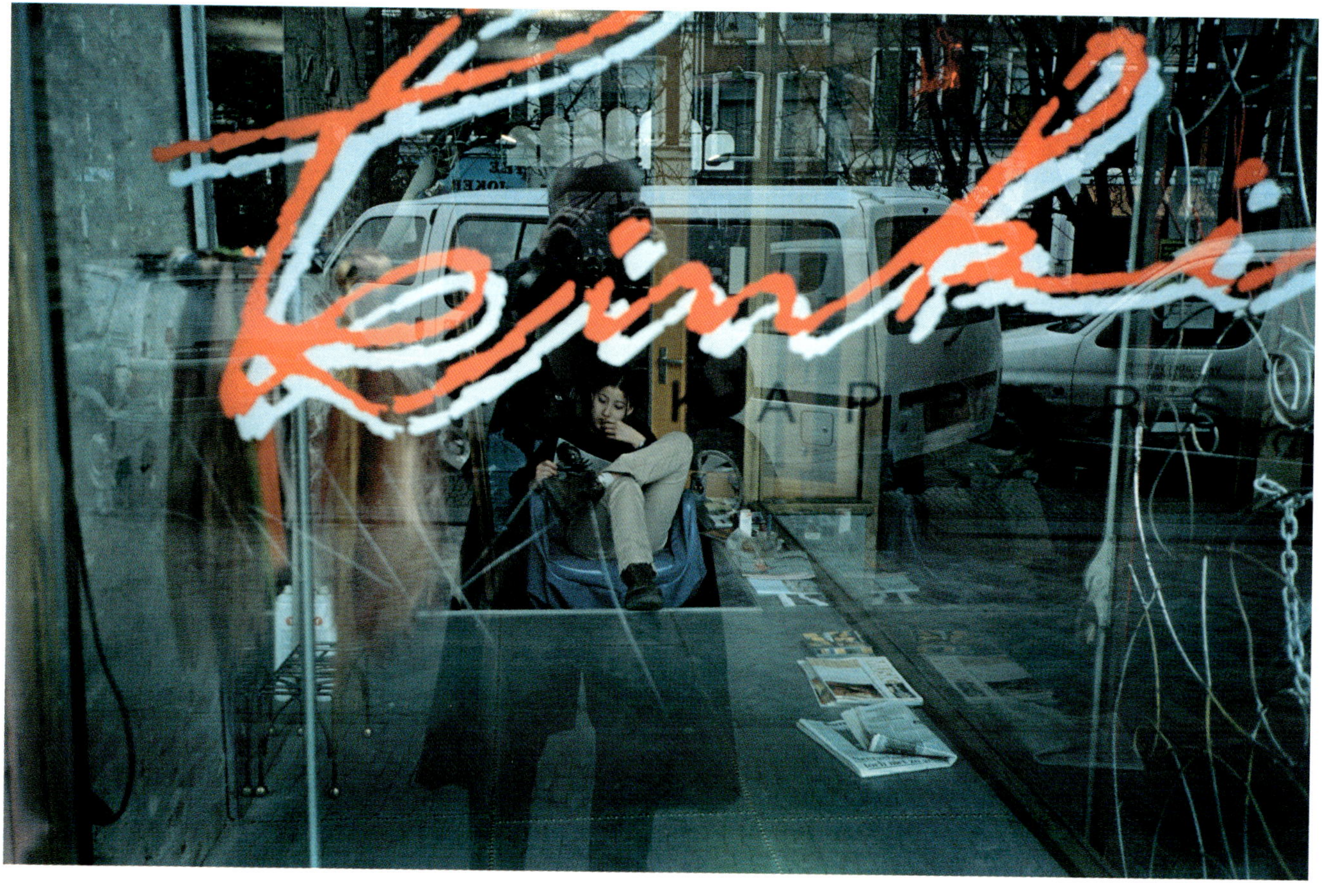

Friday, March 26. Utrecht, Netherlands. Shop window

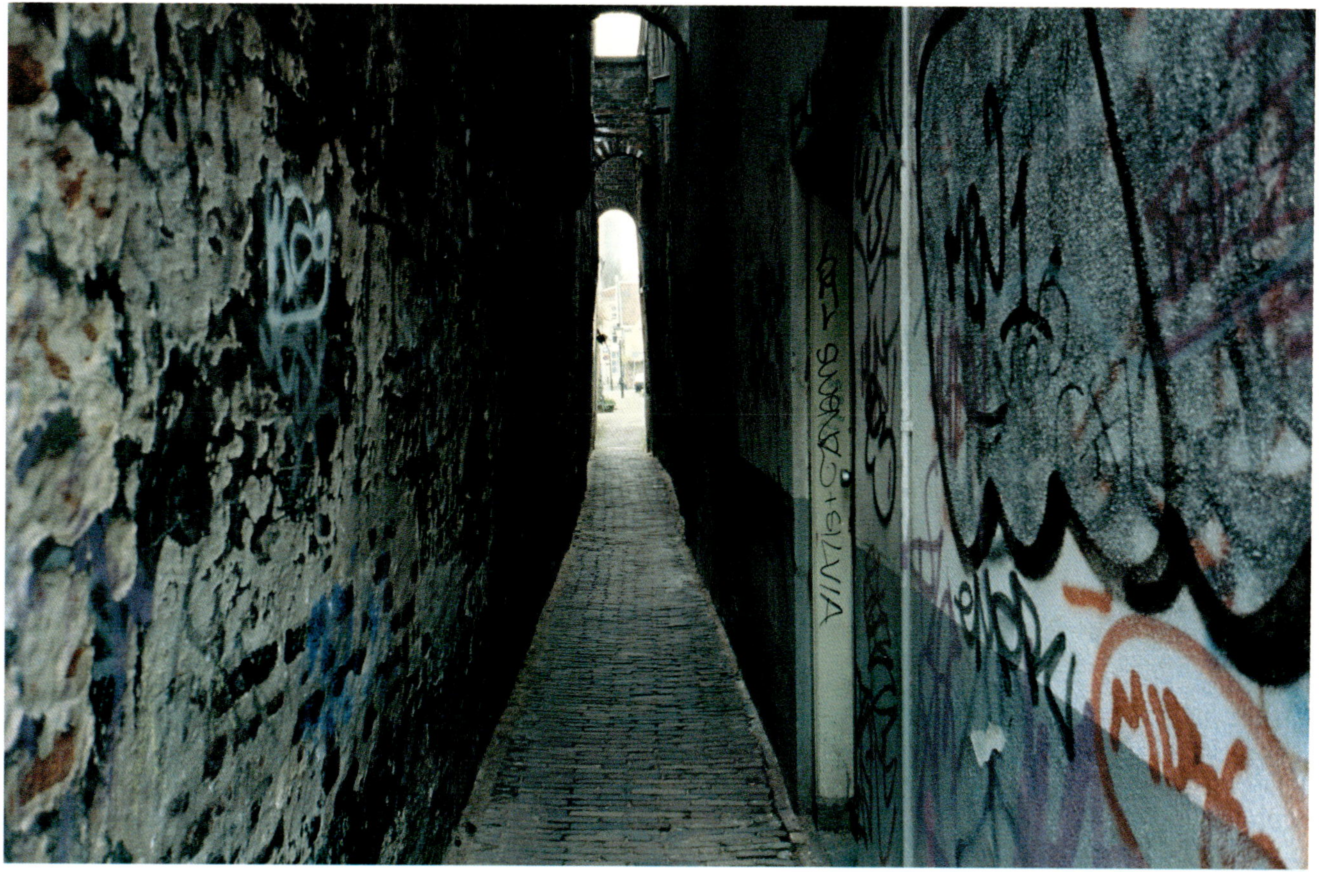

Saturday, March 27. Utrecht, Netherlands. Alleyway

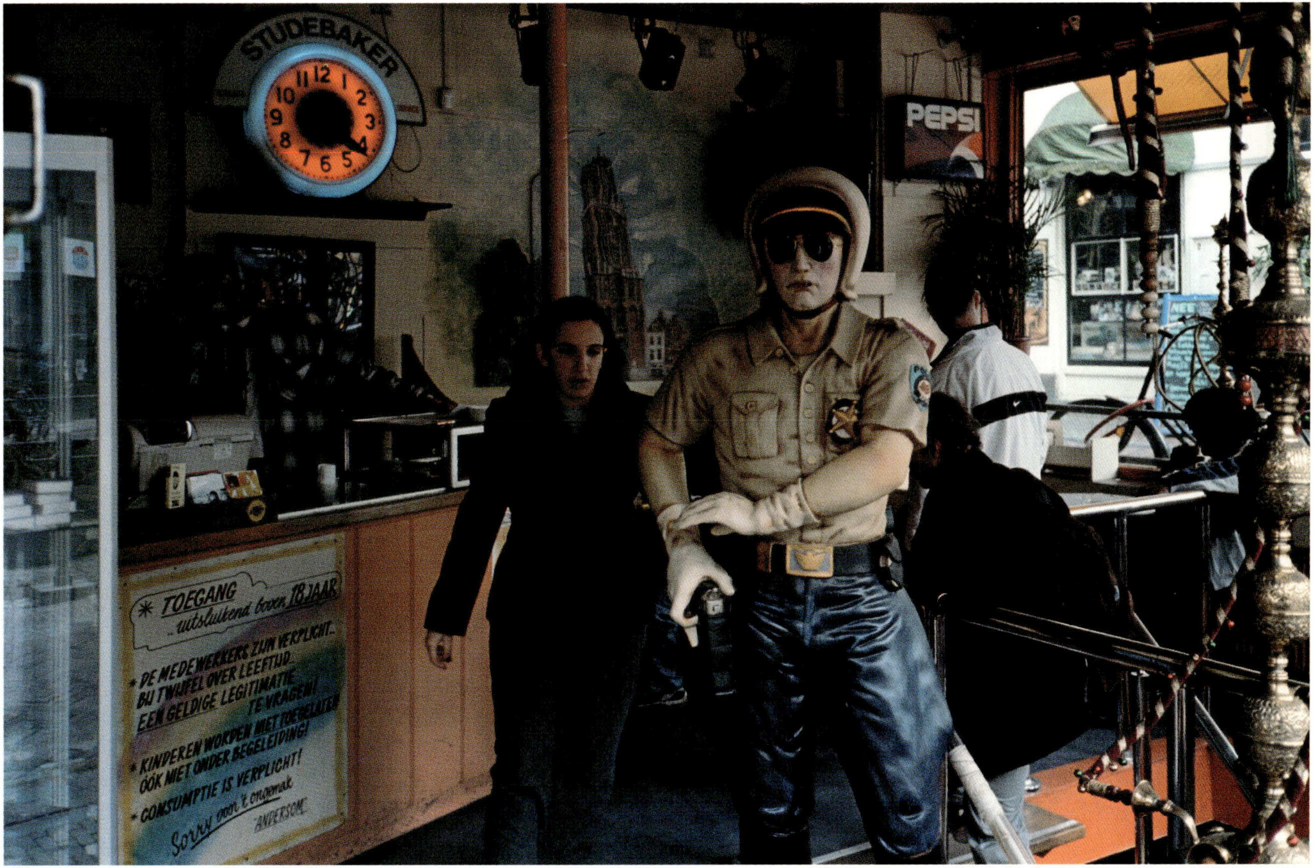

Sunday, March 28. Utrecht, Netherlands. Electronic games

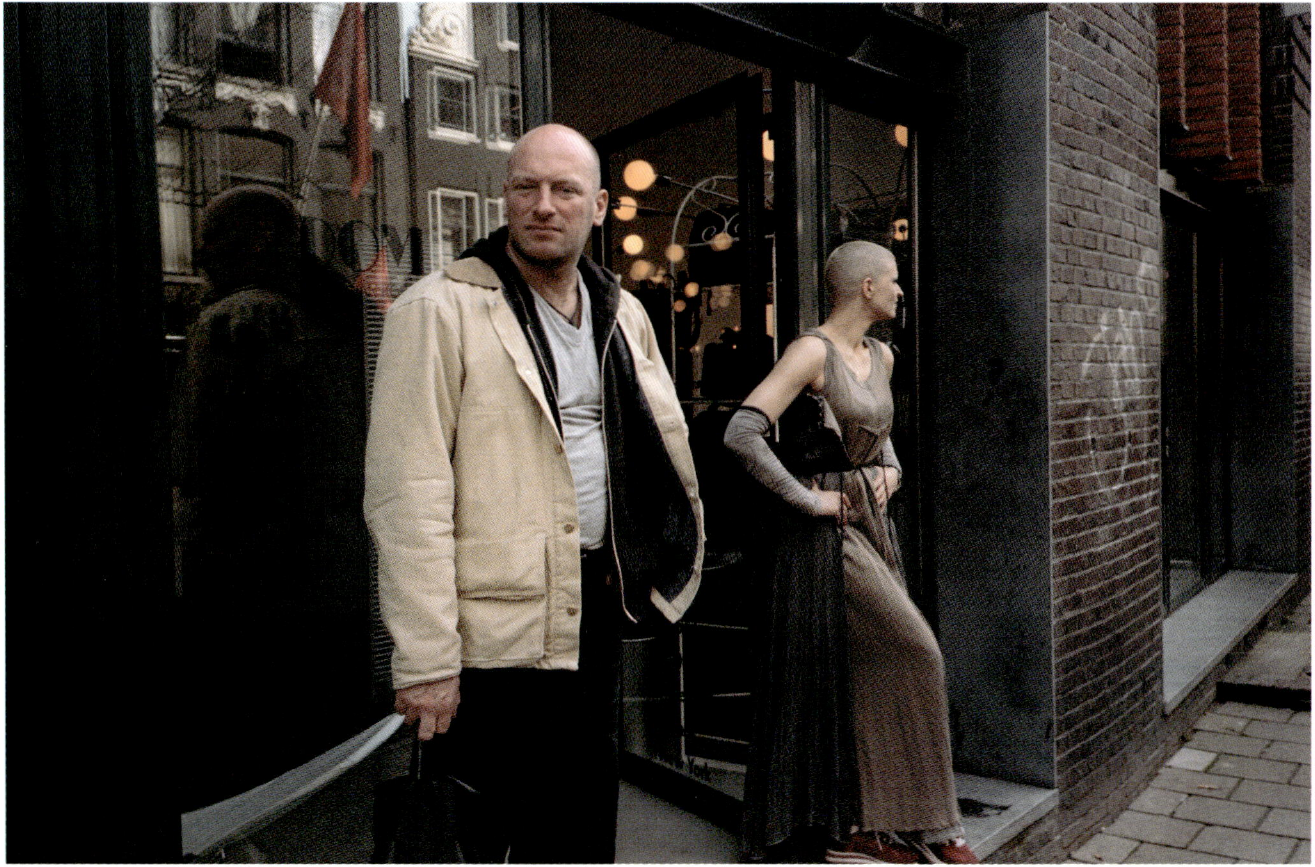

Monday, March 29. Amsterdam, Netherlands. Street scene

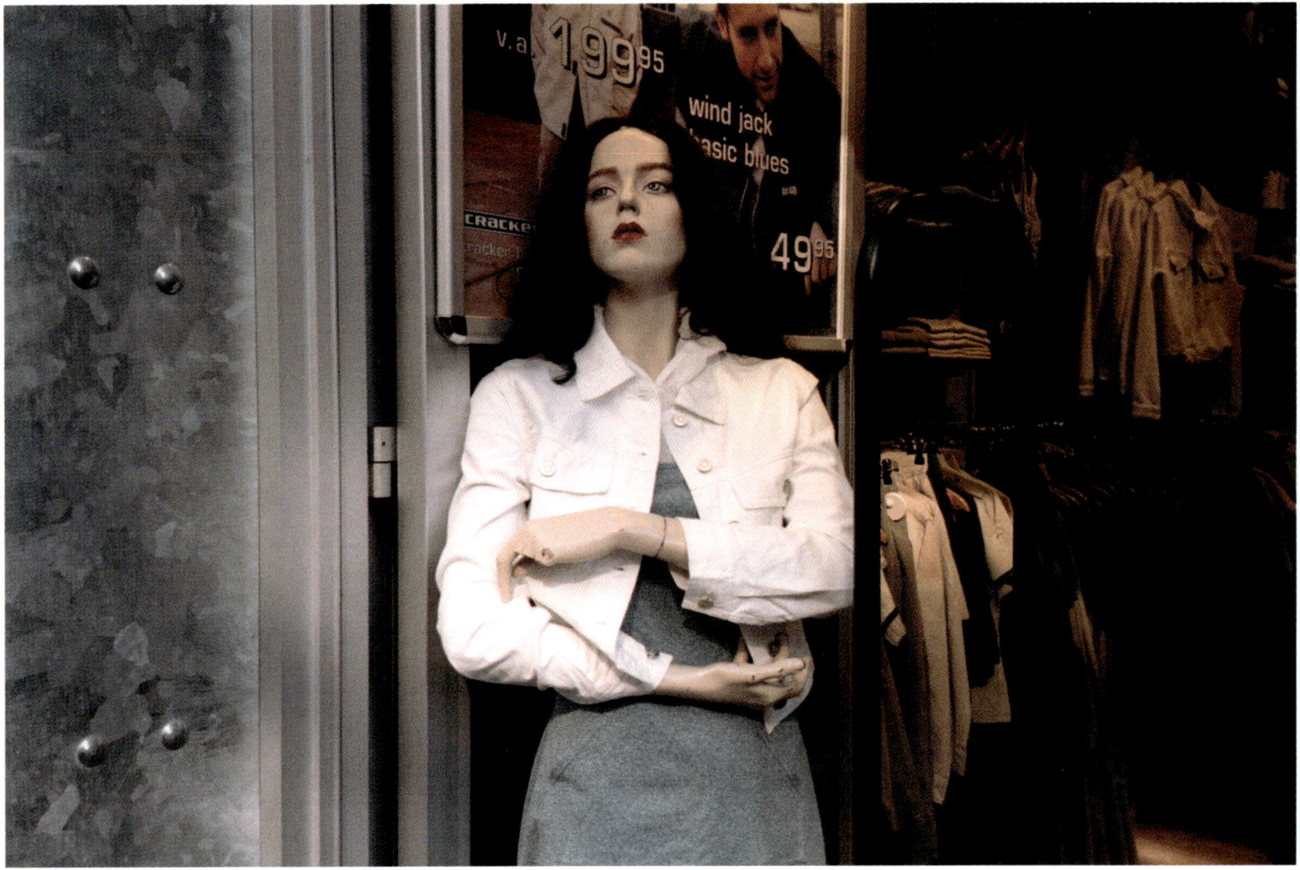

Tuesday, March 30. Amsterdam, Netherlands. Mannequin

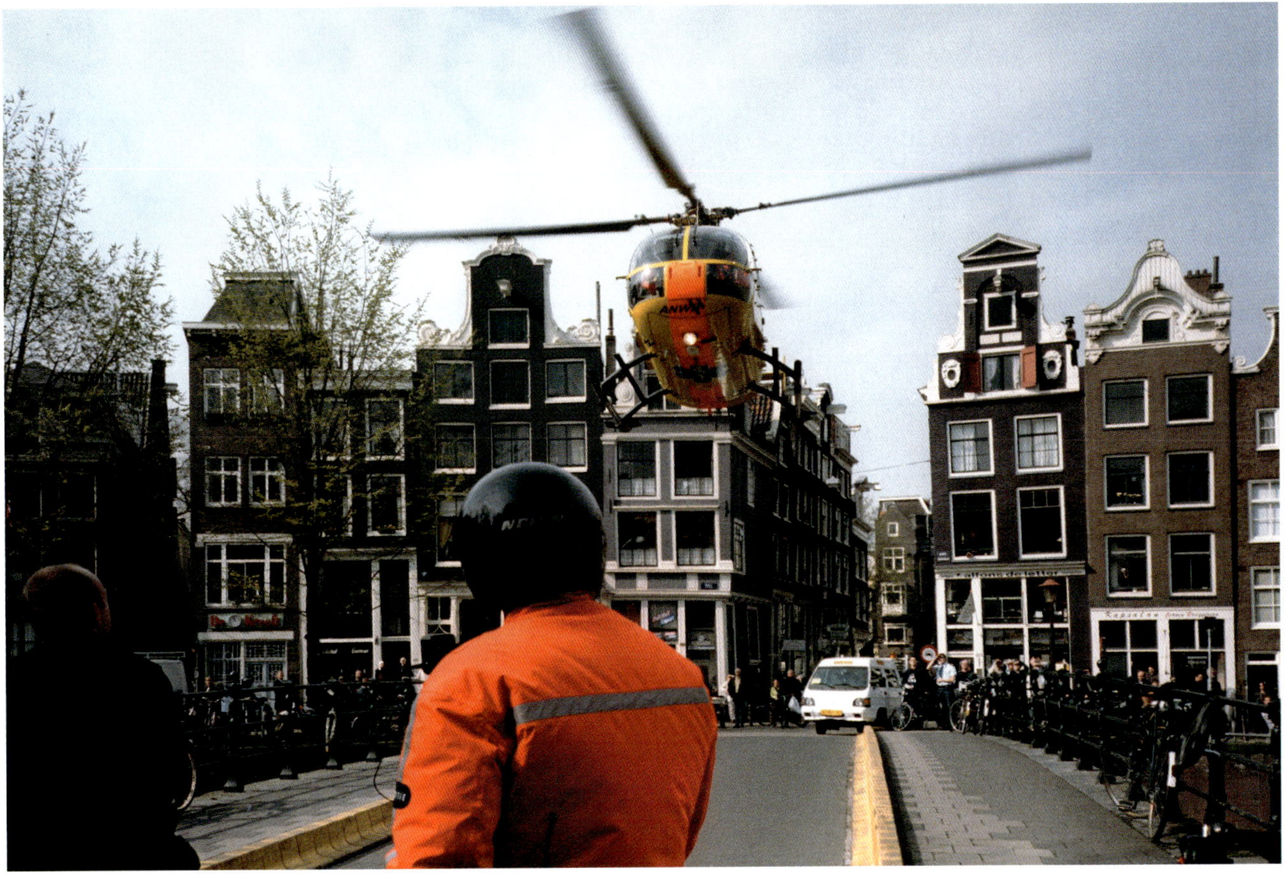

Wednesday, March 31. Amsterdam, Netherlands. Emergency helicopter

APRIL

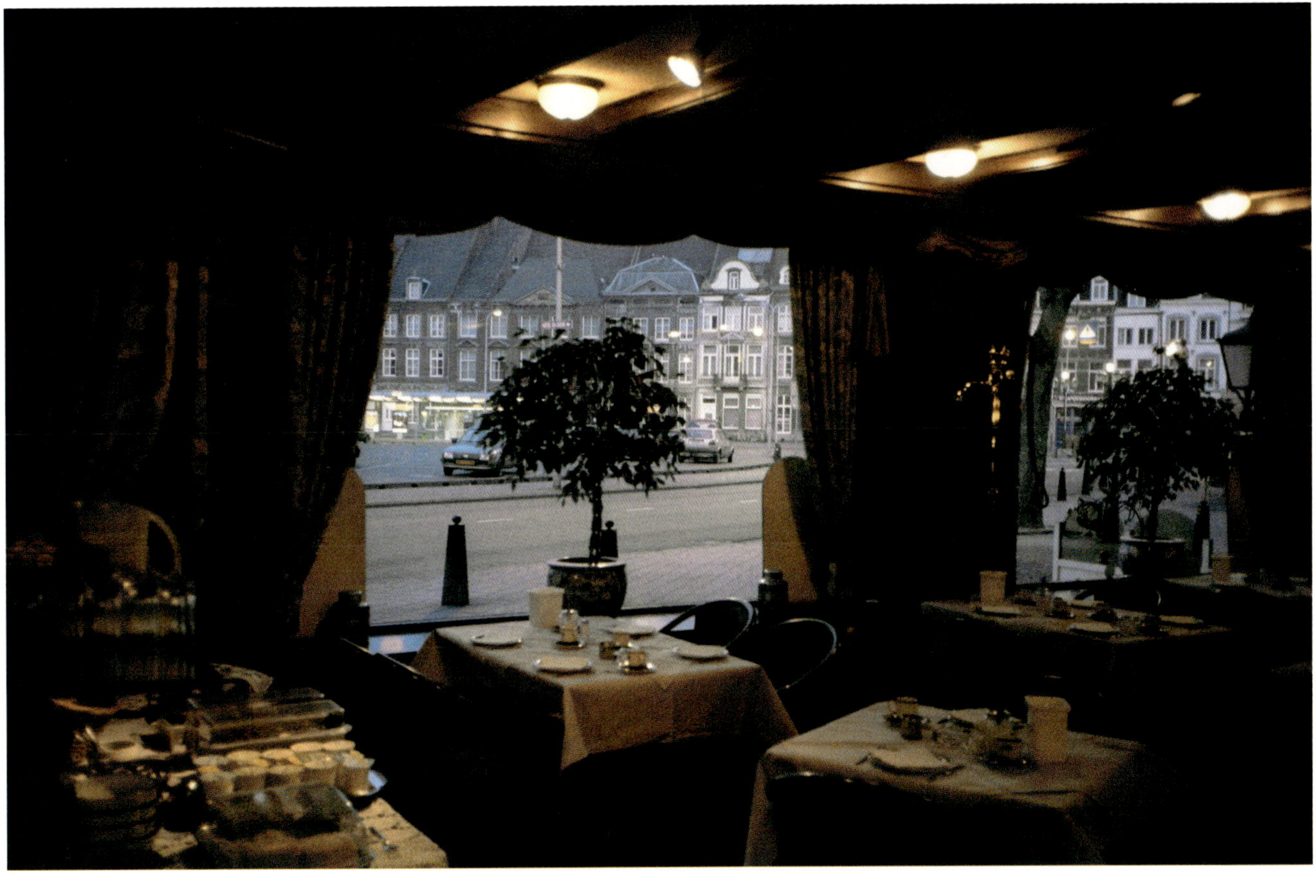

Thursday, April 1. Maastricht, Netherlands. Hotel dining room

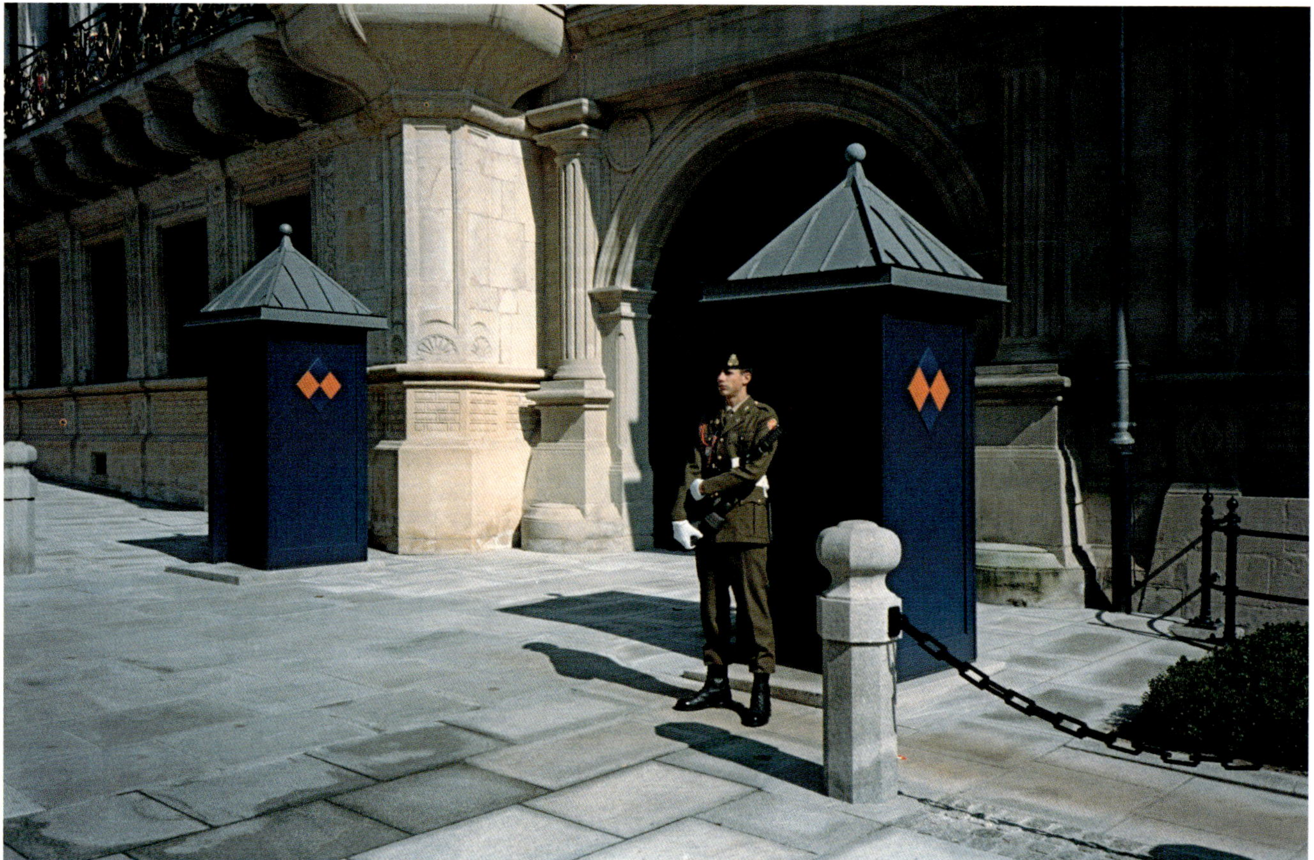

Friday, April 2. Luxembourg. The palace guard

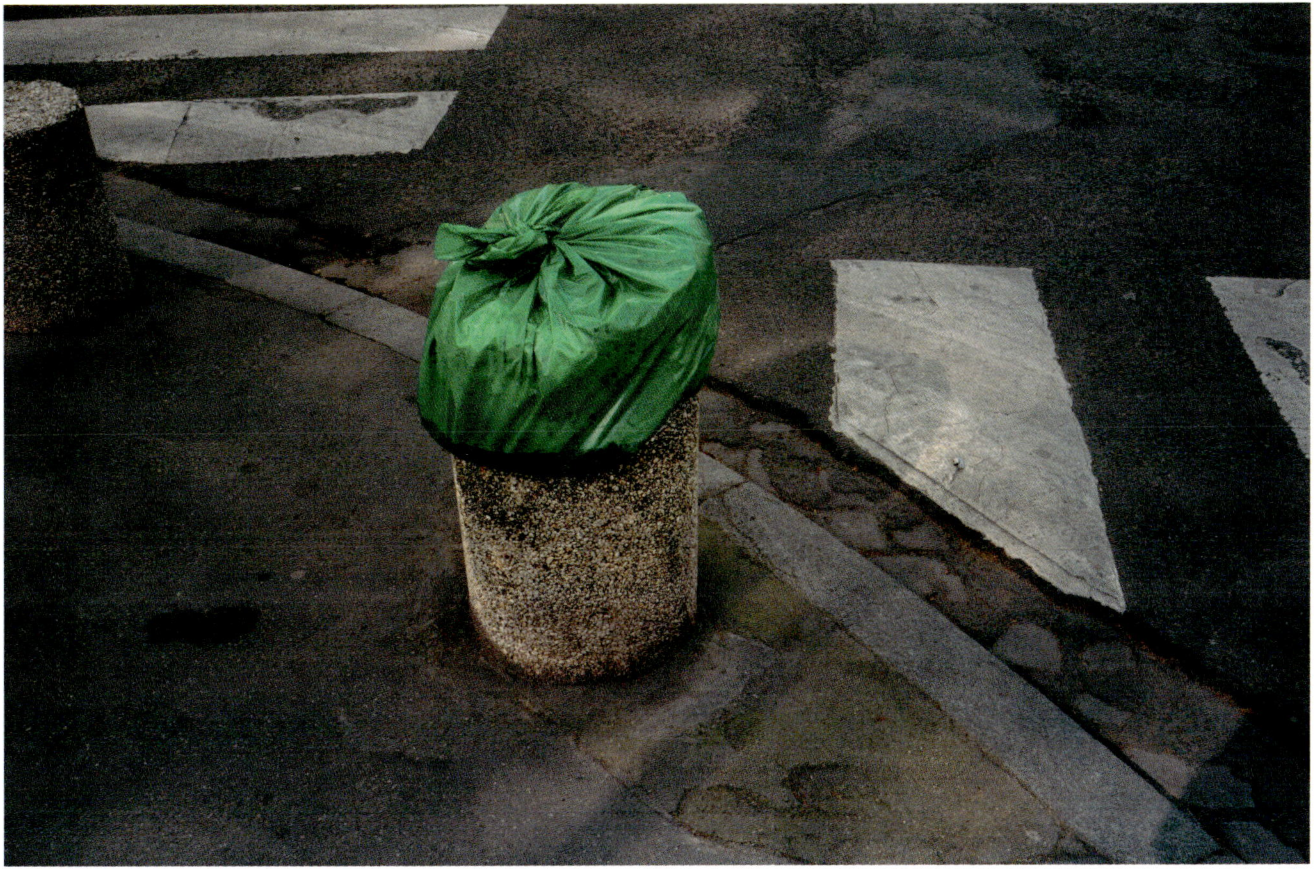

Saturday, April 3. Boulogne, France. Street corner

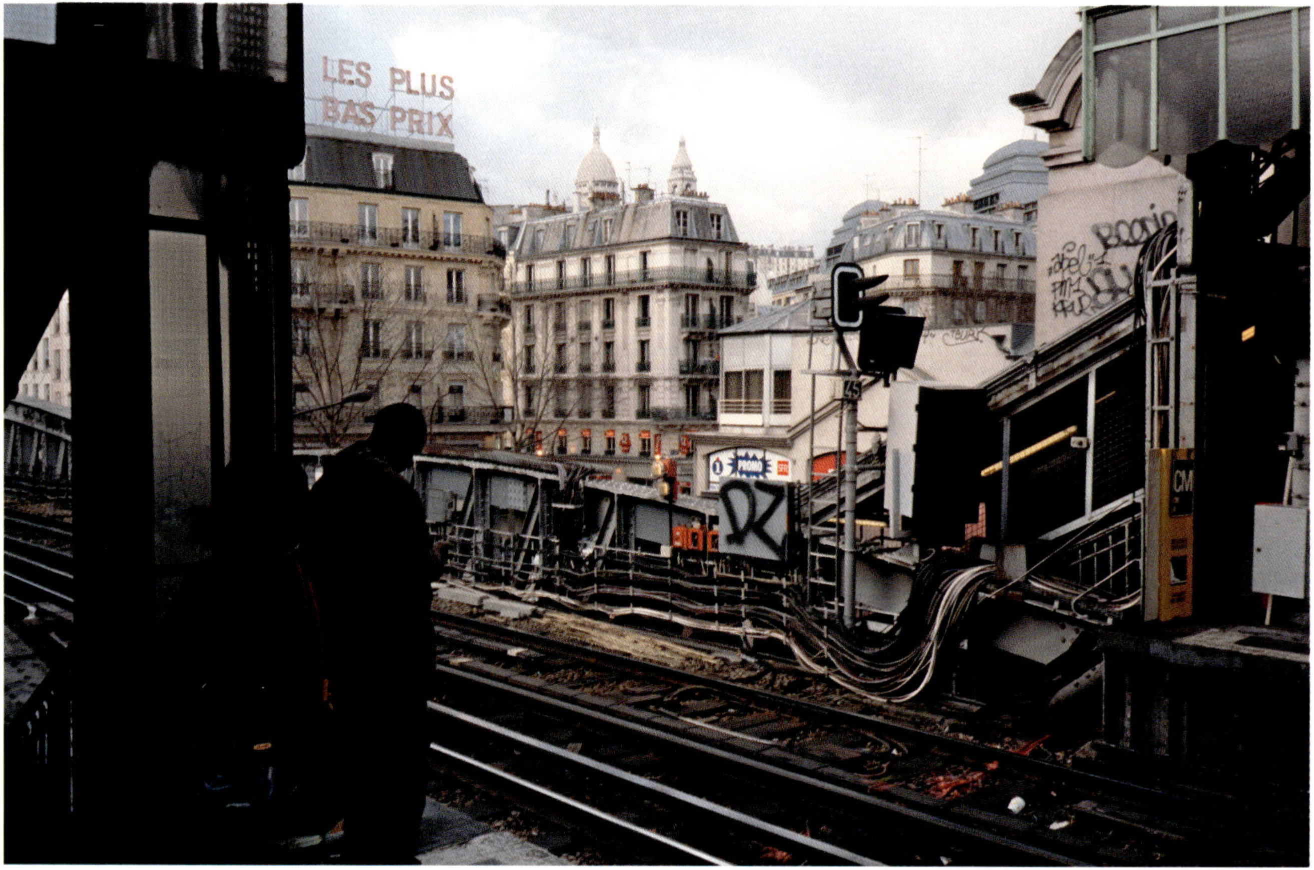

Sunday, April 4. Paris. Barbès-Rochechouart métro station

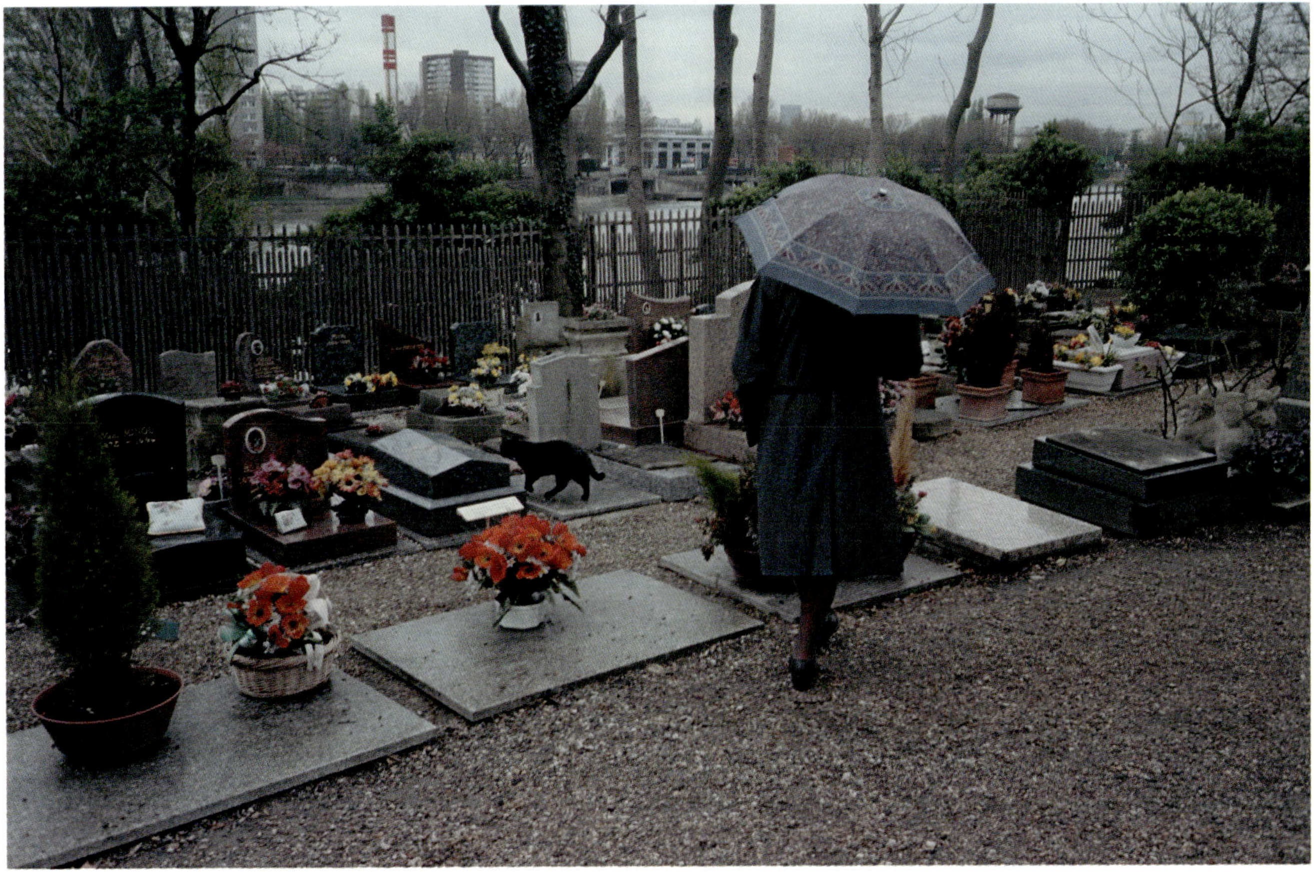

Monday, April 5. Asnières, France. Pet cemetery

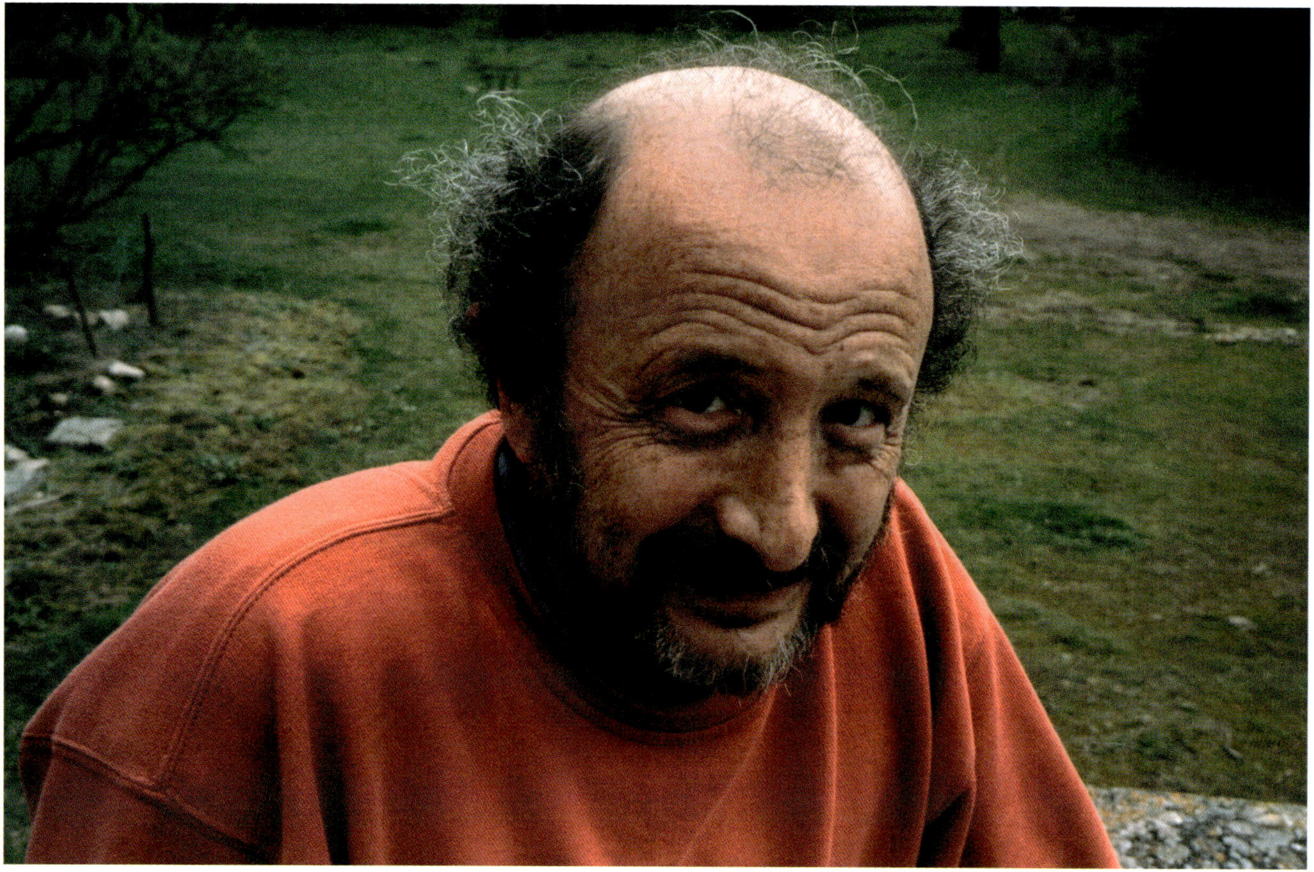

Tuesday, April 6. La Brosse, France. Dr. Alain Didier-Weill, psychoanalyst

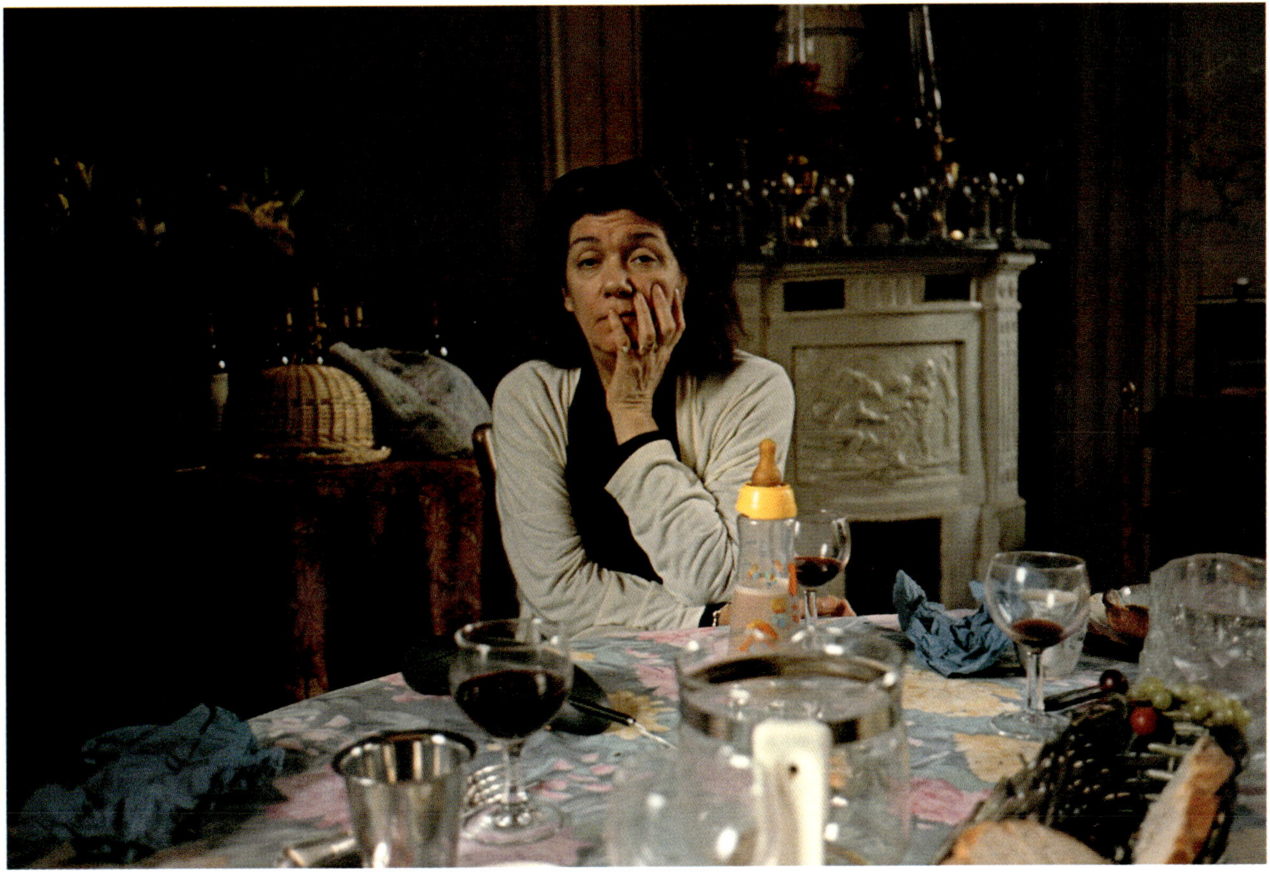

Tuesday, April 6. La Brosse, France. Marie Emmanuelle Didier-Weill, psychoanalyst, Alain's wife

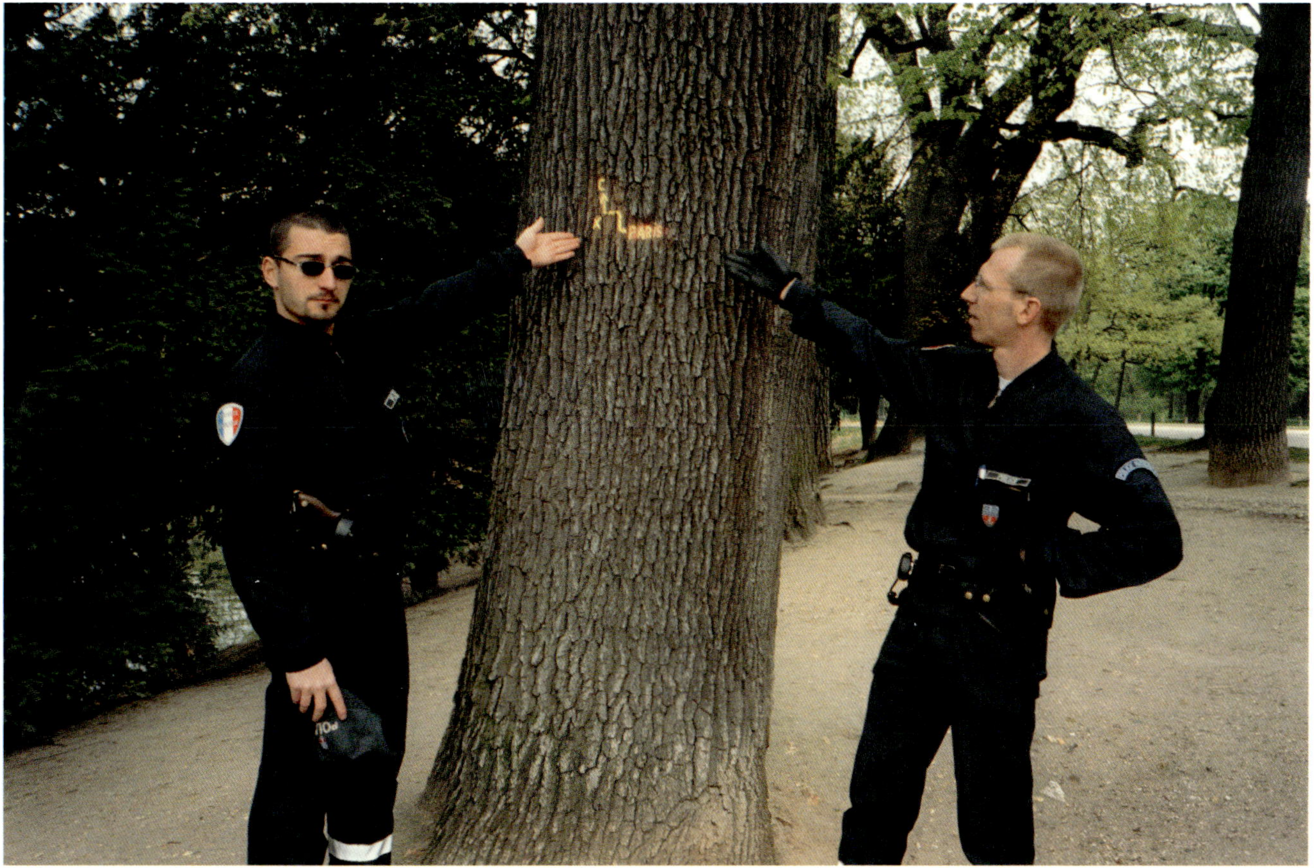

Wednesday, April 7. Paris. Bois de Boulogne. Policemen (see note)

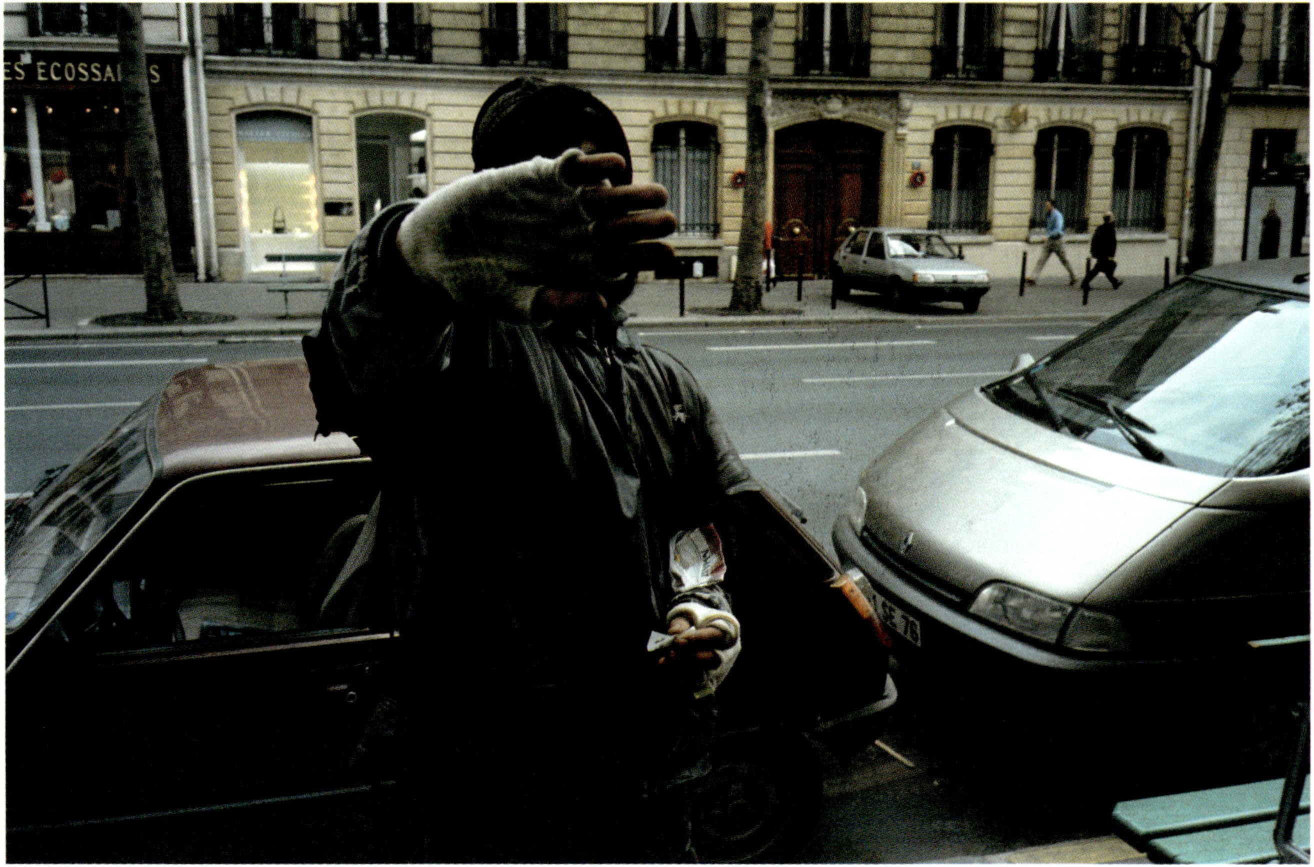

Thursday, April 8. Paris. Boulevard Saint-Germain, "no photographs, please"

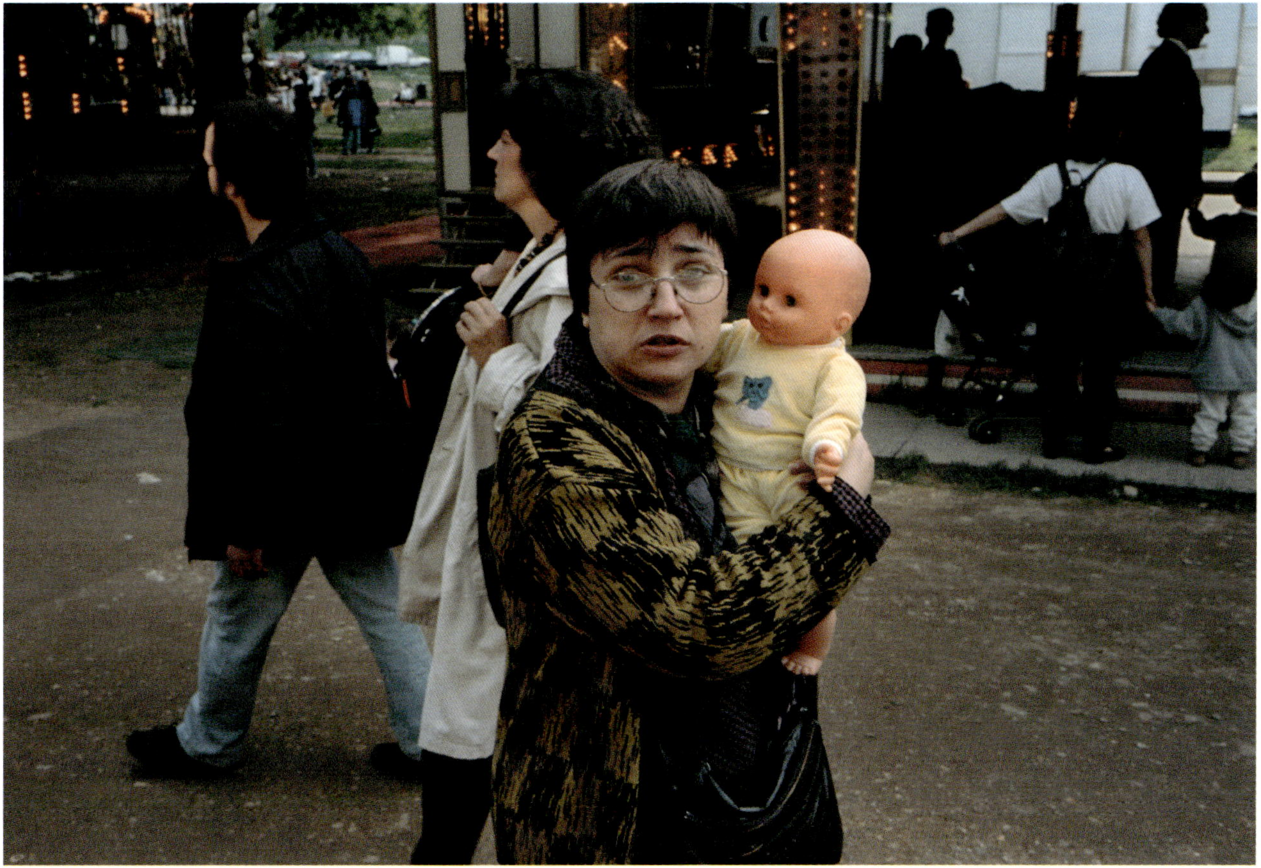

Friday, April 9. Sèvres, France. Street scene

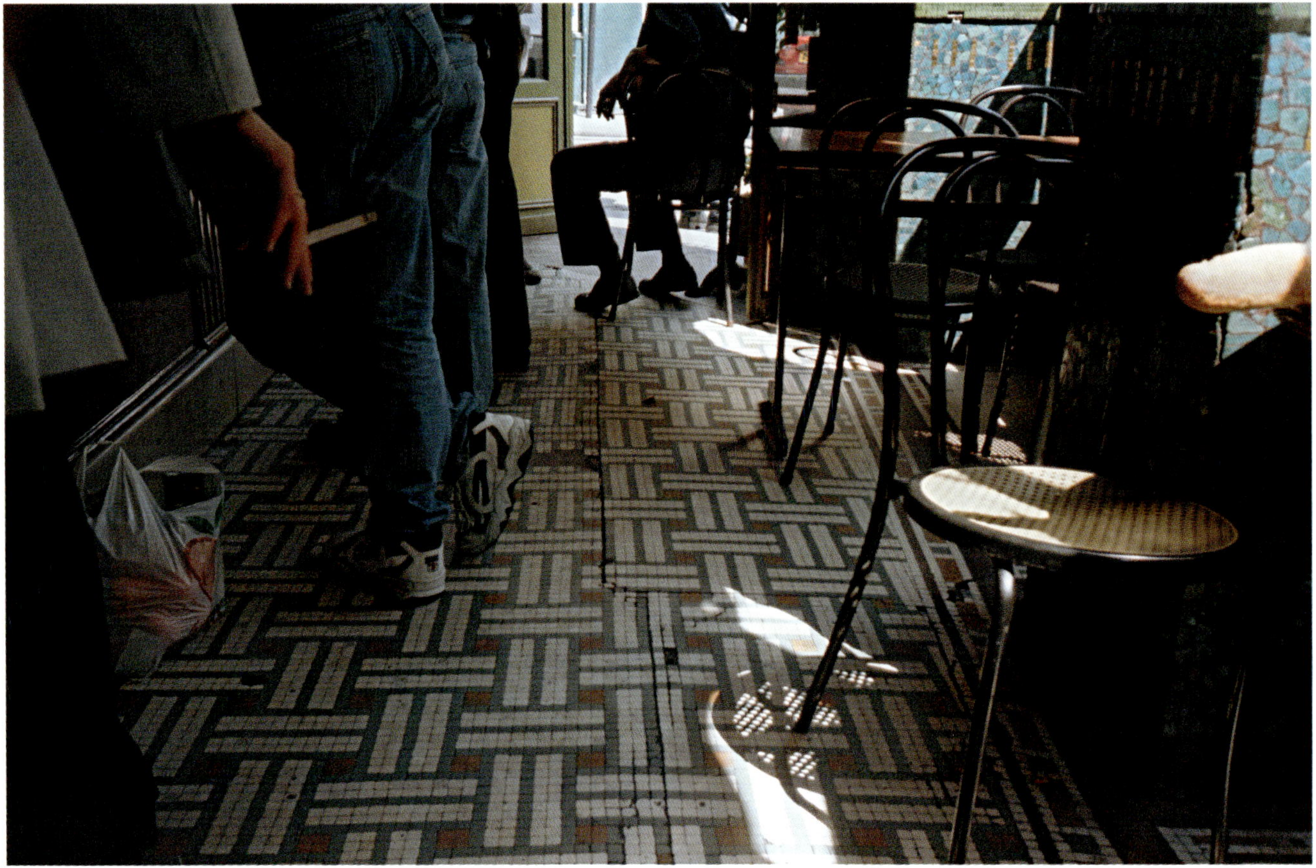

Saturday, April 10. Paris. Café, Montparnasse area

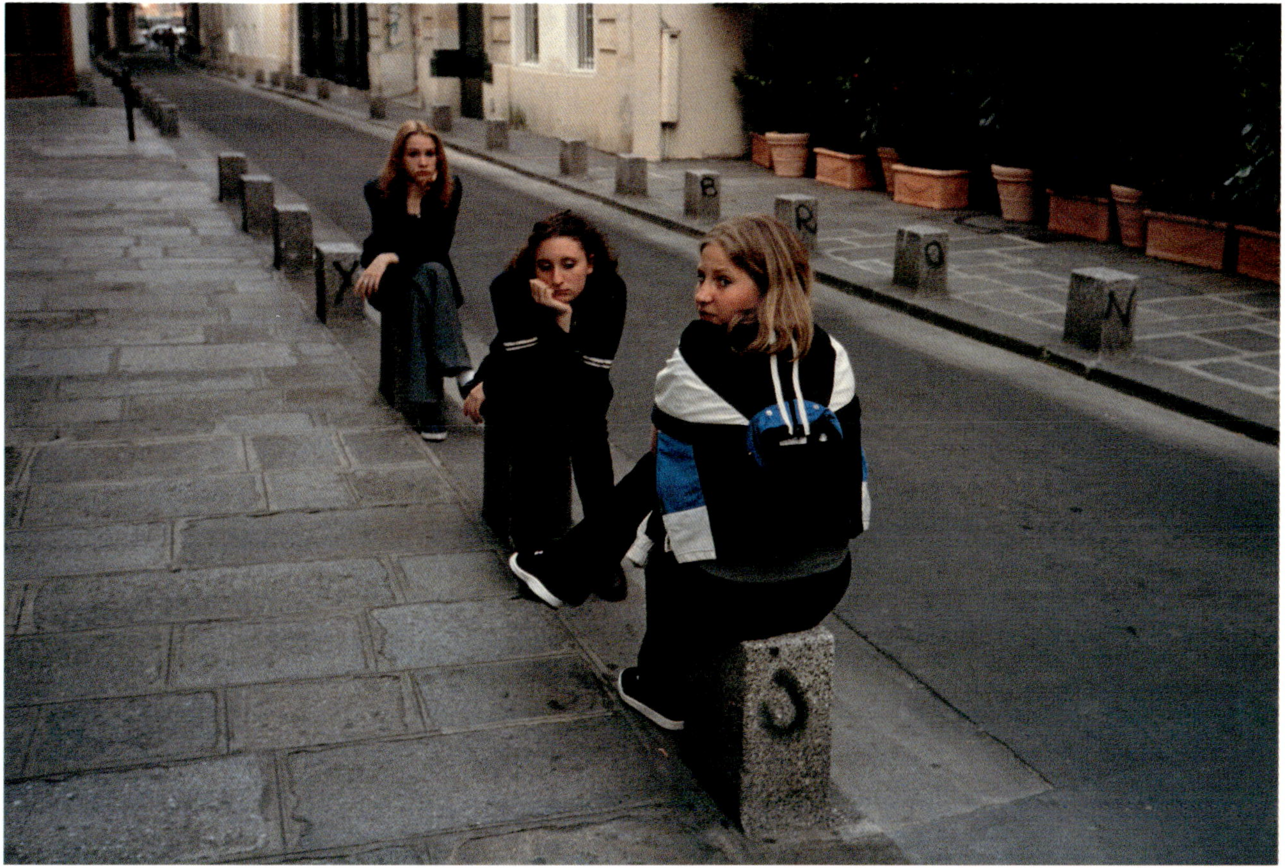

Sunday, April 11. Paris. Street scene, Latin Quarter

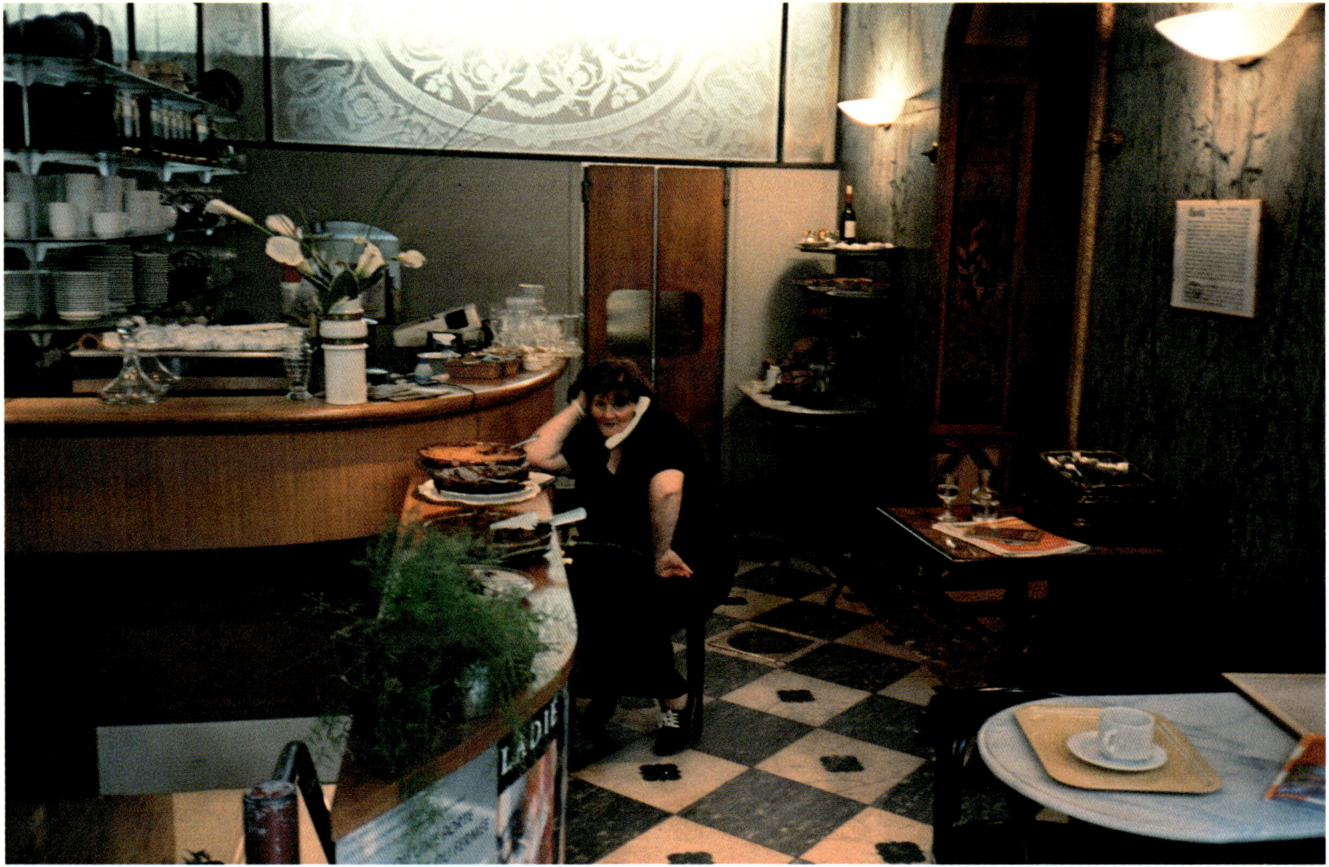

Monday, April 12. Paris. Café, in the Opéra area

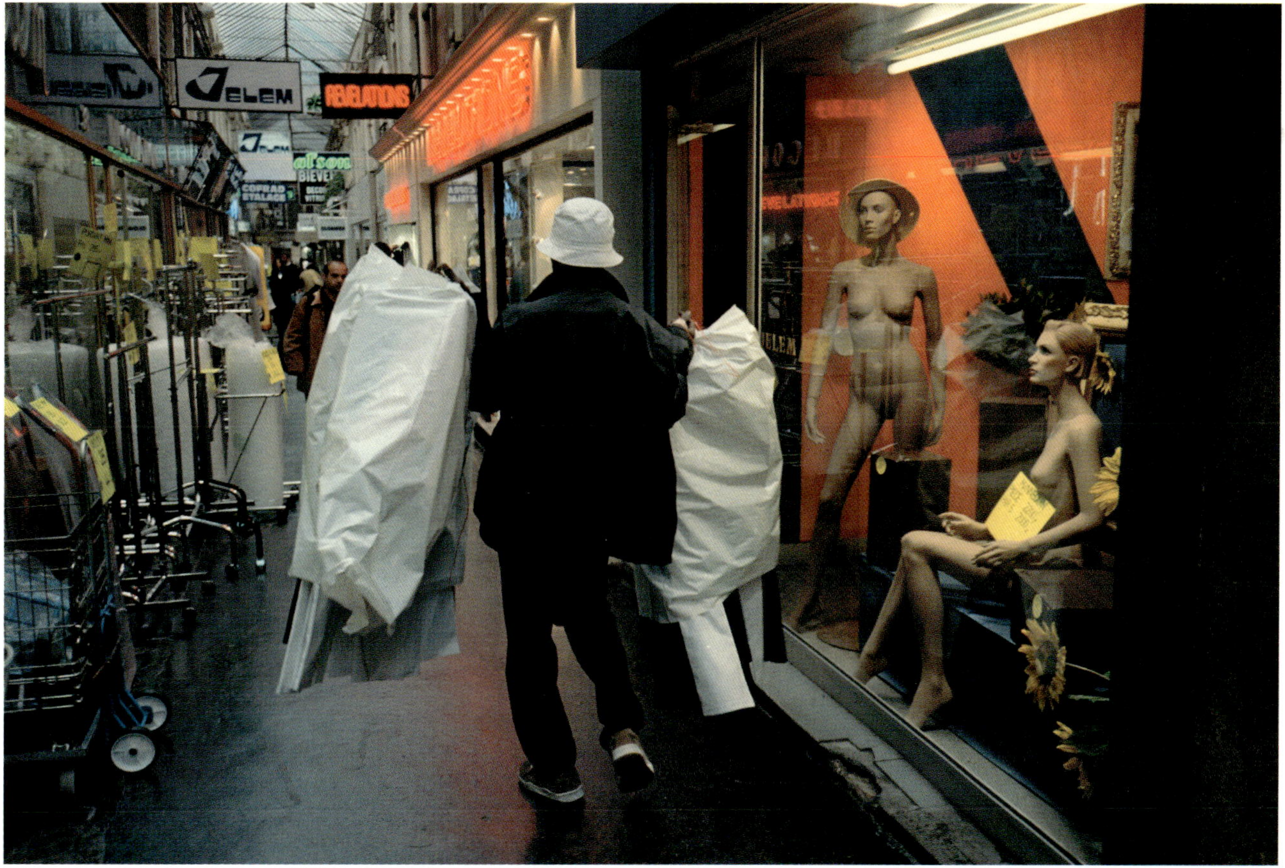

Tuesday, April 13. Paris. Galerie du Caire, in the Sentier area

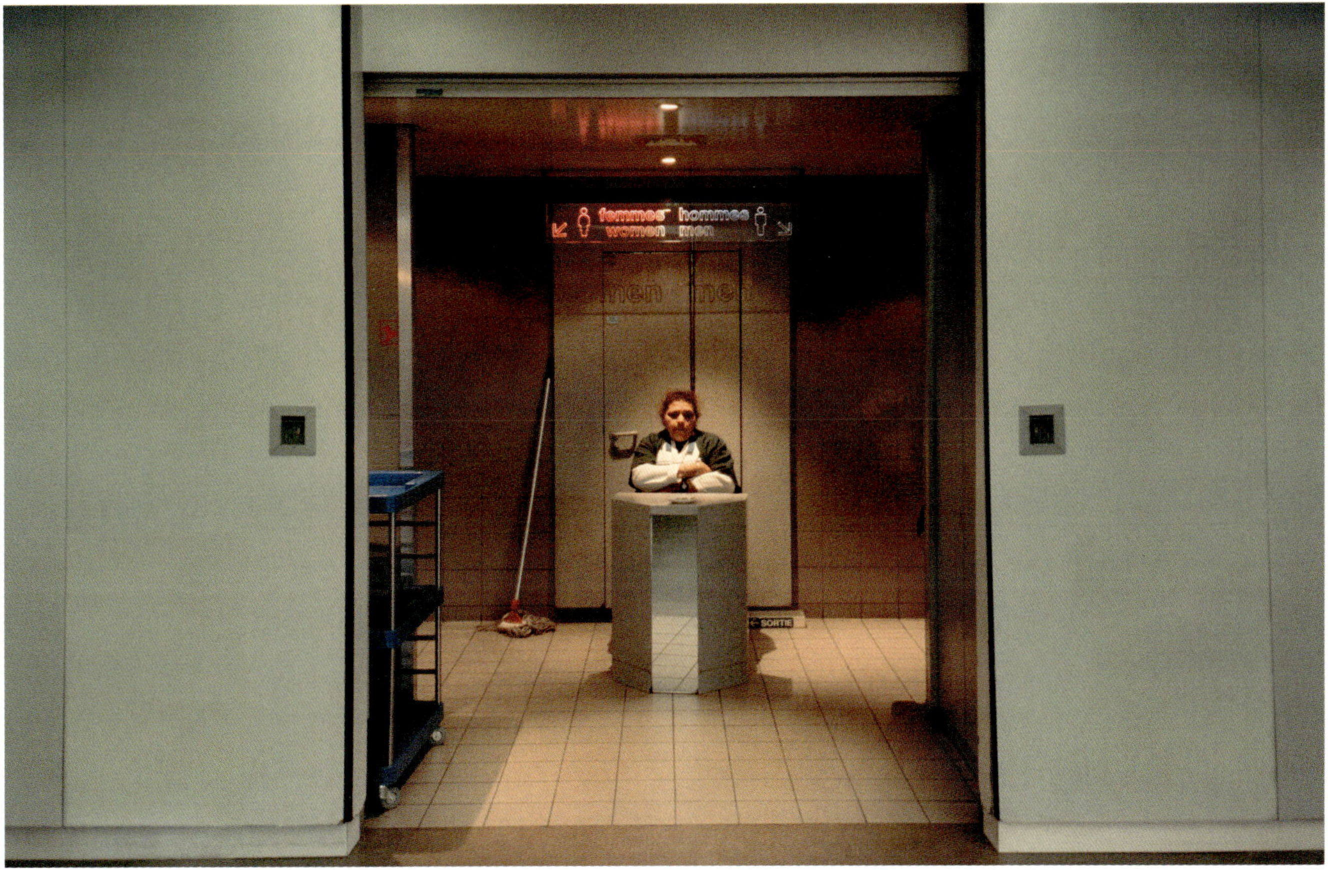

Wednesday, April 14. Paris. Orly airport

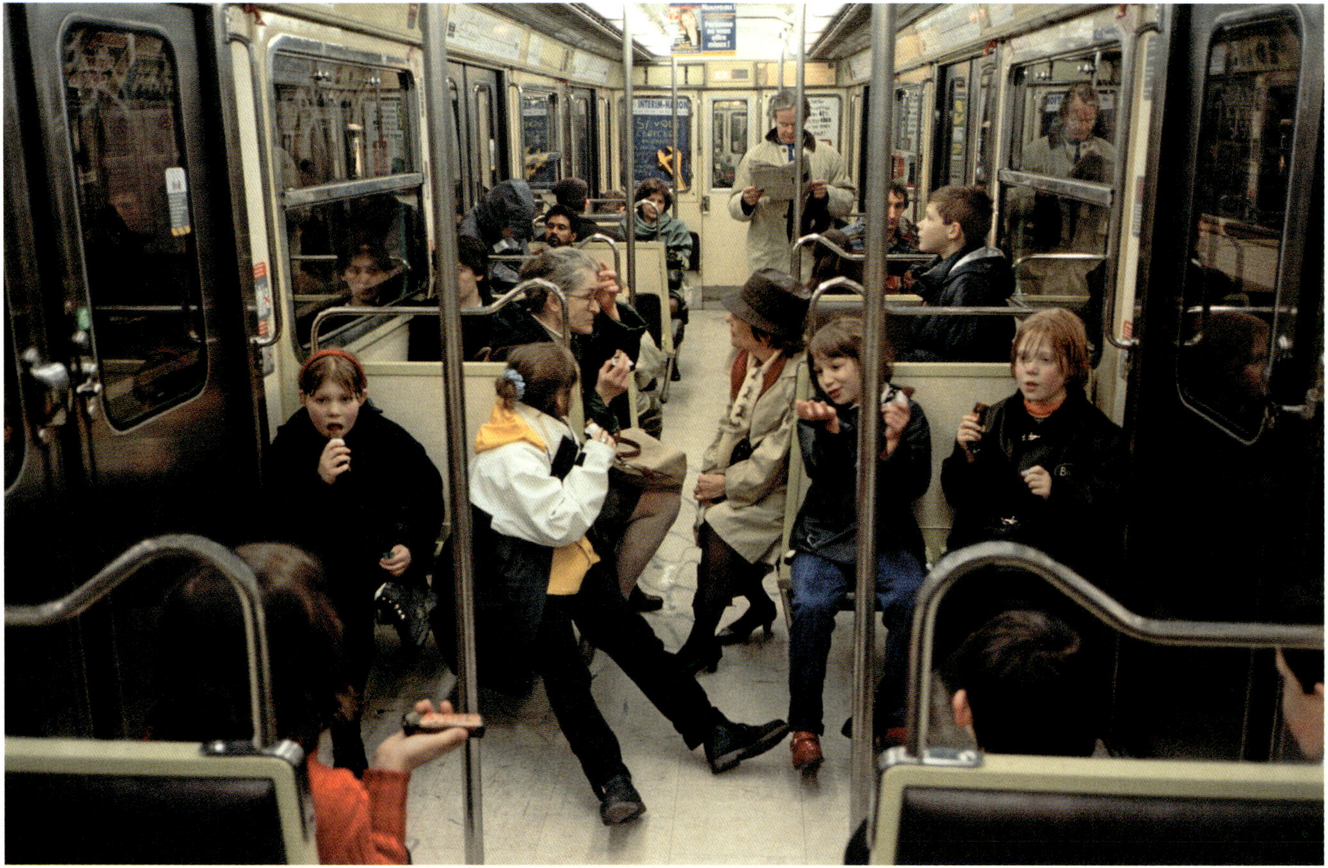

Thursday, April 15. Paris. On the métro

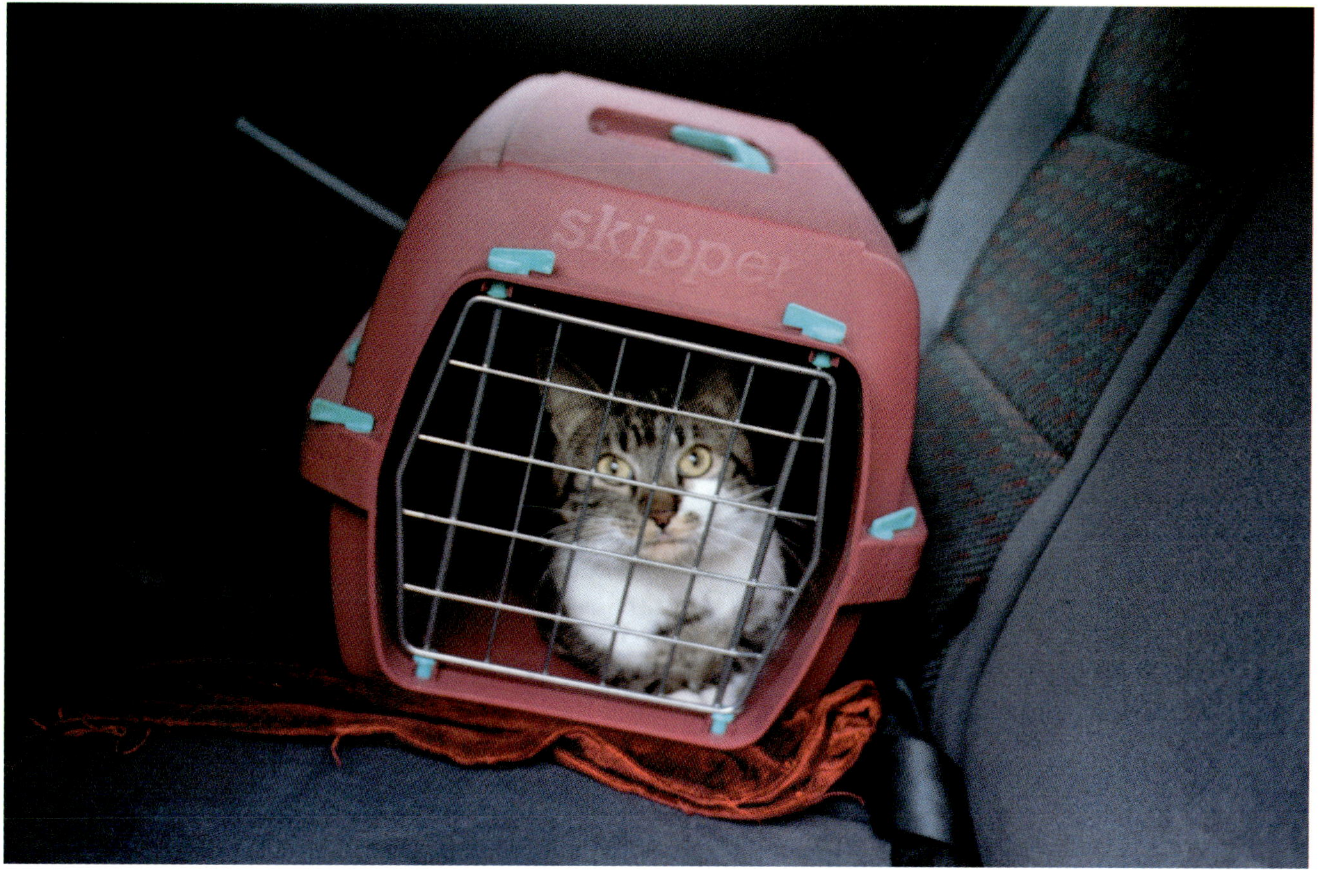

Friday, April 16. Boulogne, France. "Perdu", ready for travel

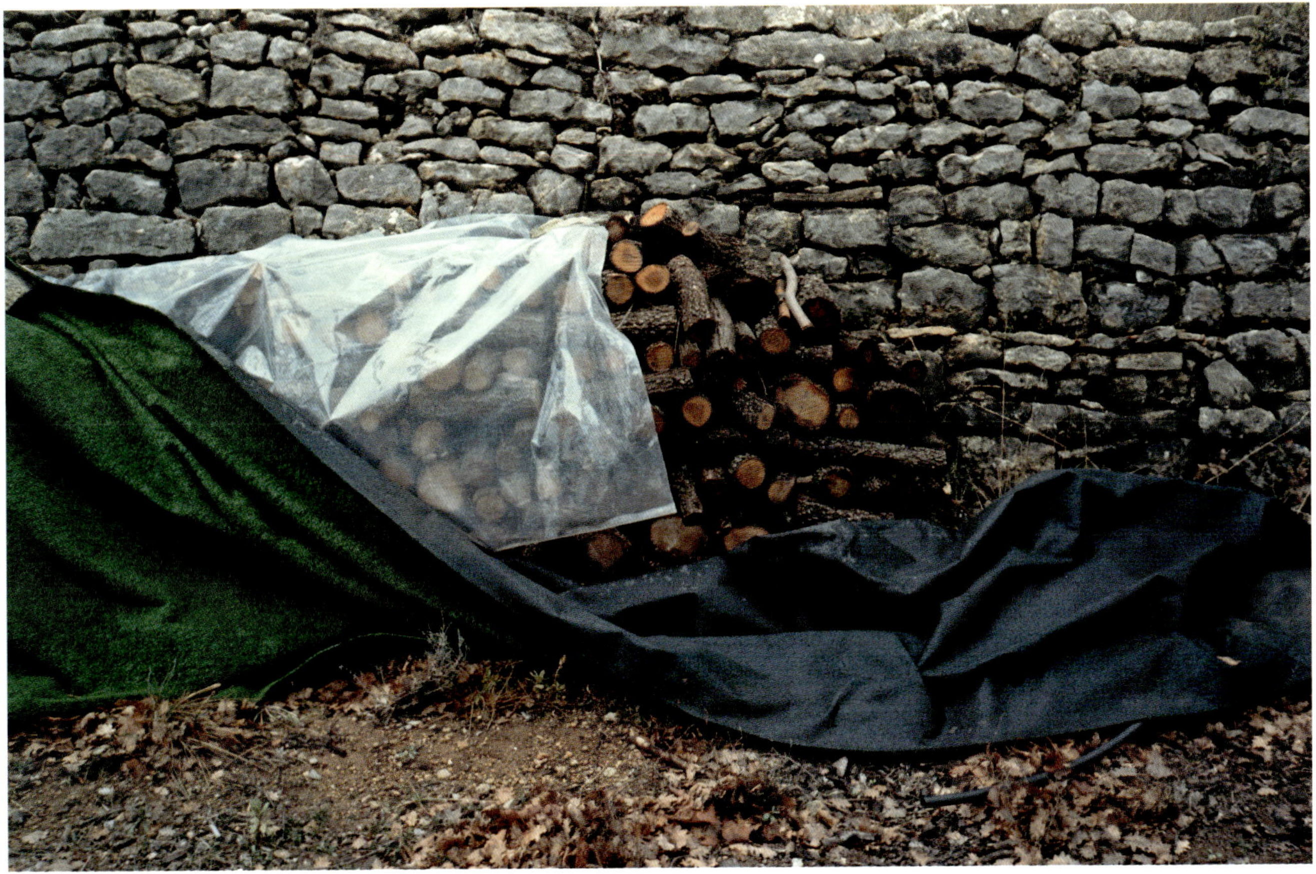

Saturday, April 17. Cotignac, France. At "La Véronique"

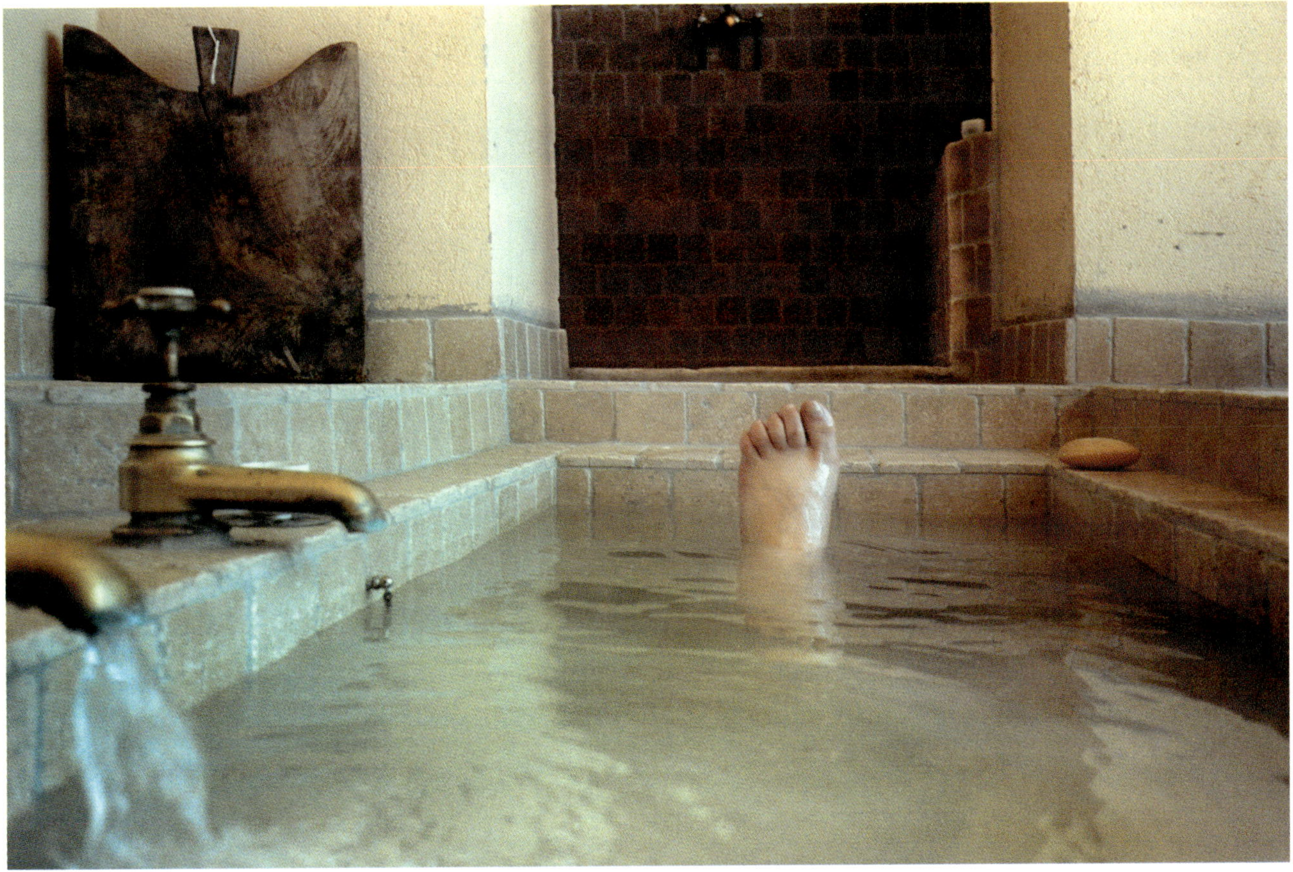

Sunday, April 18. Cotignac, France. Self-portrait in the bath

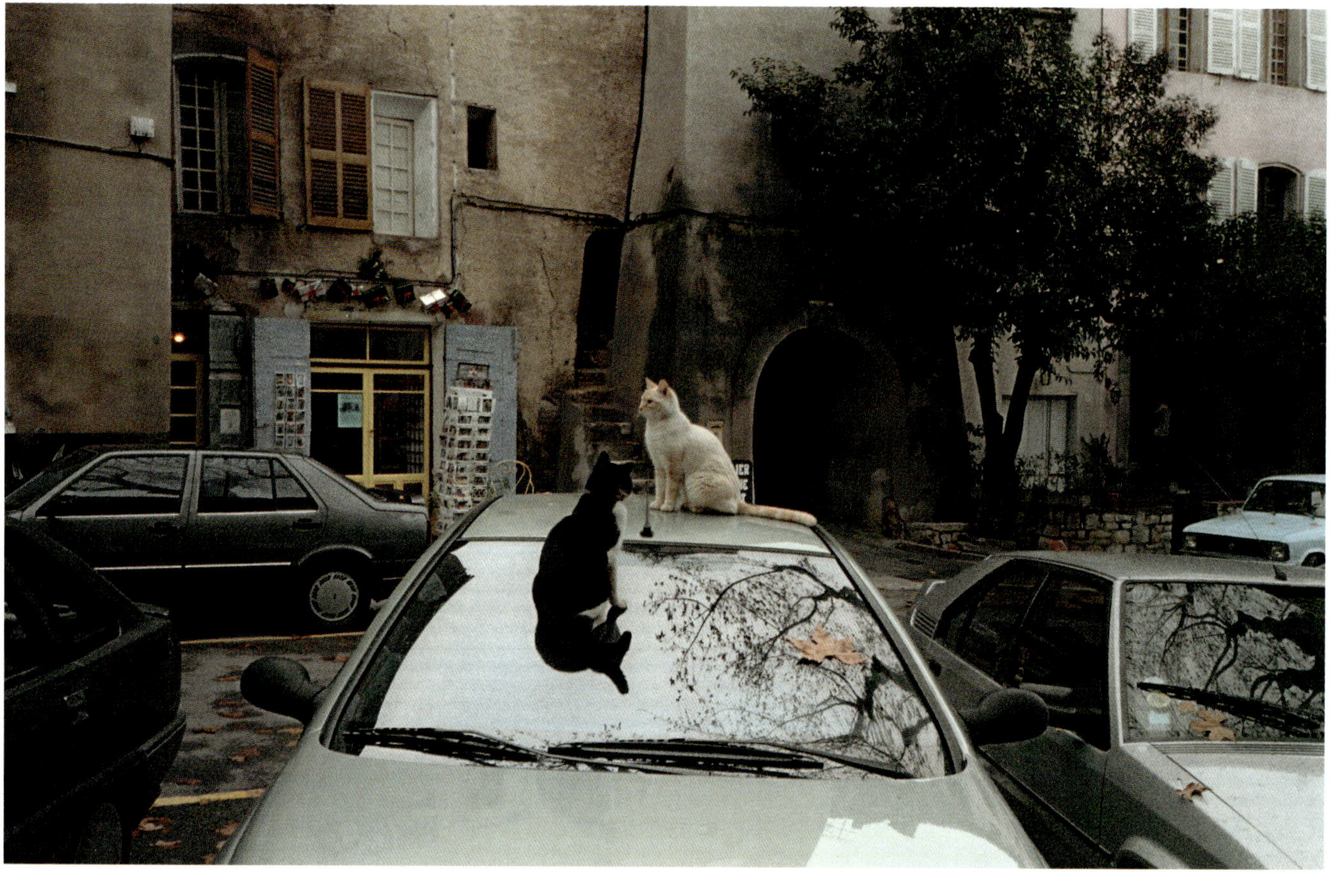

Monday, April 19. Cotignac, France. In the town hall square

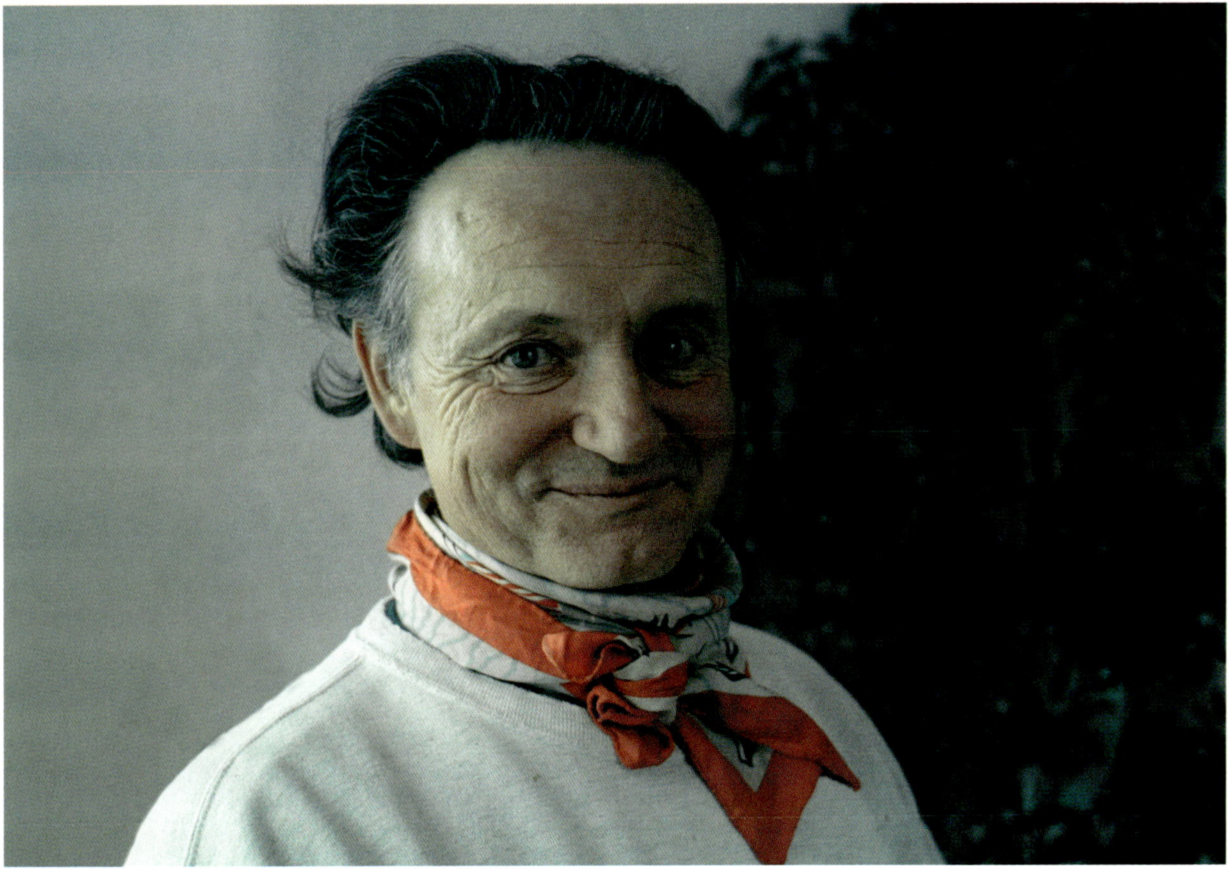

Tuesday, April 20. Cotignac, France. Nicolas Valabrègue, sculptor

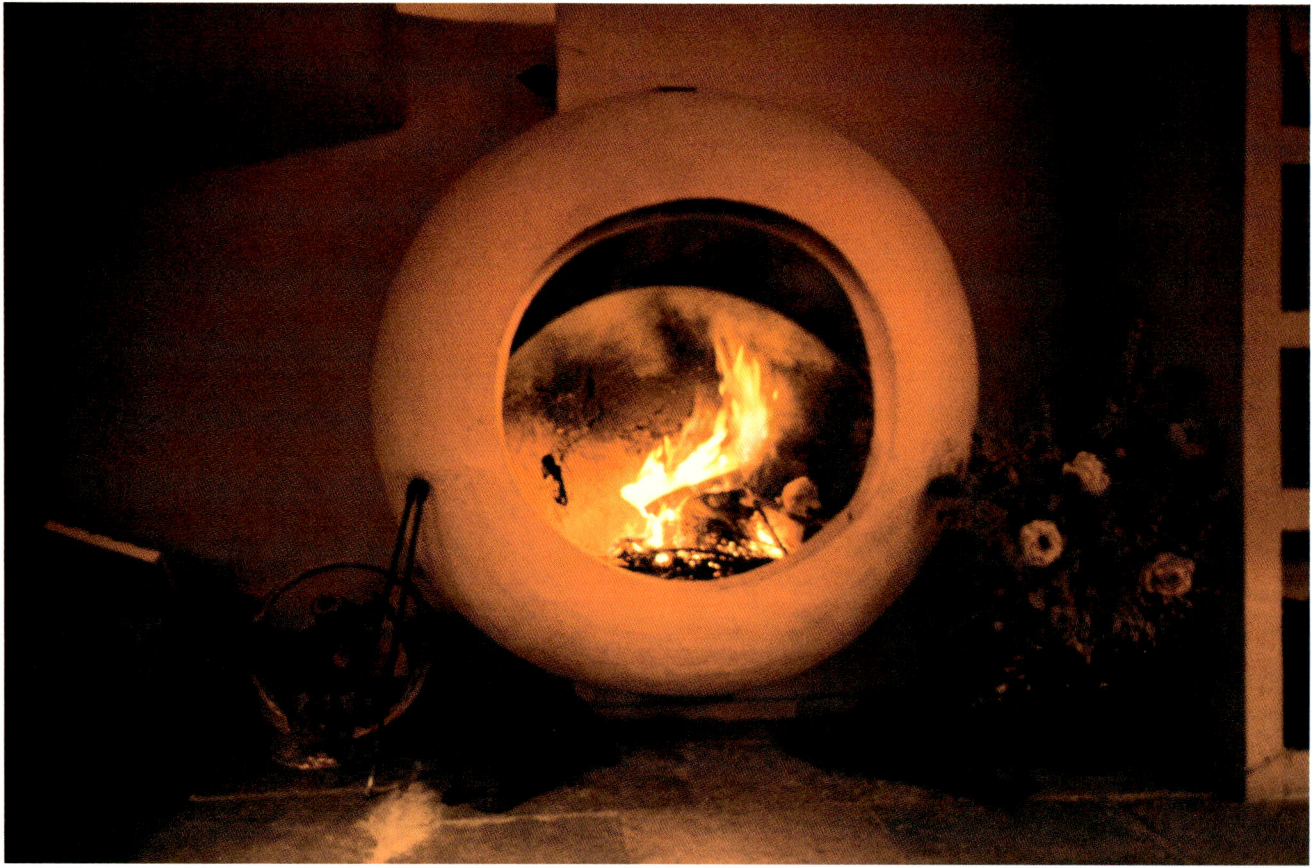

Wednesday, April 21, Cotignac, France. The fireplace at "La Véronique"

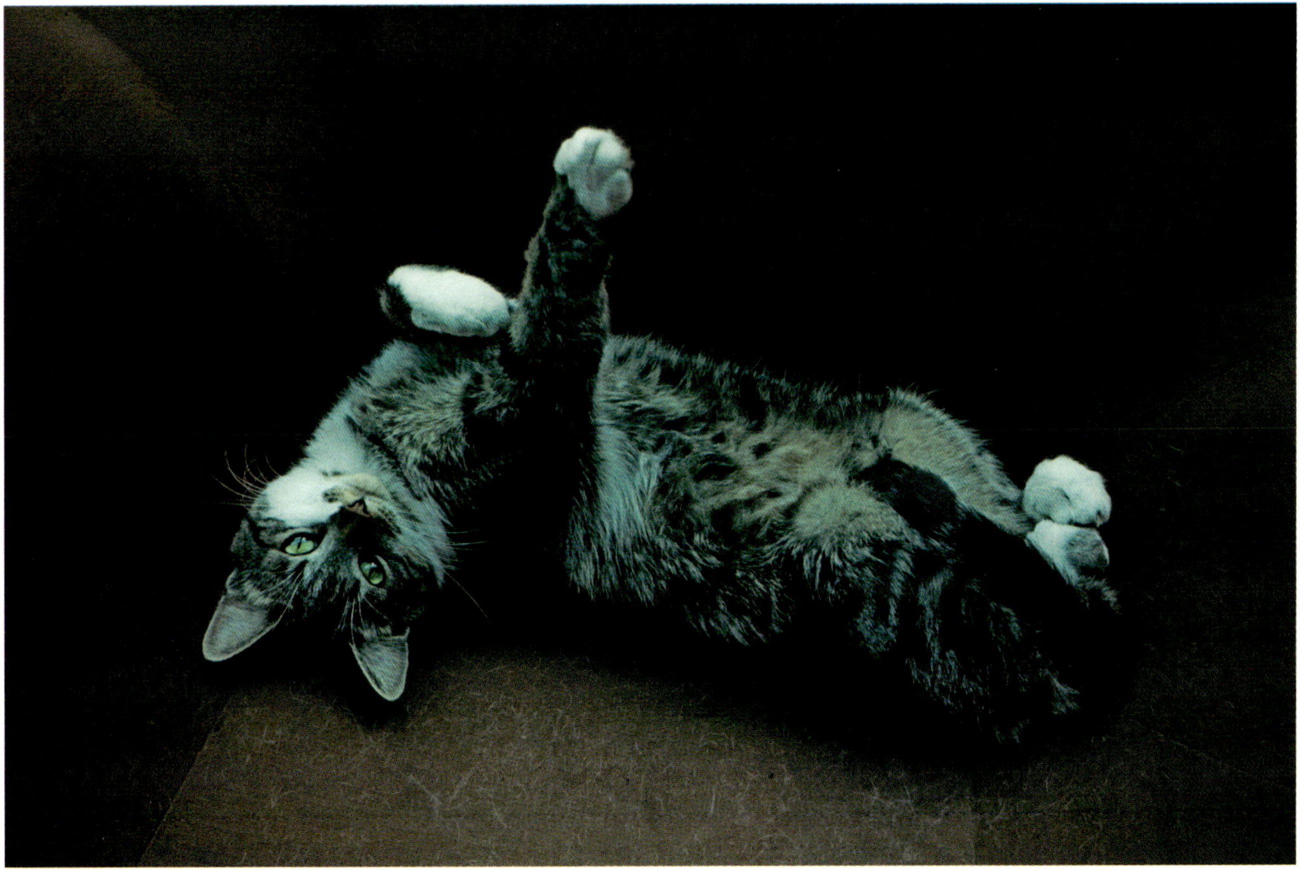

Thursday, April 22. Cotignac, France. "Perdu"

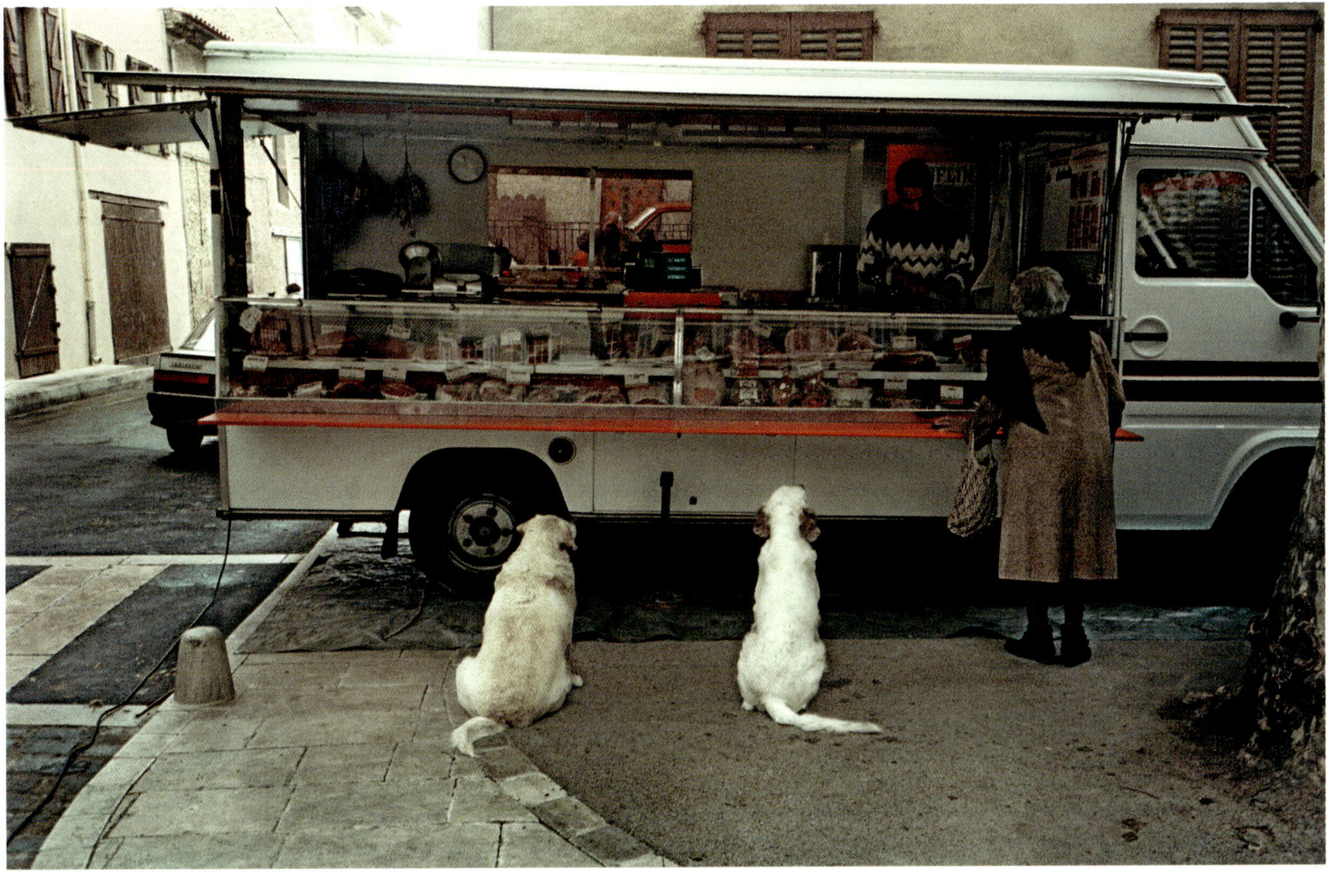

Friday, April 23. Cotignac, France. On the village square

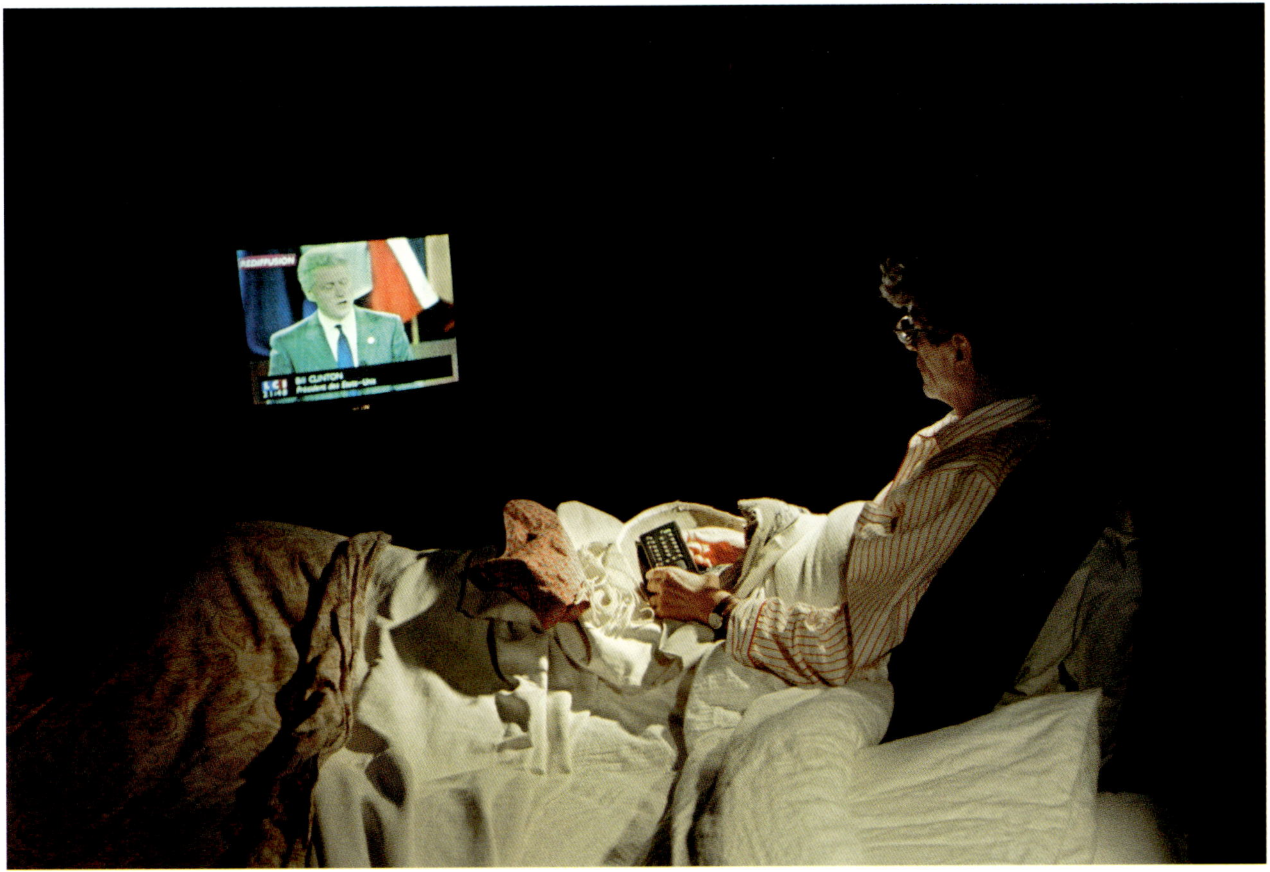

Saturday, April 24. Boulogne, France. Véronique Aubry, watching Bill Clinton

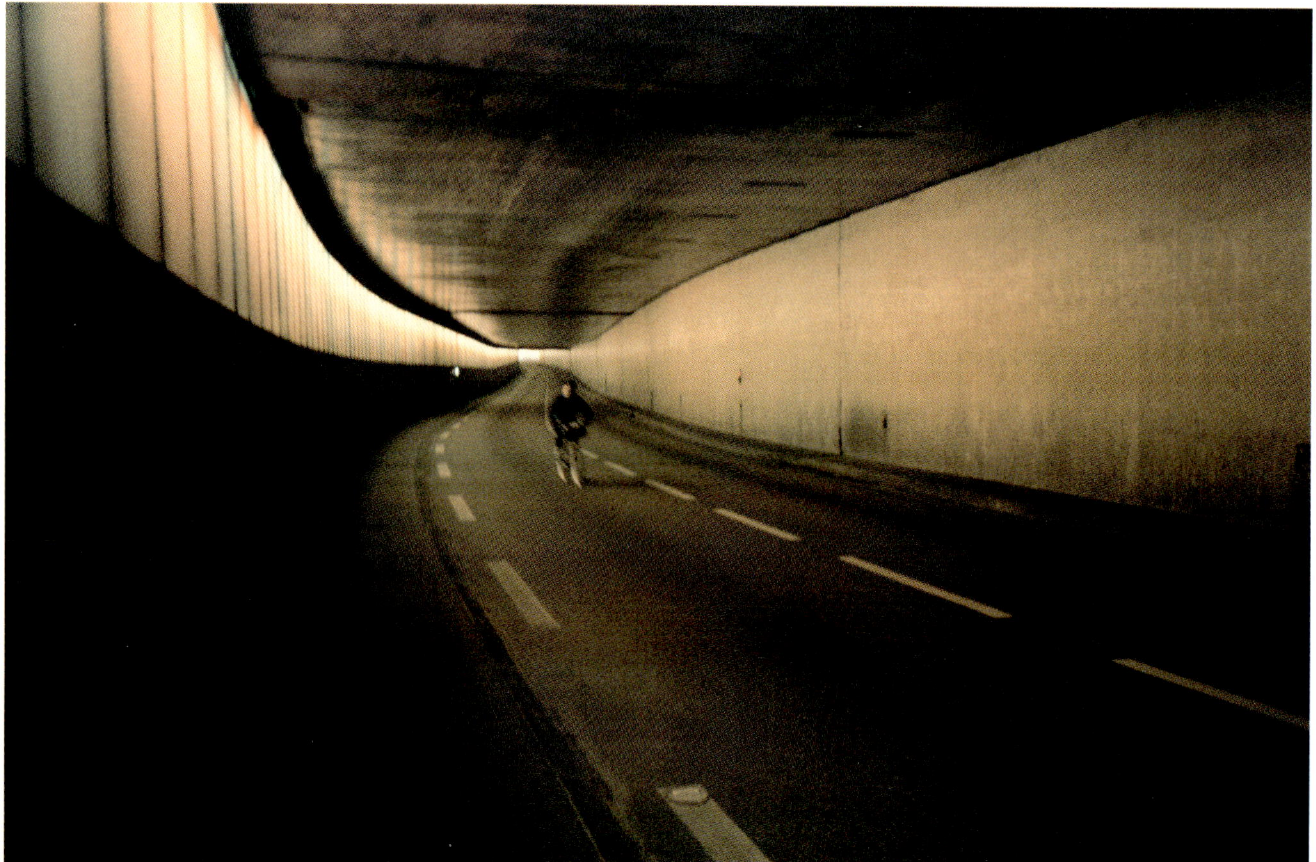

Sunday, April 25. Paris. Tunnel under the Louvre

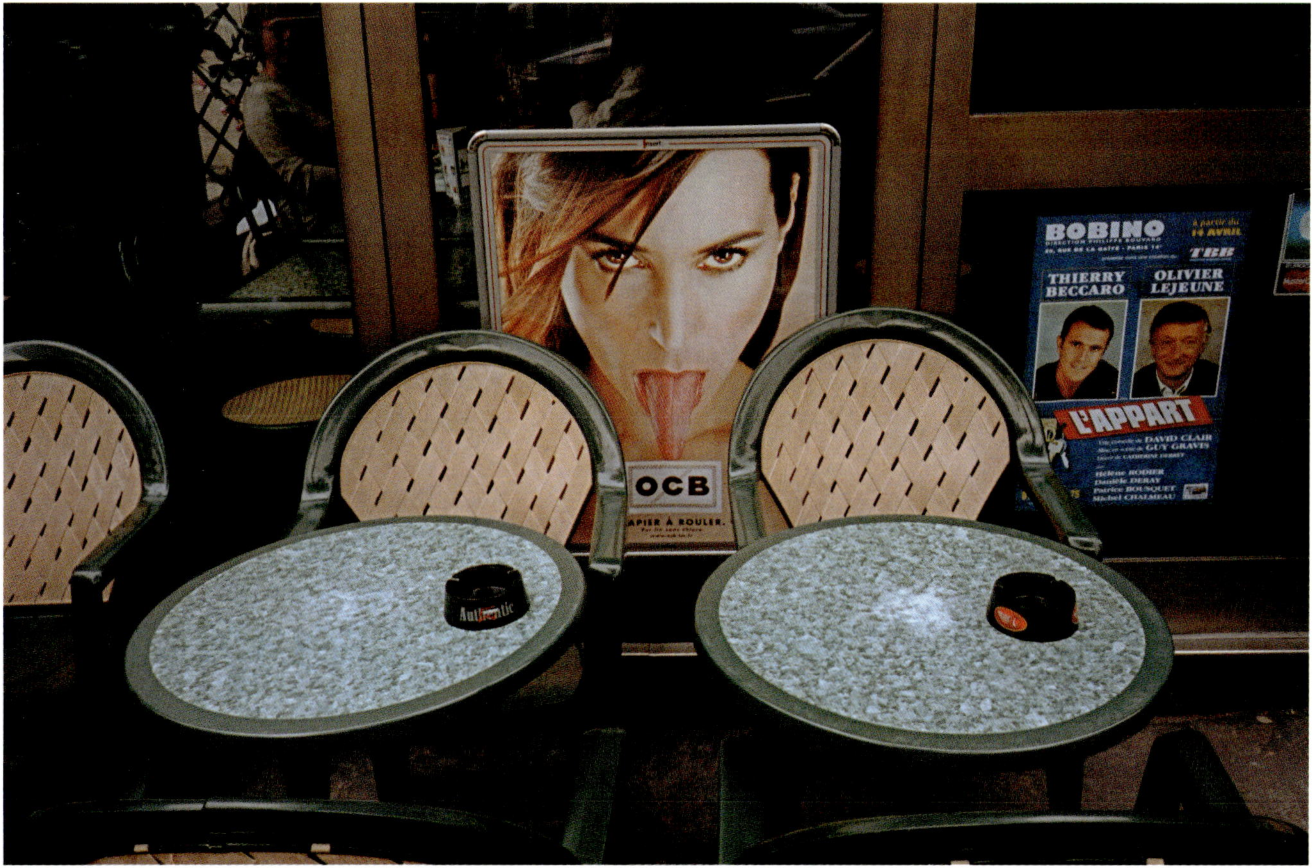

Monday, April 26. Paris. Café terrace, Champs-Elysées area

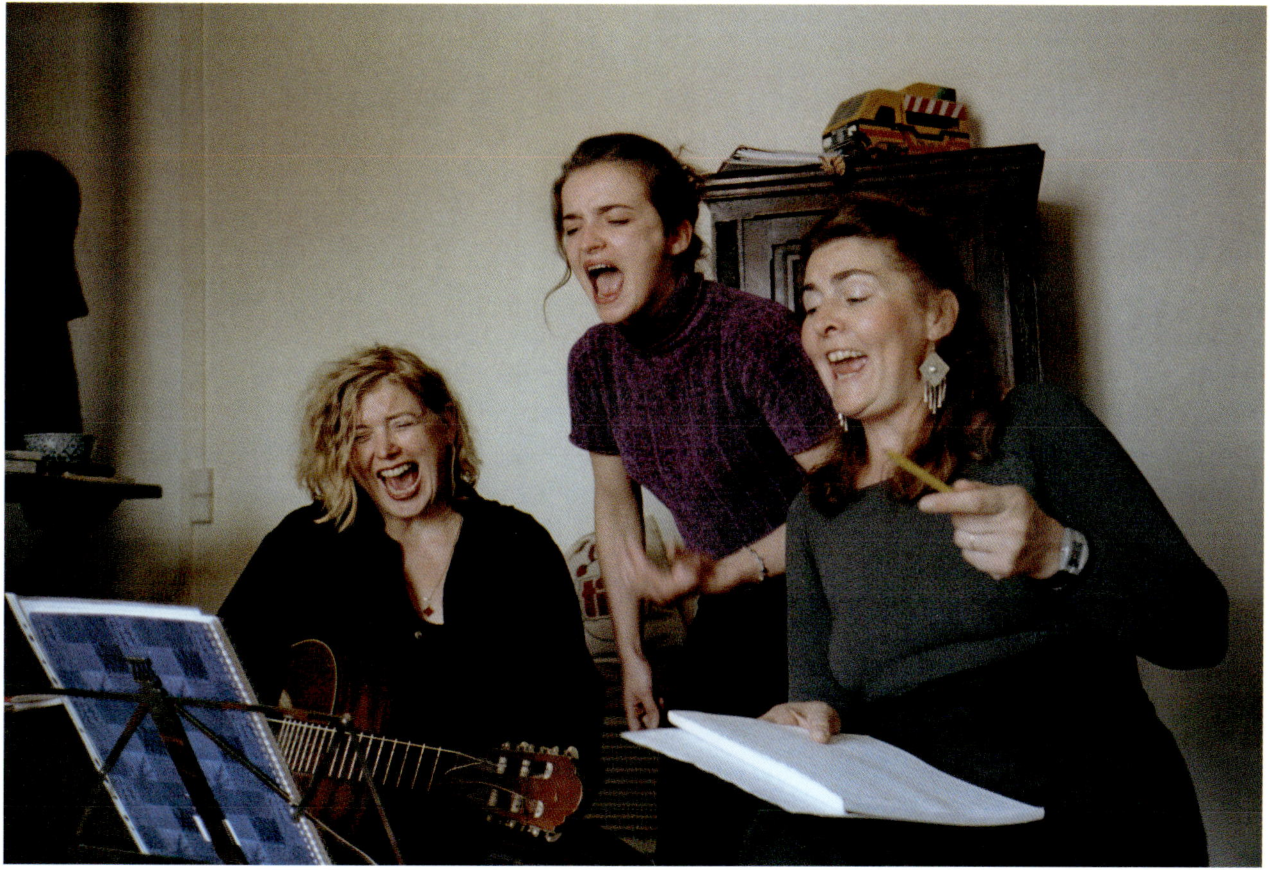

Tuesday, April 27. Paris. Susanne Schmidt, Hélène Busnel, Agnès Host, rehearsing

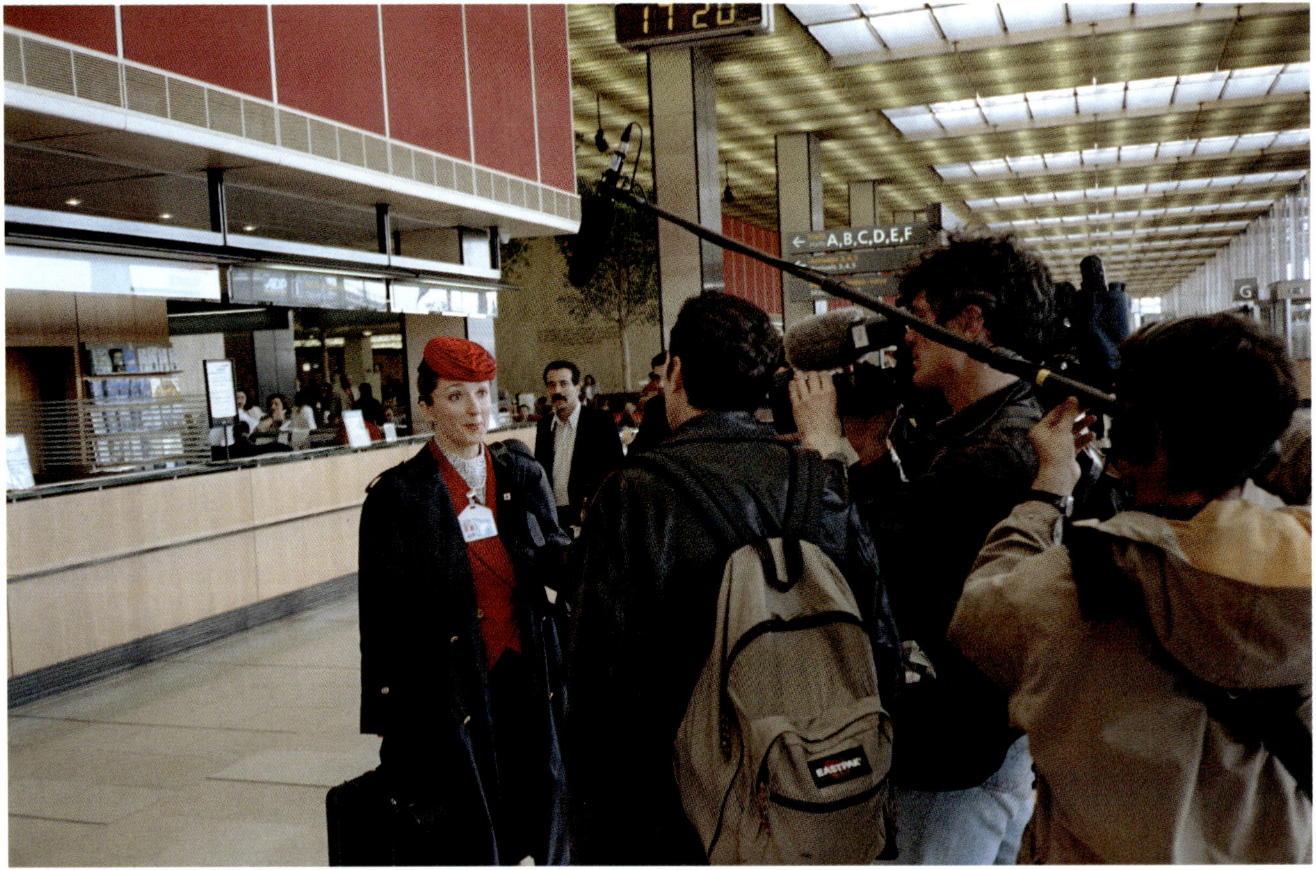

Wednesday, April 28. Paris. At Orly airport, during an Air France strike

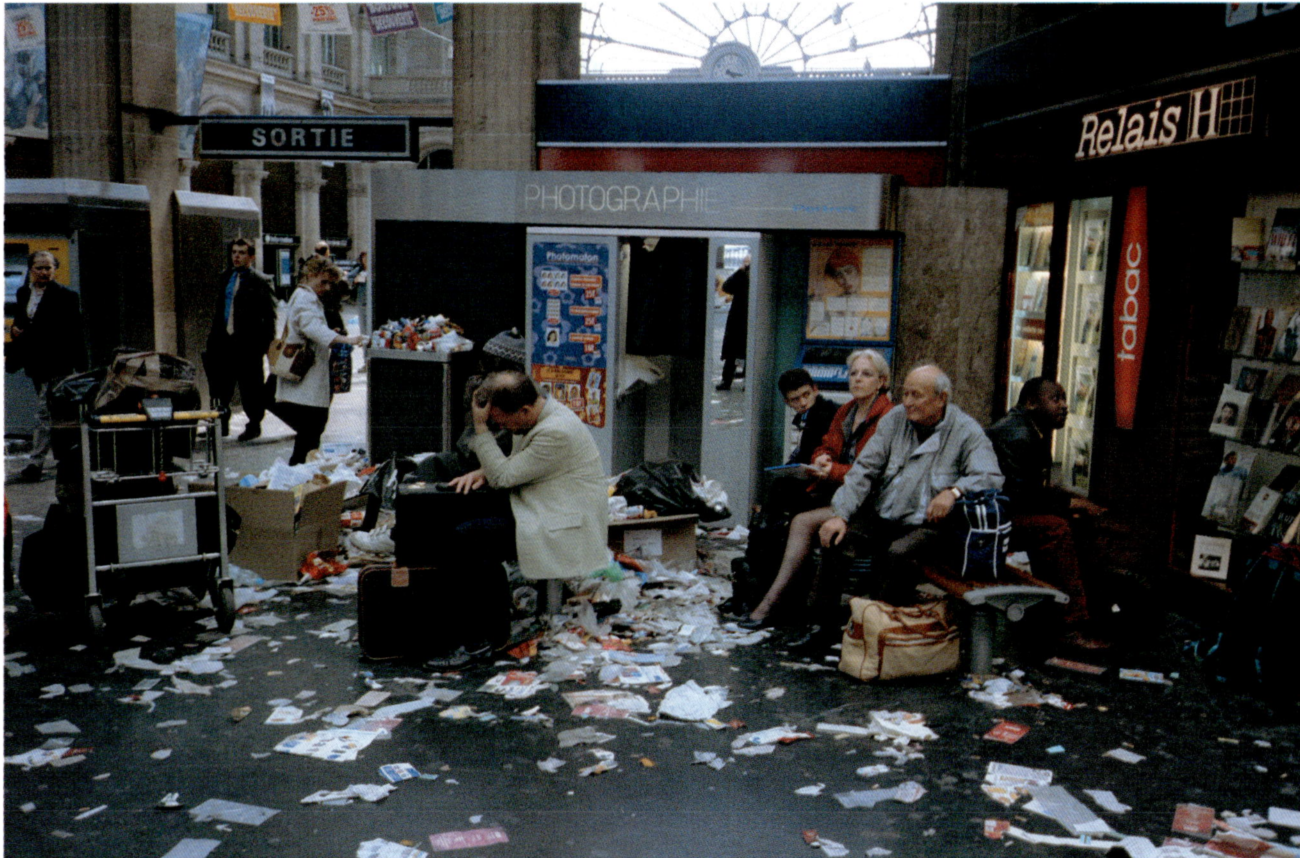

Thursday, April 29. Paris. Gare de l'Est, during a cleaners' strike

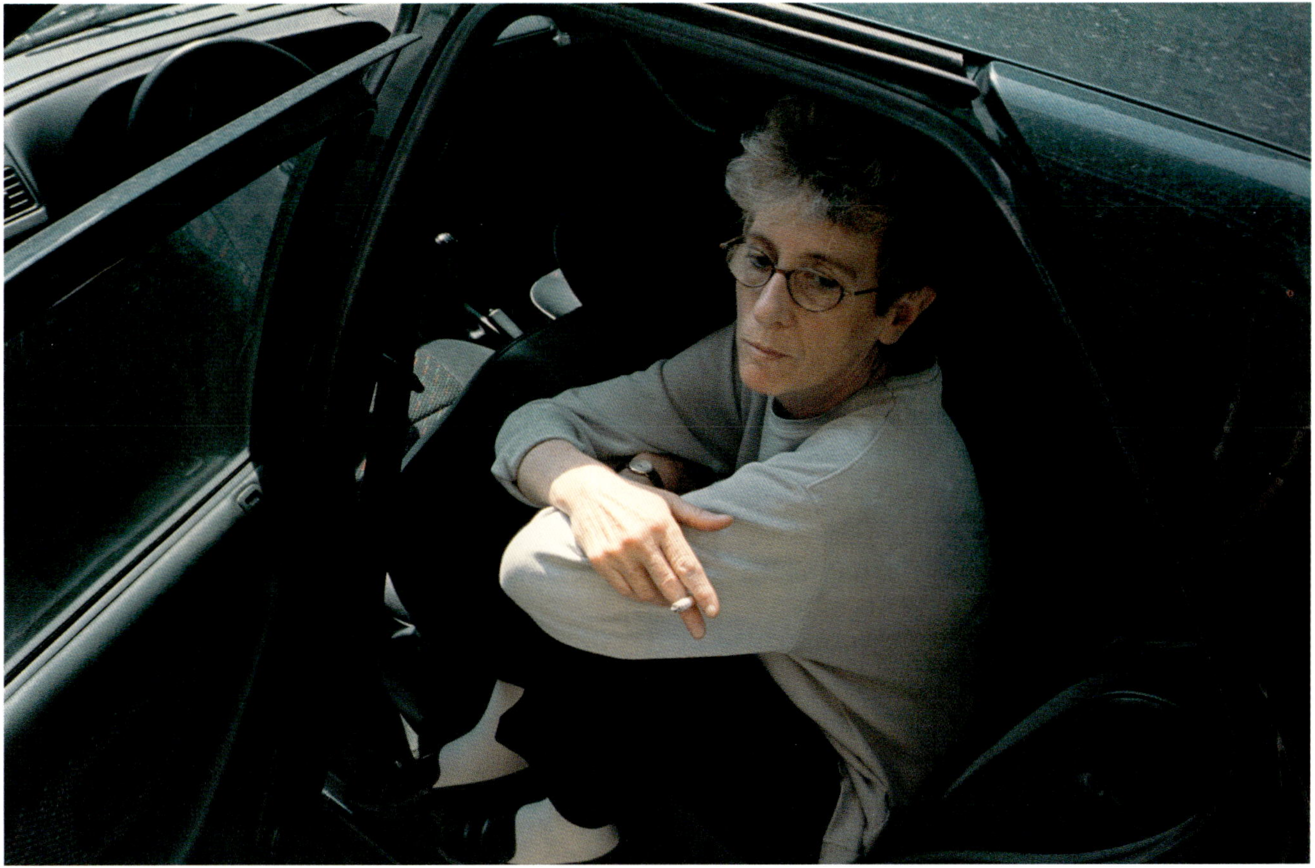

Friday, April 30. Boulogne, France. Véronique Aubry

MAY

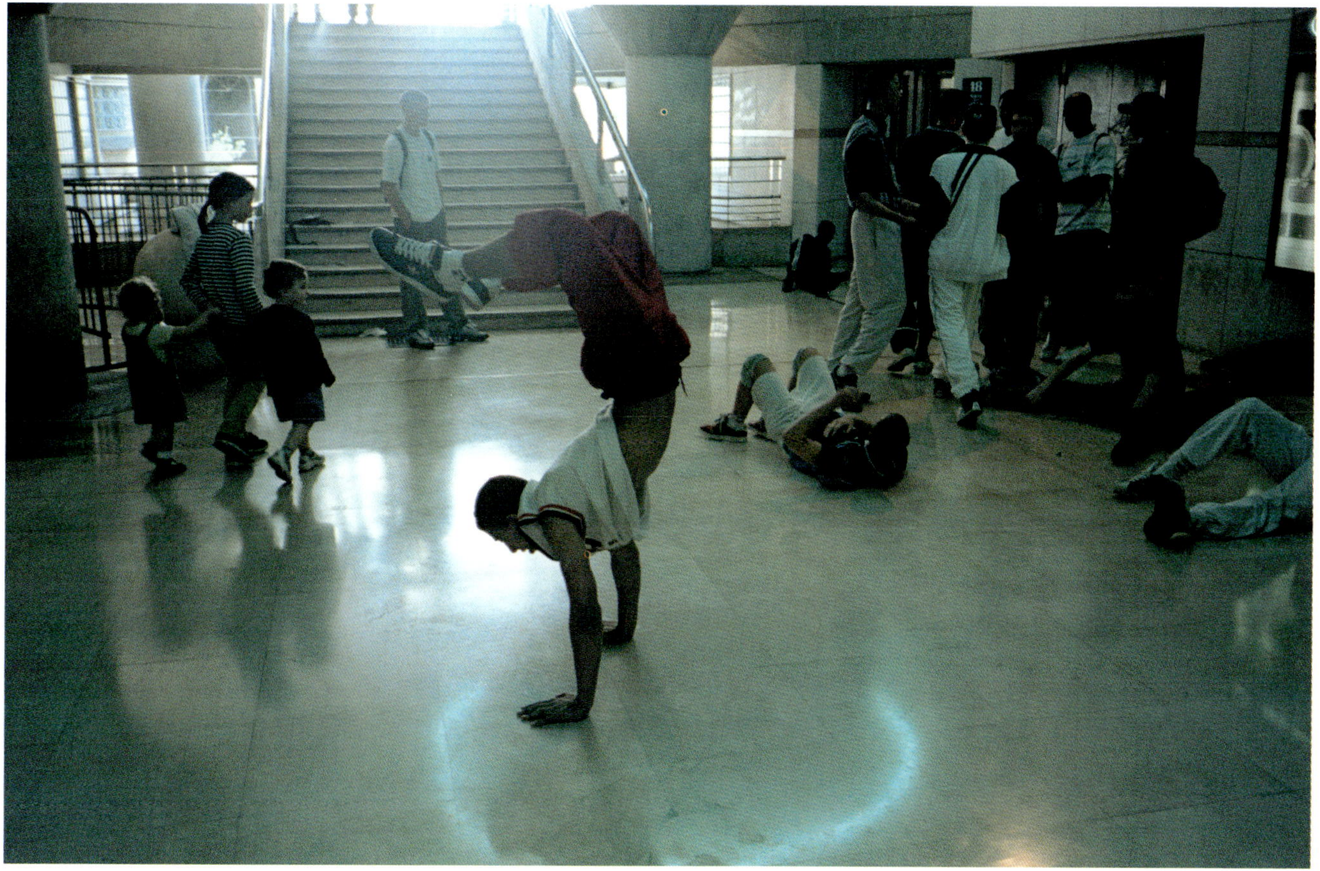

Saturday, May 1. Paris. Forum des Halles, Hip-hop dancers

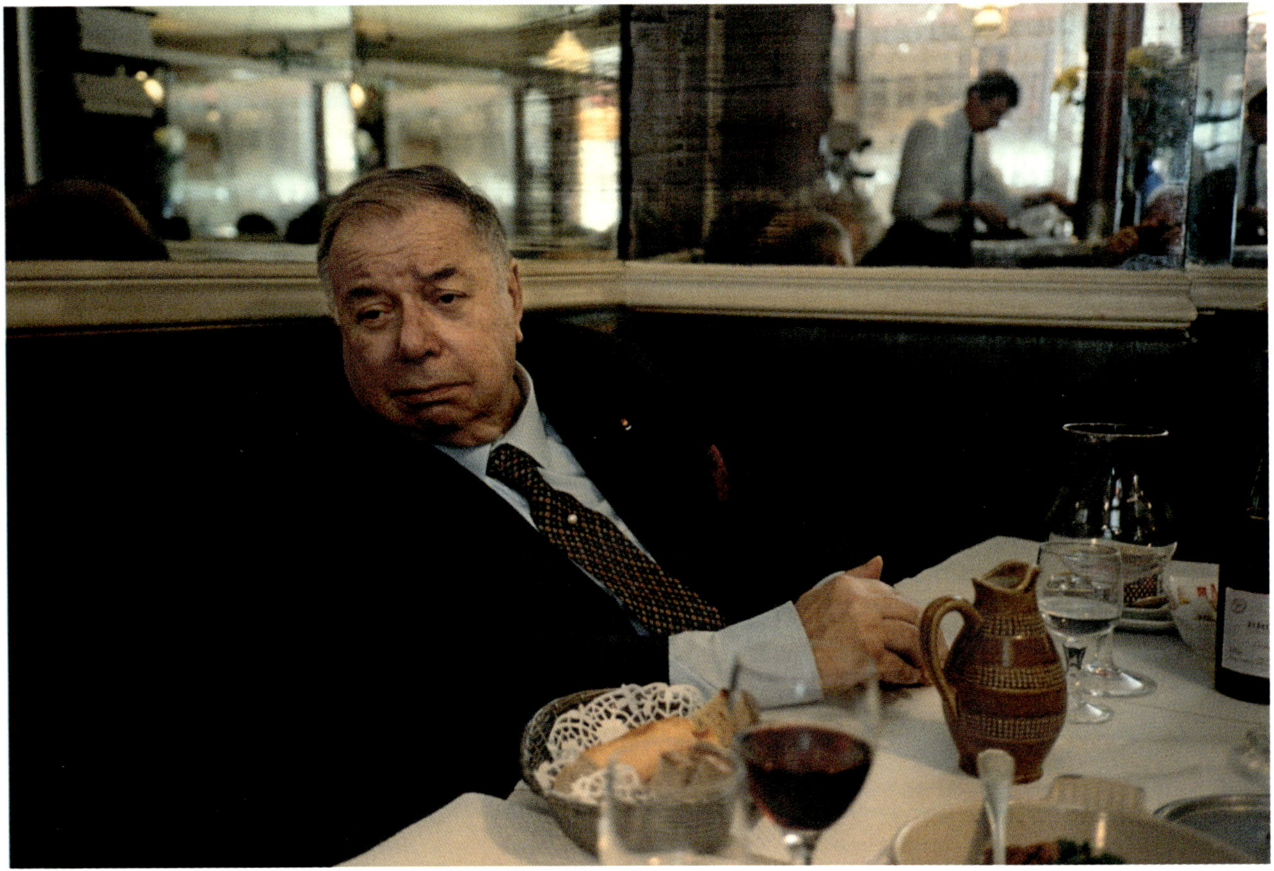

Sunday, May 2. Paris. Michel Bonnet, Grand Chancellor of the Order of Saint-Sépulchre

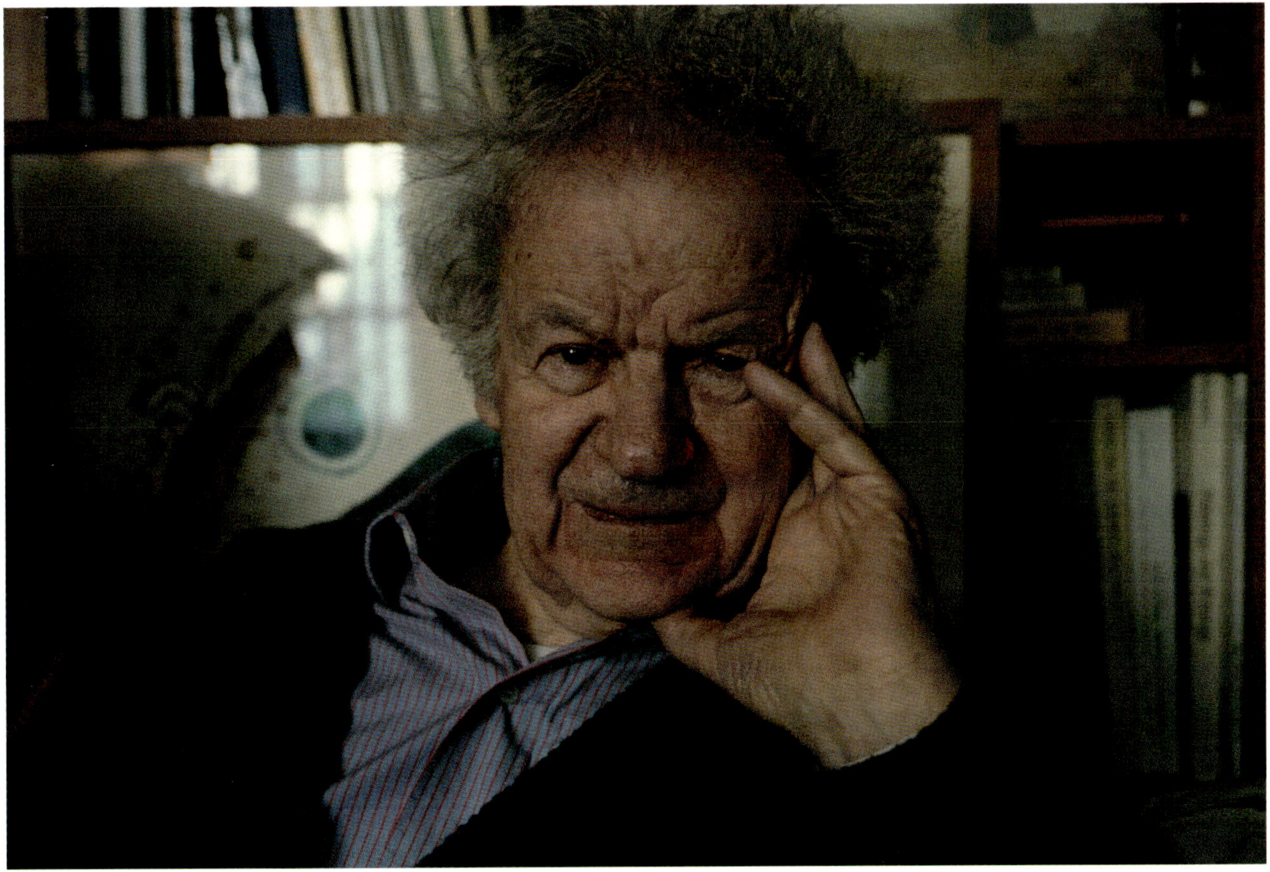

Sunday, May 2. Paris. Jean Leymarie, writer

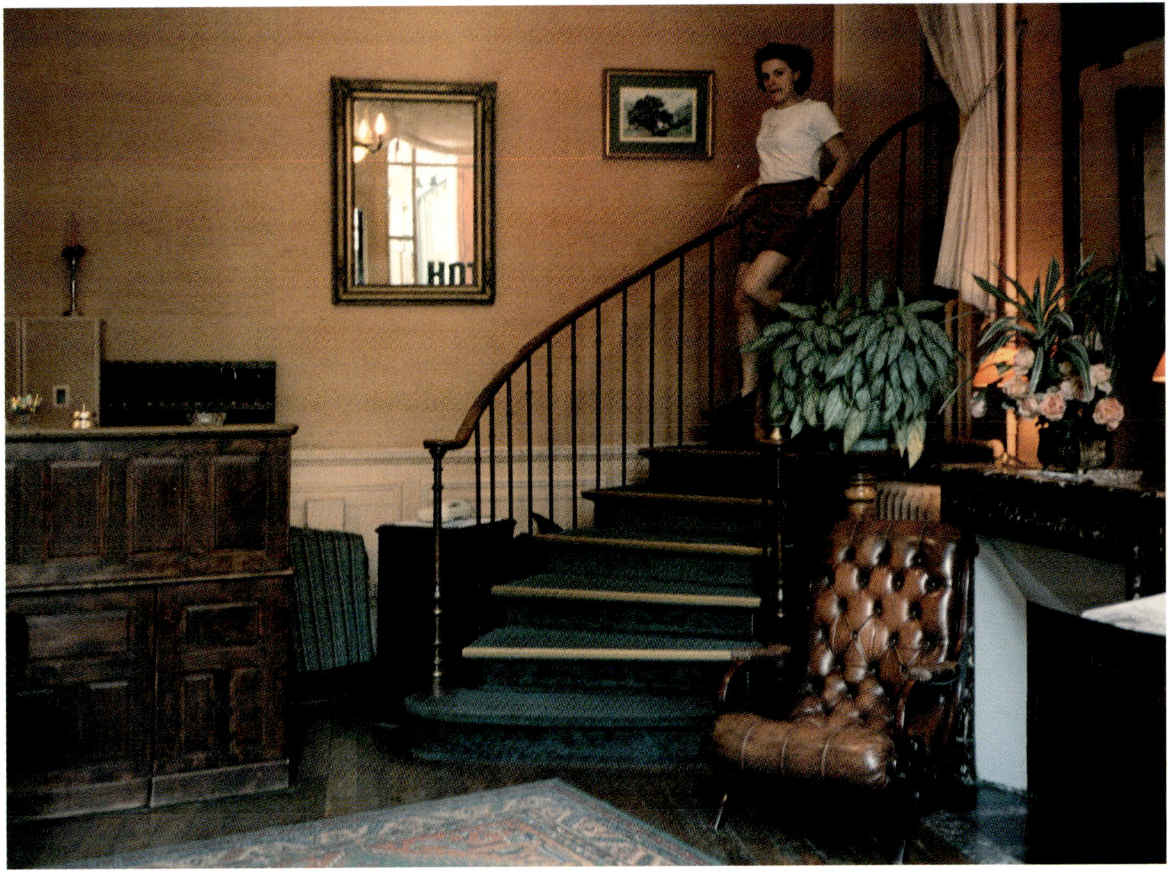

Monday, May 3. Paris. Hotel entrance, Opéra area

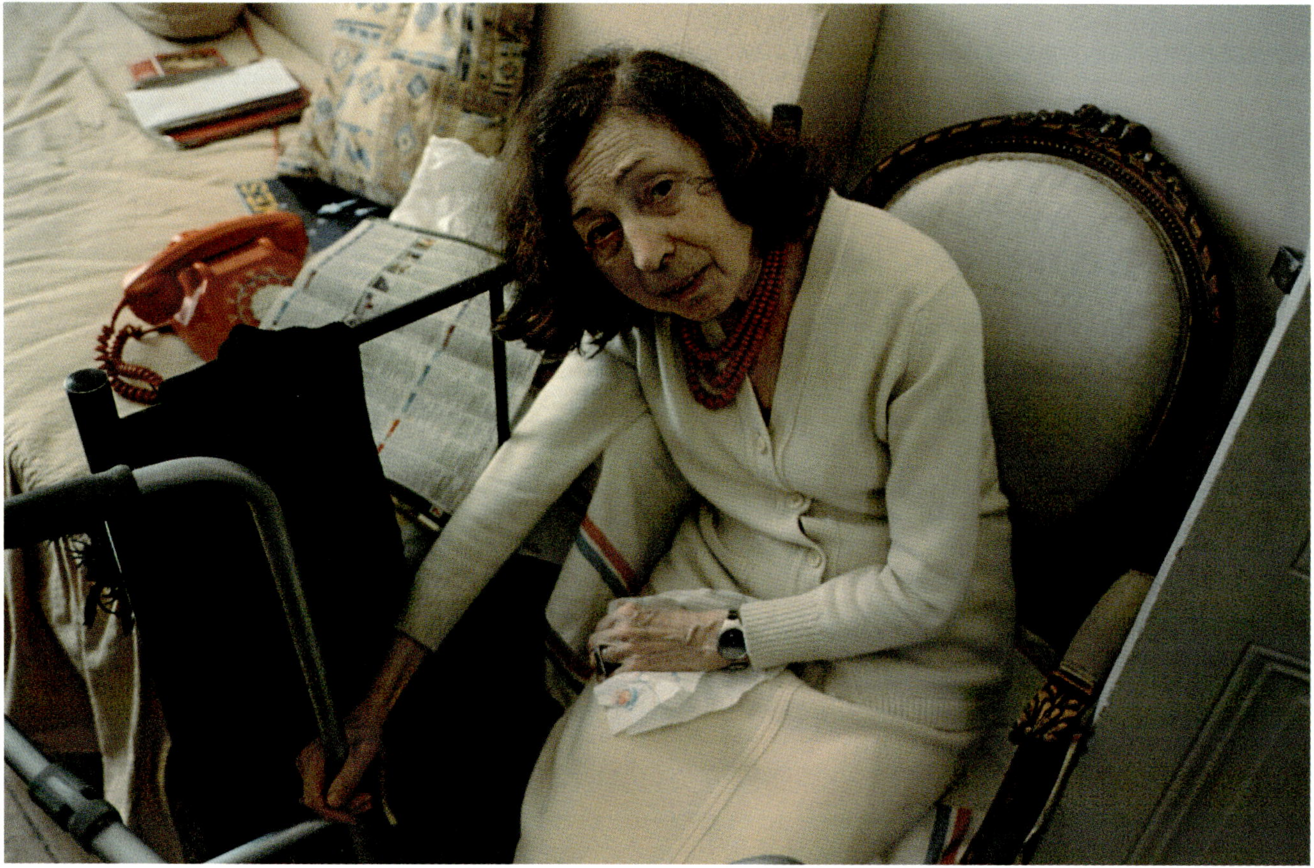

Tuesday, May 4. Paris. Sophie Boubat, Édouard's wife

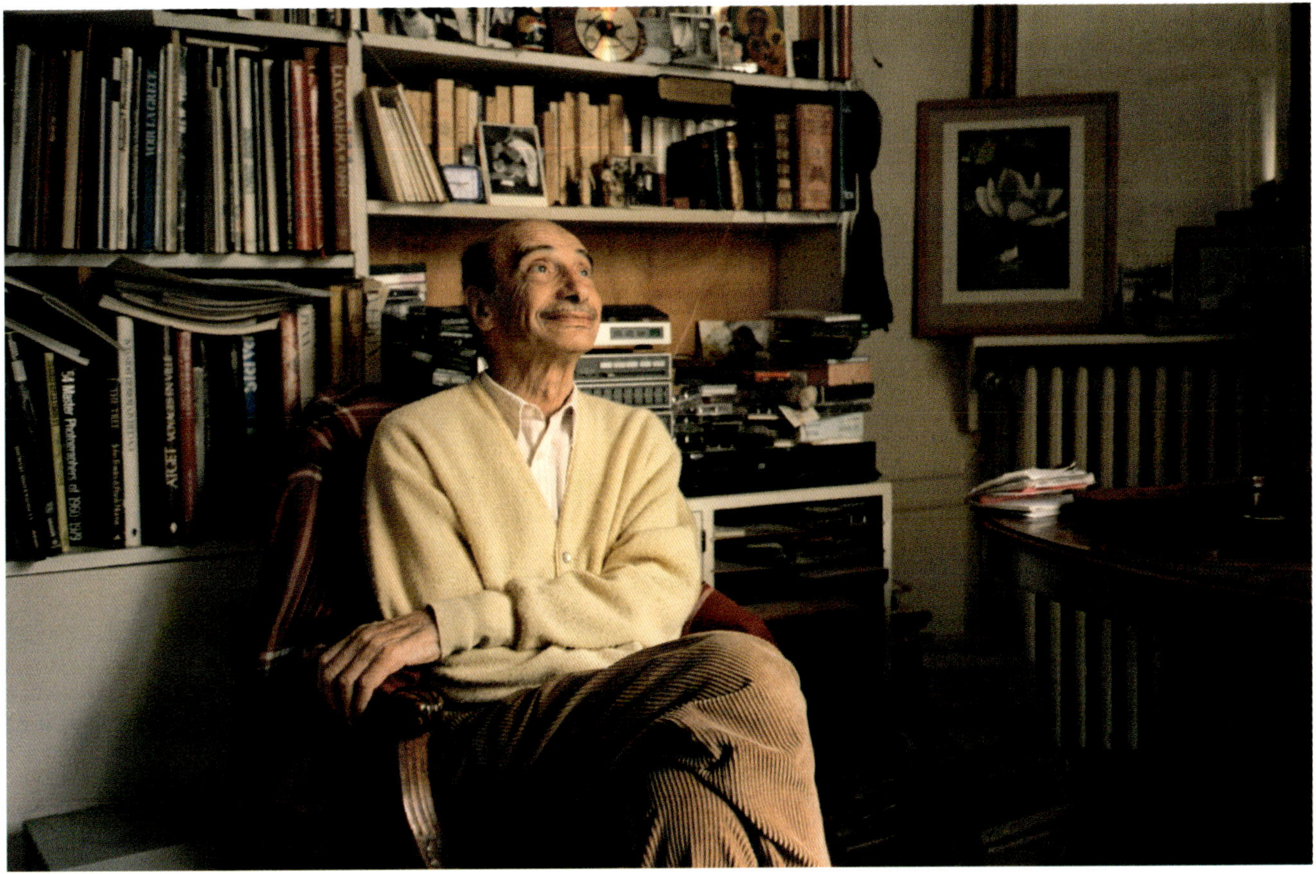

Tuesday, May 4. Paris. Édouard Boubat, photographer (see note)

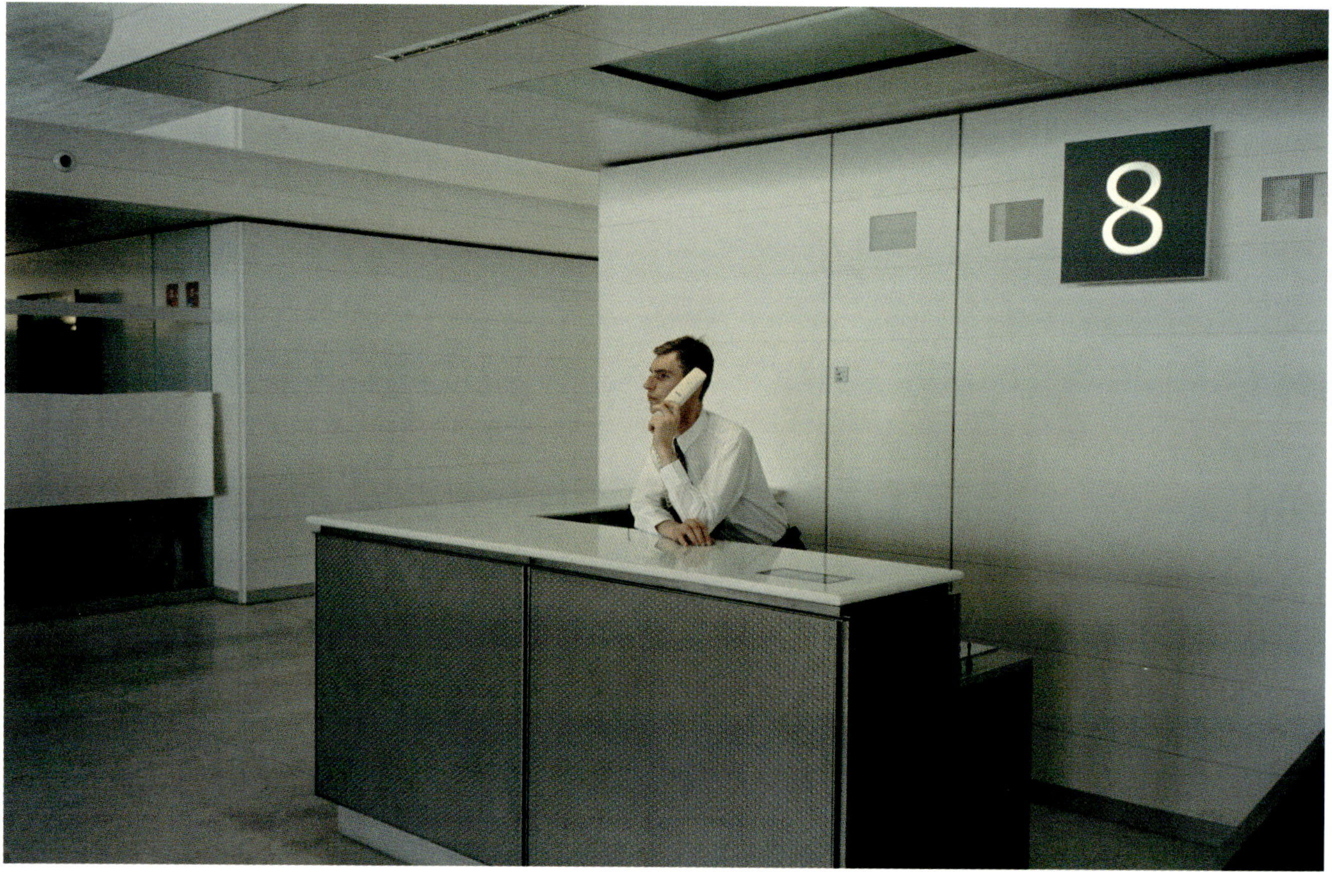

Wednesday, May 5. Paris. Charles de Gaulle airport

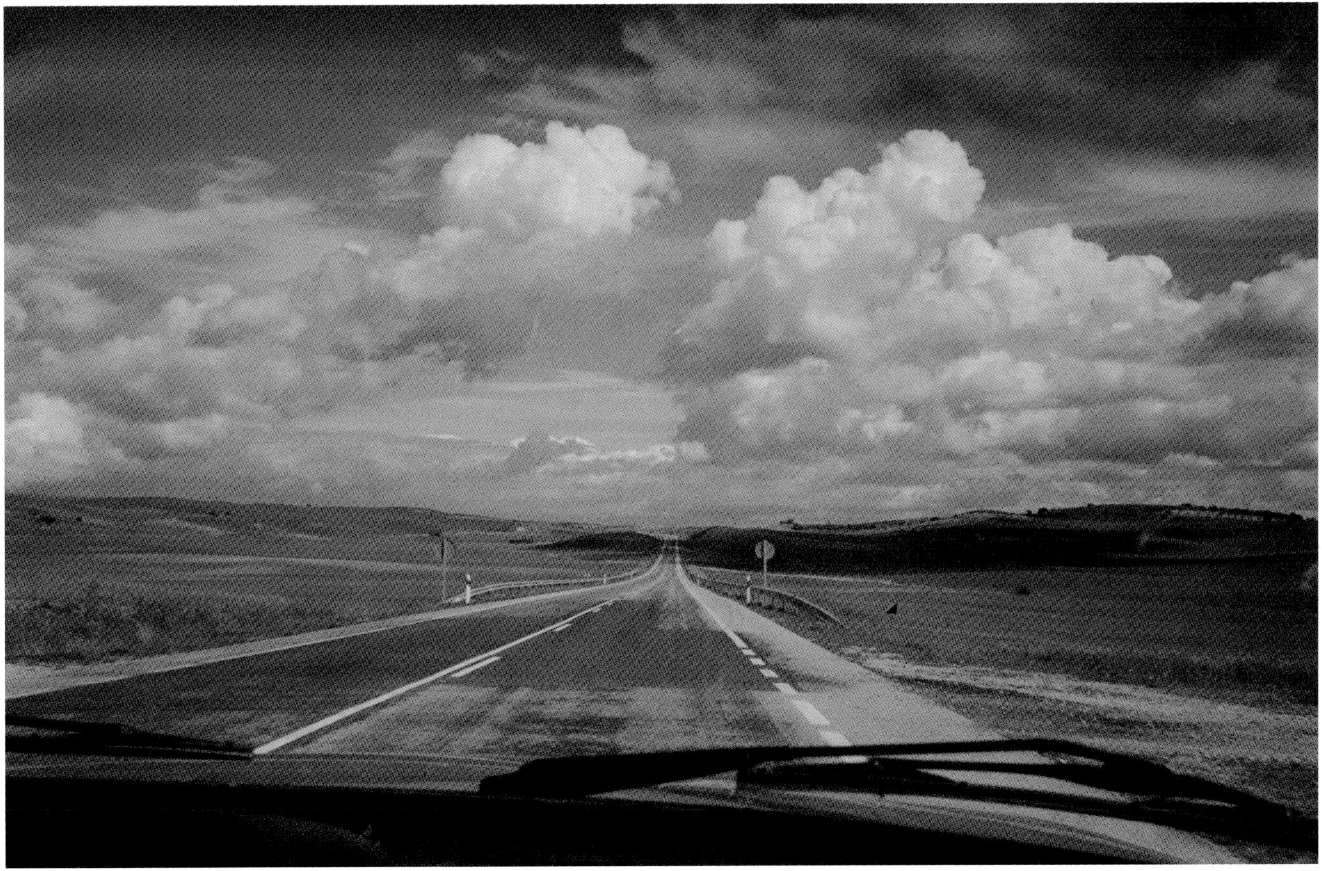

Wednesday, May 5. Spain. On the road between Madrid and Cuenca

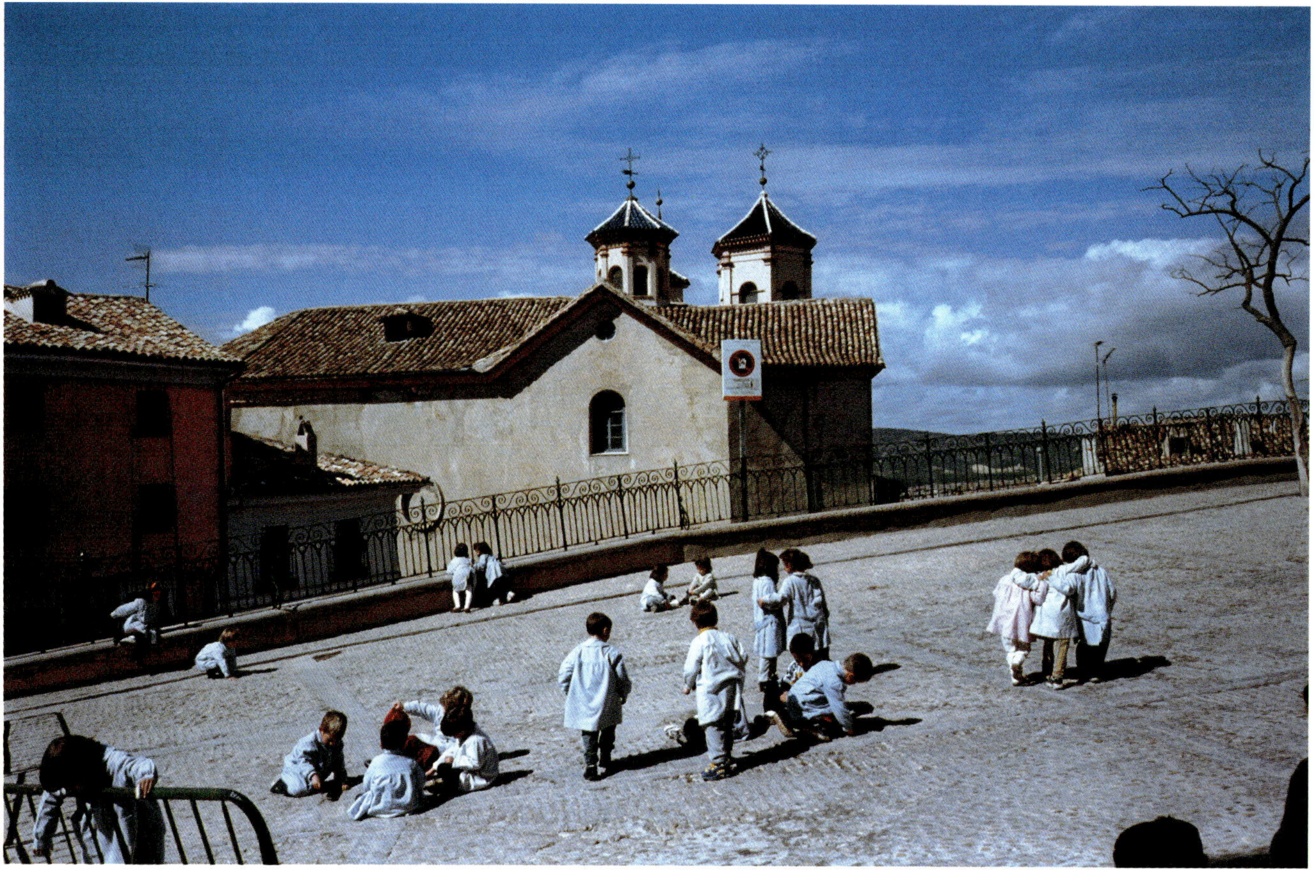

Thursday, May 6. Cuenca, Spain. Kindergarten

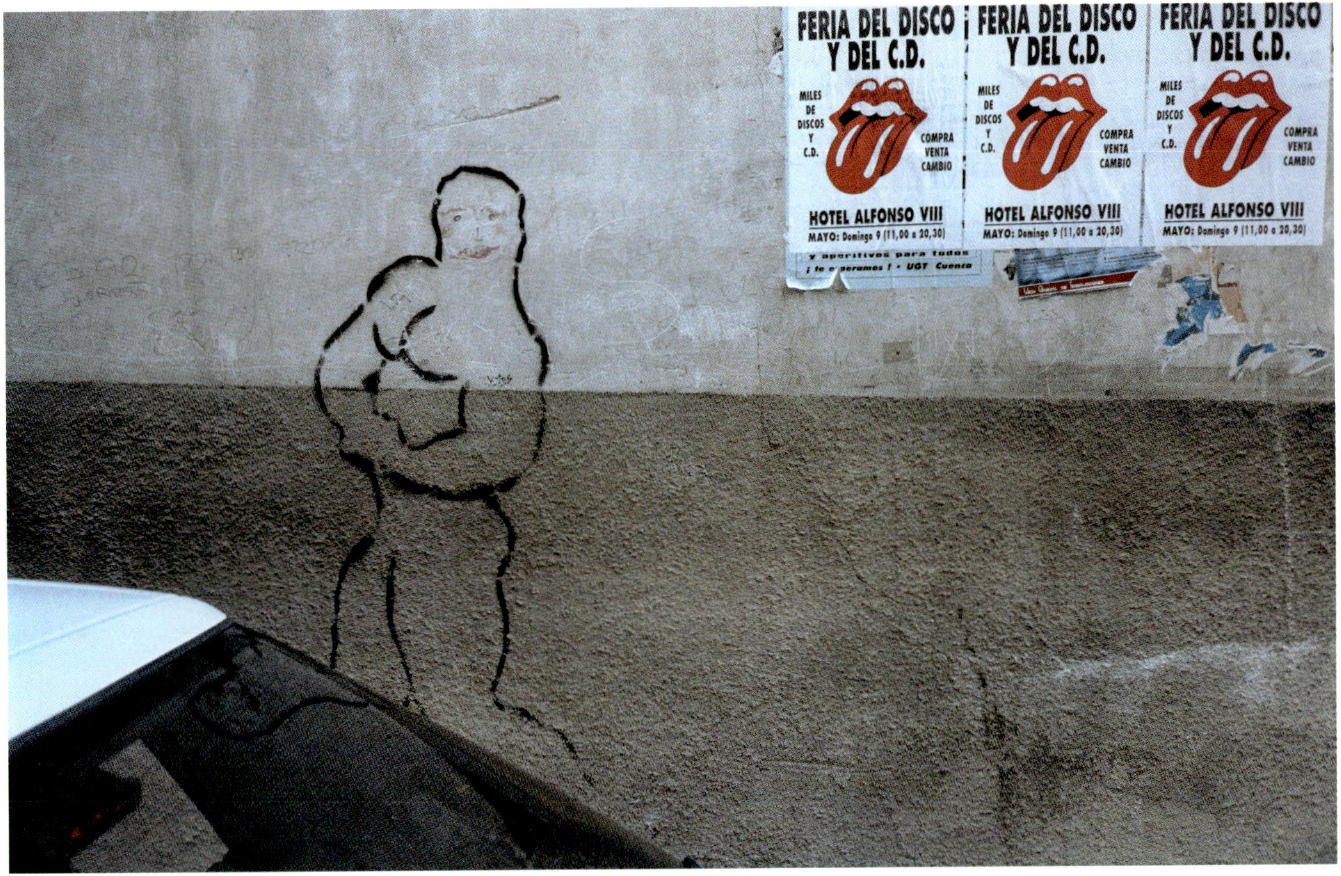

Thursday, May 6. Cuenca, Spain. Graffiti

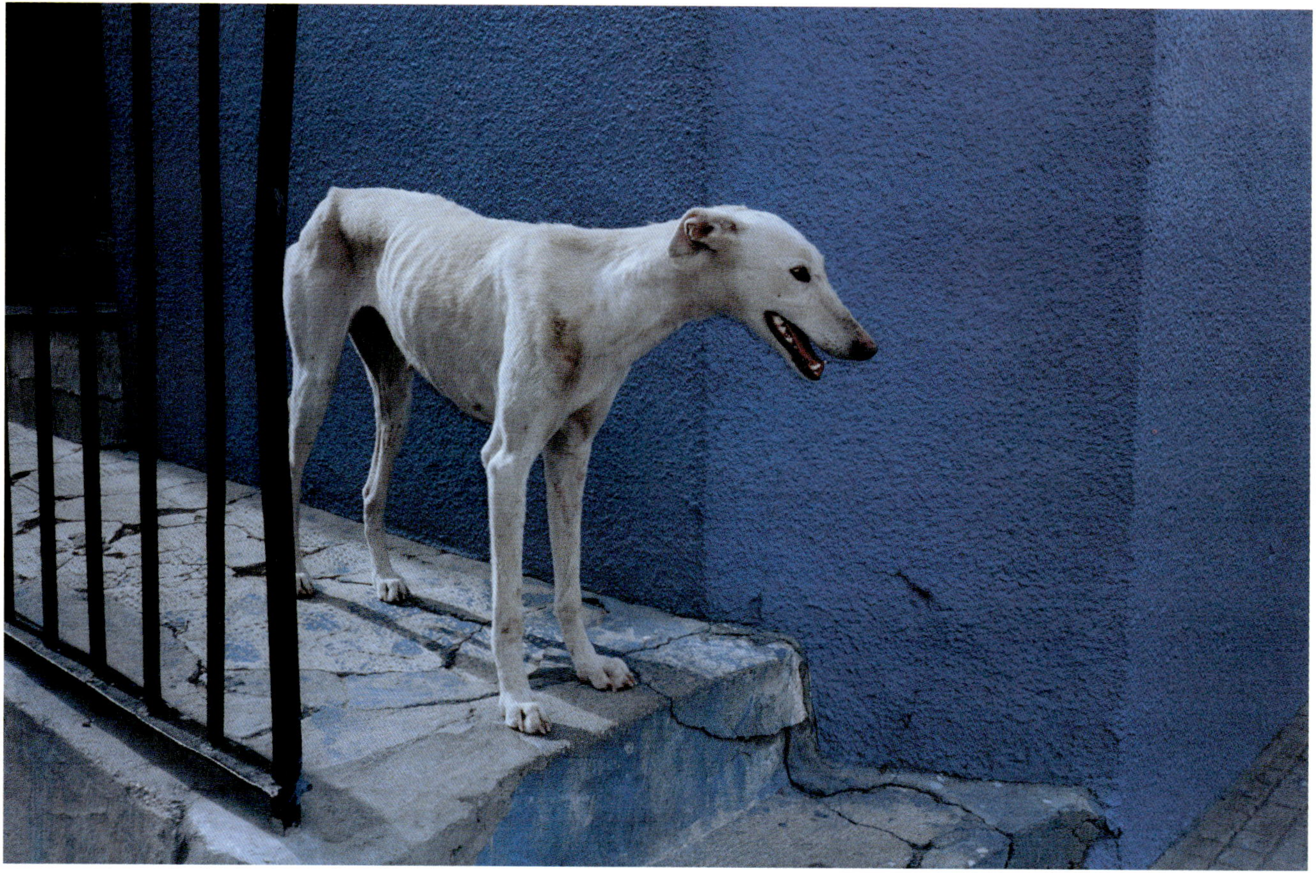

Friday, May 7. La Mancha, Spain. Stray dog

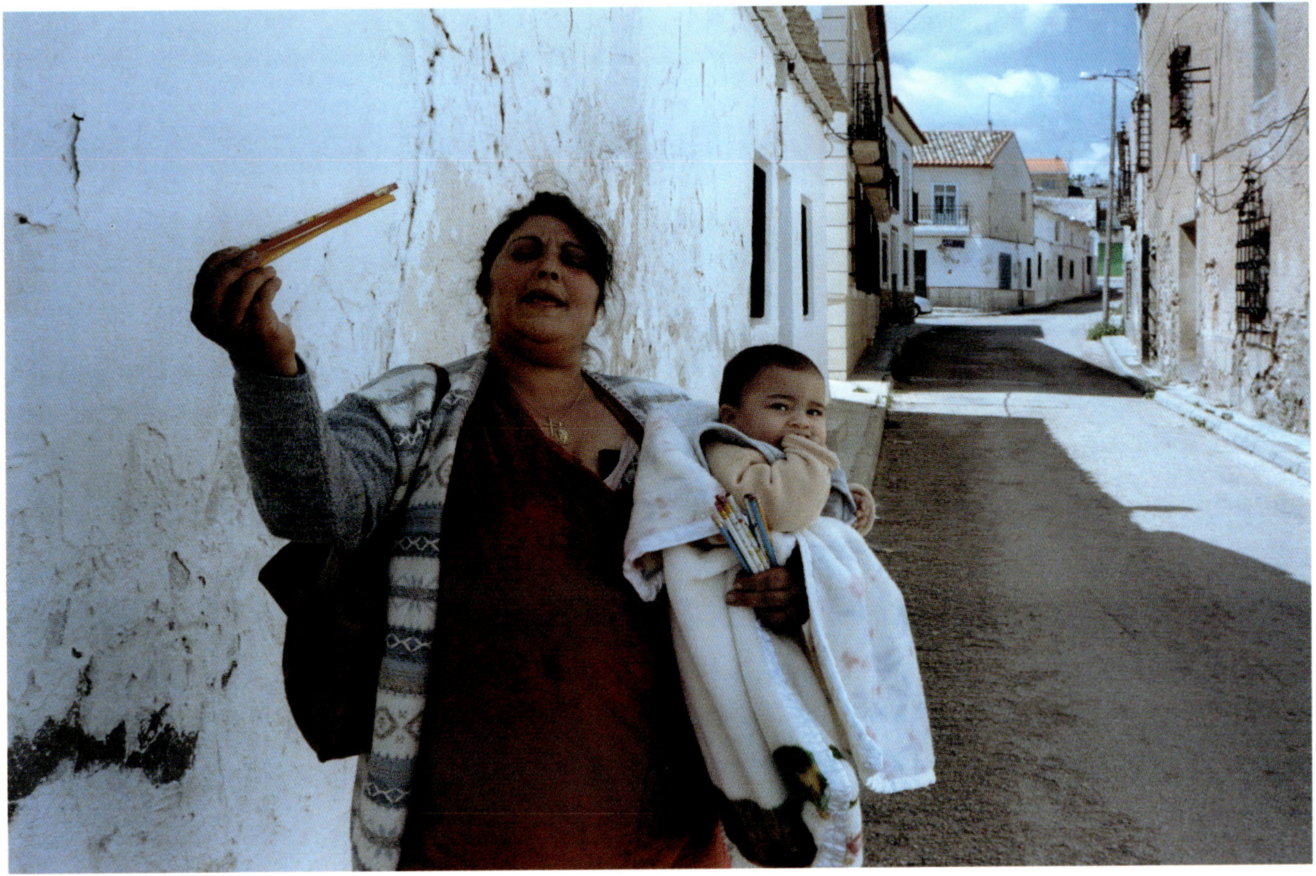

Friday, May 7. La Mancha, Spain. Gipsy woman

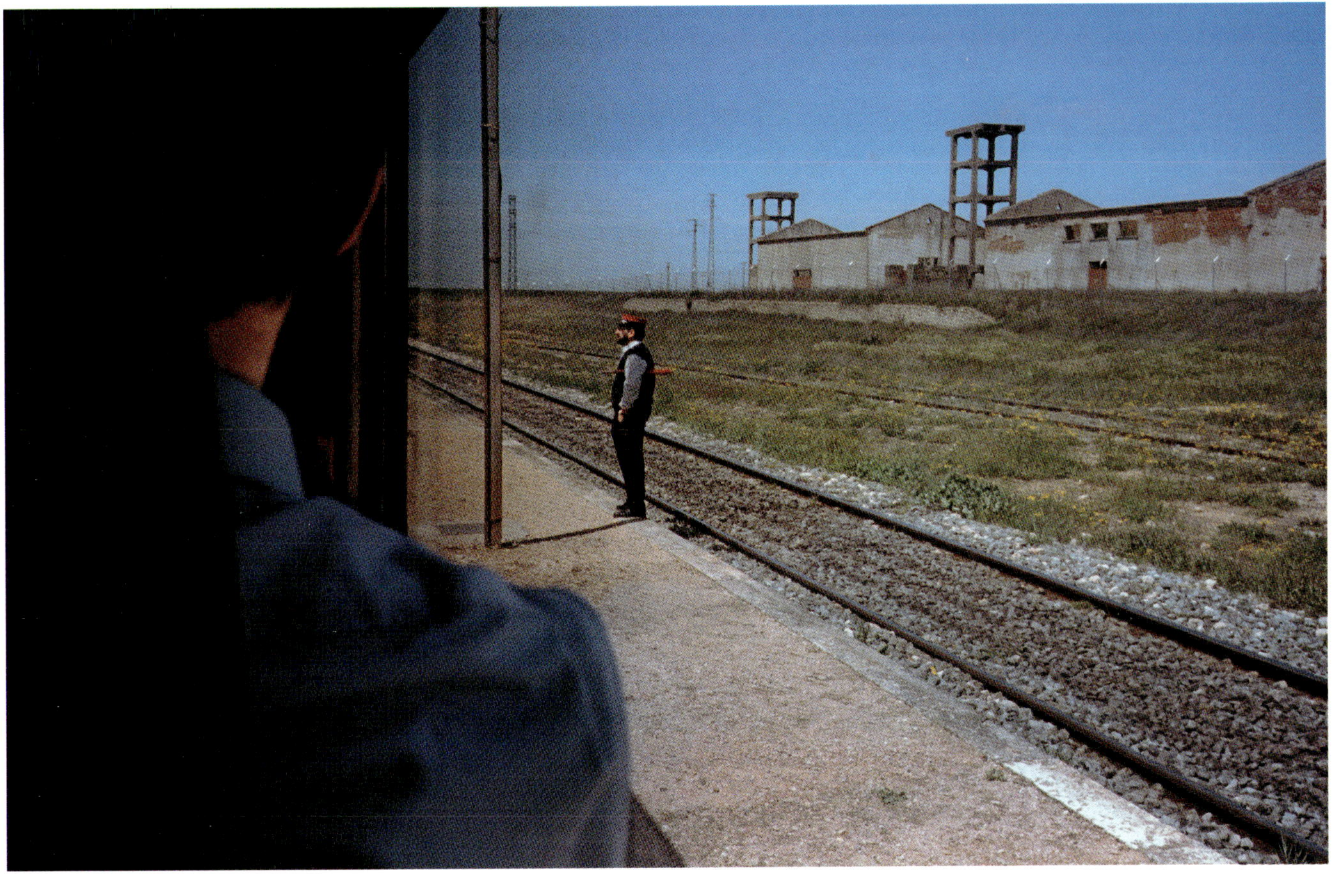

Saturday, May 8. Spain. On the railway line from Cuenca to Madrid

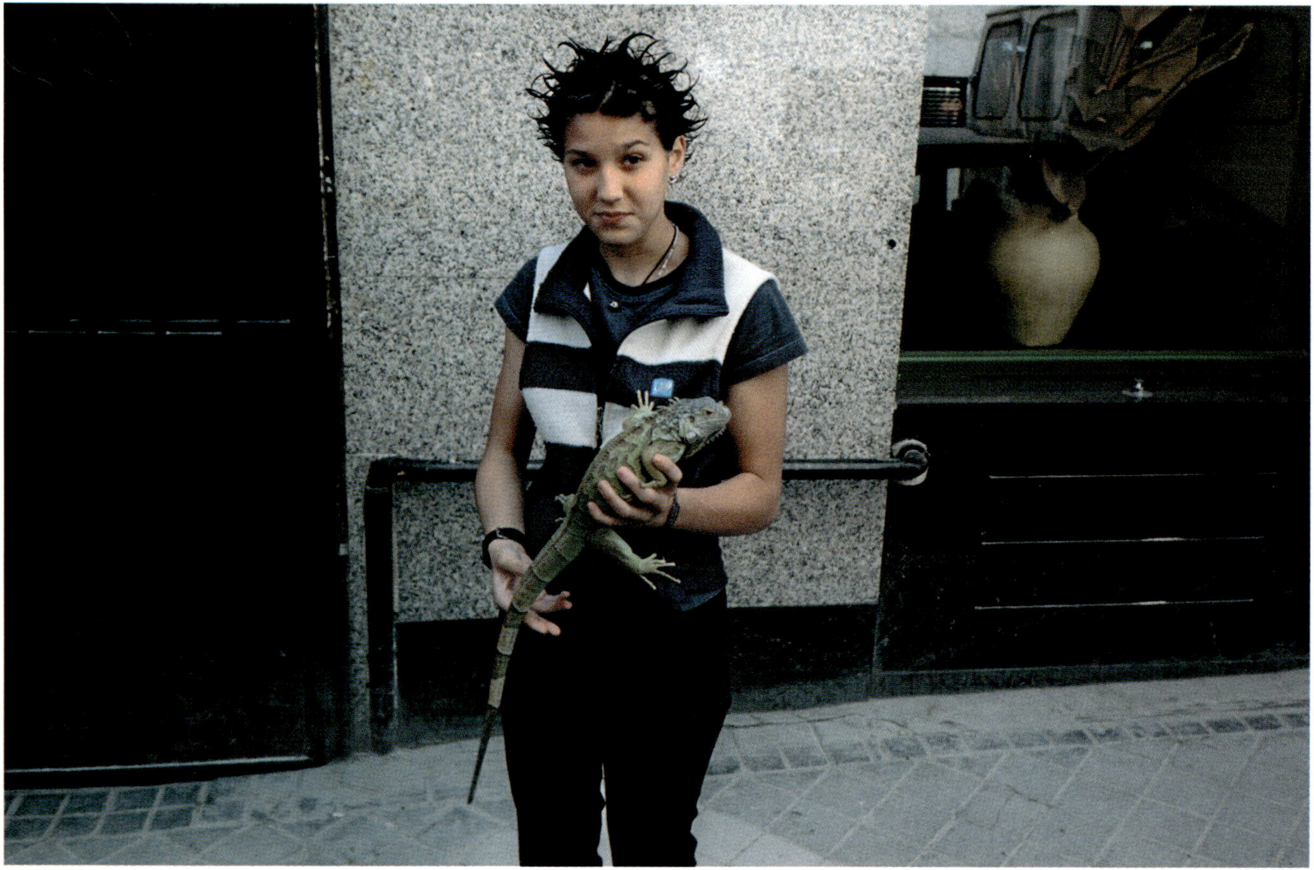

Sunday, May 9. Madrid. Street encounter

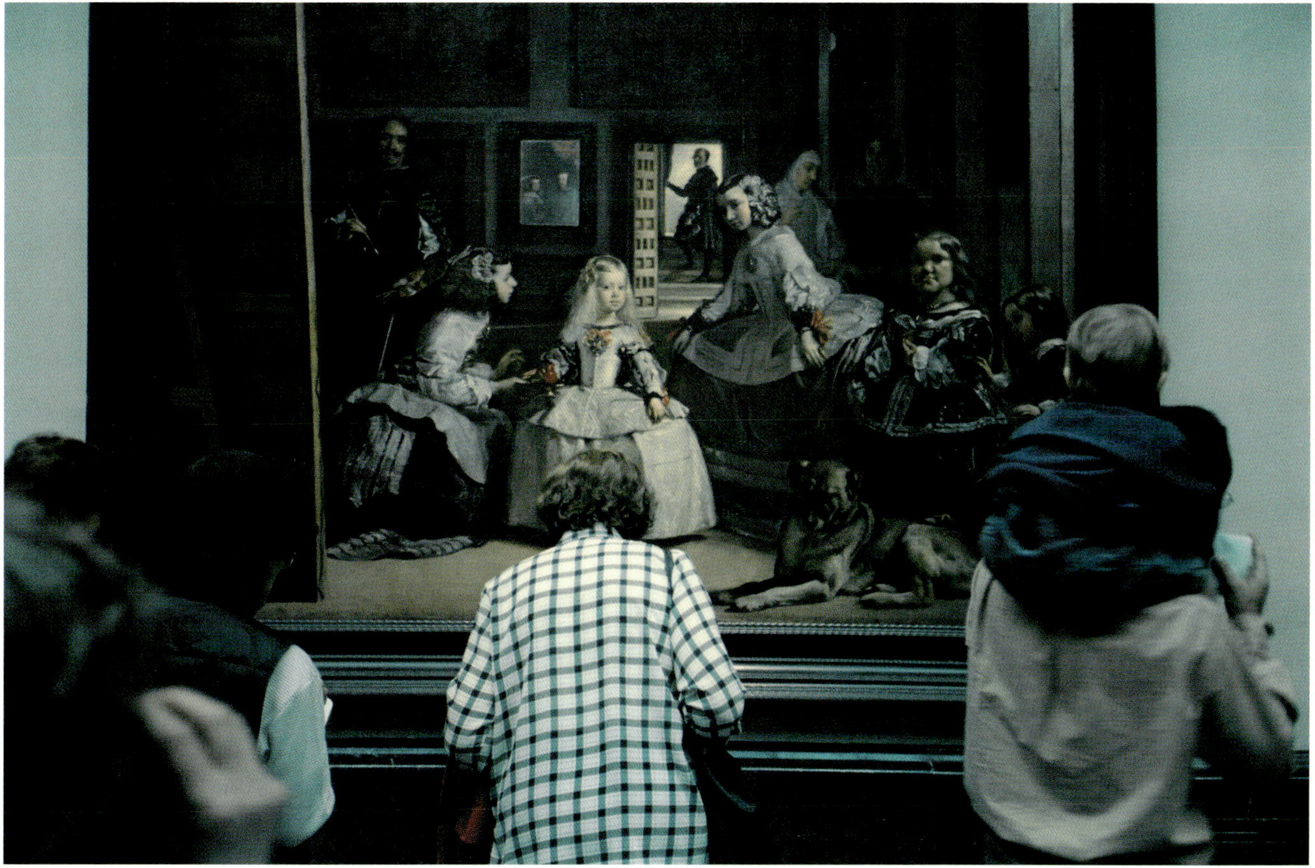

Sunday, May 9. Madrid. Prado Museum, Las Meninas

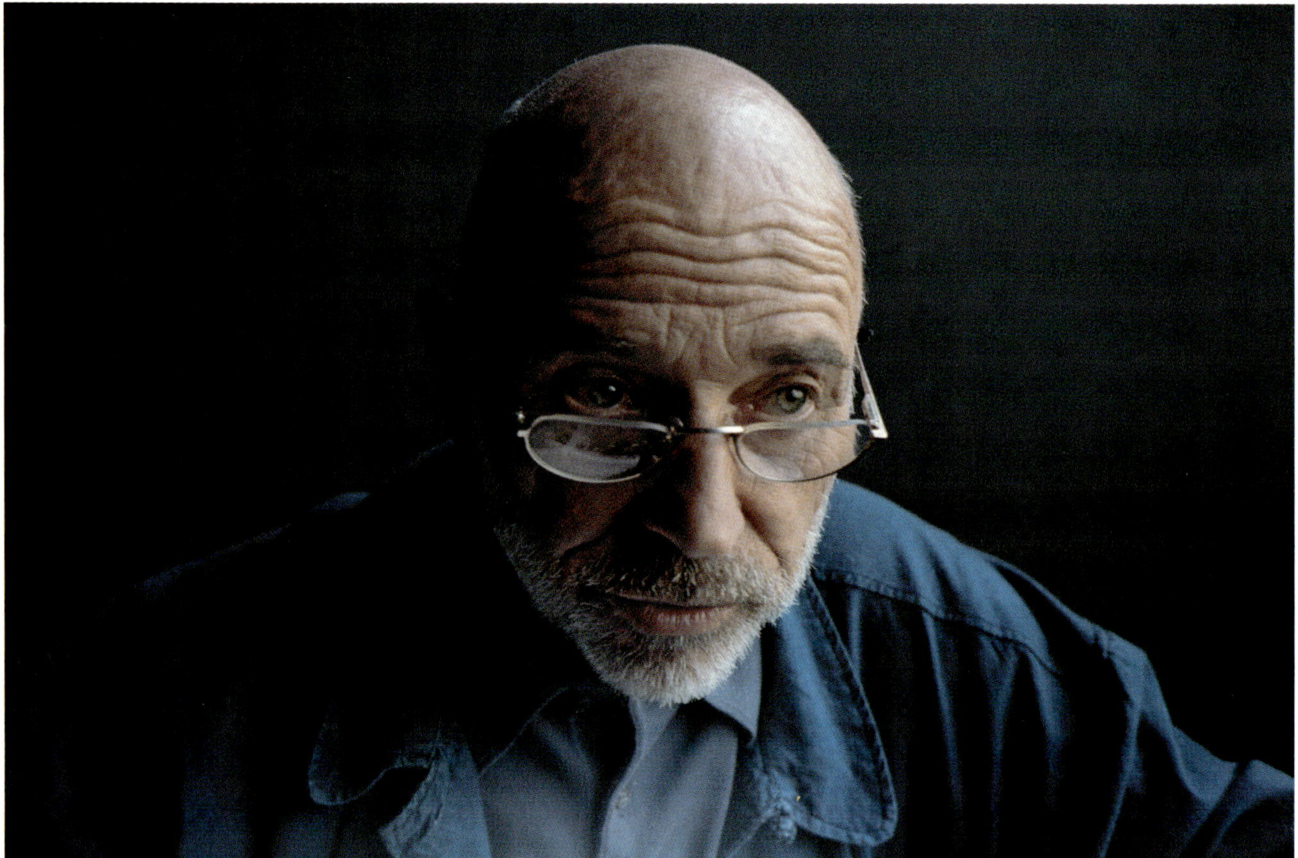

Monday, May 10. Boulogne, France. Peter Knapp, painter and photographer

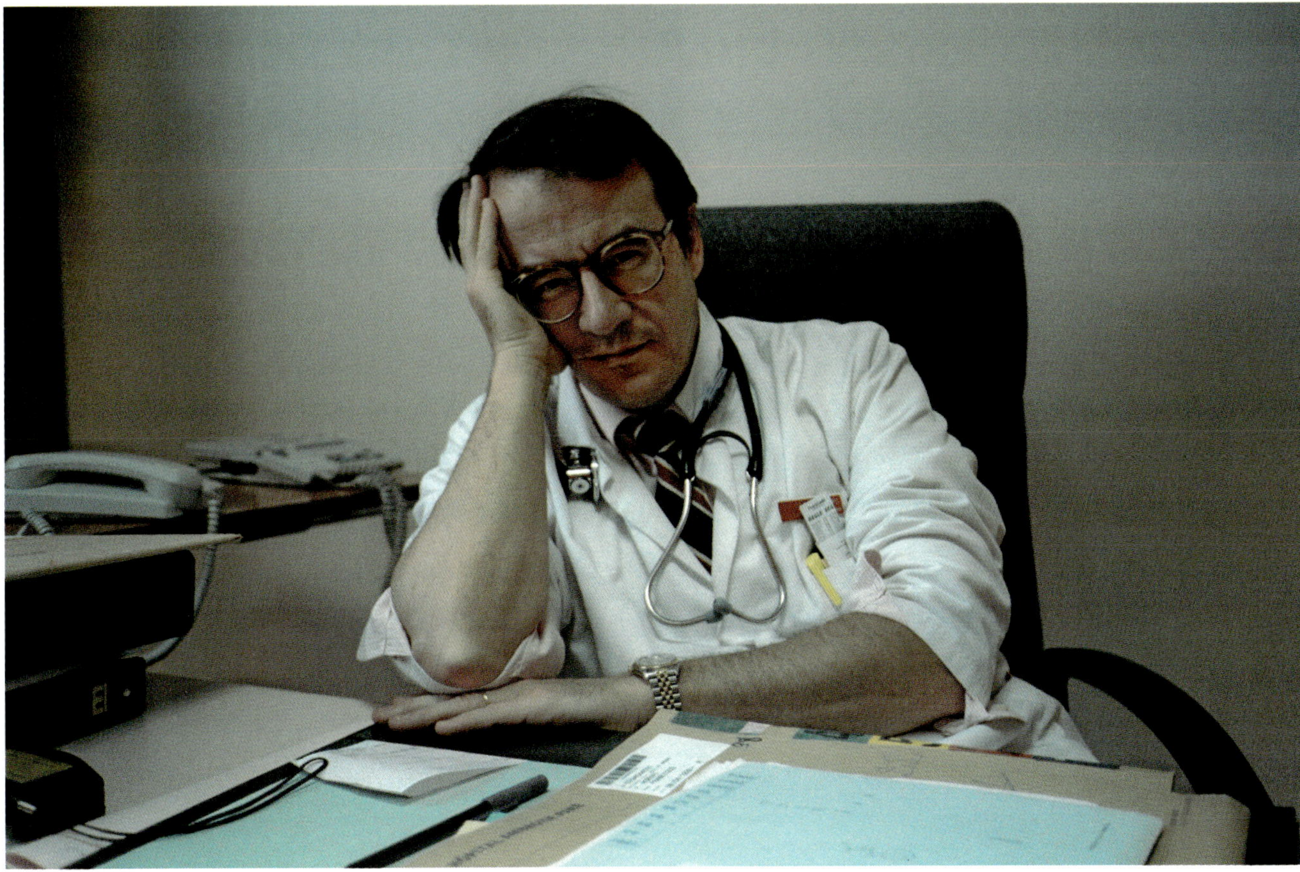

Tuesday, May 11. Boulogne, France. Professor Olivier Dubourg, cardiologist

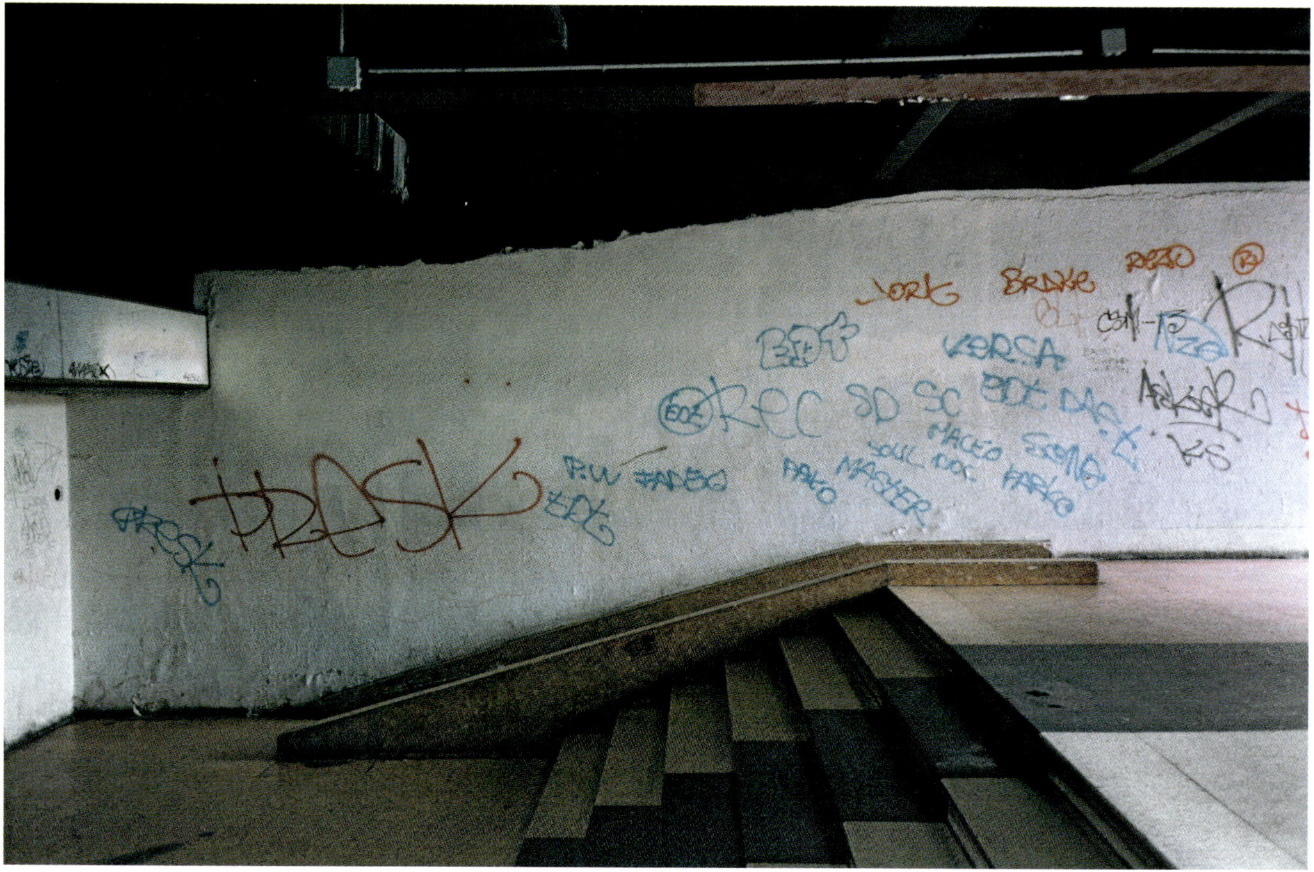

Wednesday, May 12. Paris. In the Place d'Italie area

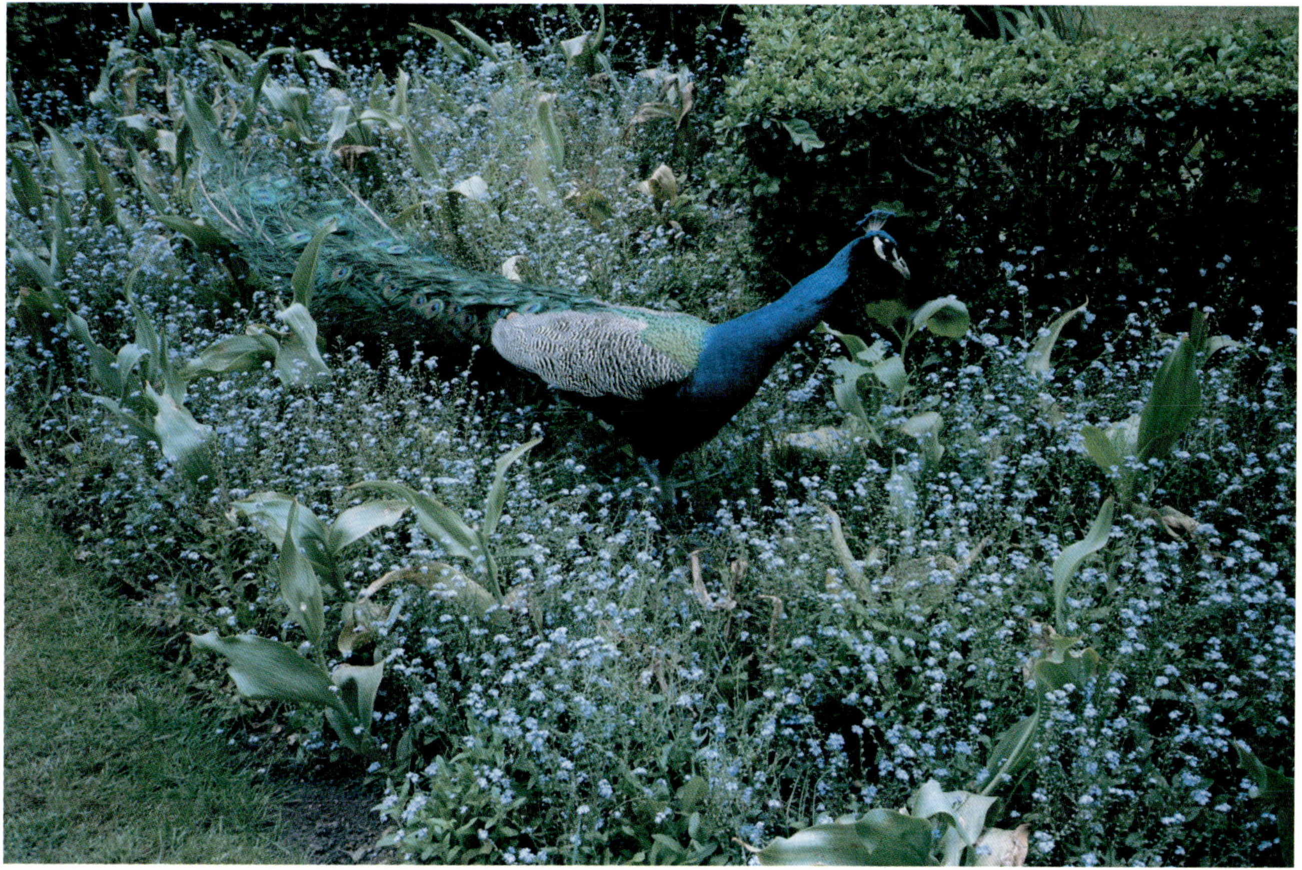

Thursday, May 13. Paris. Parc de Bagatelle

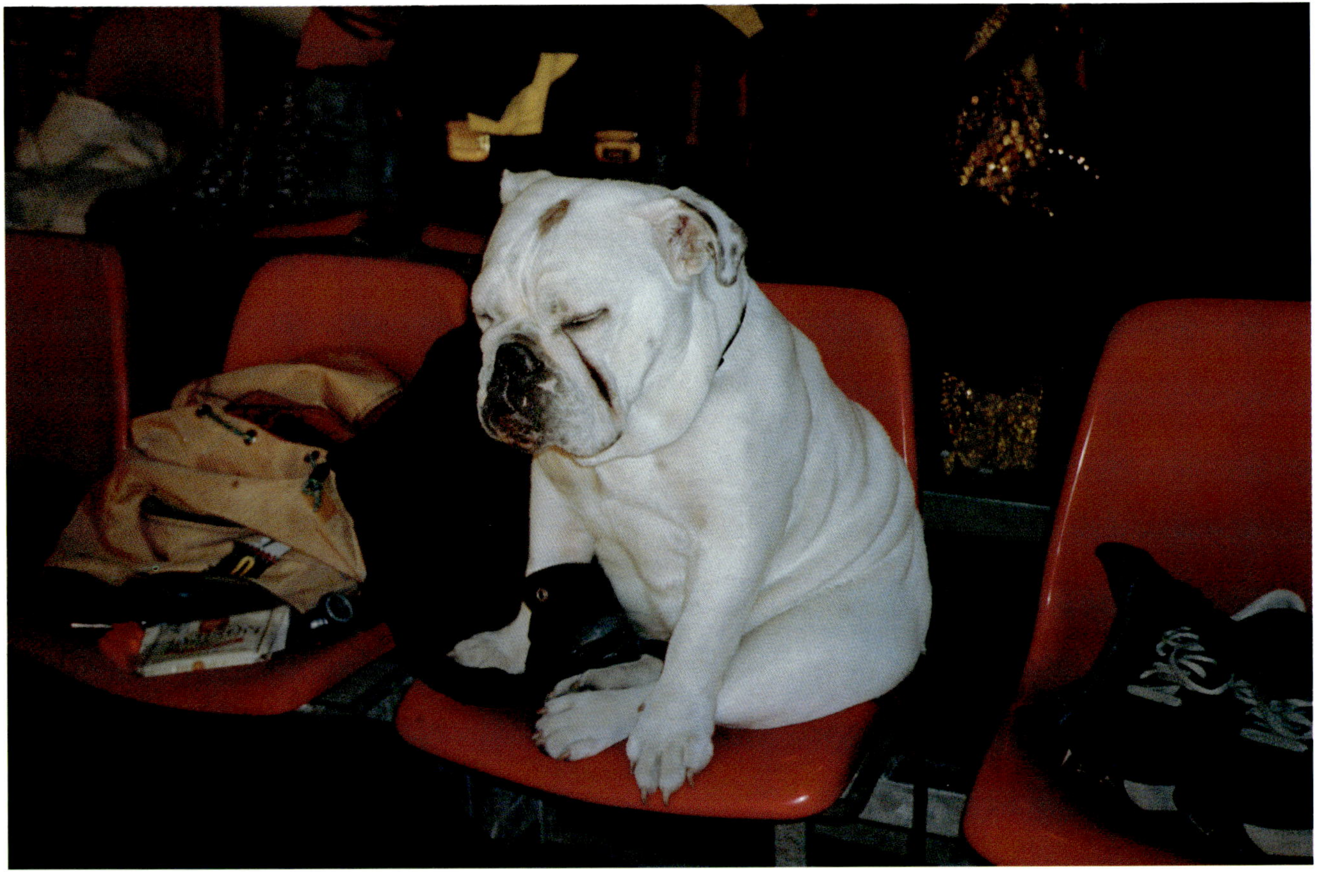

Friday, May 14. Nancy, France. "Olive"

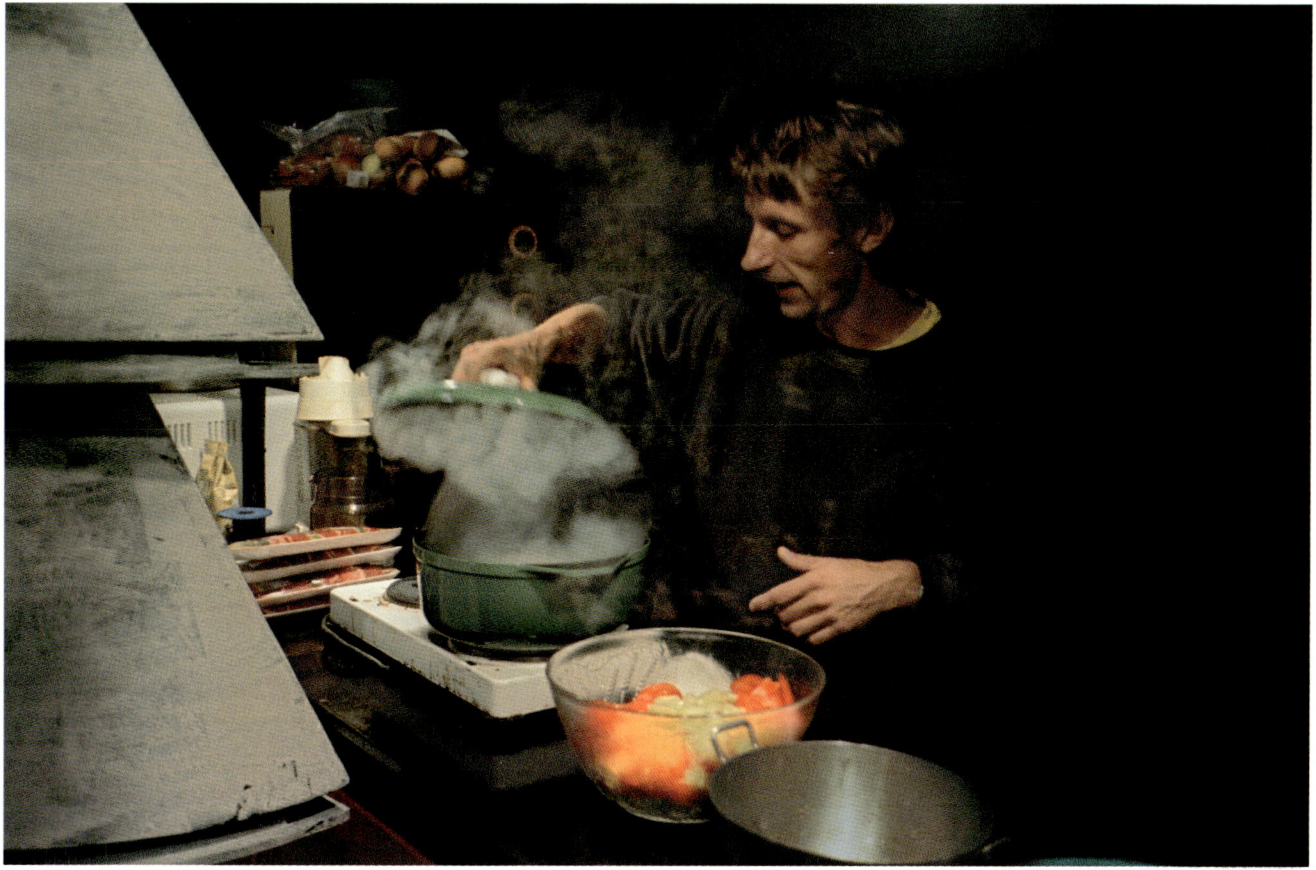

Friday, May 14. Nancy, France. Jean-Louis Laforêt, film-maker

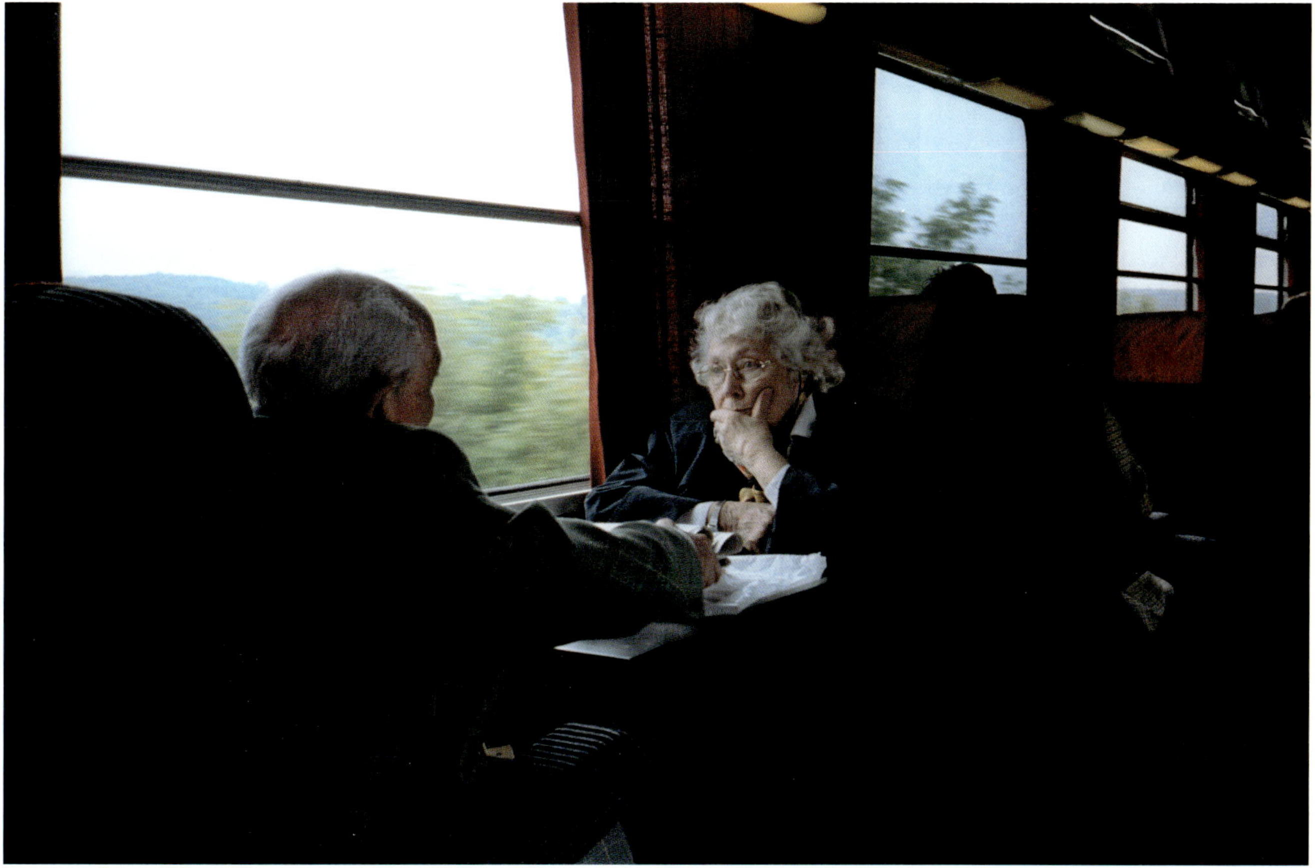

Saturday, May 15. France. On the train between Nancy and Paris

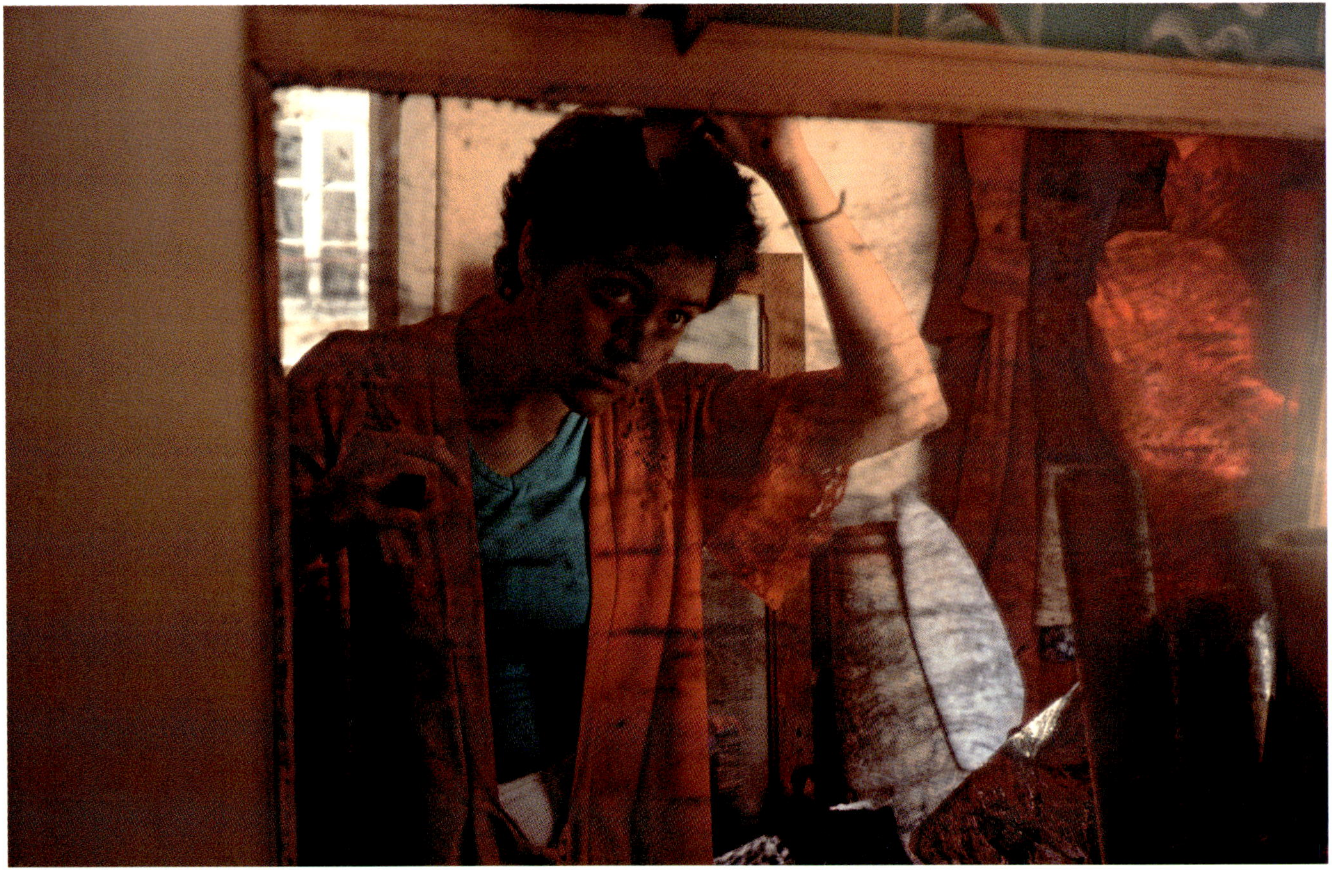

Sunday, May 16. Paris. Véronique Leyrit, photographer

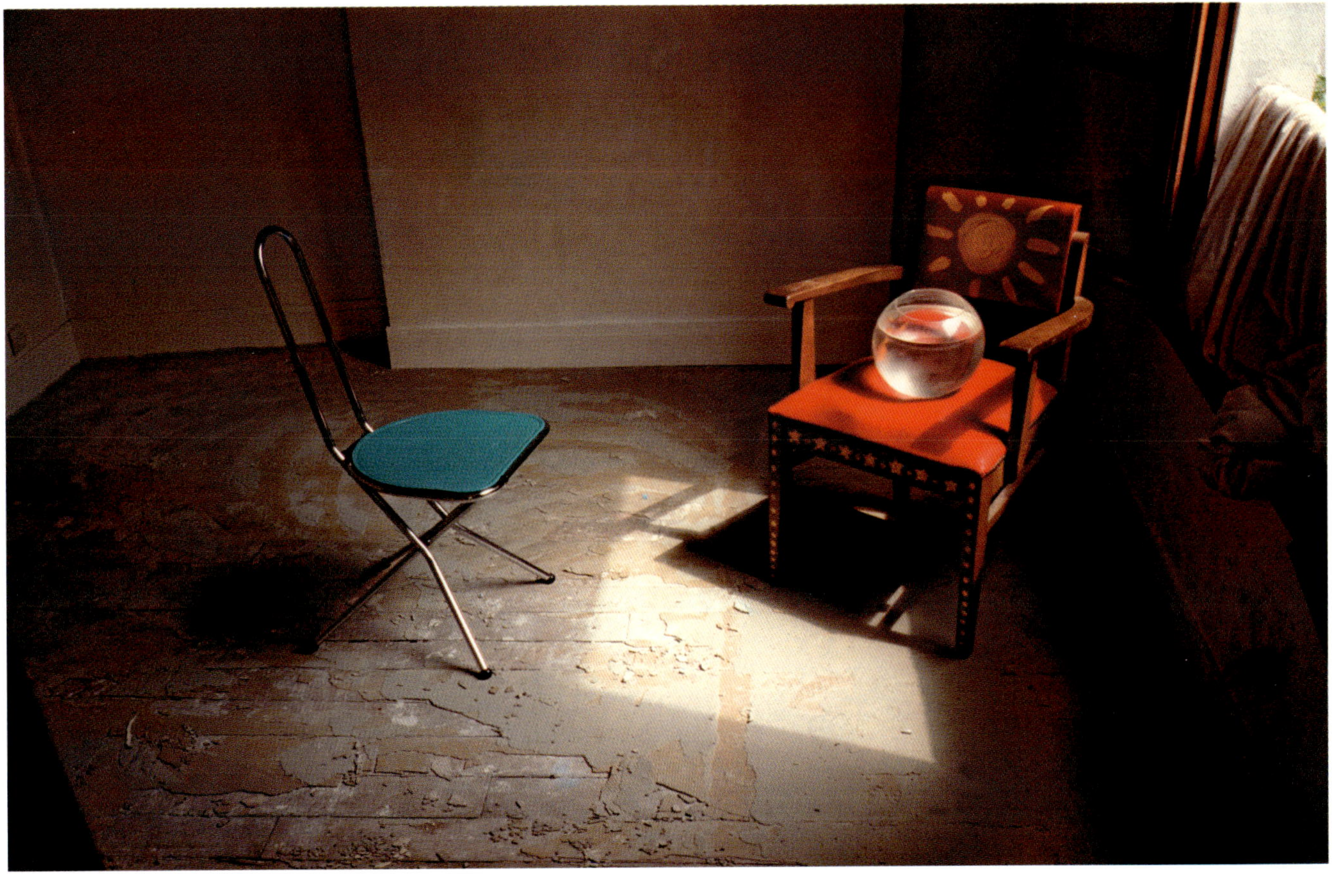

Monday, May 17. Paris. At Véronique Leyrit's home

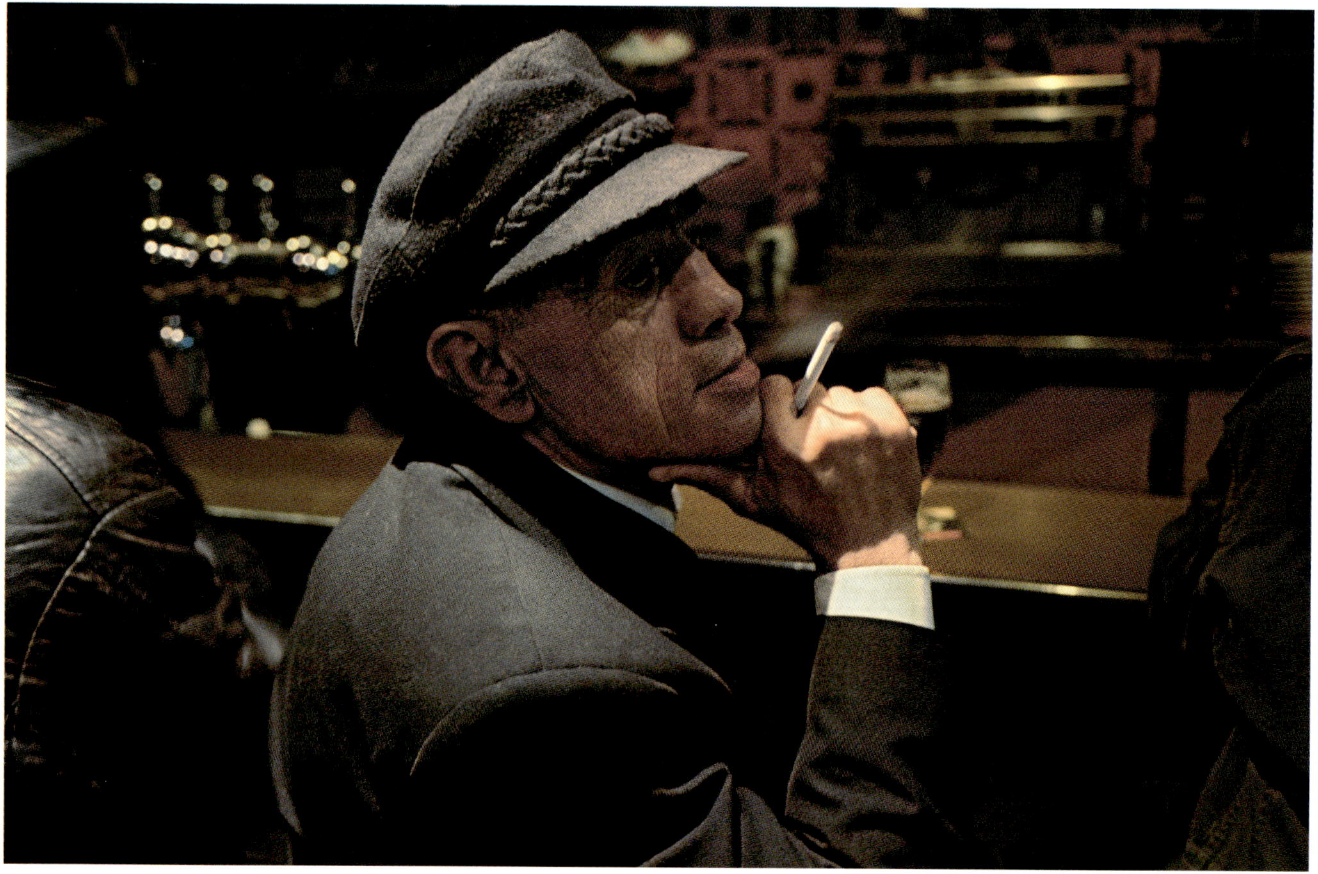

Tuesday, May 18. Paris. A bar in the Bastille area

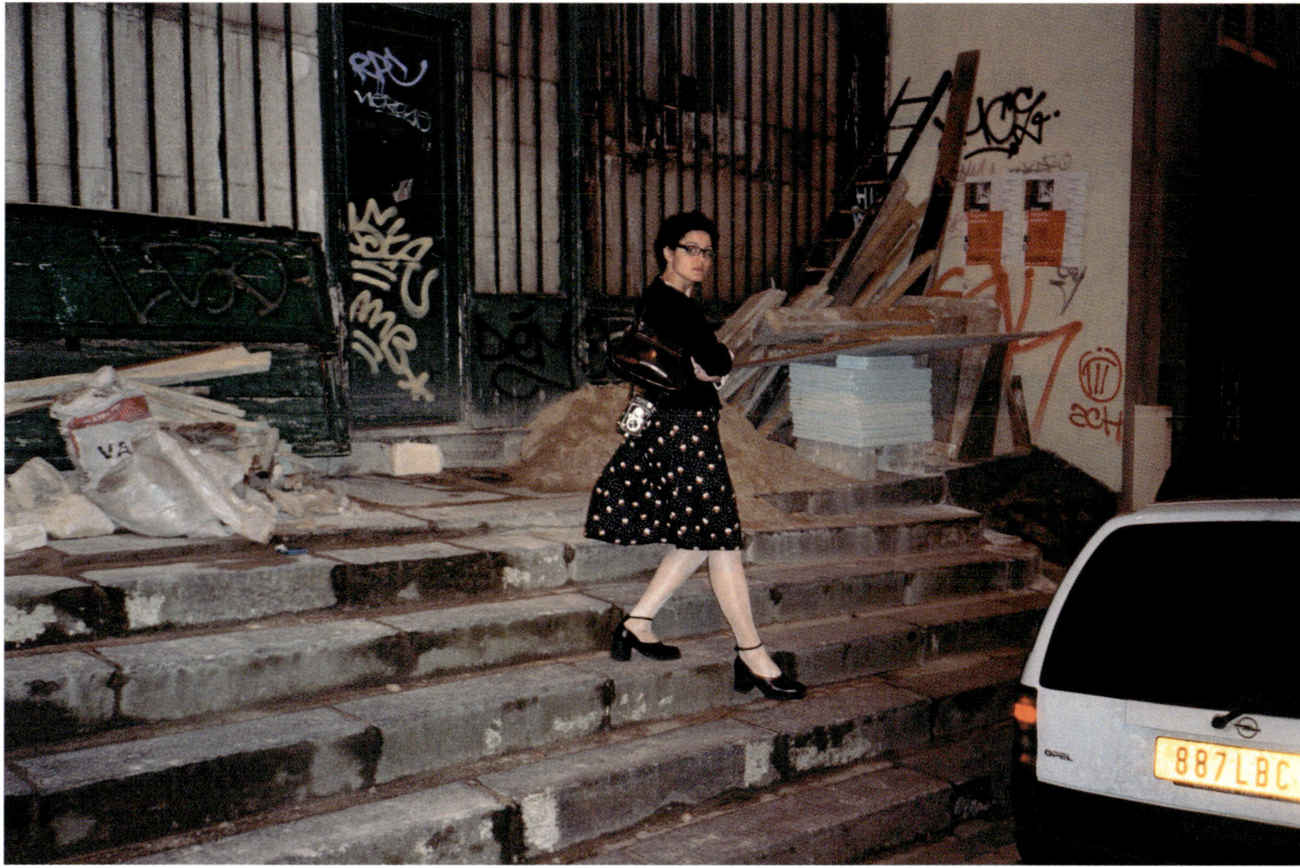

Wednesday, May 19. Paris. Véronique Leyrit, photographer

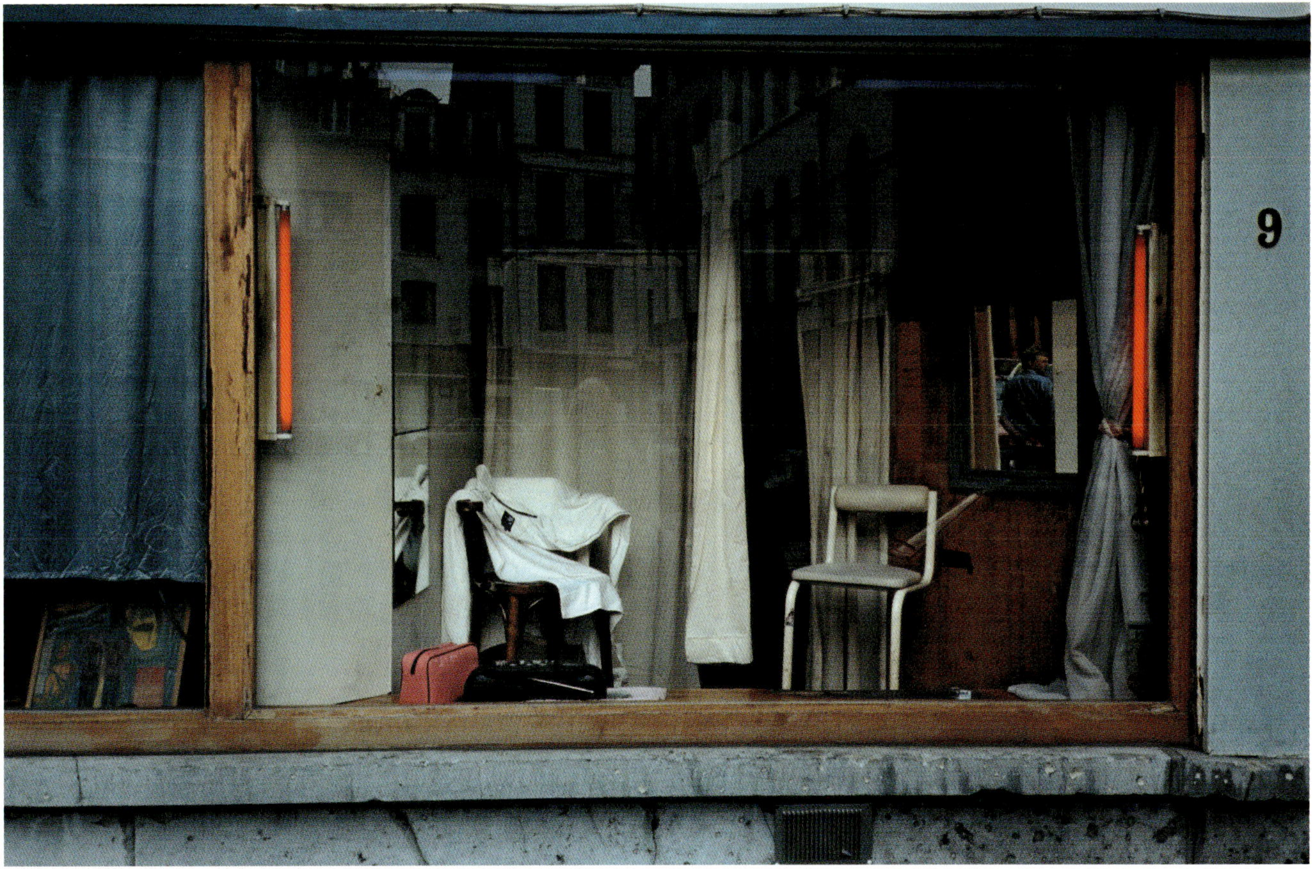

Thursday, May 20. Antwerp, Belgium. Prostitute's shop window

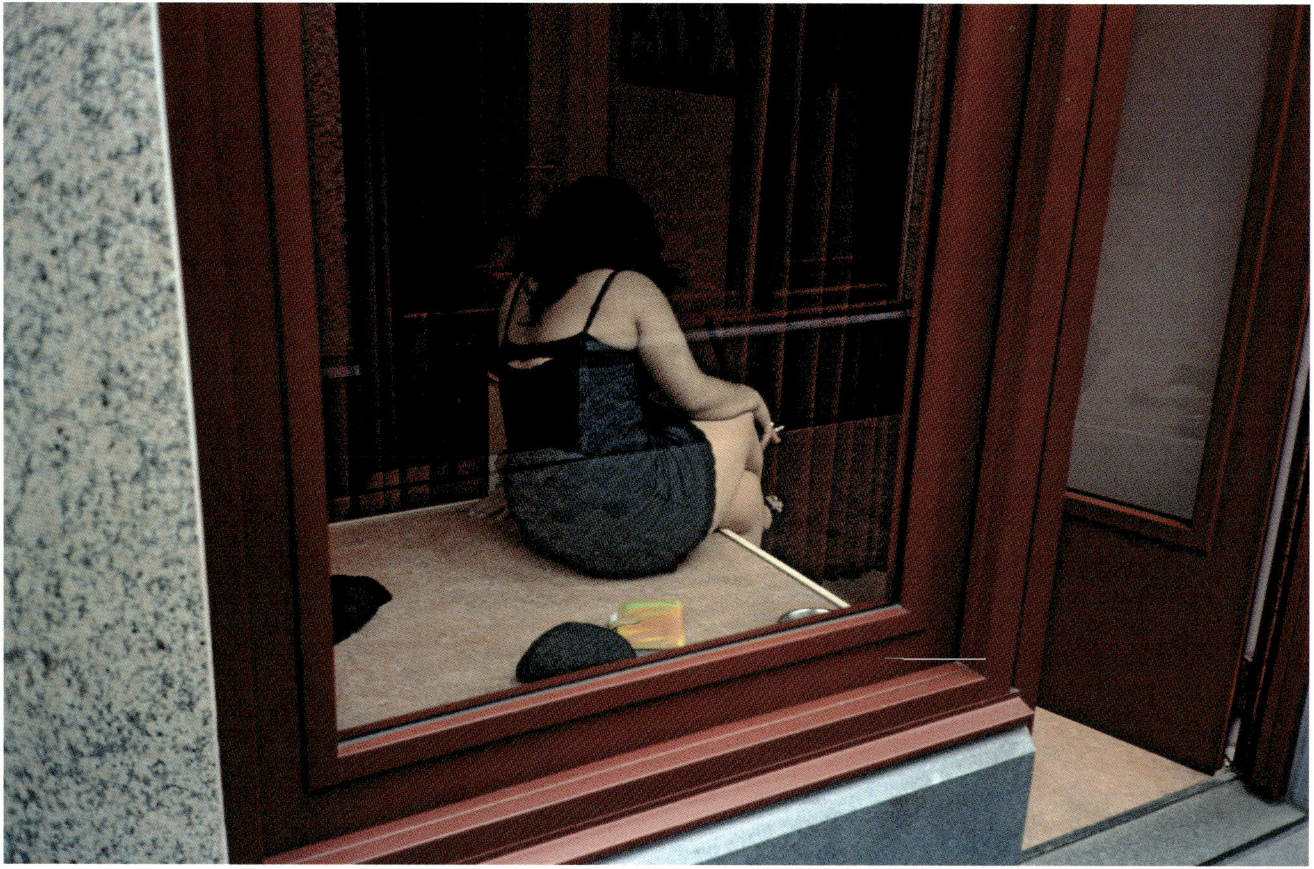

Friday, May 21. Antwerp, Belgium. Prostitute

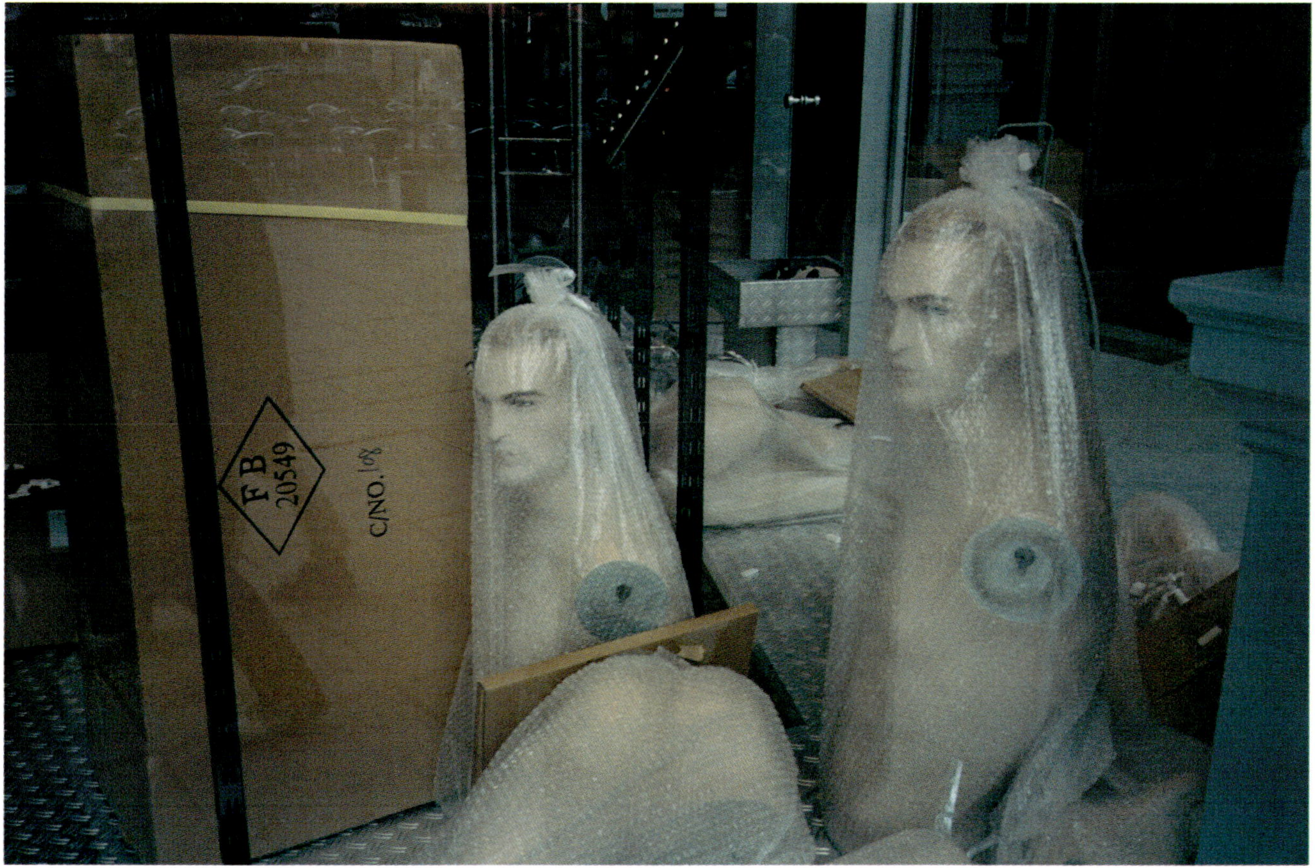

Saturday, May 22. Antwerp, Belgium. Mannequins

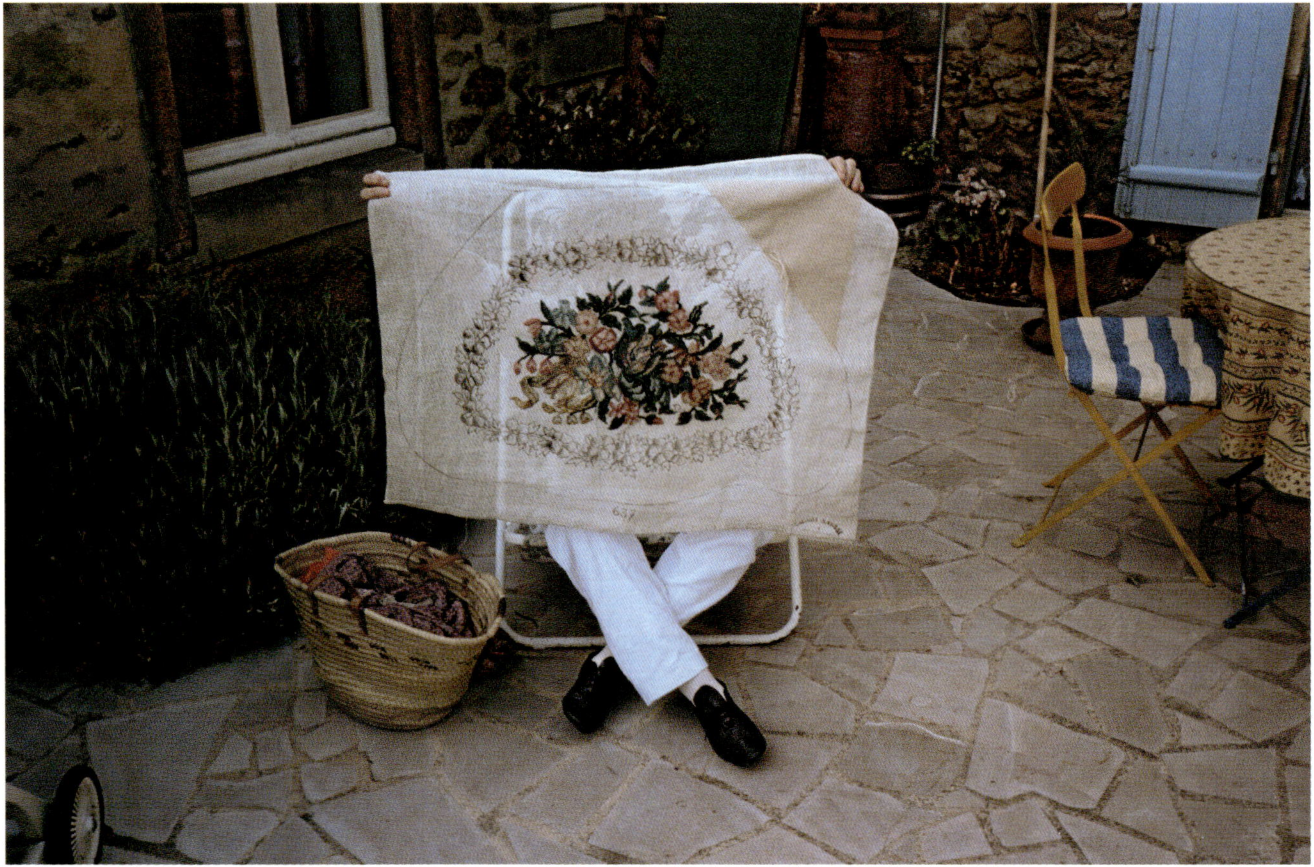

Sunday, May 23. Le Dunet, France. Véronique Aubry behind her tapestry work

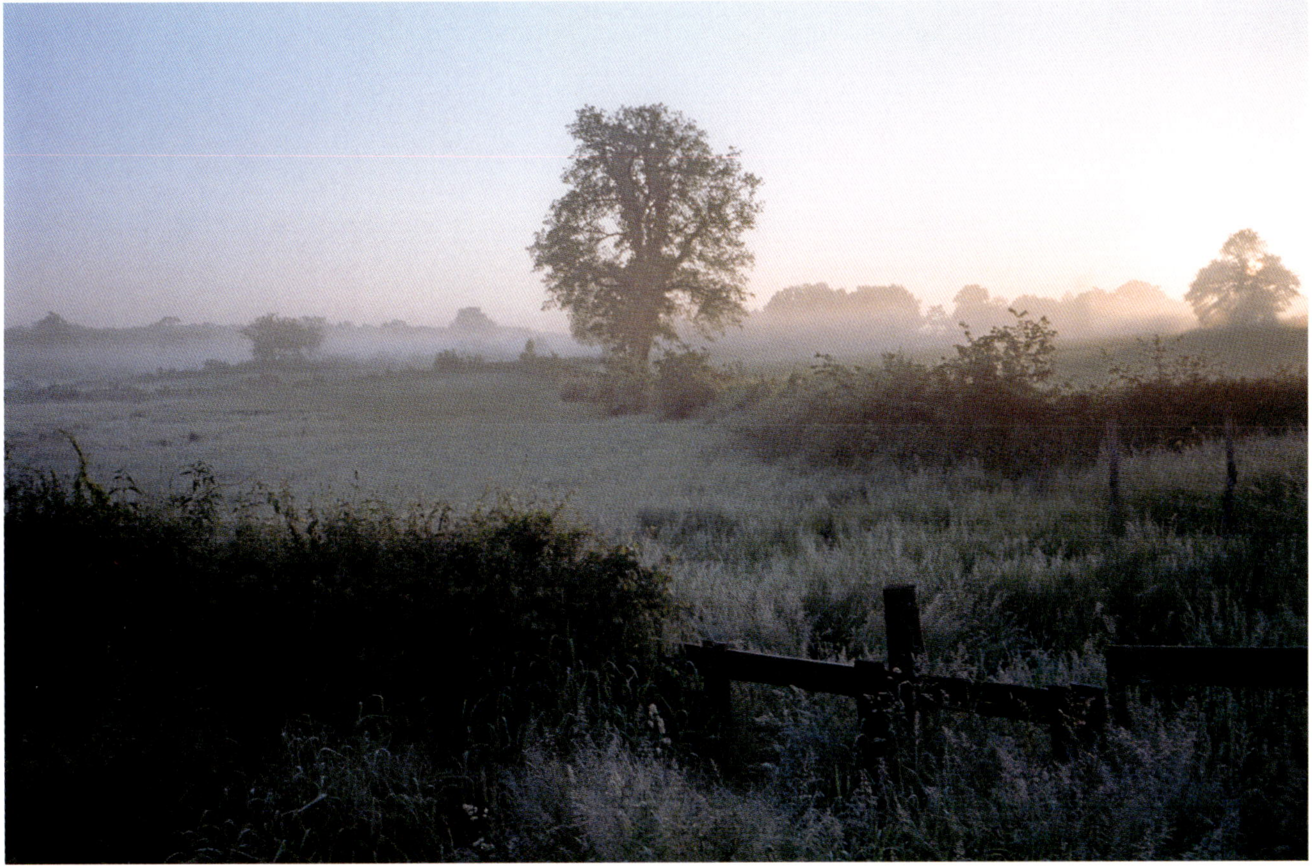

Monday, May 24. Le Dunet, France. Early morning

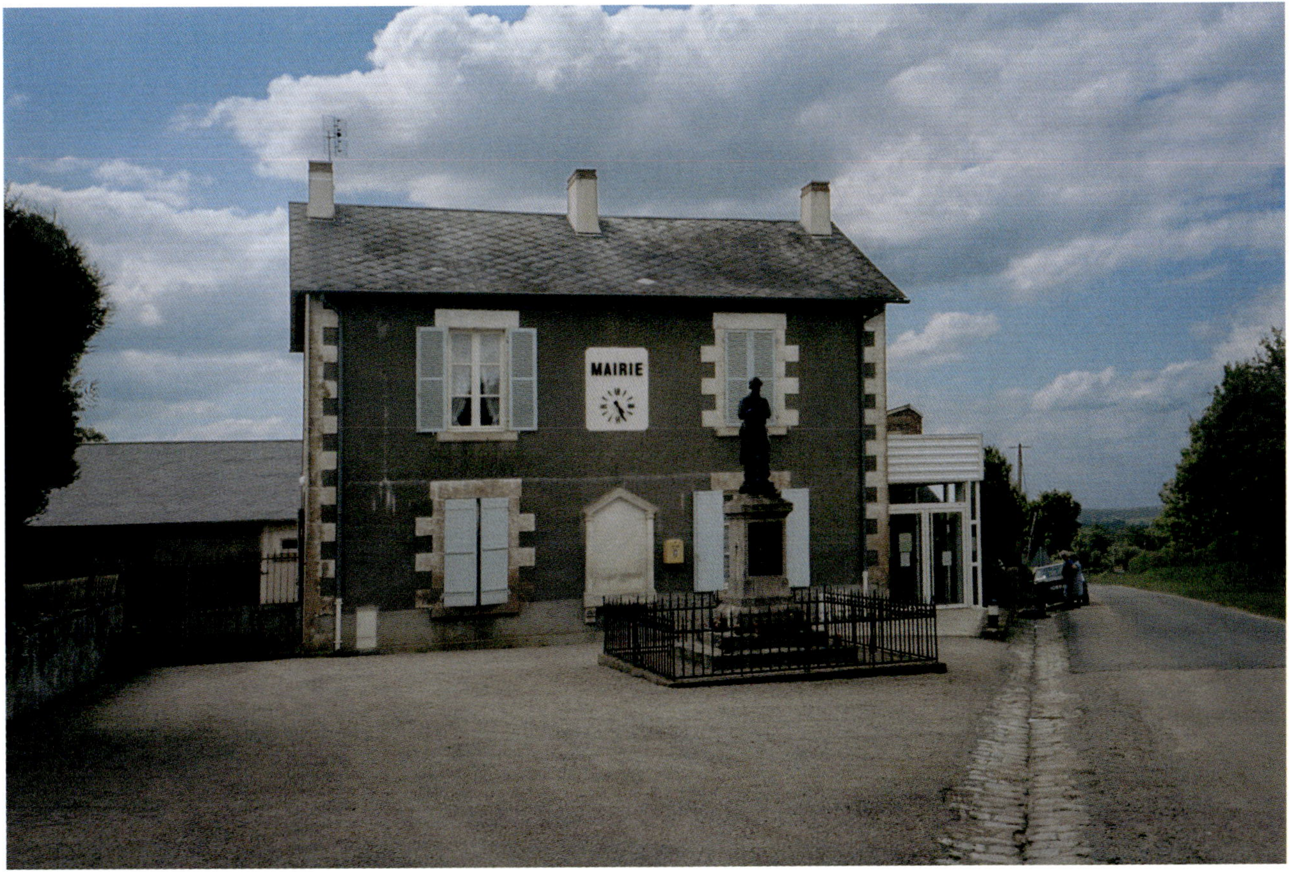

Tuesday, May 25. Le Dunet, France. The town hall

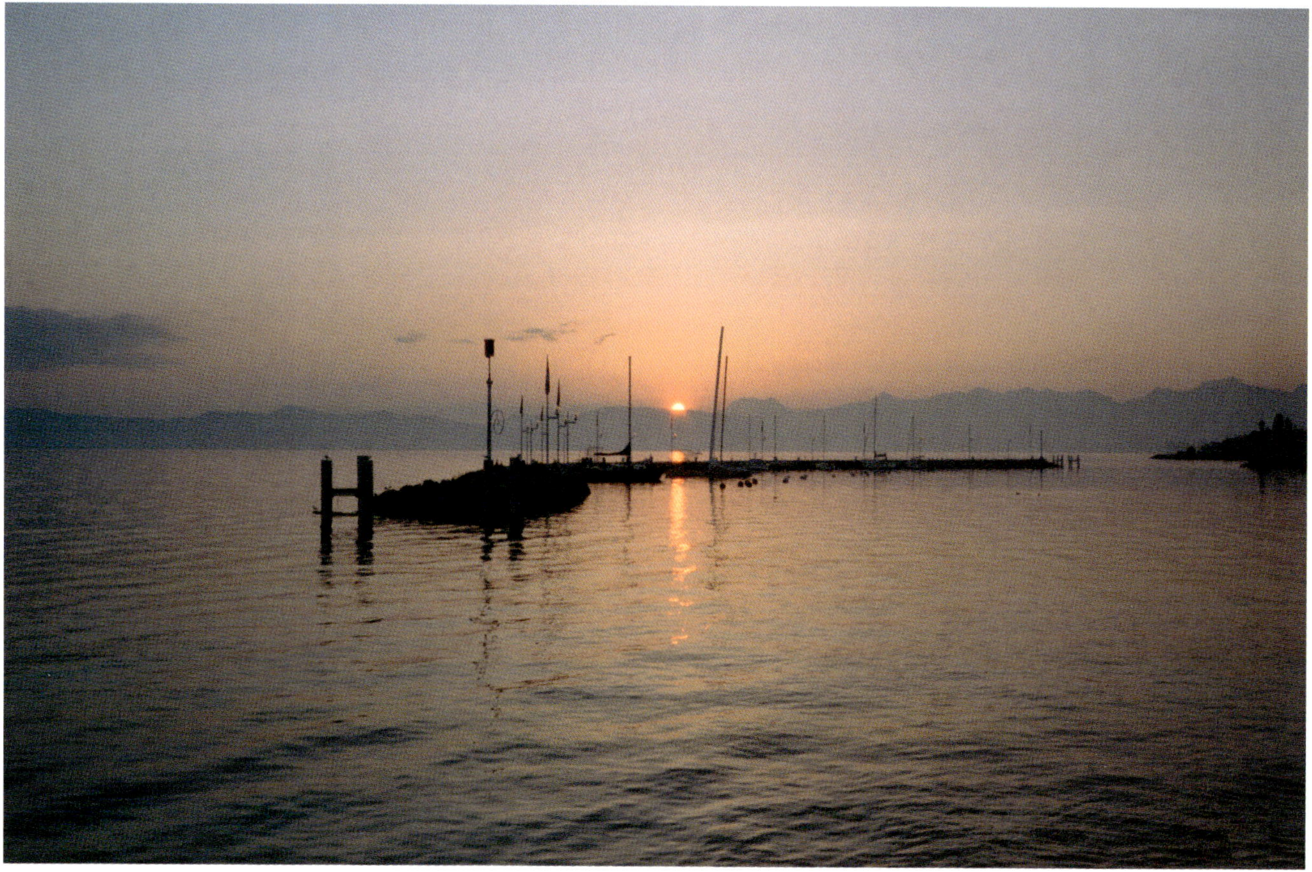

Wednesday, May 26. Evian, France. Sunrise

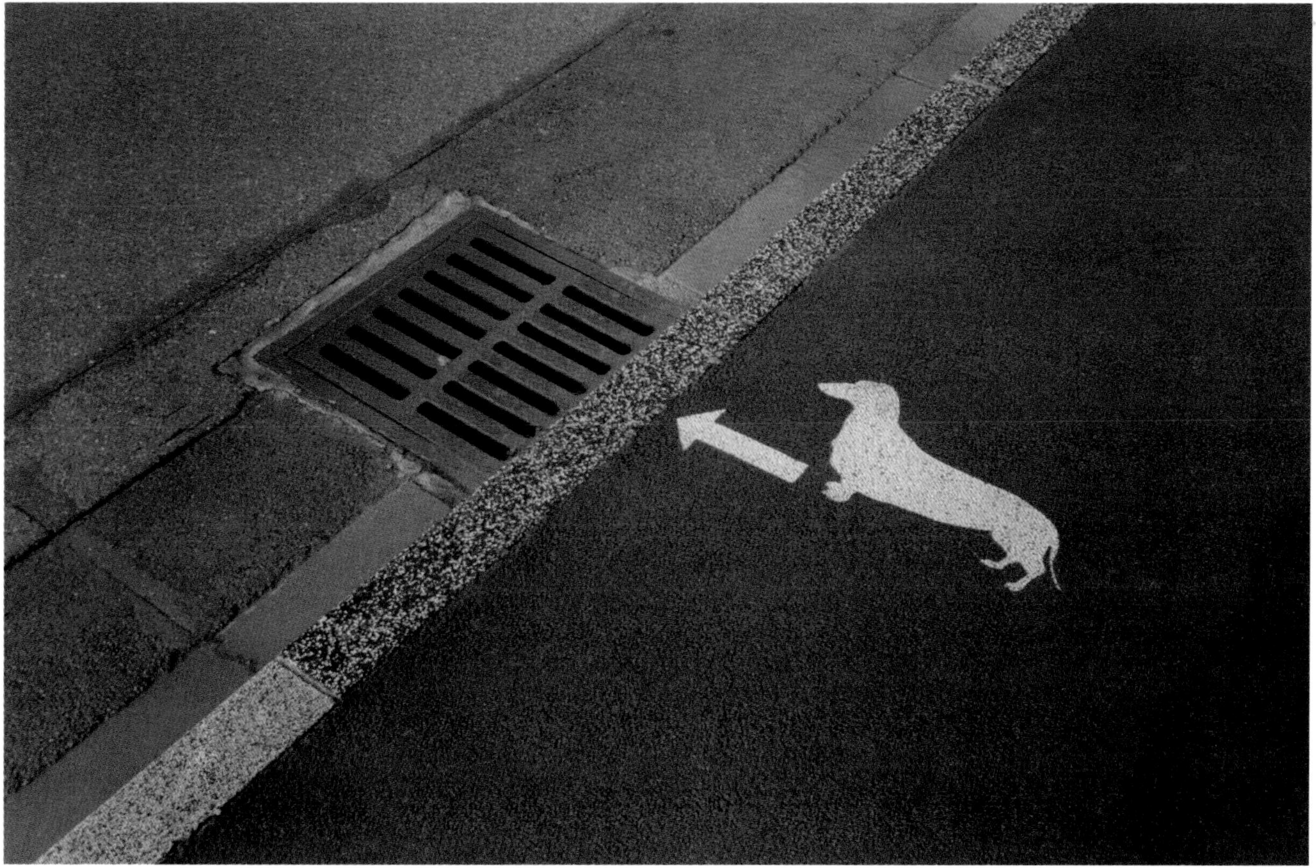

Thursday, May 27. Evian, France. Footpath

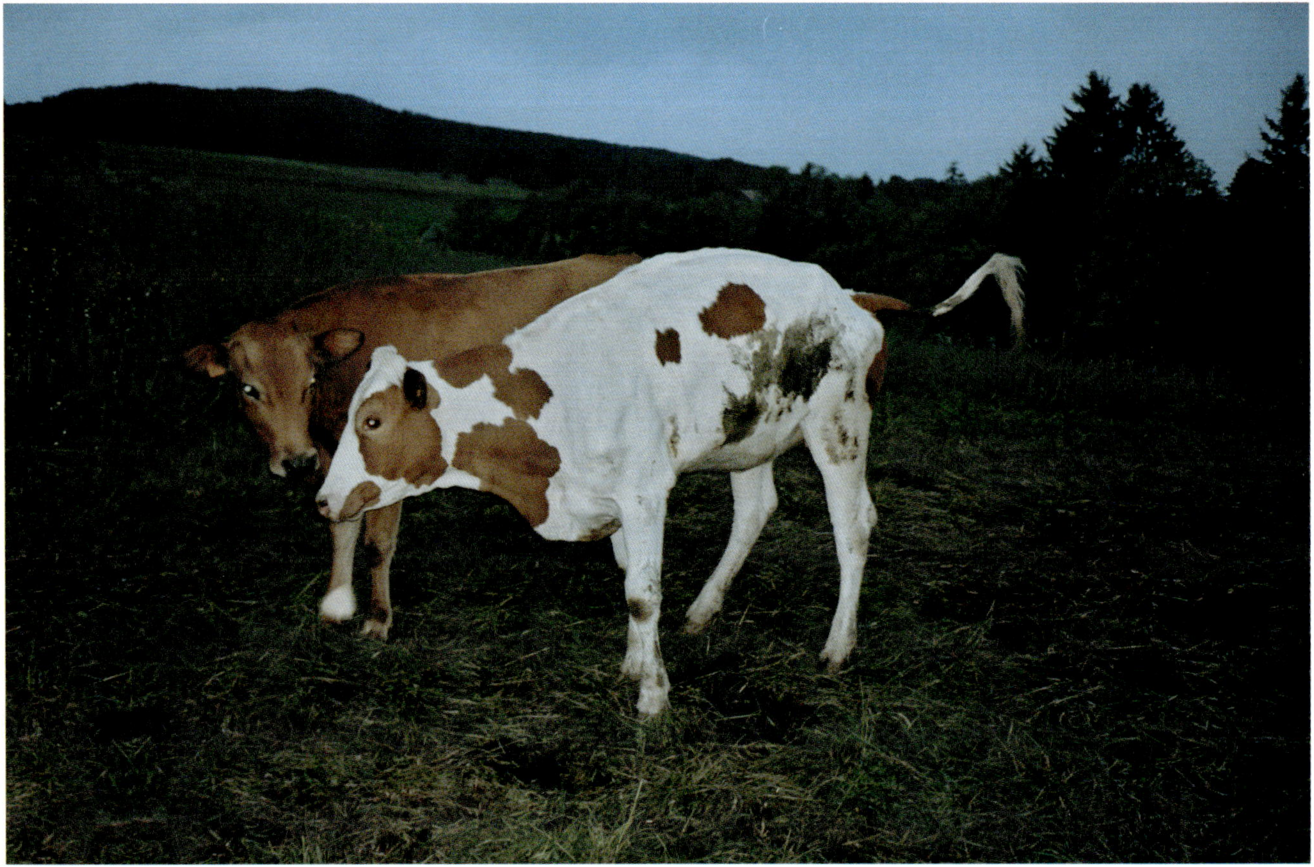

Friday, May 28. Vaulruz, Switzerland. Nightfall

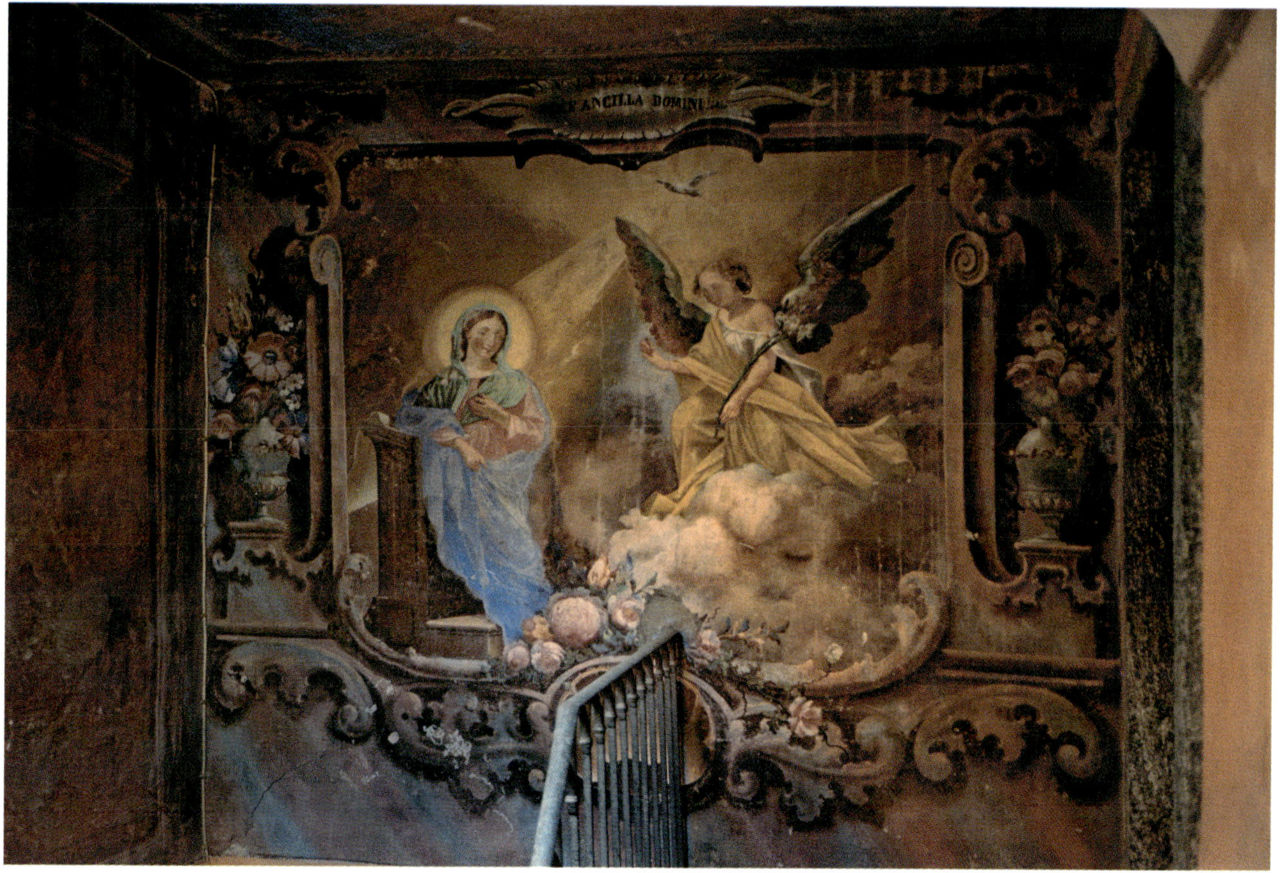

Saturday, May 29. Intragna, Switzerland. In the house of my adolescence (see note)

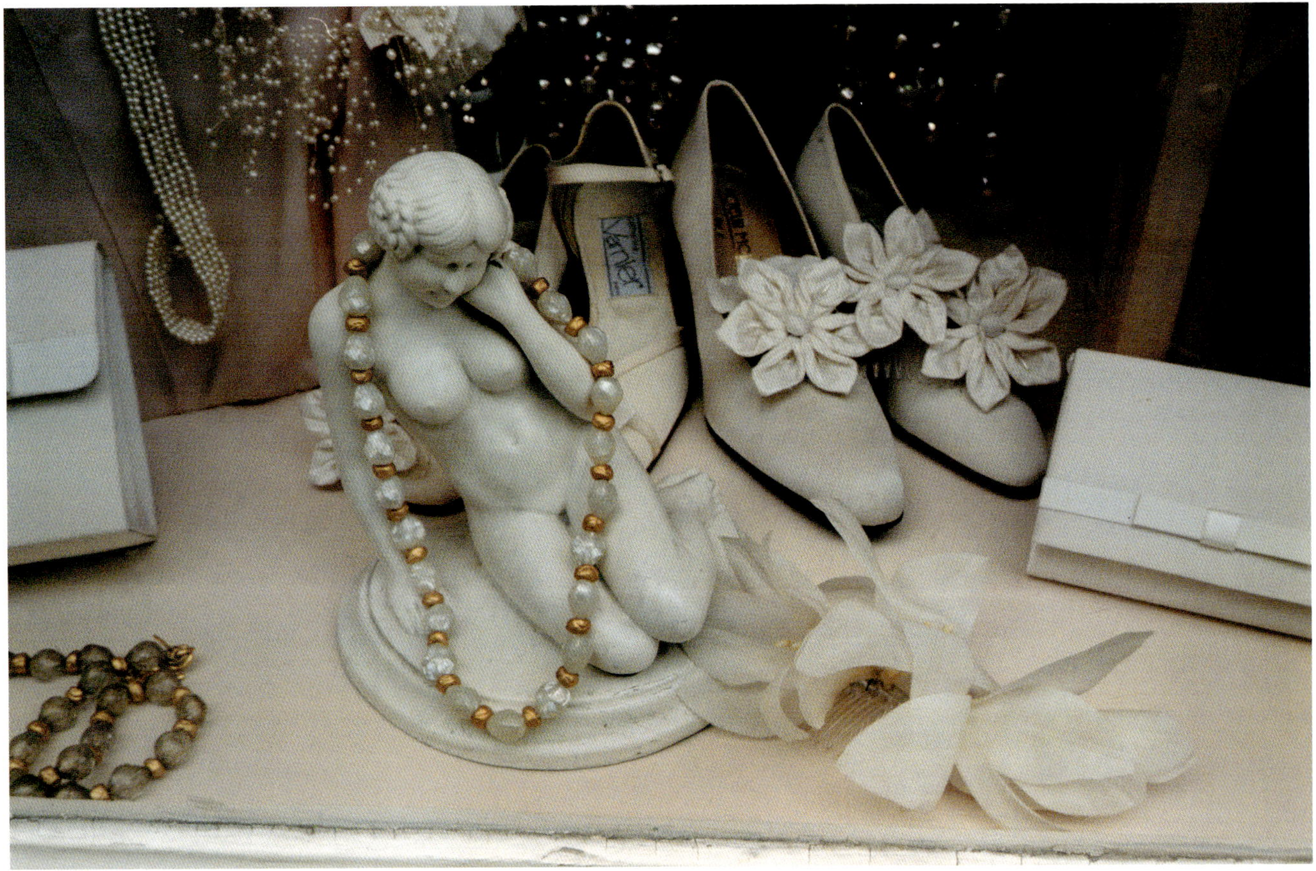

Sunday, May 30. Paris. Detail of a window display, near the home of Édouard Boubat

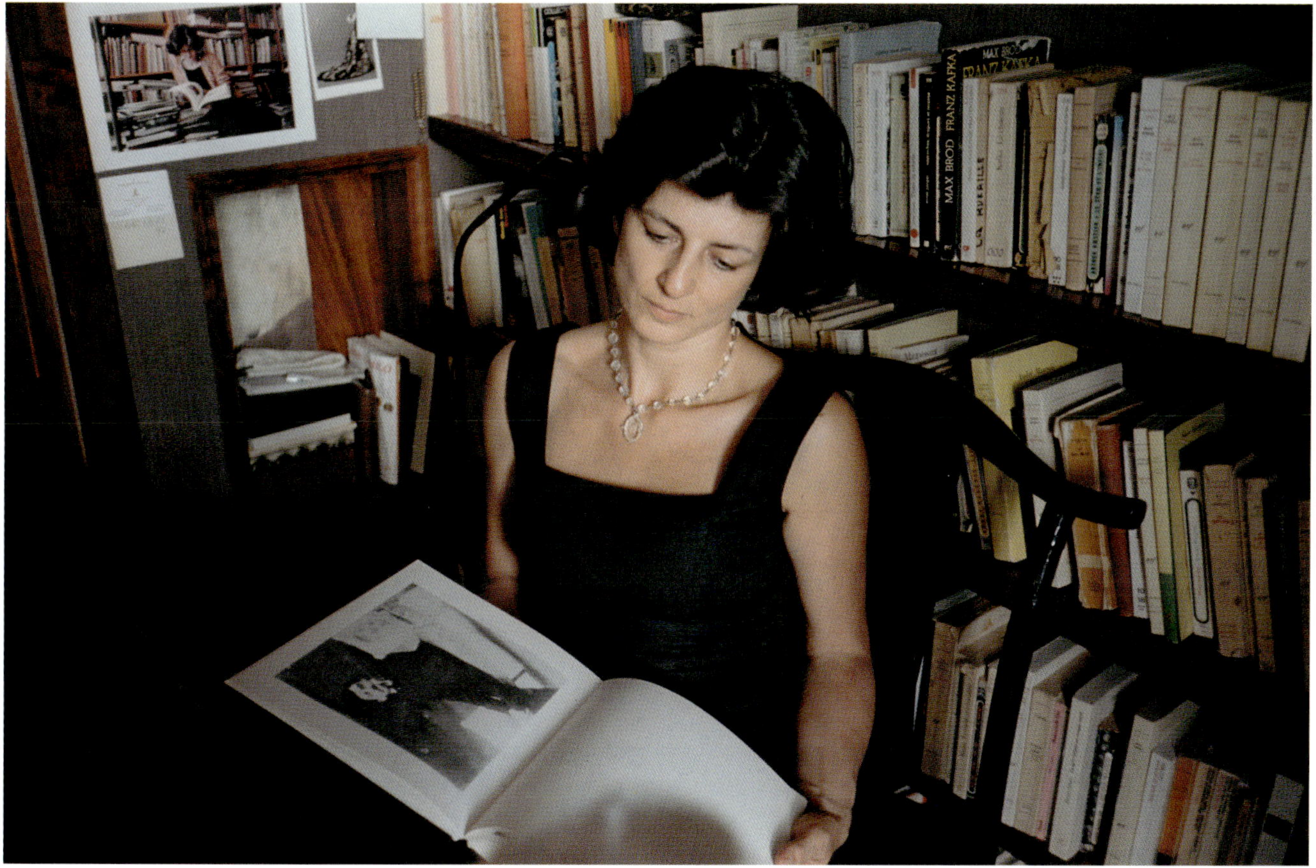

Monday, May 31. Paris. Alexandra de Leal, photographer

JUNE

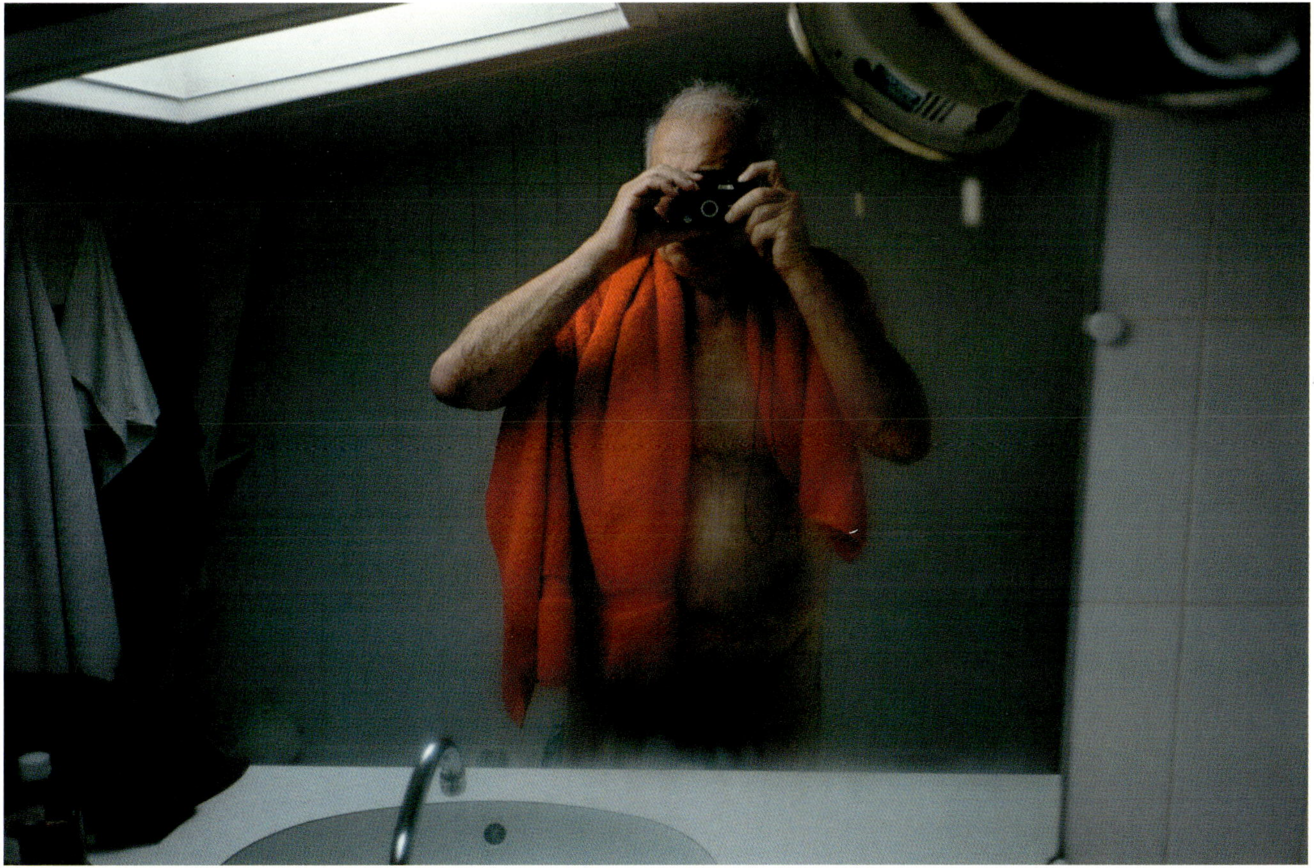

Tuesday, June 1. Boulogne, France. Self-portrait

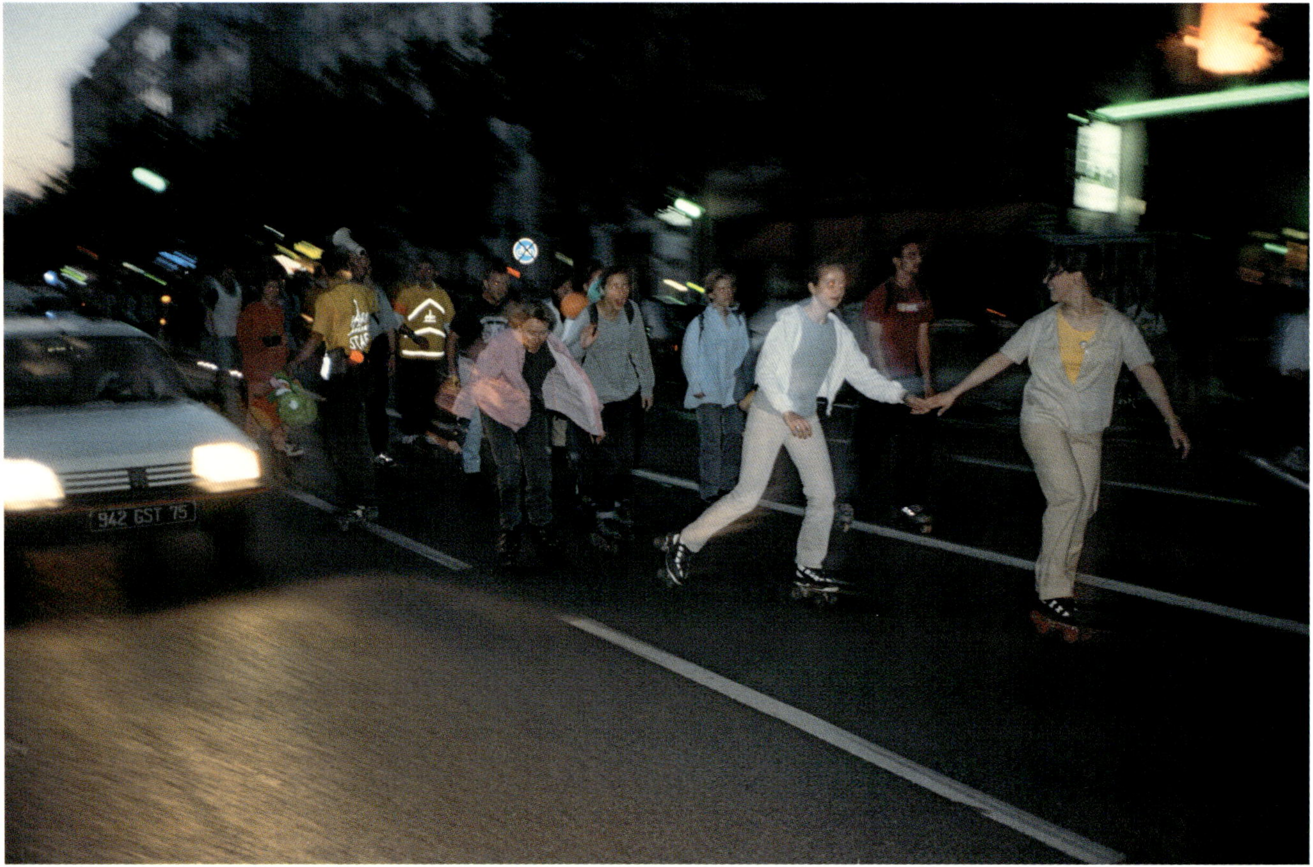

Wednesday, June 2. Paris. Rollers parade

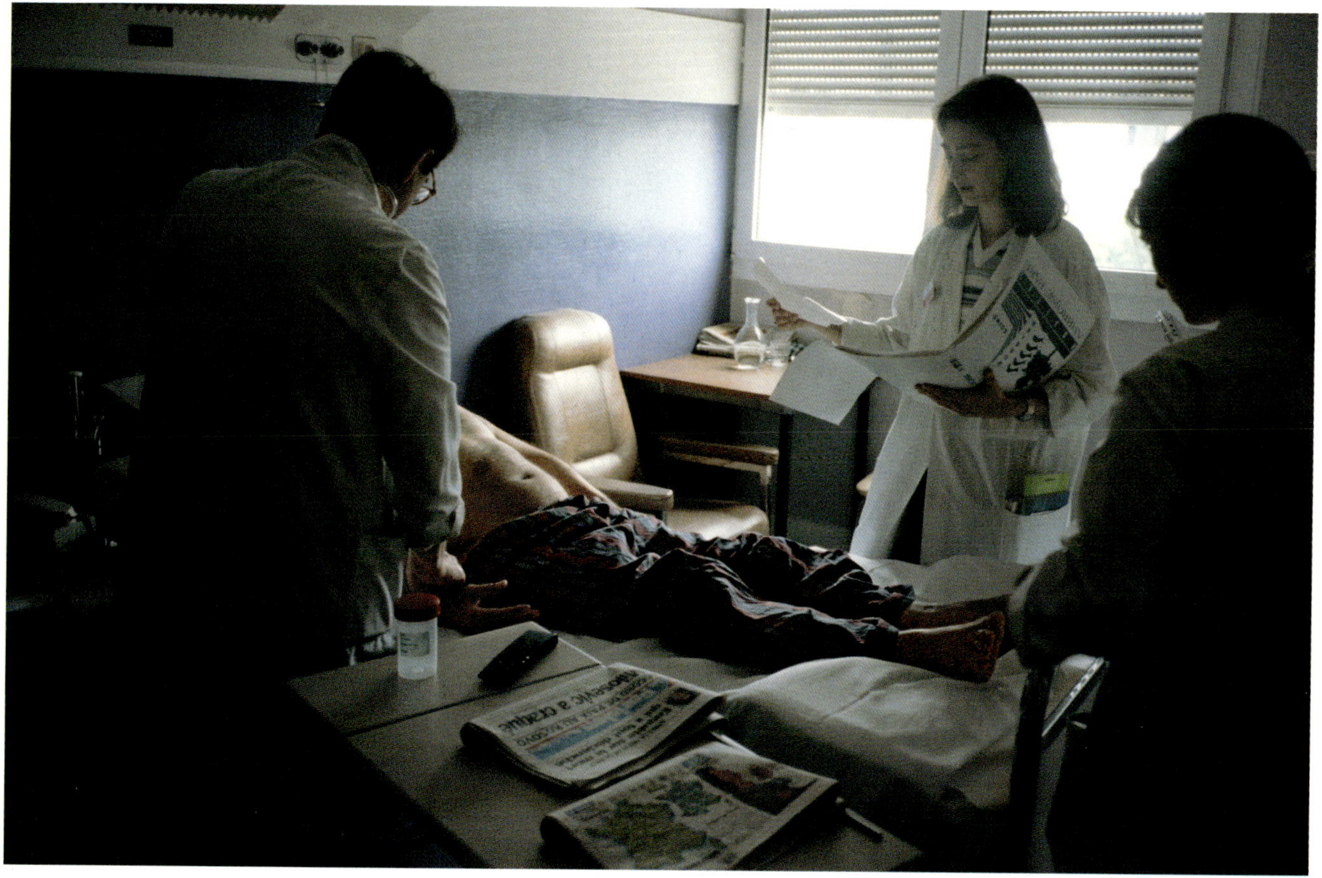

Thursday, June 3. Boulogne, France. Professor Olivier Dubourg with patient, Ambroise Paré hospital

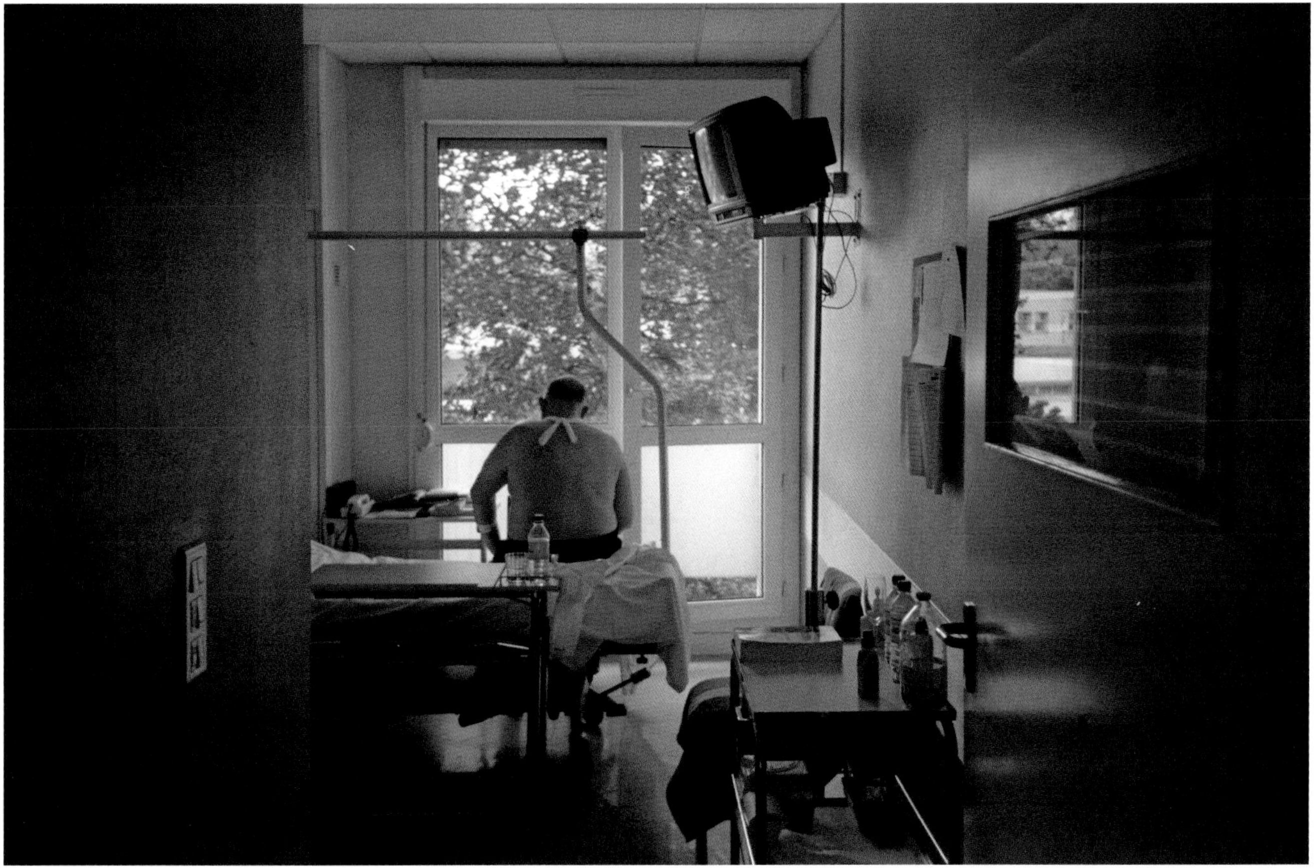

Friday, June 4. Boulogne, France. A patient, Ambroise Paré hospital

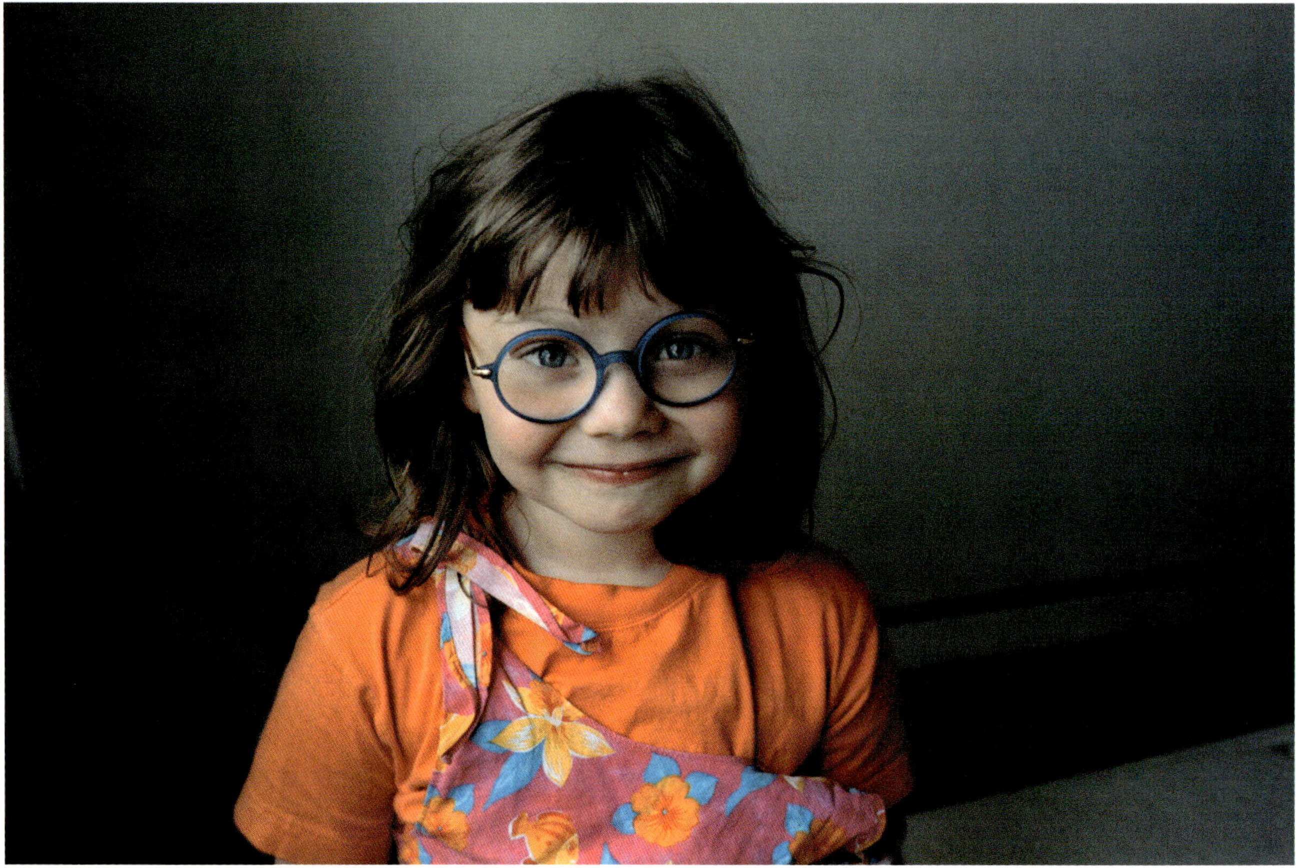

Saturday, June 5. Paris. Rose, a friend of my granddaughter Louise

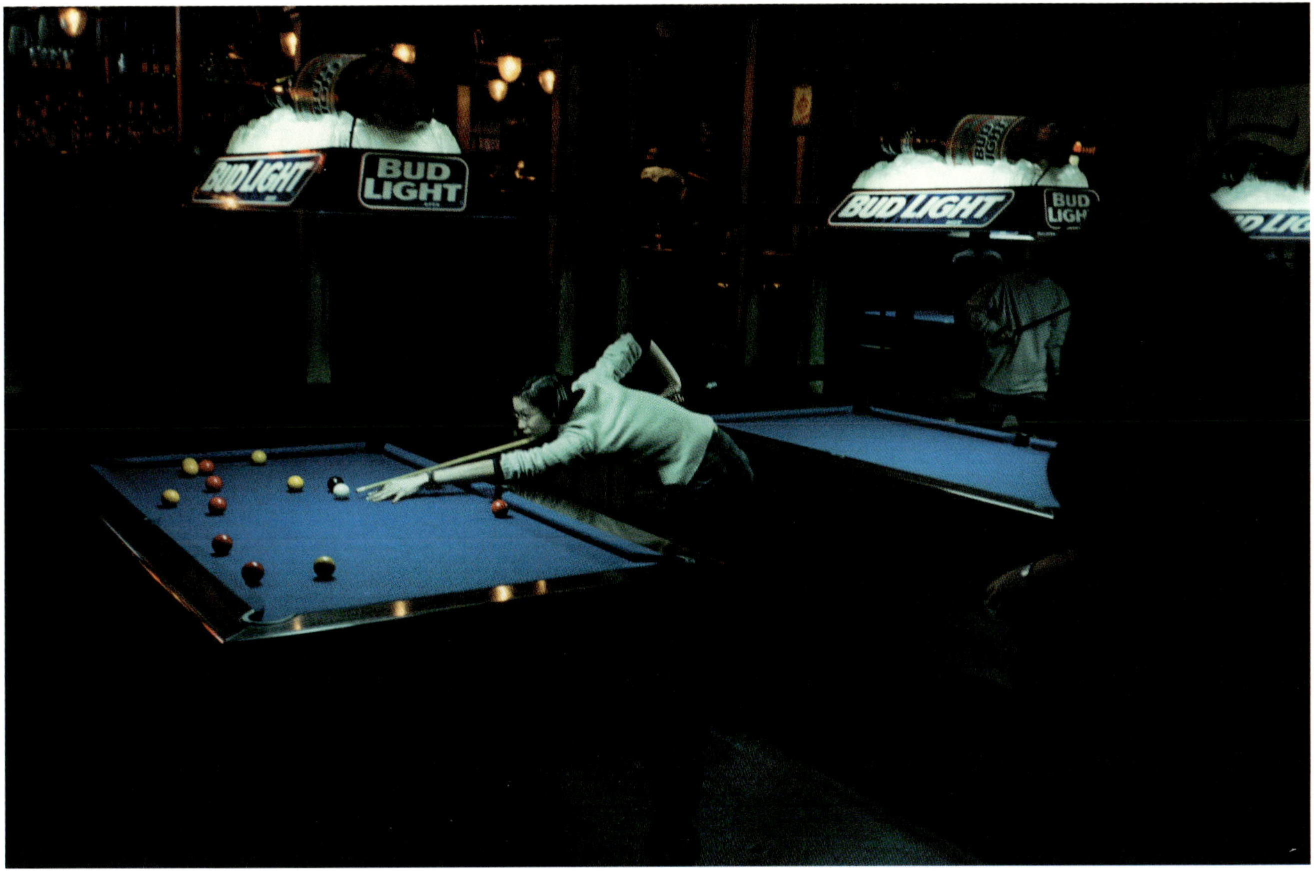

Sunday, June 6. Paris. Billiards club, in the République area

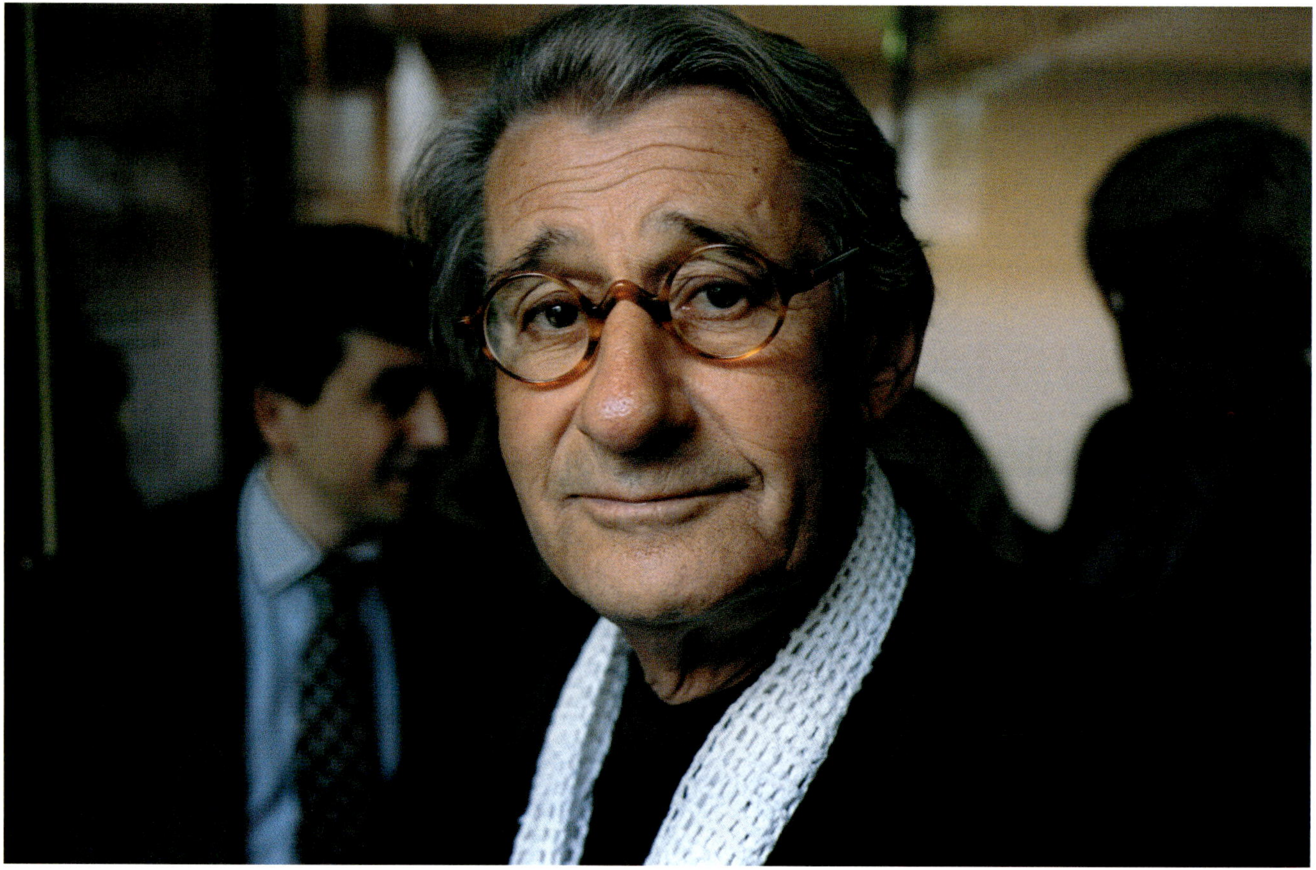

Monday, June 7. Paris. Helmut Newton, photographer

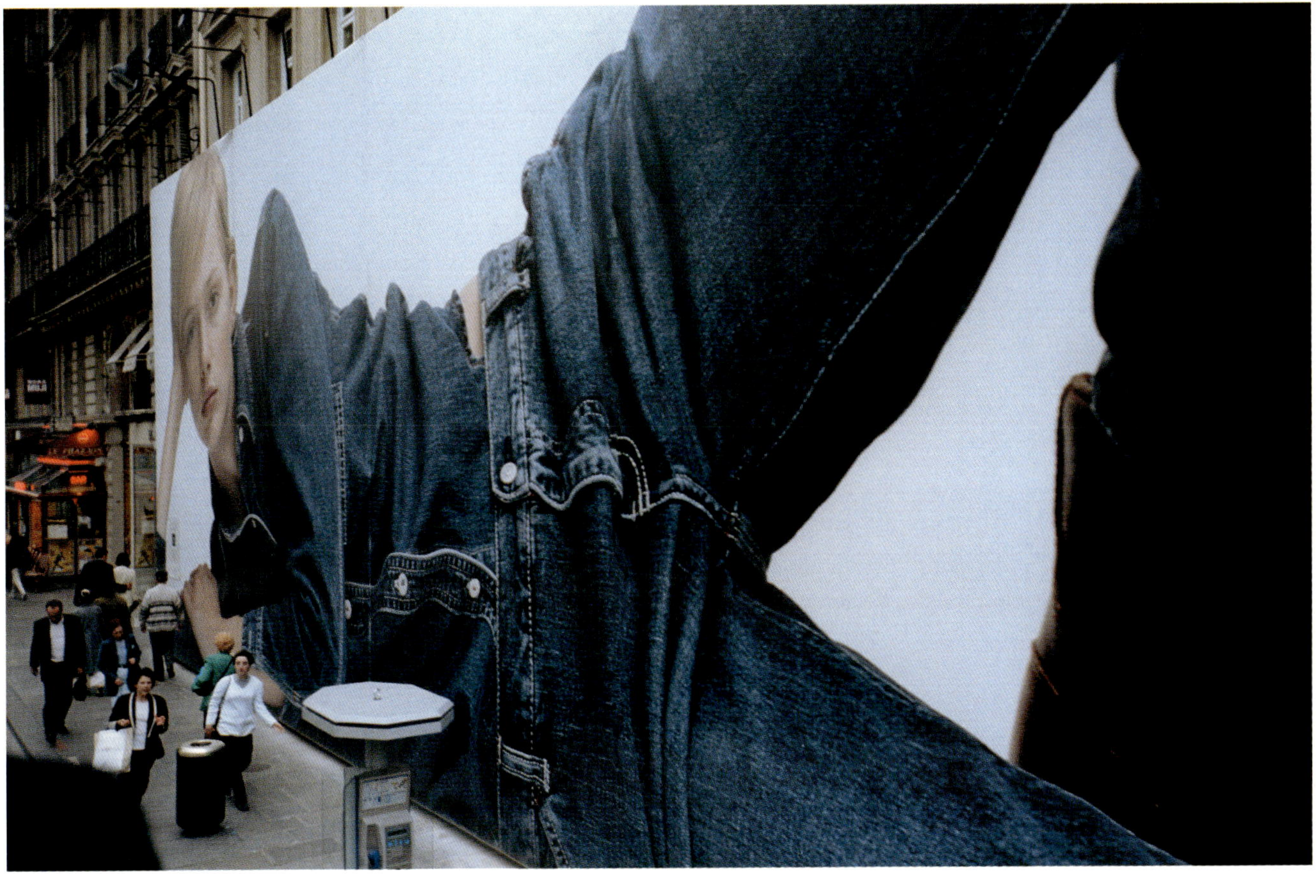

Tuesday, June 8. Paris. Poster, in the Opéra area

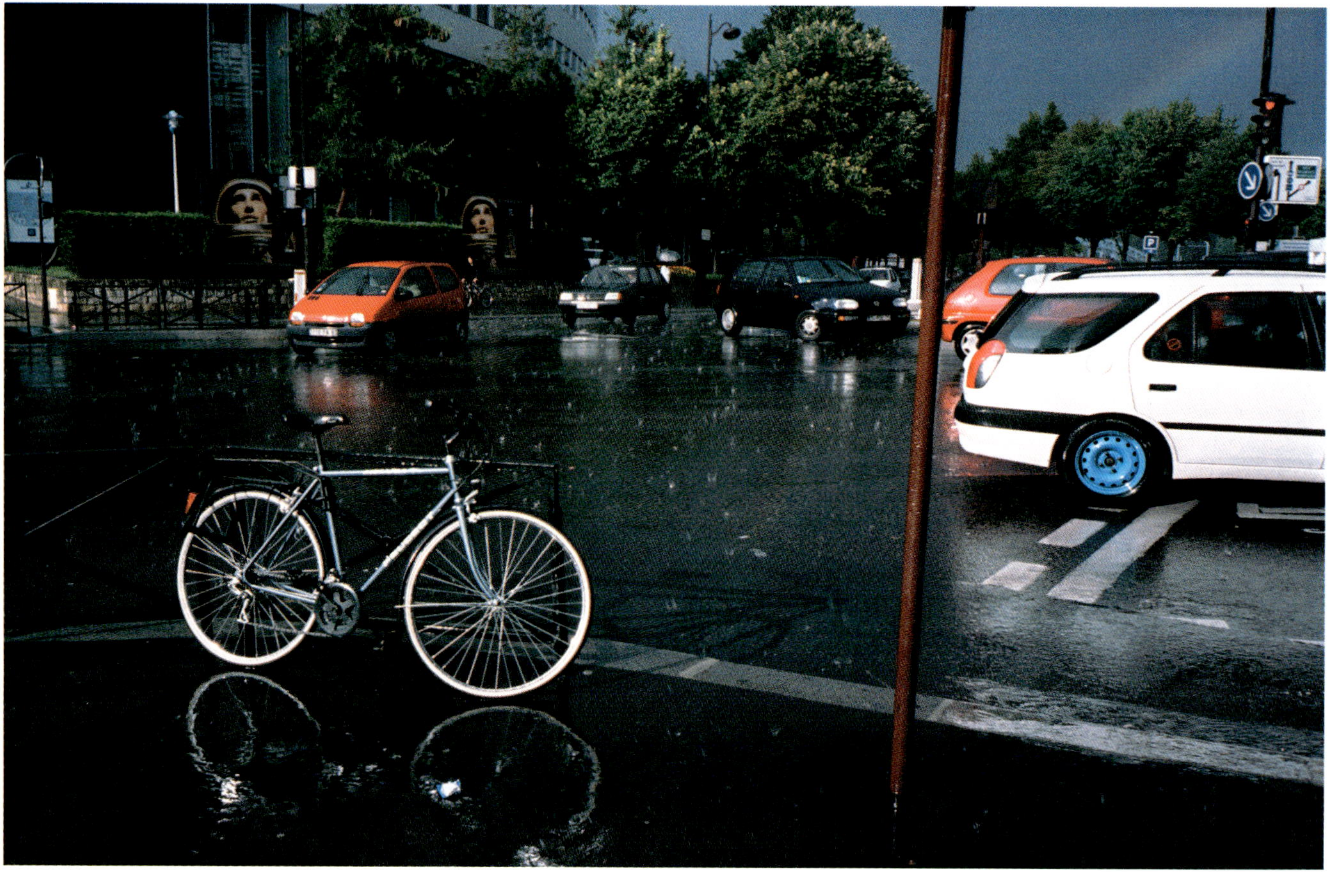

Wednesday, June 9. Paris. After the rain

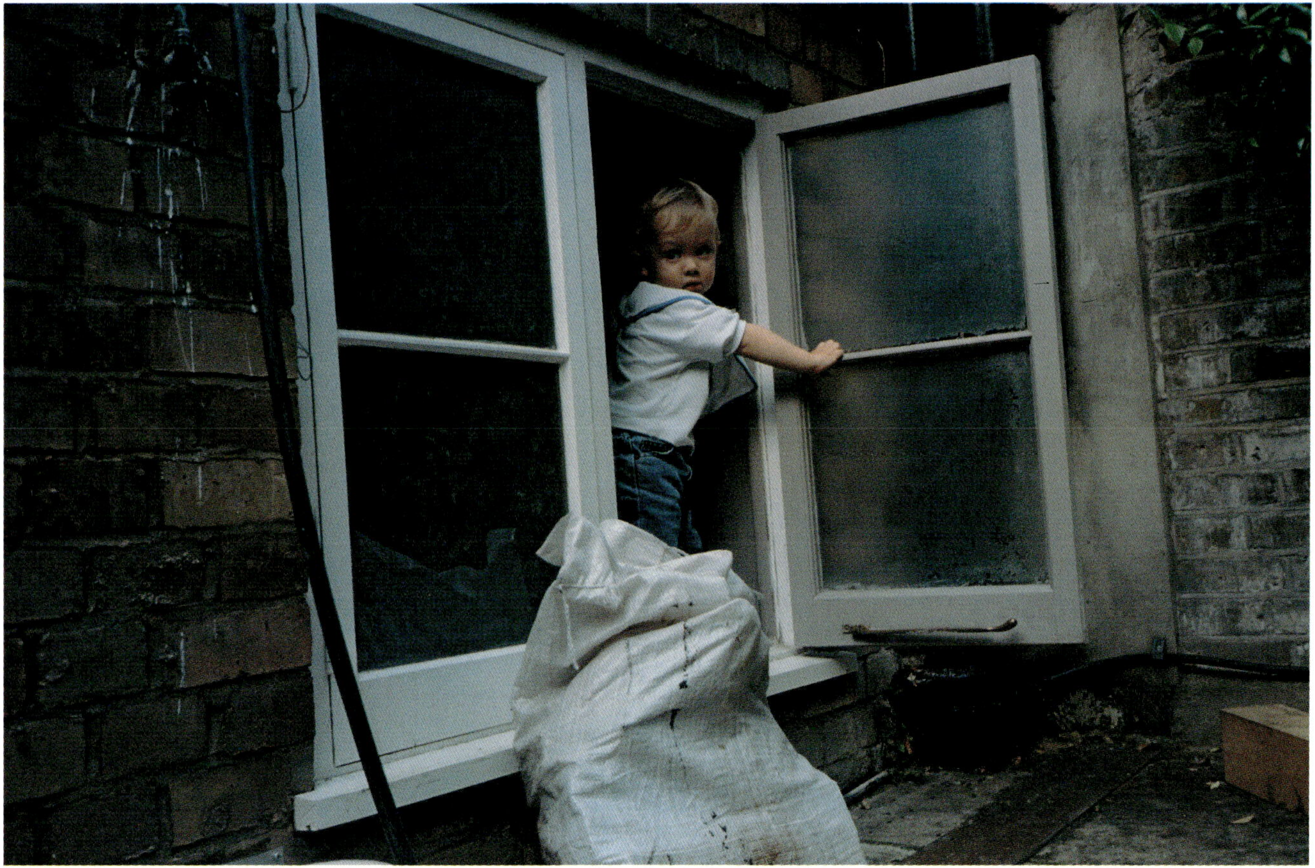

Thursday, June 10. London. Christopher Bury, son of Sascha Hackel and Marcus Bury

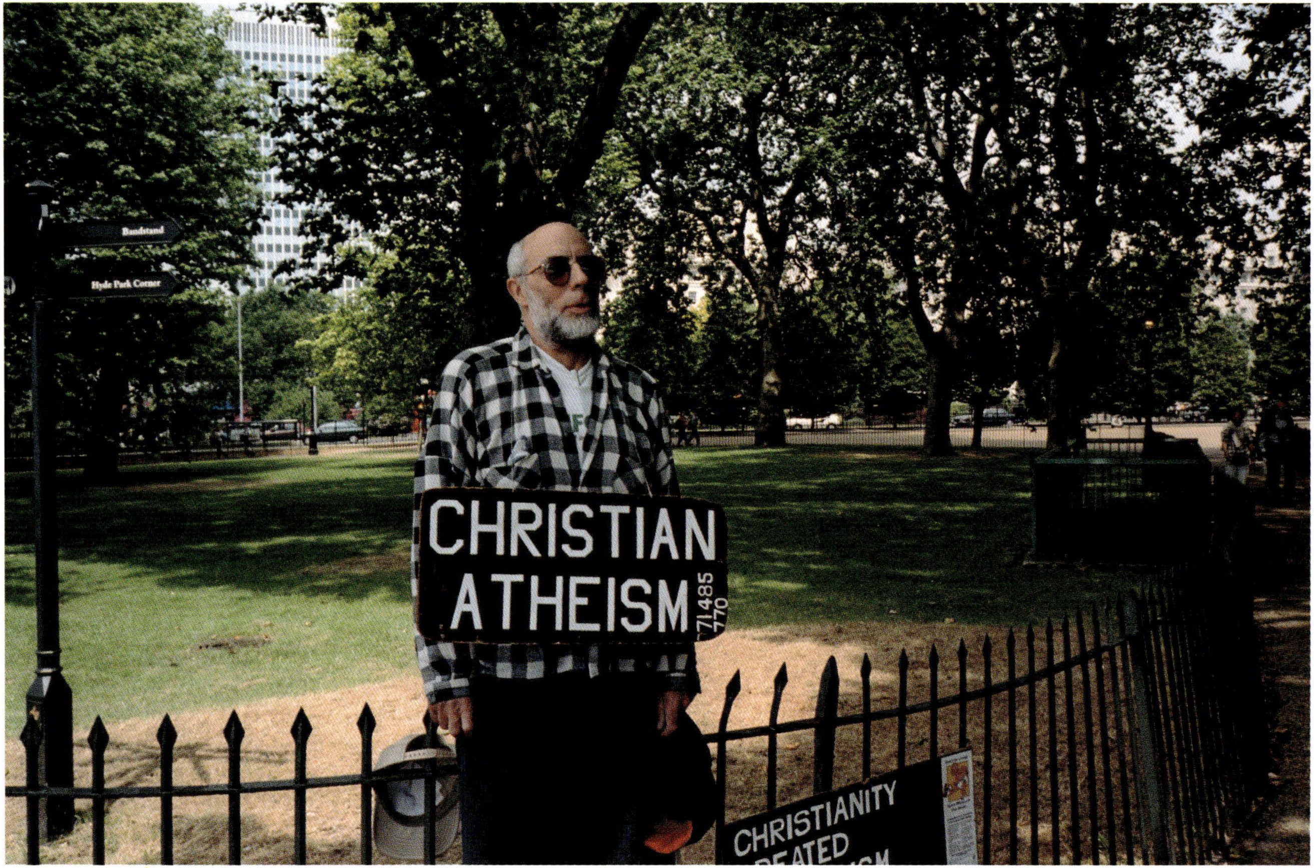

Friday, June 11. London. Hyde Park, Speaker's Corner

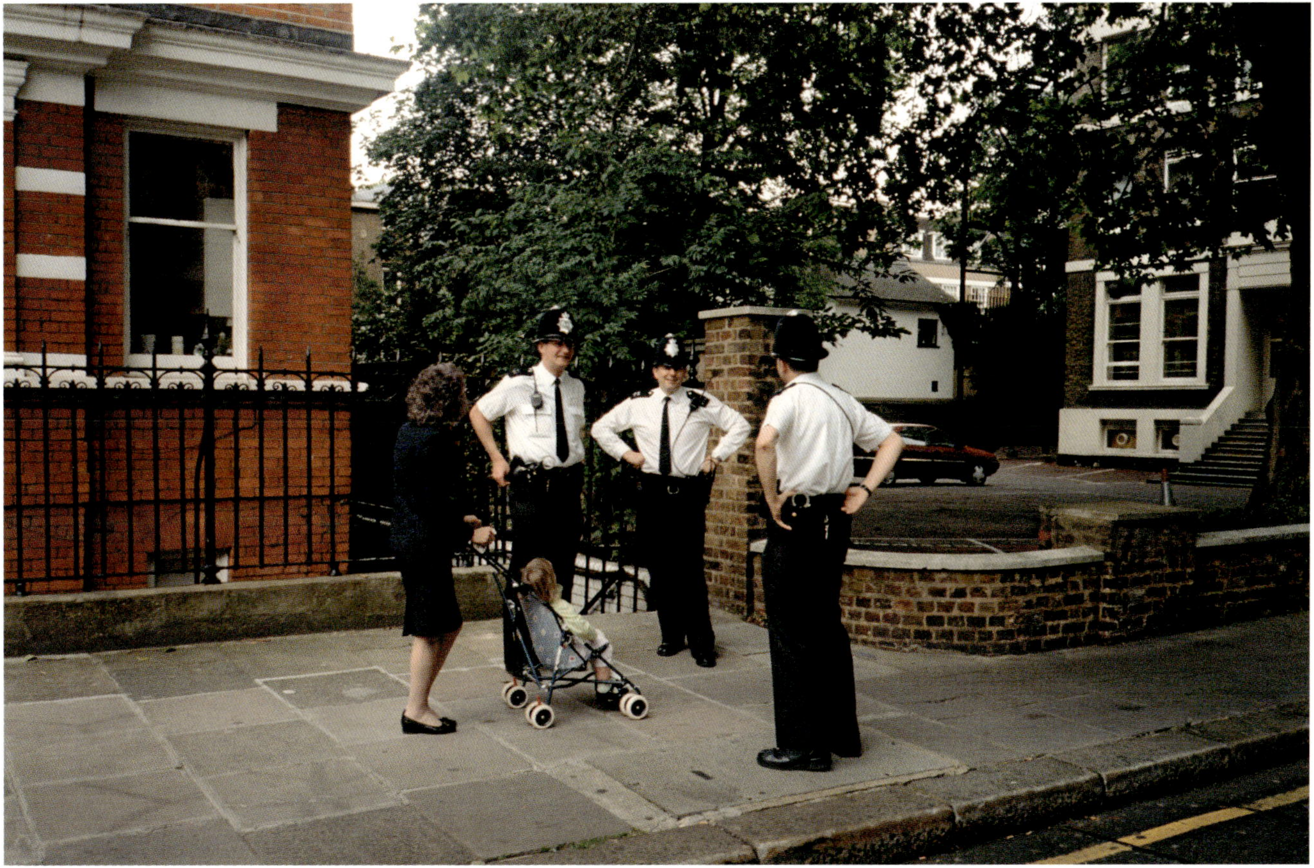

Friday, June 11. London. Street scene, South Kensington

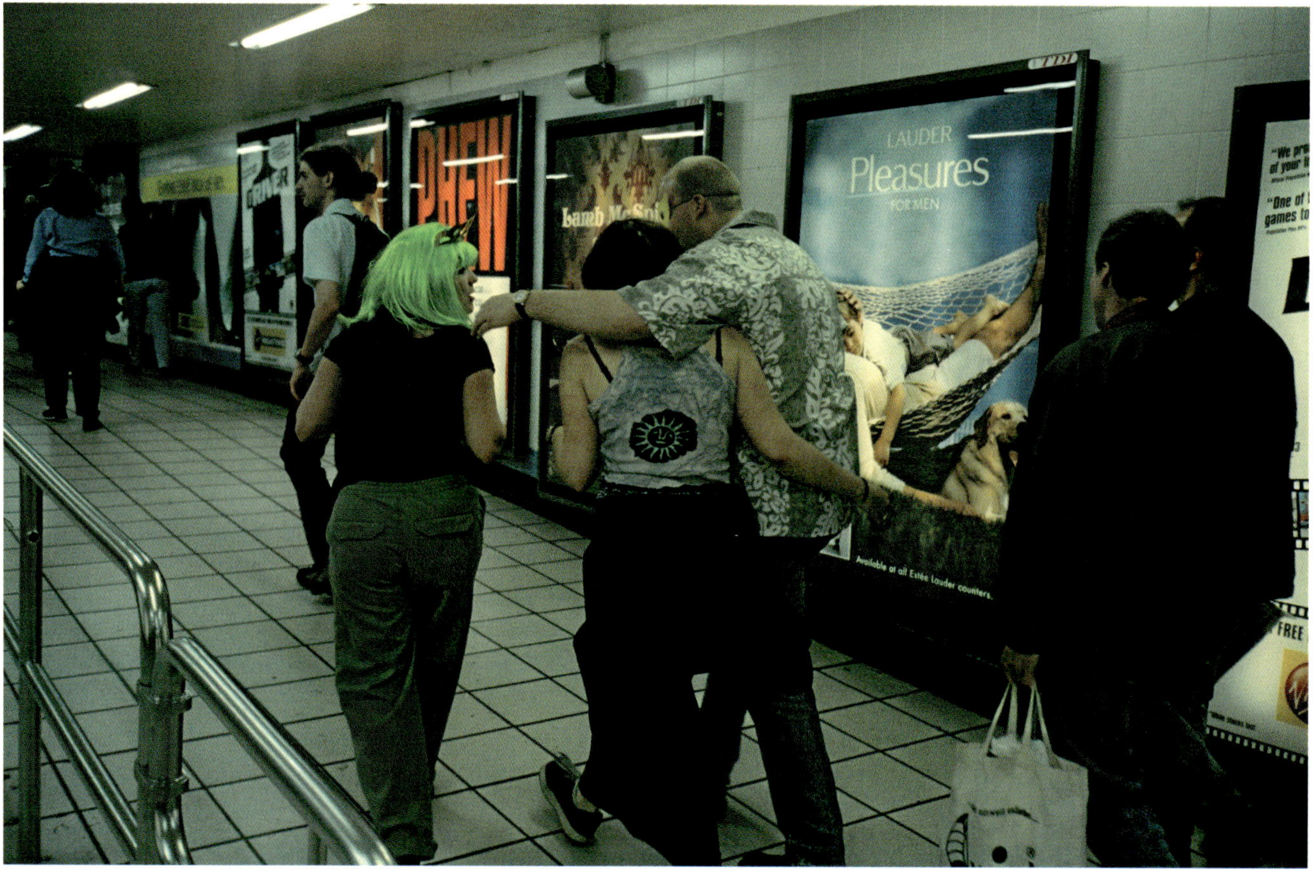

Saturday June 12. London. Underground scene, Piccadilly Station

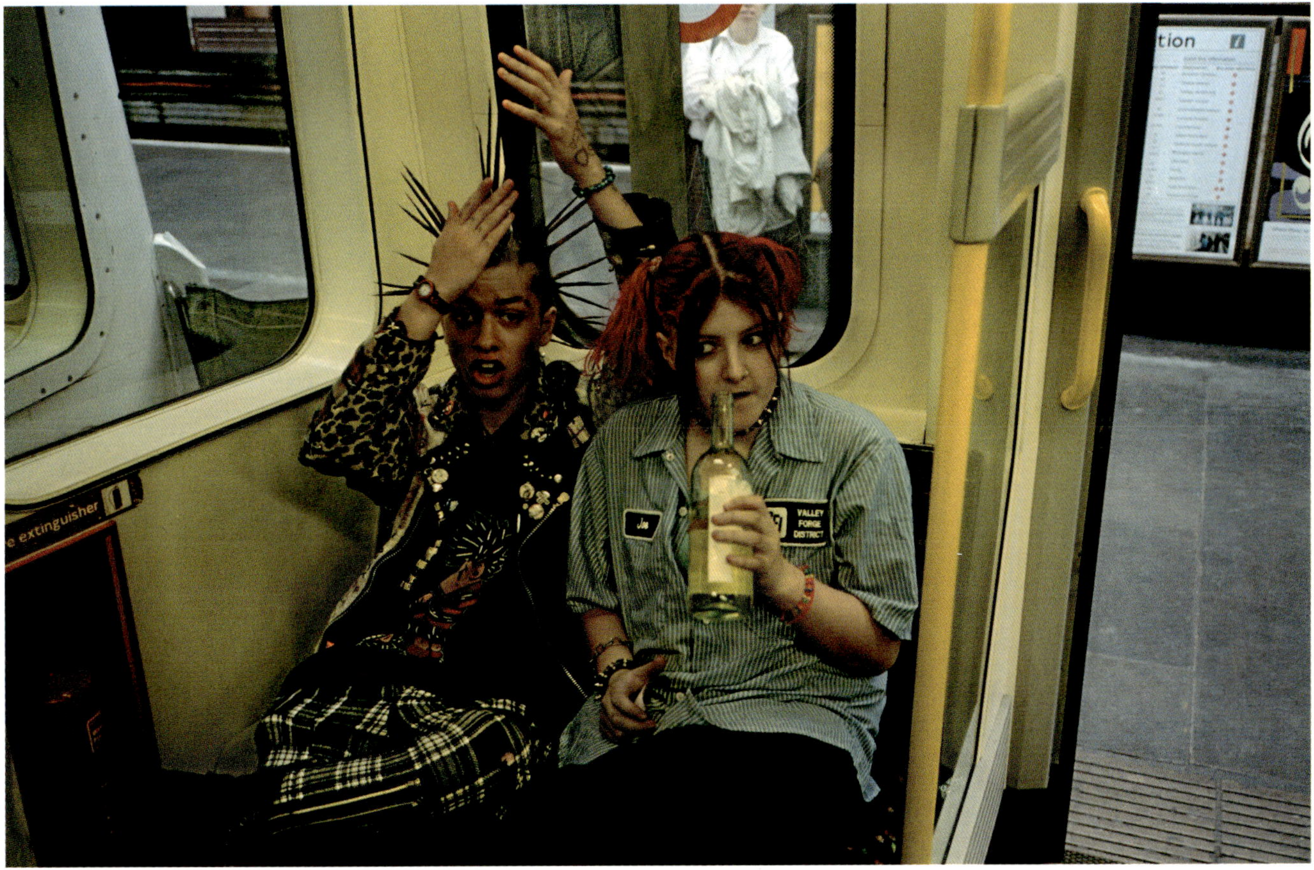

Saturday June 12. London. Underground scene, Circle Line

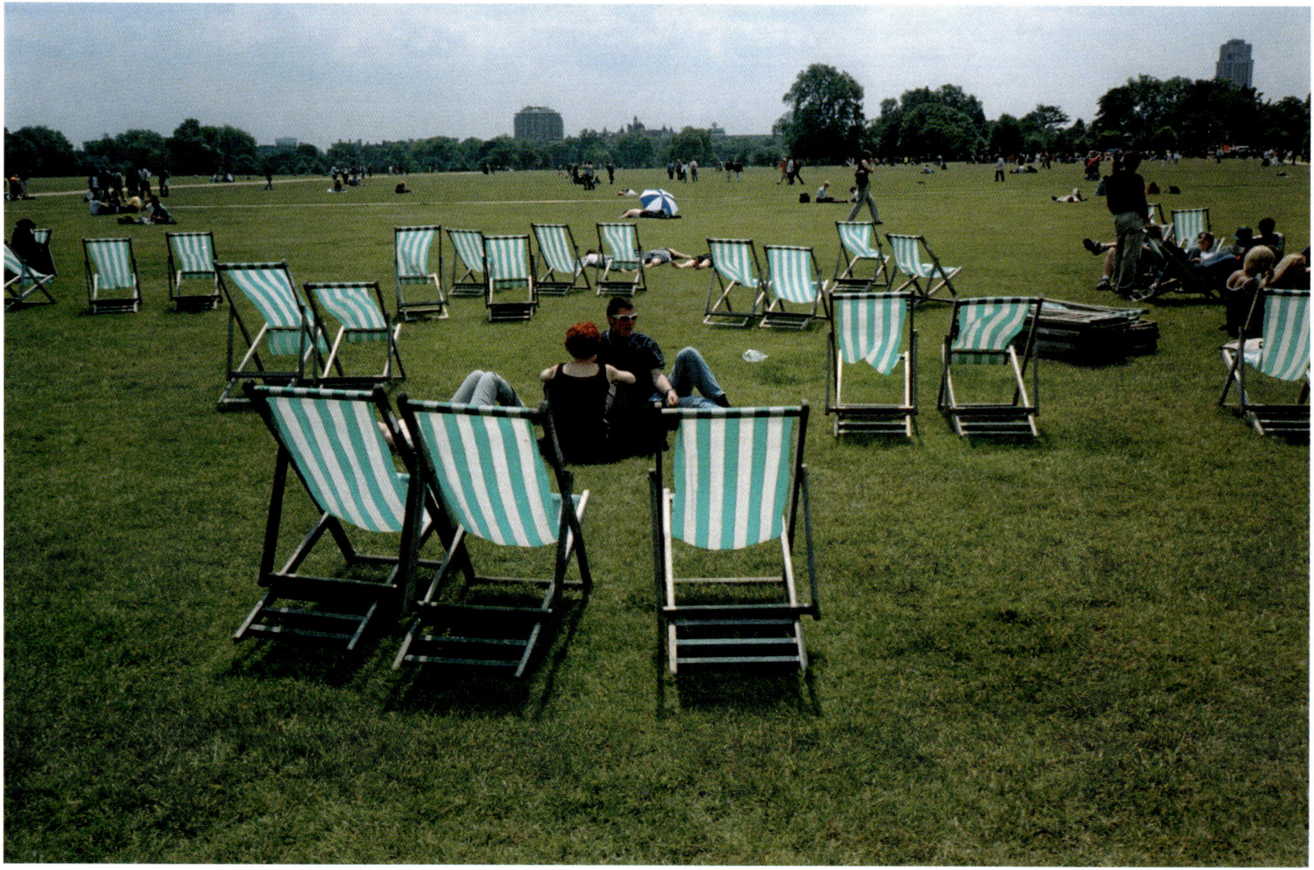

Sunday, June 13. London. In Hyde Park

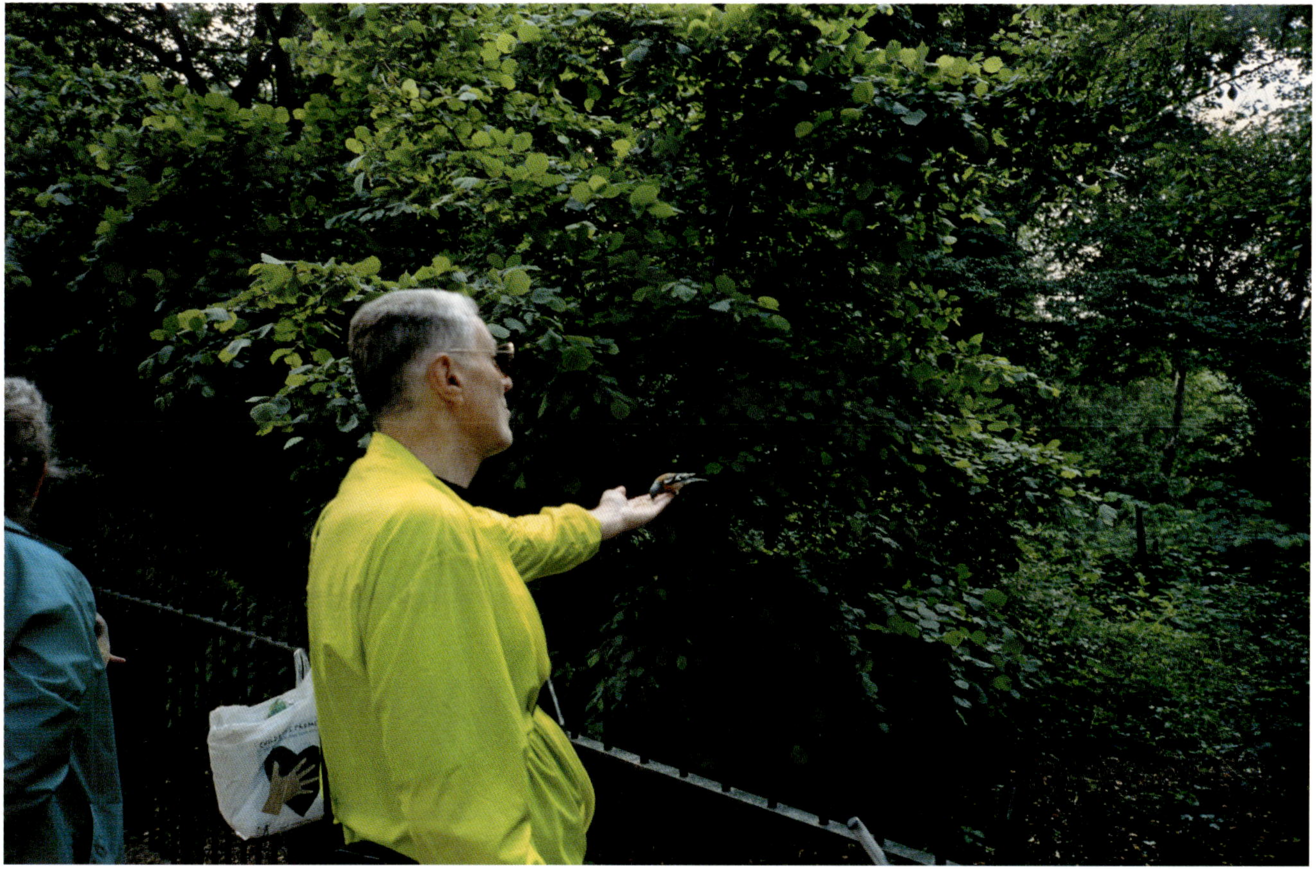

Sunday, June 13. London. Blind man, in Hyde Park

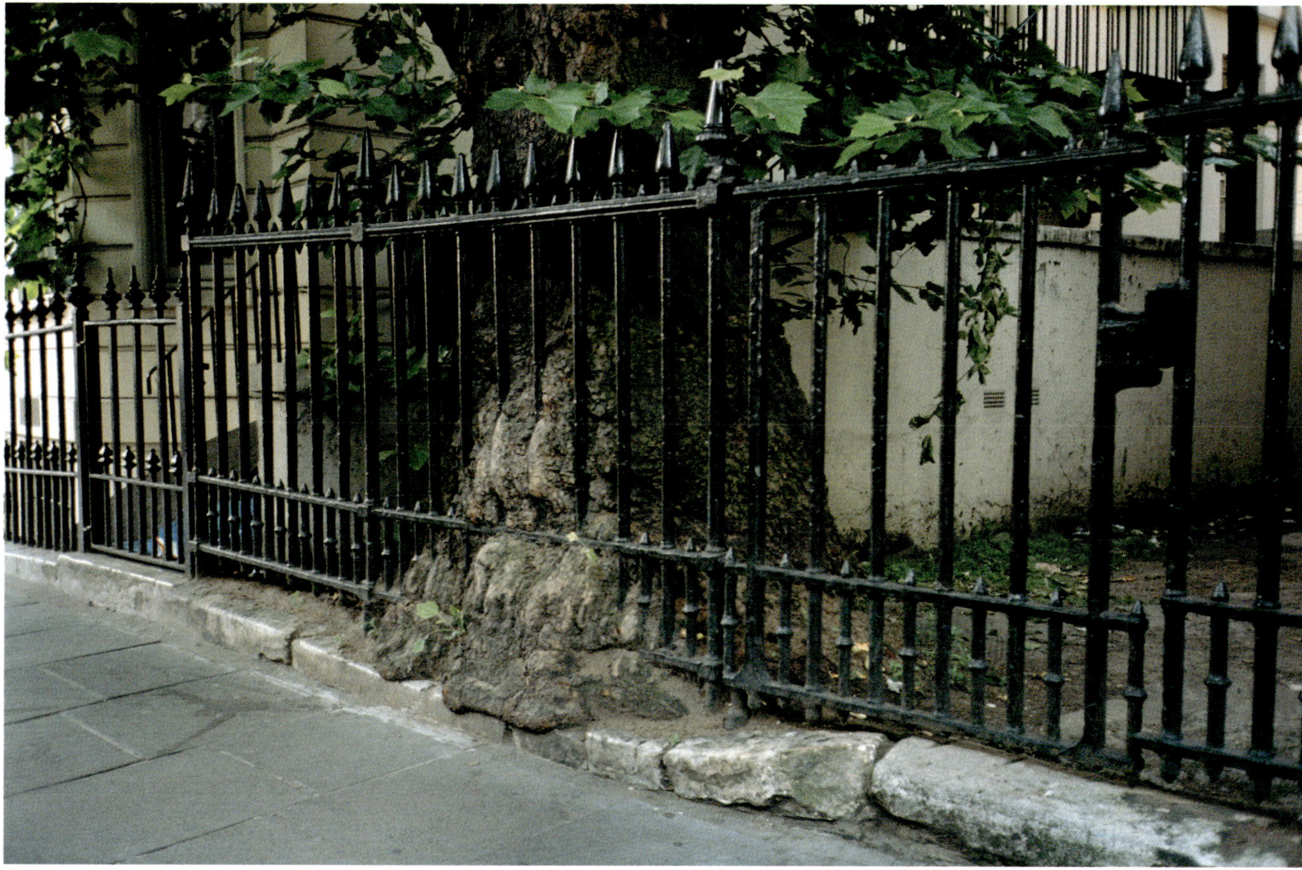

Monday, June 14. London. Plane tree, South Kensington

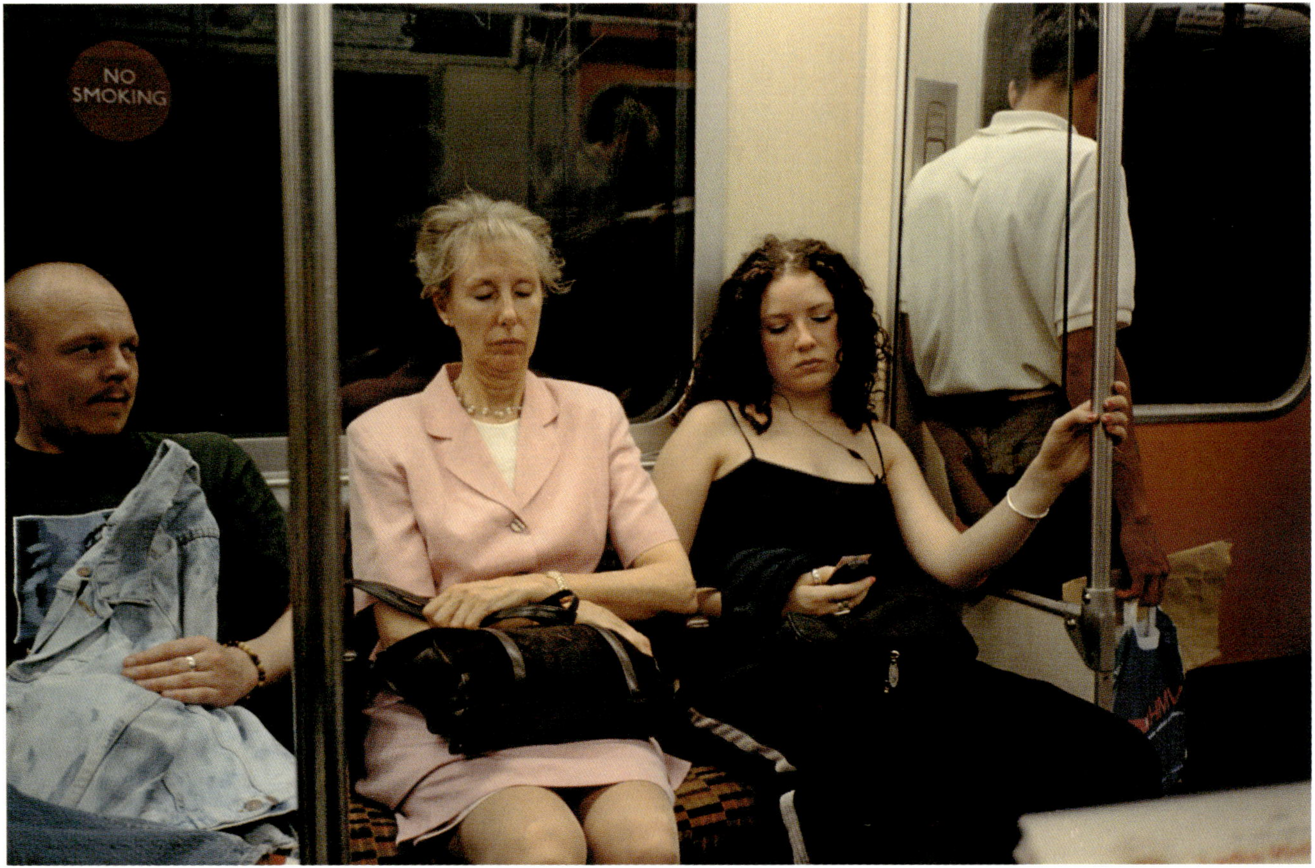

Tuesday, June 15. London. Underground scene, Central Line

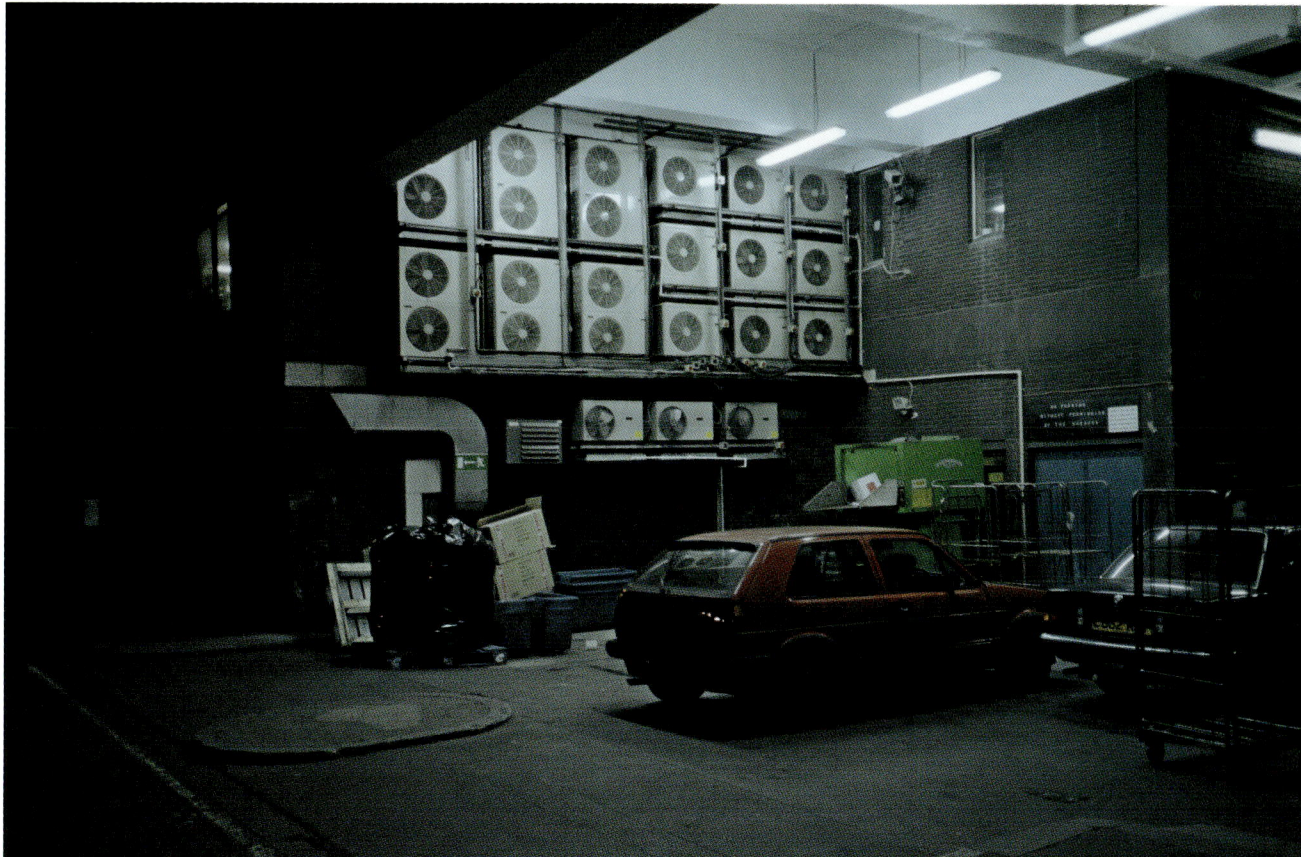

Wednesday, June 16. London. Night scene, Regent's Park area

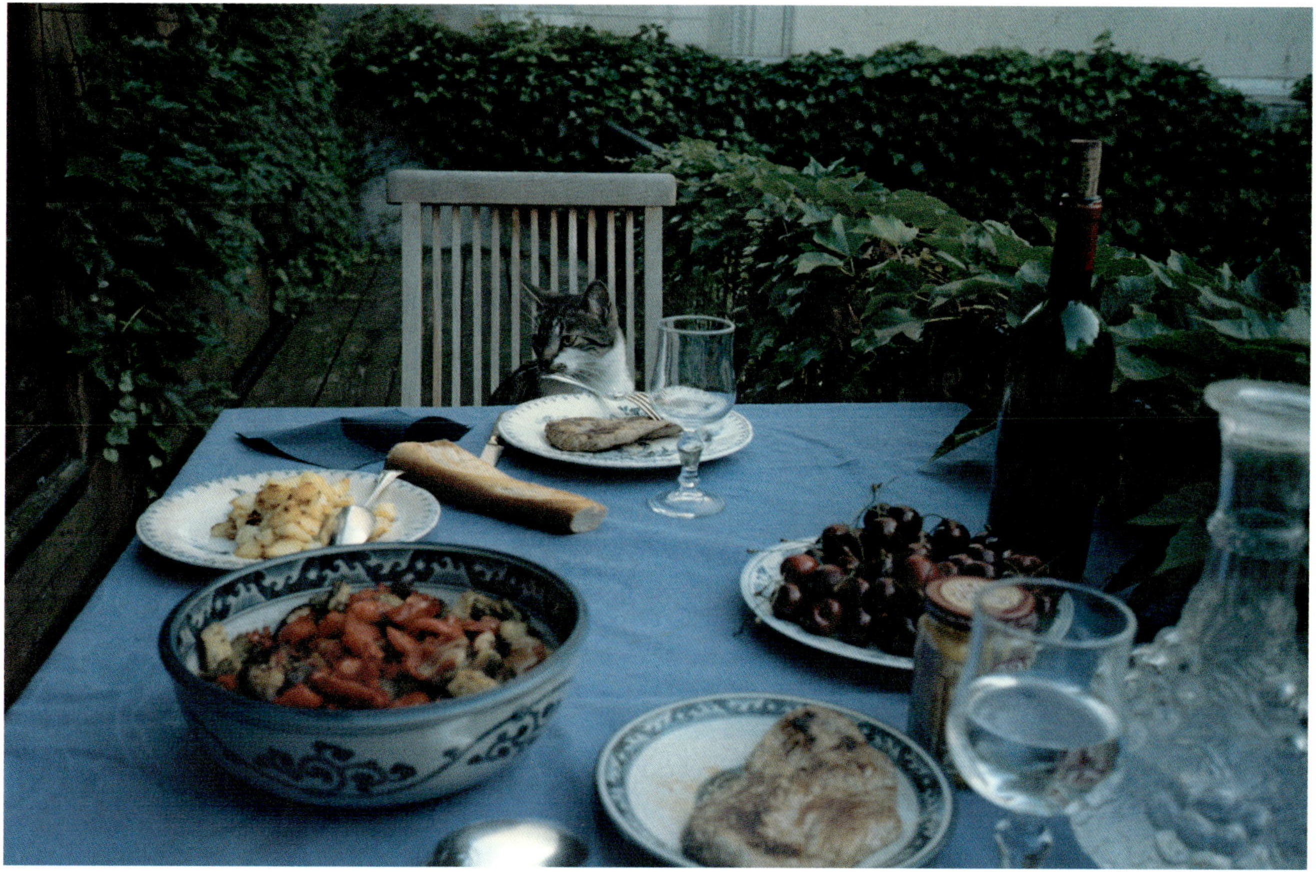

Thursday, June 17. Boulogne, France. Dinner on the terrace

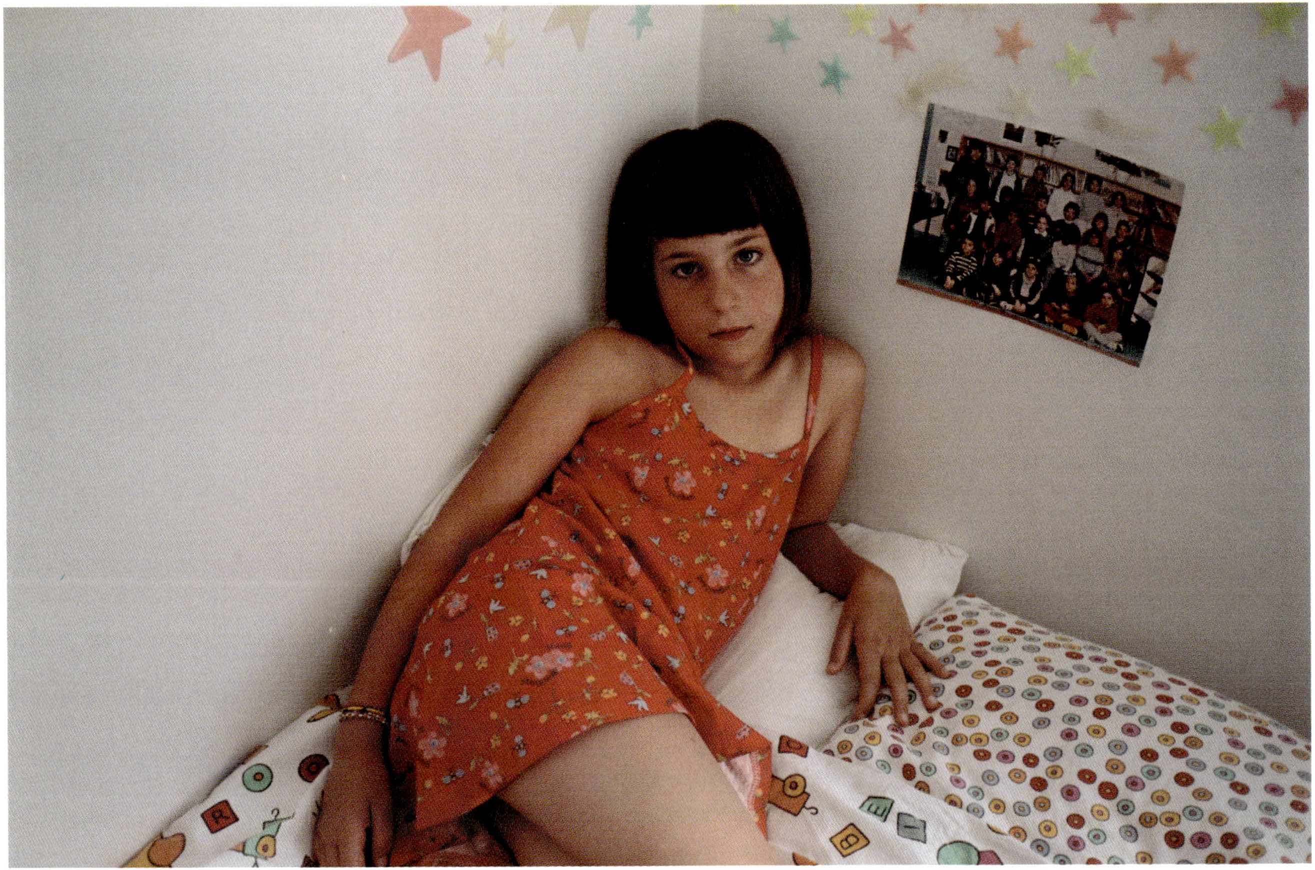

Friday, June 18, Paris. Louise (daughter of Jean-Michel Horvat), with make-up

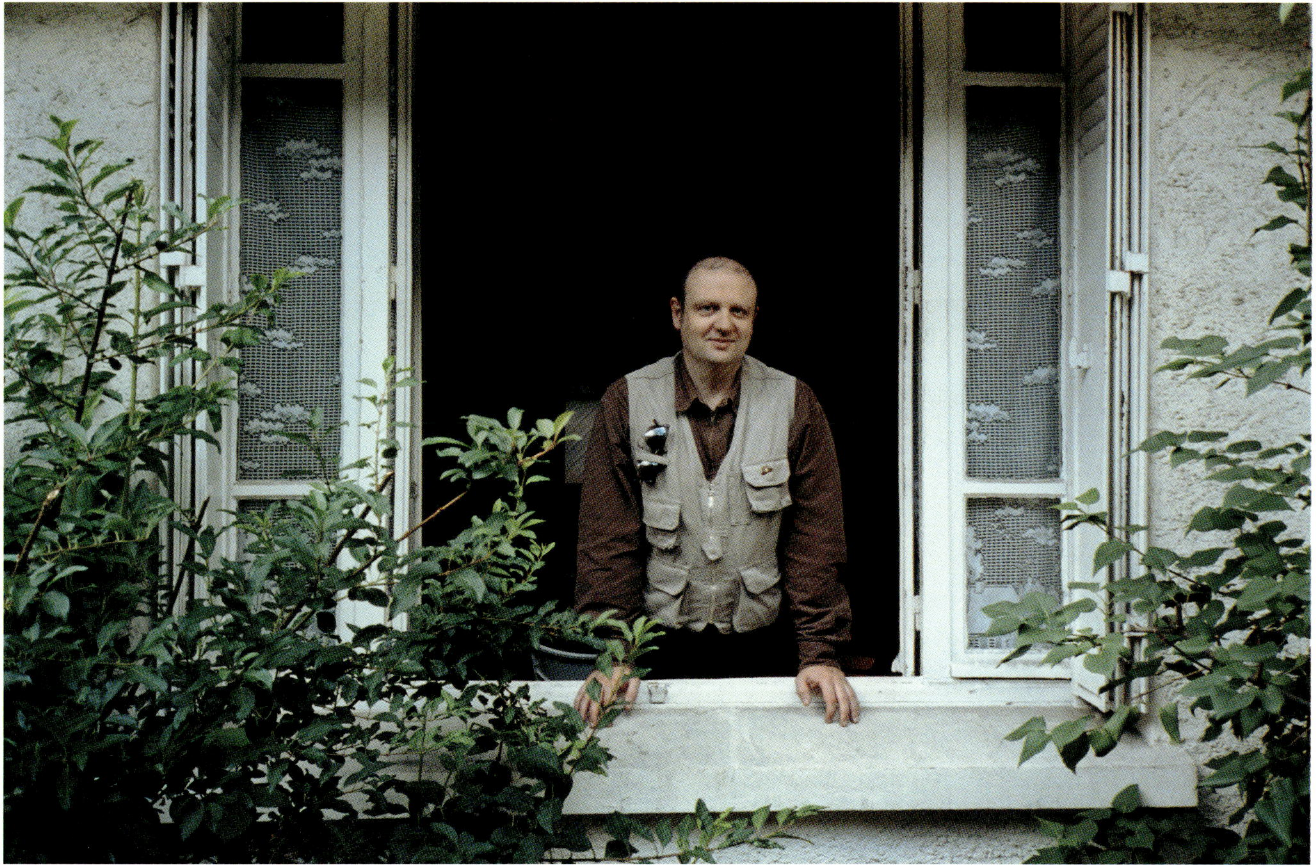

Saturday, June 19. Paris. Jean-Michel Horvat

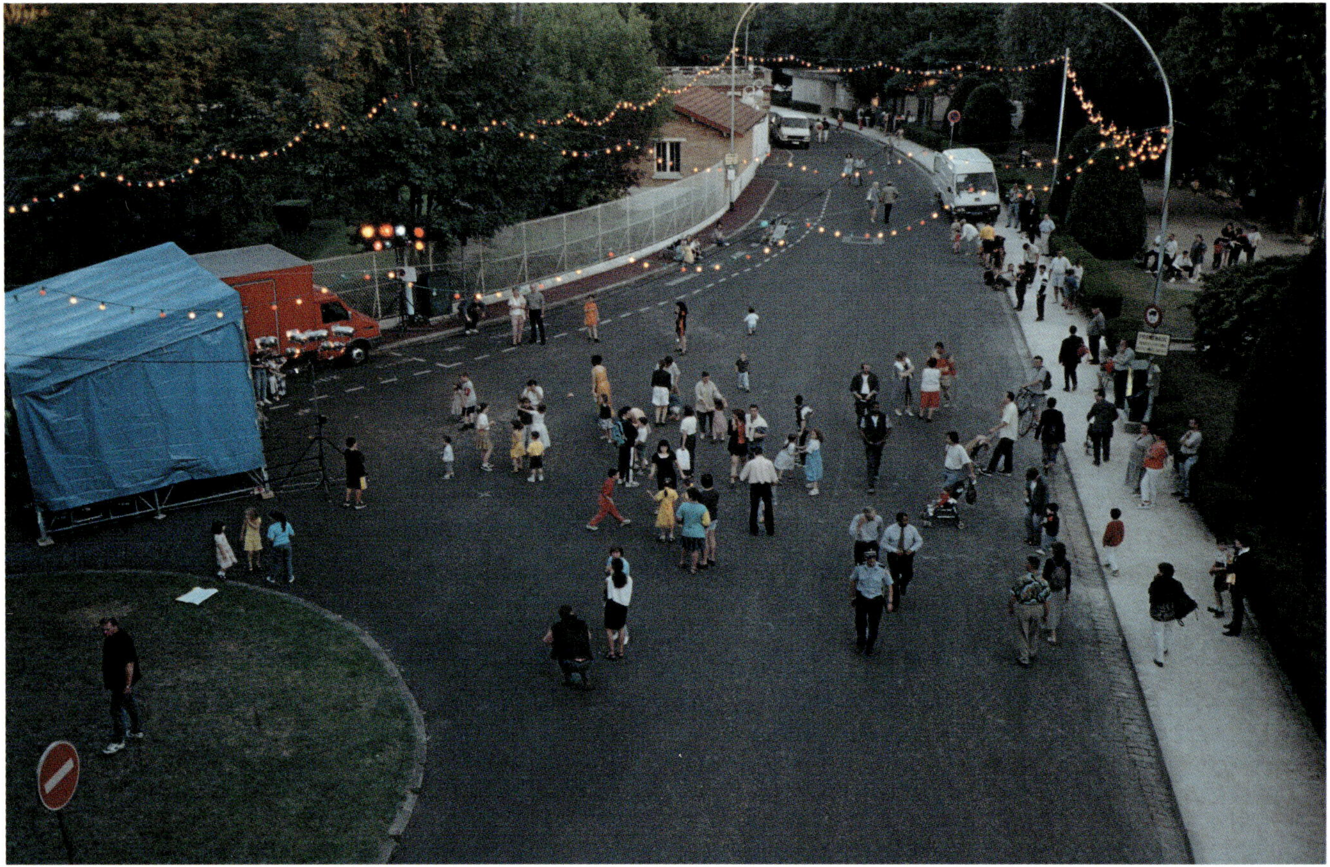

Sunday, June 20. Joinville, France. Amusement park

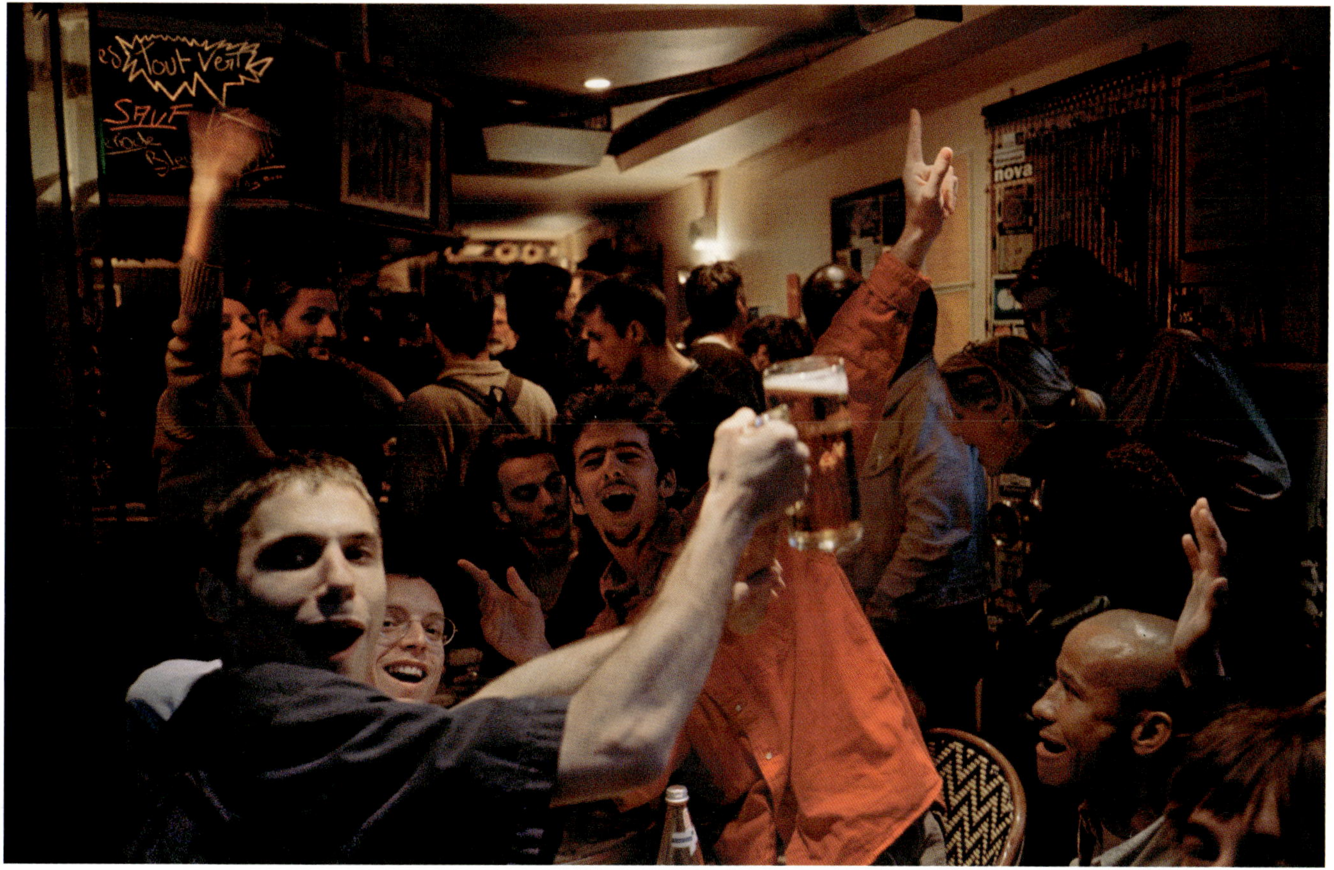

Monday, June 21. Paris. Bastille area, Fête de la Musique

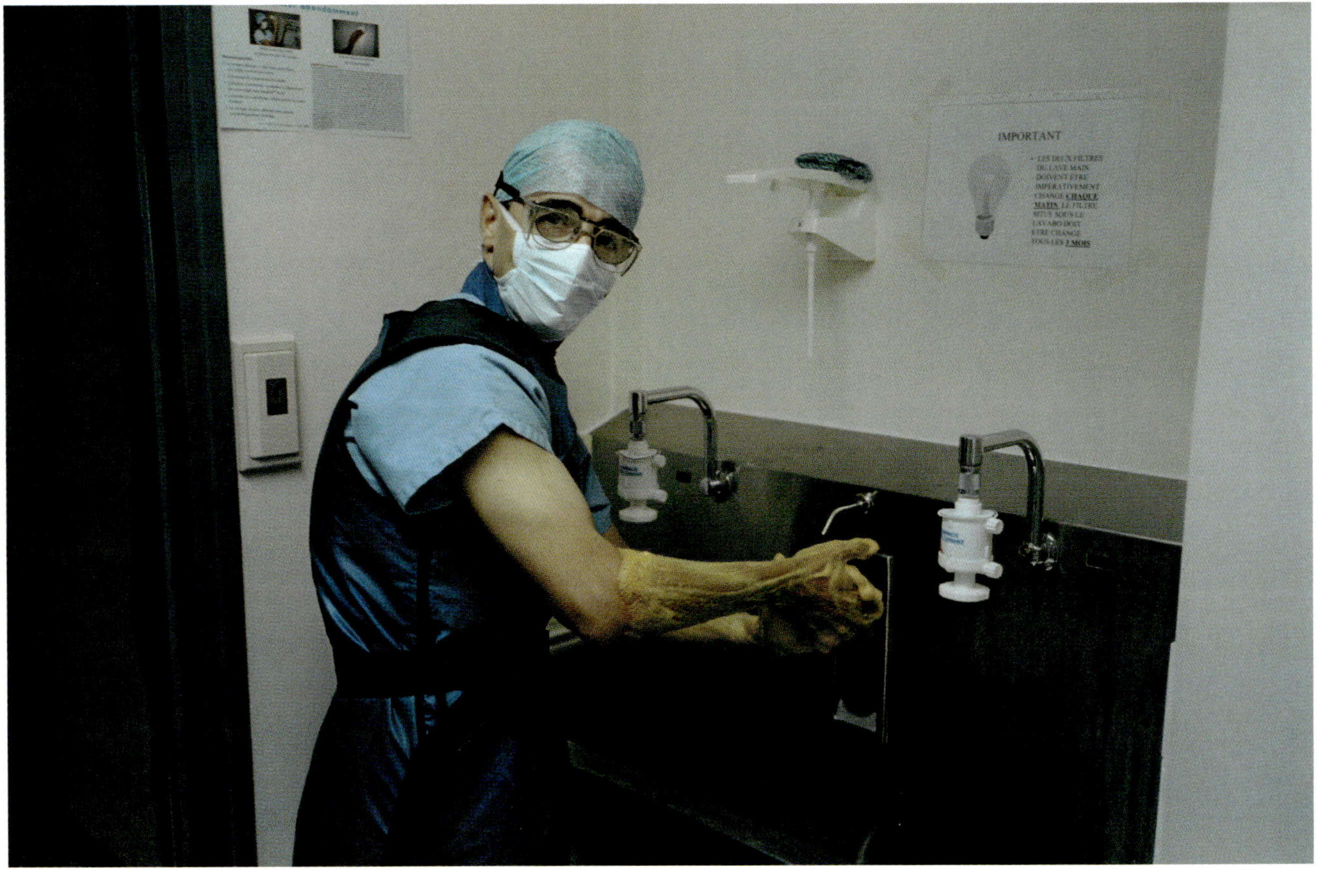

Tuesday, June 22. Boulogne, France. Professor Pascal Lacombe, at Ambroise Paré Hospital

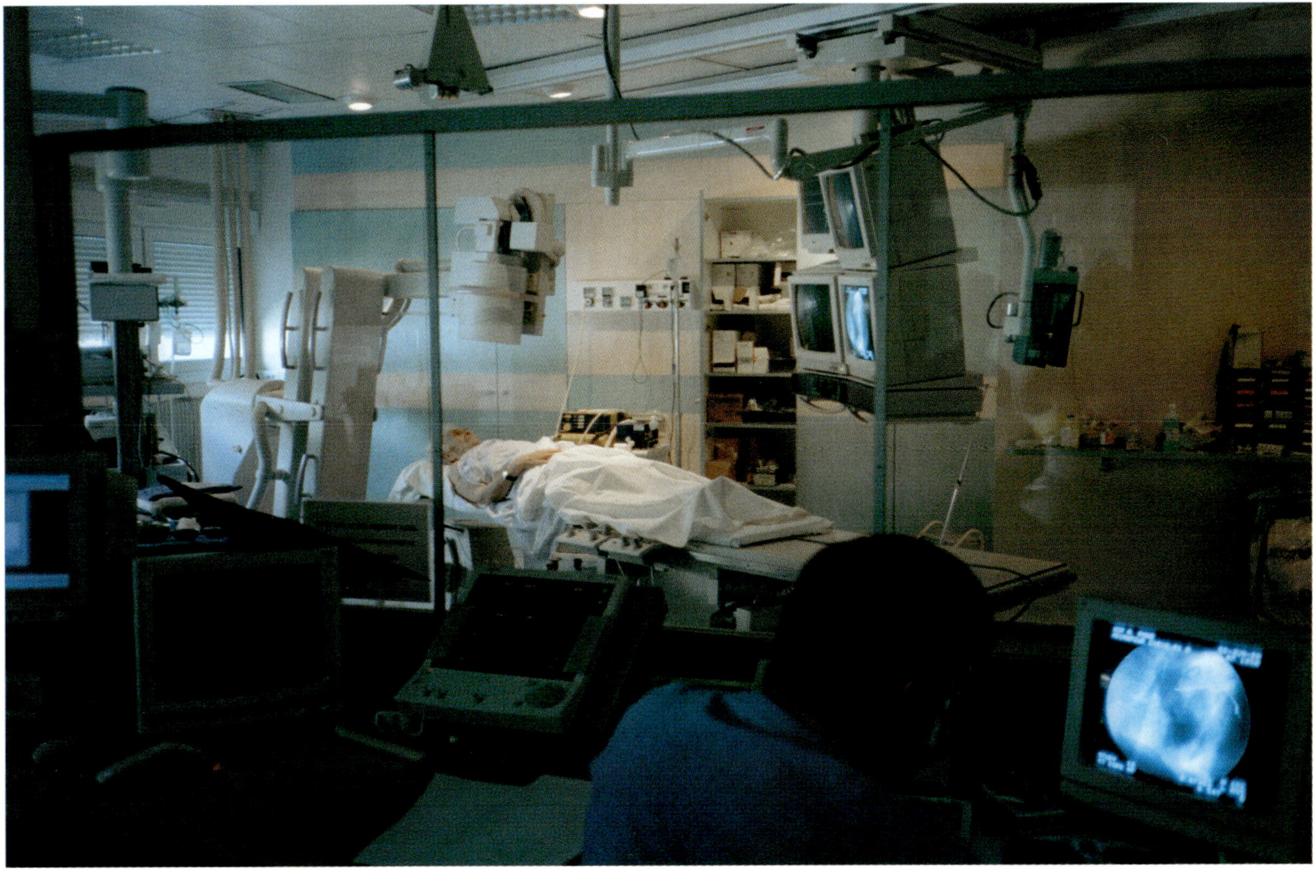

Wednesday, June 23. Boulogne, France. Operating room, at Ambroise Paré Hospital

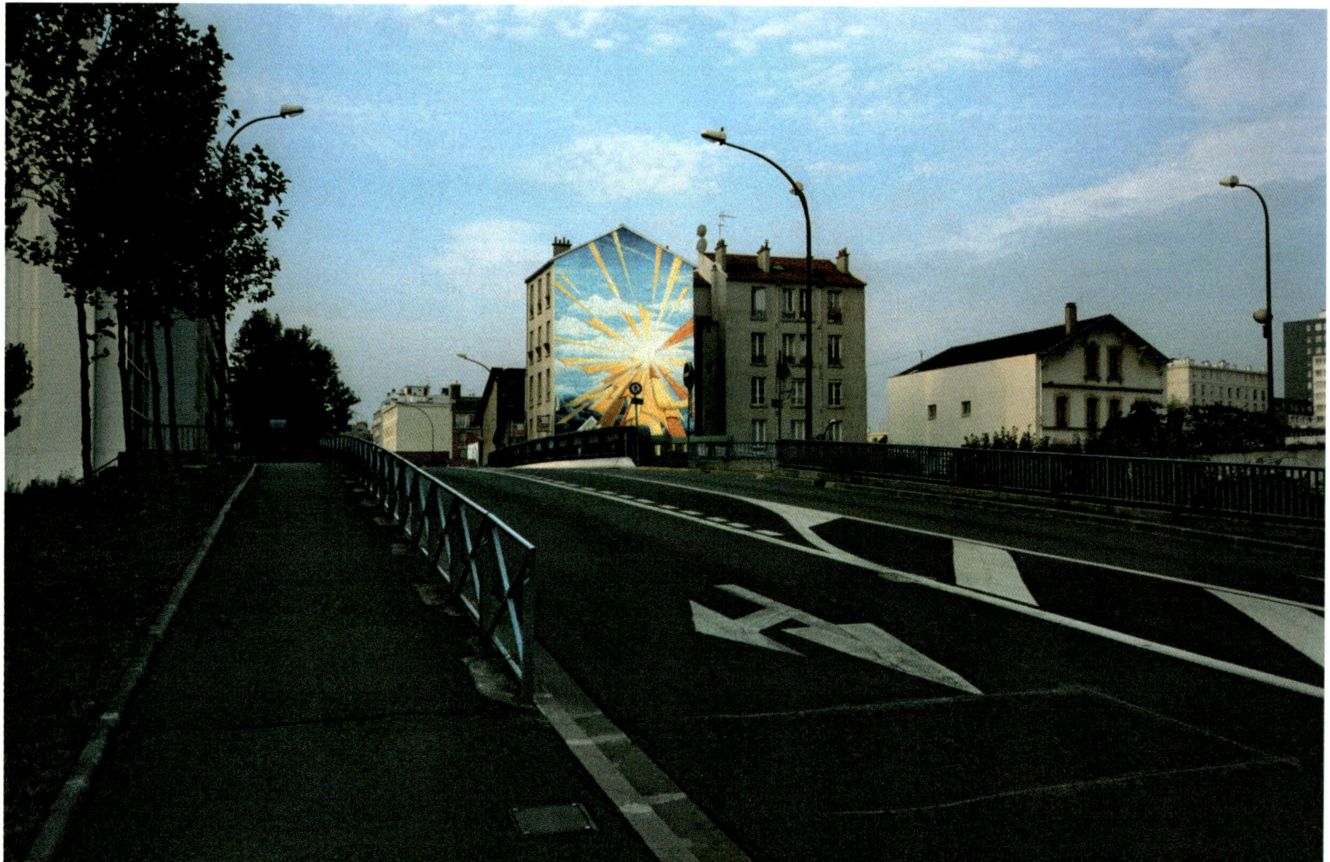

Thursday, June 24. Bobigny, France. Cityscape

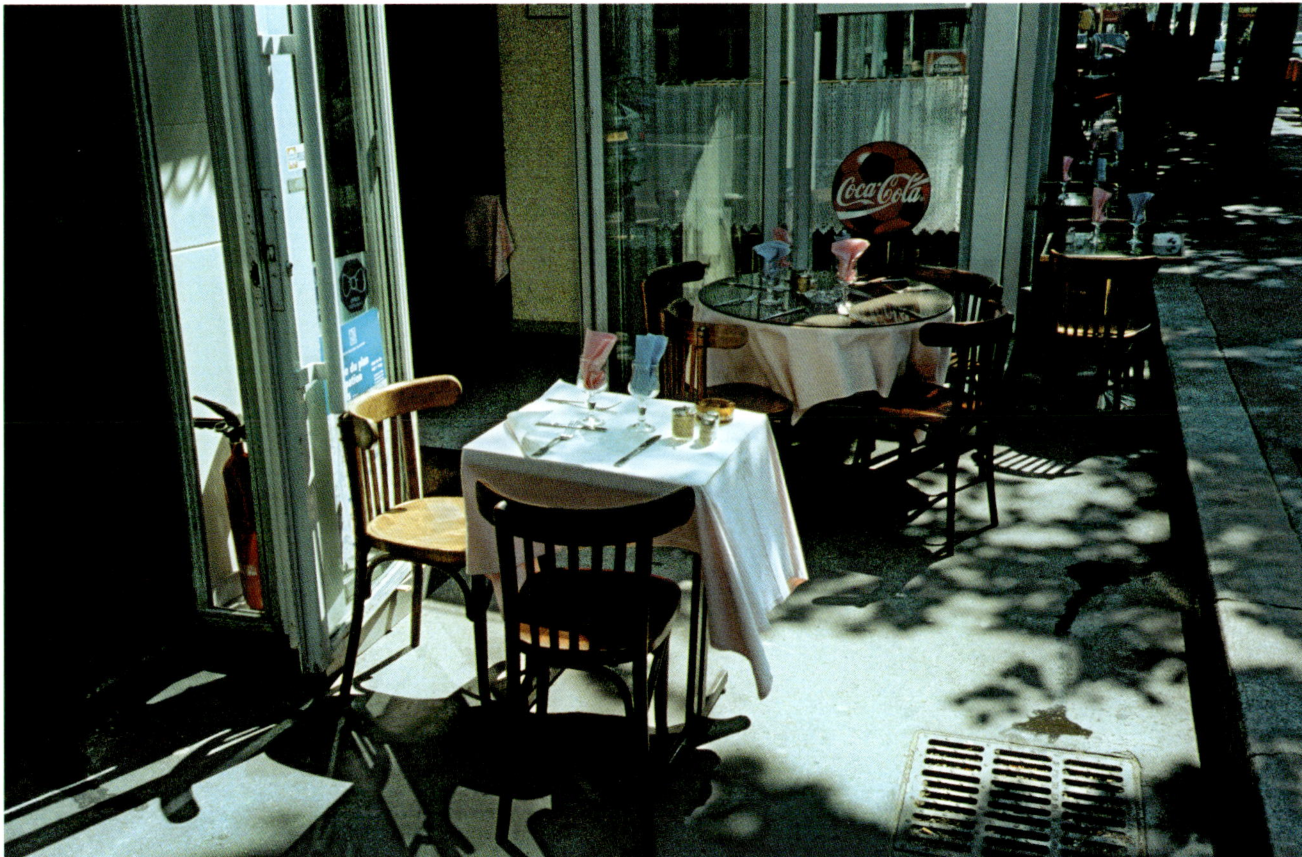

Friday, June 25. Boulogne, France. Street scene

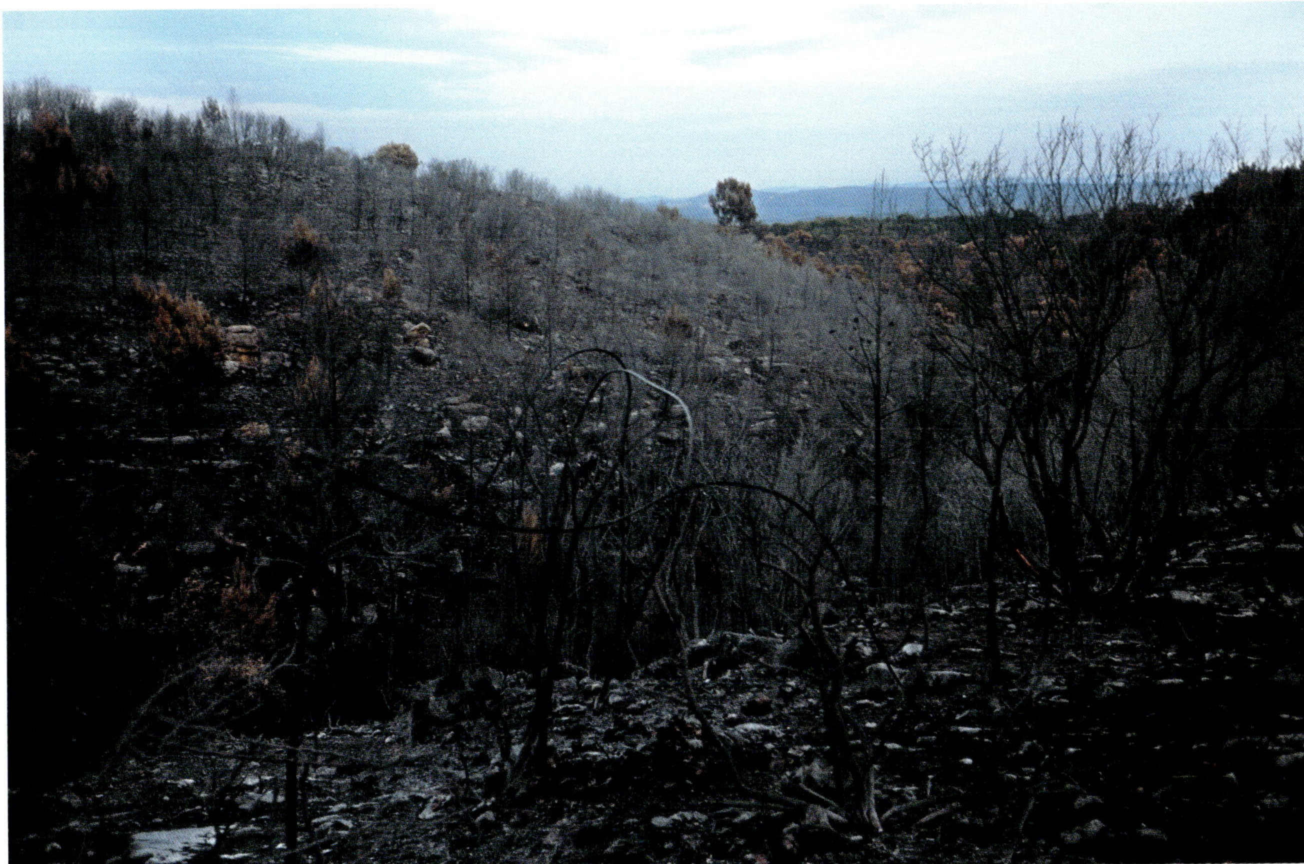

Saturday, June 26. Cotignac, France. After the fire (see note)

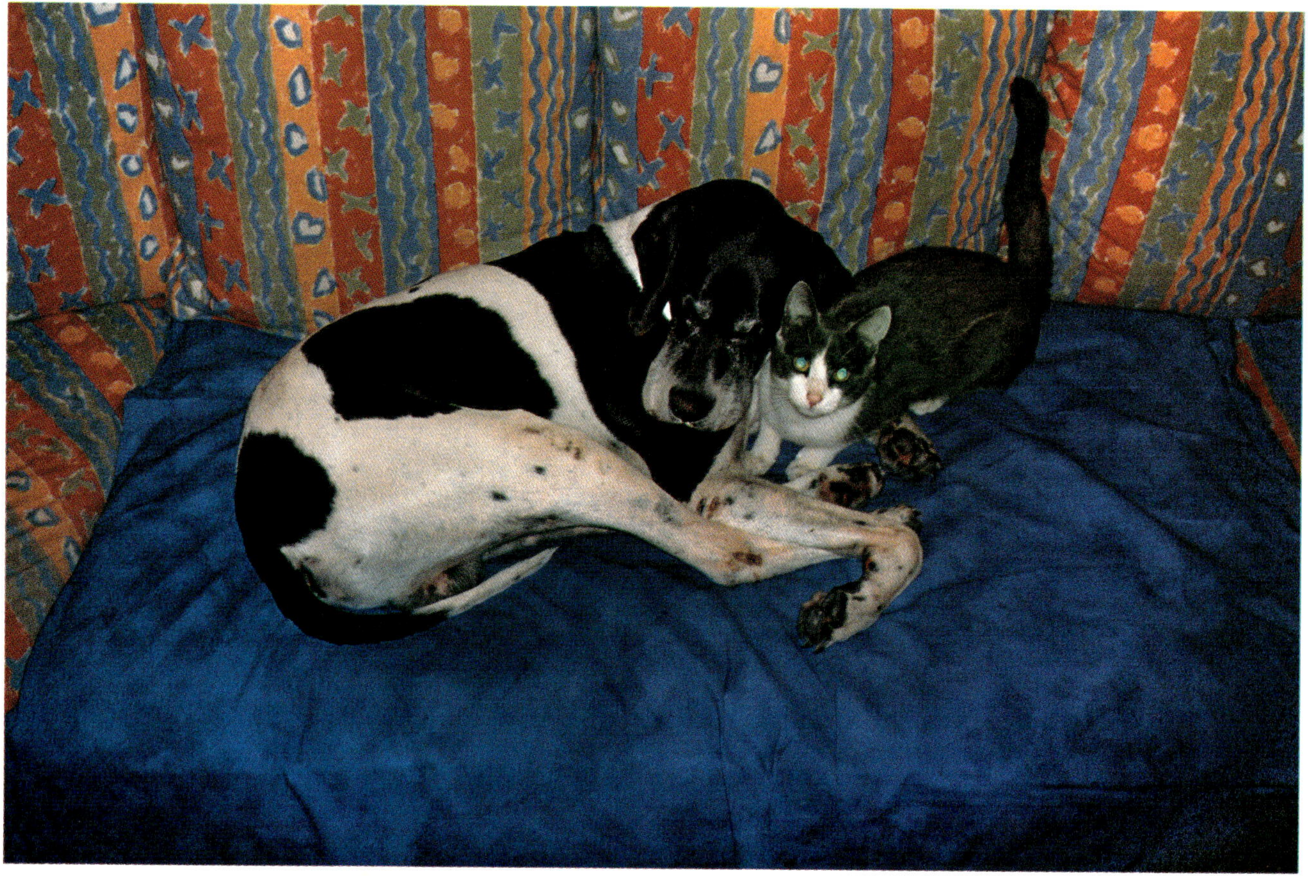

Sunday, June 27. Avignon, France. Love scene

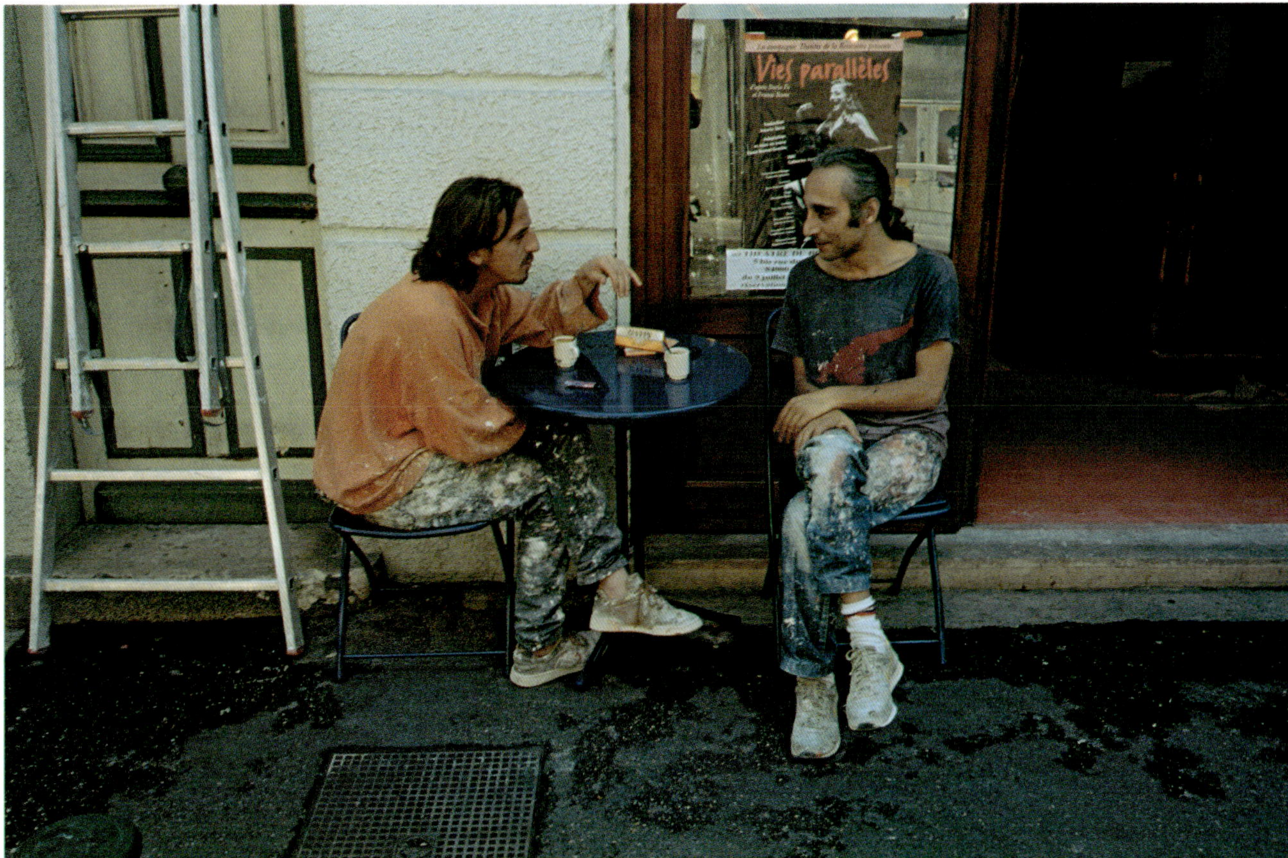

Monday, June 28. Avignon, France. Street scene

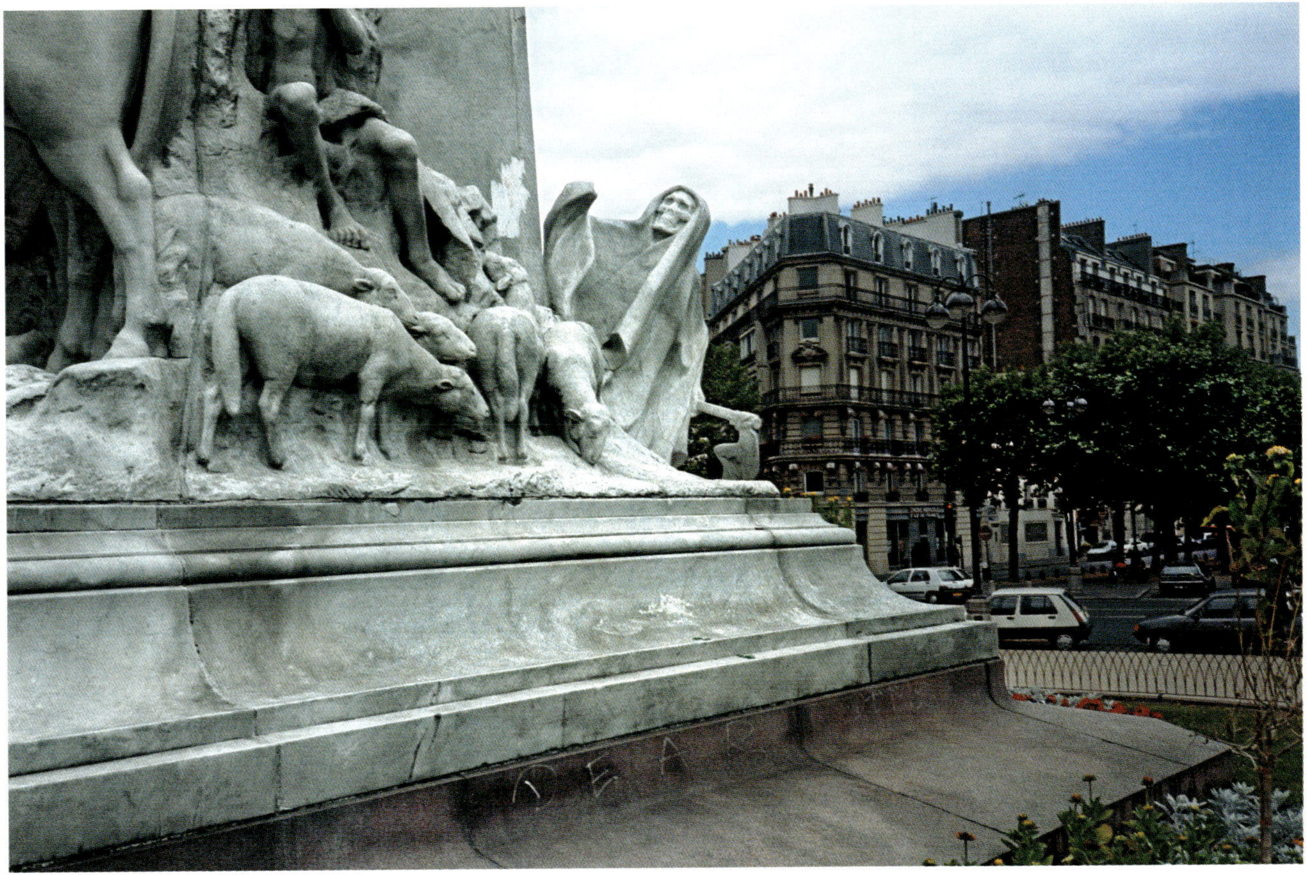

Tuesday, June 29, Paris. In the Invalides area, near Édouard Boubat's home (see note)

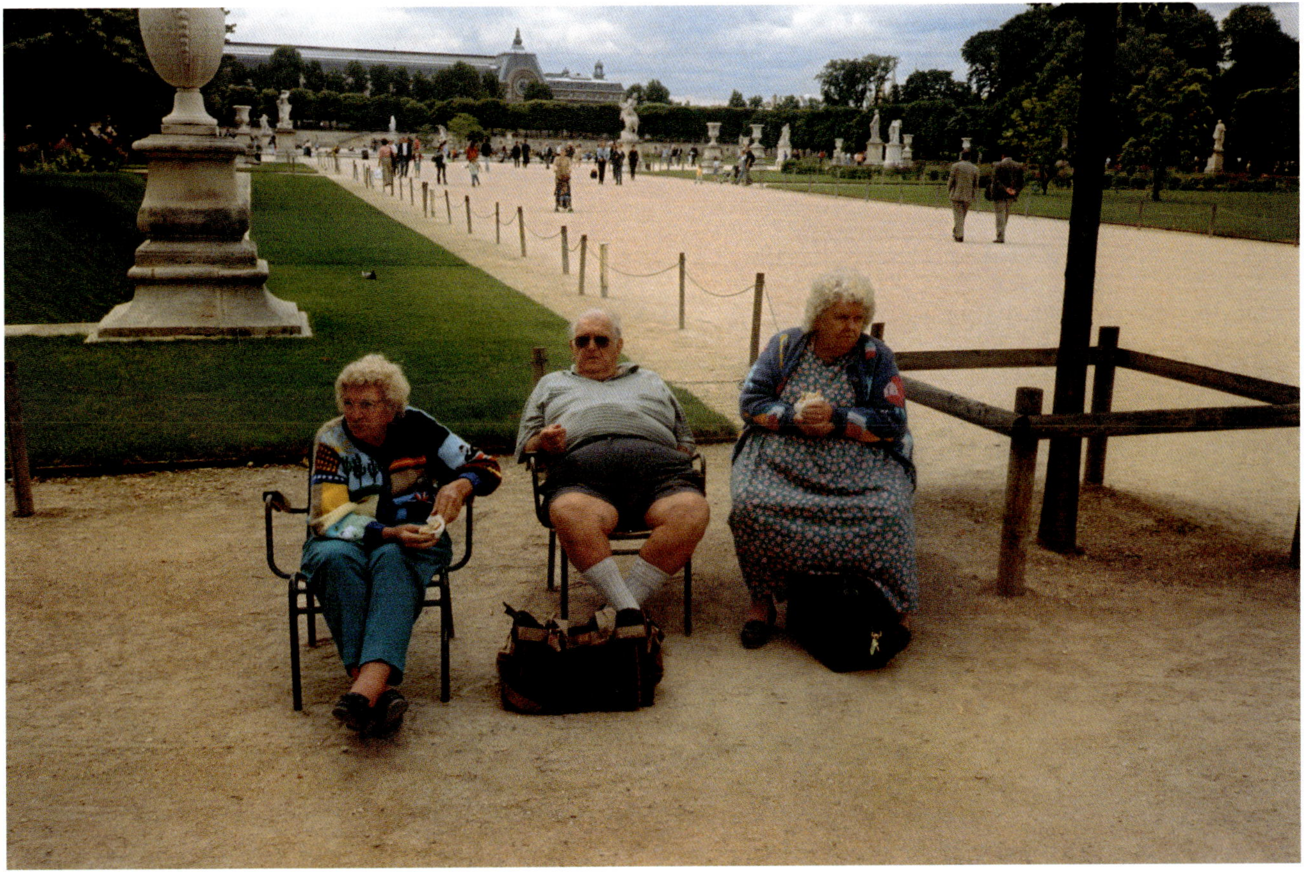

Wednesday, June 30. Paris. In the Tuileries garden

JULY

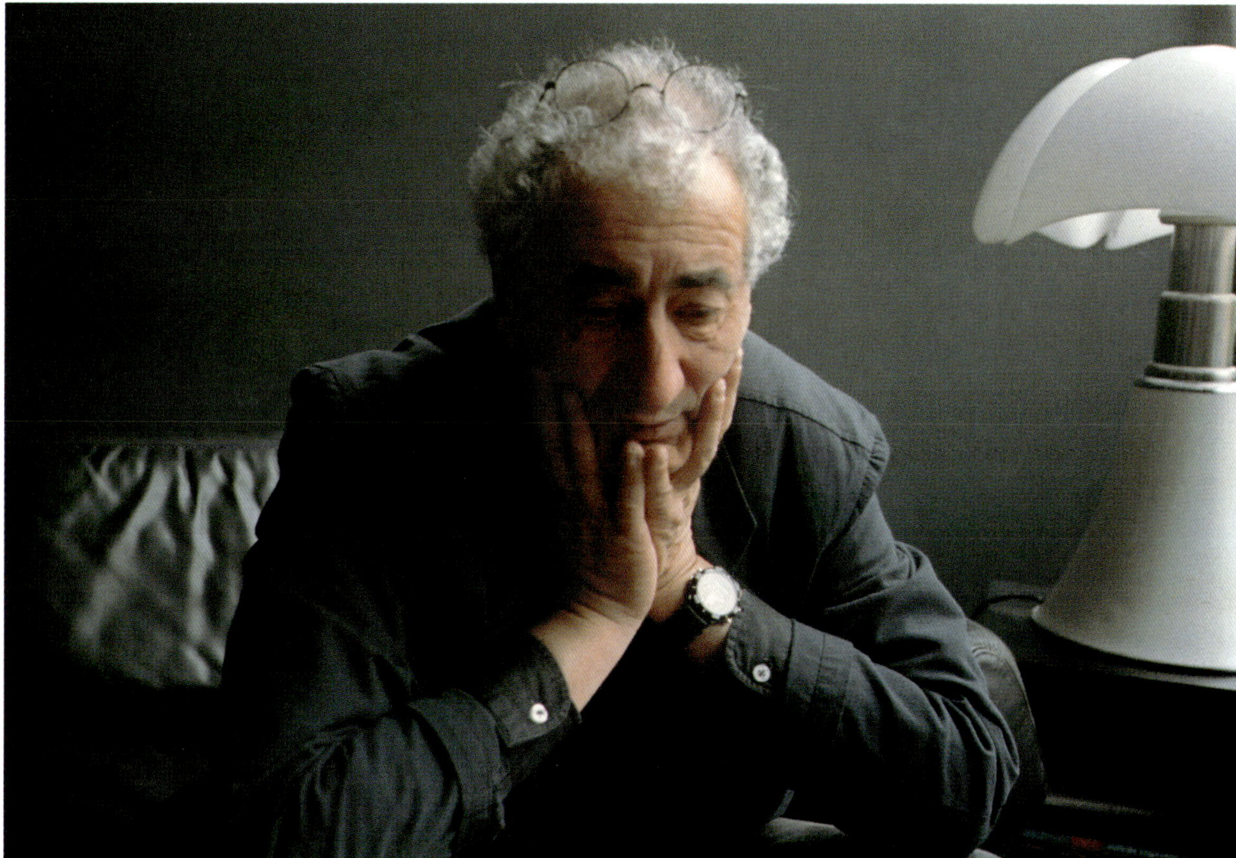

Thursday, July 1. Paris. Doctor Jean-Jacques Touati, a friend of Édouard Boubat

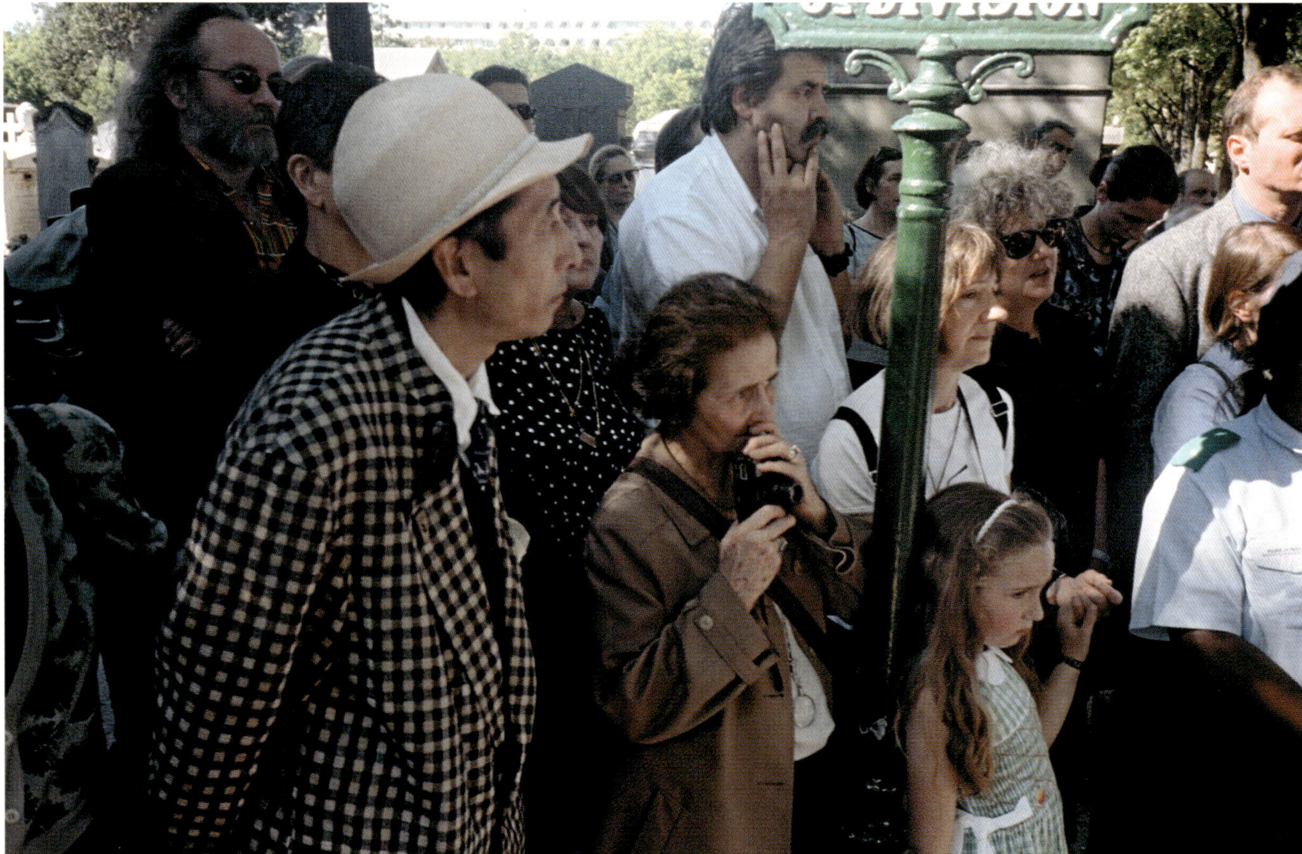

Friday, July 2. Paris. At Édouard Boubat's funeral

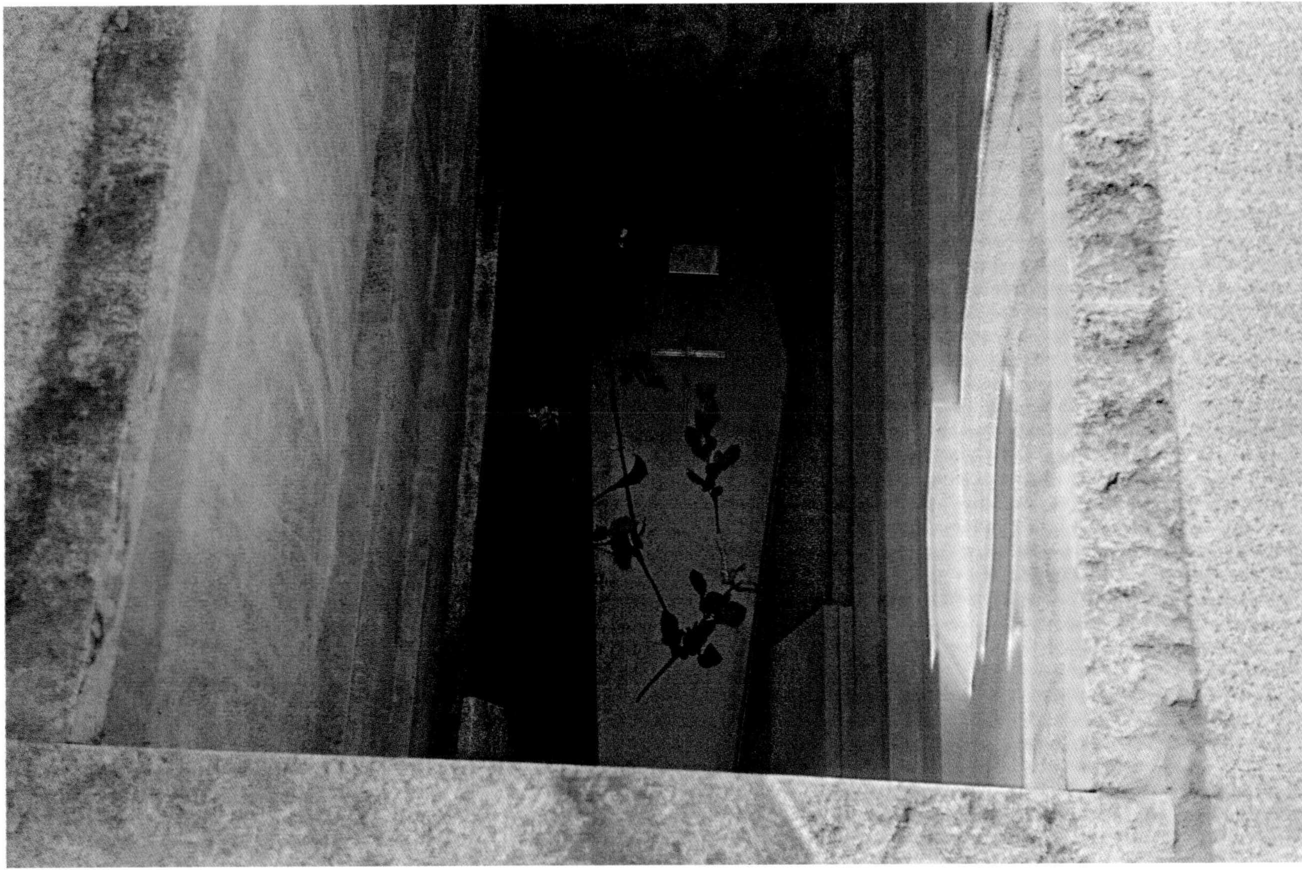

Friday, July 2. Paris. Édouard Boubat's grave

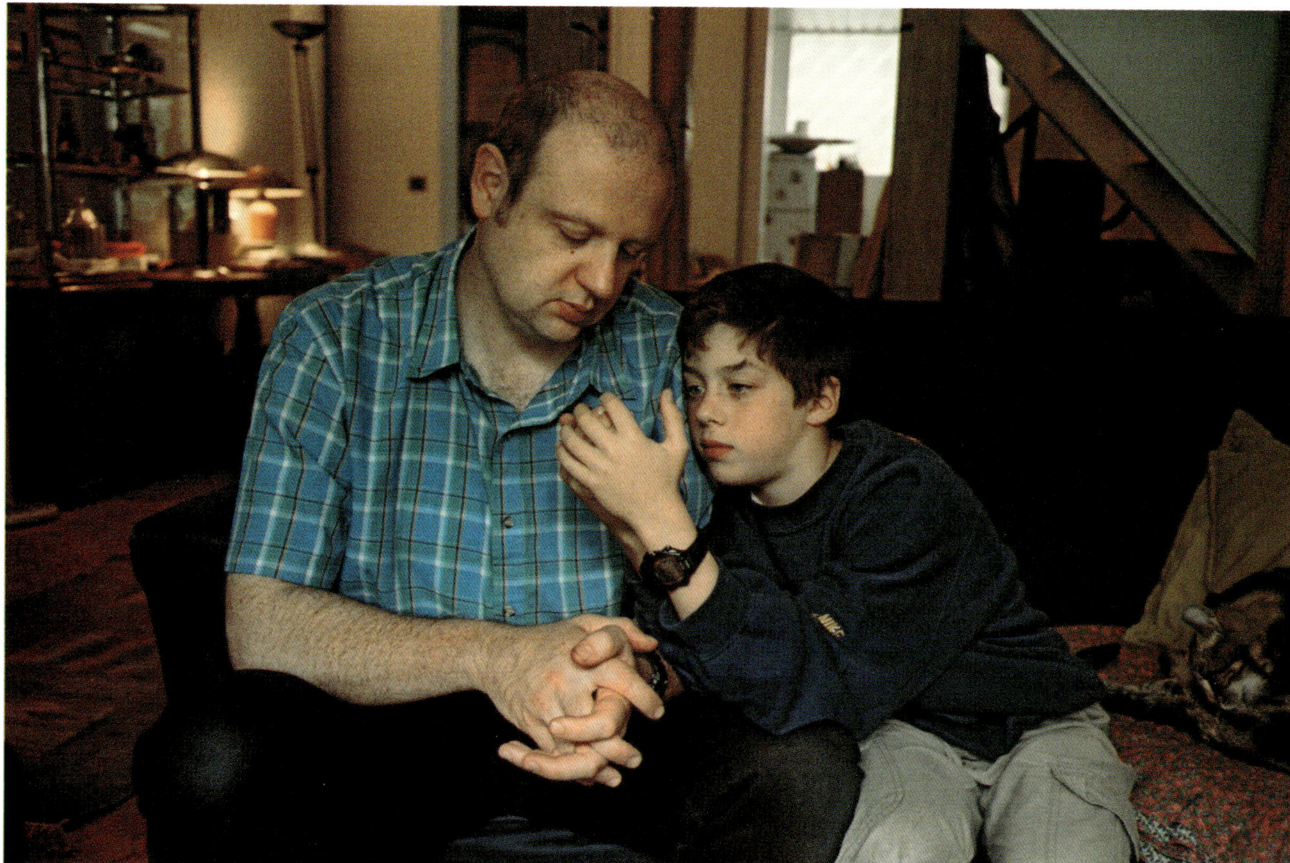

Saturday, July 3. Paris. Jean-Michel Horvat with his son Grégoire

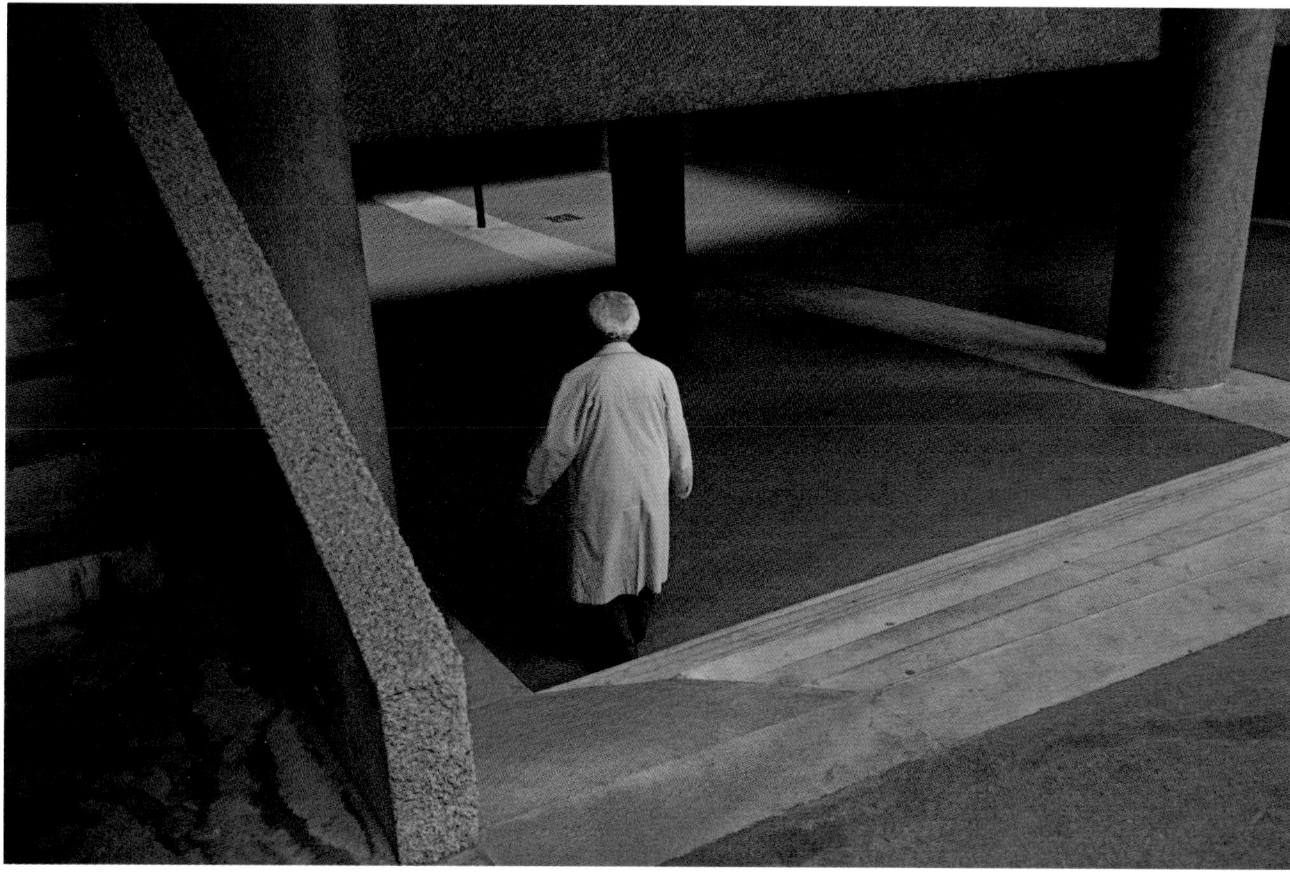

Sunday, July 4. Paris. Street scene, in La Défense area

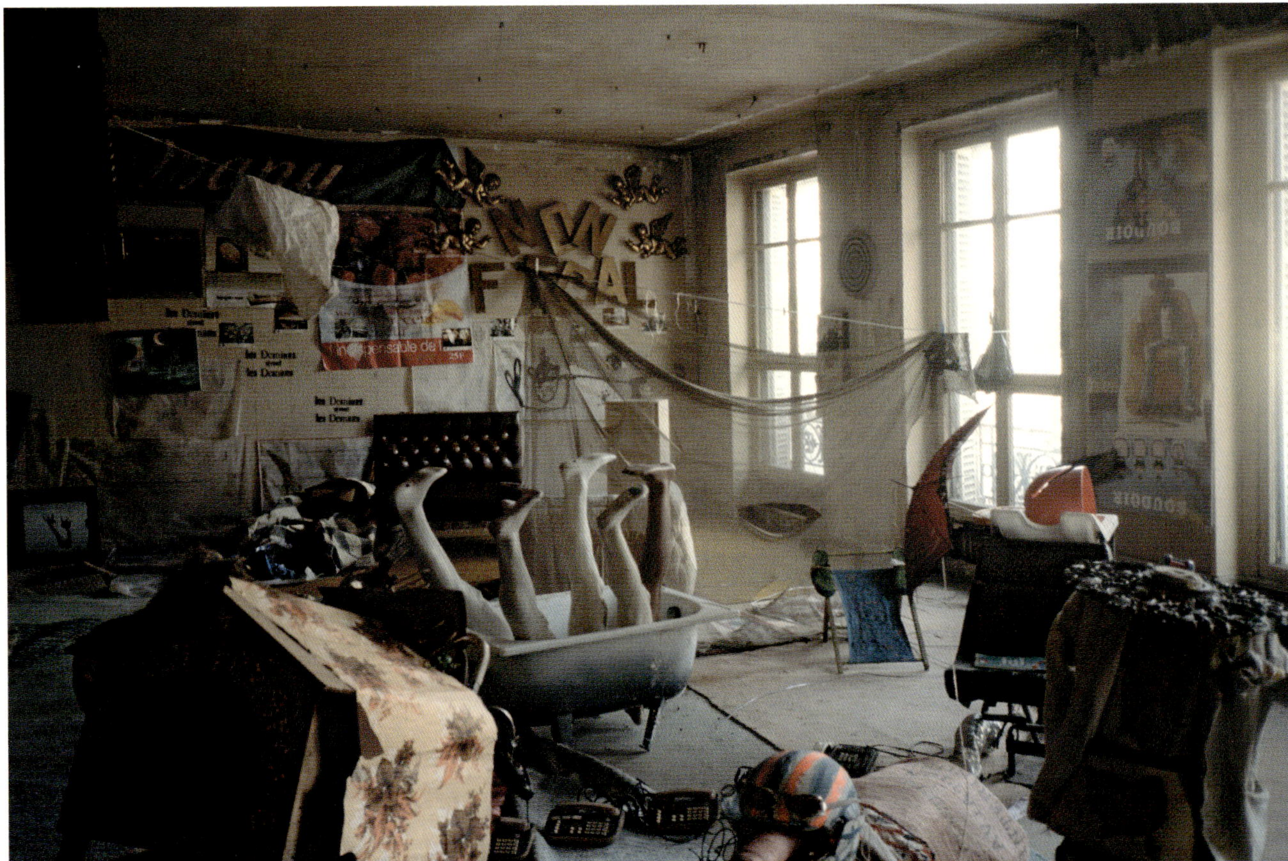

Monday, July 5. Paris. Artist's squat, in the Bourse area

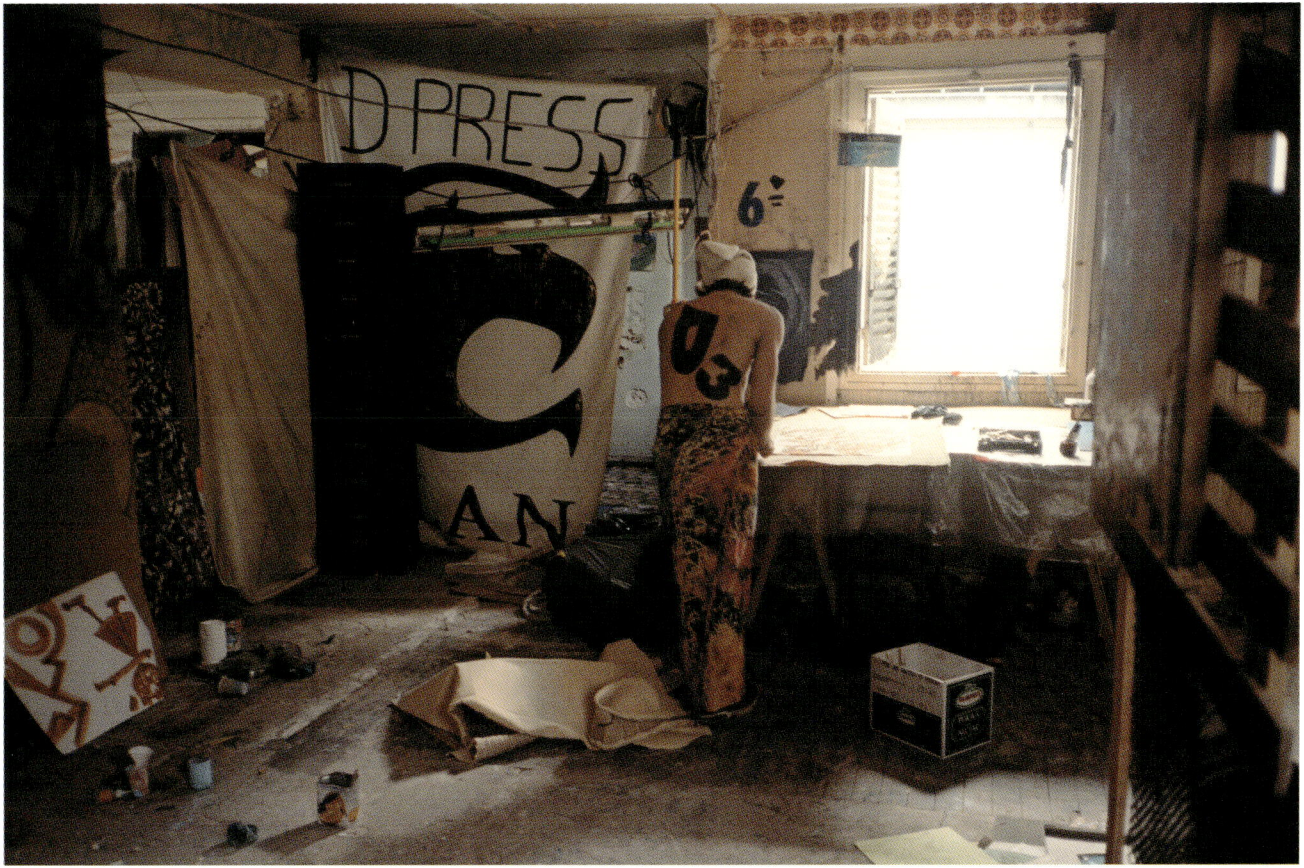

Monday, July 5. Paris. Artist's squat, in the Bourse area

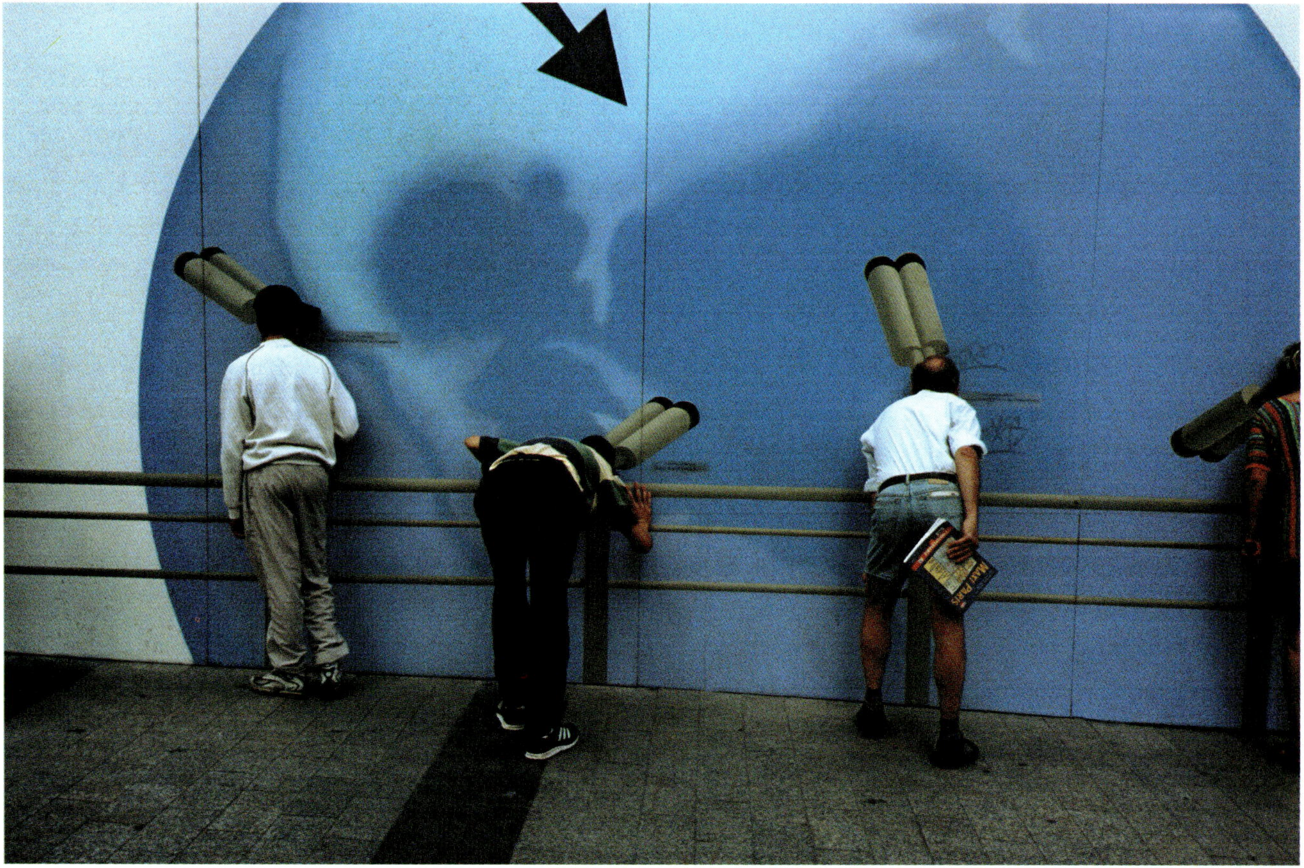

Tuesday, July 6. Paris. On the Champs Élysées, shop renovation

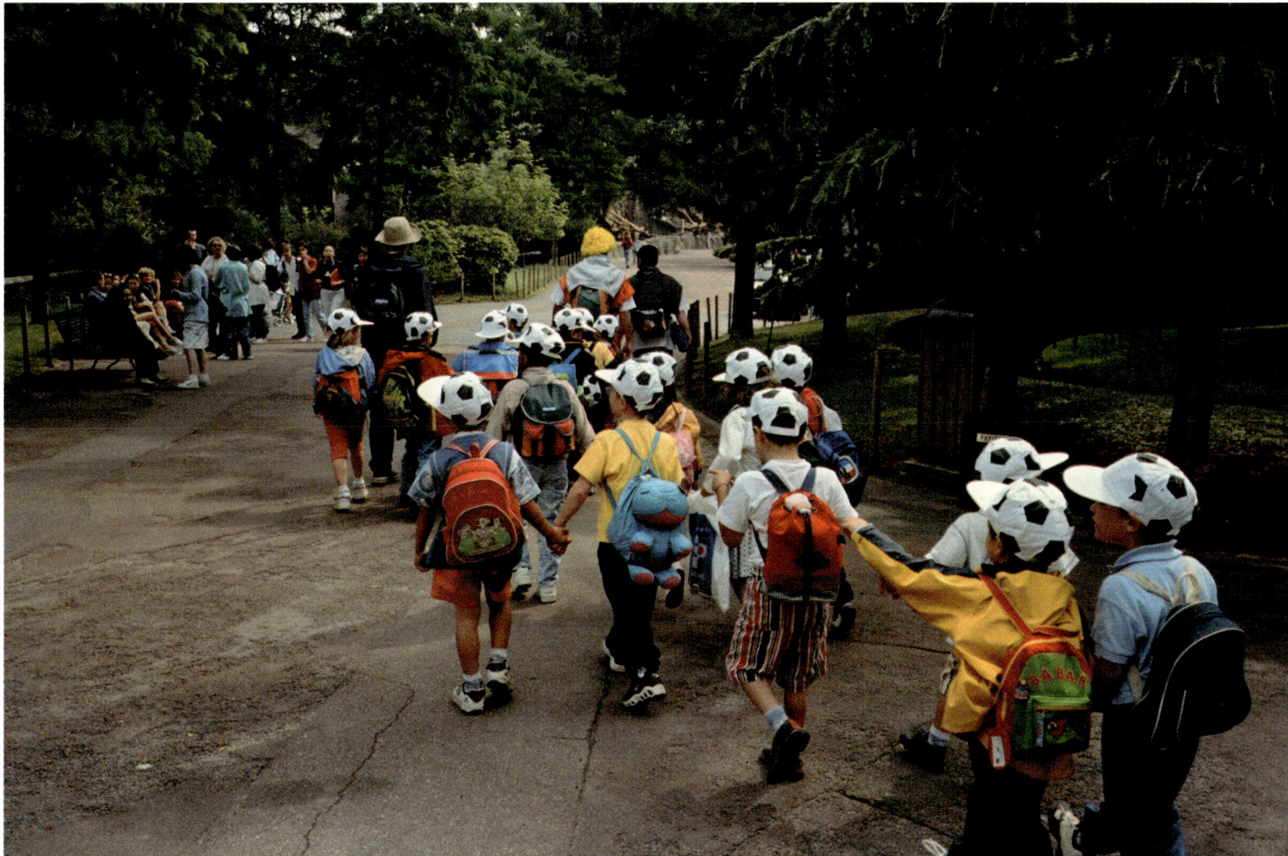

Wednesday, July 7. Paris. Bois de Vincennes, children at the zoo

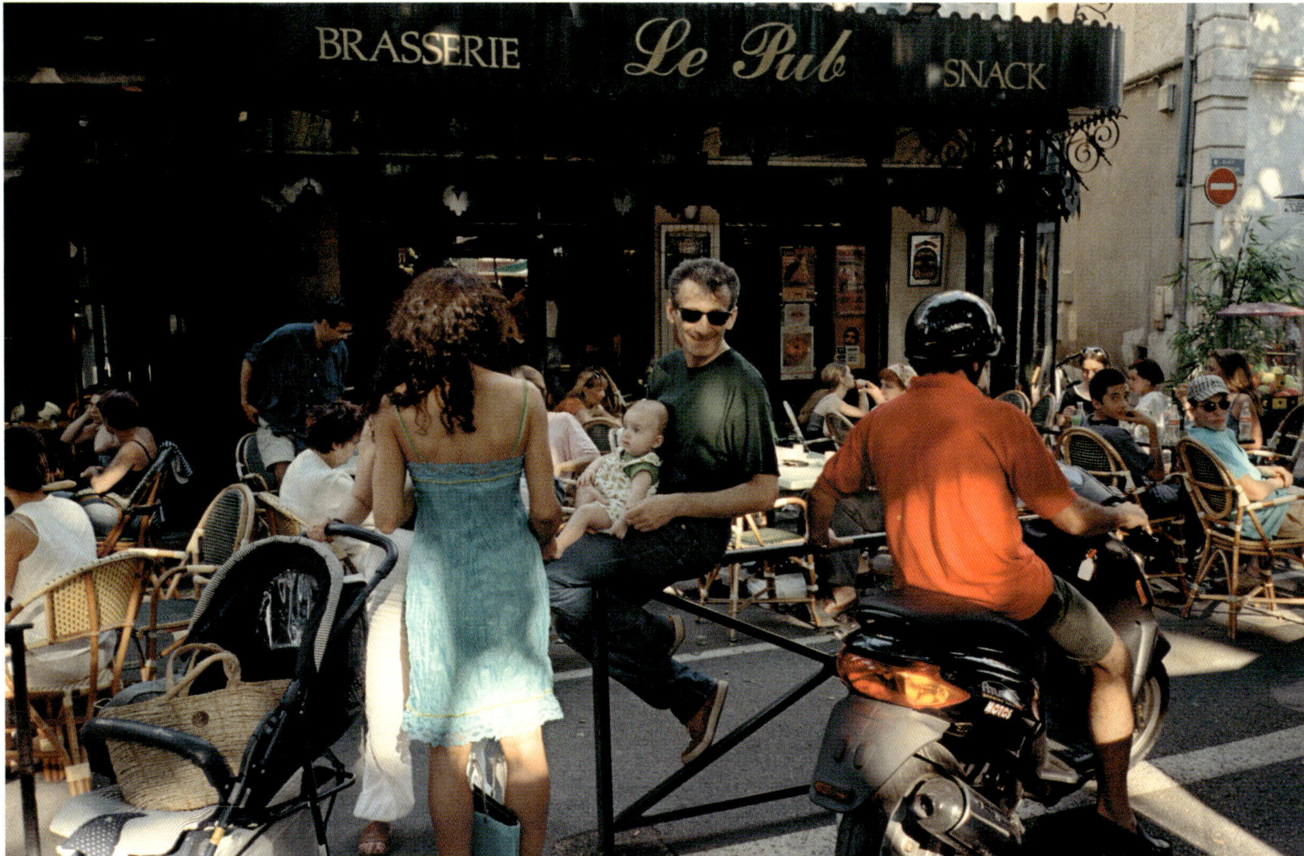

Thursday, July 8. Arles, France. Place du Forum, during the Rencontres de la Photo

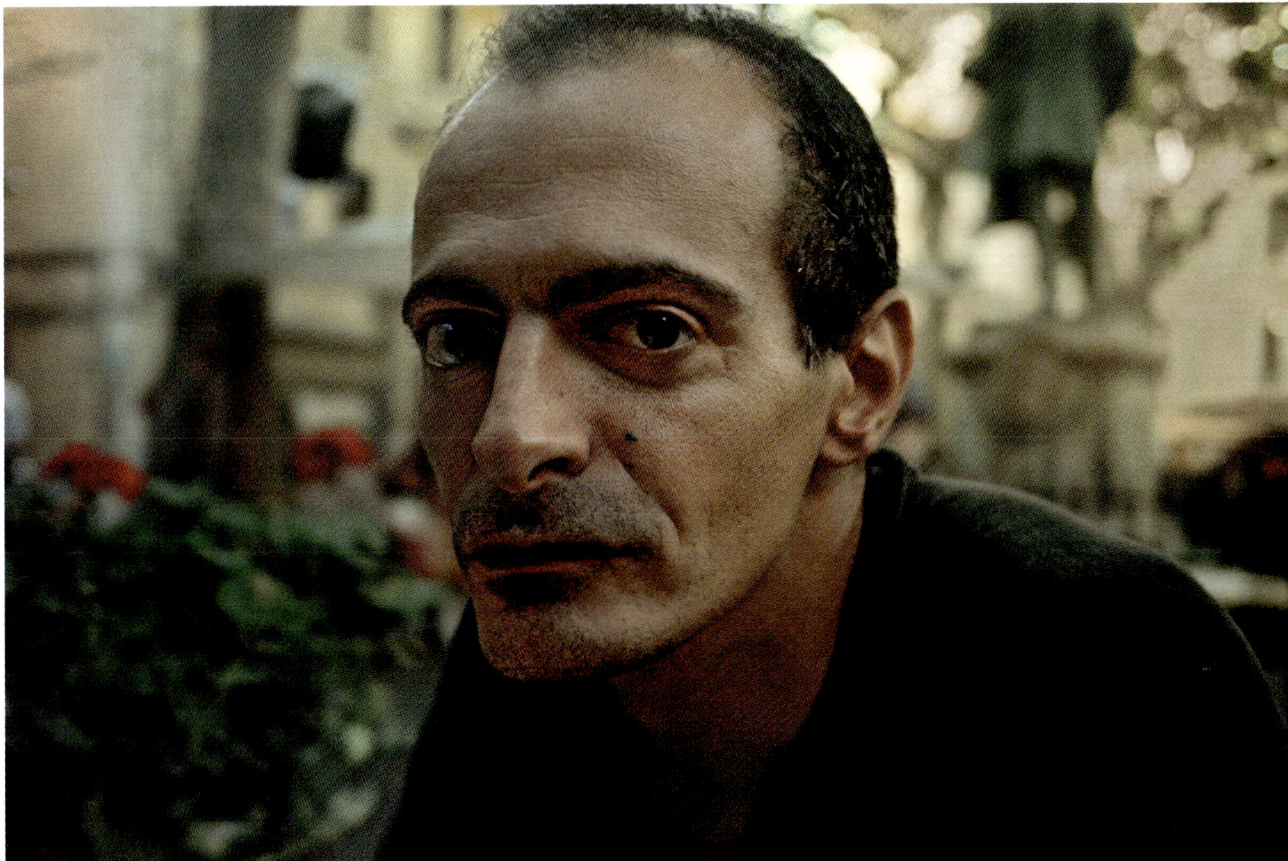

Friday, July 9. Arles, France. Antoine d'Agata, photographer

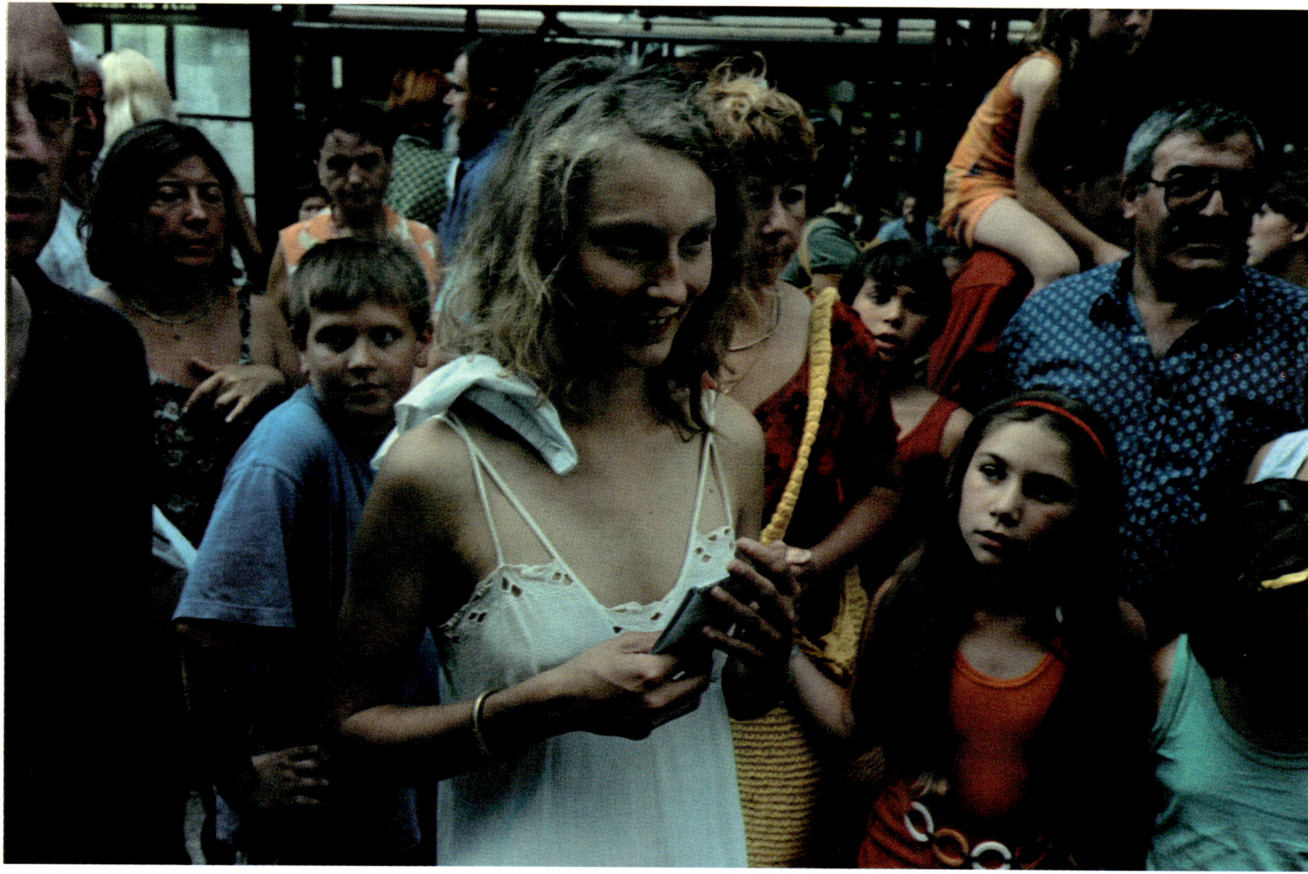

Saturday, July 10. Avignon, France. Street scene, during the Theatre Festival

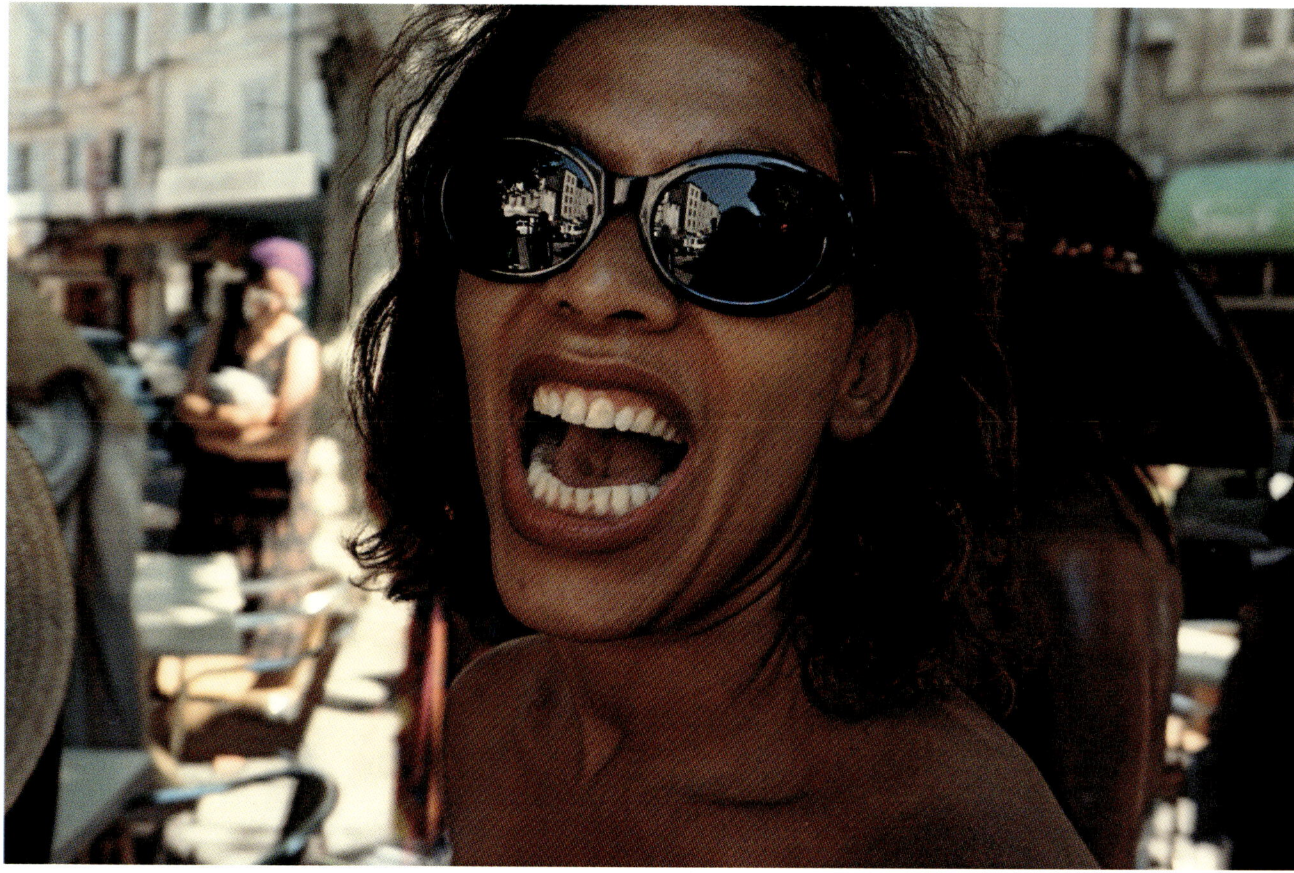

Saturday, July 10. Avignon, France. Street scene, during the Theatre Festival

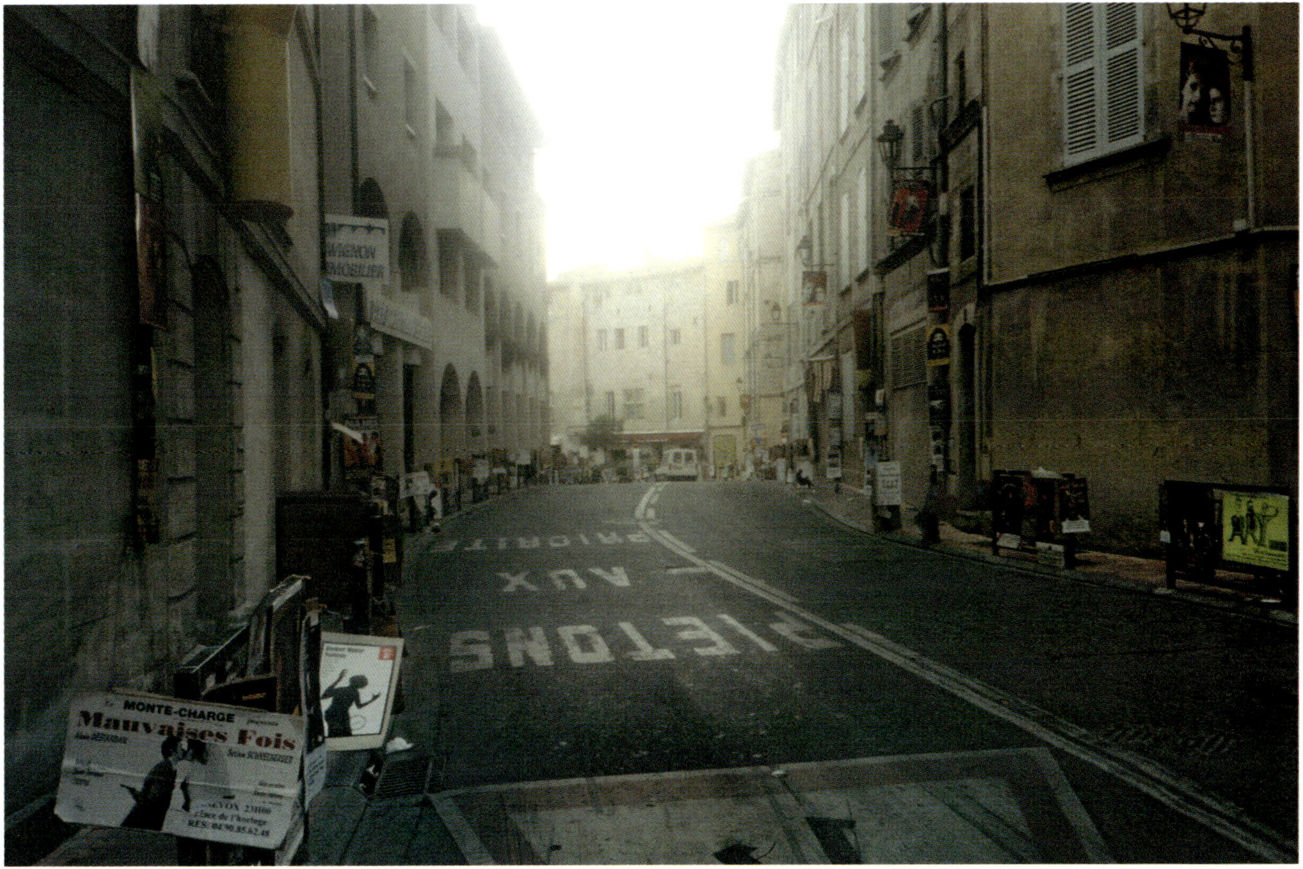

Sunday, July 11. Avignon, France. Early morning

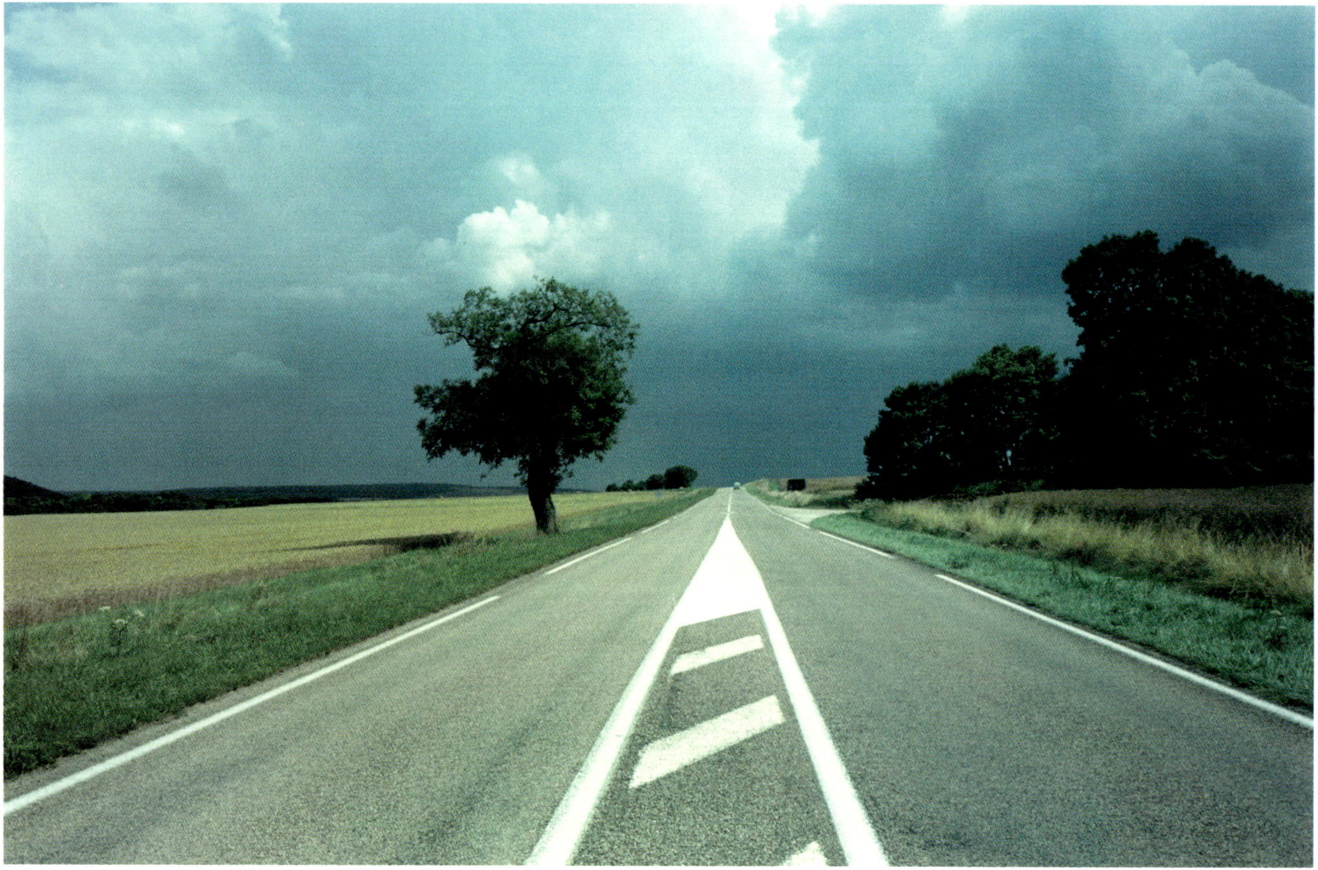

Monday, July 12. Bourgogne, France. Summer landscape

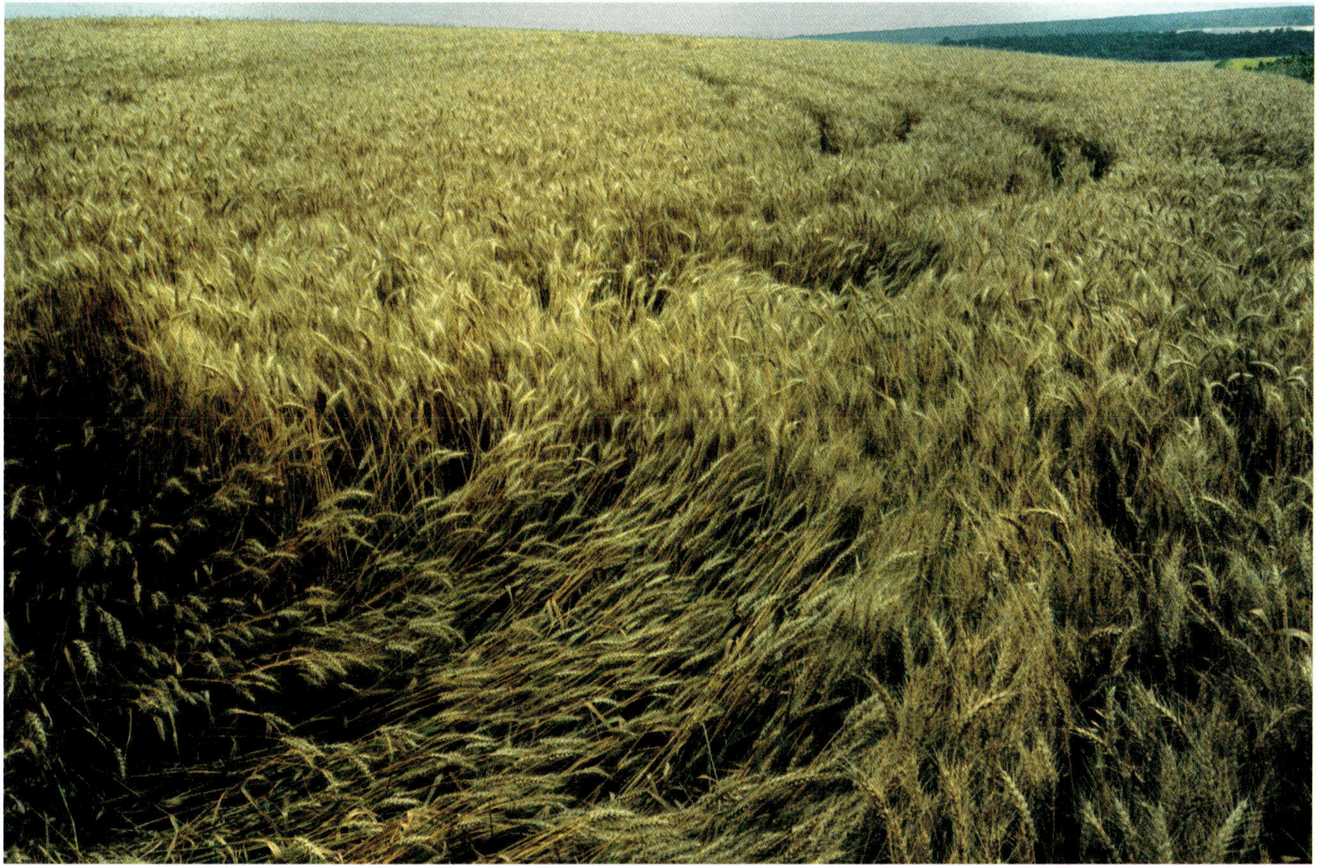

Monday, July 12. Bourgogne, France. Summer landscape

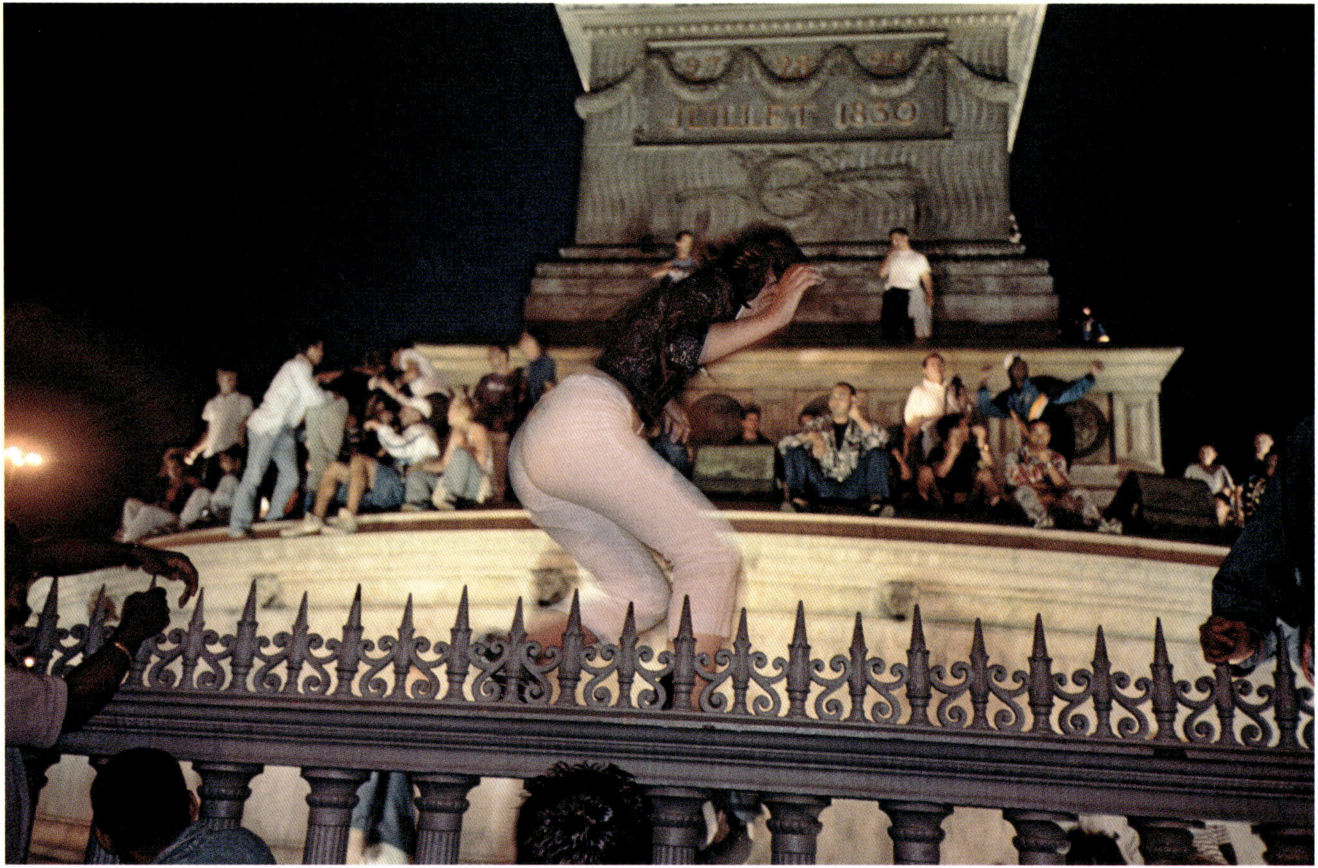

Tuesday, July 13. Paris. National holiday celebration, Place de la Bastille

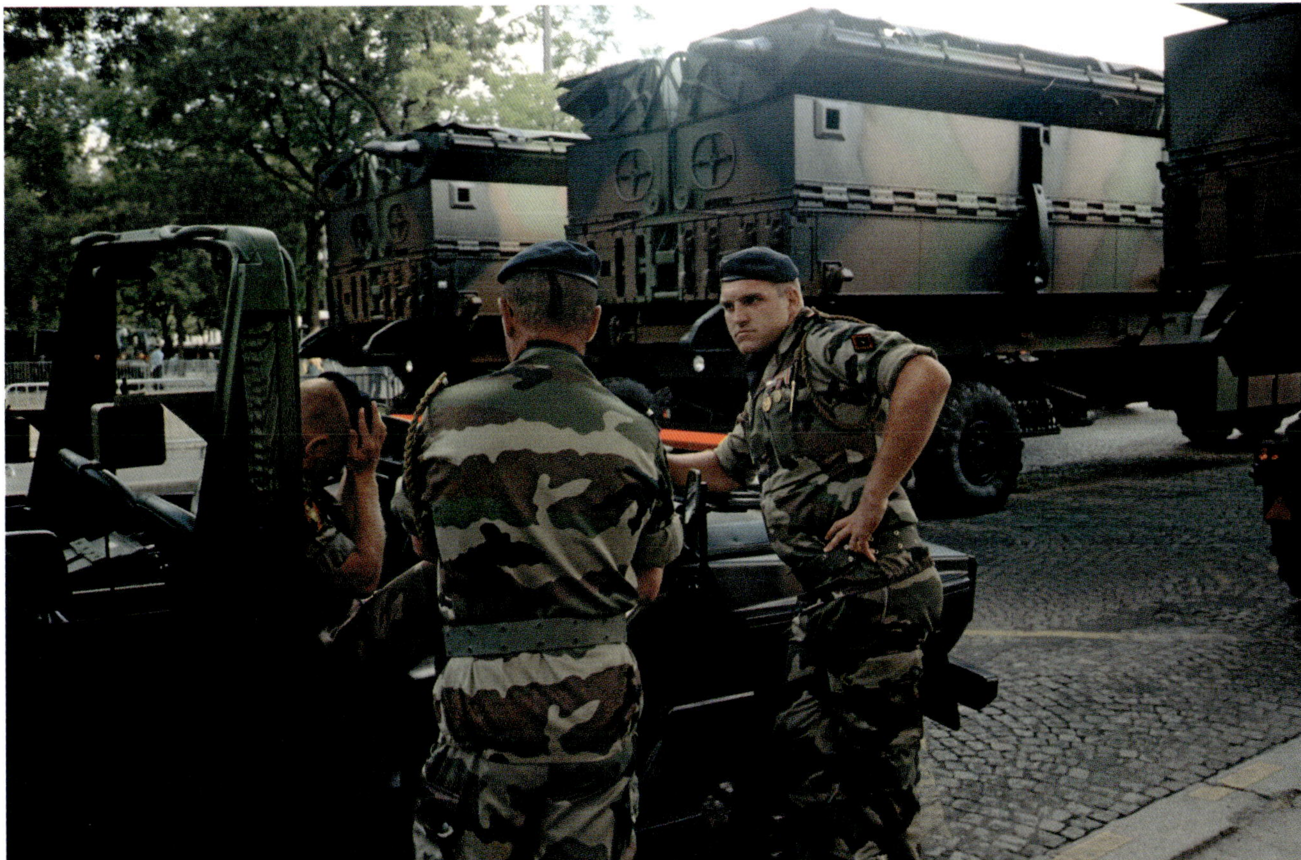

Wednesday, July 14. Paris. Near the Champs Élysées, before the parade

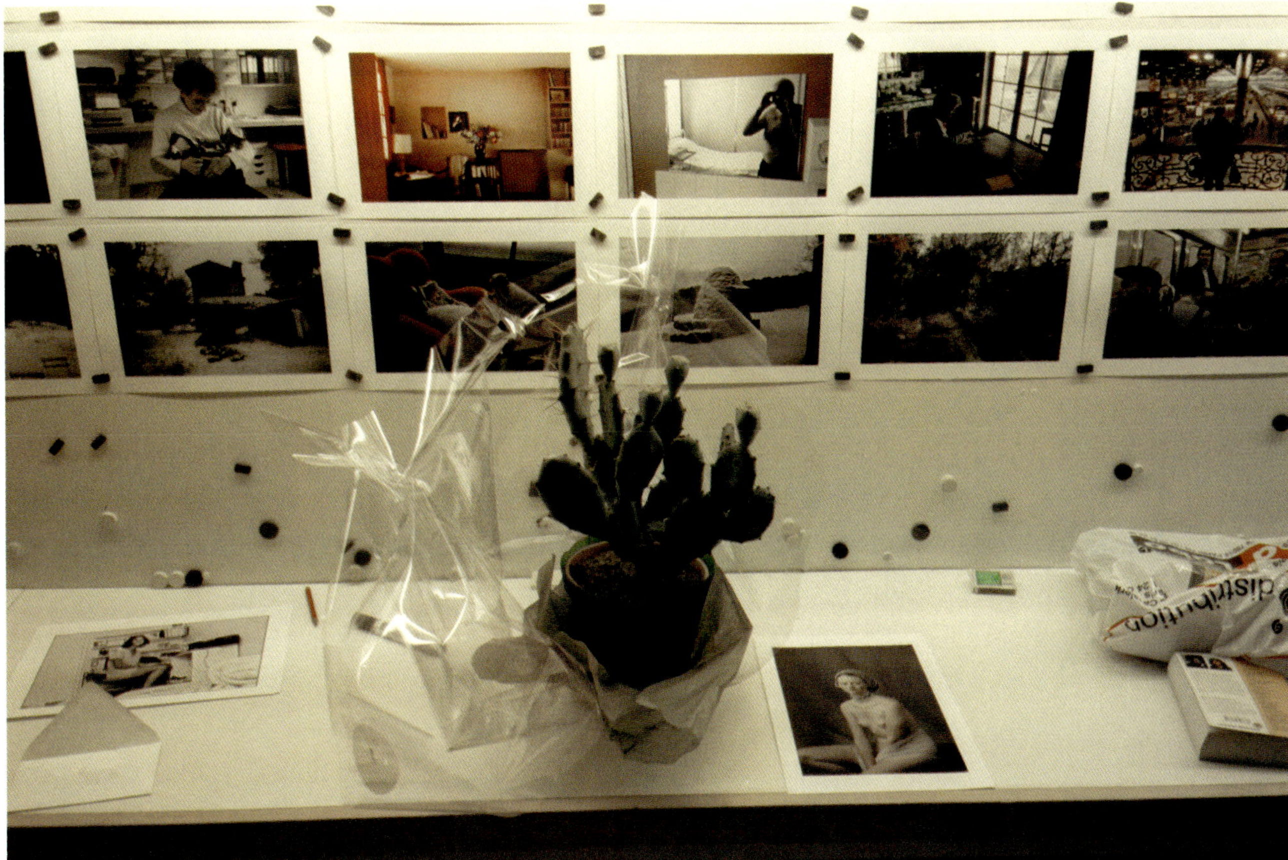

Thursday, July 15. Boulogne, France. In my studio

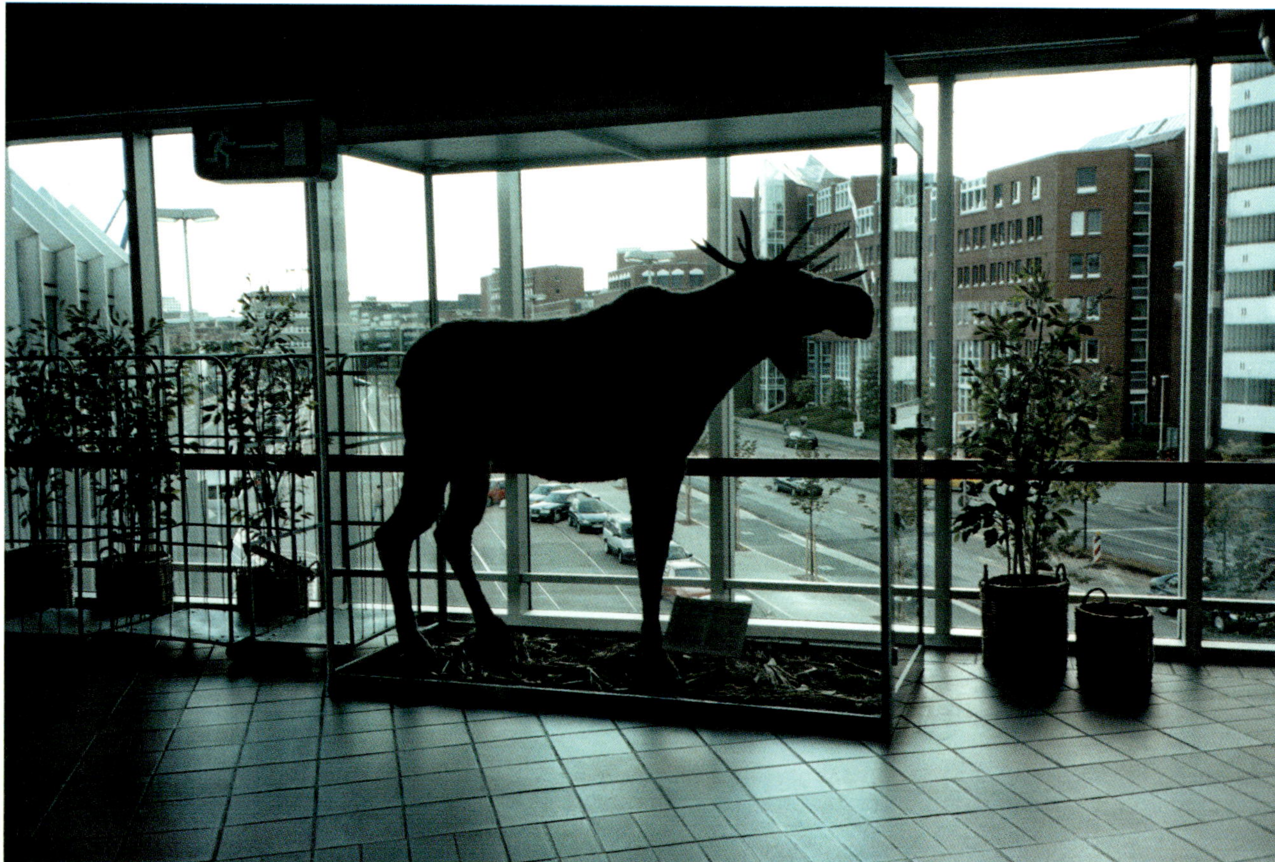

Friday, July 16. Kiel, Germany. The embarkation hall for the ferry to Scandinavia

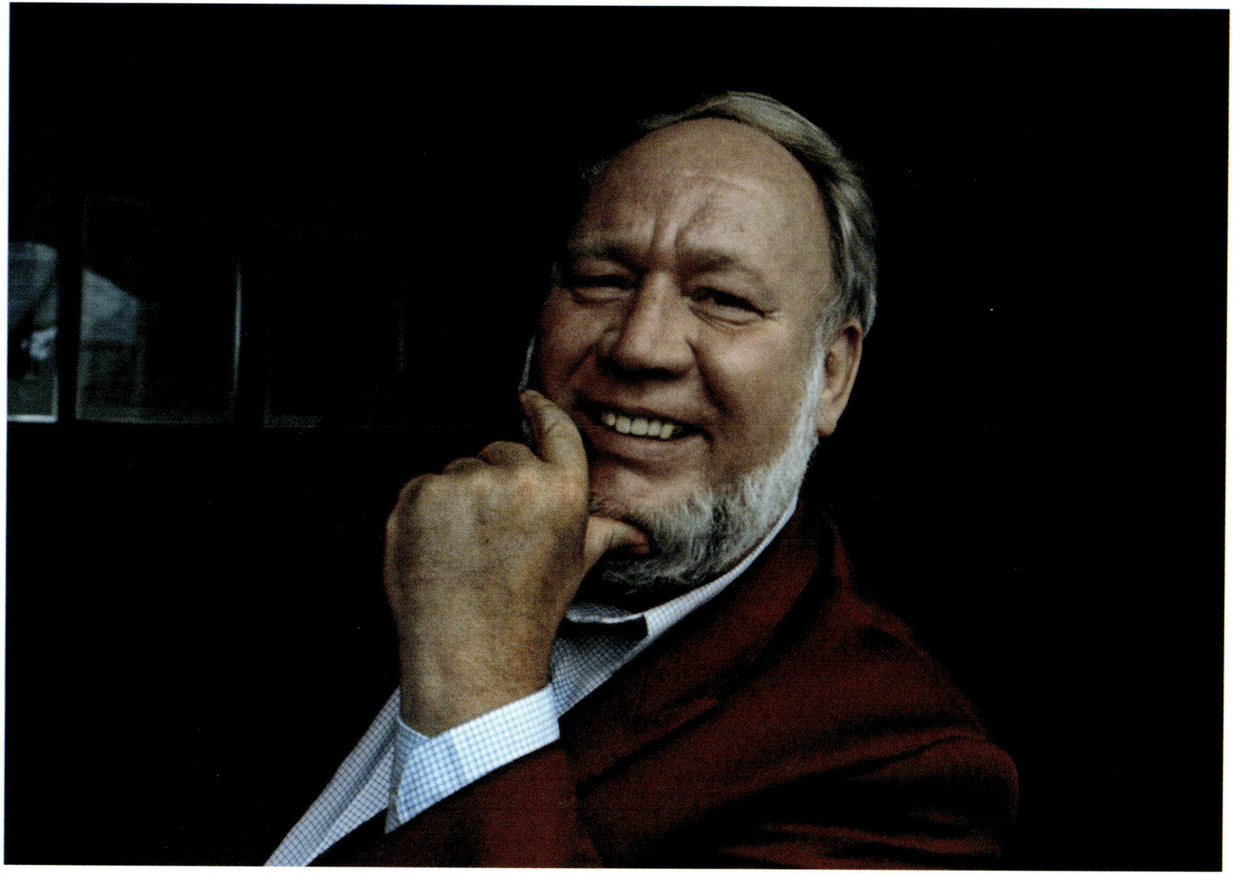

Friday, July 16. Kiel, Germany. Dr. Wolfgang Dreyer, Director of the Zoological Museum

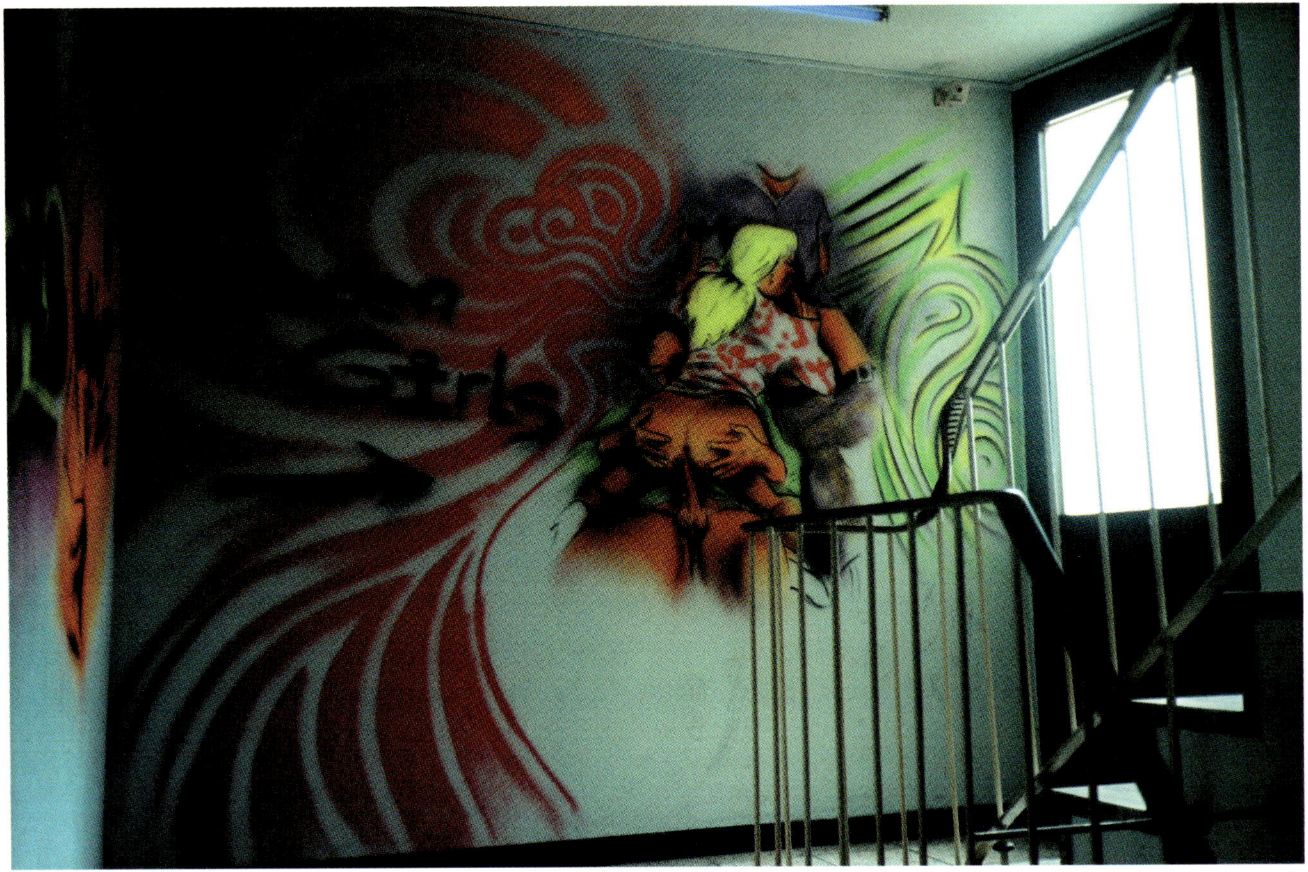

Saturday, July 17. Kiel, Germany. In the Eros Center

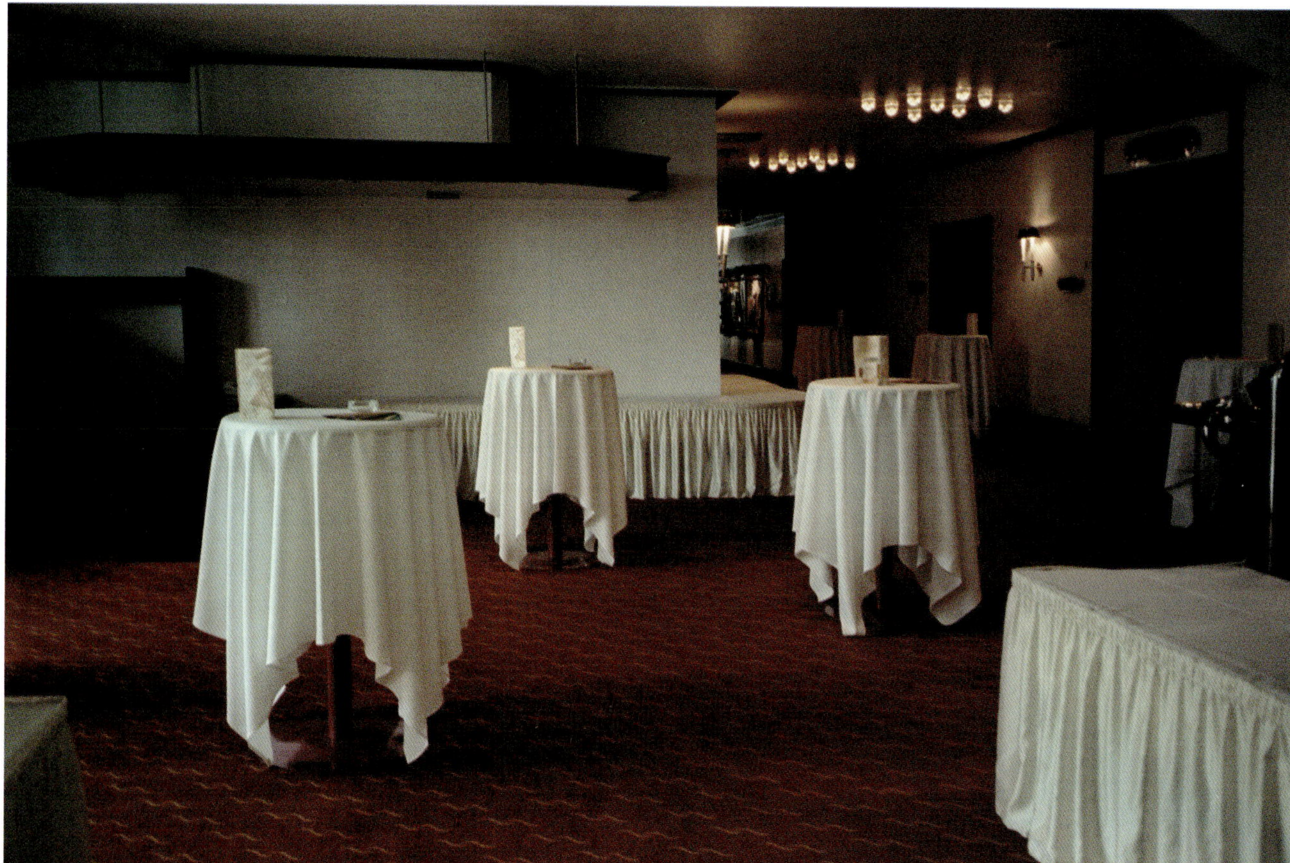

Sunday, July 18. Kiel, Germany. Hotel lobby

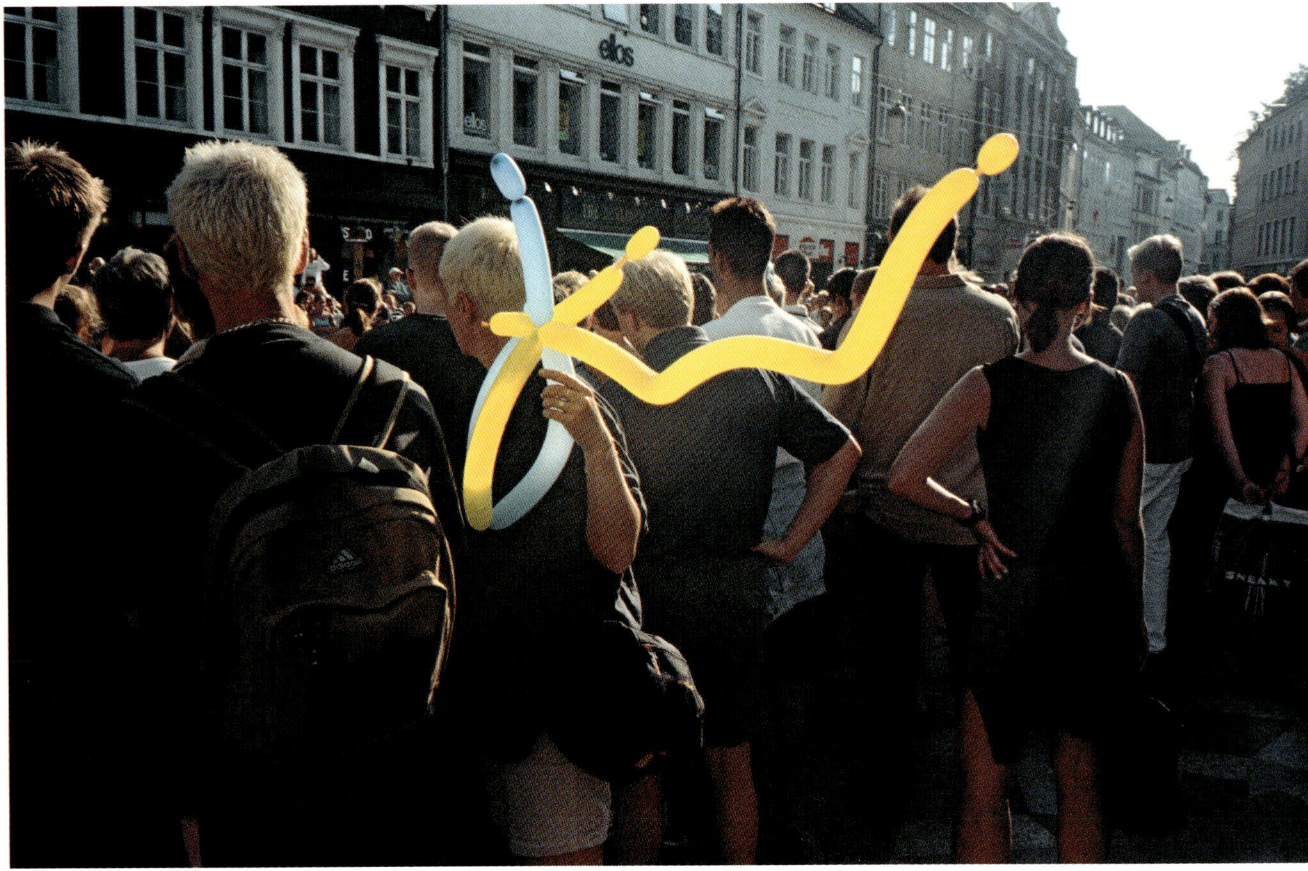

Monday, July 19. Copenhagen. Street scene

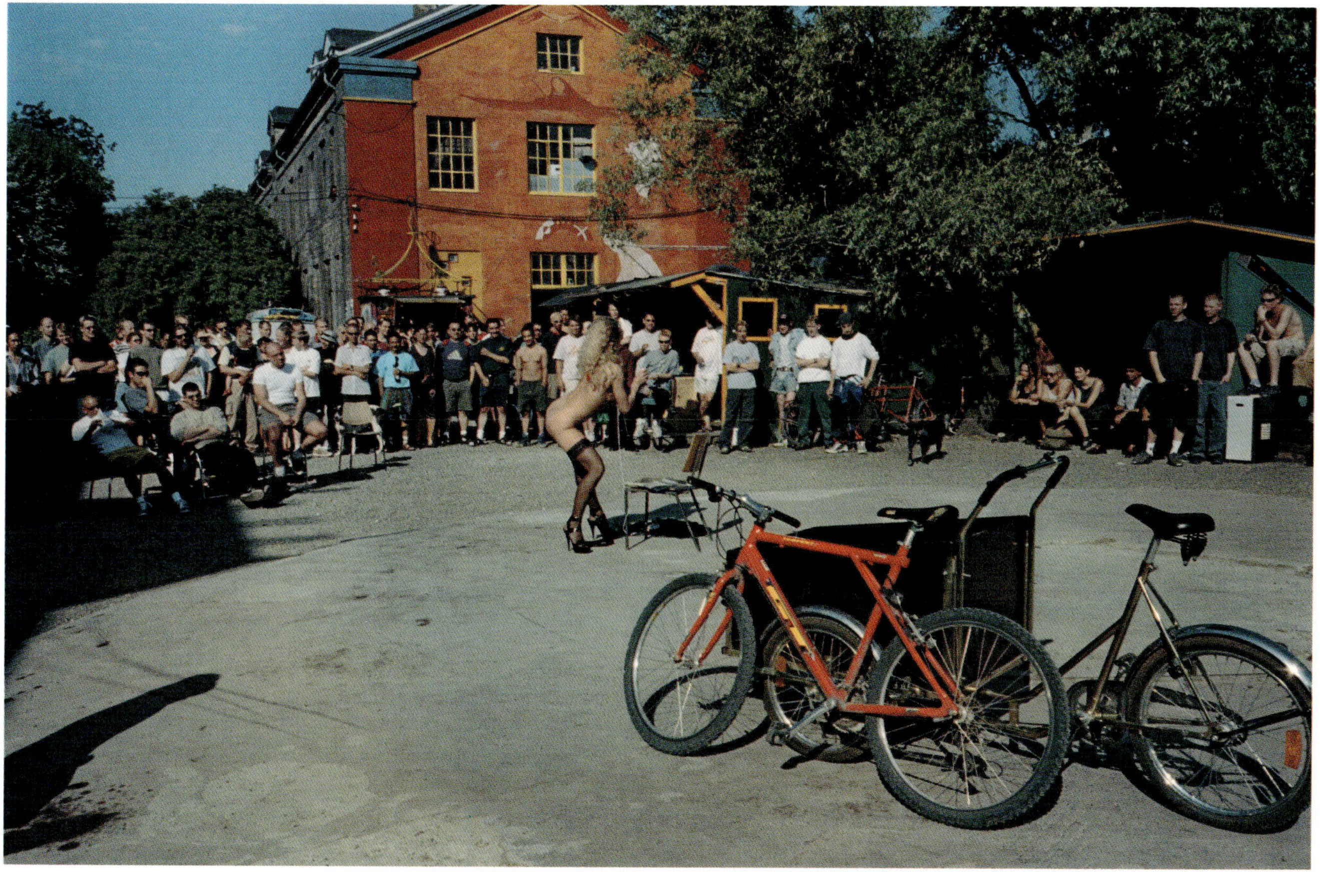

Monday, July 19. Copenhagen. Striptease in the Christiania area

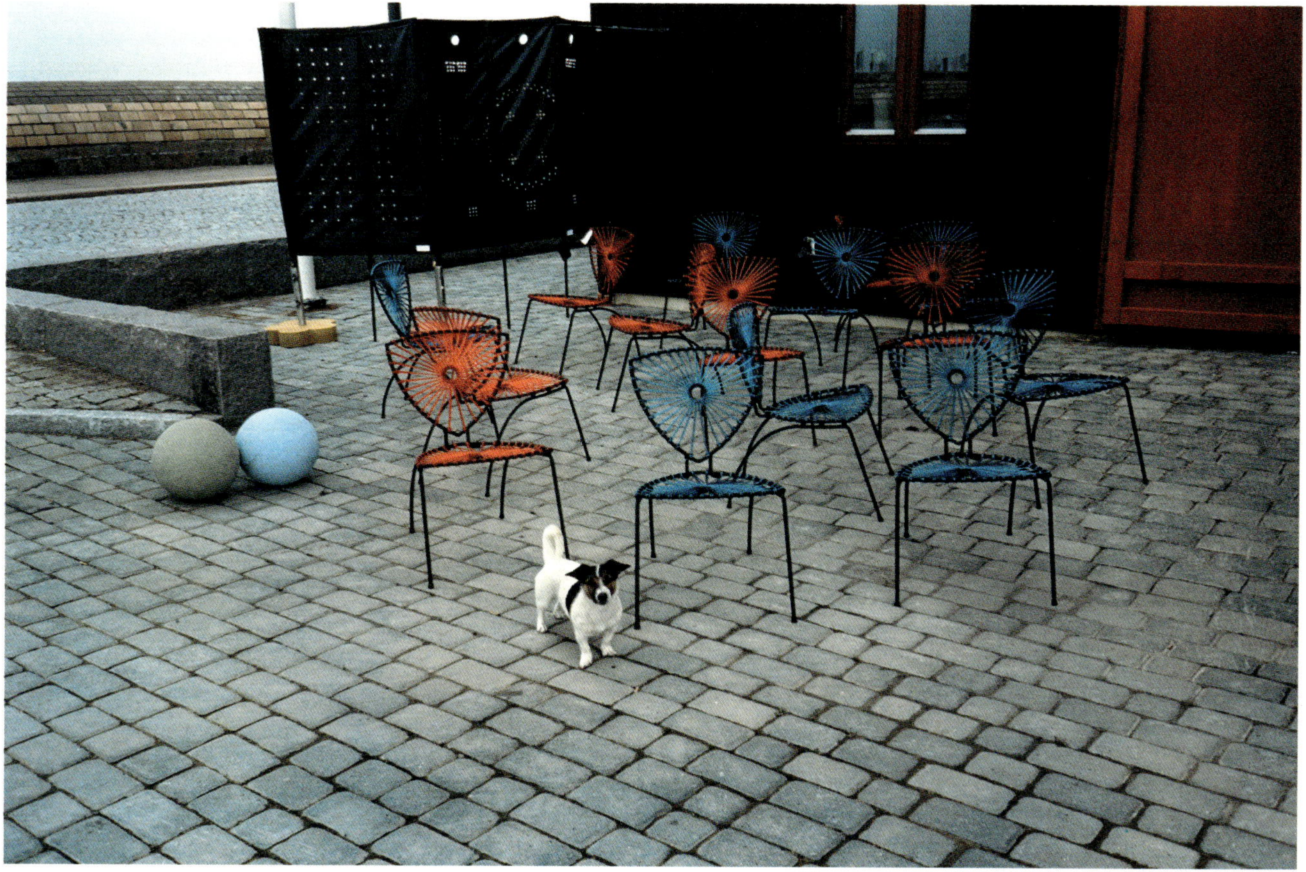

Tuesday, July 20. Helsingborg, Sweden. Street scene

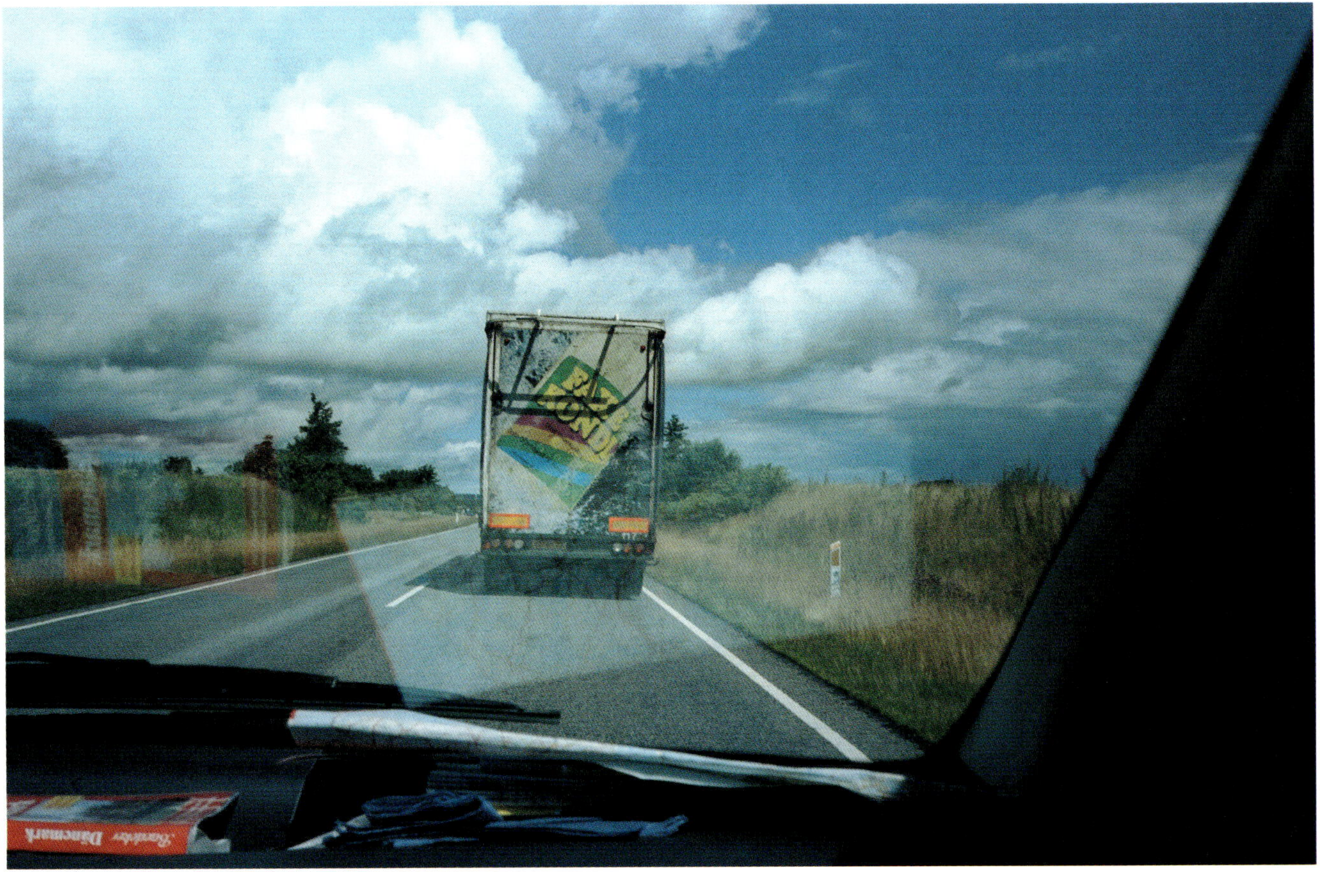

Wednesday, July 21. Jutland, Denmark. Road scene

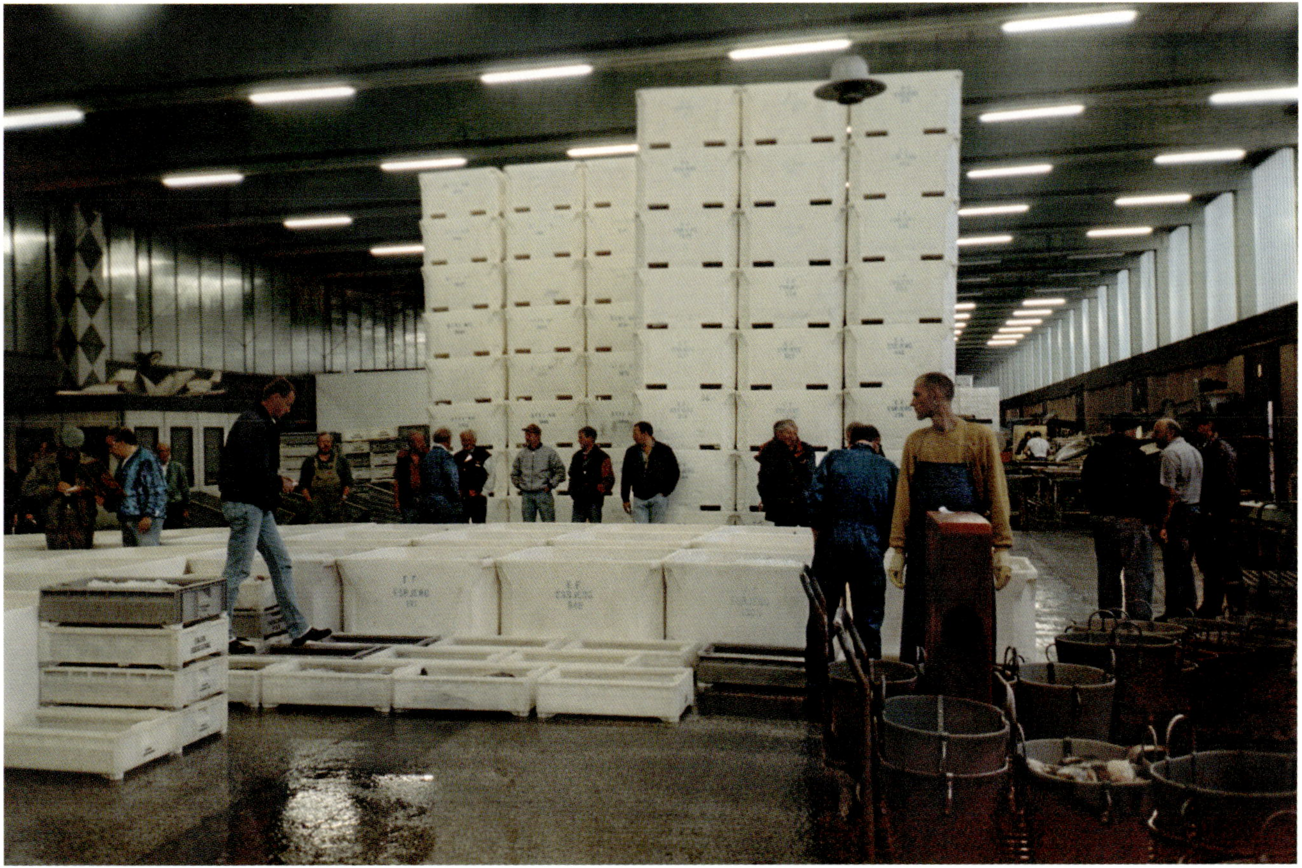

Thursday, July 22. Esbjerg, Denmark, fish market

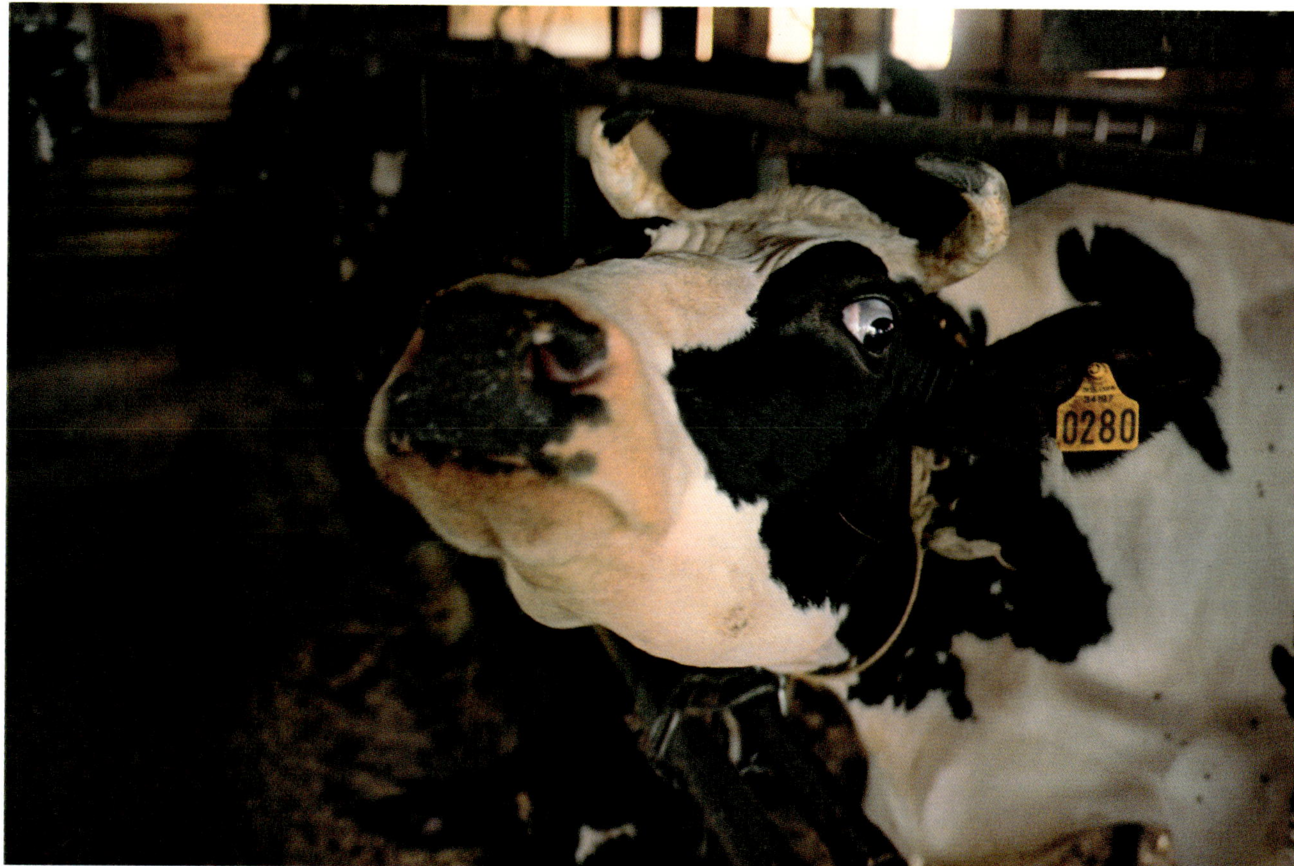

Friday, July 23. Jutland, Denmark. Farm scene

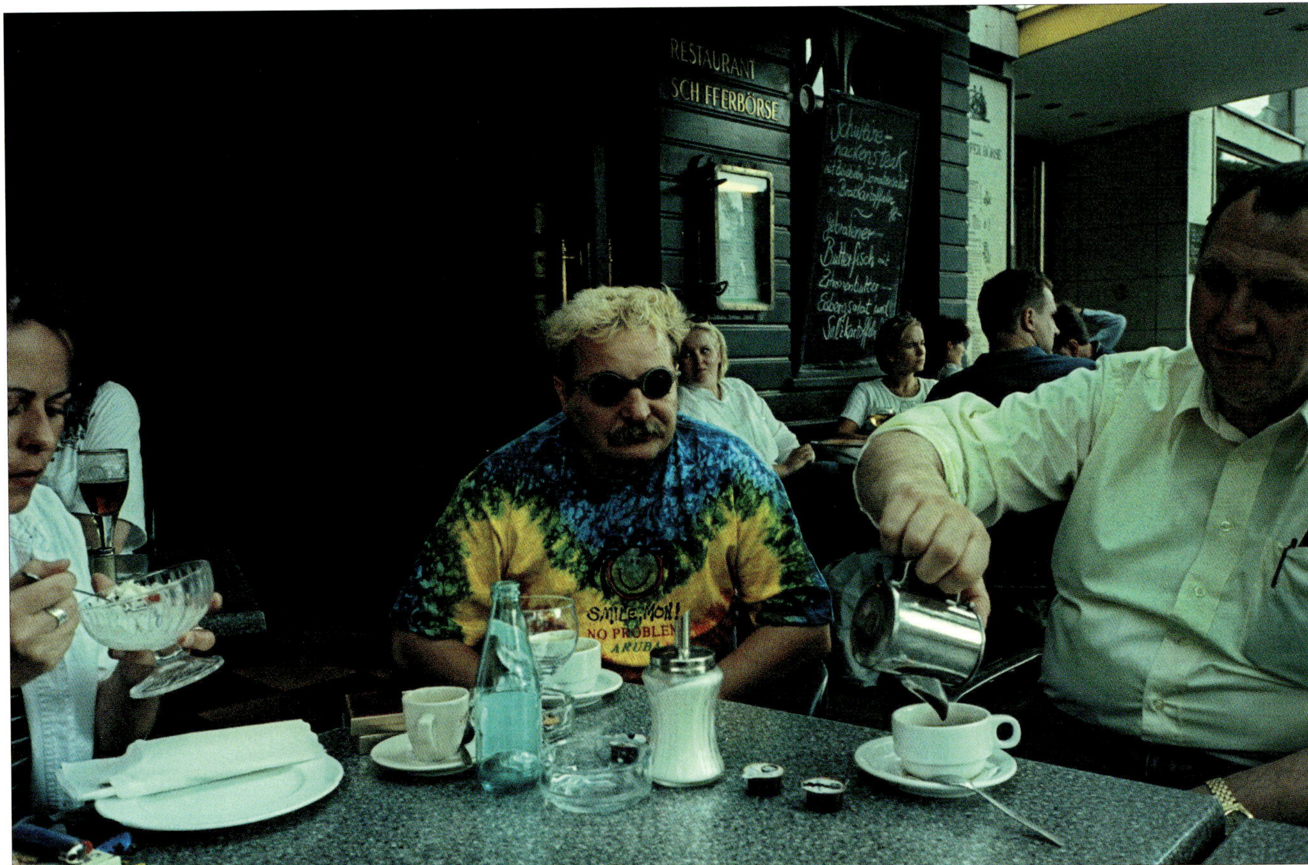

Saturday, July 24. Hamburg, Germany. On a café terrace

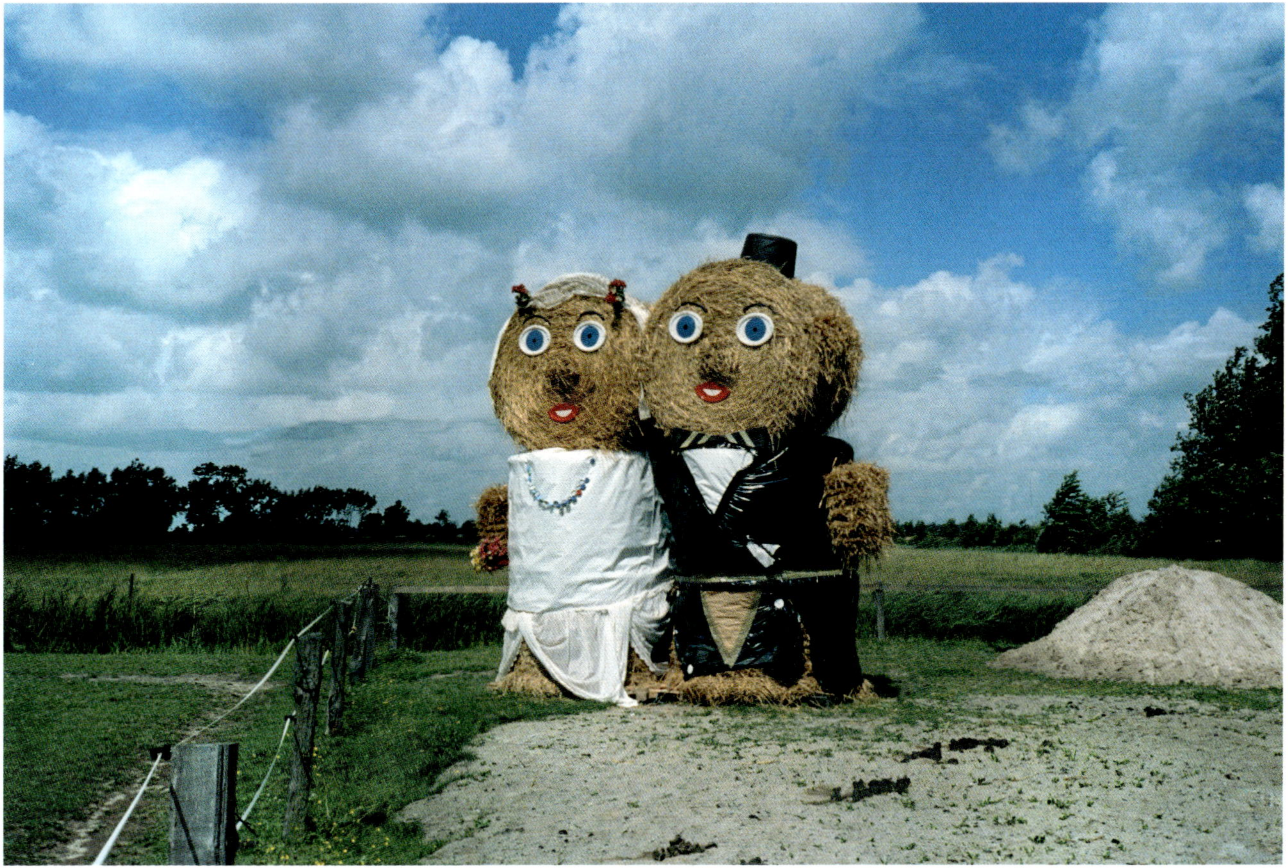

Saturday, July 24. Schleswig-Holstein, Germany. Farm scene: newly-weds announce their marriage

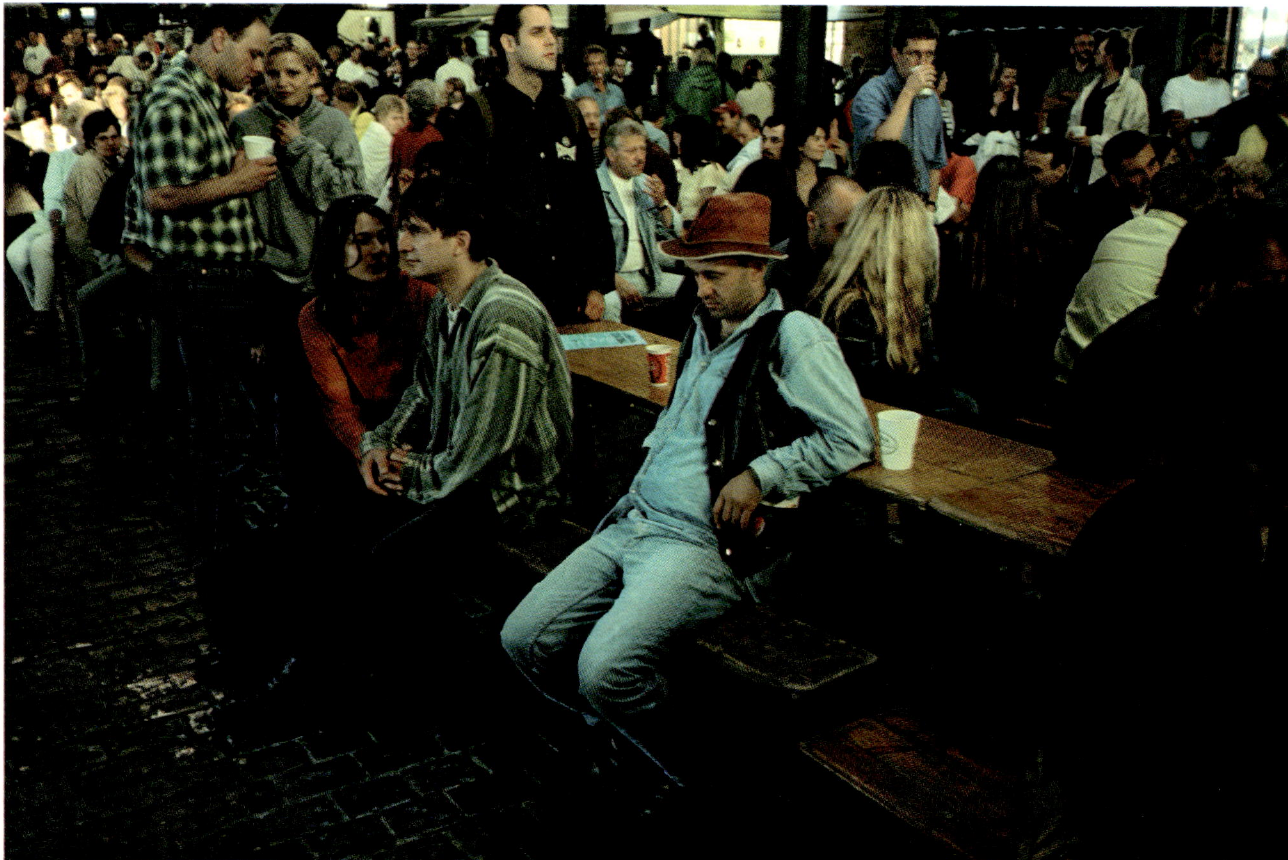

Sunday, July 25. Hamburg, Germany. In the Fisch-Halle, early Sunday morning

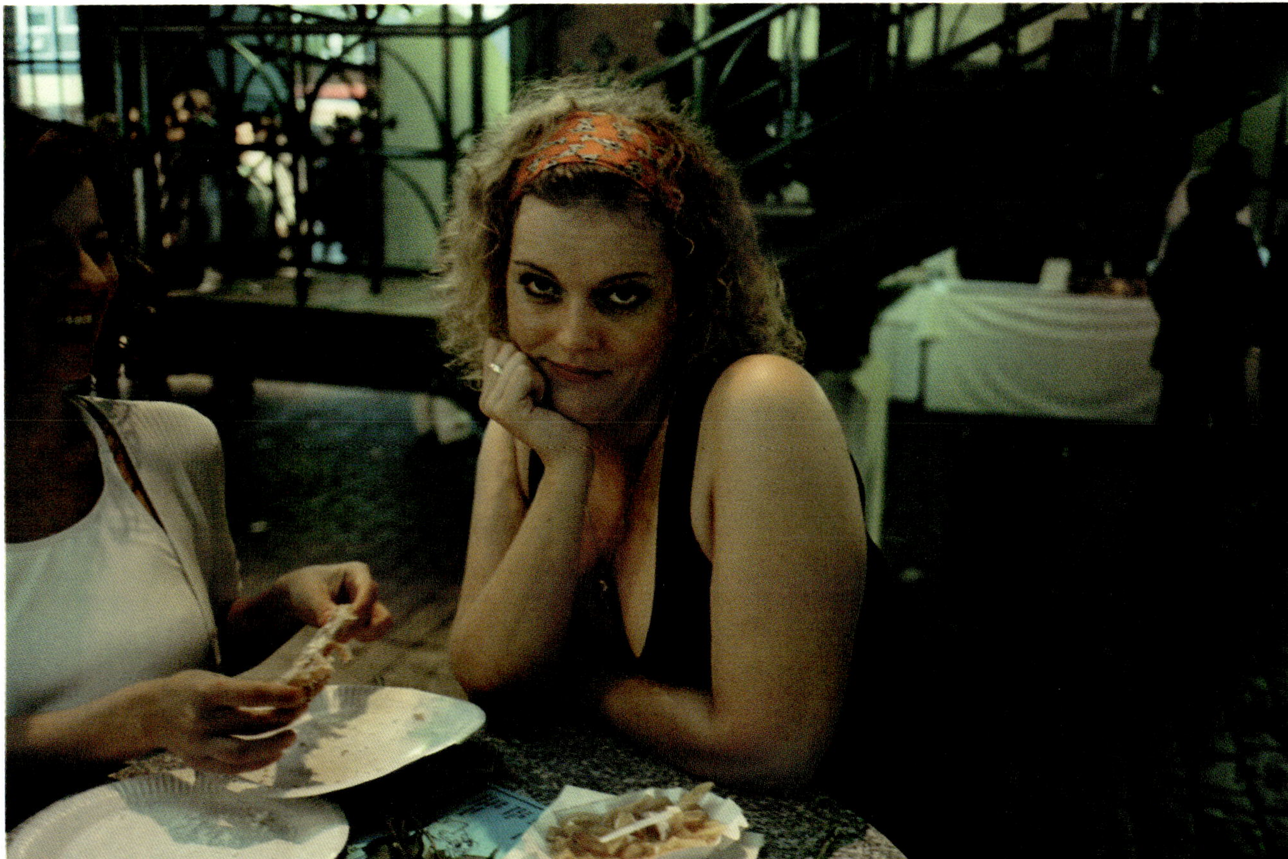

Sunday, July 25. Hamburg, Germany. In the Fisch-Halle, early Sunday morning

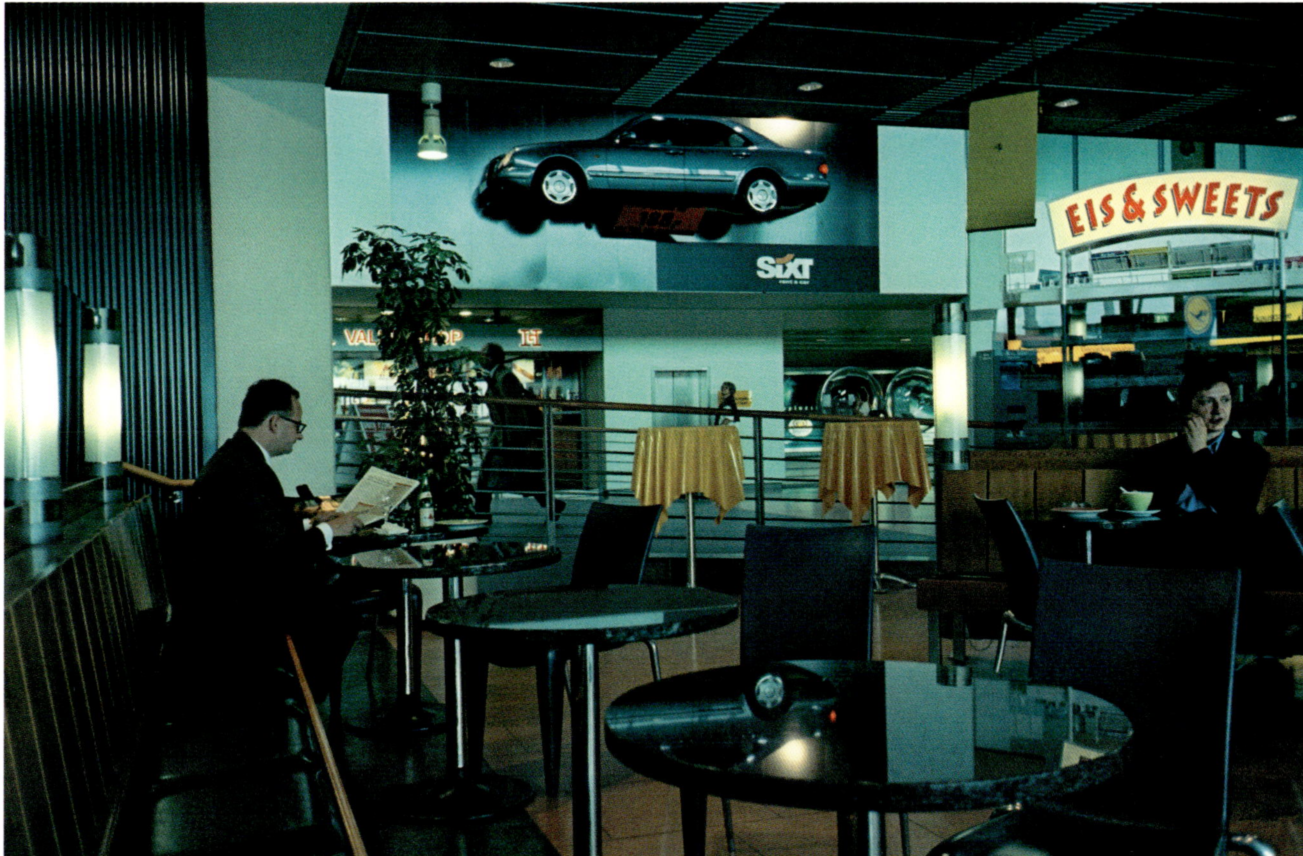

Monday, July 26. Hamburg, Germany. Airport scene

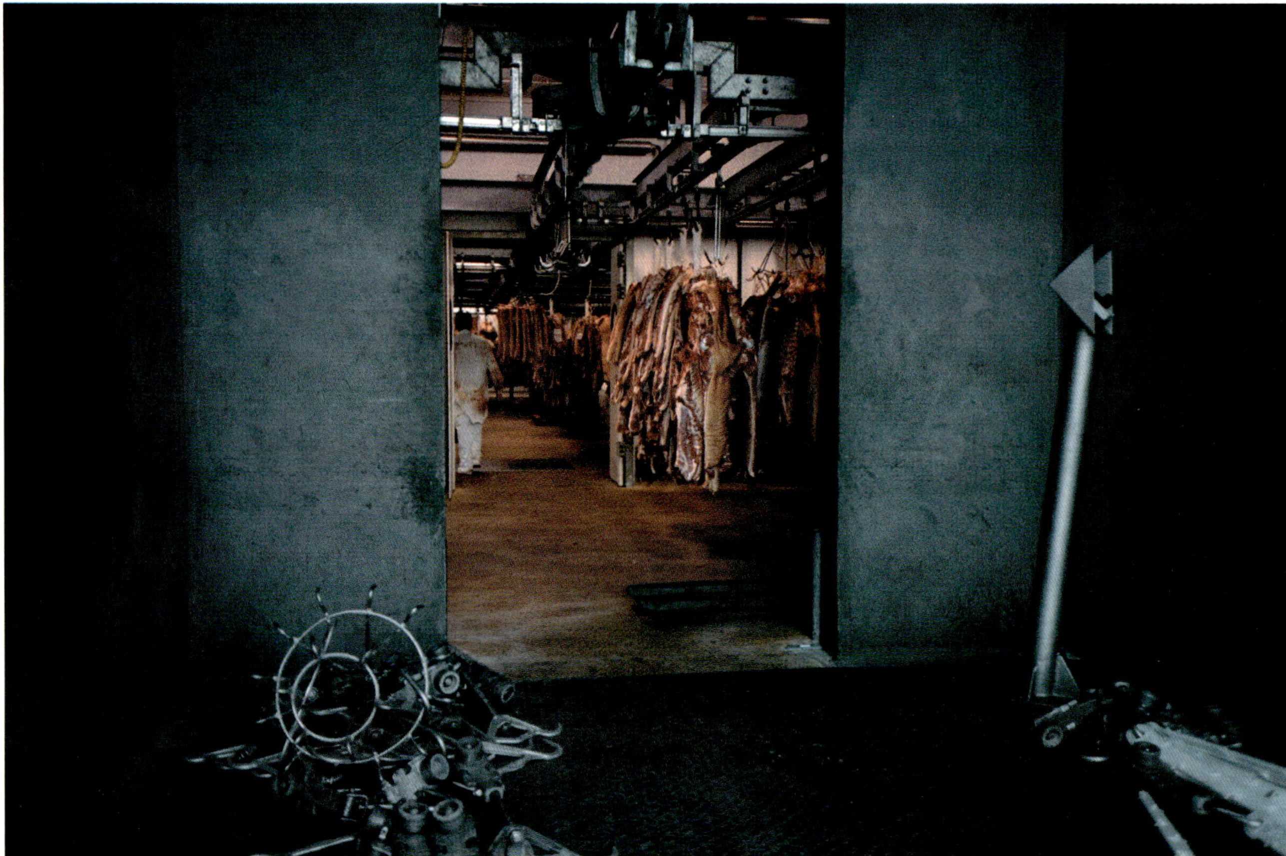

Tuesday, July 27. Paris. In the wholesale meat market, Paris-Rungis

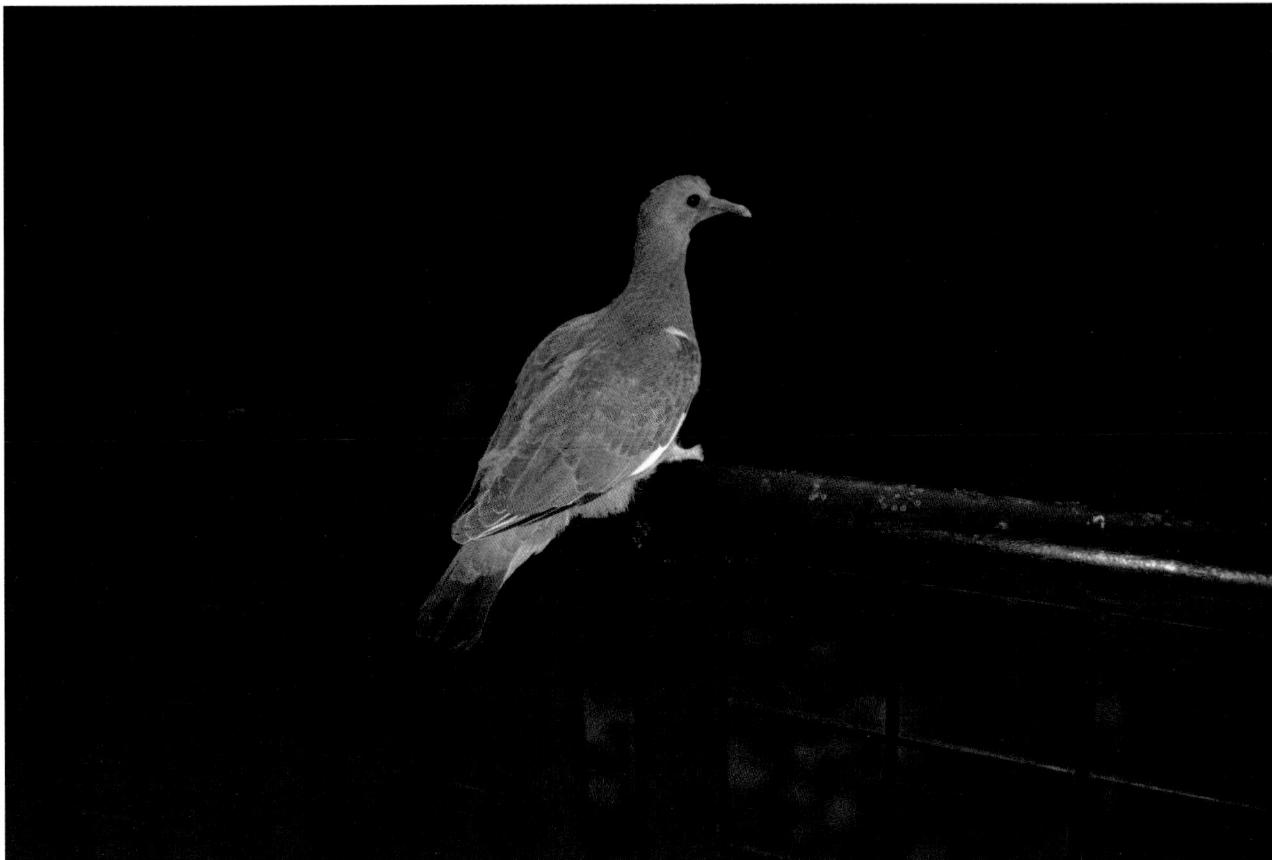

Wednesday, July 28. Boulogne, France. A dying pigeon (see note)

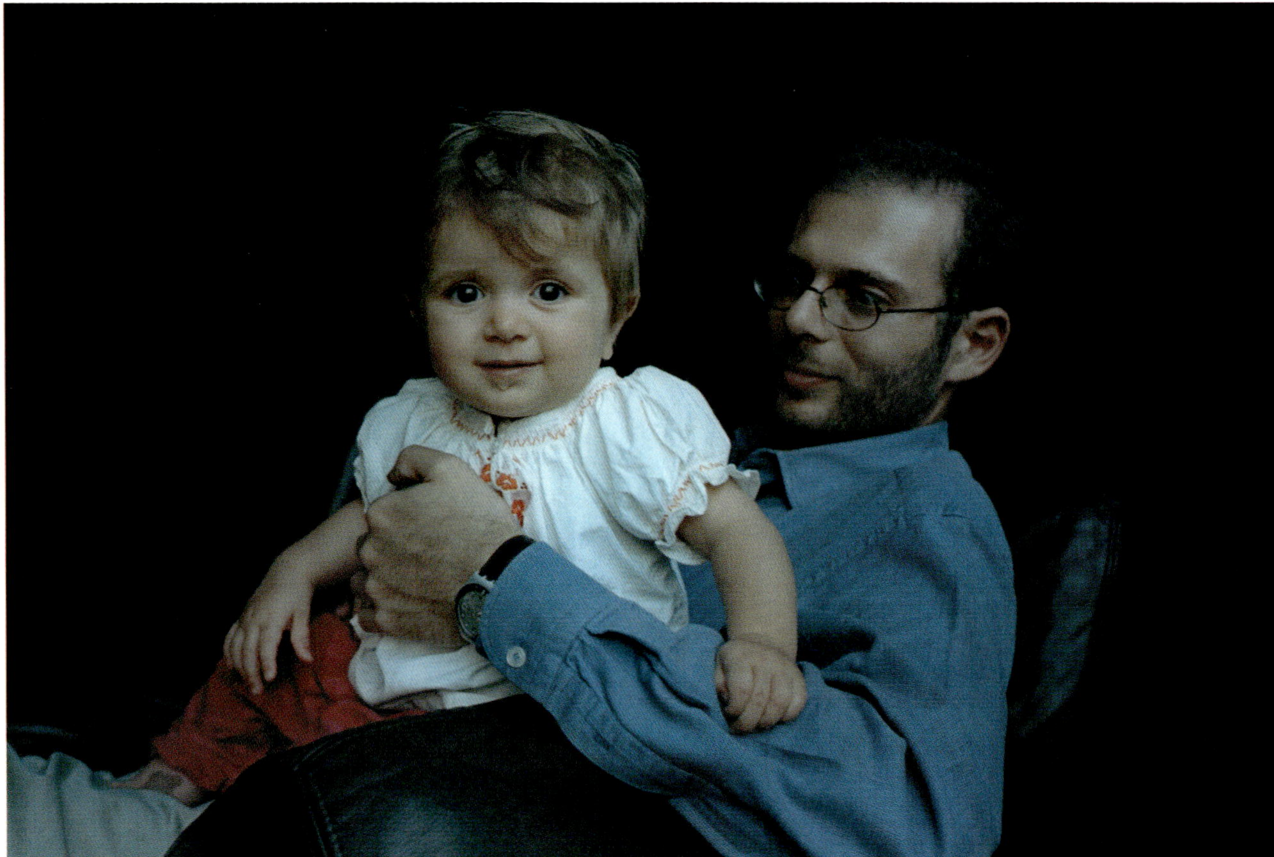

Thursday, July 29. Boulogne, France. David Horvat with his daughter Saskia

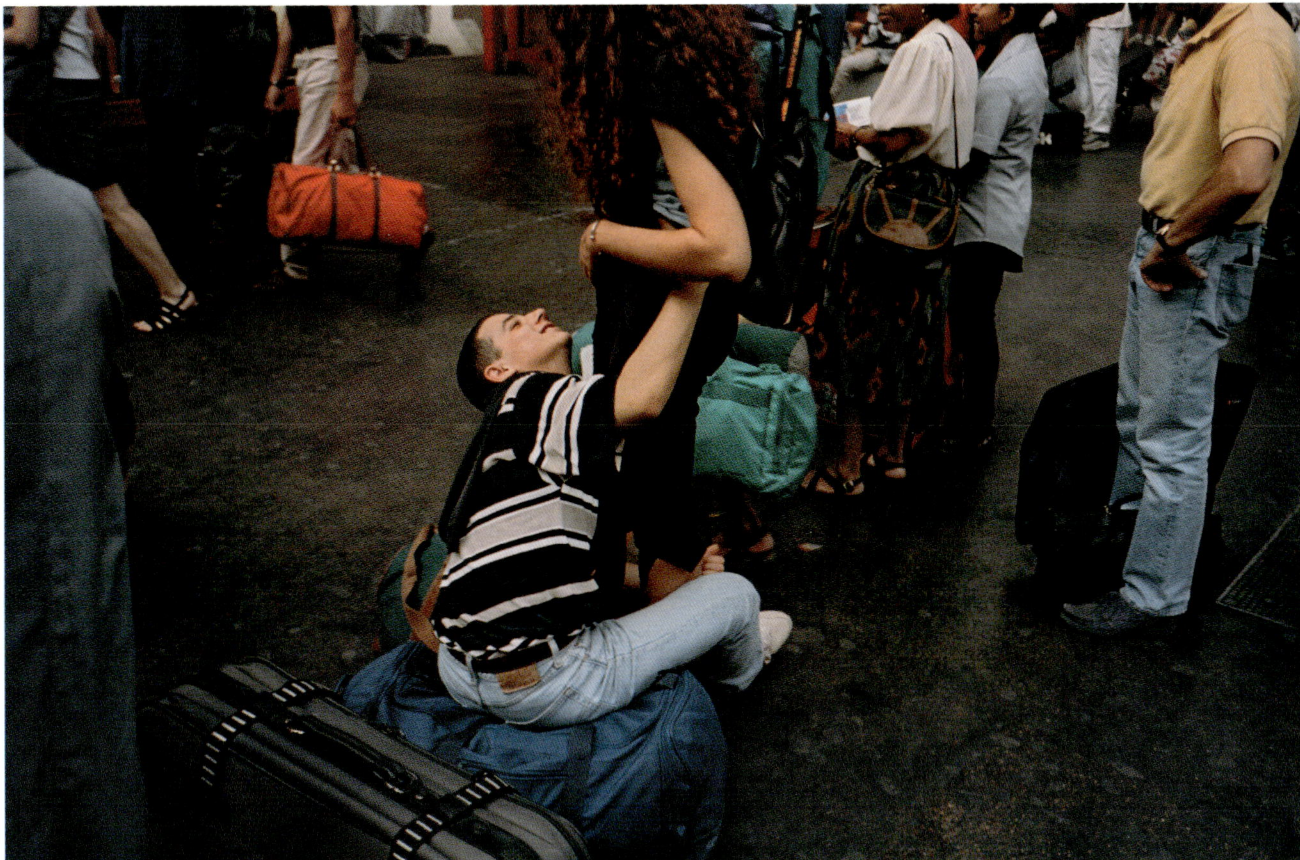

Friday, July 30. Paris. Gare de Lyon, holiday departures

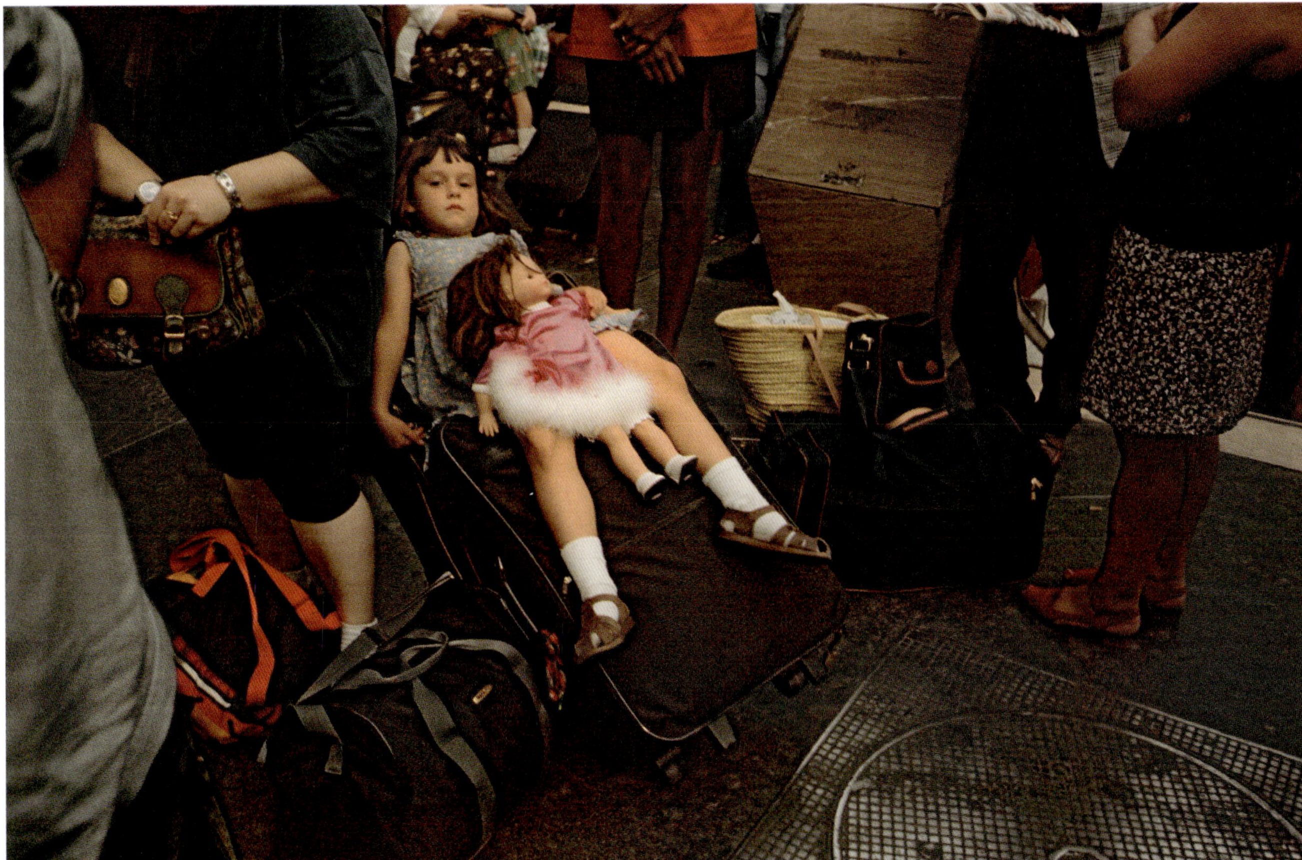

Saturday, July 31. Paris. Gare de Lyon, holiday departures

AUGUST

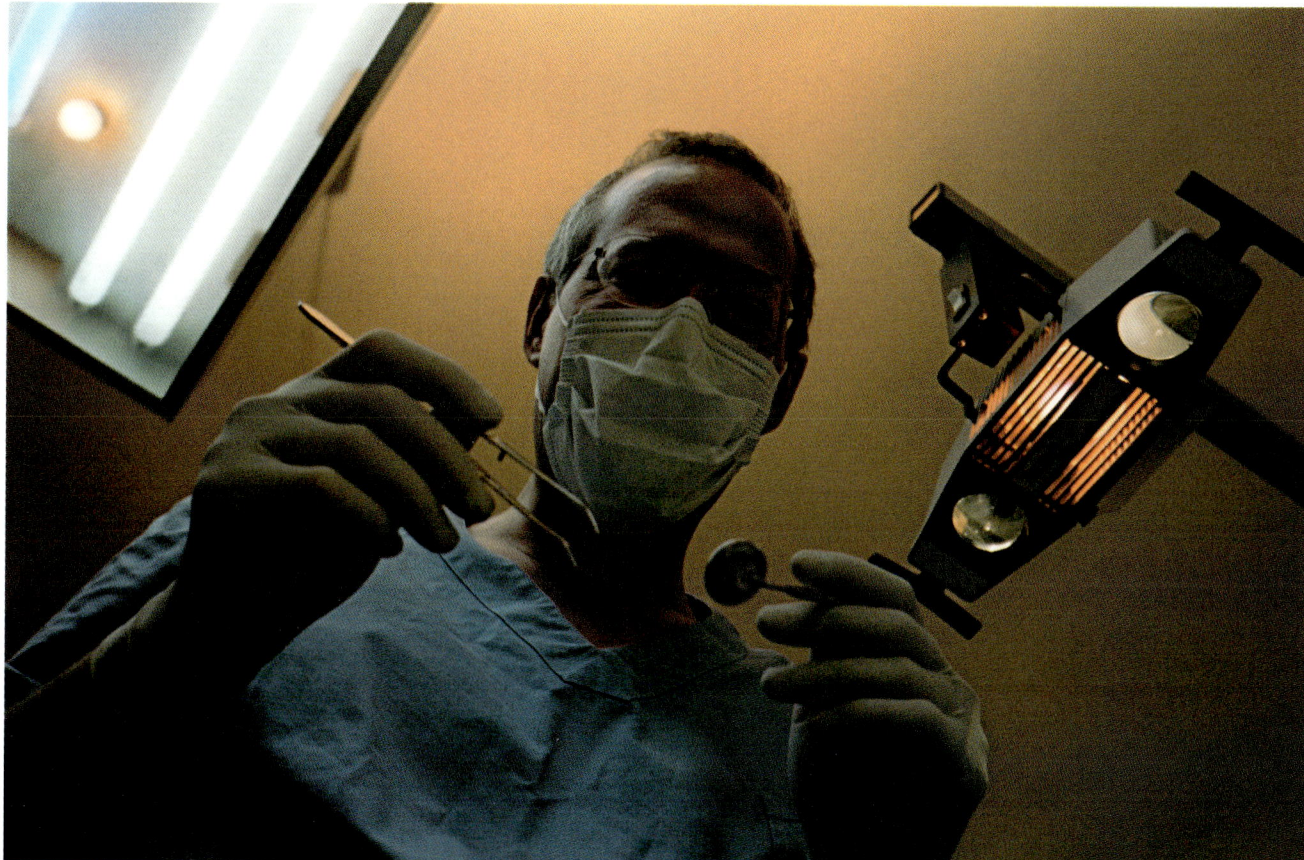

Sunday, August 1. Paris. Dr. Dominique Boës, my dentist (who occasionally works Sundays)

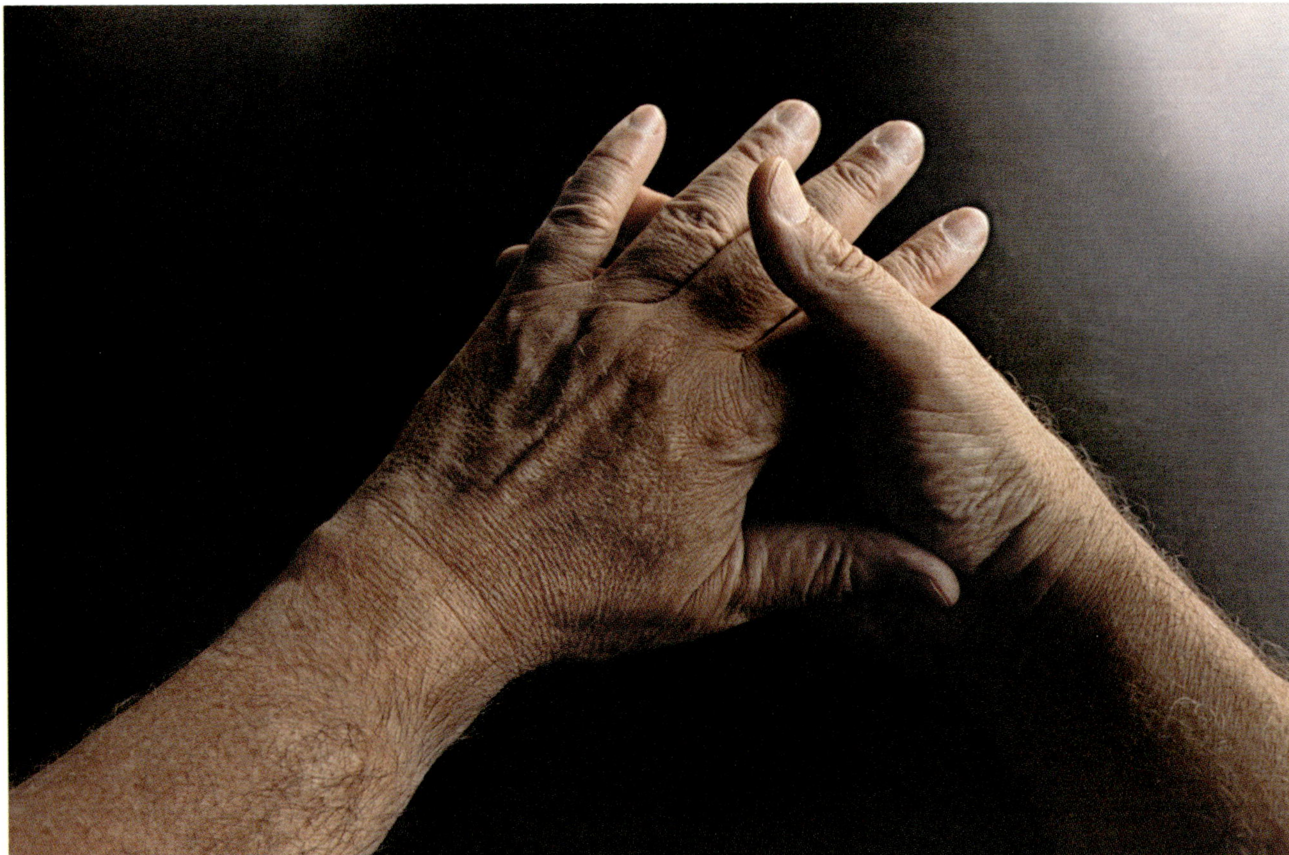

Monday, August 2. Boulogne, France. Self-portrait

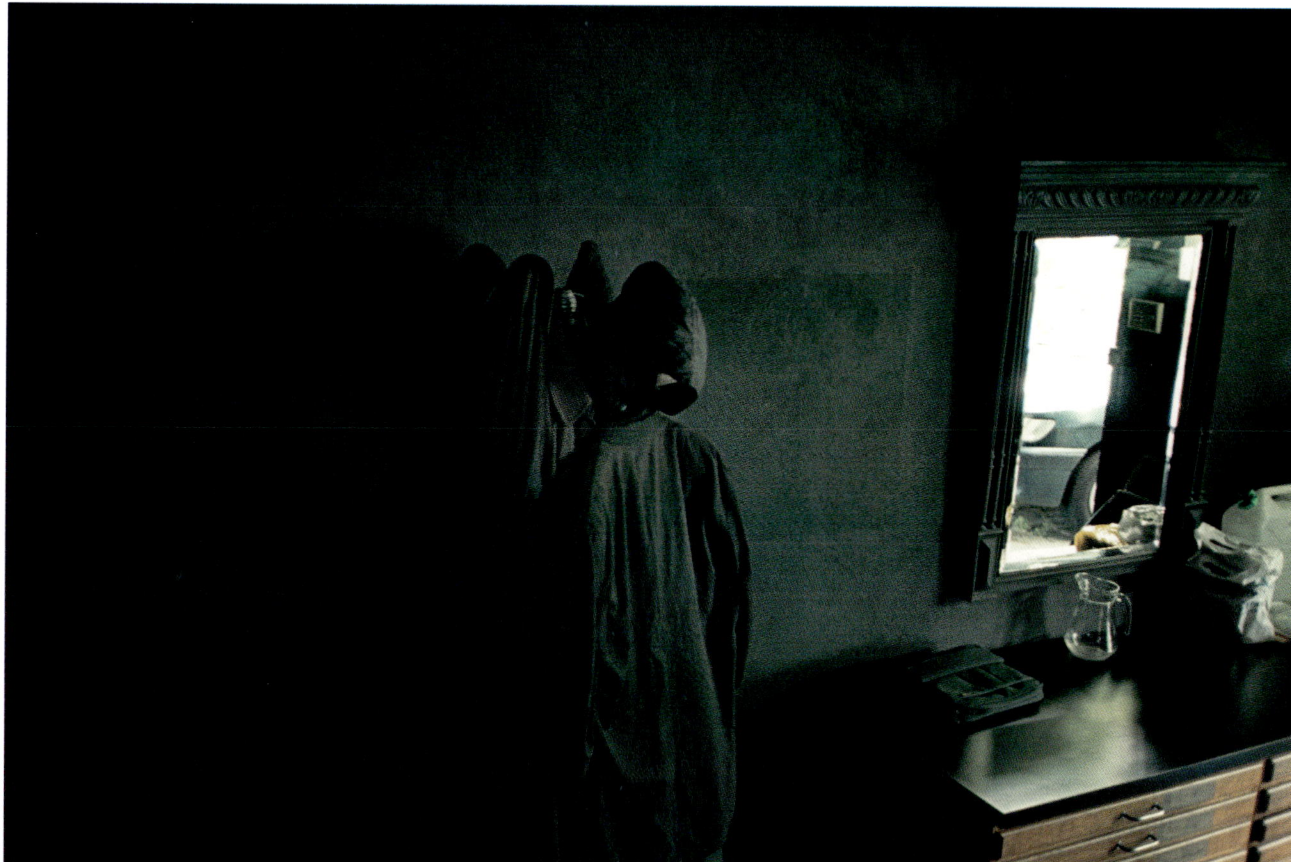

Tuesday, August 3. Boulogne, France. The entrance to my studio

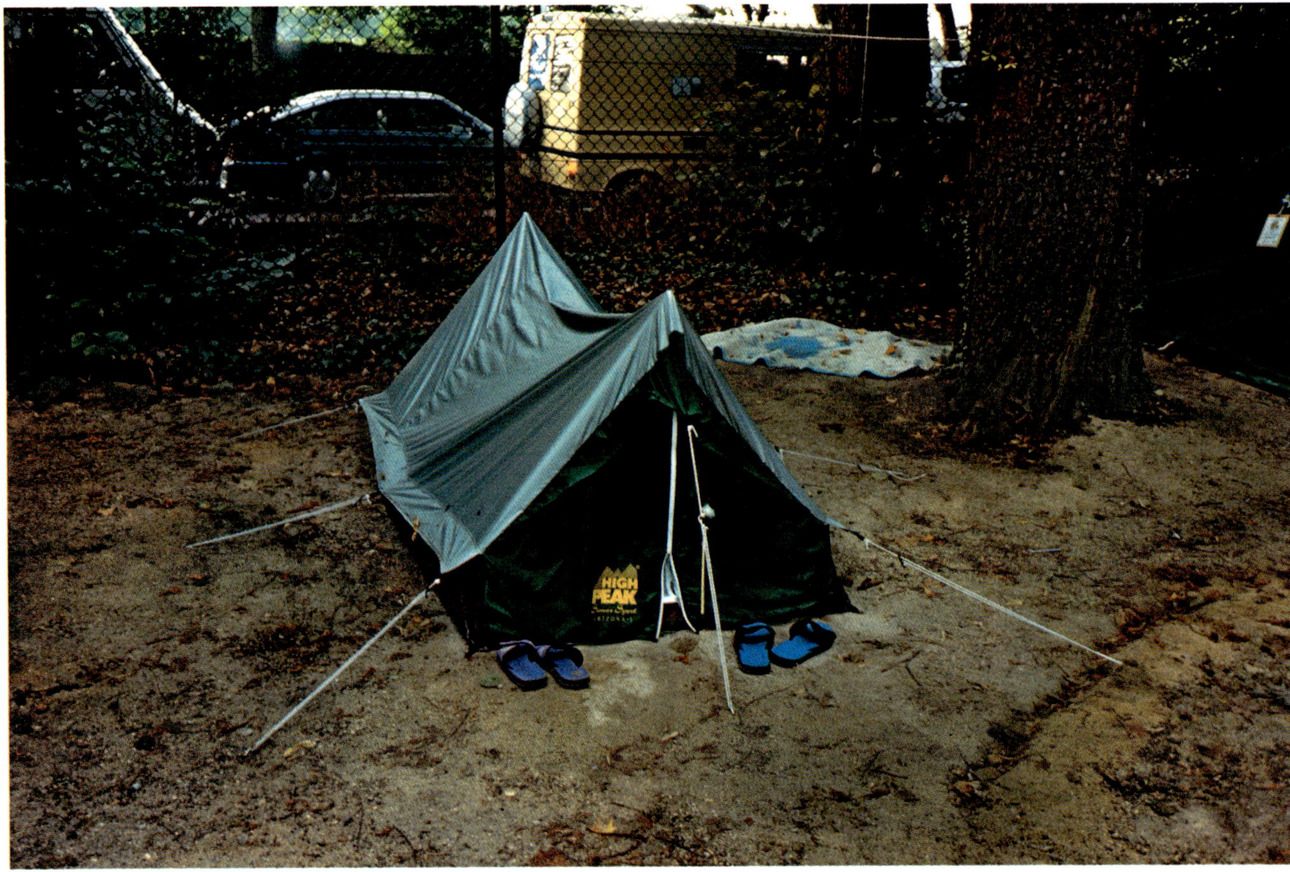

Wednesday, August 4. Paris. In the camping area of the Bois de Boulogne

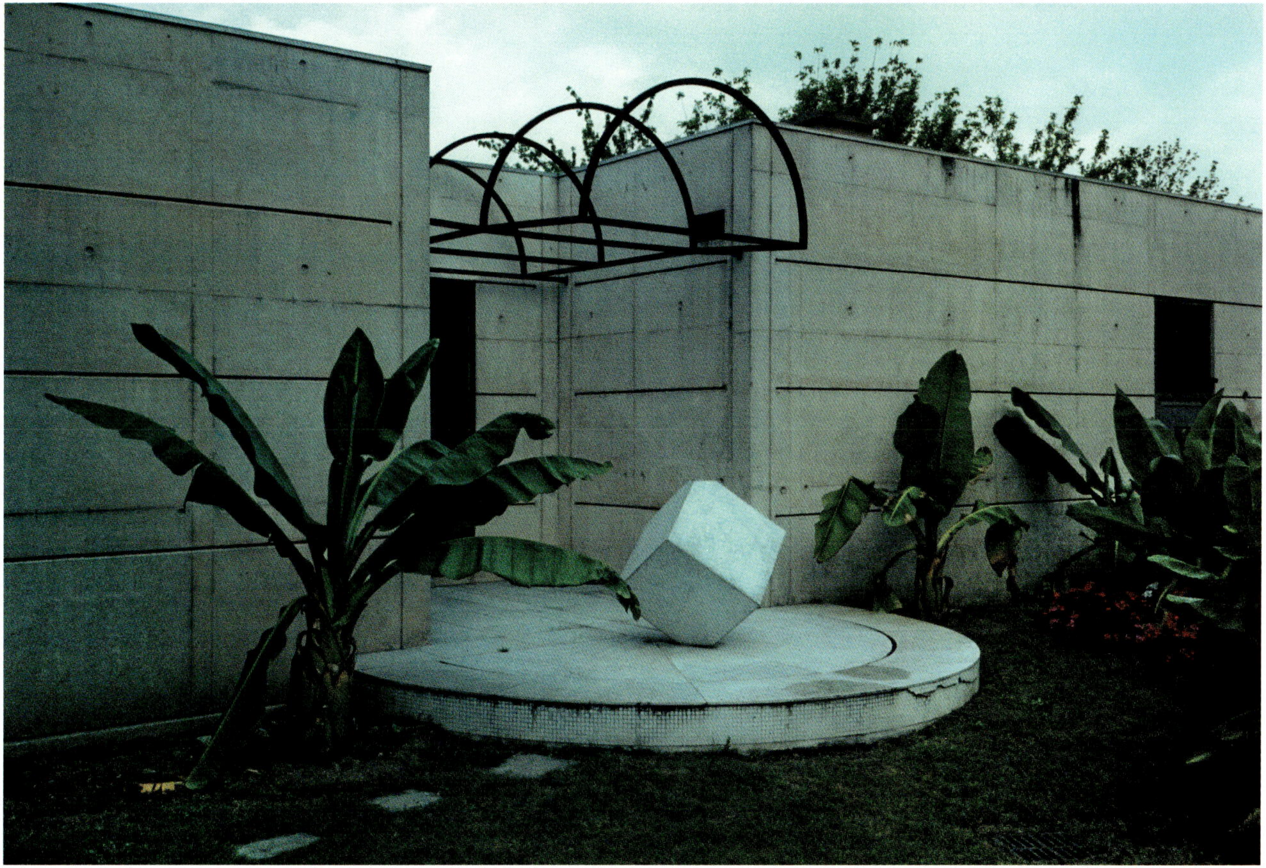

Thursday, August 5. Cergy-Pontoise, France. A piece of contemporary art

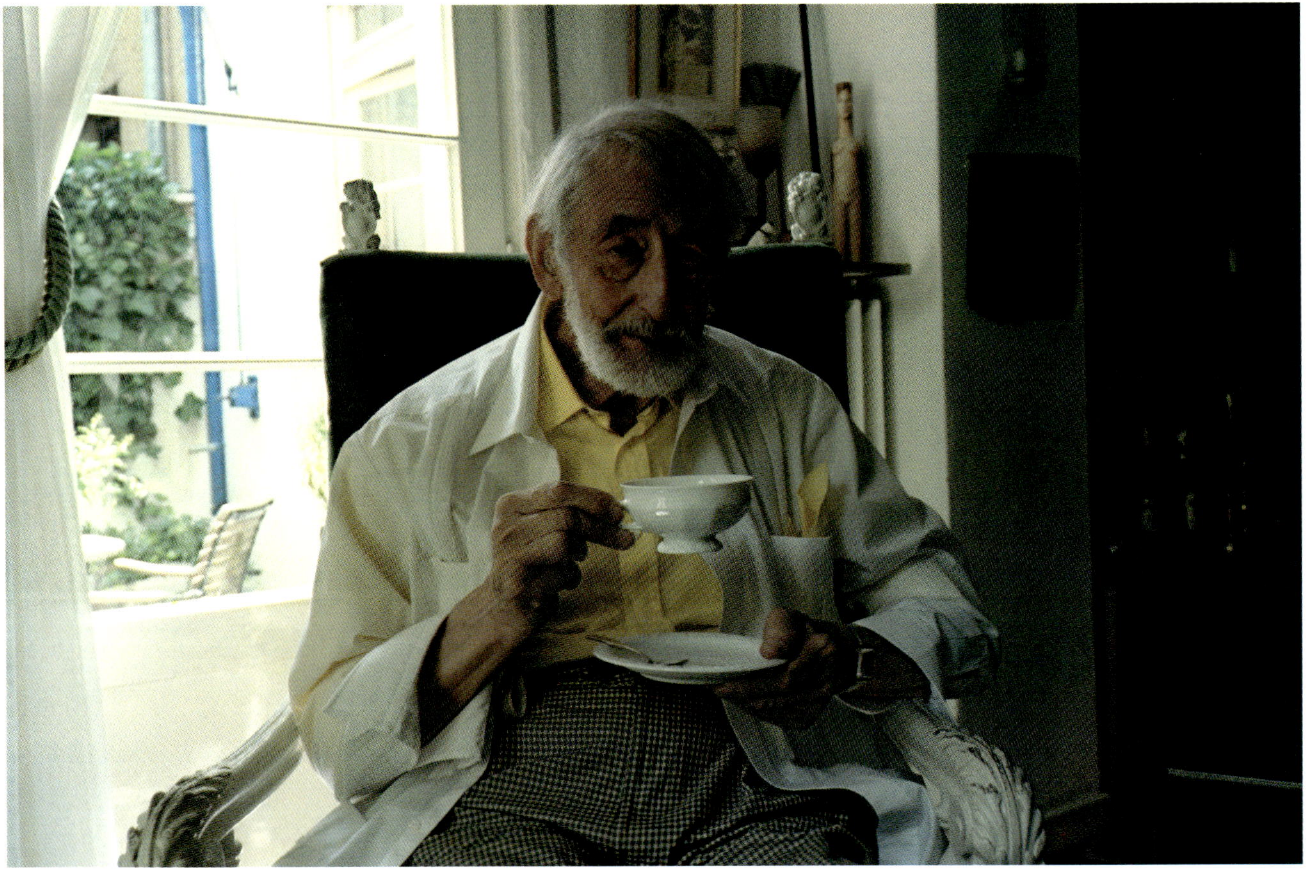

Friday, August 6. Cologne, Germany. Professor Fritz Gruber, at his home

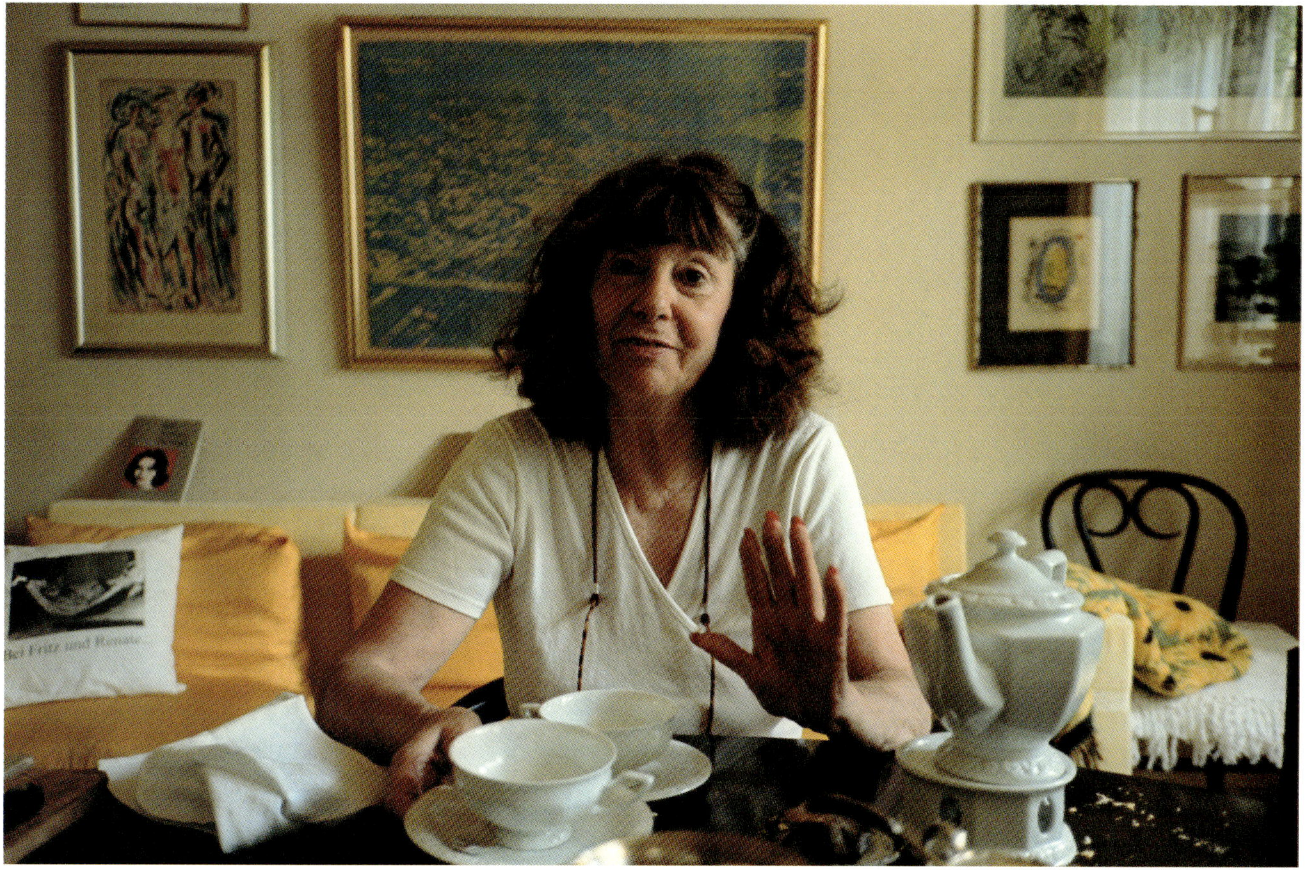

Friday, August 6. Cologne, Germany. Renate Gruber, Fritz Gruber's wife

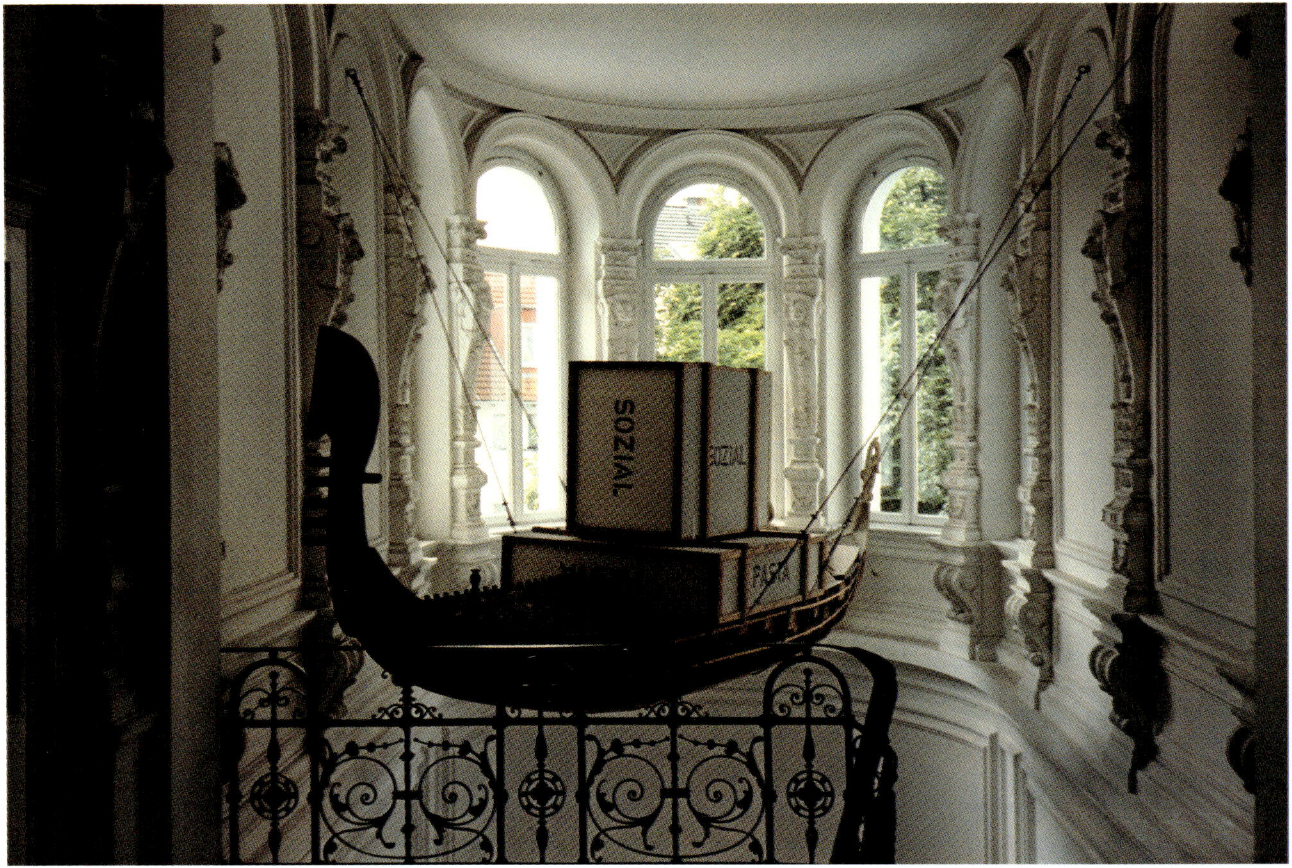

Saturday, August 7. Cologne, Germany. Work from the collection of publisher Benedikt Taschen

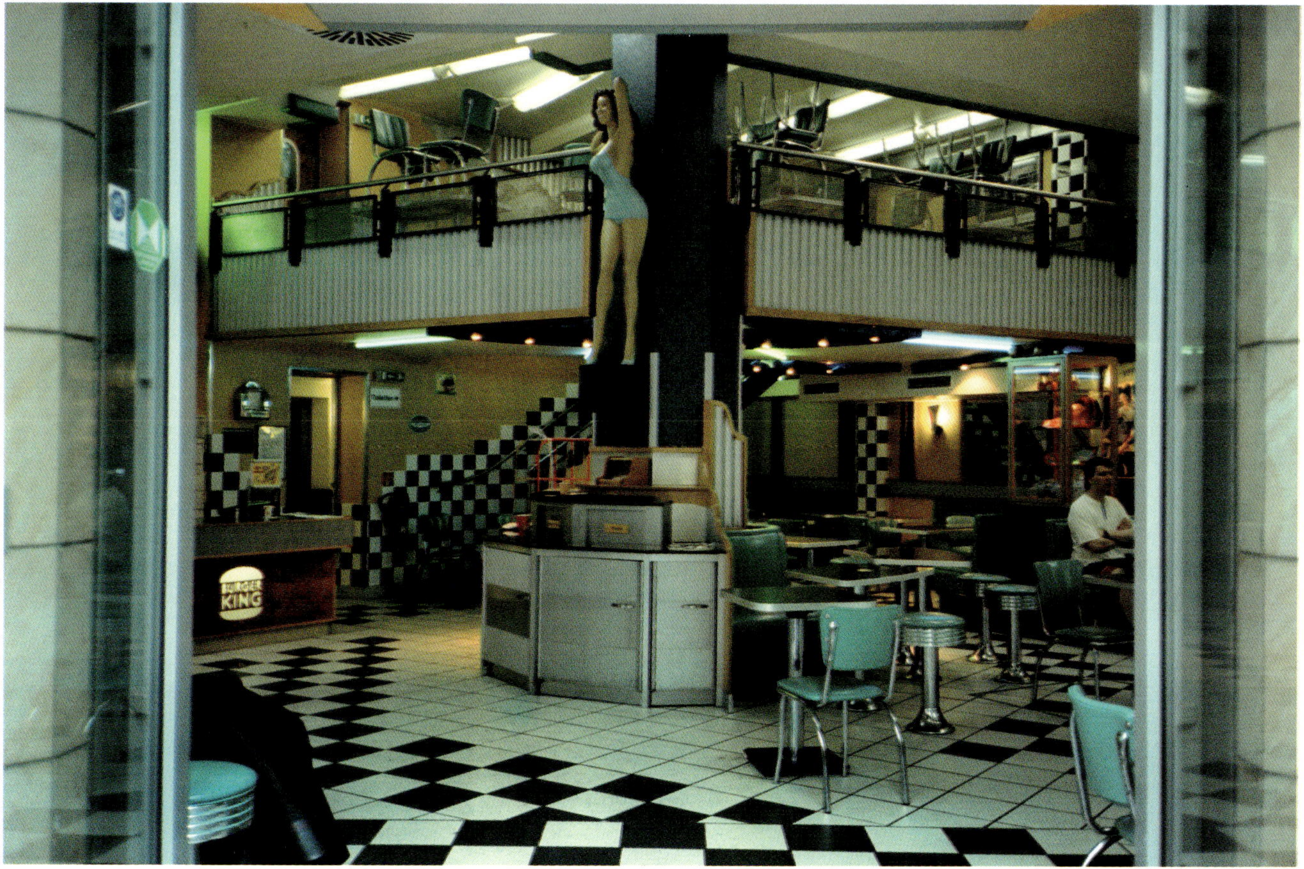

Sunday, August 8. Cologne, Germany. A snack bar on Hohenzoller-Ring

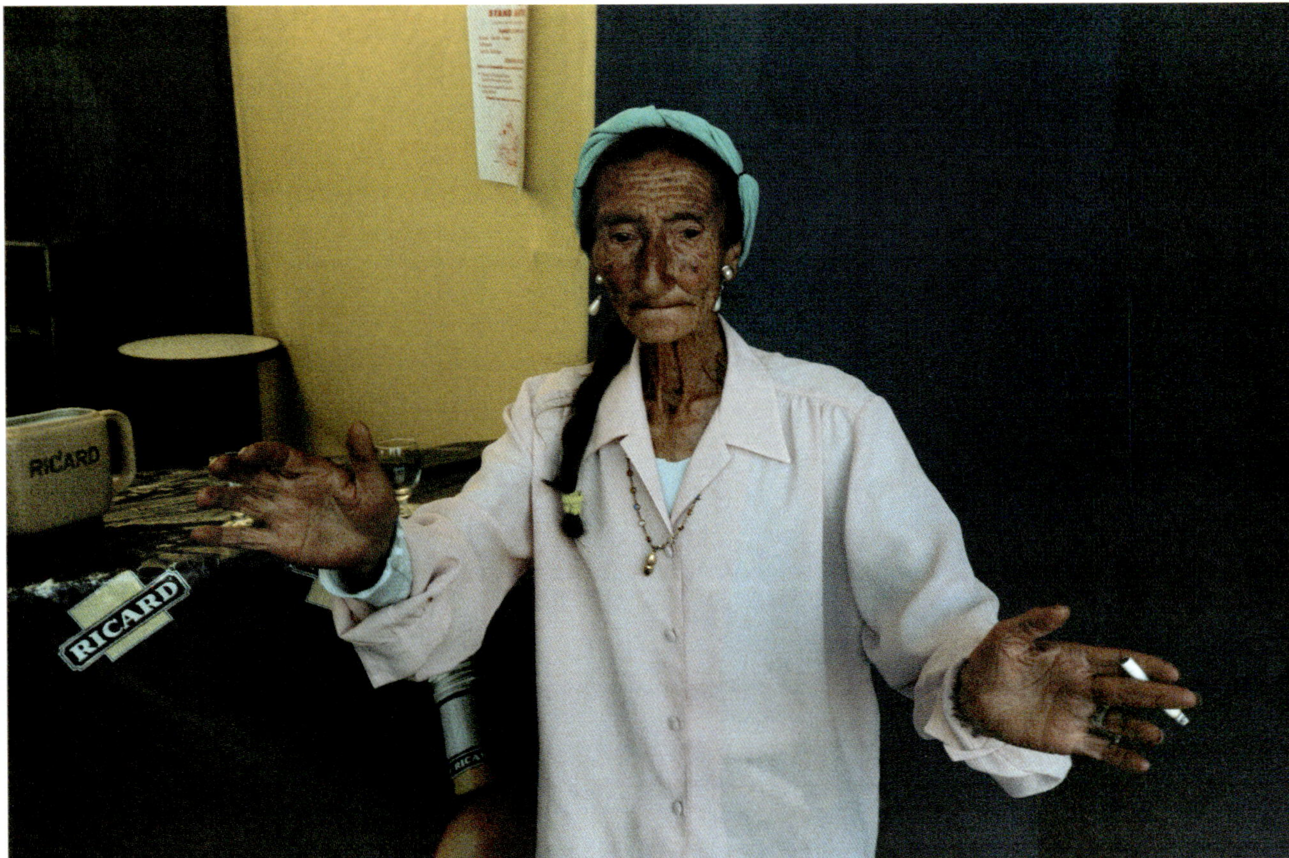

Monday, August 9. La Courneuve, France. Street encounter

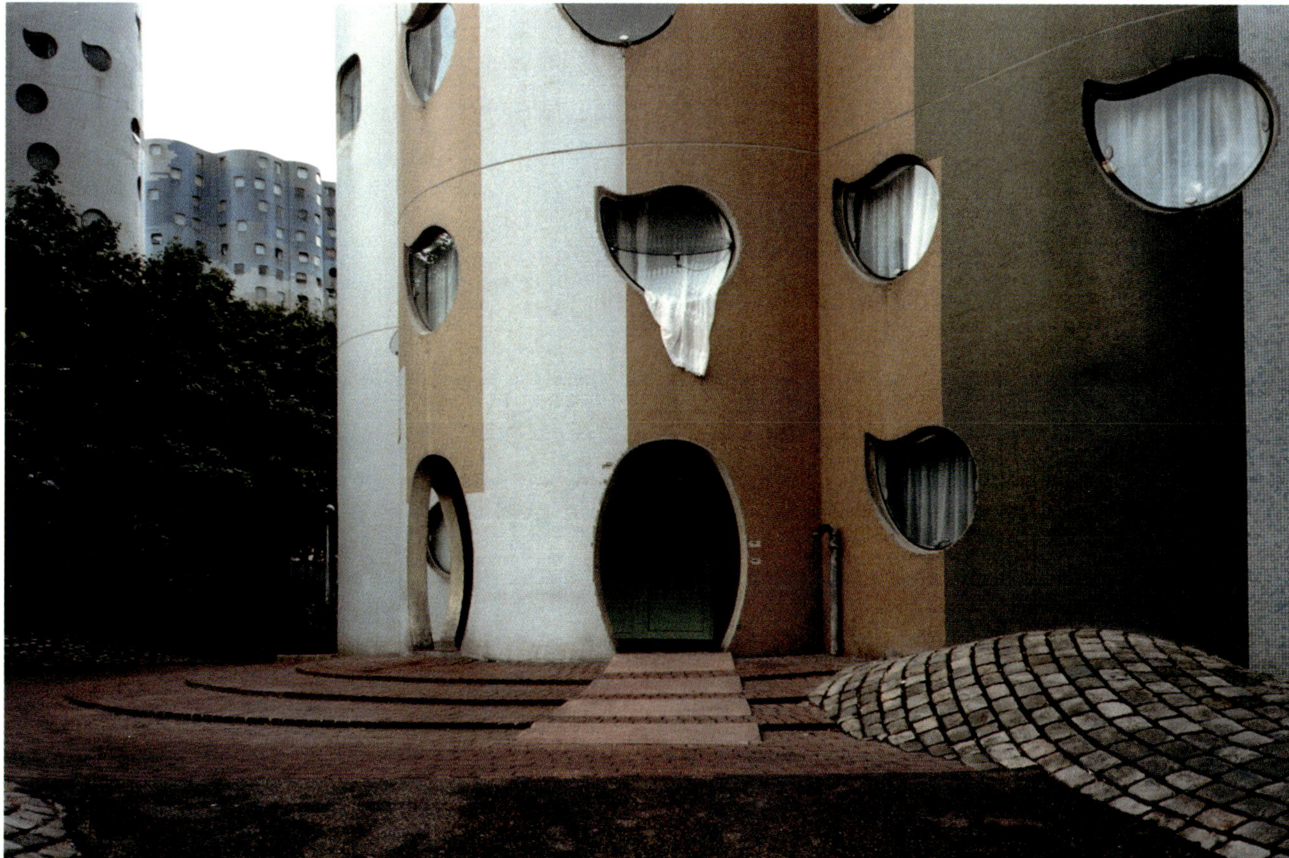

Tuesday, August 10. Puteaux, France. Les Nuages apartment buildings

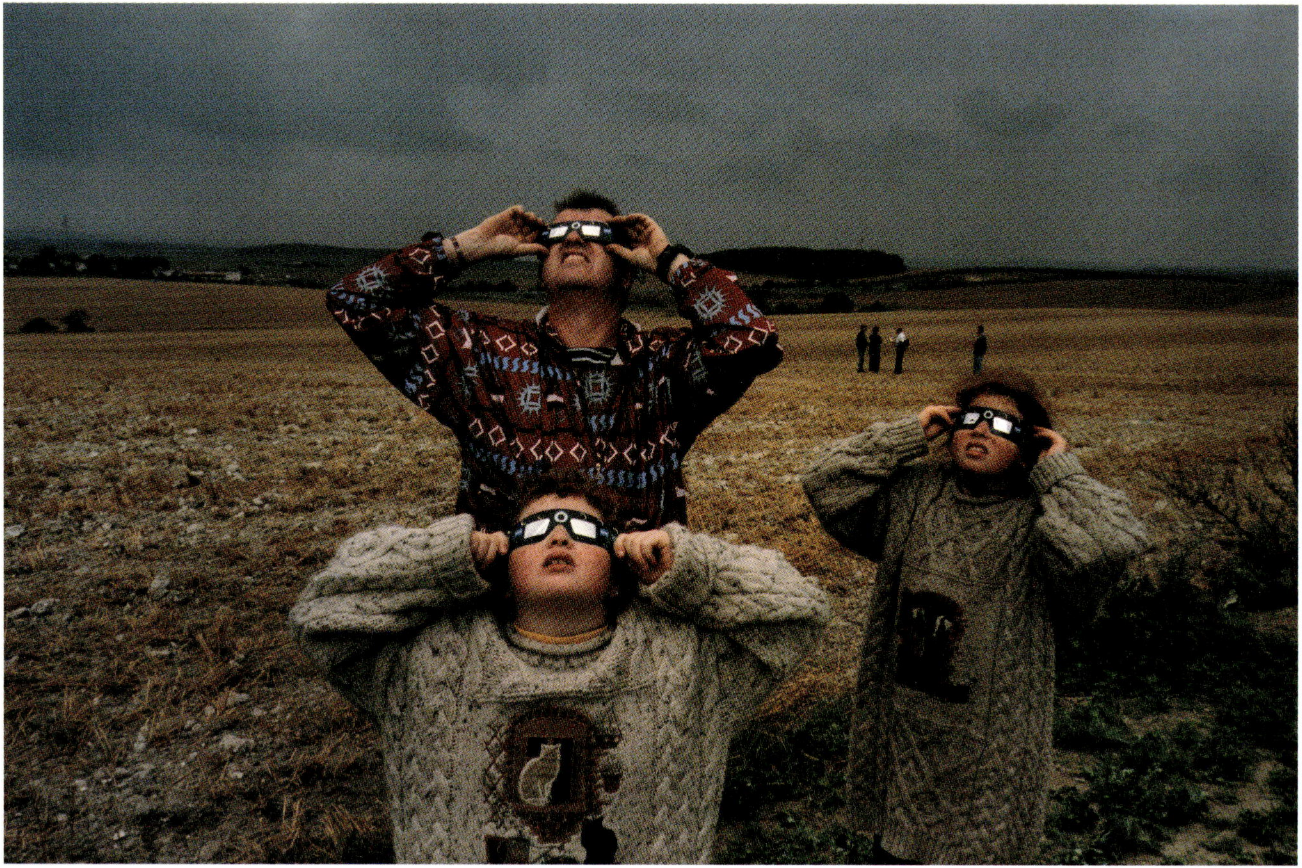

Wednesday, August 11. Near Reims, France. Watching the eclipse

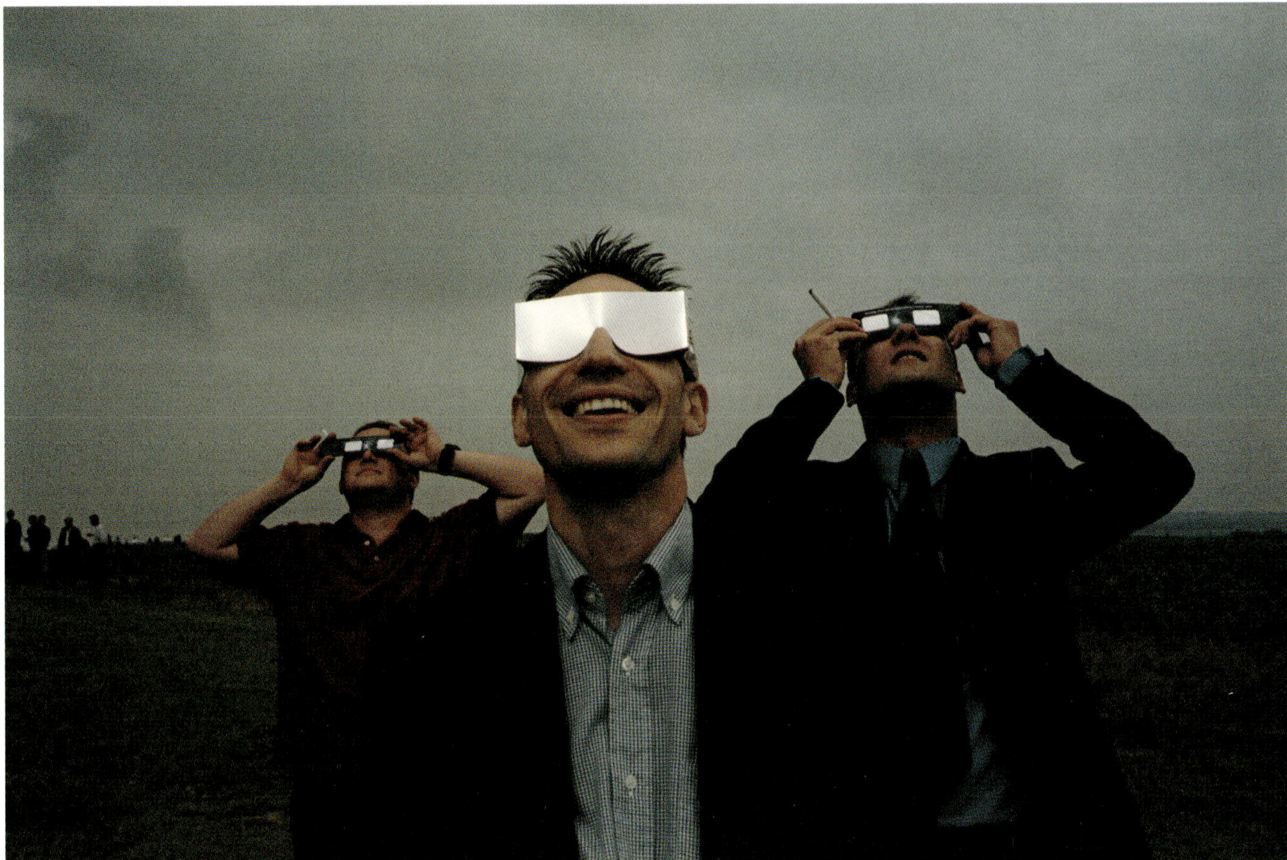

Wednesday, August 11. Near Reims, France. Watching the eclipse

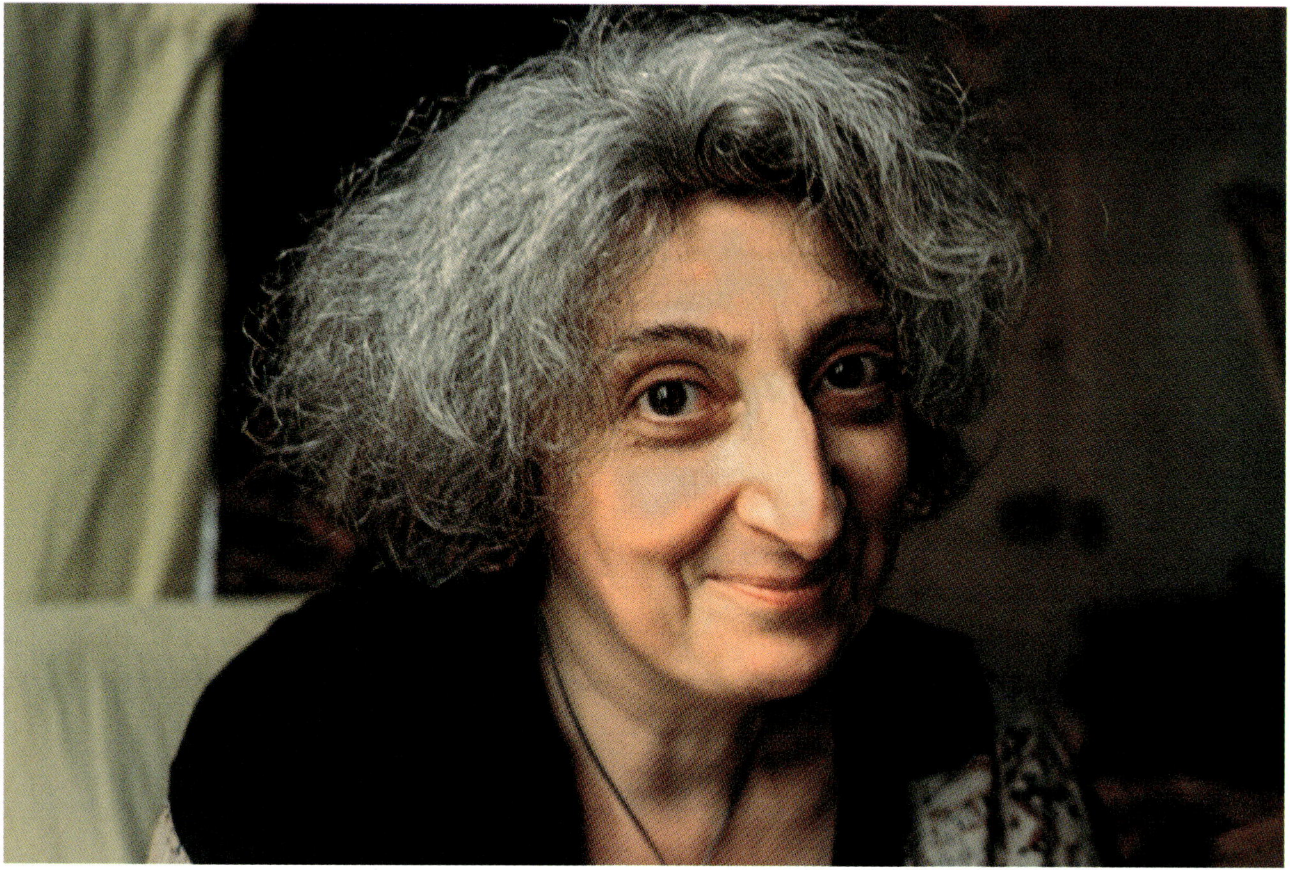

Thursday, August 12. Paris. Araxie Toutghalian, art expert

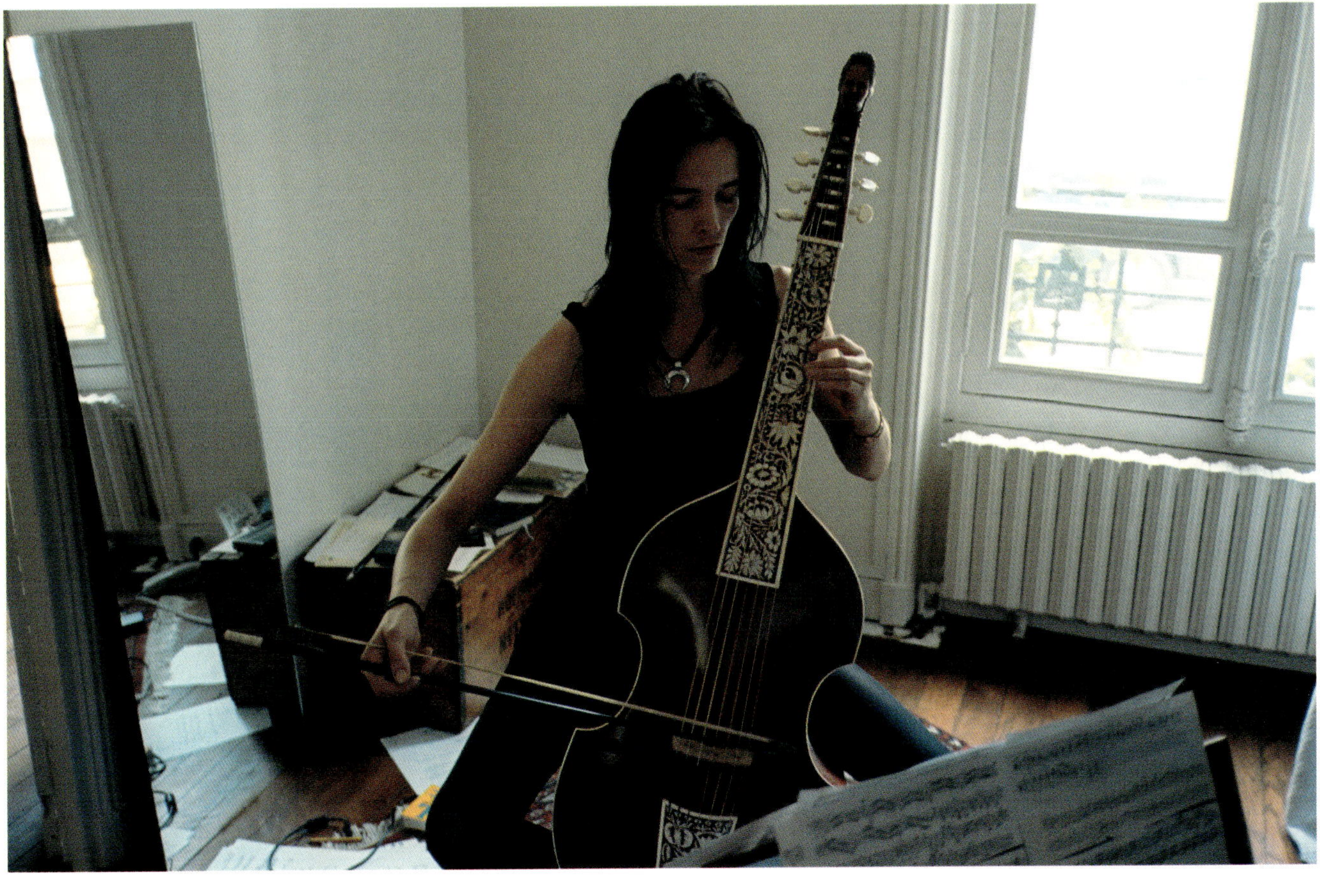

Friday, August 13. Boulogne, France. Hille Perl, musician

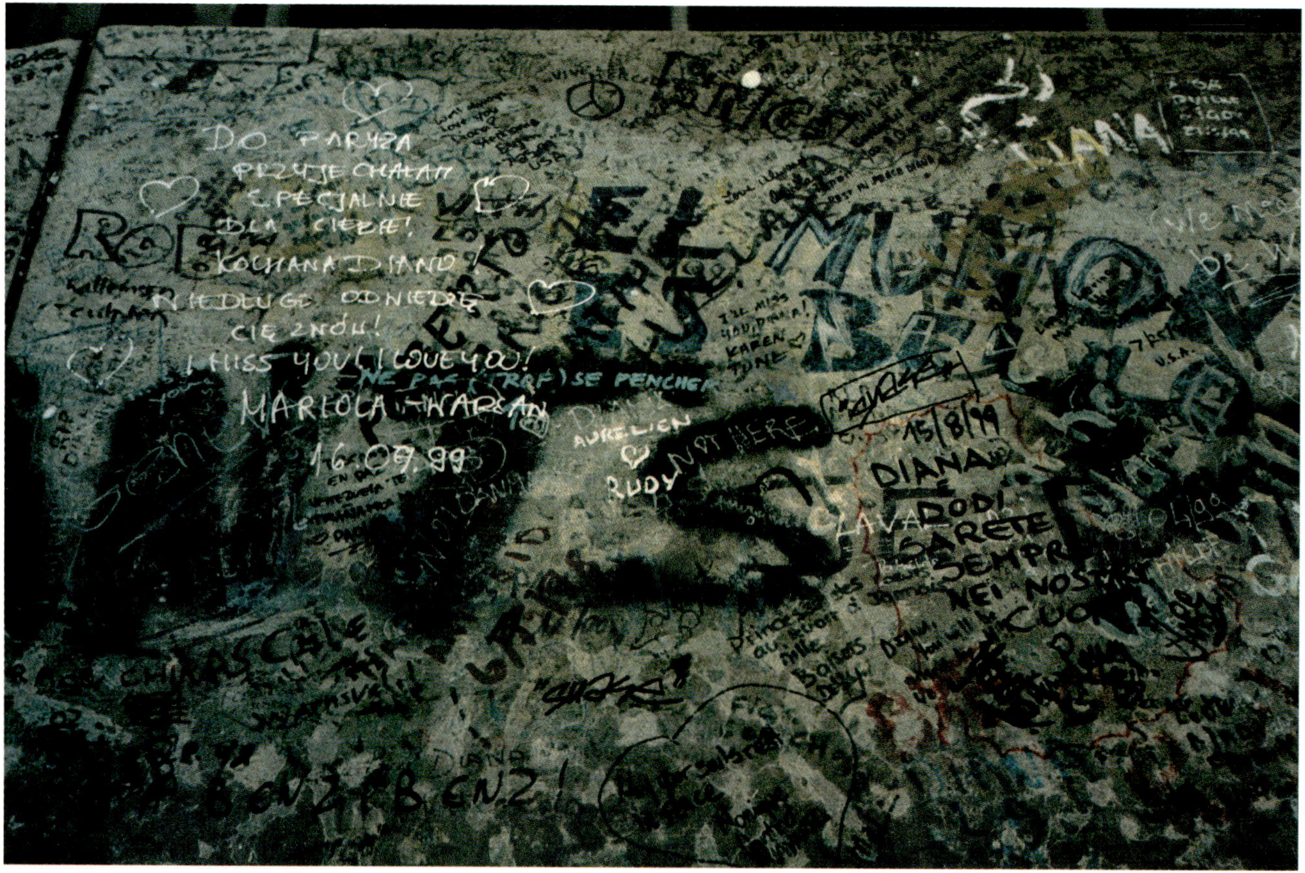

Saturday, August 14. Paris. A memorial to Princess Diana

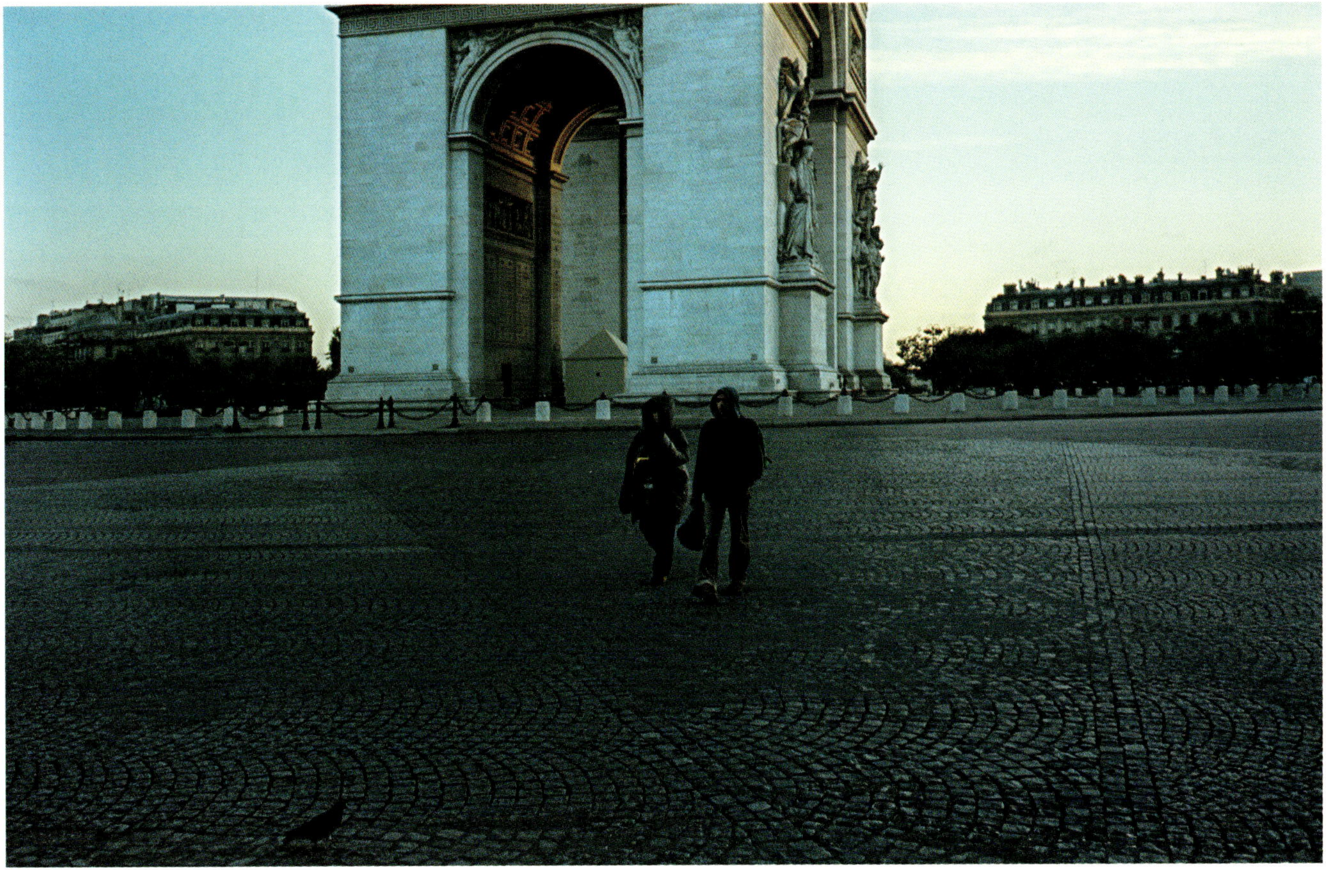

Sunday, August 15. Paris. Arc de Triomphe, early morning

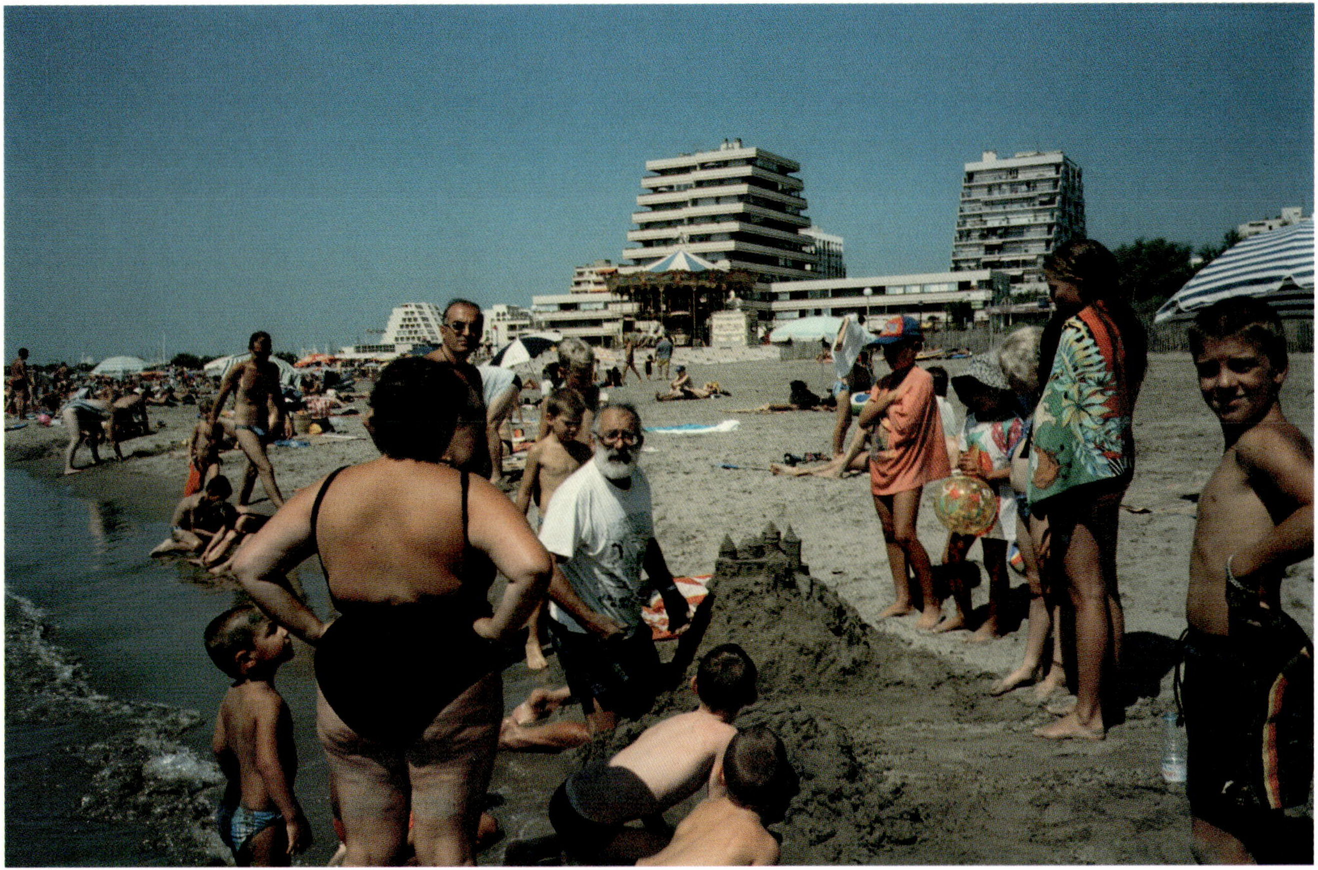

Monday, August 16. La Grande Motte, France. On the beach

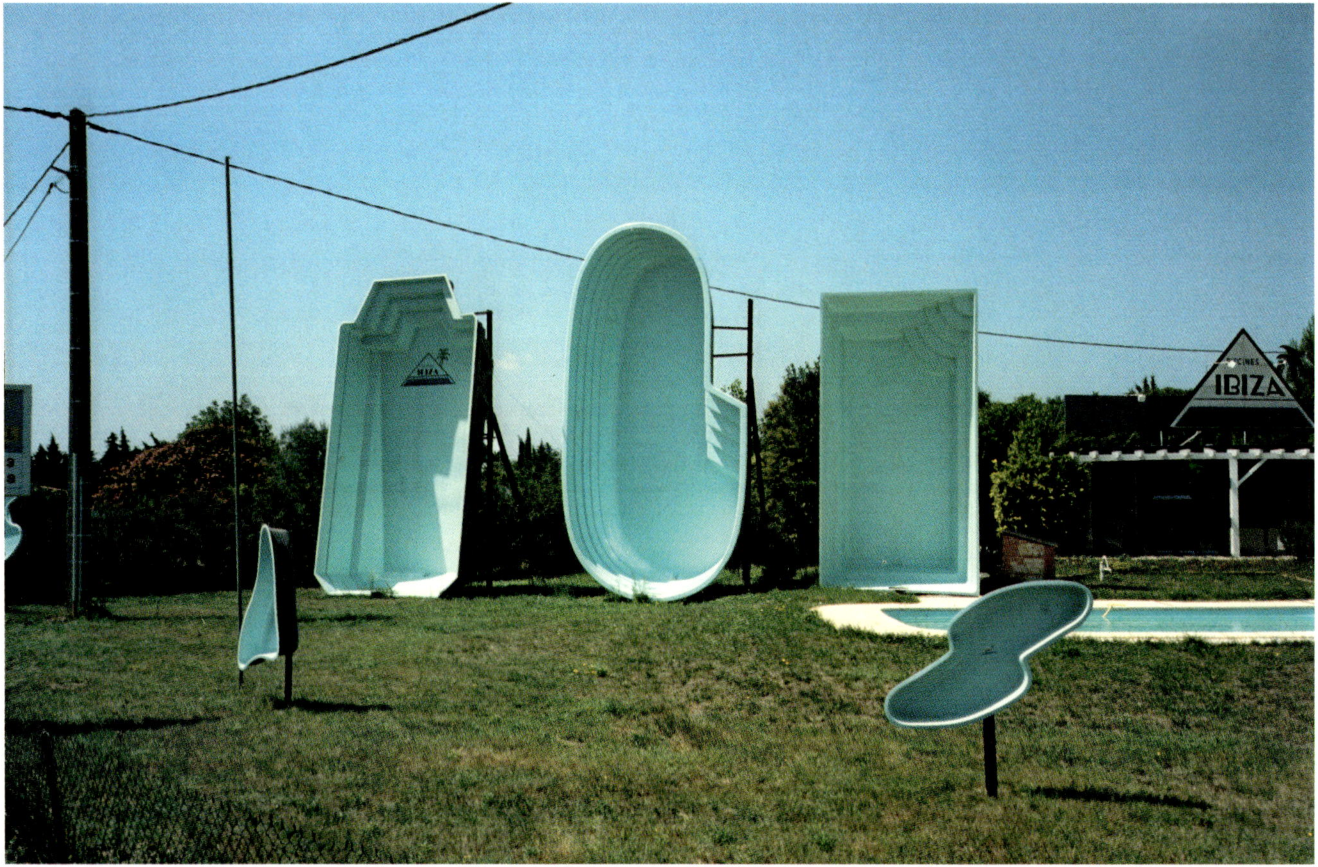

Tuesday, August 17. La Grande Motte, France. Swimming pools on sale

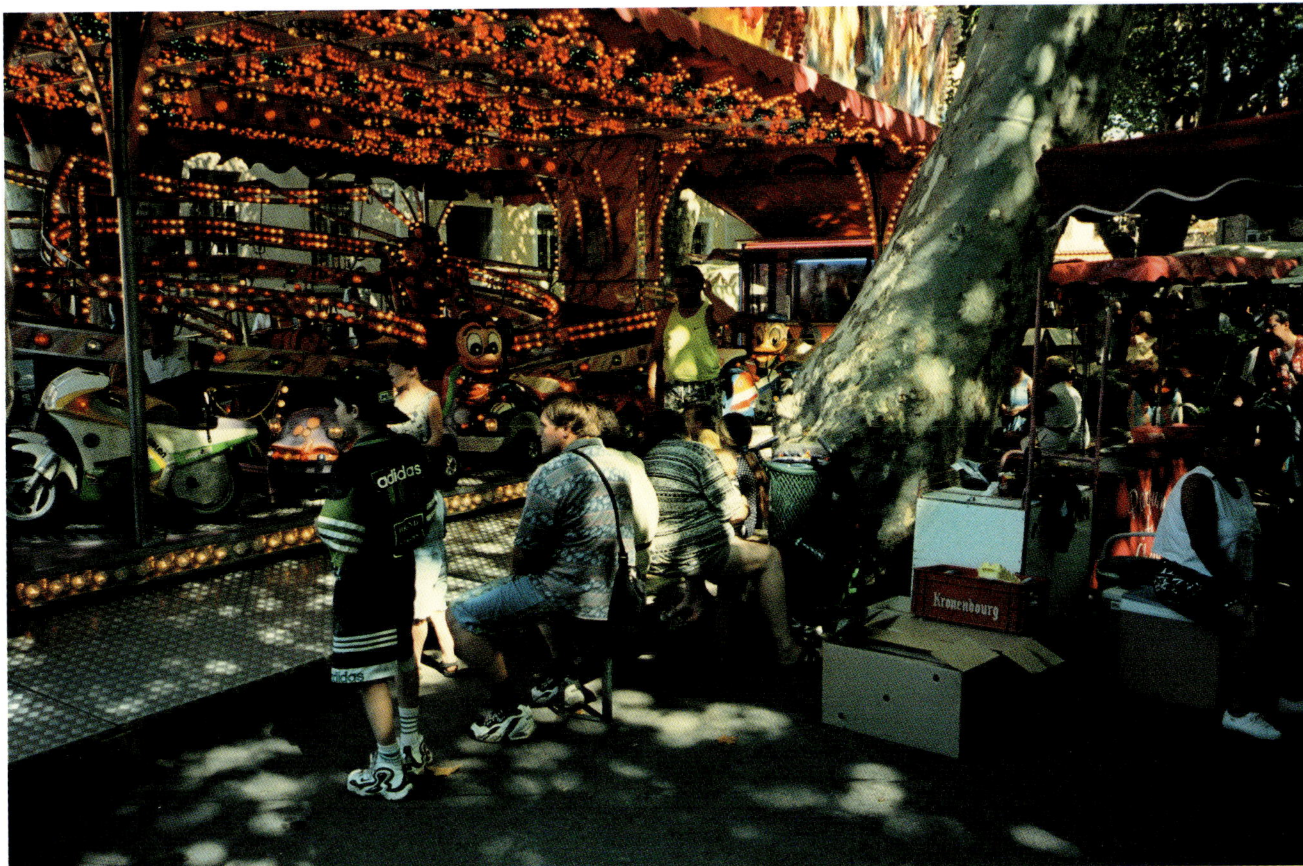

Wednesday, August 18. Aups, France. Amusement park

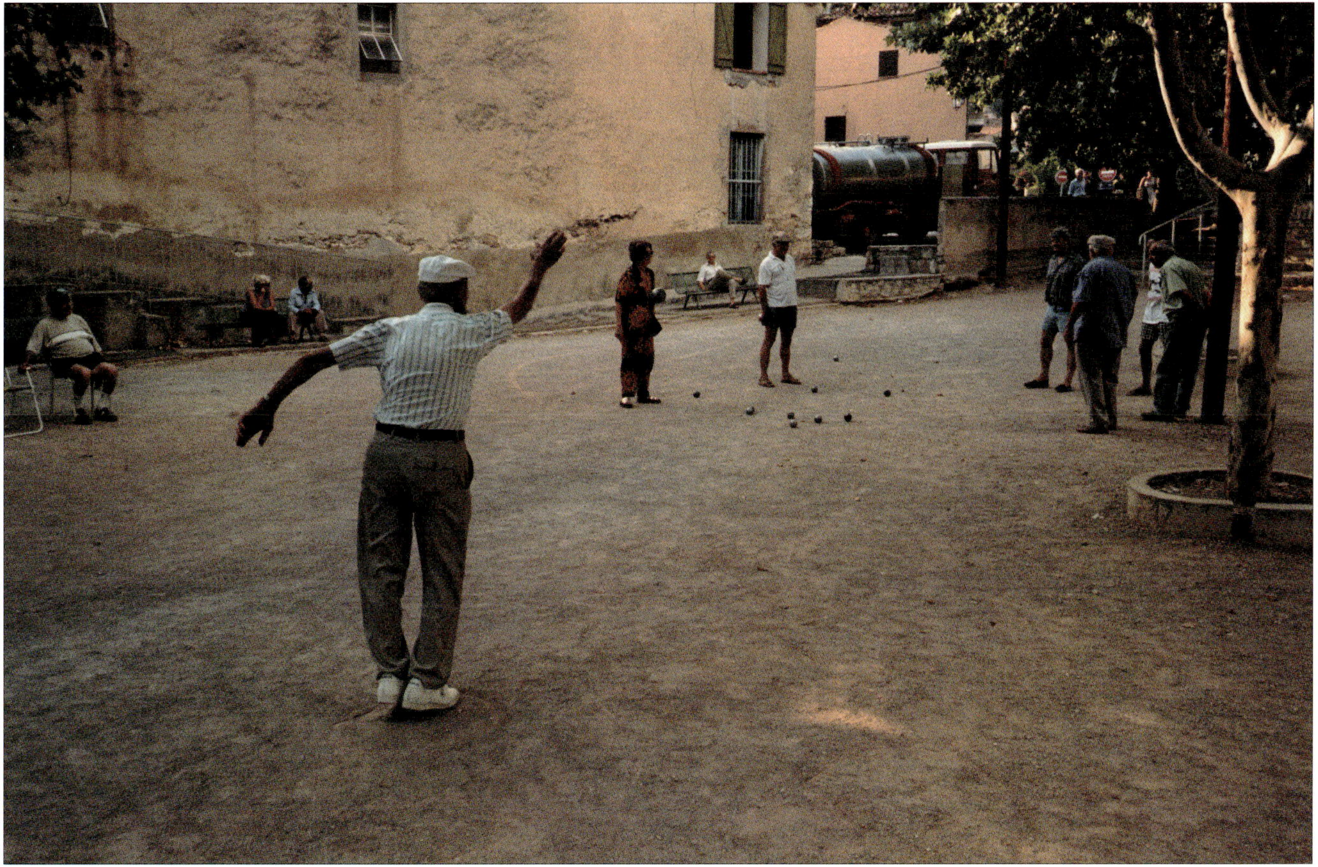

Thursday, August 19. Cotignac, France. Boule players

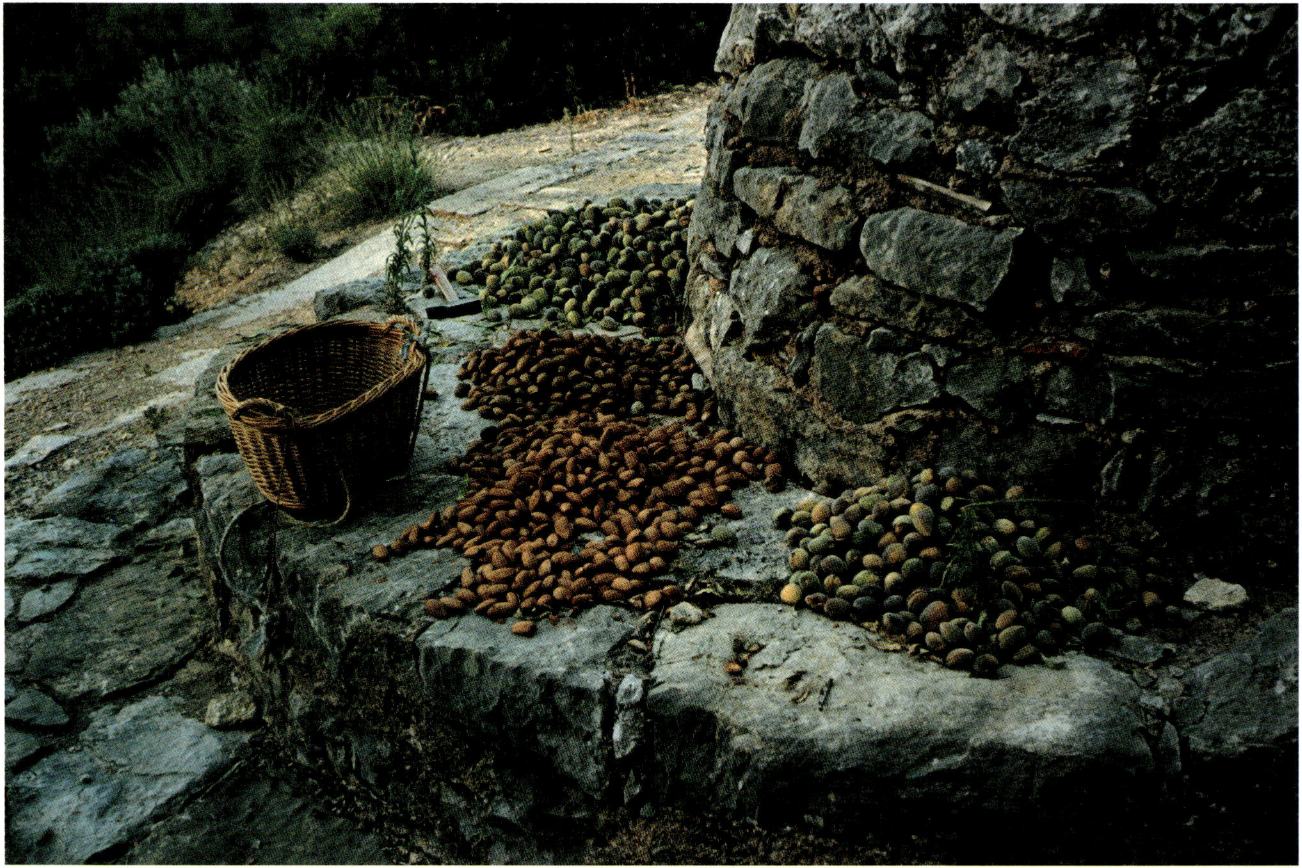

Friday, August 20. Cotignac, France. Our almond harvest, "La Véronique"

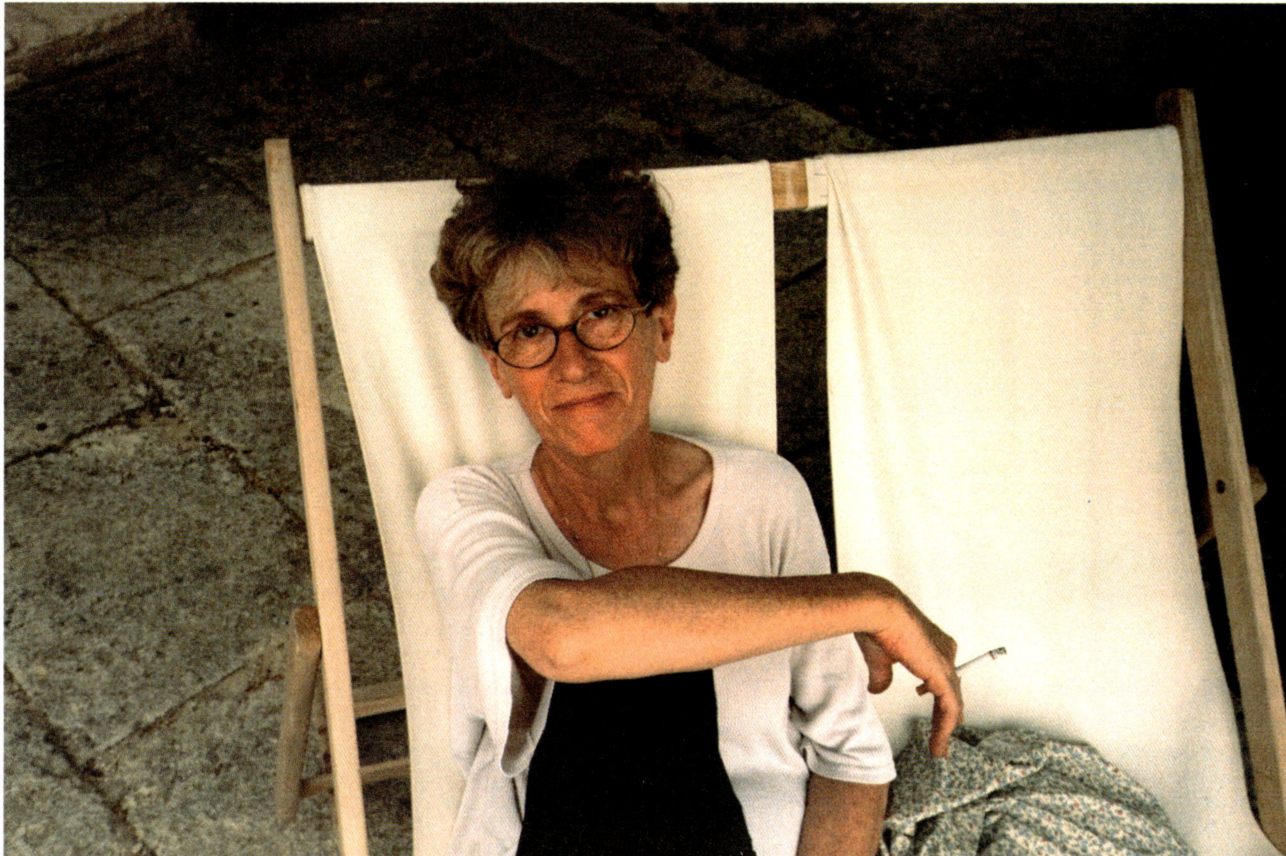

Saturday, August 21. Cotignac, France. Véronique Aubry

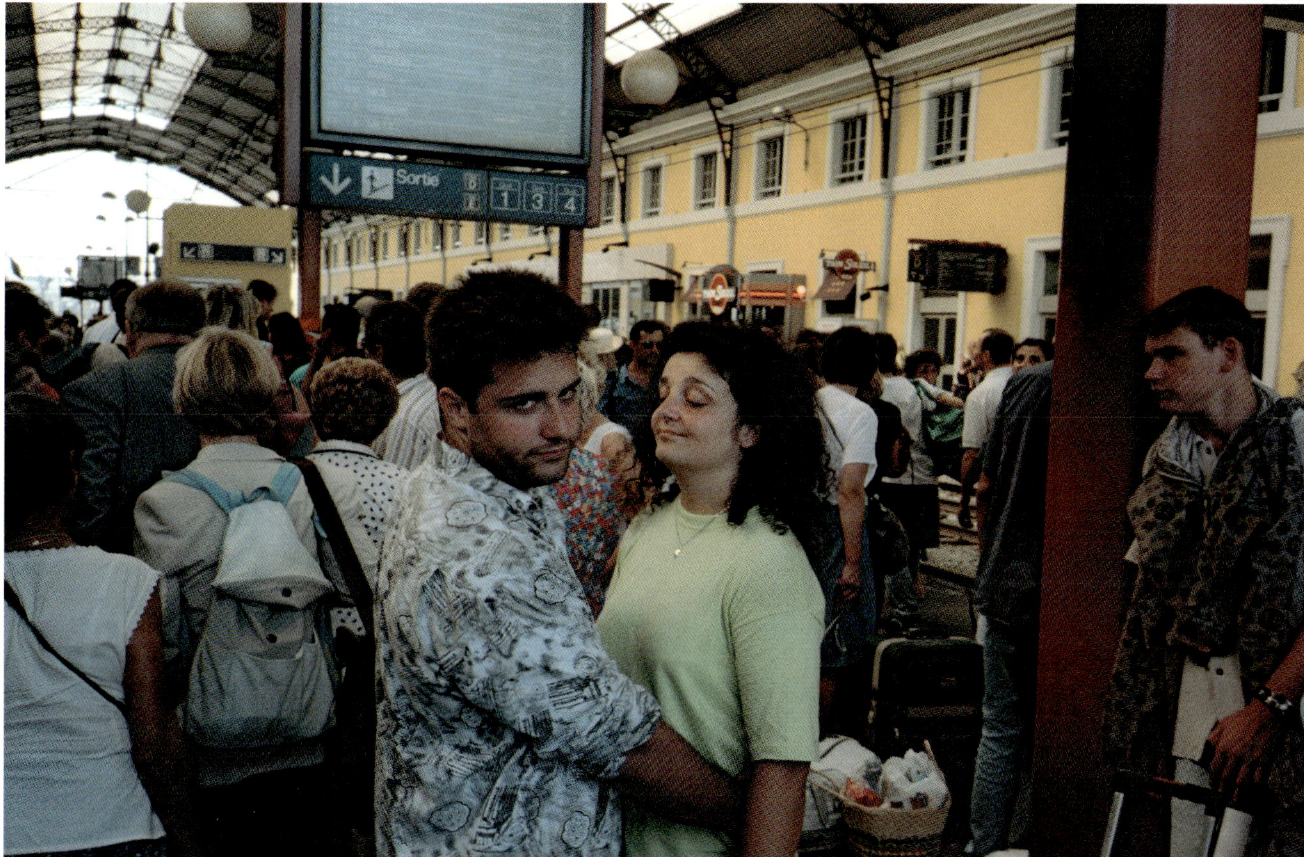

Sunday, August 22. Avignon, France. Scene at the railway station

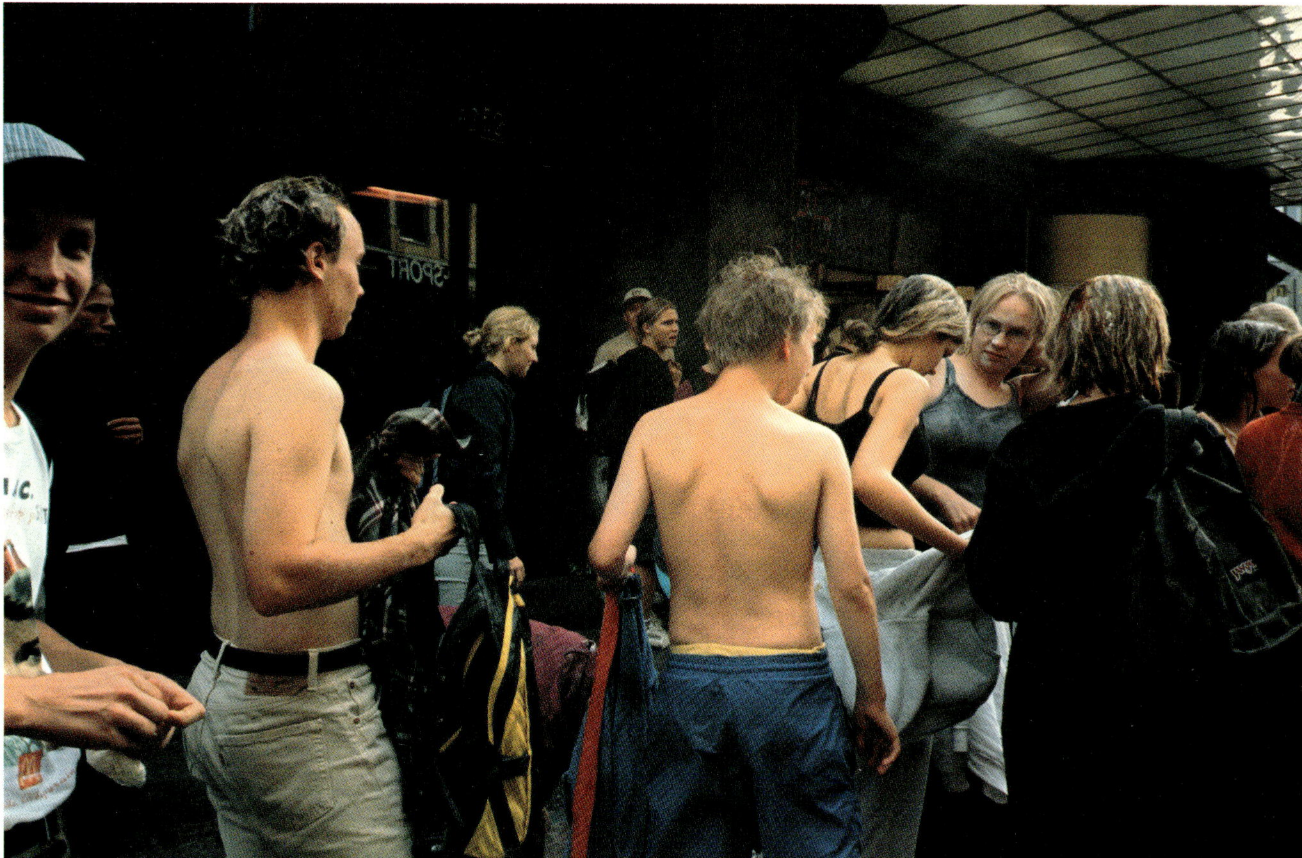

Monday, August 23. Helsinki. Street scene

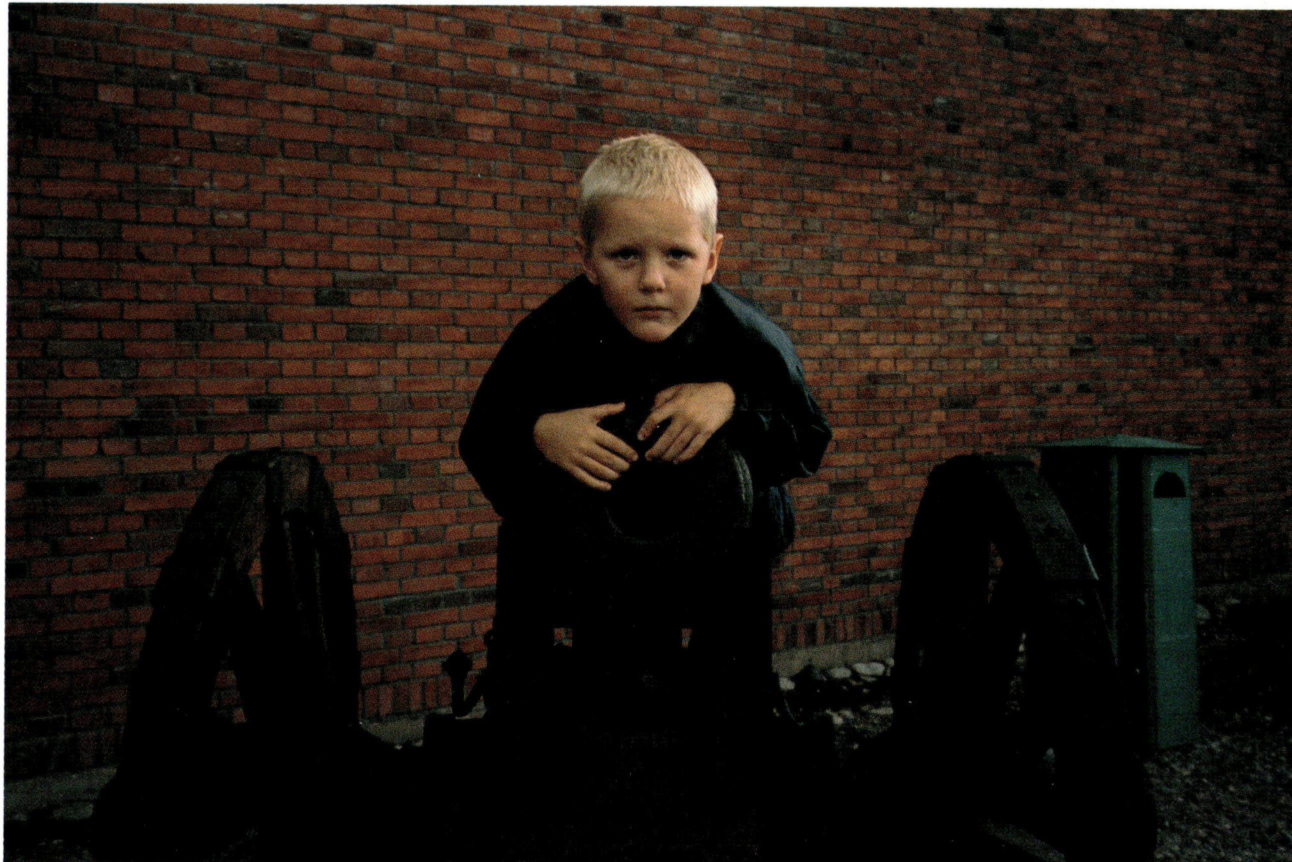

Tuesday, August 24. Helsinki. At the Old Fort

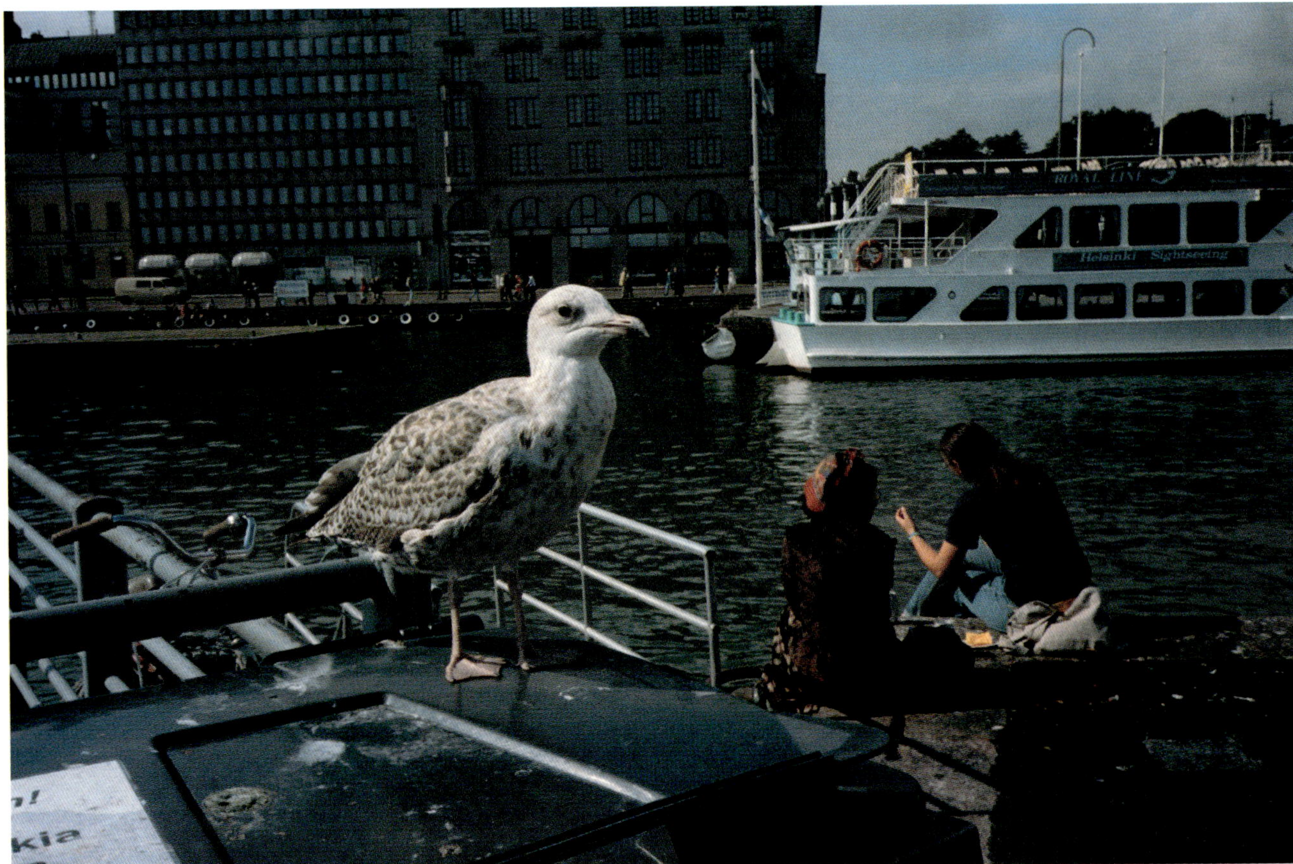

Wednesday, August 25. Helsinki. At the port

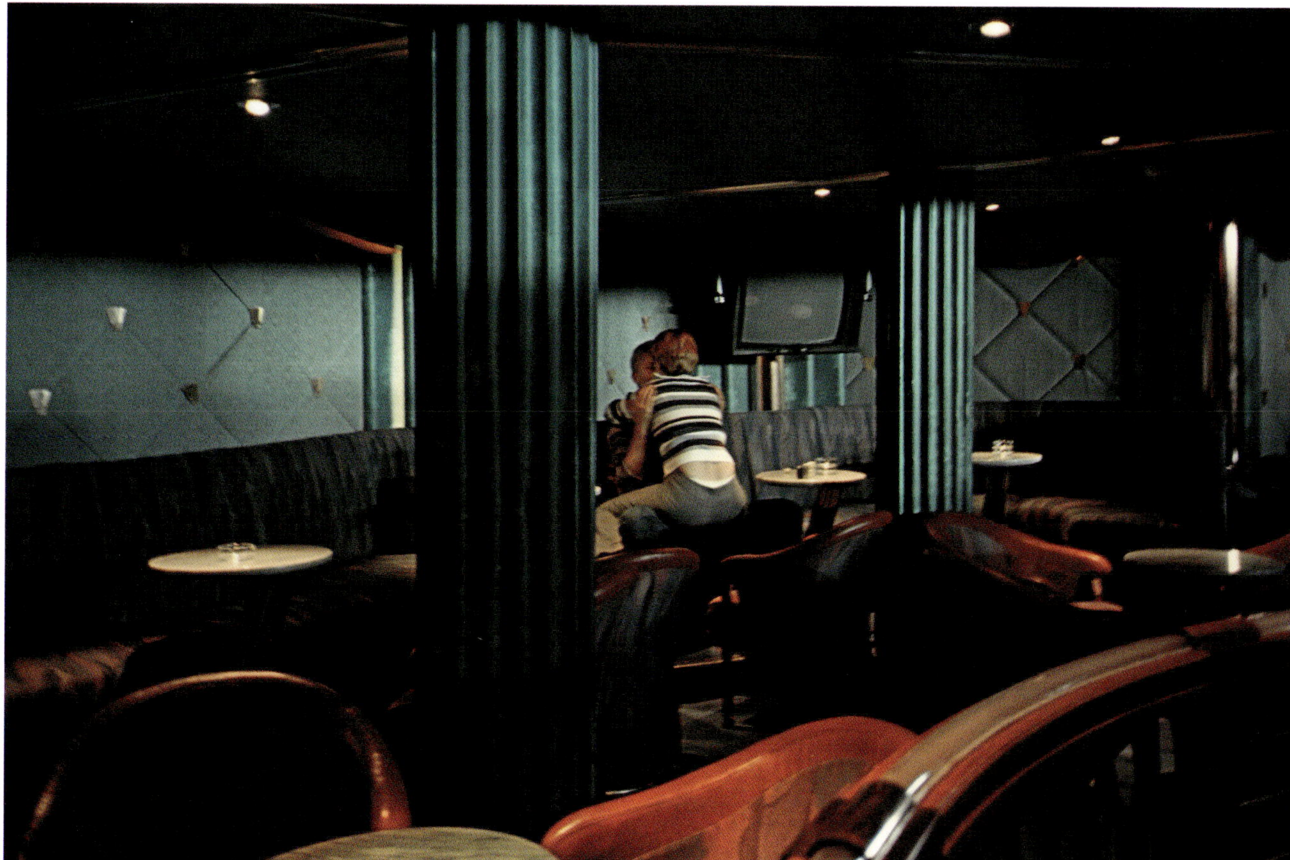

Thursday, August 26. Helsinki. Bar scene

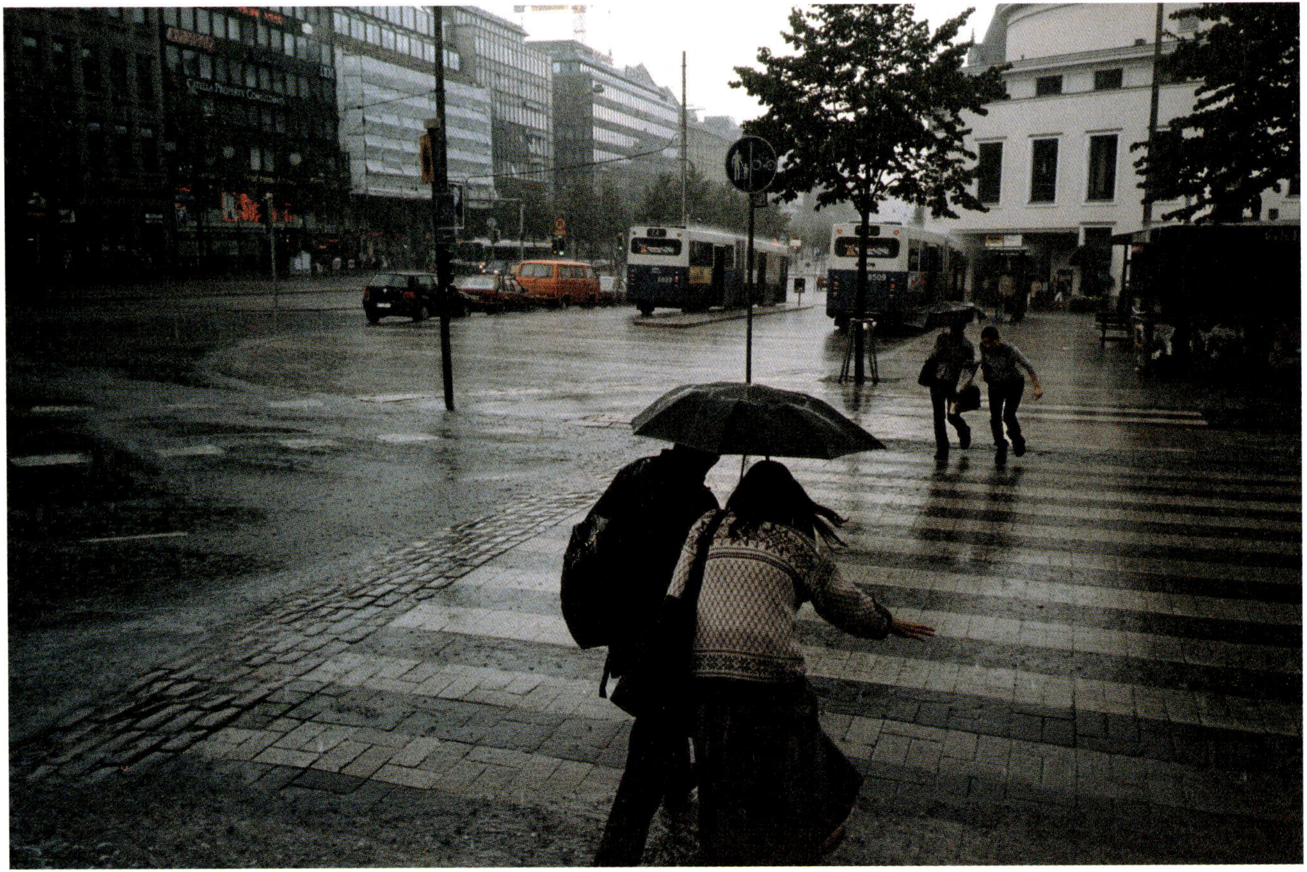

Friday, August 27. Helsinki. Street scene

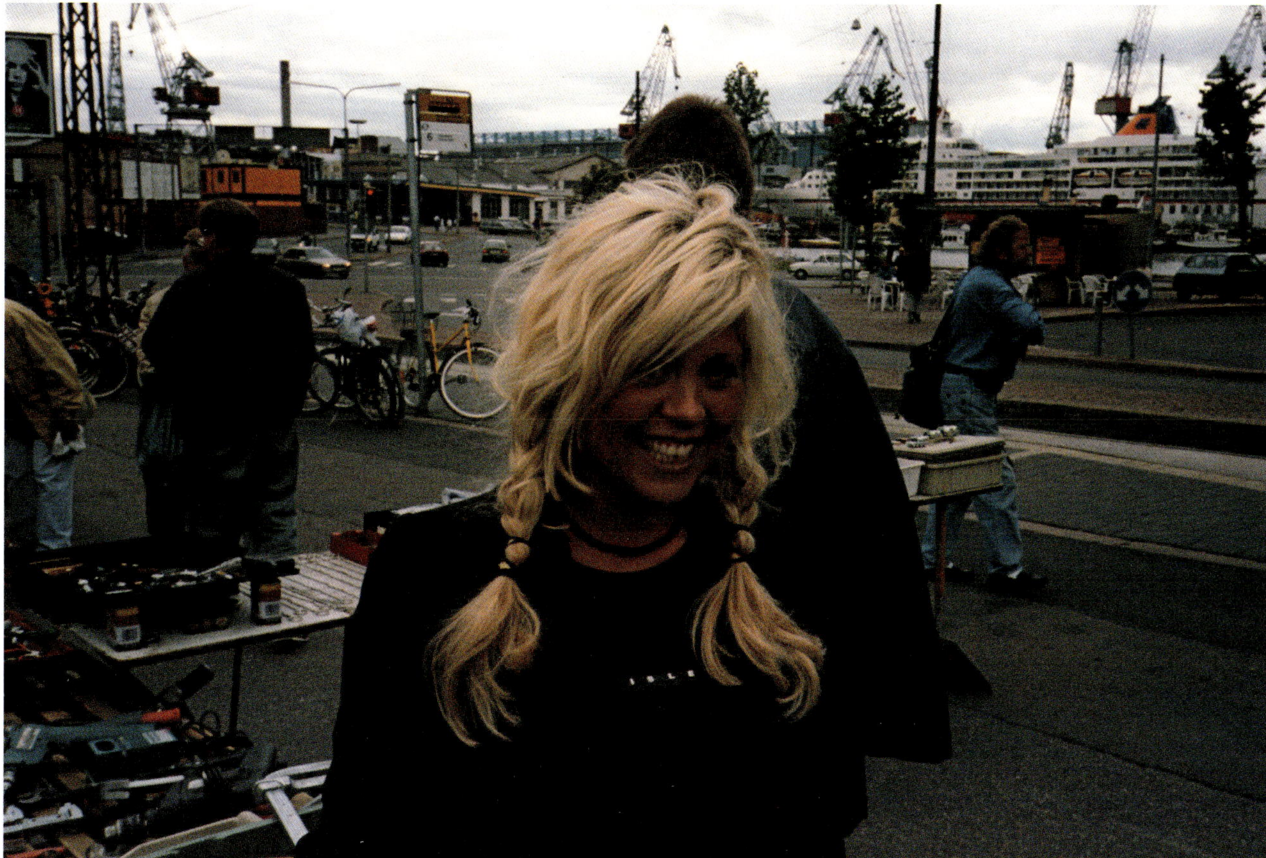

Saturday, August 28. Helsinki. In the flea market

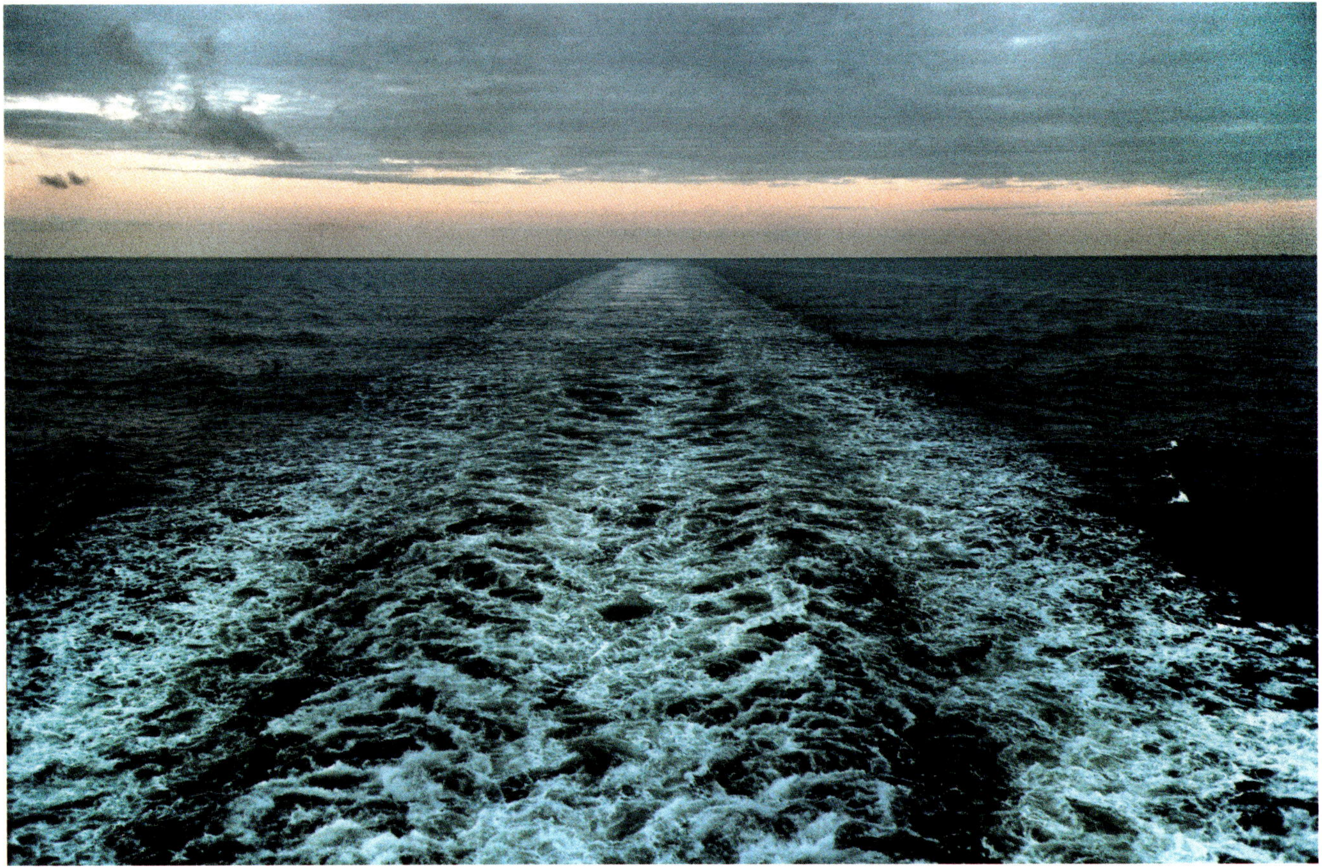

Sunday, August 29. Helsinki-Stockholm ferry. Seascape

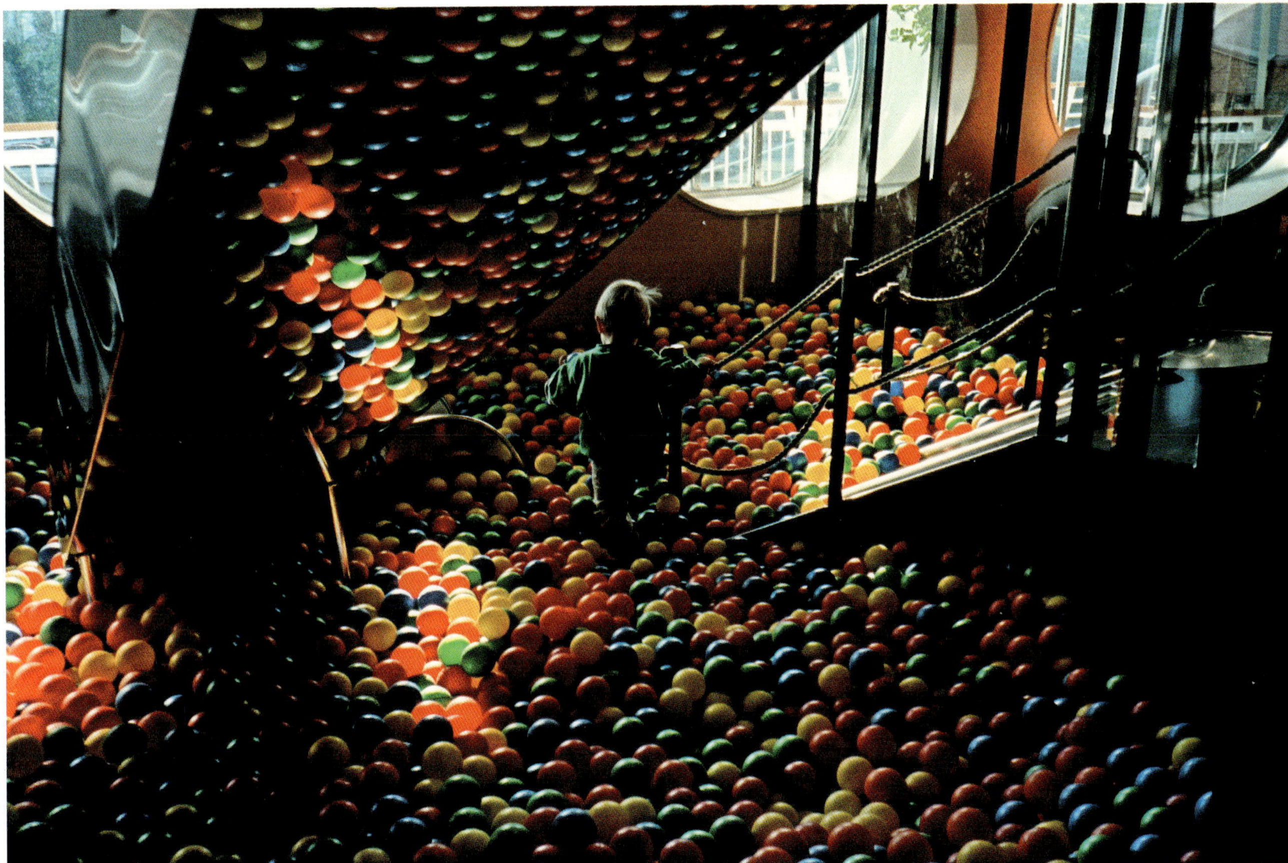

Sunday, August 29. Helsinki-Stockholm ferry. Children's playroom

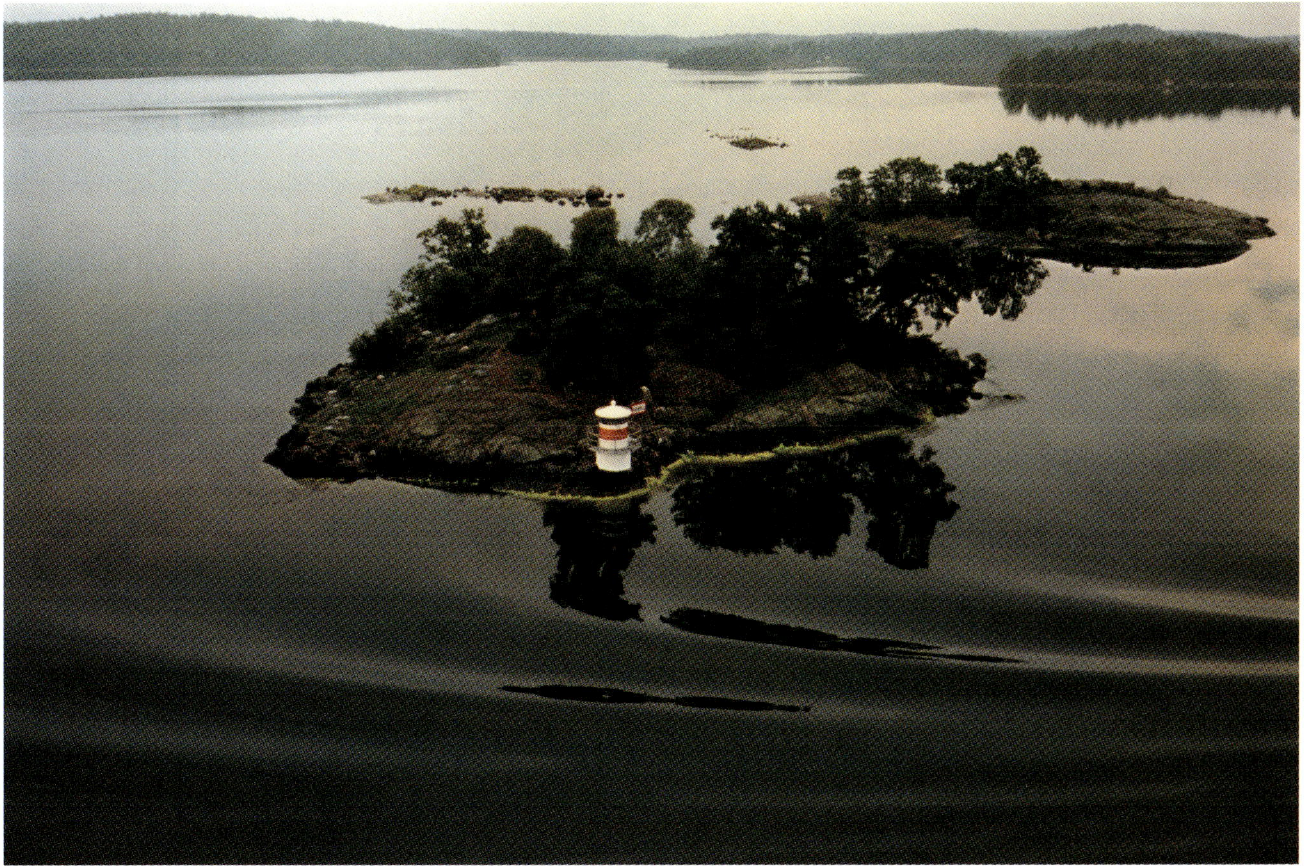

Monday, August 30. Helsinki-Stockholm ferry. Swedish landscape

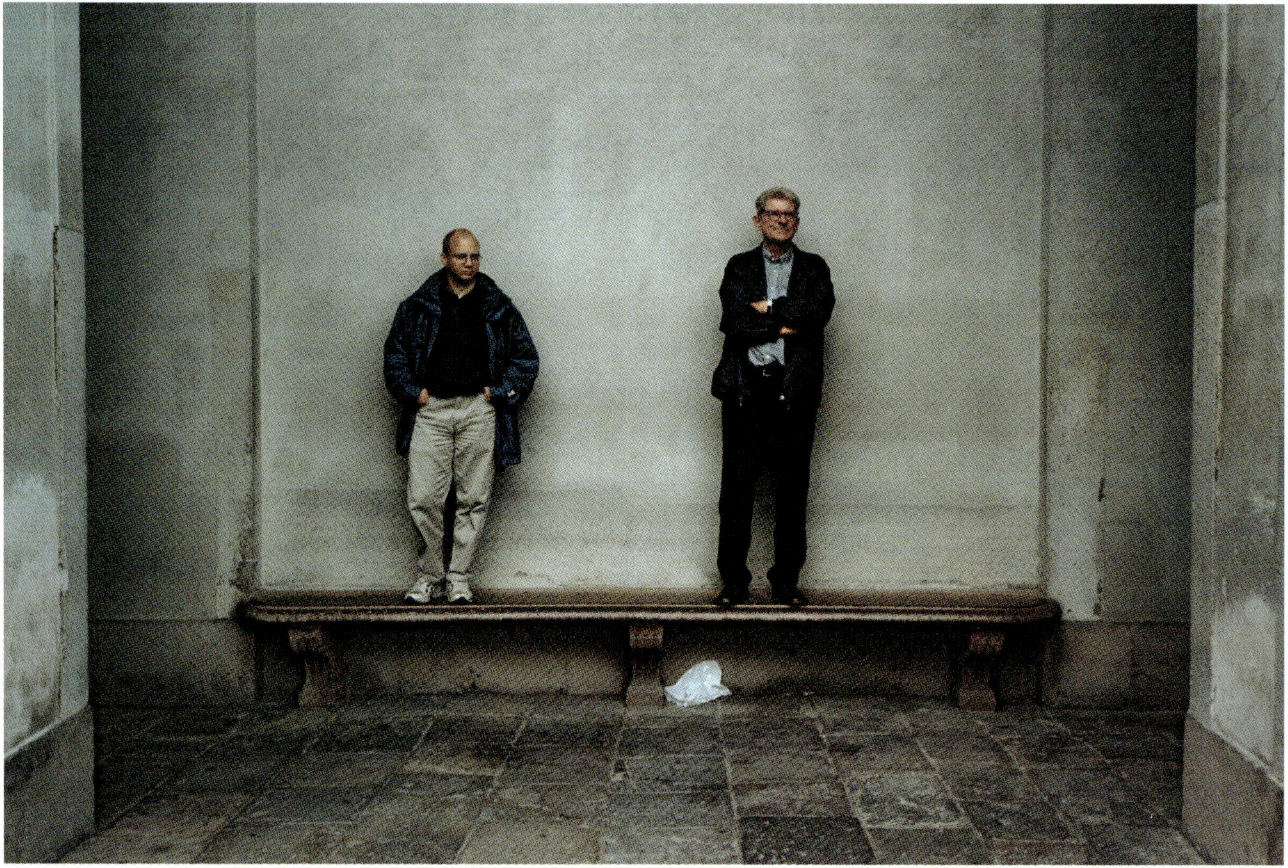

Tuesday, August 31. Stockholm. Onlookers at the changing of the guard, at the Royal Palace

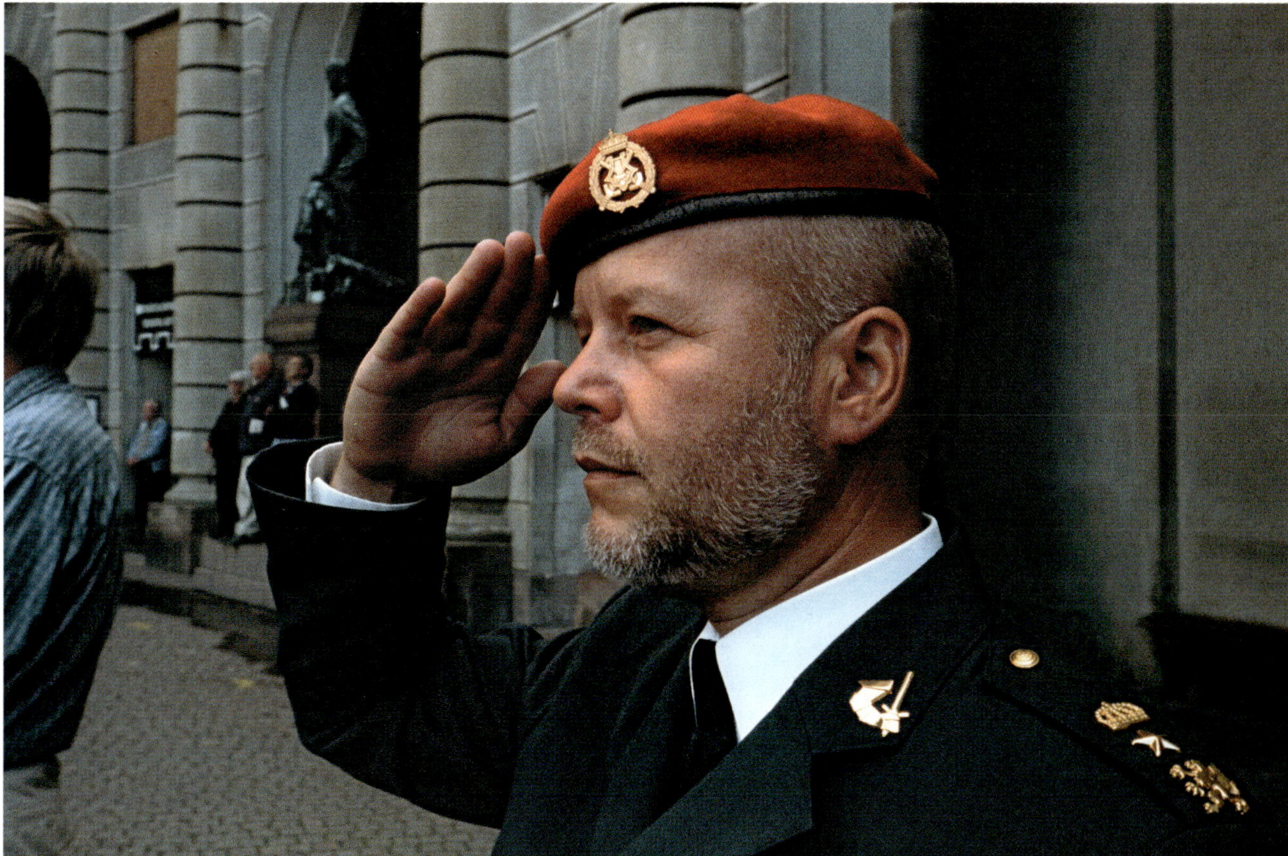

Tuesday, August 31. Stockholm. The changing of the guard, at the Royal Palace

SEPTEMBER

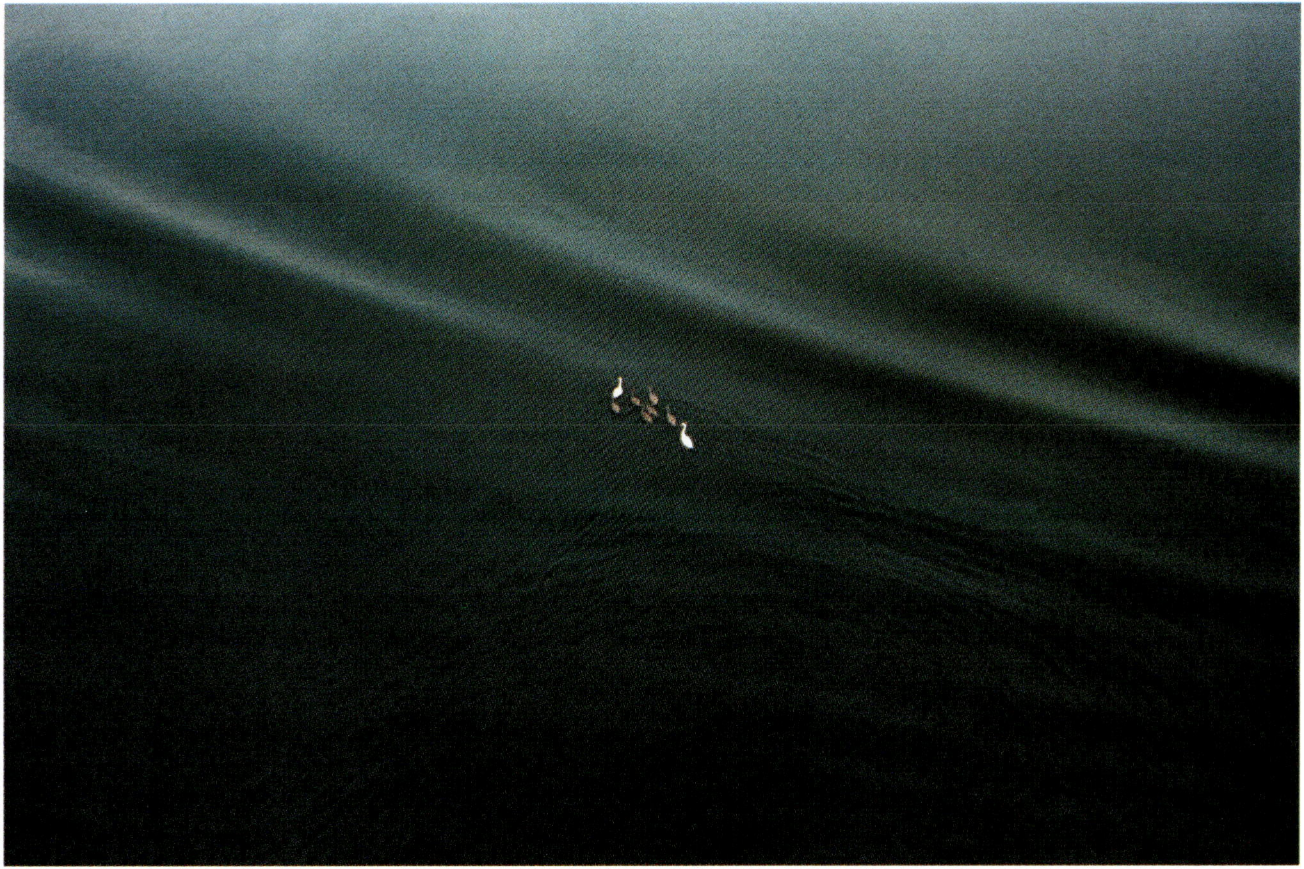

Wednesday, September 1. Helsinki-Stockholm ferry. Swans

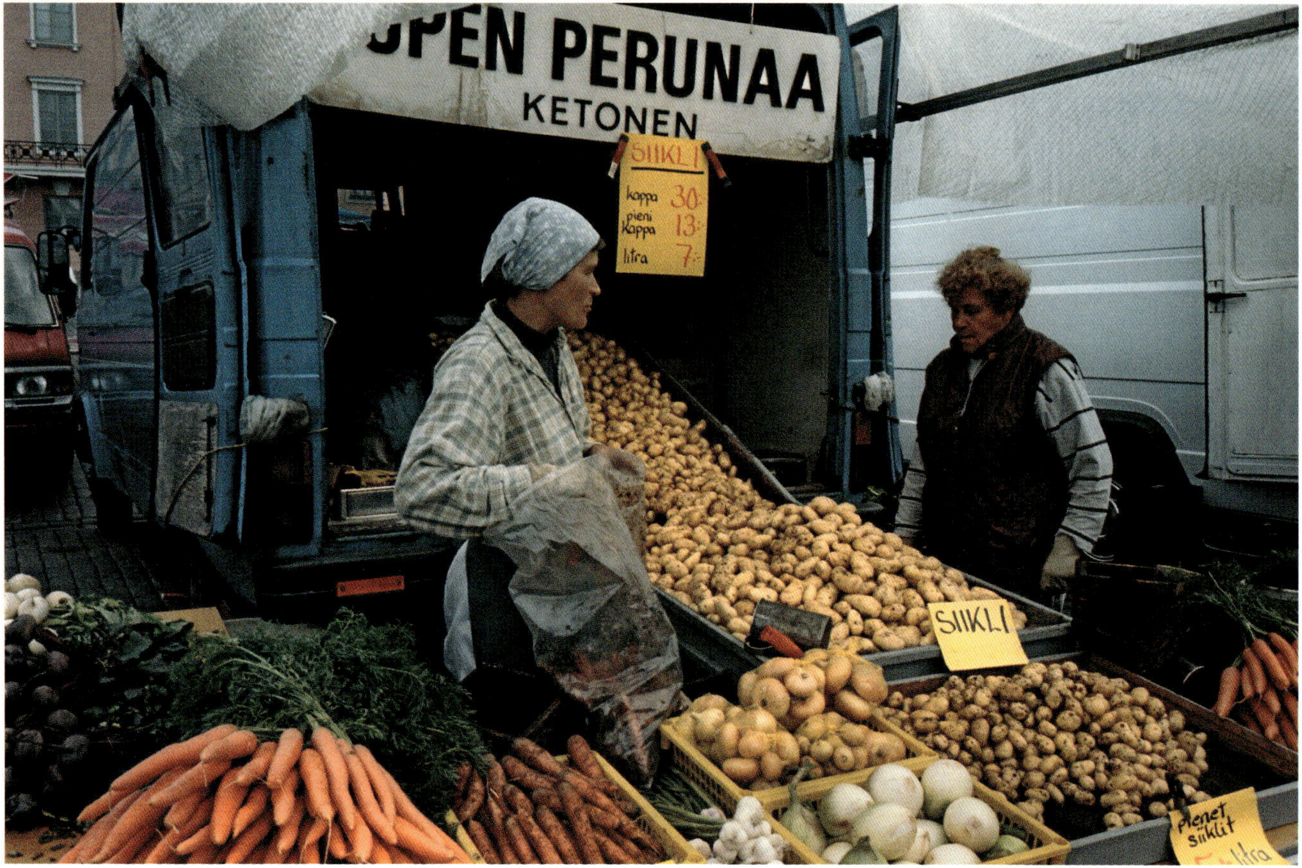

Thursday, September 2. Helsinki. At the market

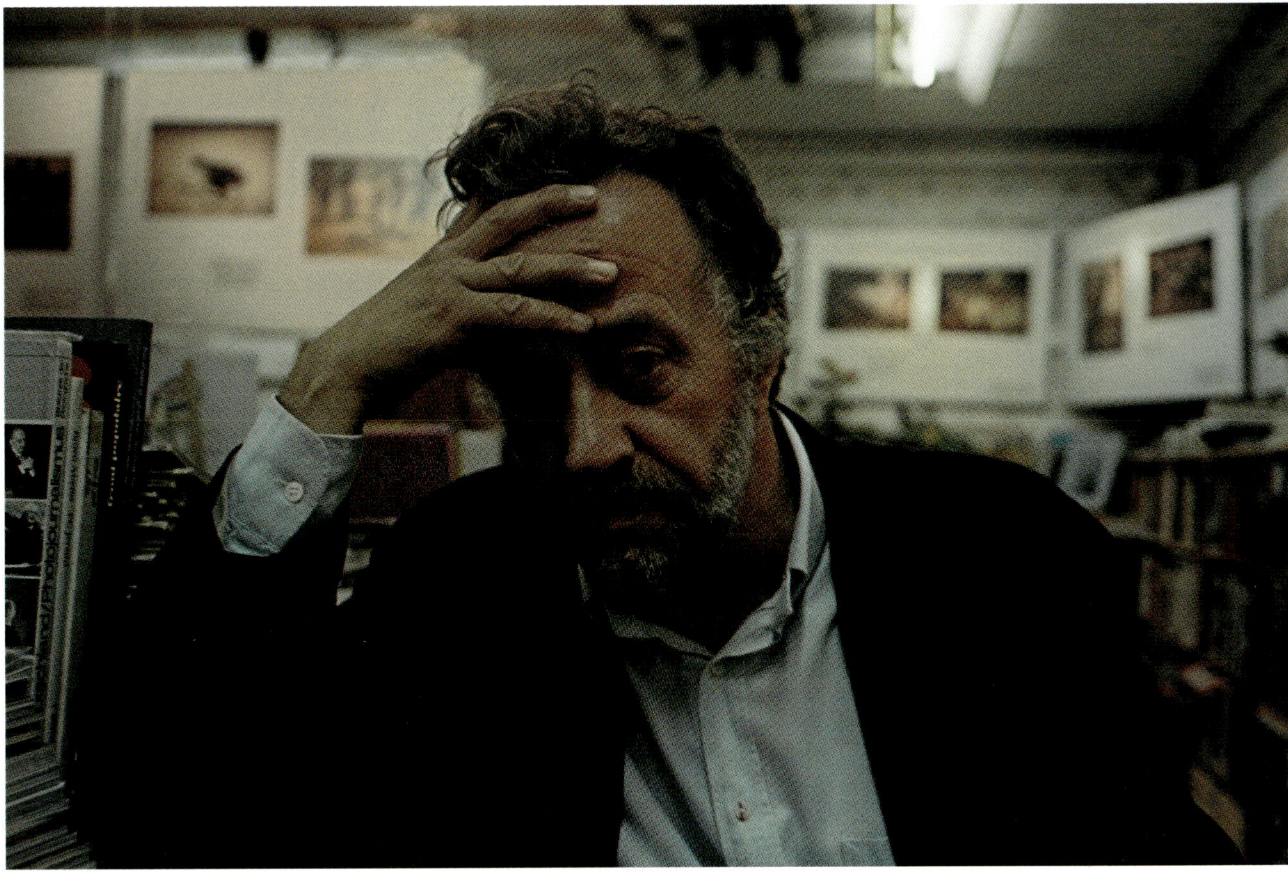

Thursday, September 2. Helsinki. Pentti Samallahti, photographer

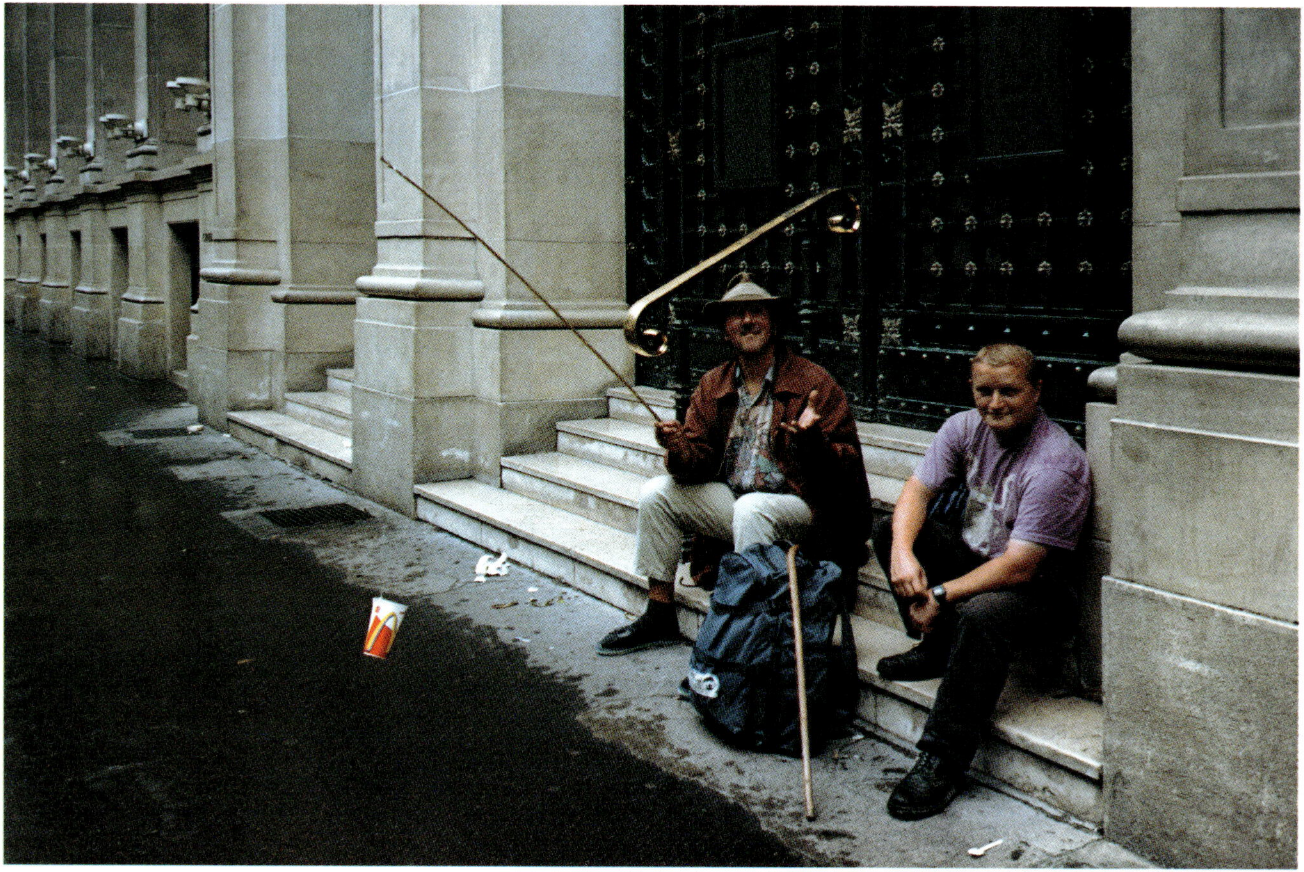

Friday, September 3. Paris. Beggars, in the Opéra area

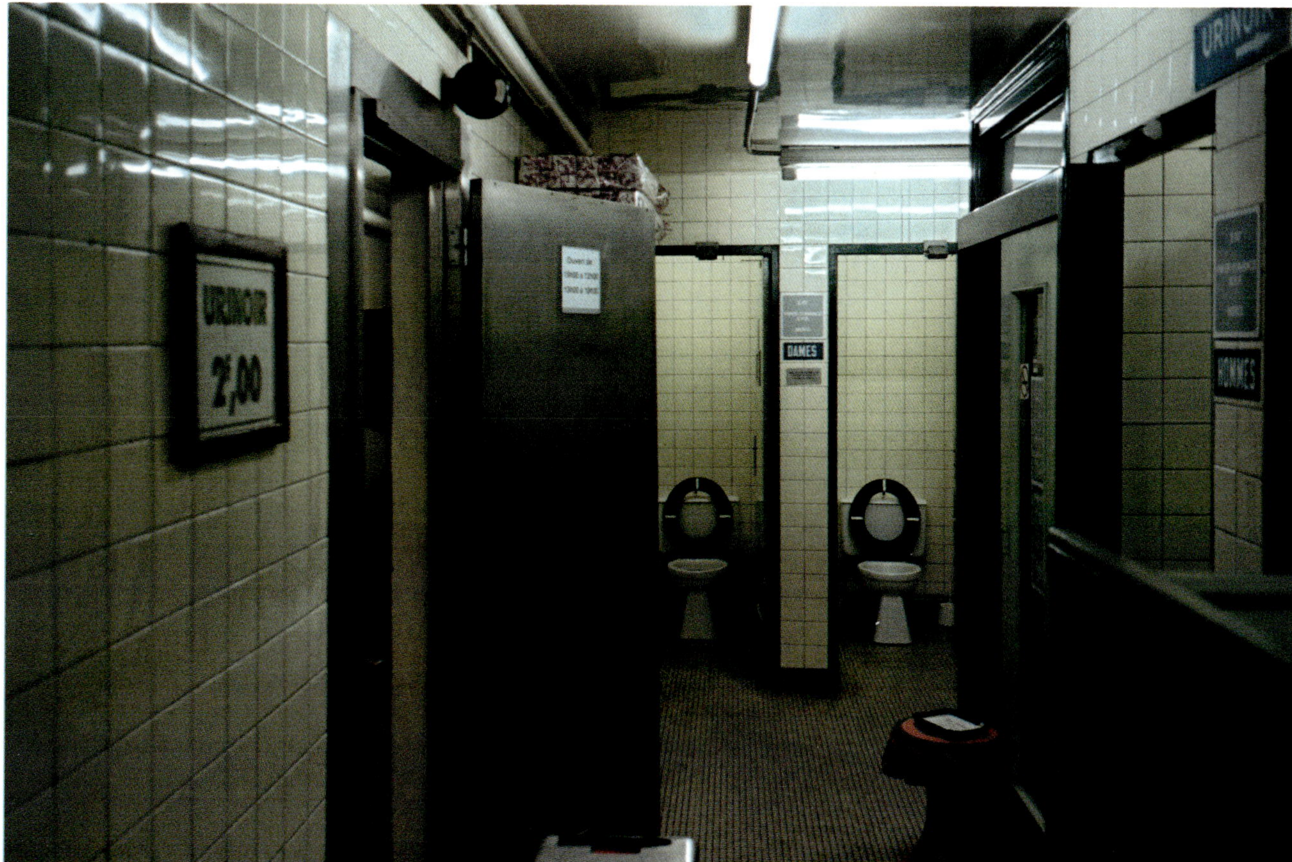

Saturday, September 4. Paris. Public toilets, in the Opéra area

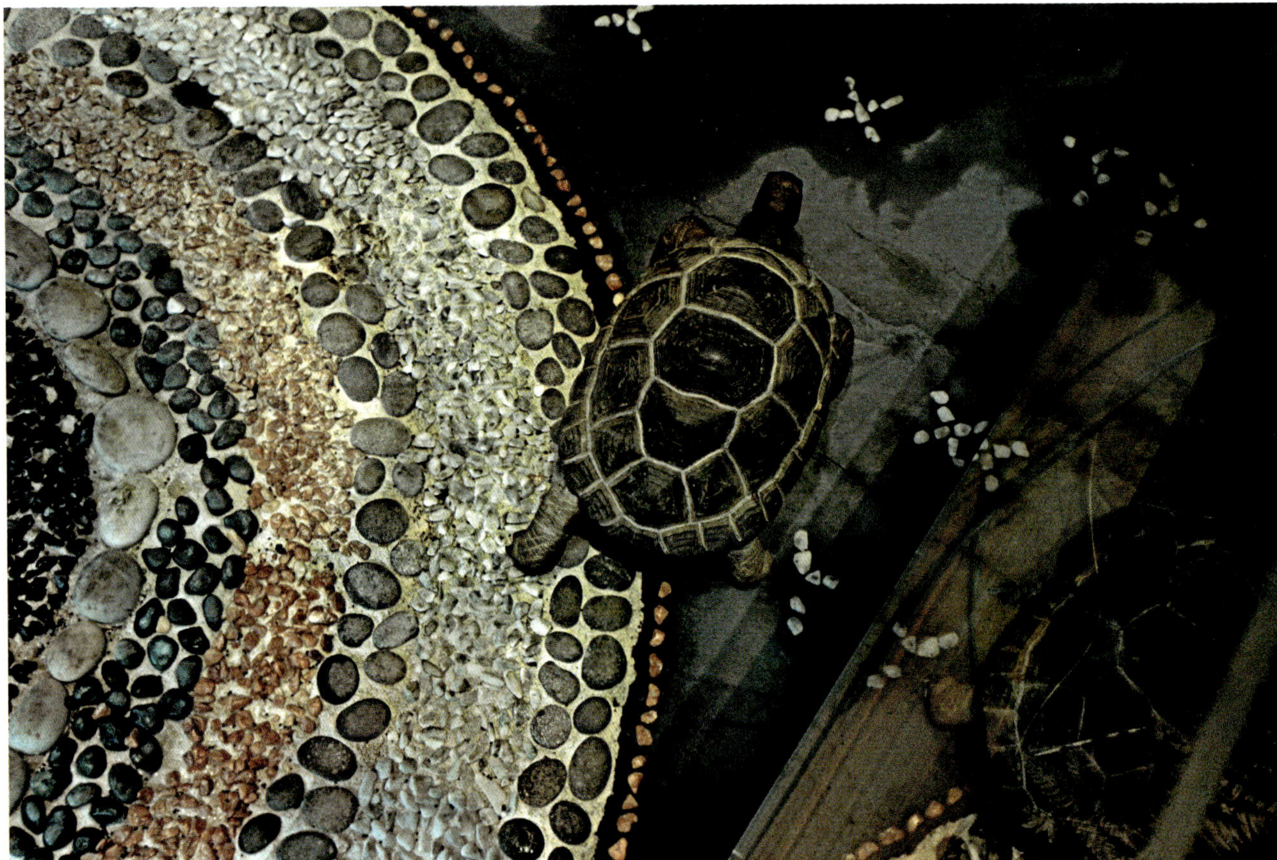

Sunday, September 5. Paris. A turtle, Parc de la Villette

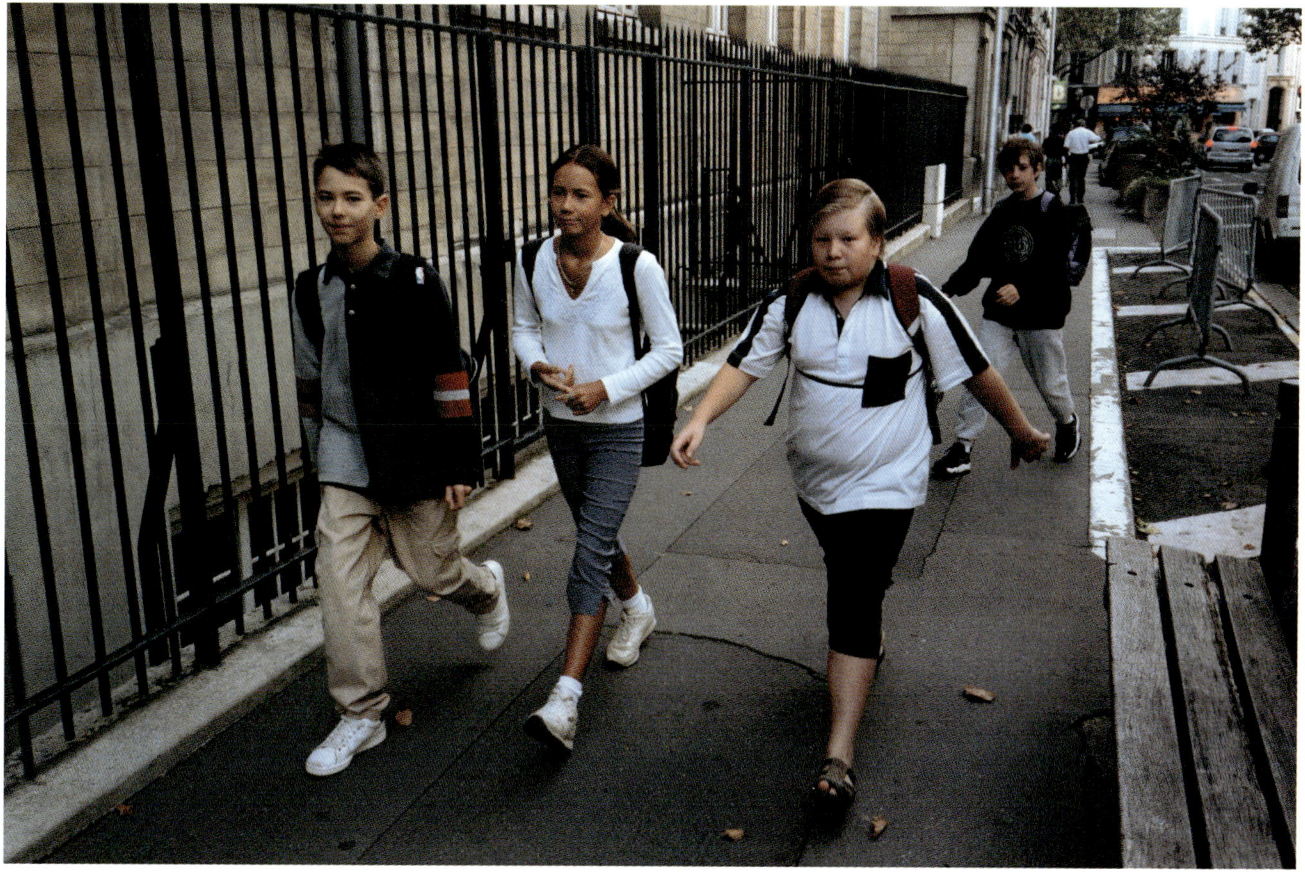

Monday, September 6. Boulogne, France. The first day of school

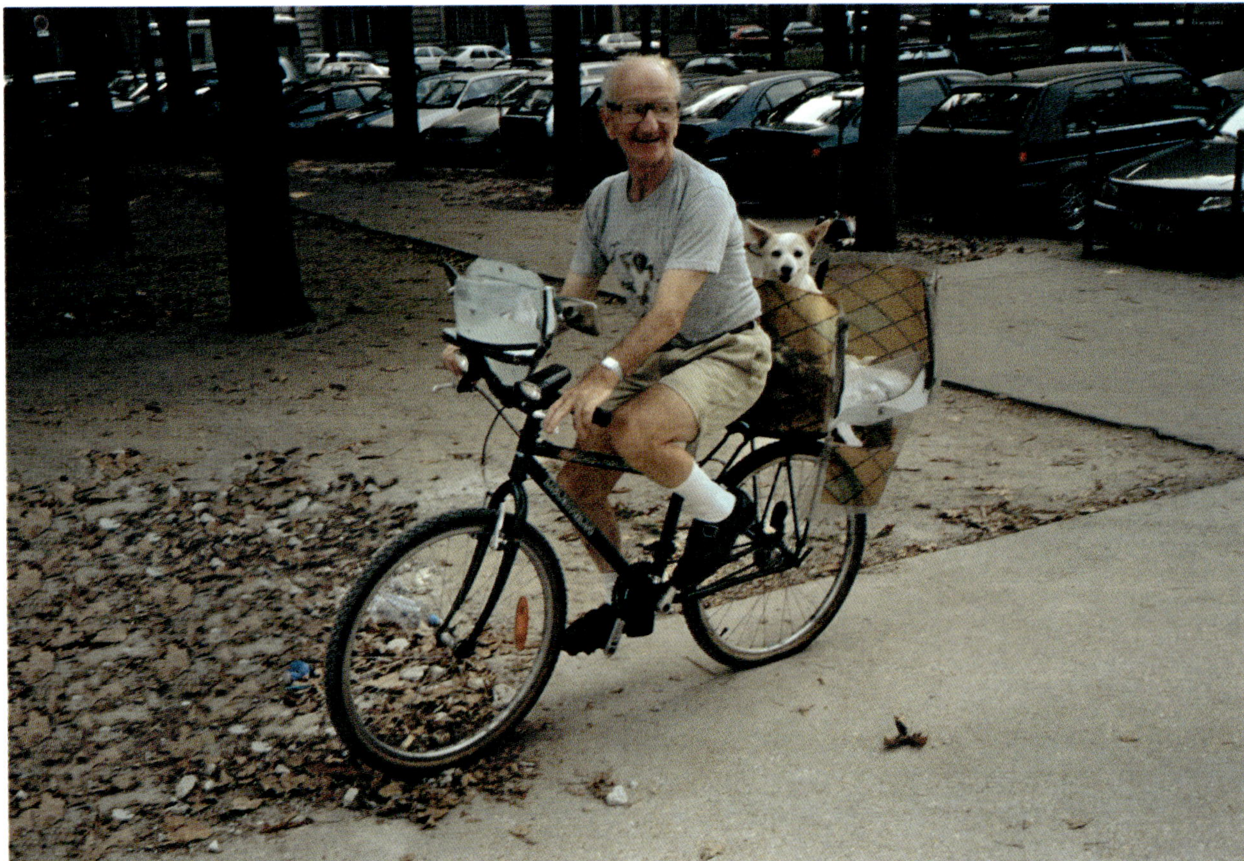

Tuesday, September 7. Paris. Street scene, on the Champs Élysées

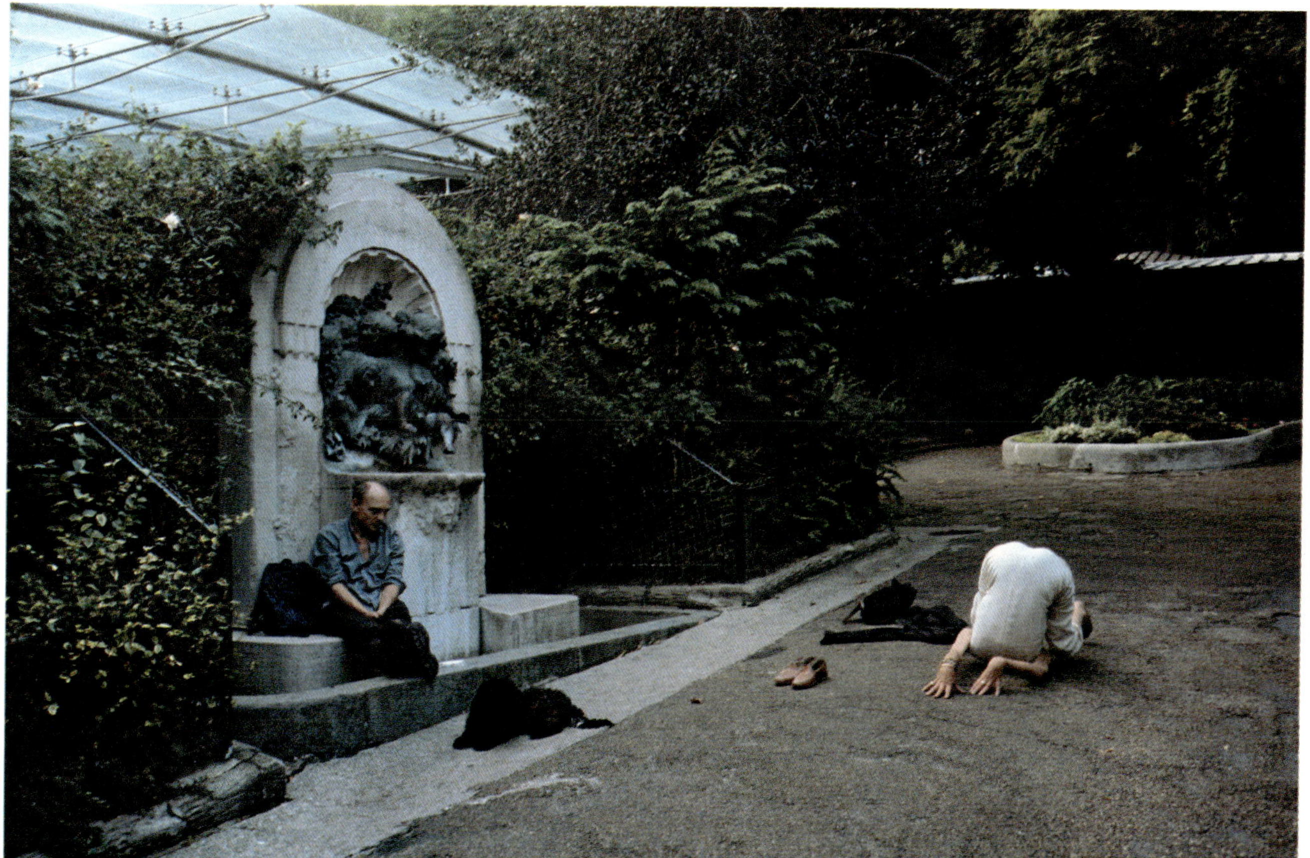

Wednesday, September 8. Paris. Public park in Montmartre

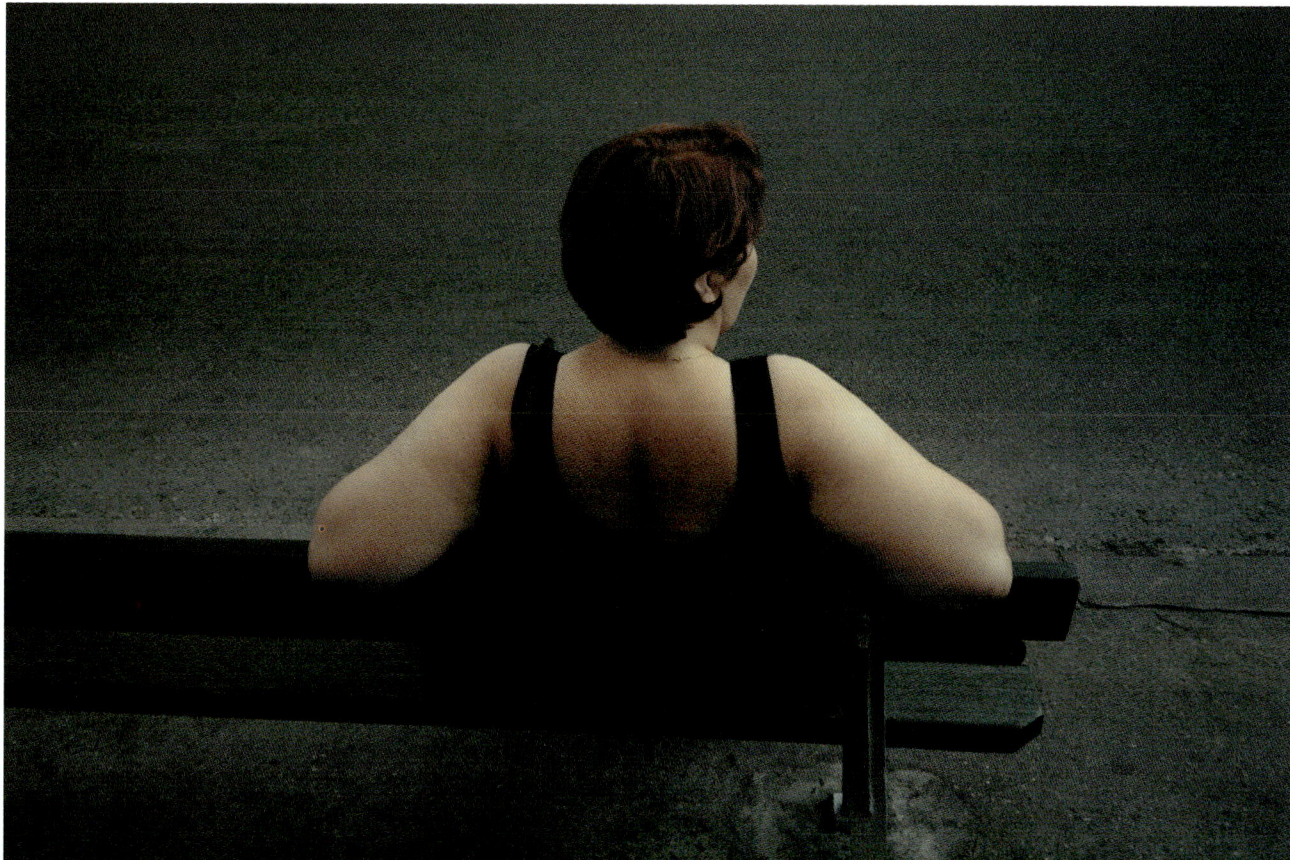

Thursday, September 9. Paris. Street scene, Bastille area

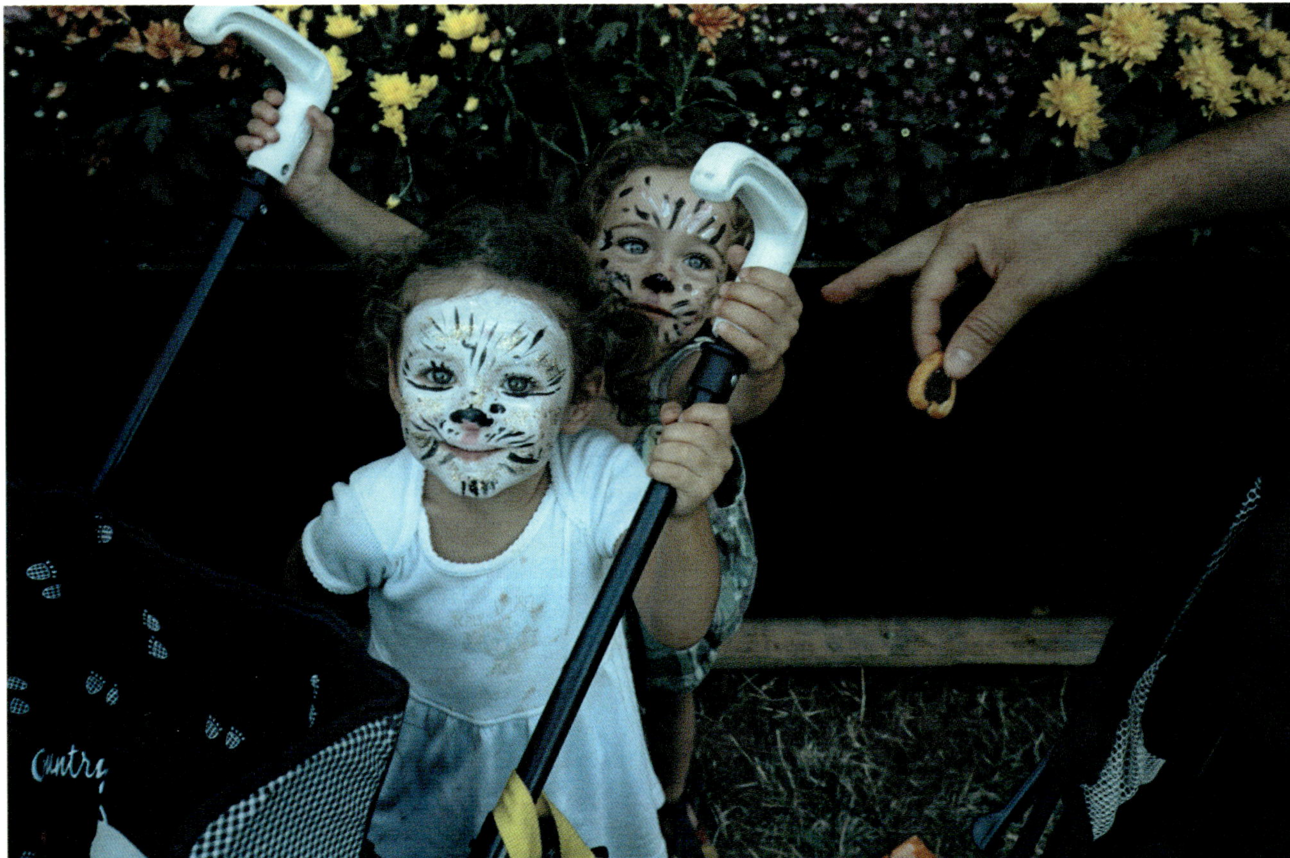

Friday, September 10. La Courneuve, France. Preparations for La Fête de L'Humanité

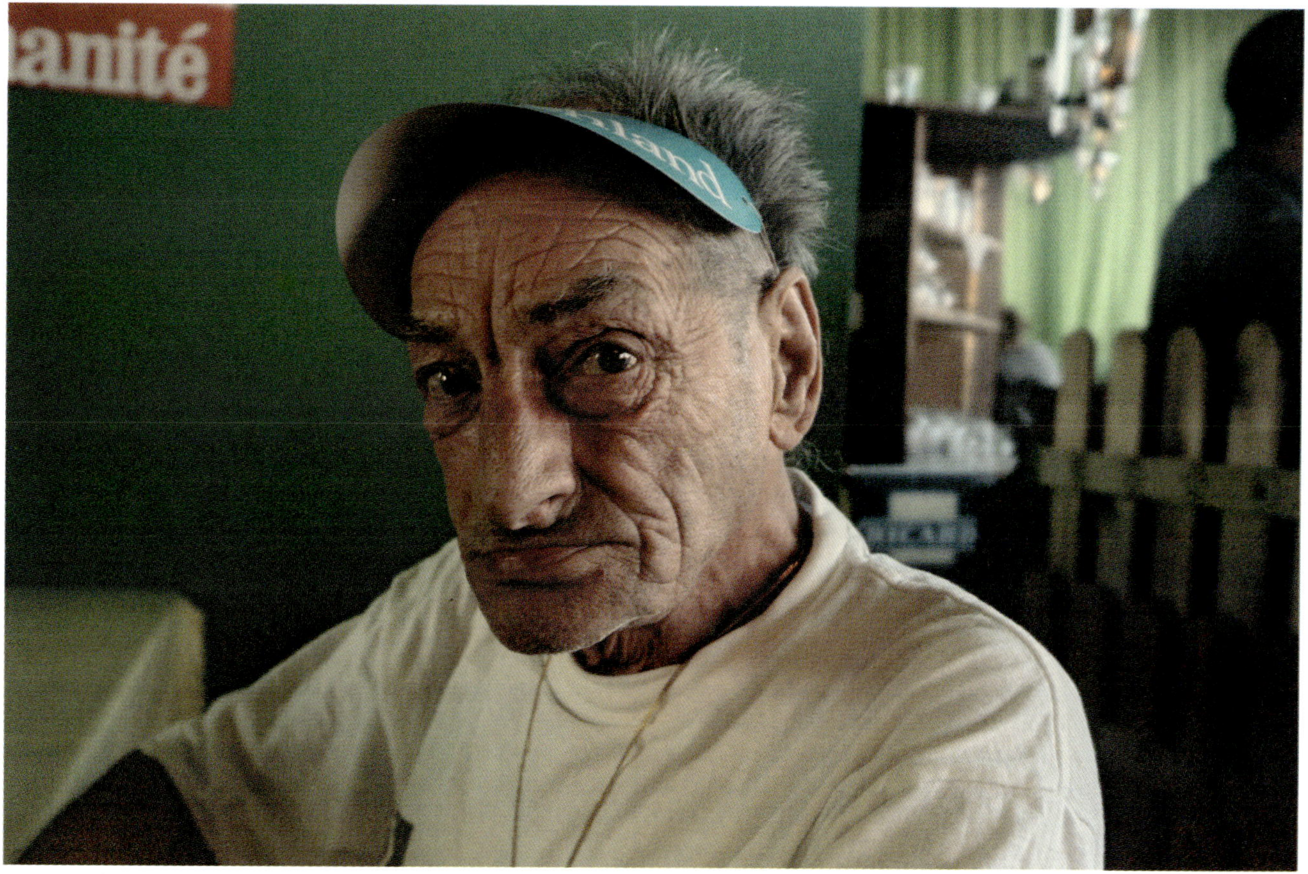

Saturday, September 11. La Courneuve, France. At La Fête de L'Humanité

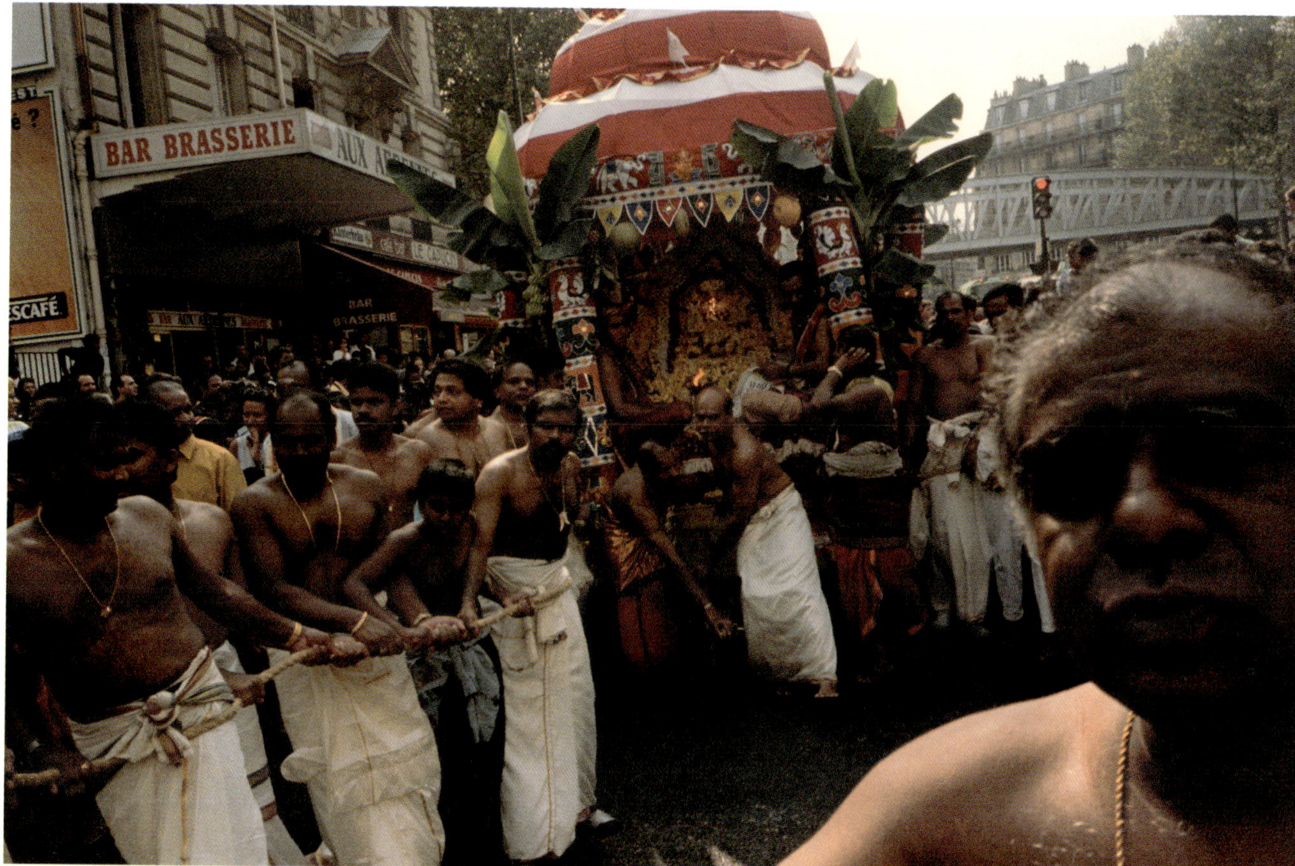

Sunday, September 12. Paris. Gare du Nord area, South Indian community celebration

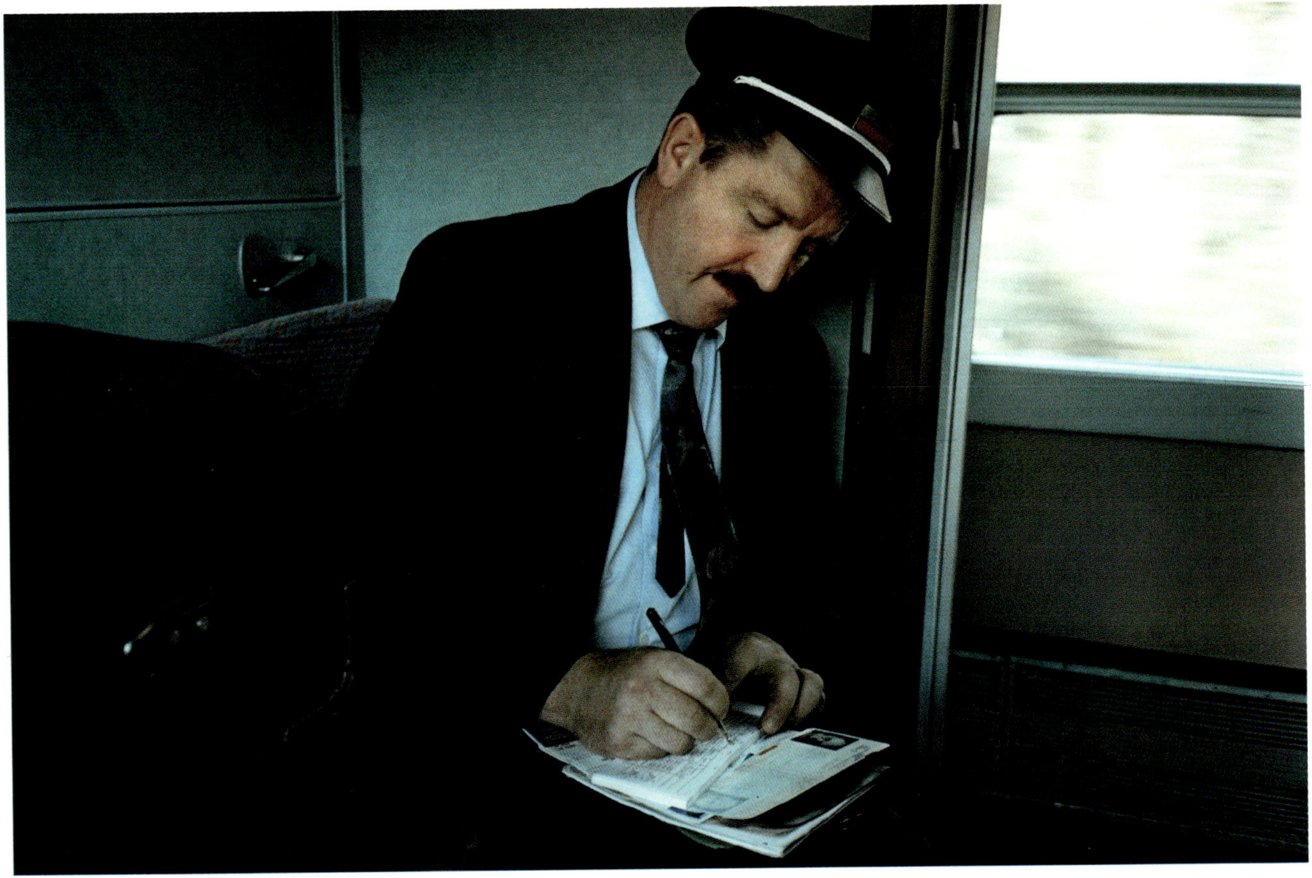

Monday, September 13. Paris-Vienna train. I had forgotten my discount card

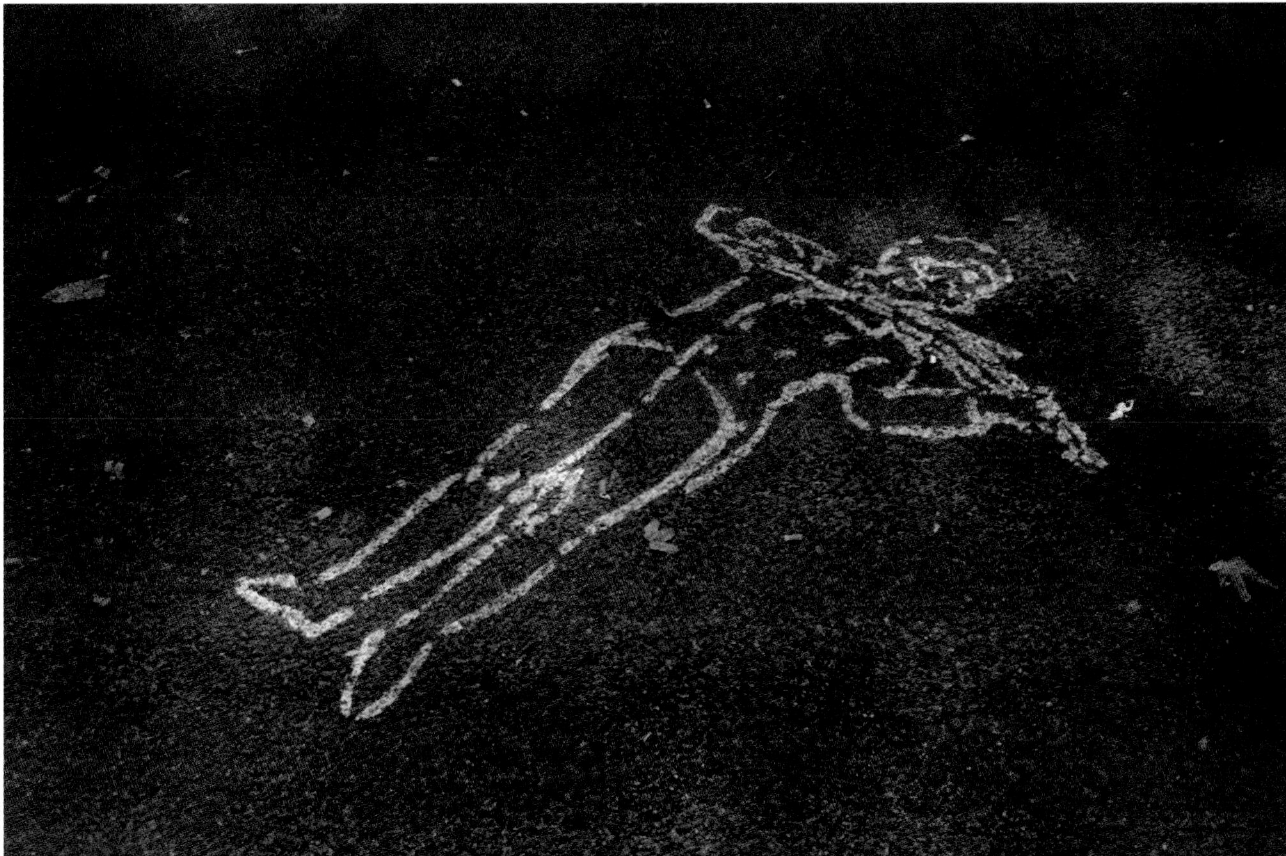

Tuesday, September 14. Vienna. Musical pavement

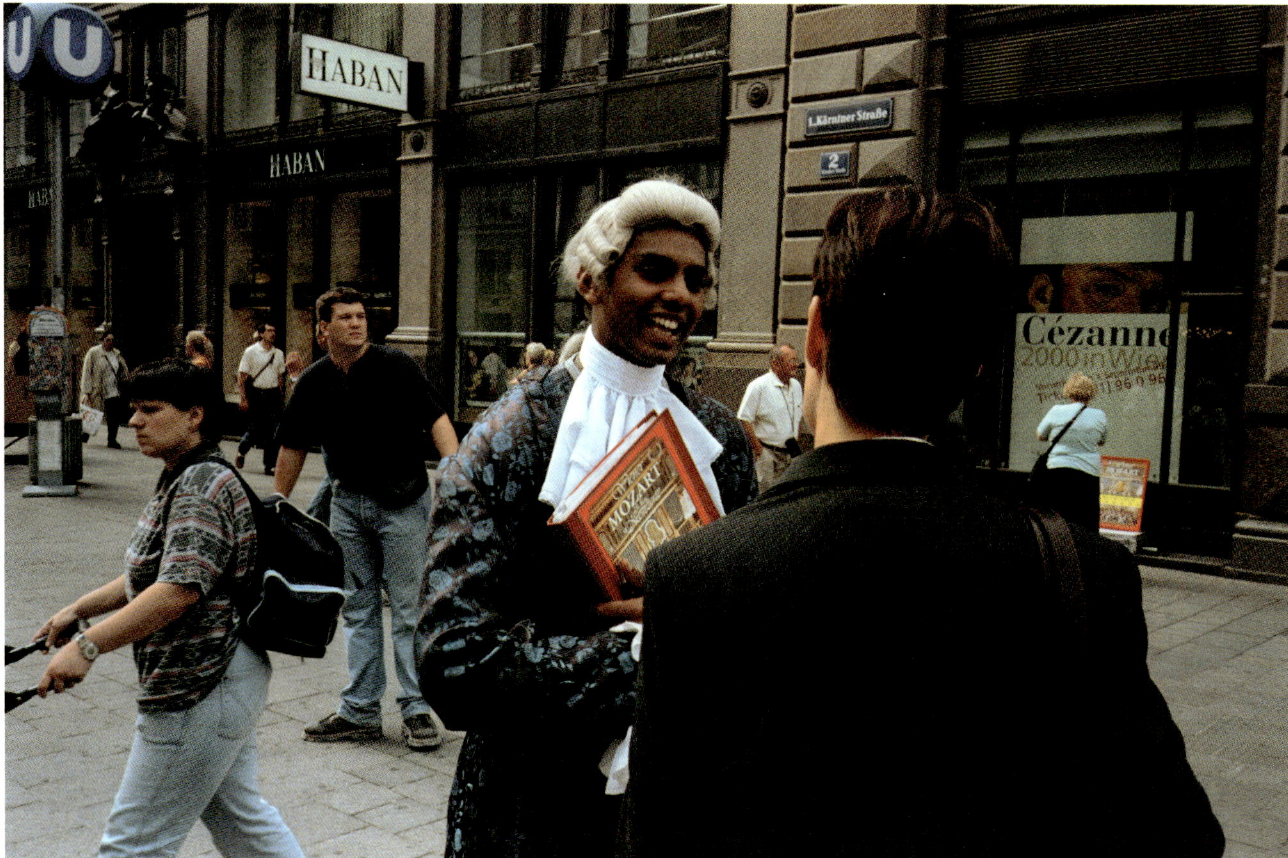

Wednesday, September 15. Vienna. Street scene

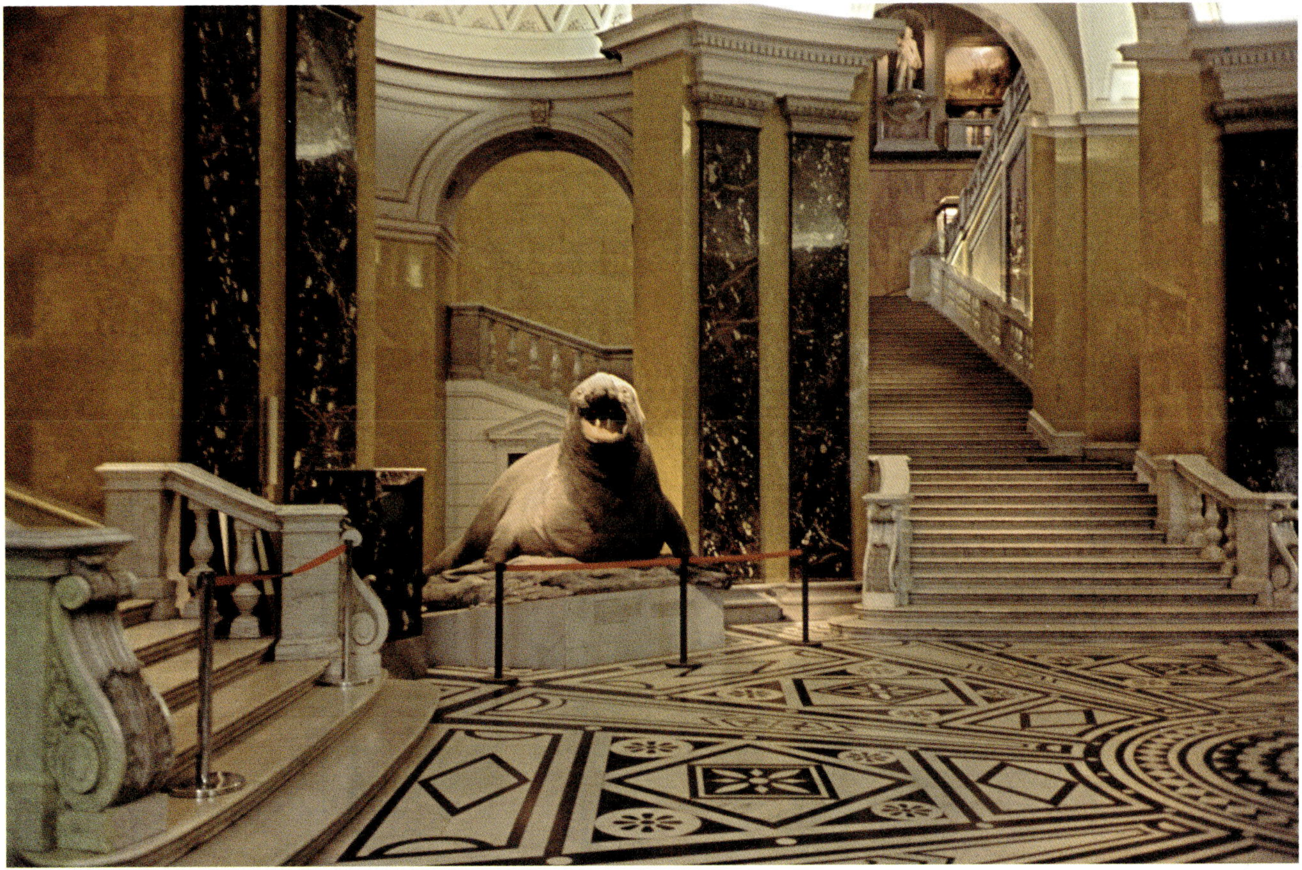

Wednesday, September 15. Vienna. At the Natural History Museum

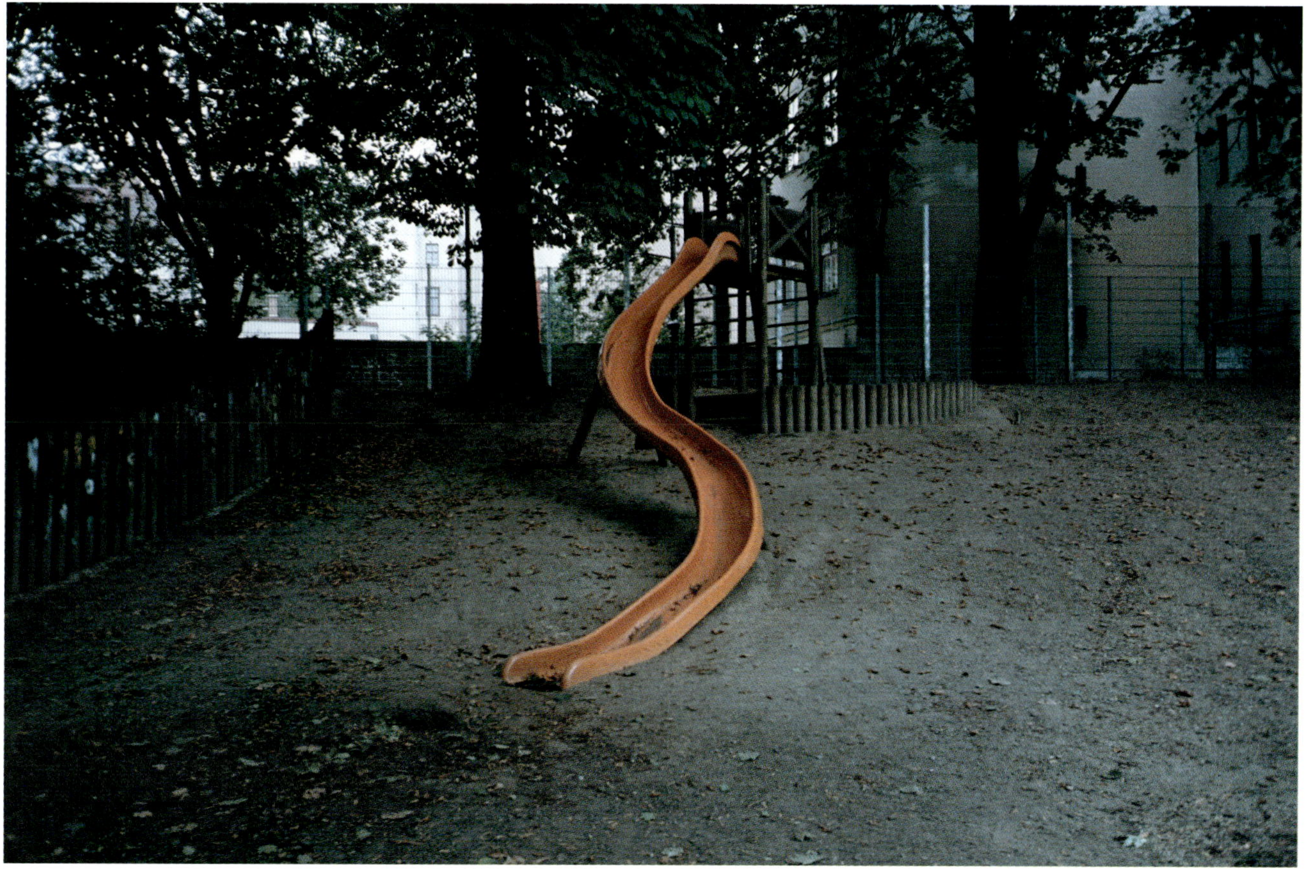

Thursday, September 16. Vienna. In a public garden

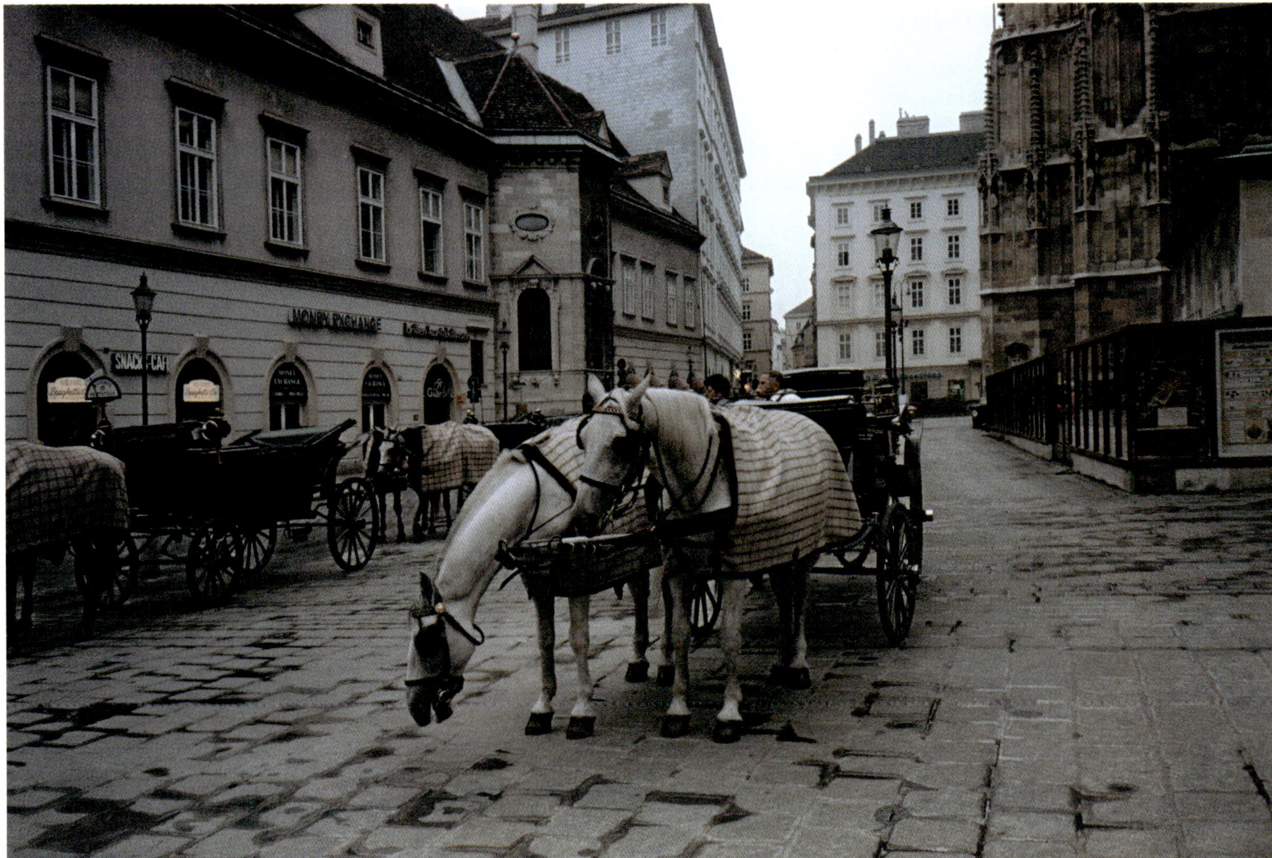

Friday, September 17. Vienna. In front of Saint Stephan cathedral

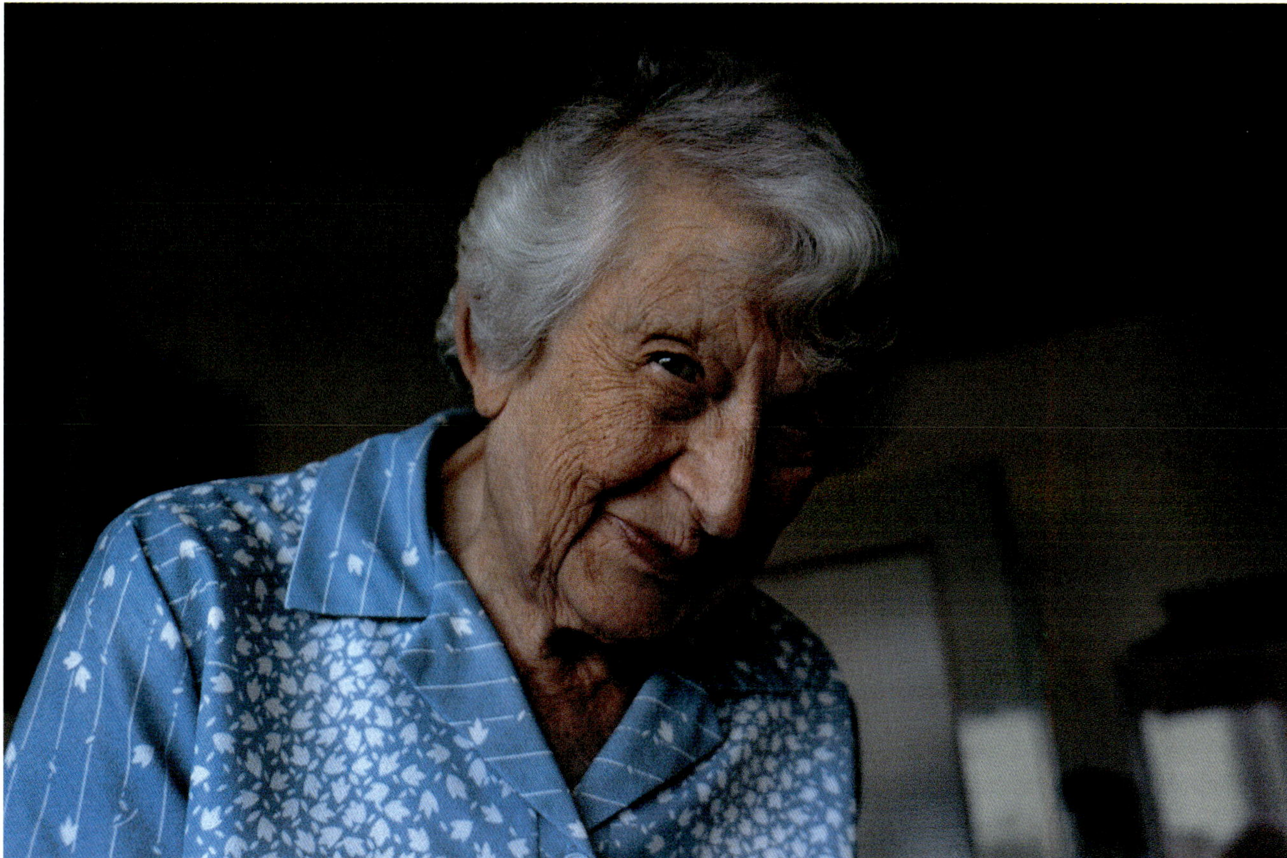

Saturday, September 18. Vienna. Olga Jaul, my mother's cousin

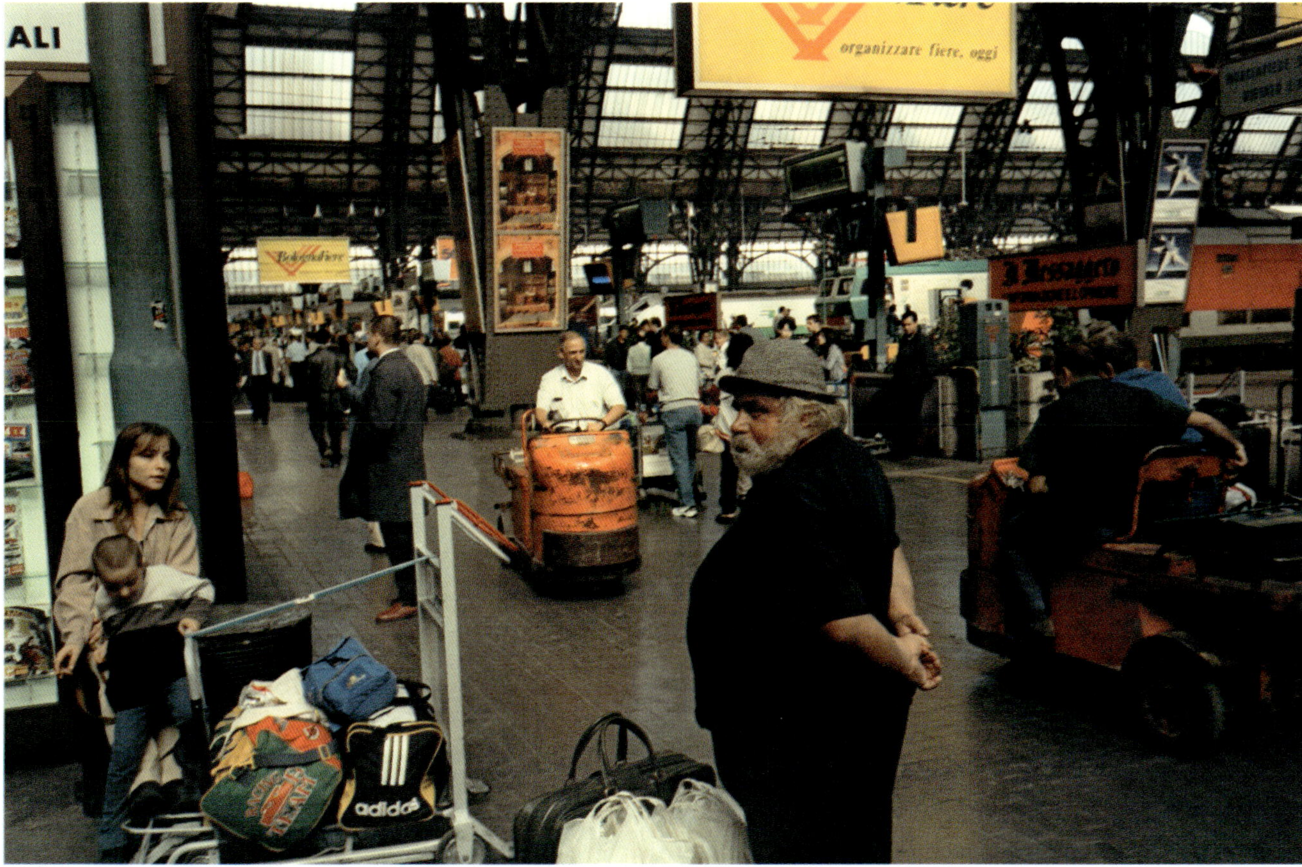

Sunday, September 19. Milan, Italy. Stazione Centrale

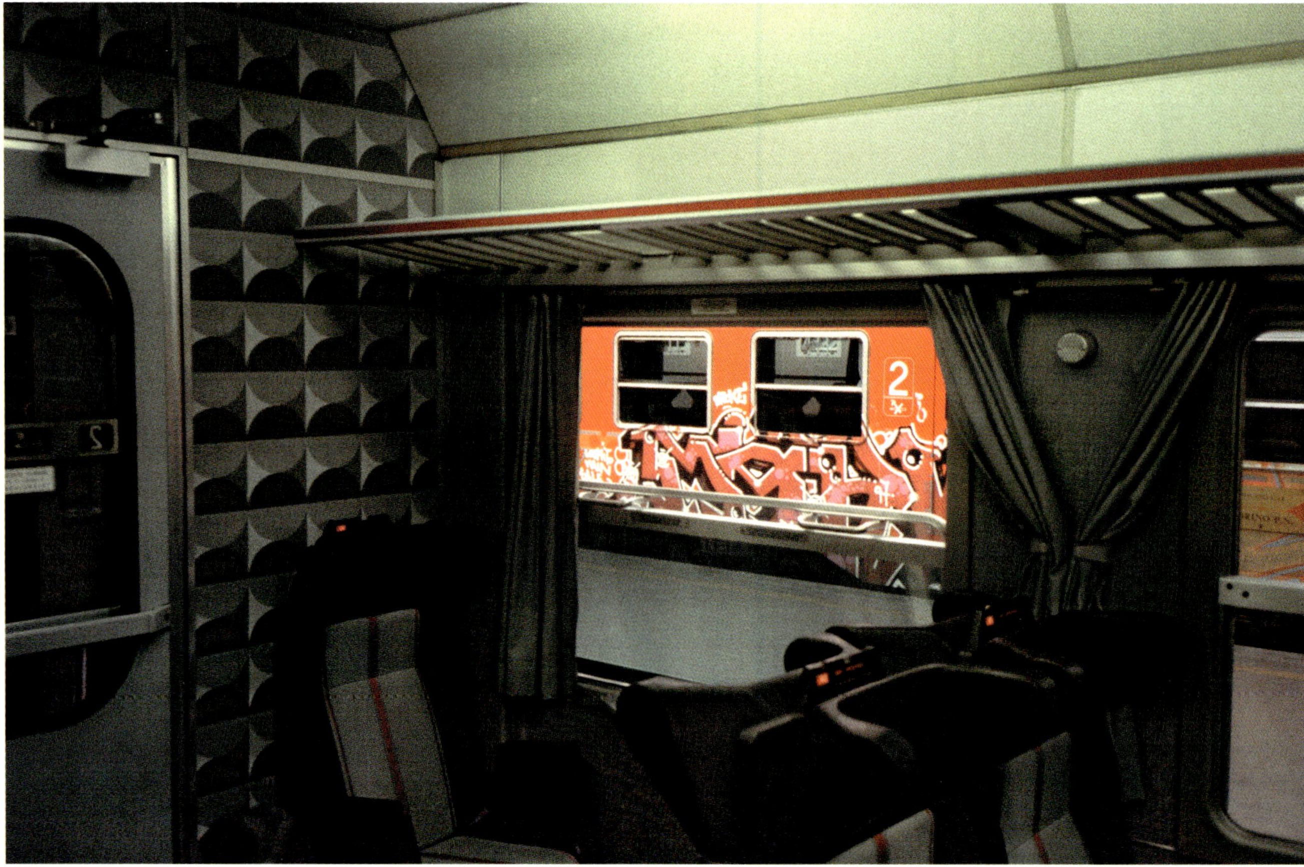

Monday, September 20. Milan, Italy. Railway scene

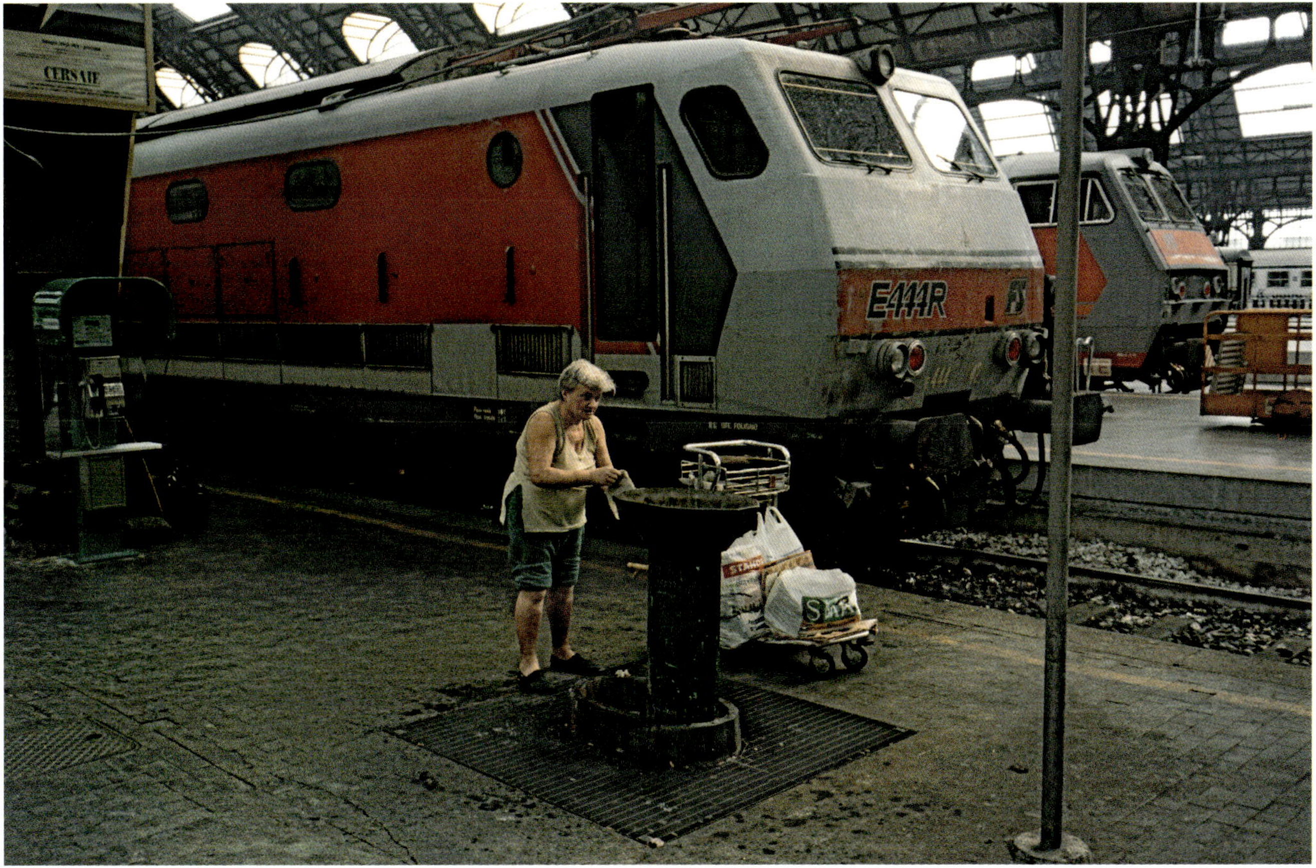

Monday, September 20. Milan, Italy. Railway scene

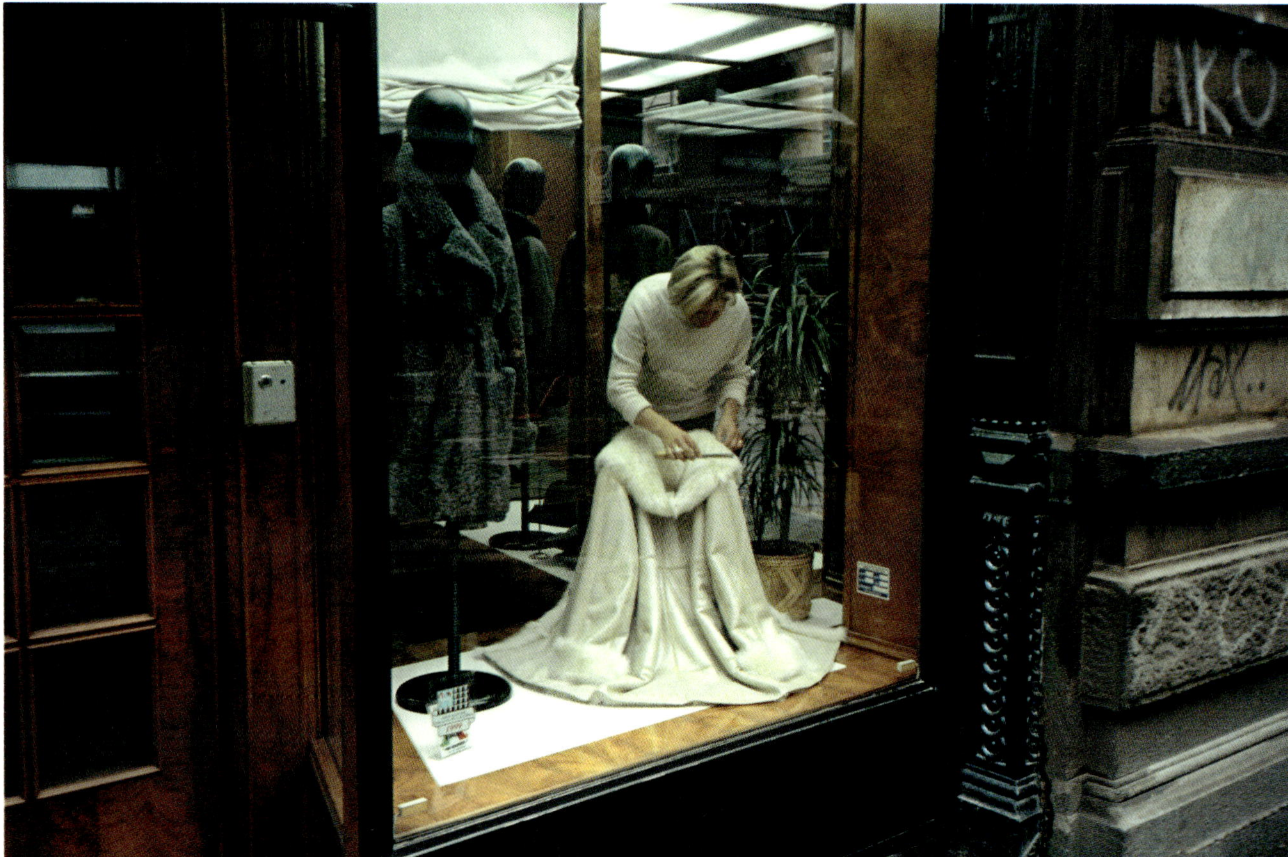

Tuesday, September 21. Milan, Italy. Street scene

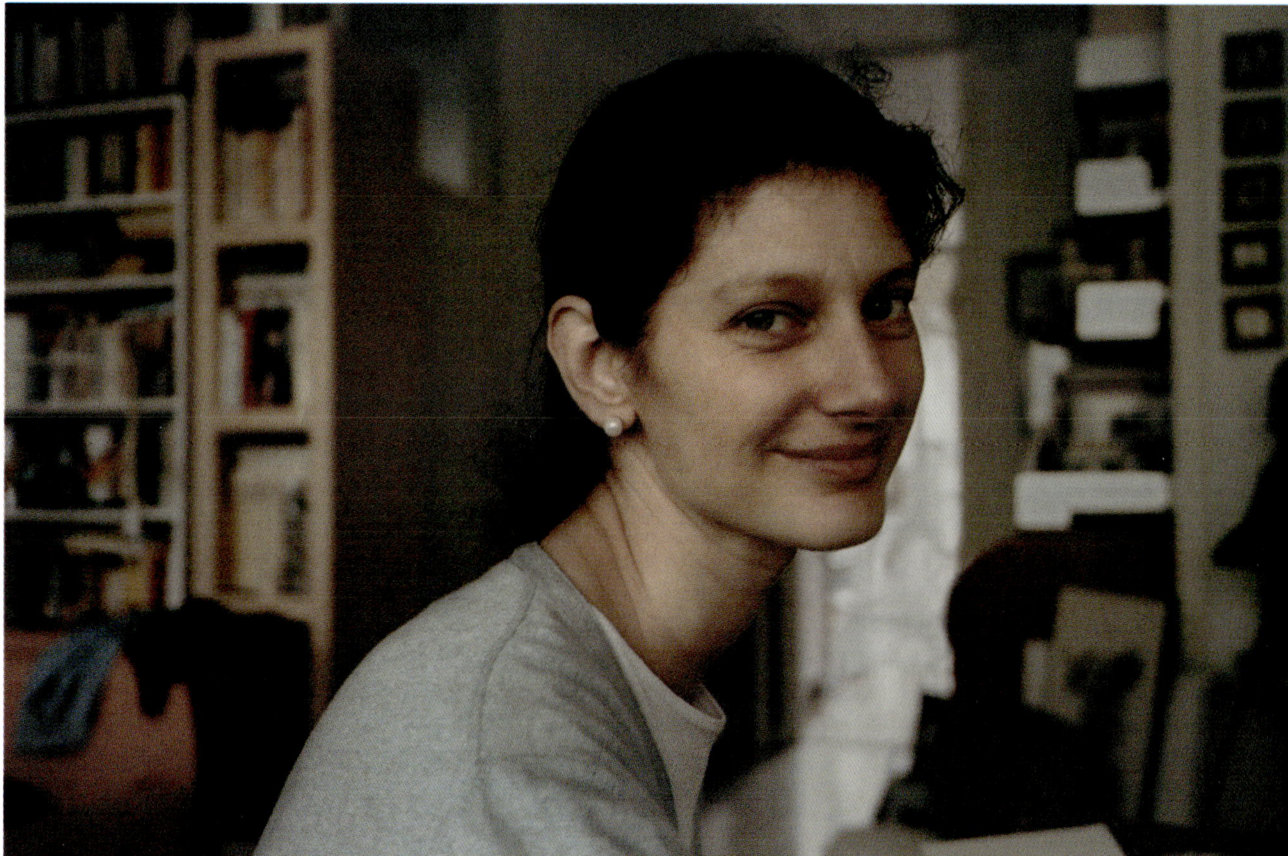

Wednesday, September 22. Milan, Italy. Alessandra Ceretti

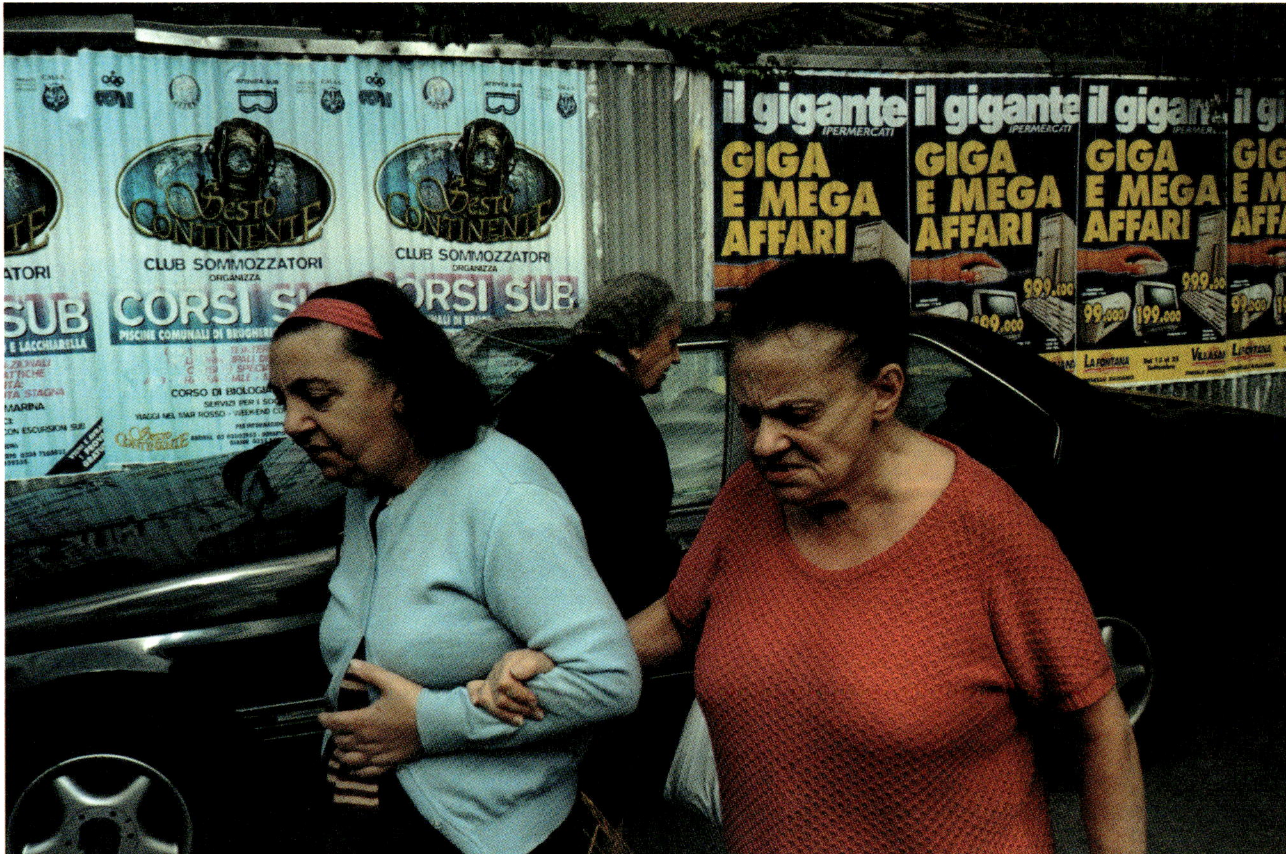

Thursday, September 23. Milan, Italy. Street scene

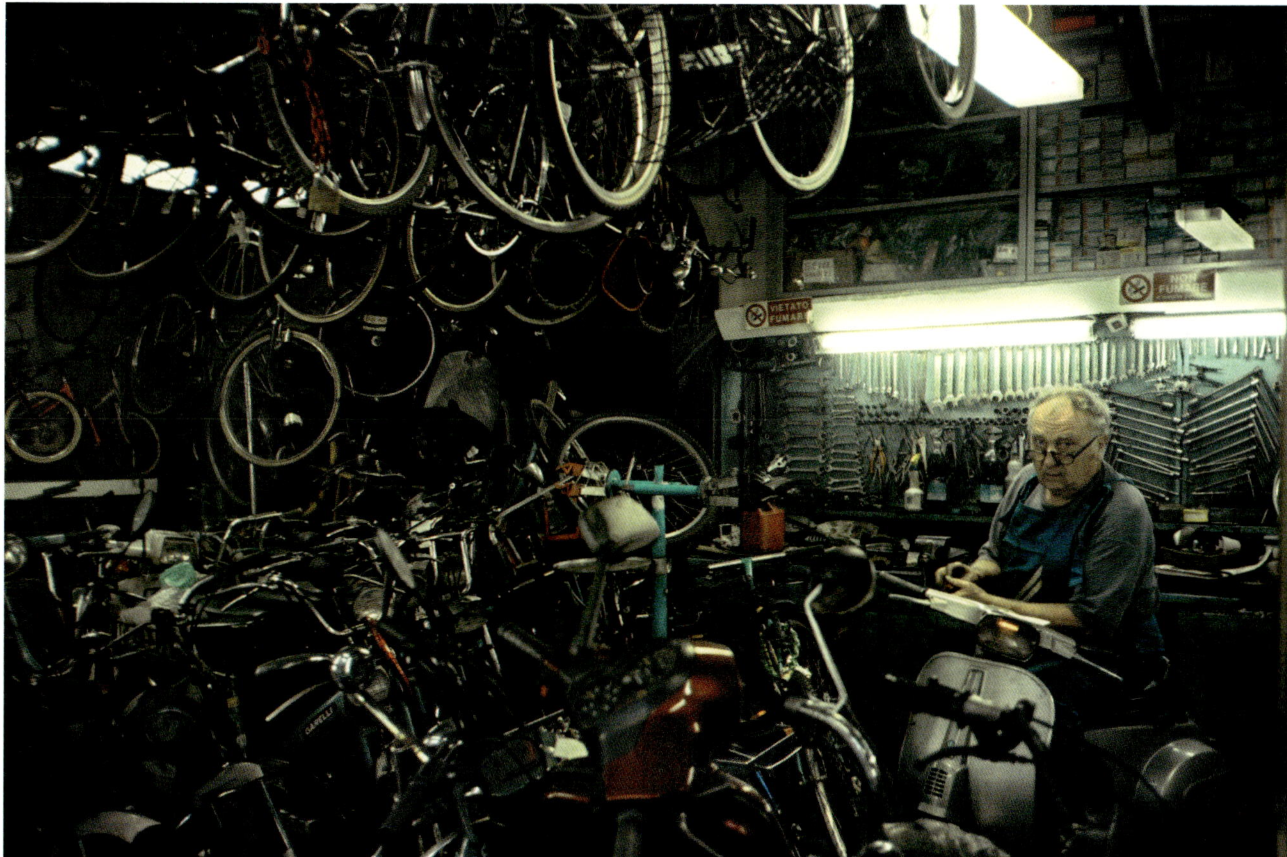

Thursday, September 23. Milan, Italy. Bicycle repair shop

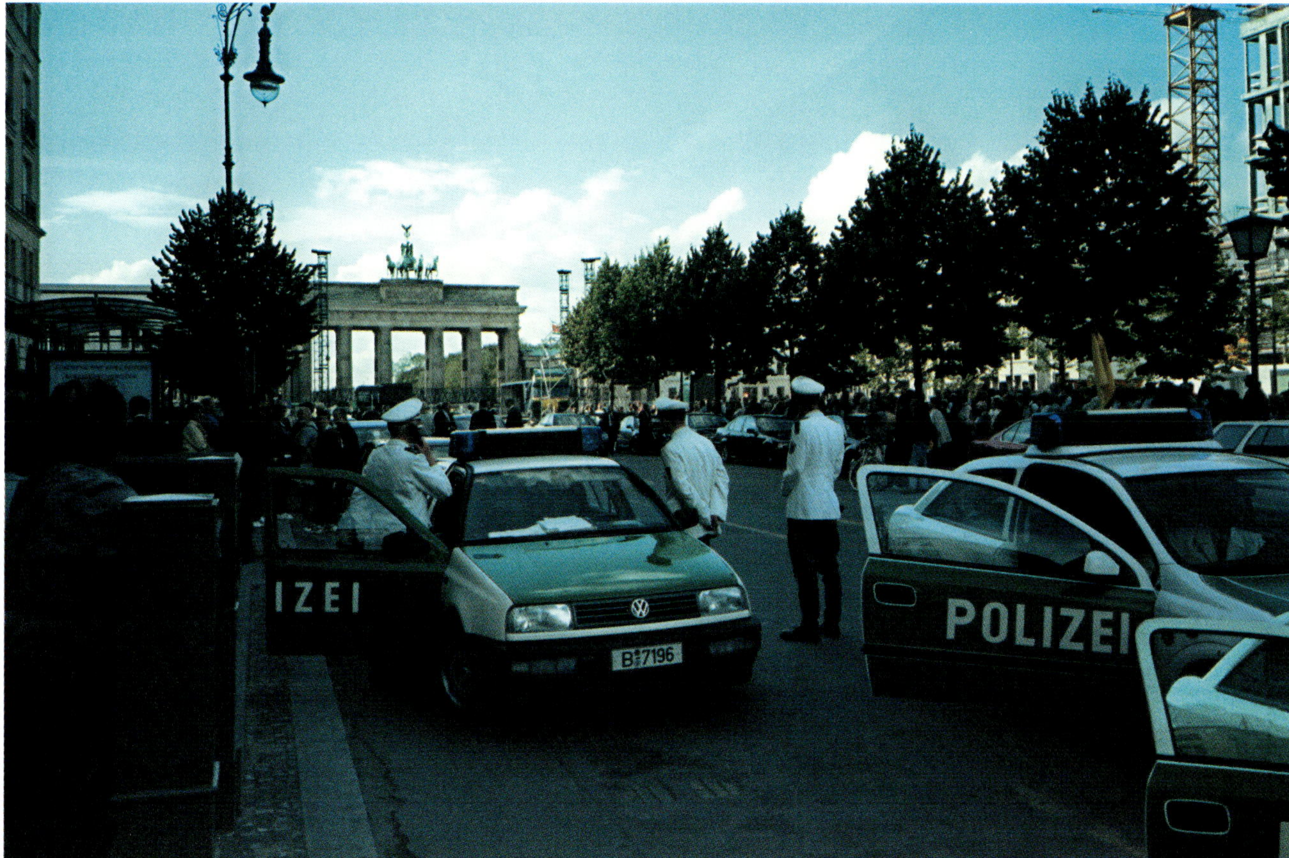

Friday, September 24. Berlin. Unter den Linden

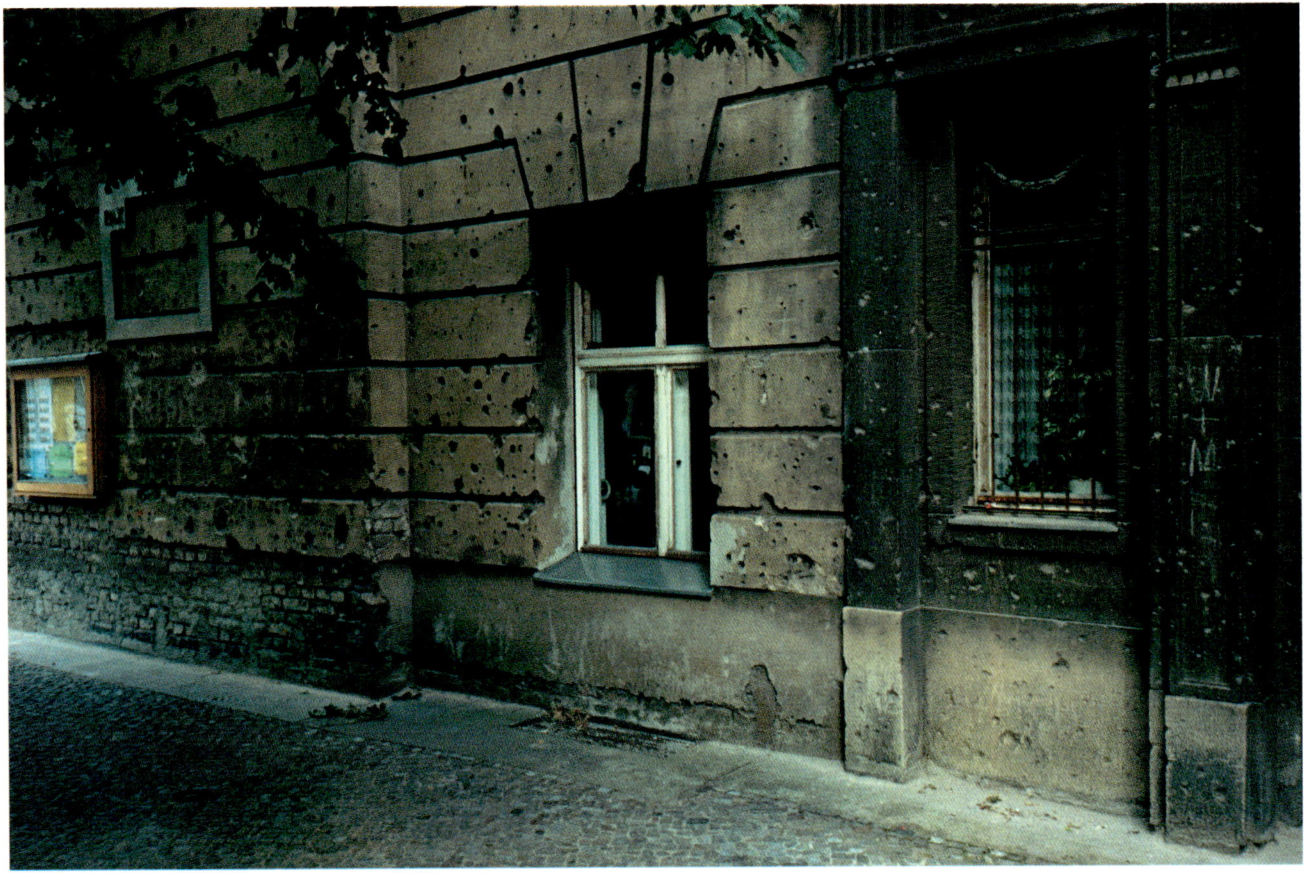

Saturday, September 25. Berlin. Bullet marks from 1945, in the former eastern sector

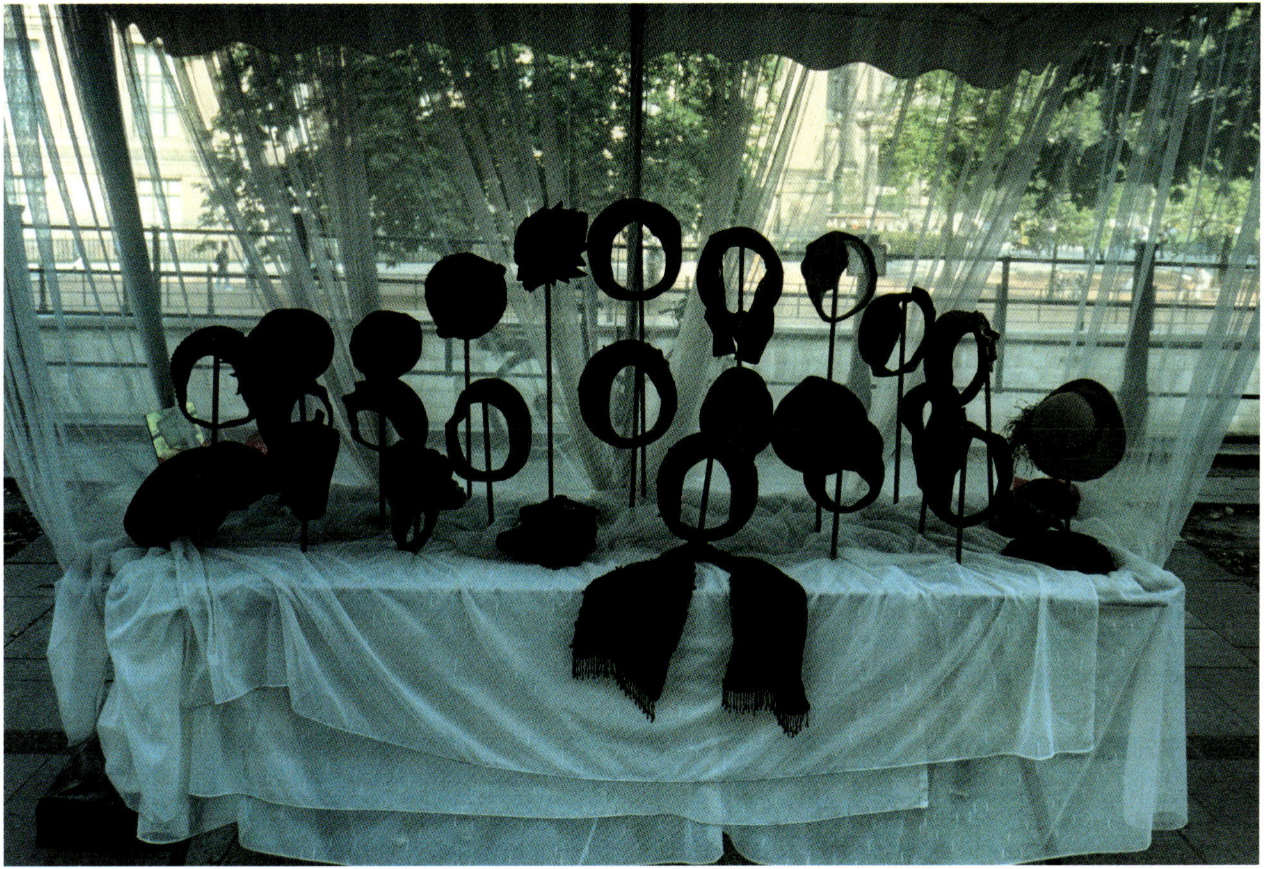

Sunday, September 26. Berlin. Street market, in the former eastern sector

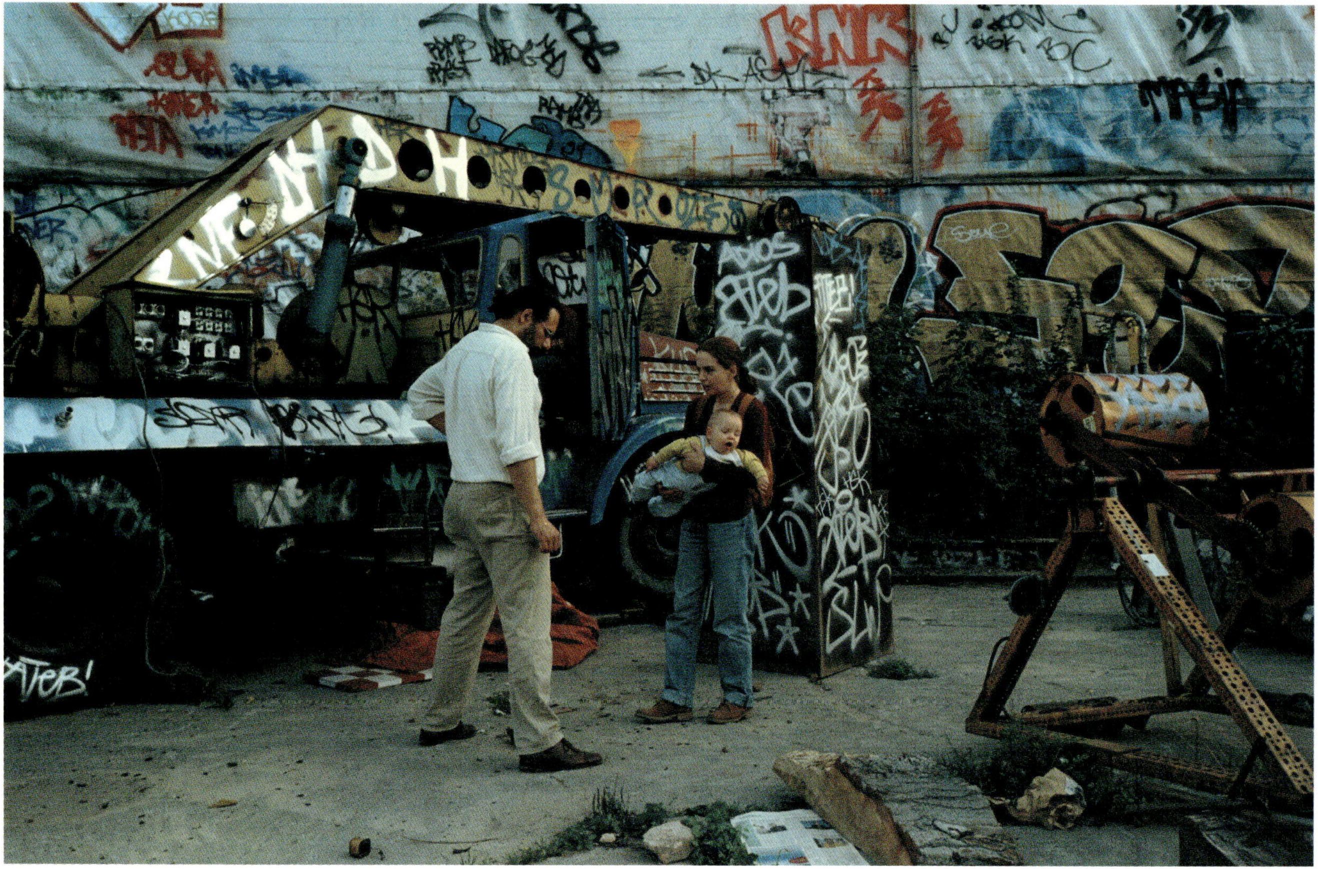

Monday, September 27. Berlin. Artist's squat, in the former eastern sector

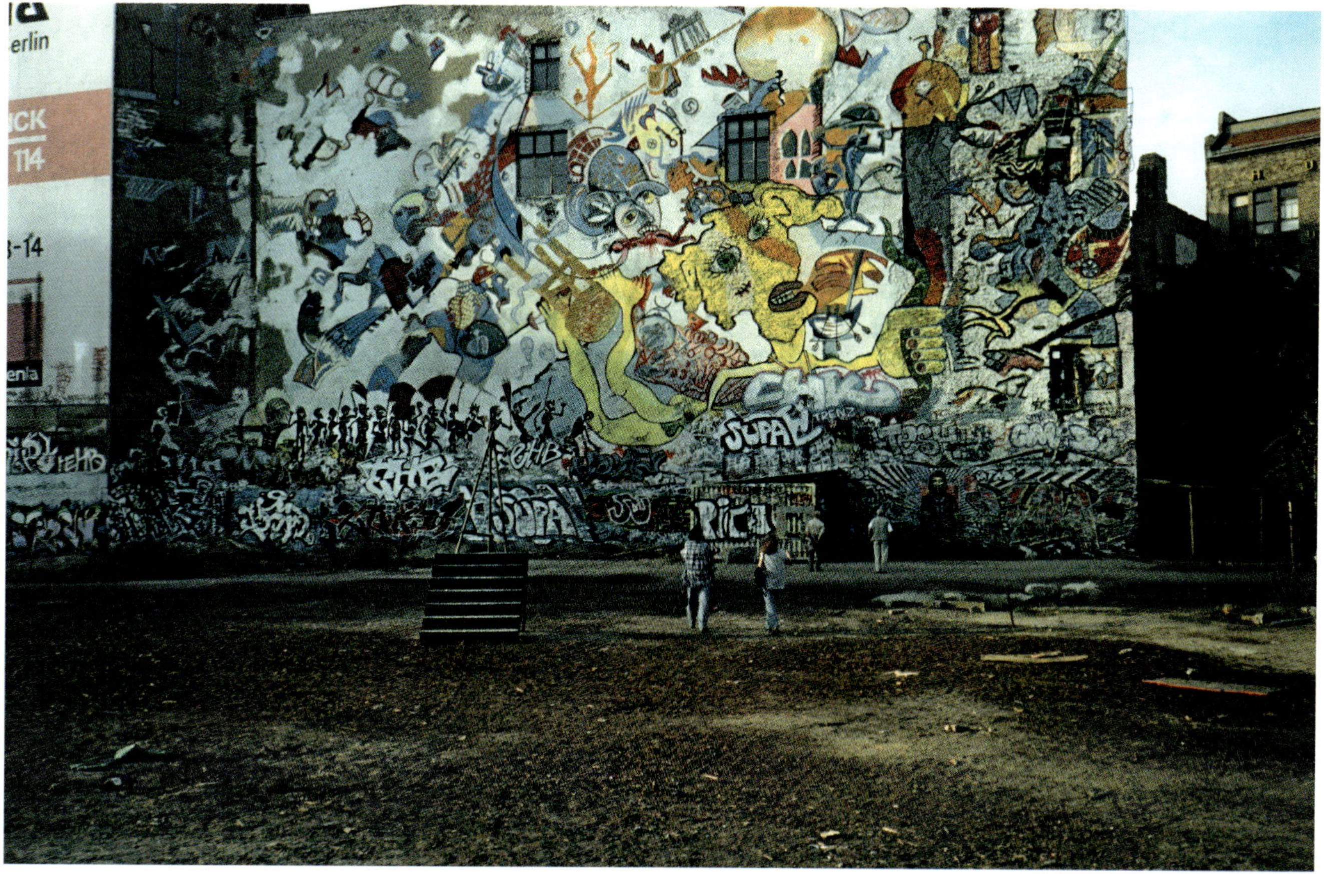

Tuesday, September 28. Berlin. Artist's squat, in the former eastern sector

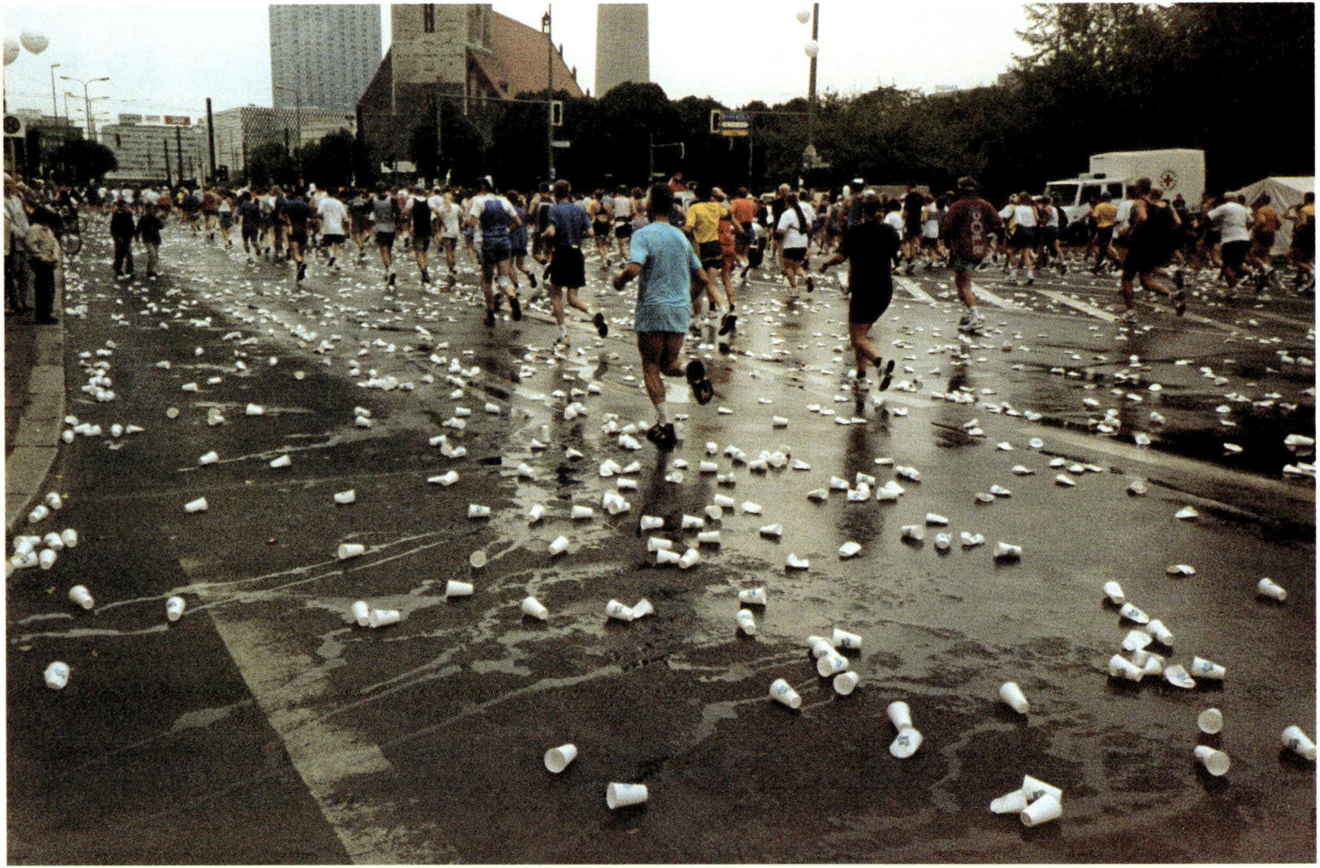

Wednesday, September 29. Berlin. Unter den Linden, end of a marathon

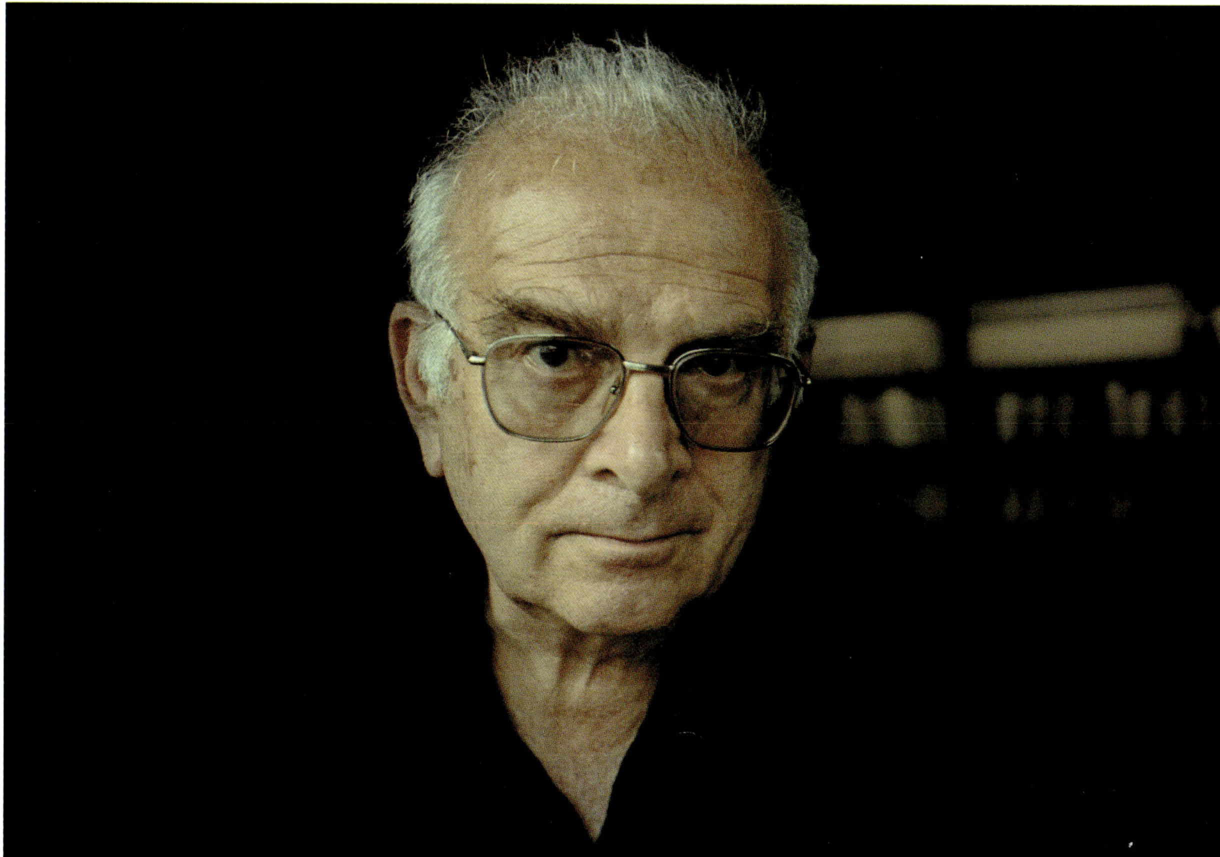

Thursday, September 30. Boulogne, France. Self-portrait

OCTOBER

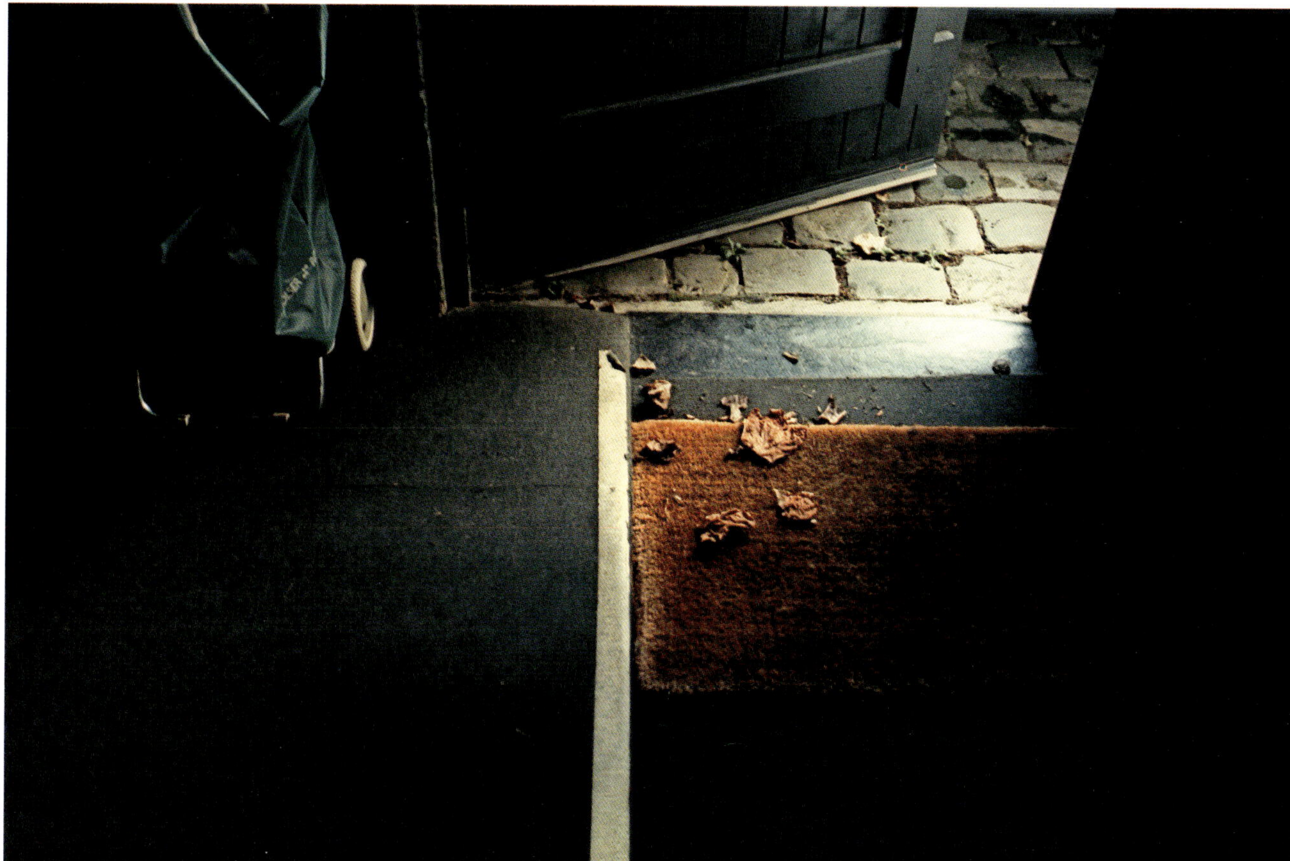

Friday, October 1. Boulogne, France. The entrance to my studio

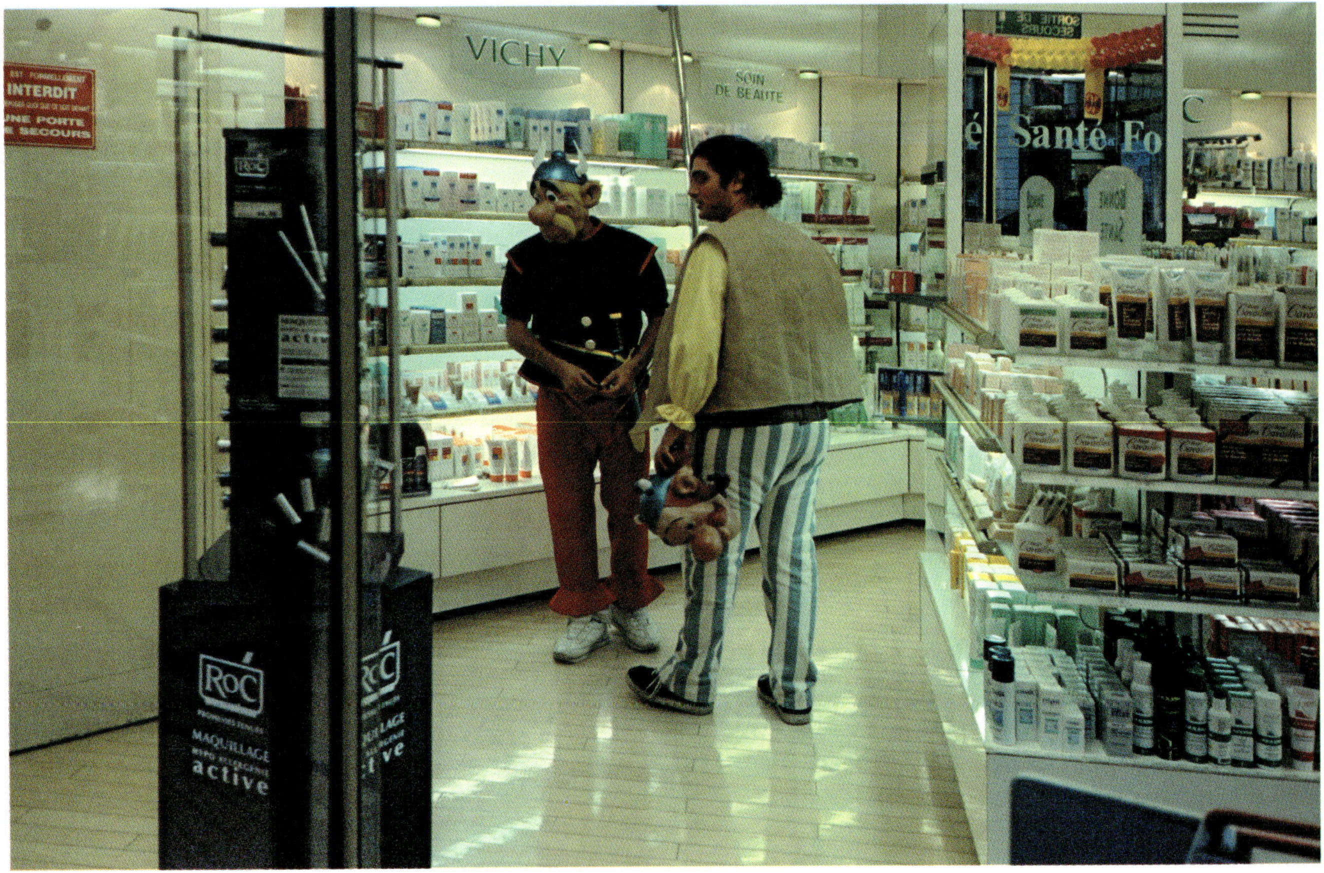

Saturday, October 2. Paris. Shop scene

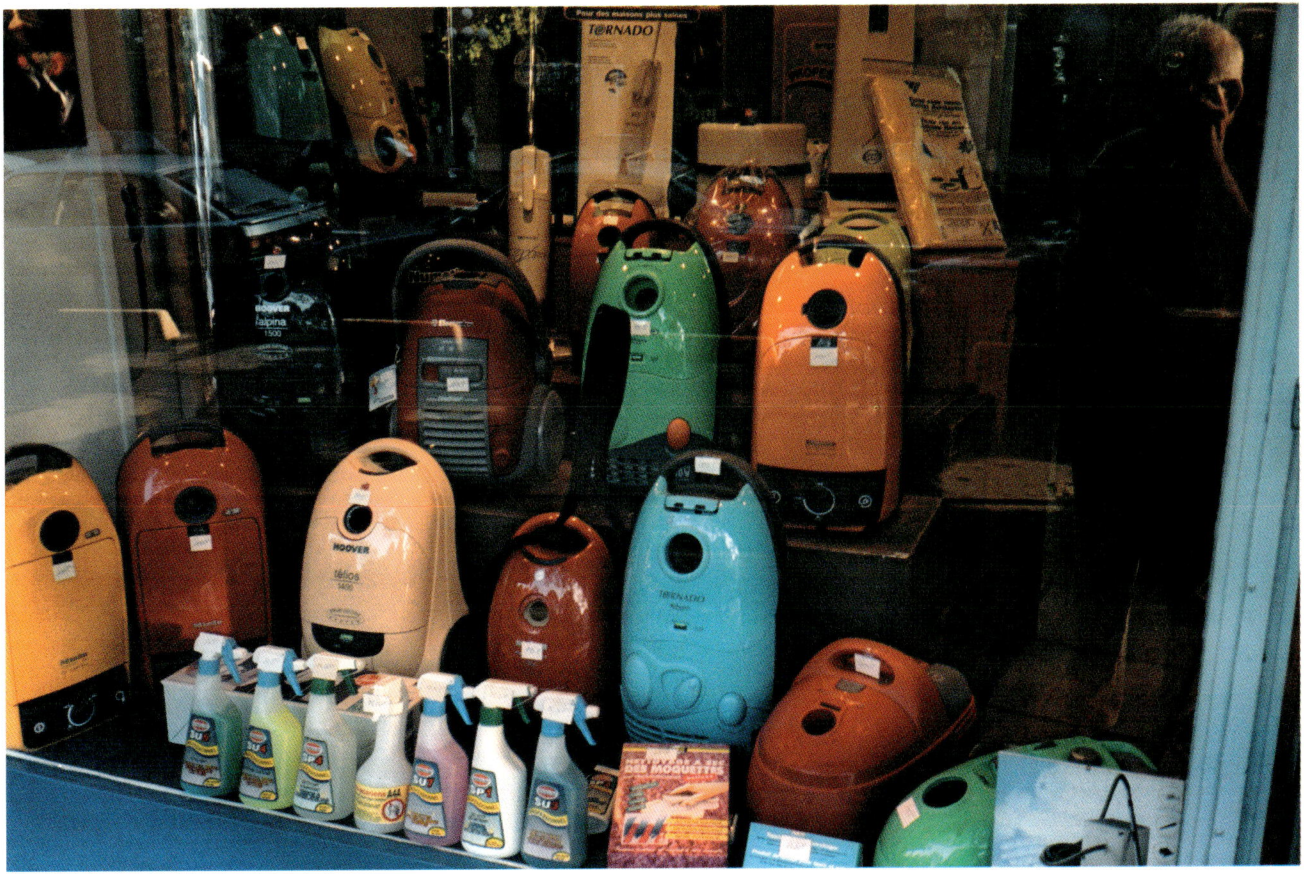

Sunday, October 3. Boulogne, France. Window display

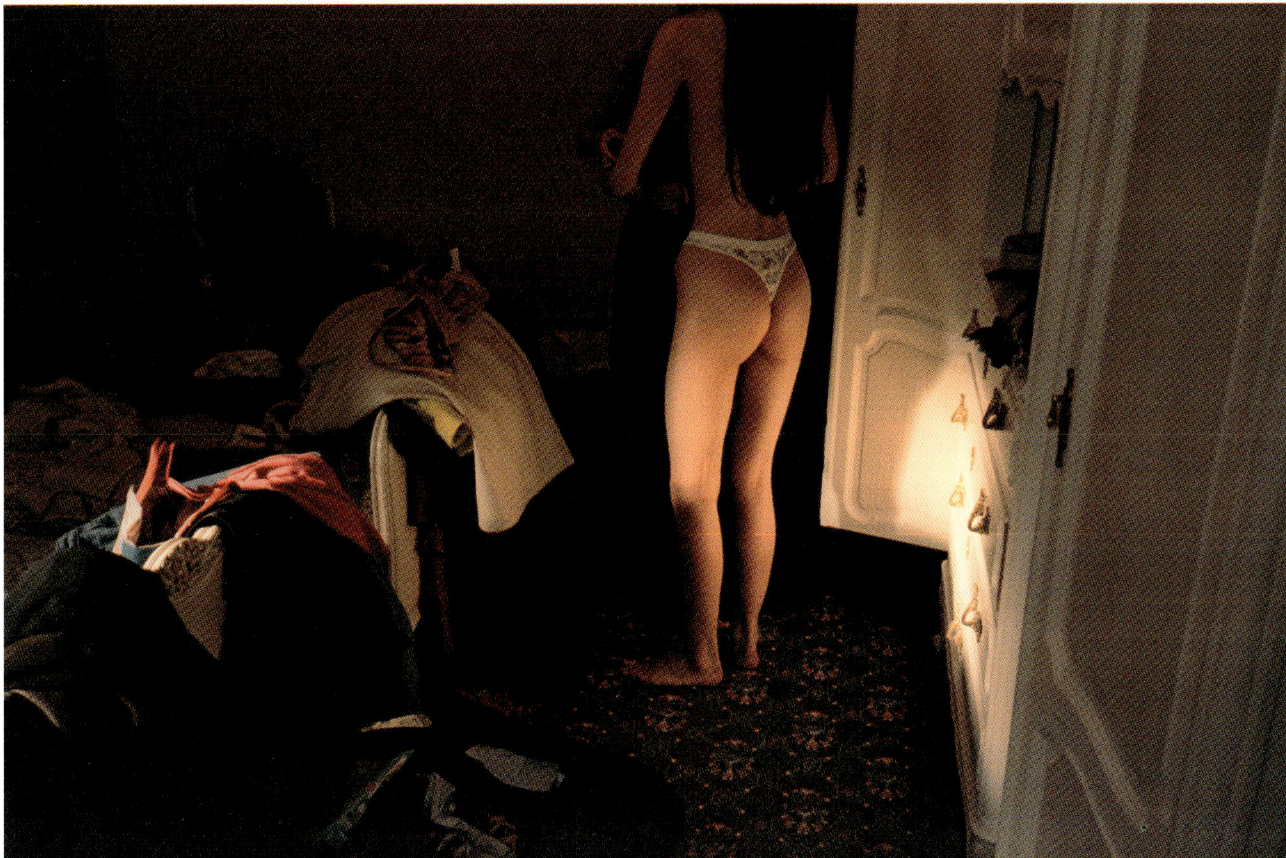

Monday, October 4. Paris. Fitting for fashion photographs, for Donna magazine, Milan

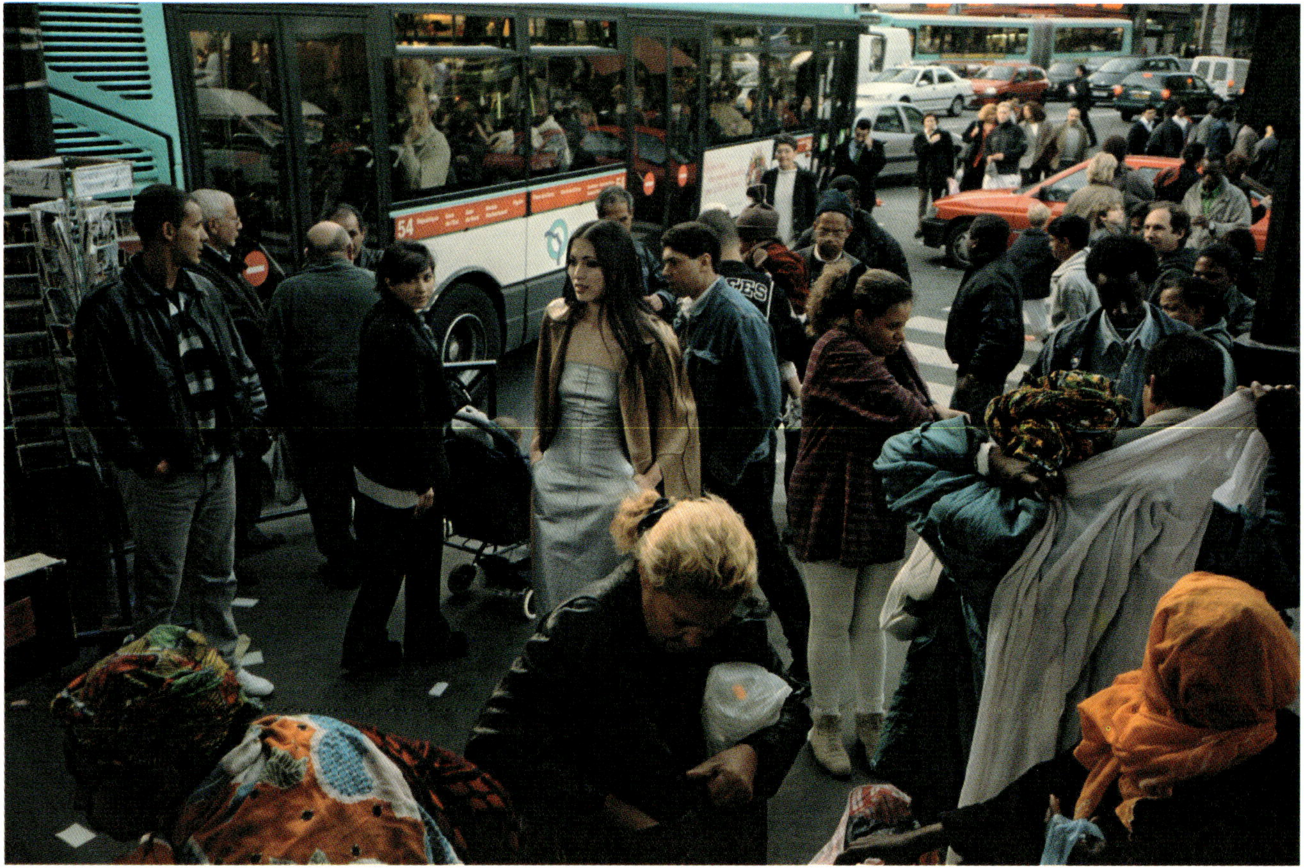

Tuesday, October 5. Paris. Fashion photograph for Donna, Milan

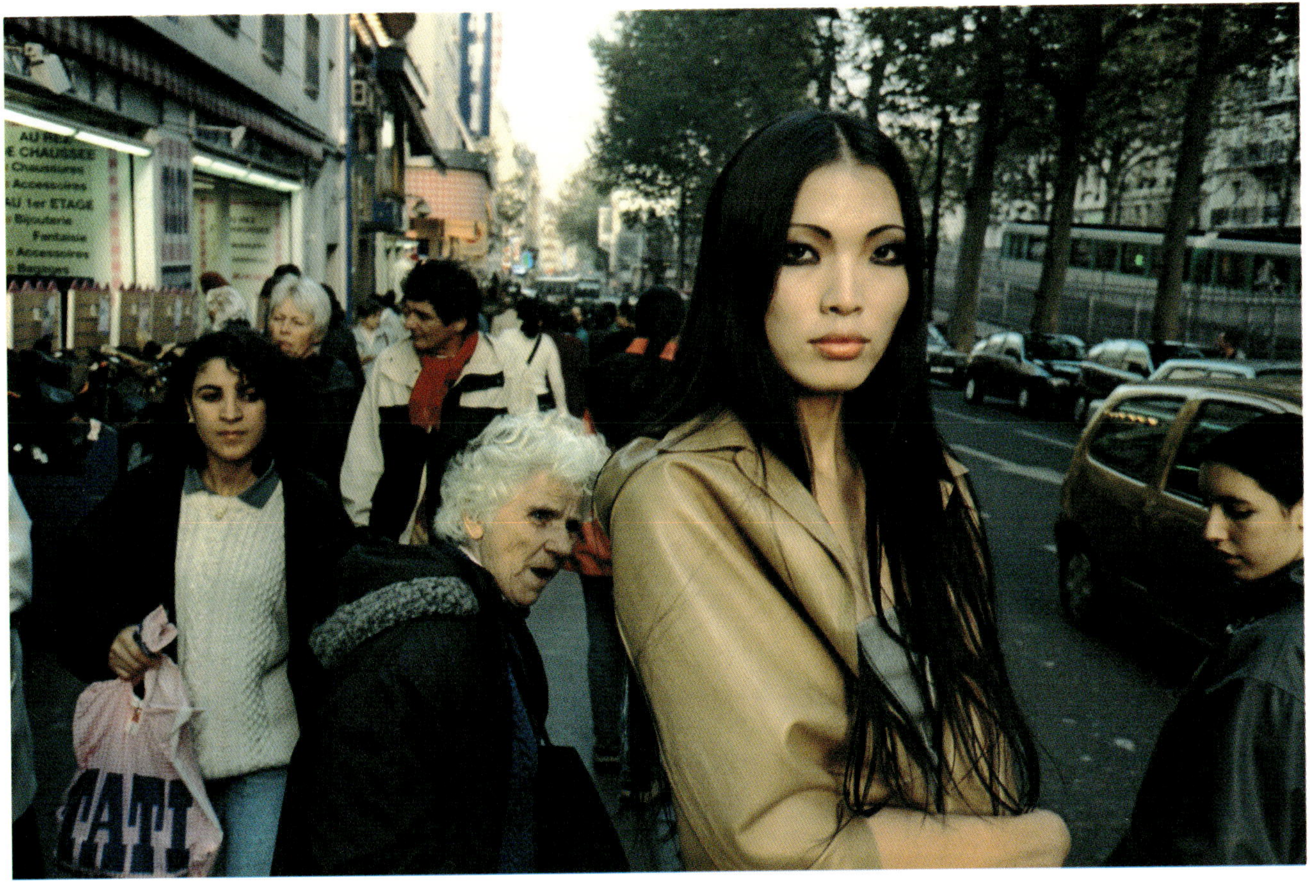

Tuesday, October 5. Paris. Fashion photograph for Donna, Milan

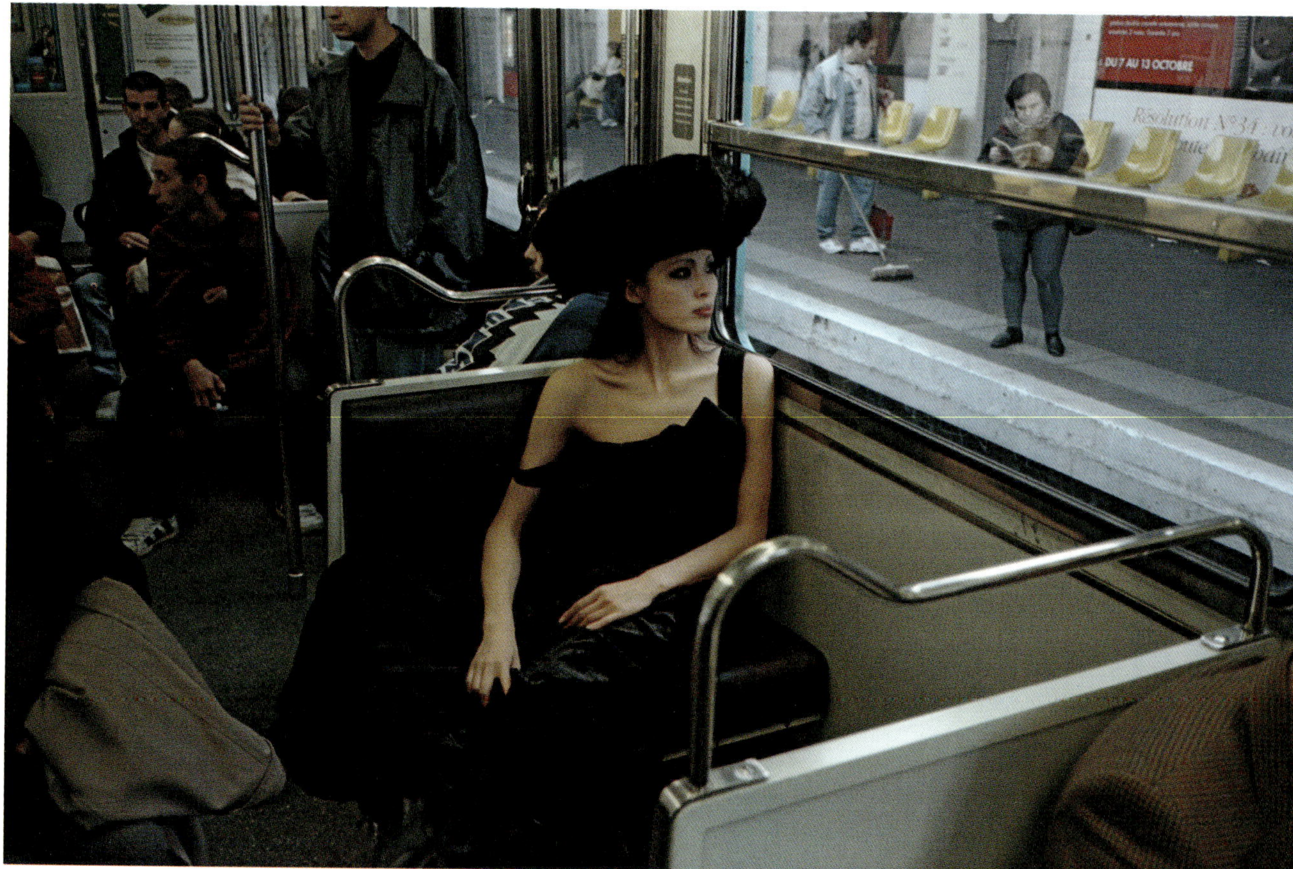

Wednesday, October 6. Paris. Fashion photograph for Donna, Milan

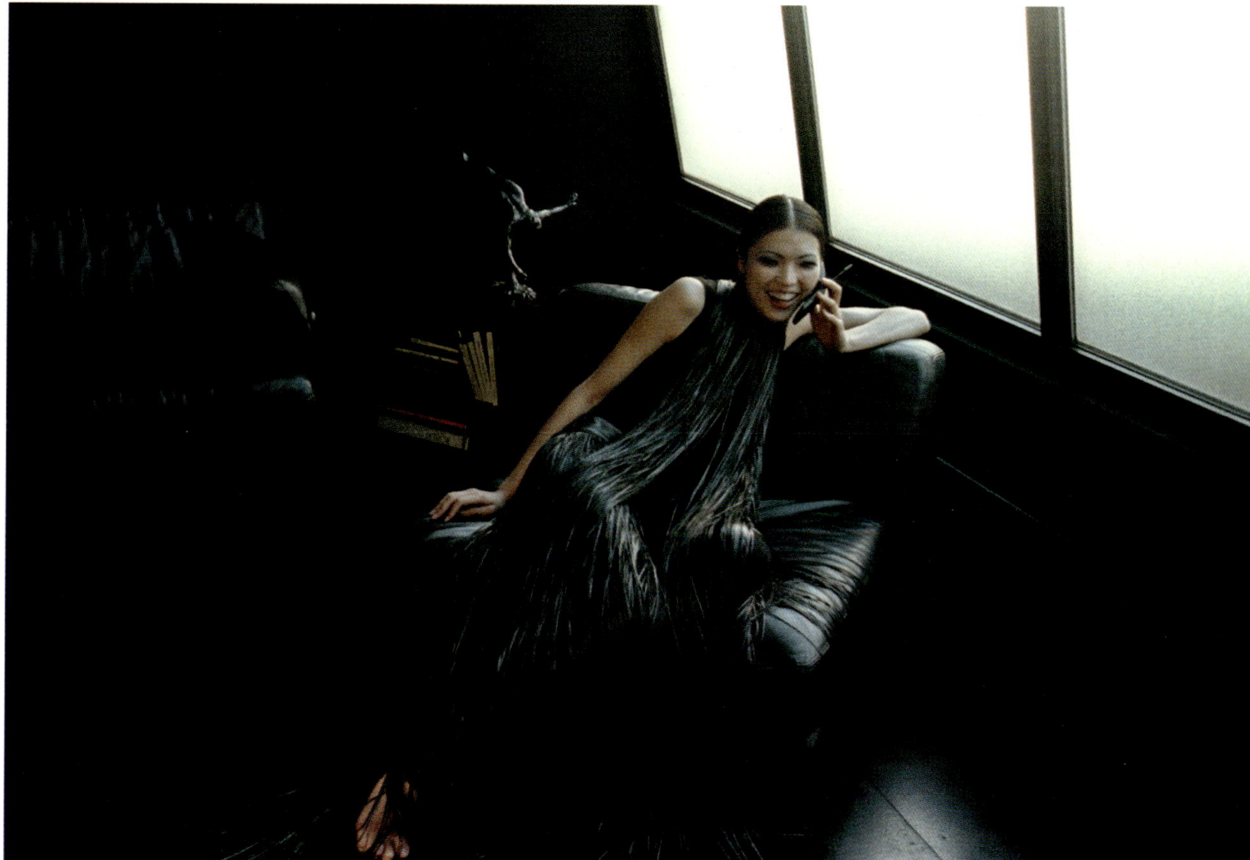

Wednesday, October 6. Paris. Fashion photograph for Donna, Milan

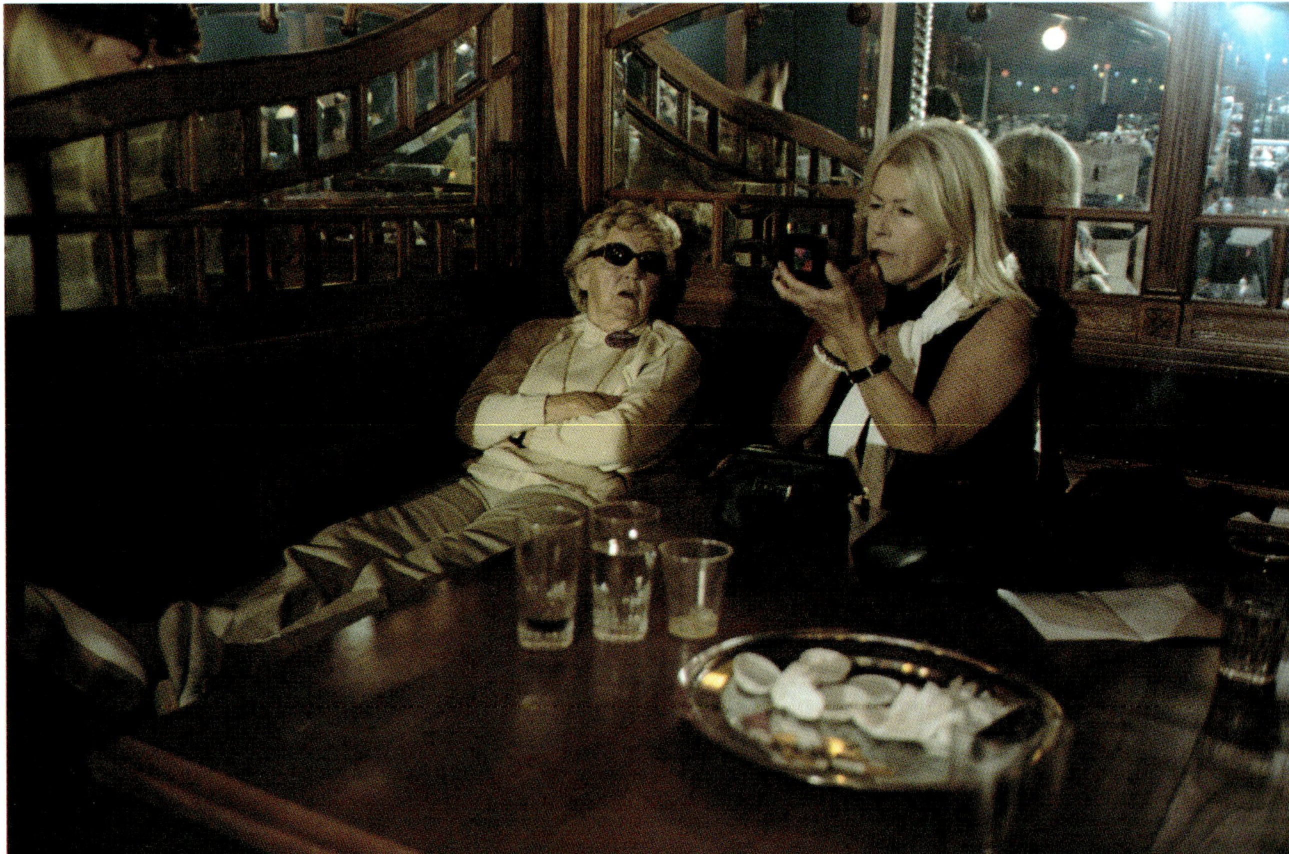

Thursday, October 7. Paris. Kenzo fashion show, Parc de La Villette

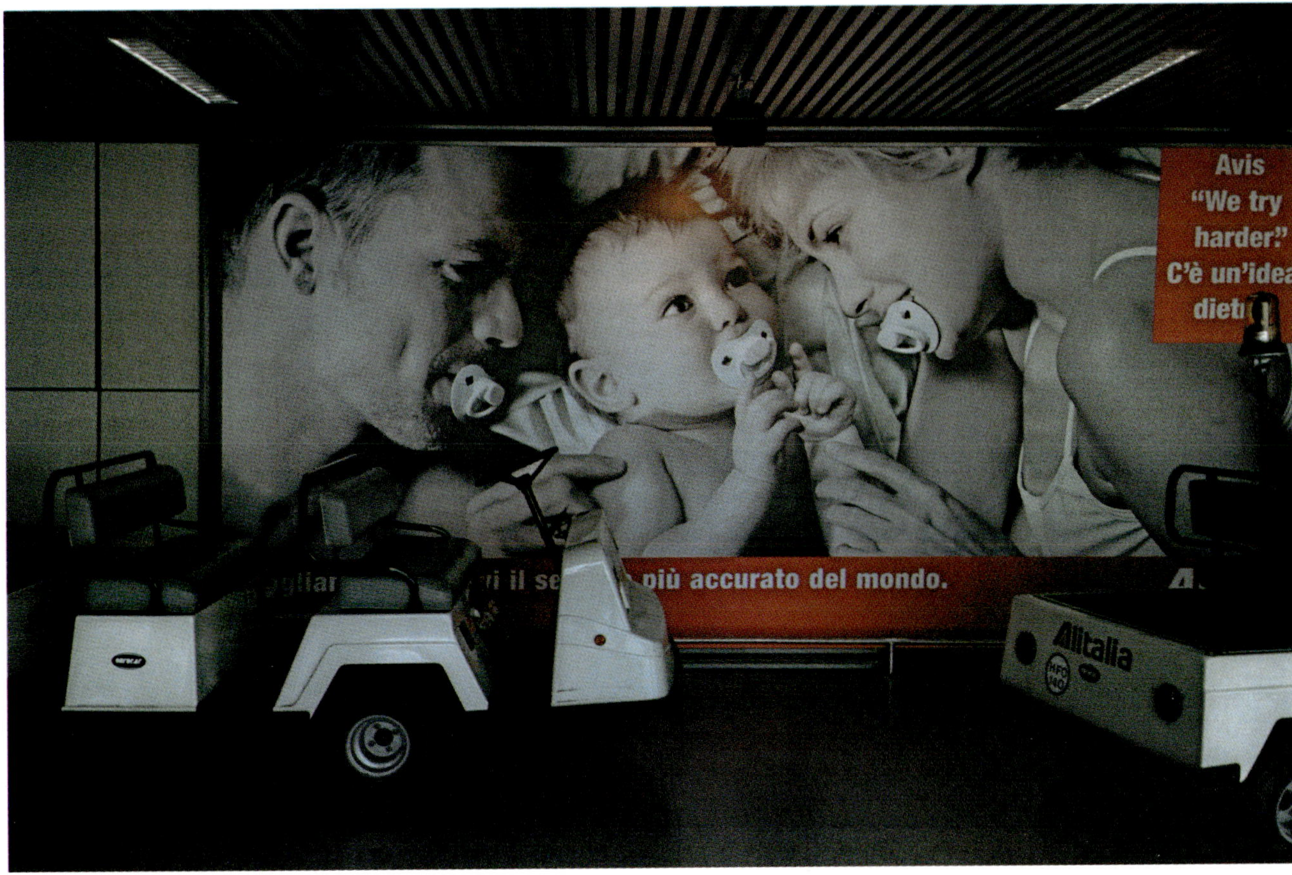

Friday, October 8. Rome. Leonardo da Vinci airport

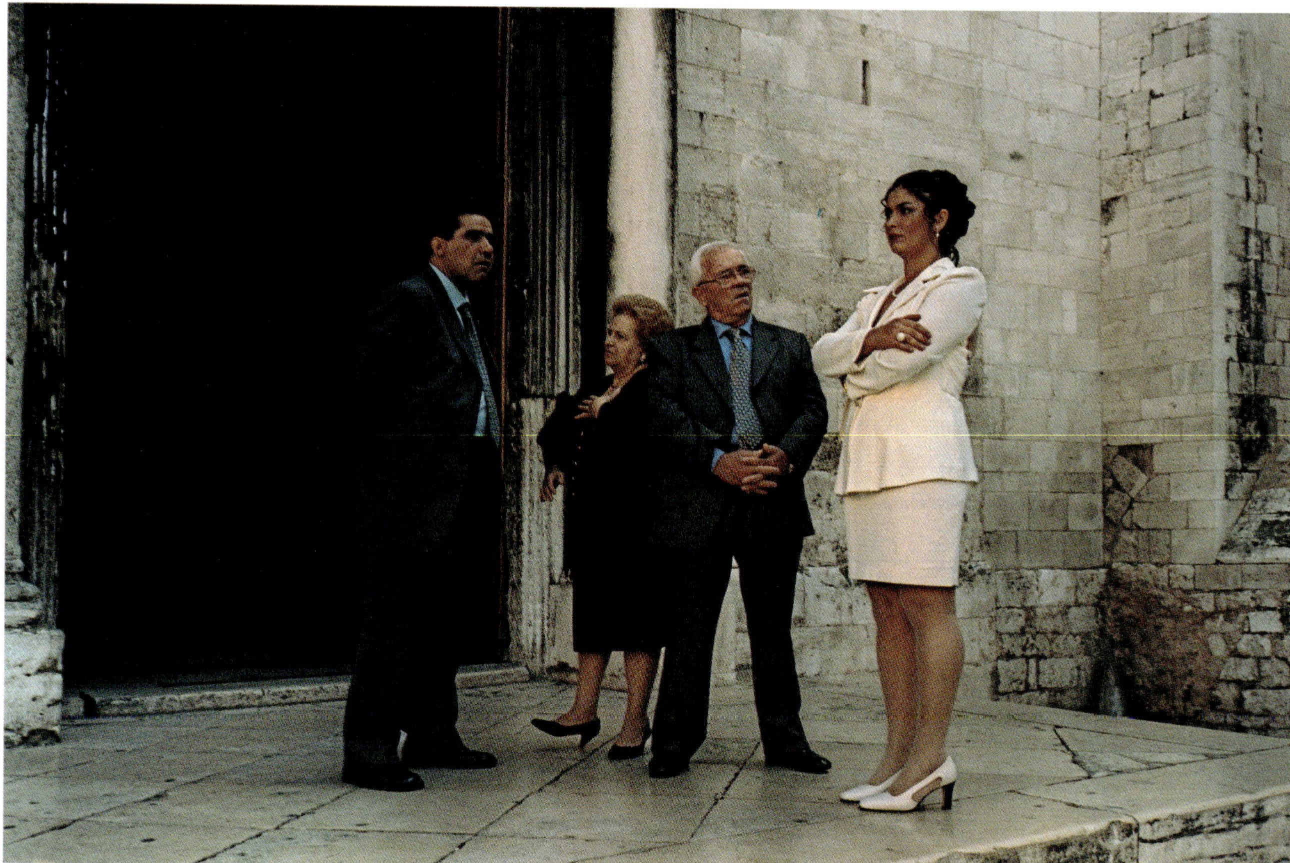

Saturday, October 9. Bari, Italy. Street scene

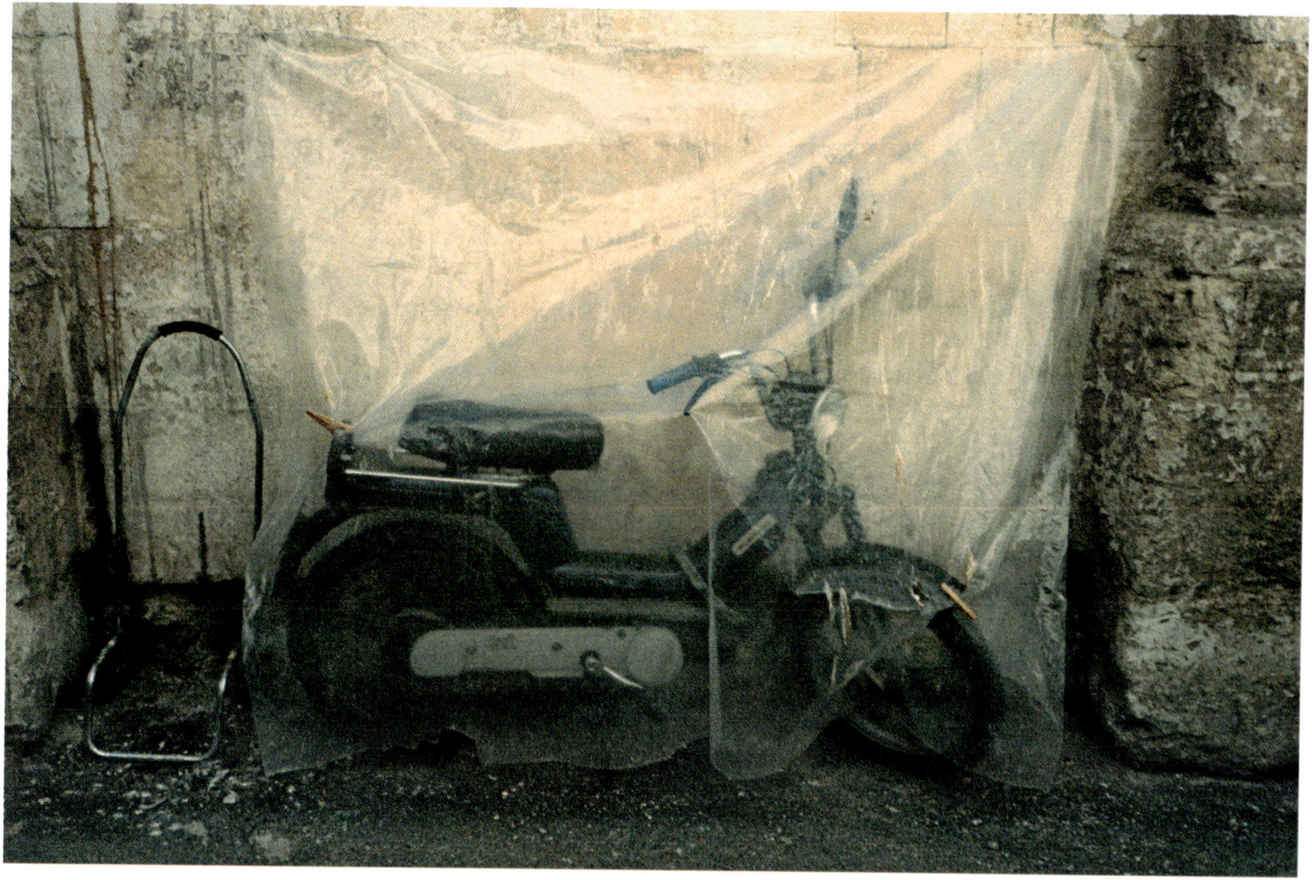

Saturday, October 9. Monopoli, Italy. Still life

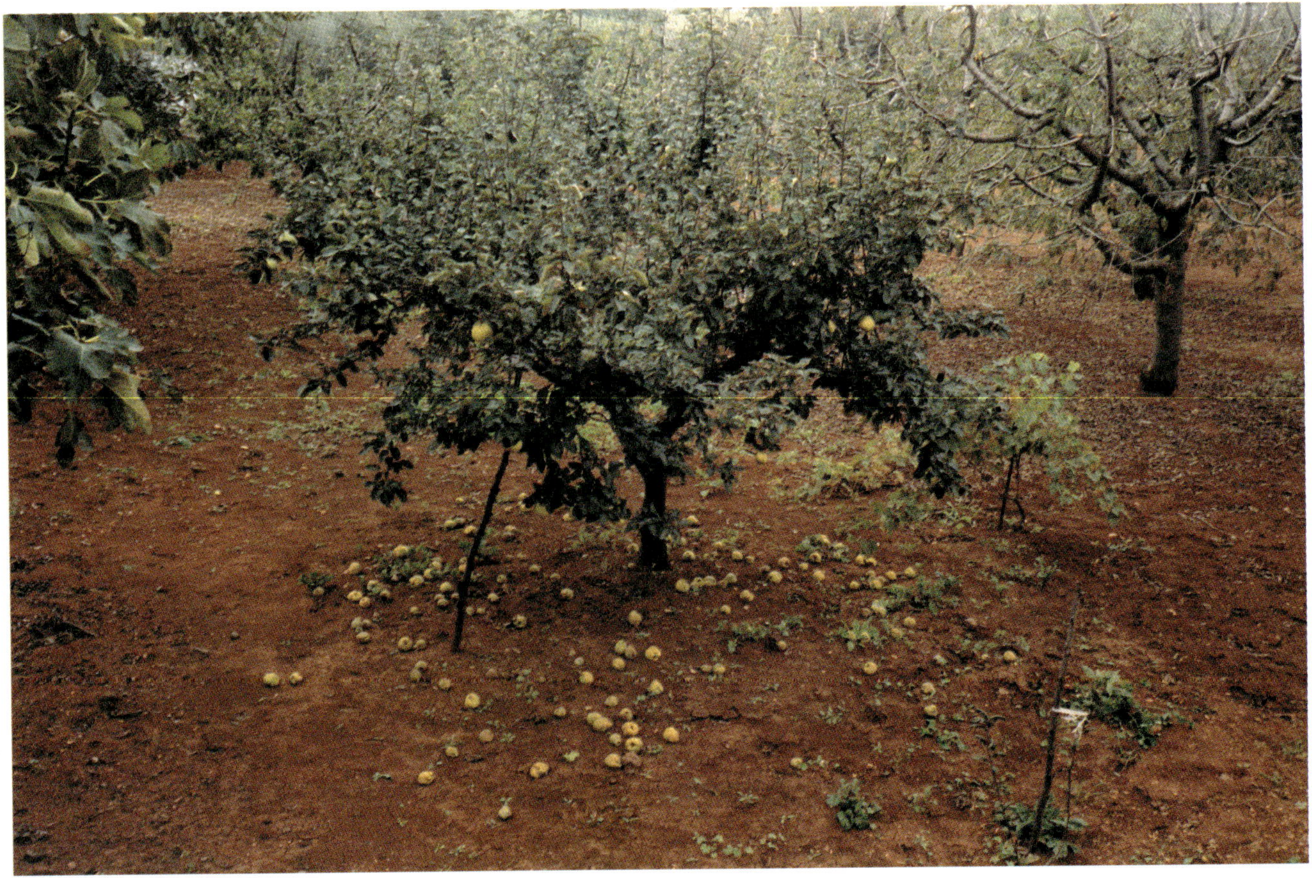

Sunday, October 10. Alberobello, Italy. Orchard

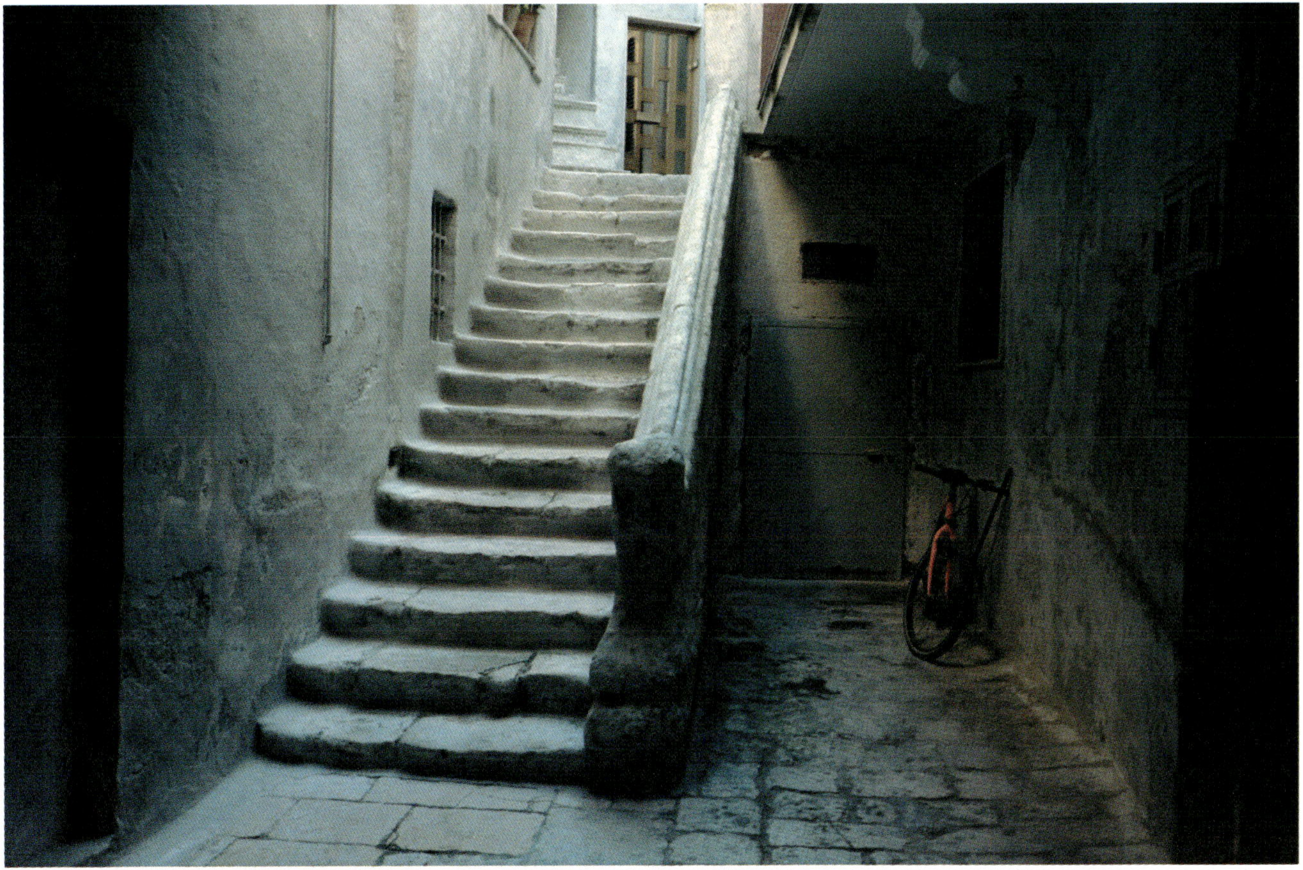

Sunday, October 10. Monopoli, Italy. Courtyard

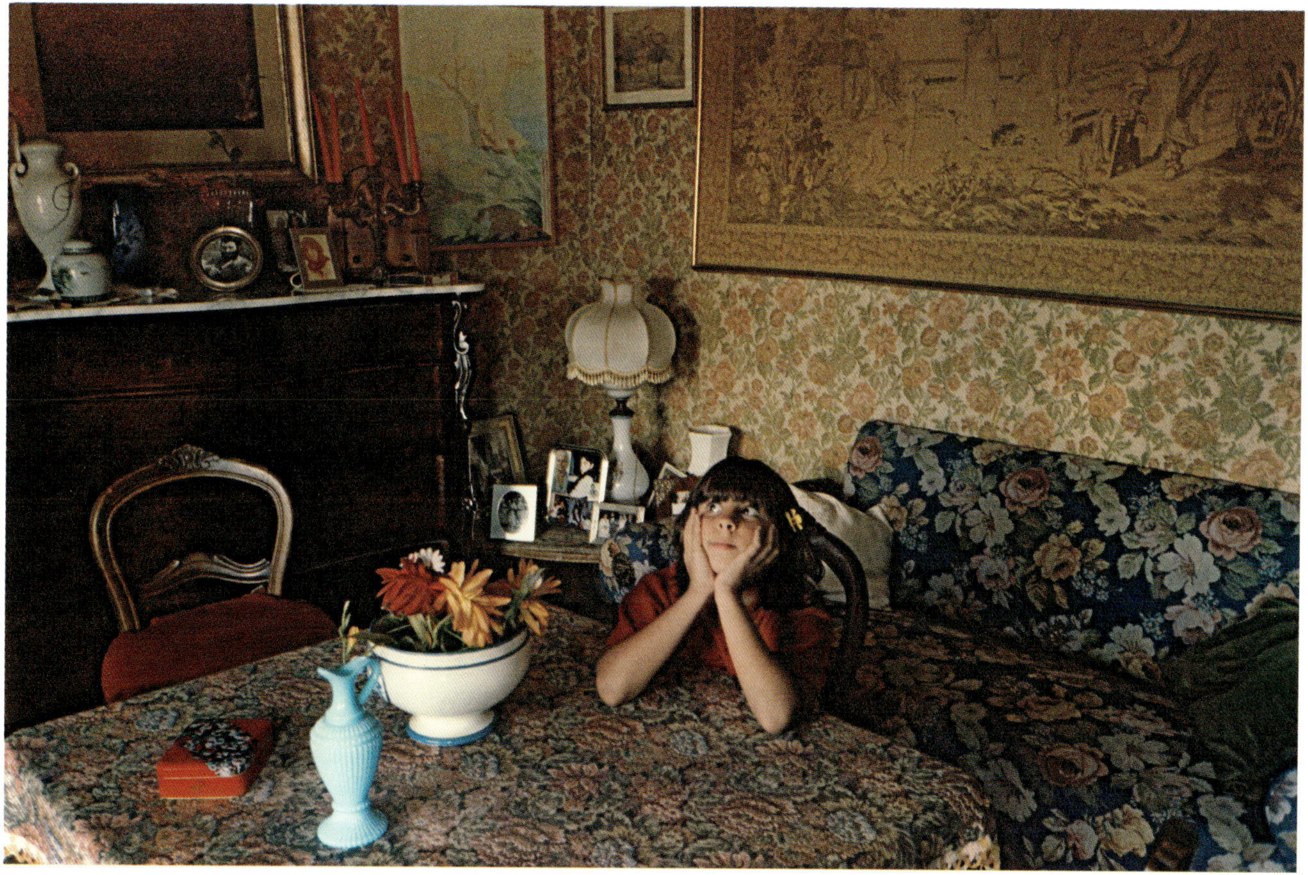

Monday, October 11. Bari, Italy. Living room

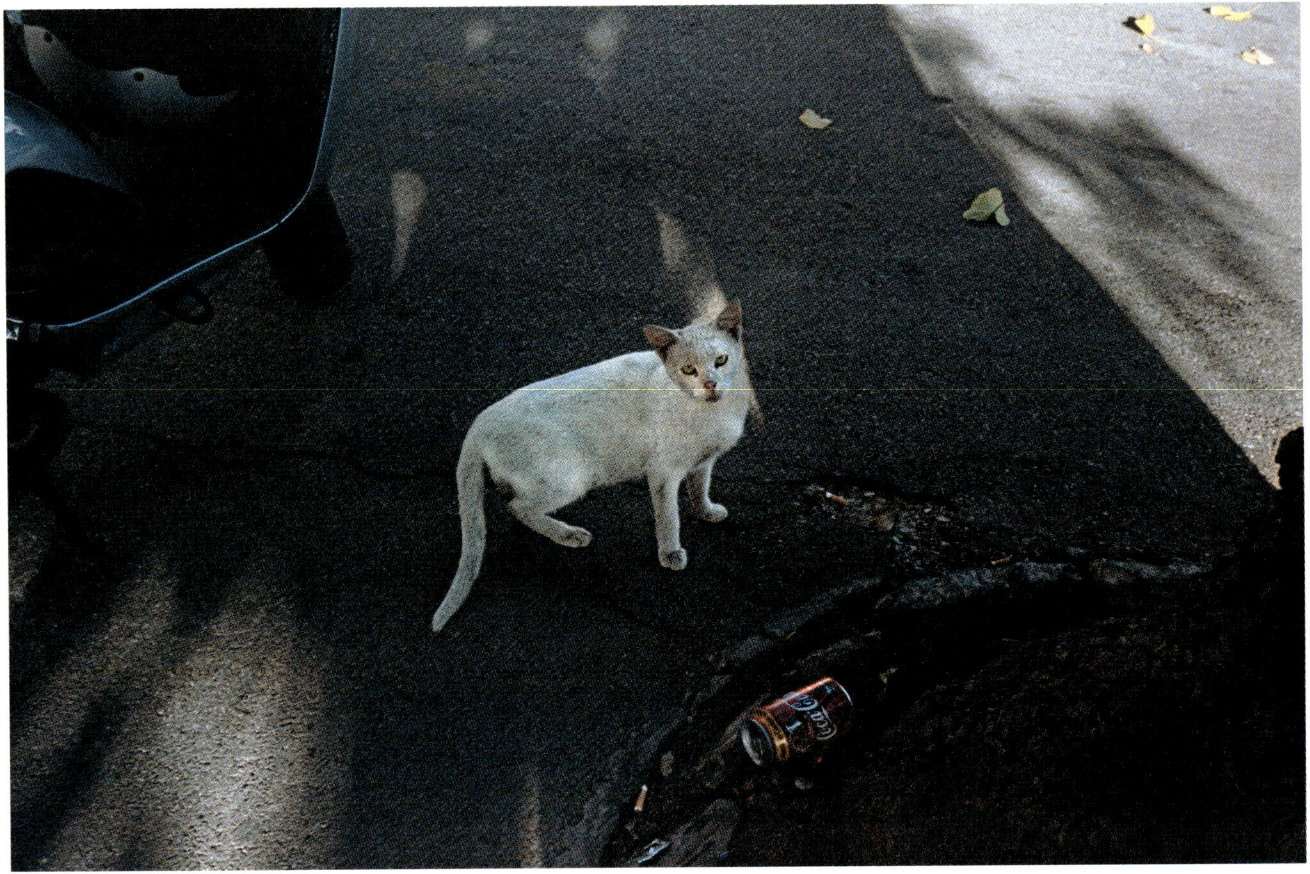

Tuesday, October 12. Alberobello, Italy. Stray cat

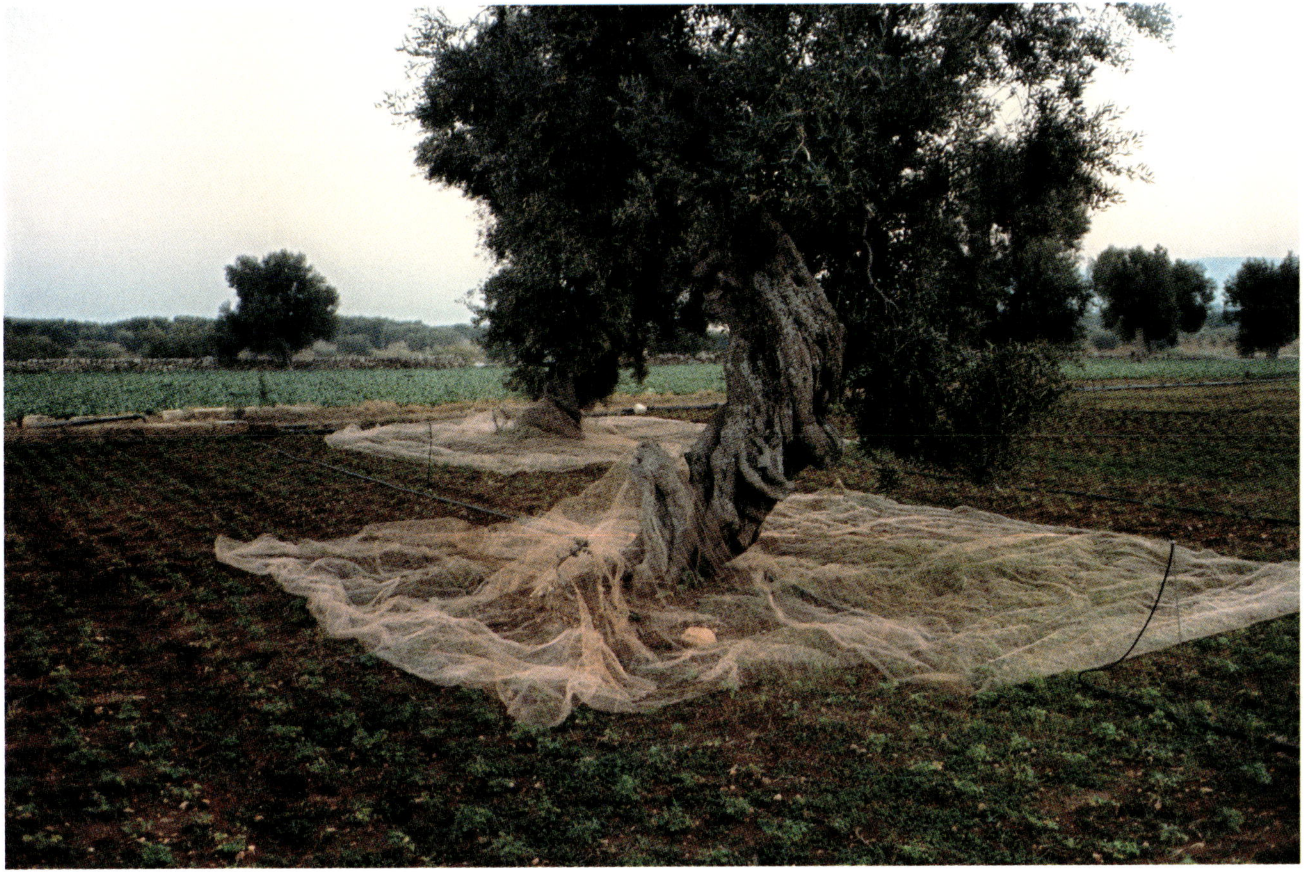

Wednesday, October 13. Monopoli, Italy. Olive harvest

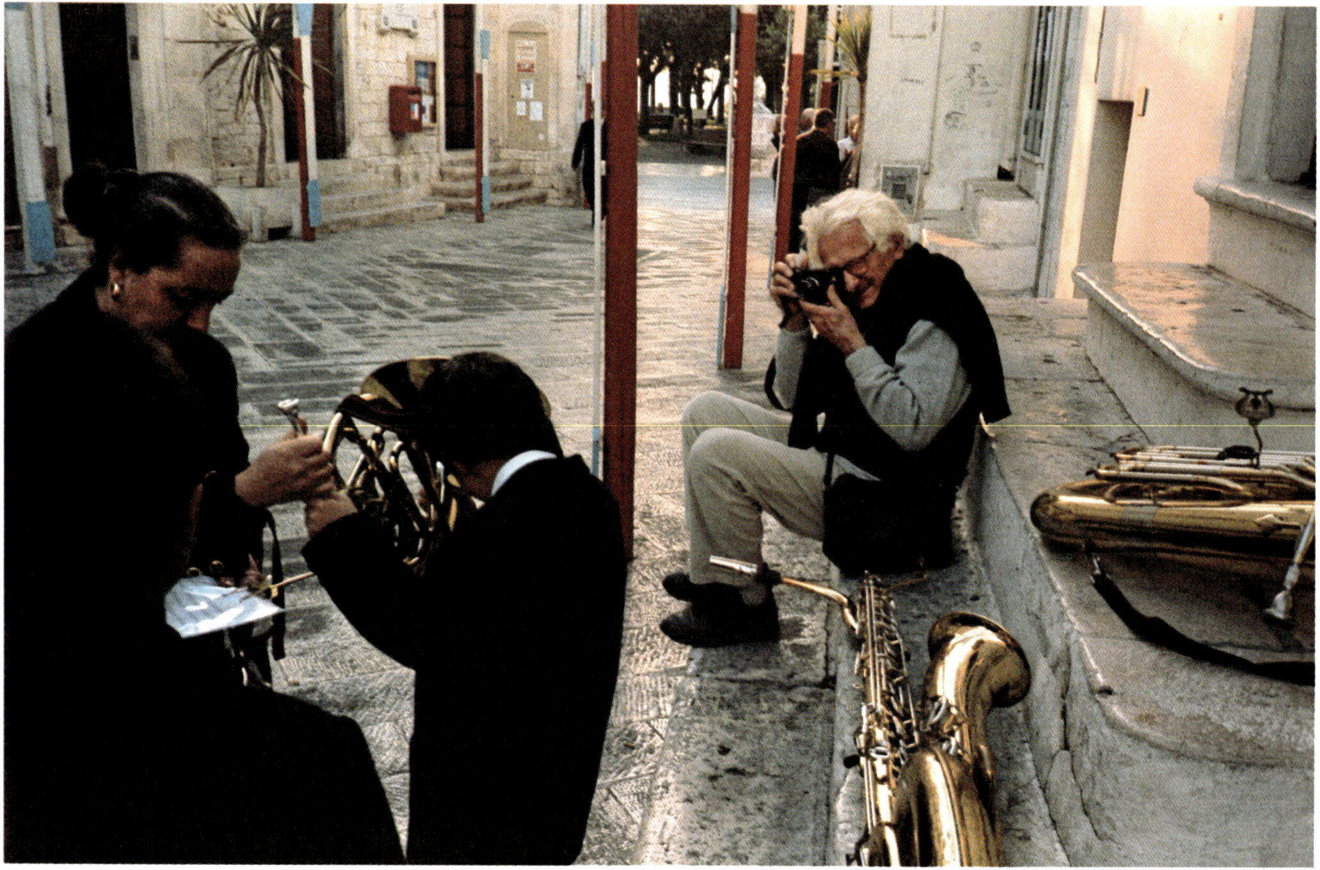

Thursday, October 14. Locorotondo, Italy. Marc Riboud, photographer

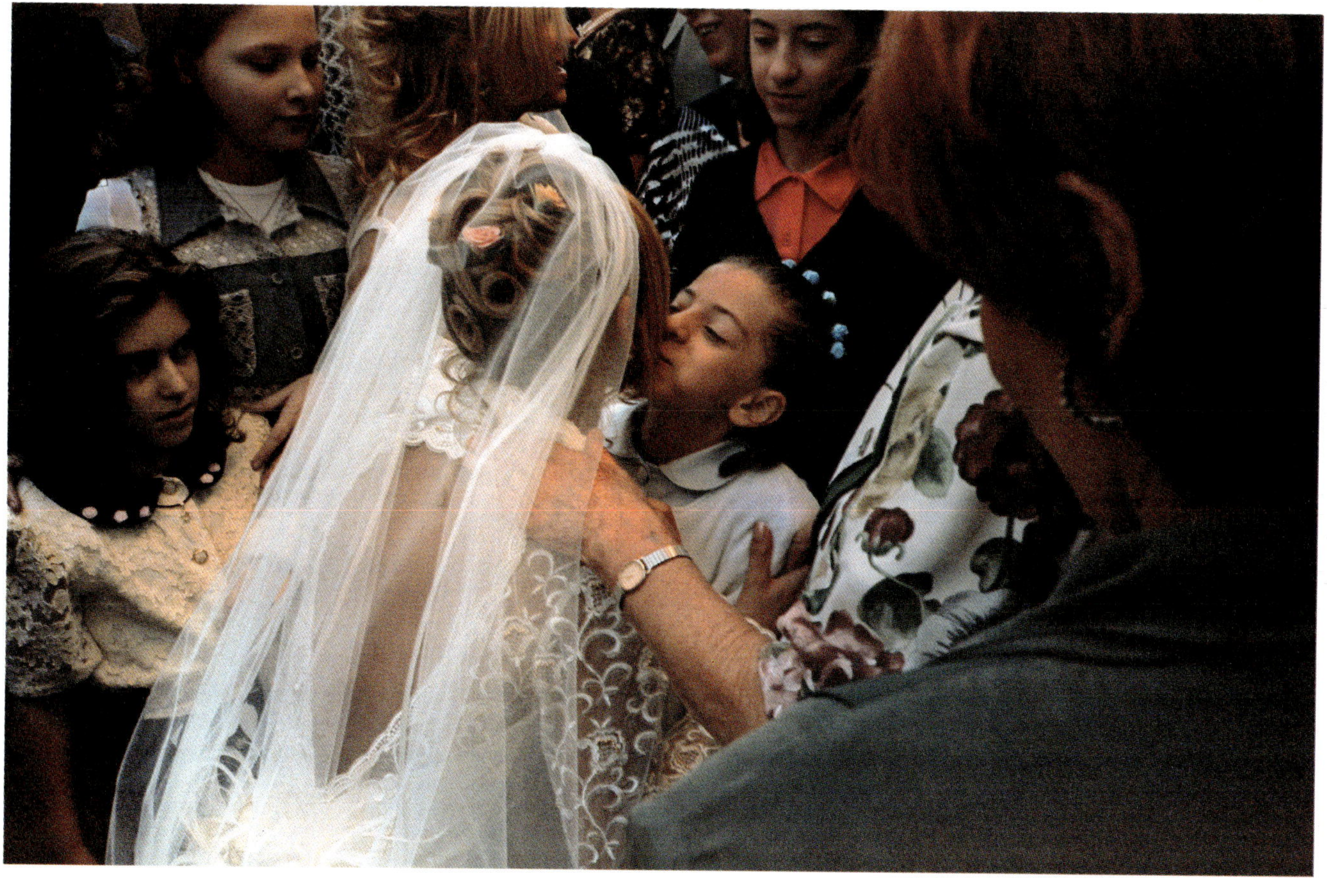

Thursday, October 14. Monopoli, Italy. A wedding

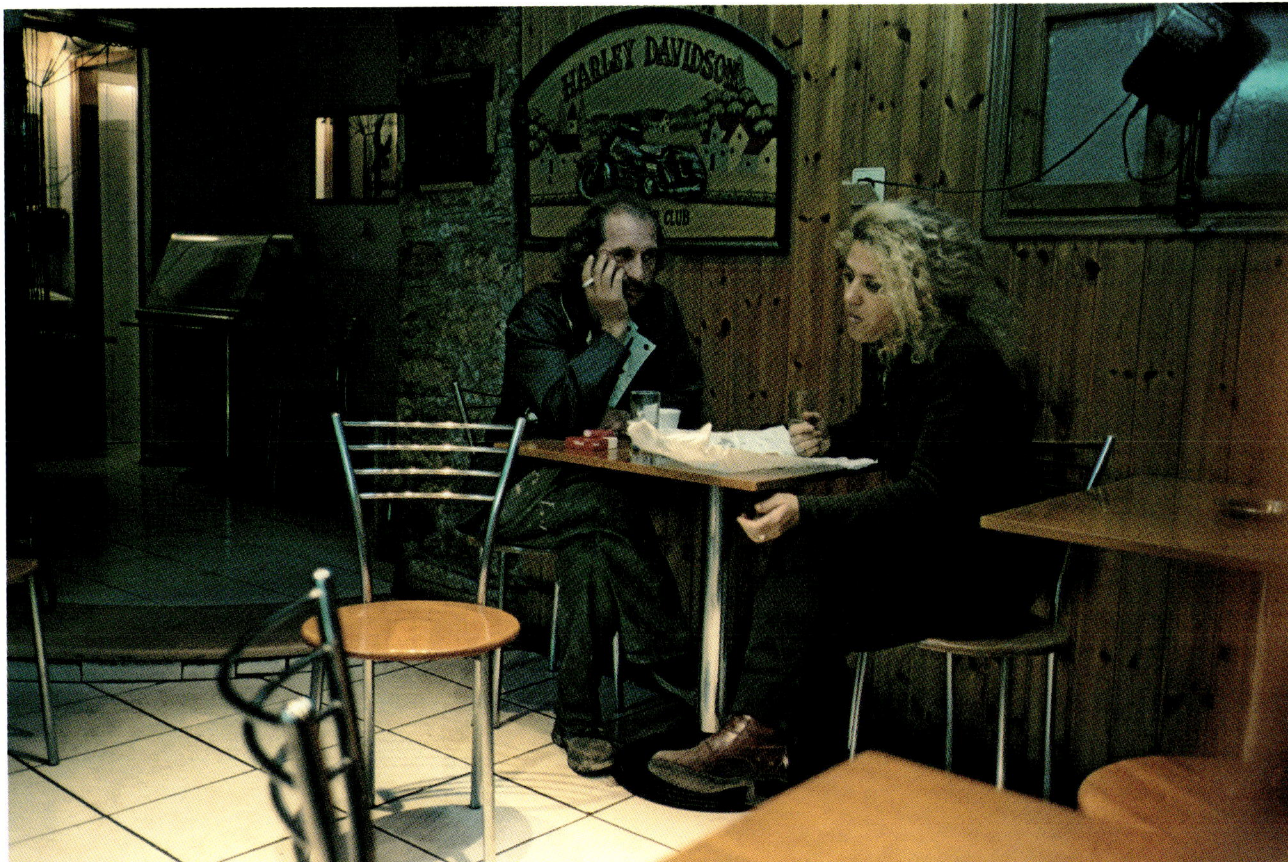

Friday, October 15. Igoumenitza, Greece. Bar scene

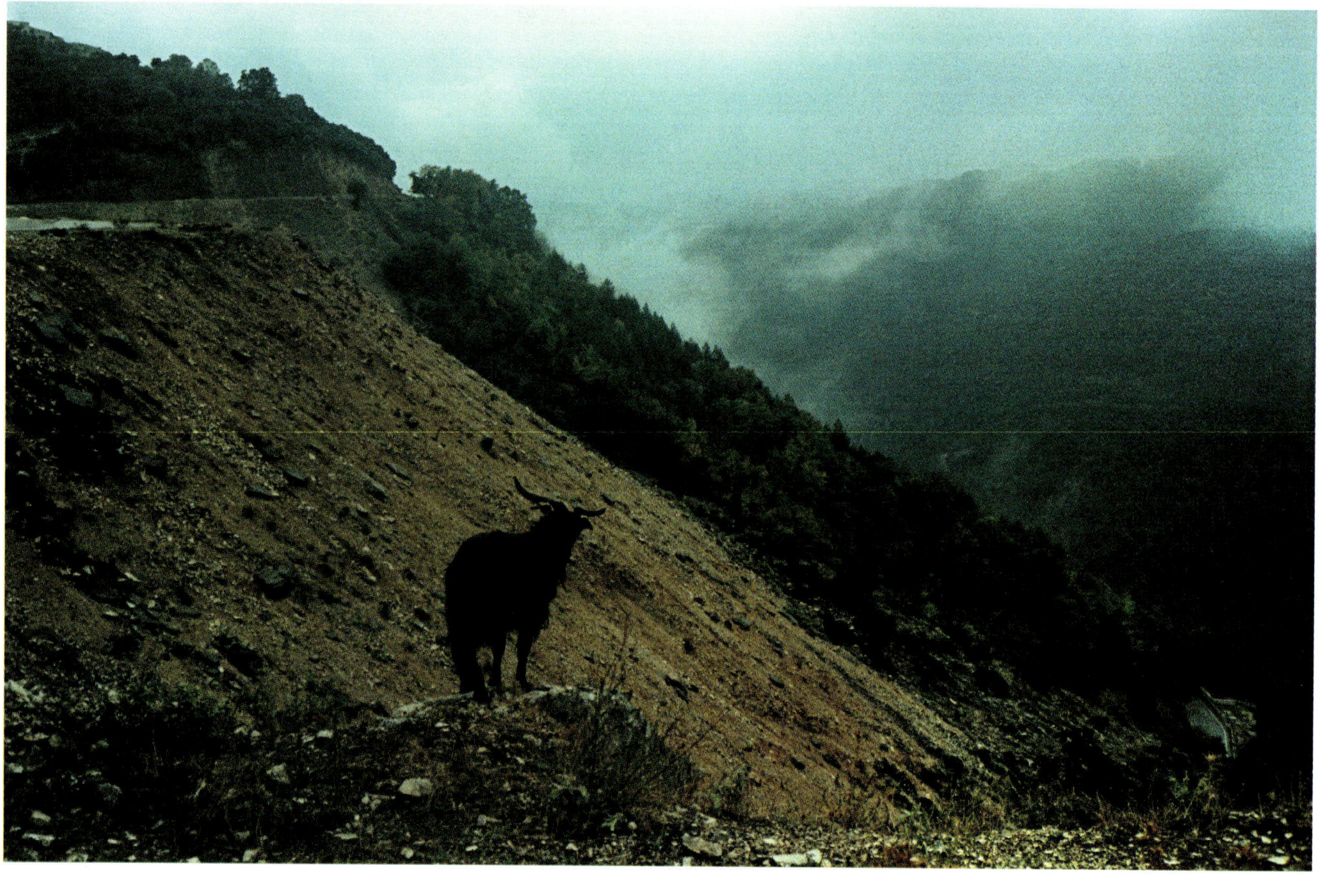

Saturday, October 16. Road from Igoumenitza to Jenina, Greece. Mountain landscape

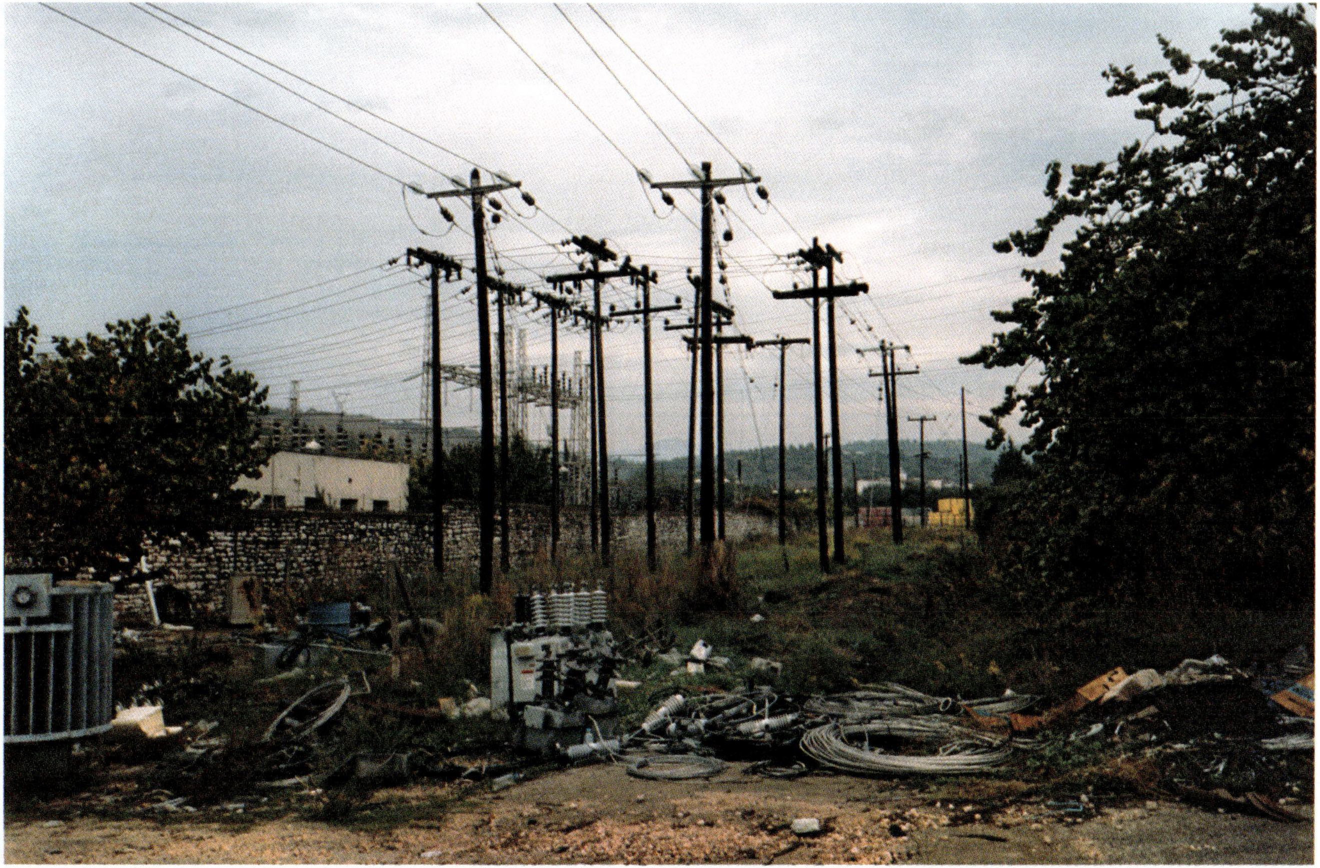

Saturday, October 16. Road from Igoumenitza to Jenina, Greece. Suburban landscape

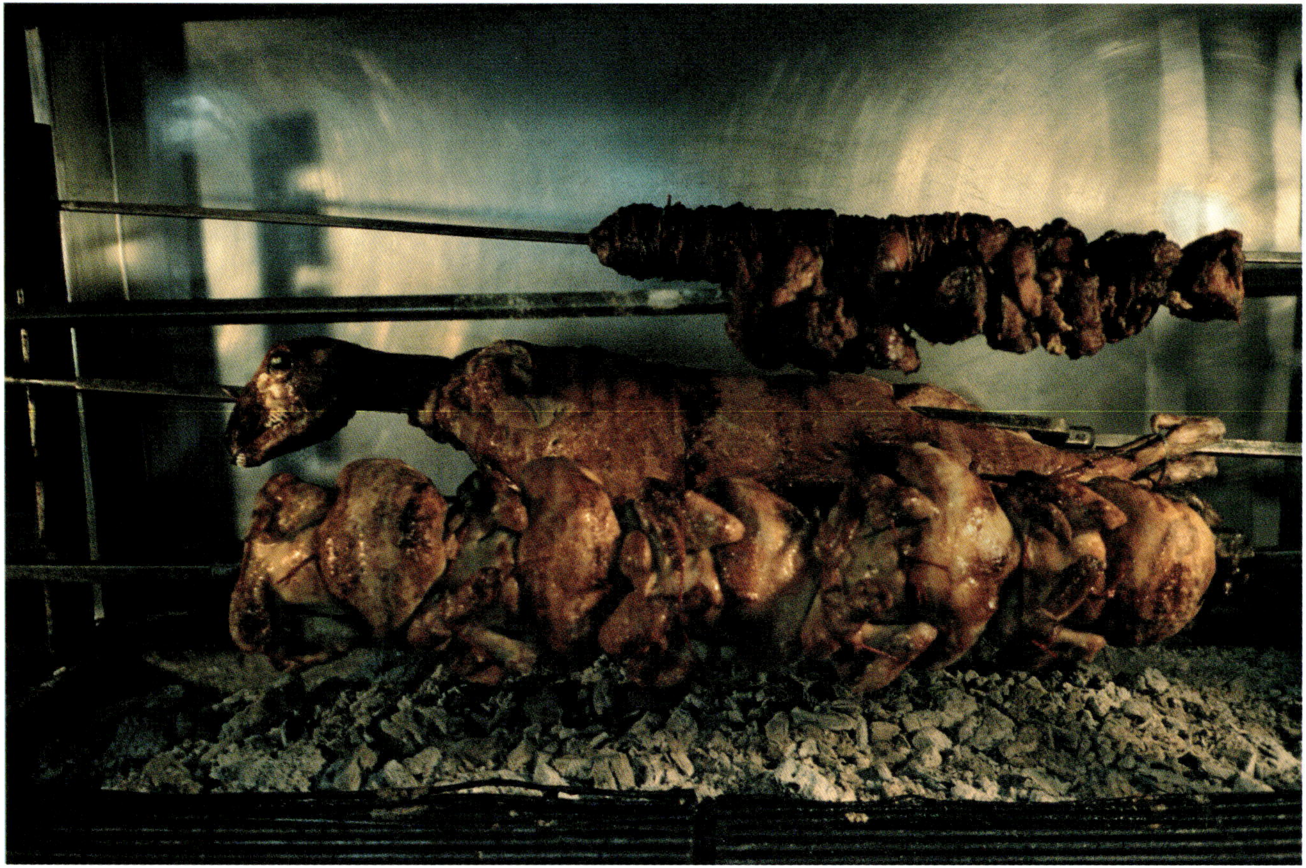

Sunday, October 17. Jenina, Greece. Roast lamb

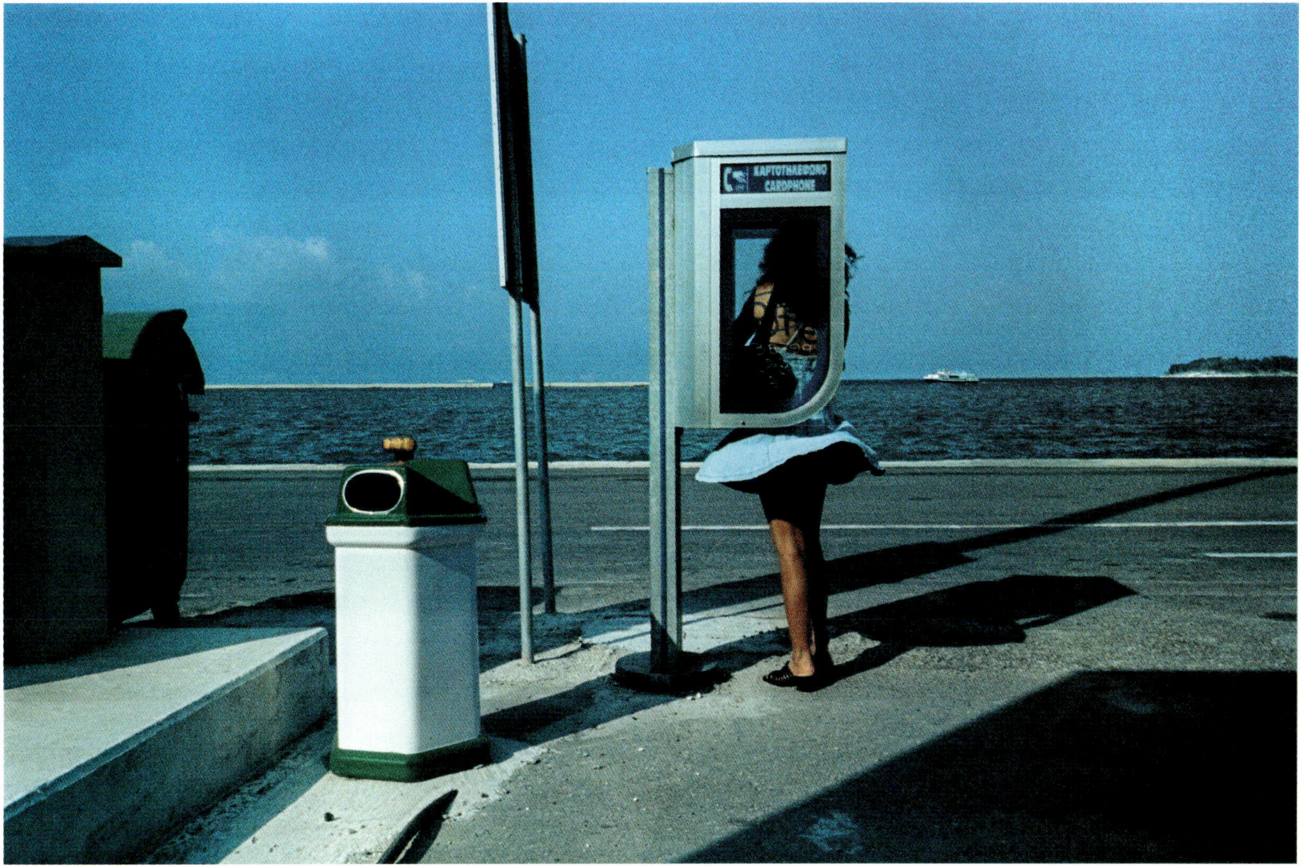

Monday, October 18. Corfu, Greece. Beach scene

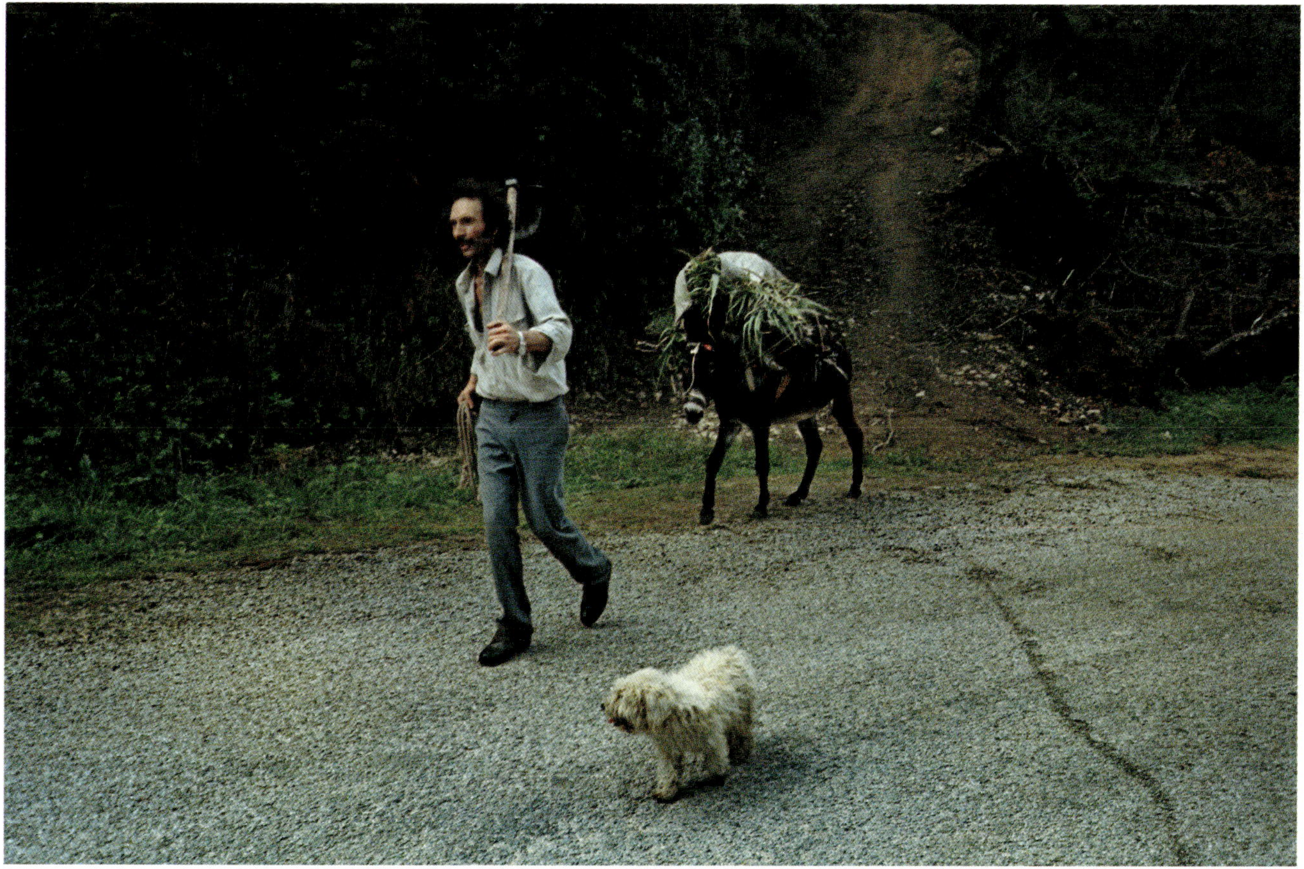

Tuesday, October 19. Corfu, Greece. Country scene

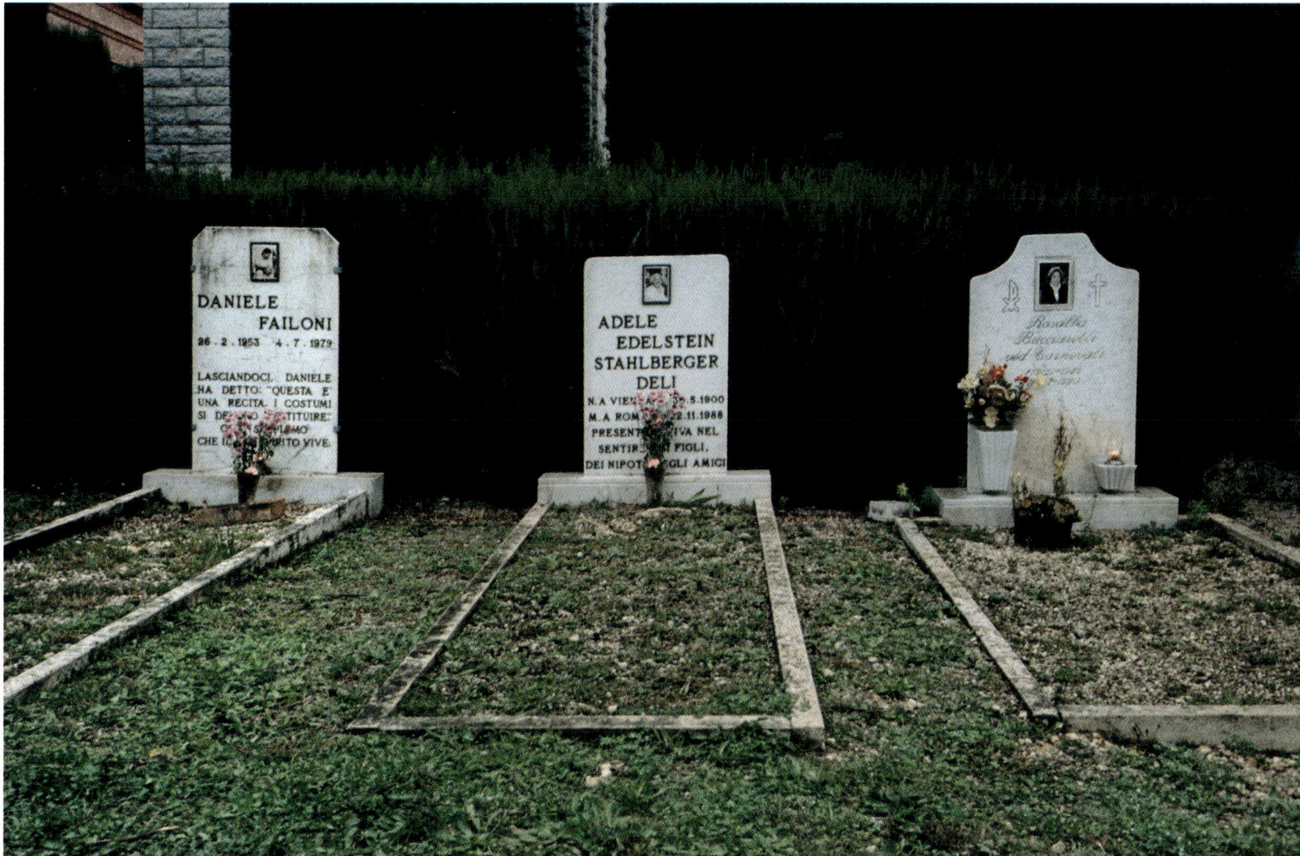

Wednesday, October 20. Serra San Quirico, Italy. The graves of my mother, Adele Edelstein, and my nephew, Daniele Failoni

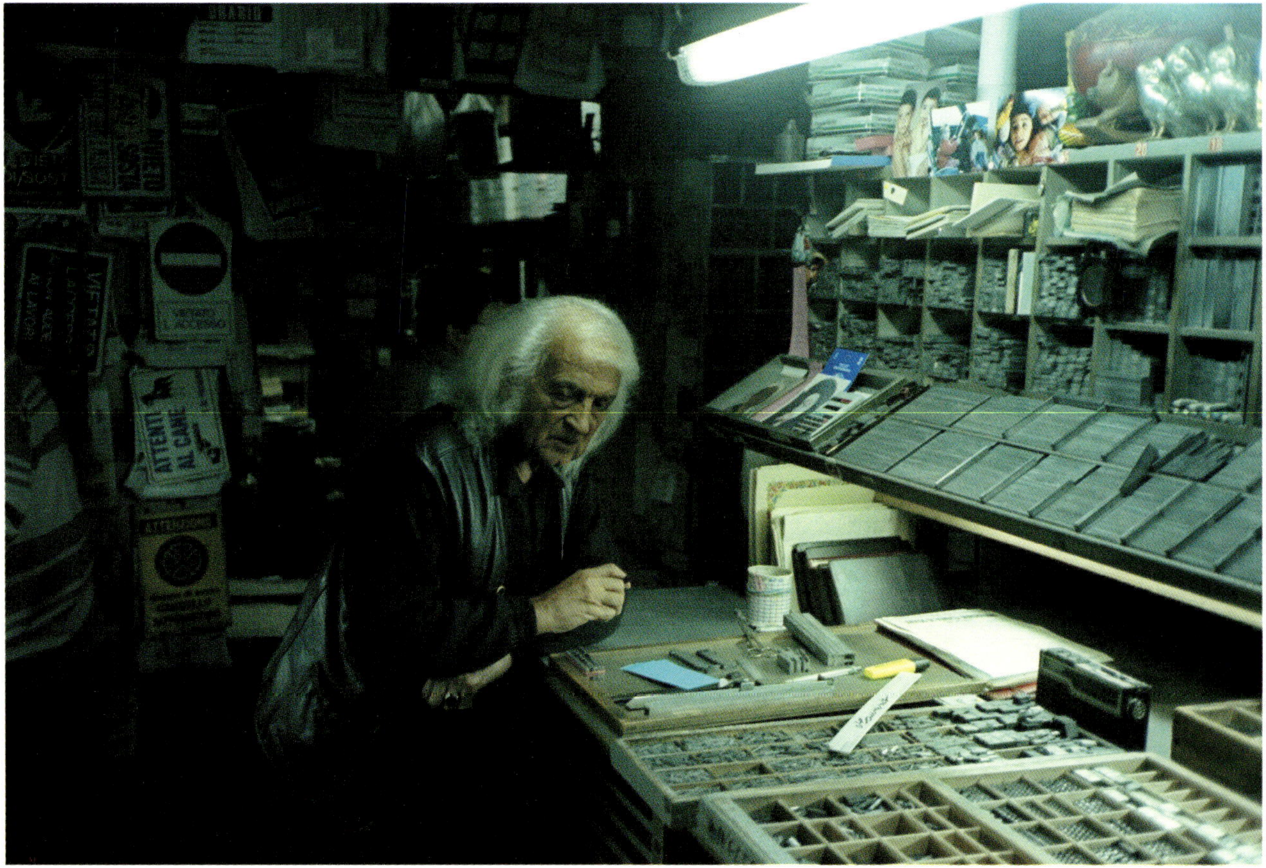

Wednesday, October 20. Sinigallia, Italy. Mario Giacomelli, photographer, in his printing shop

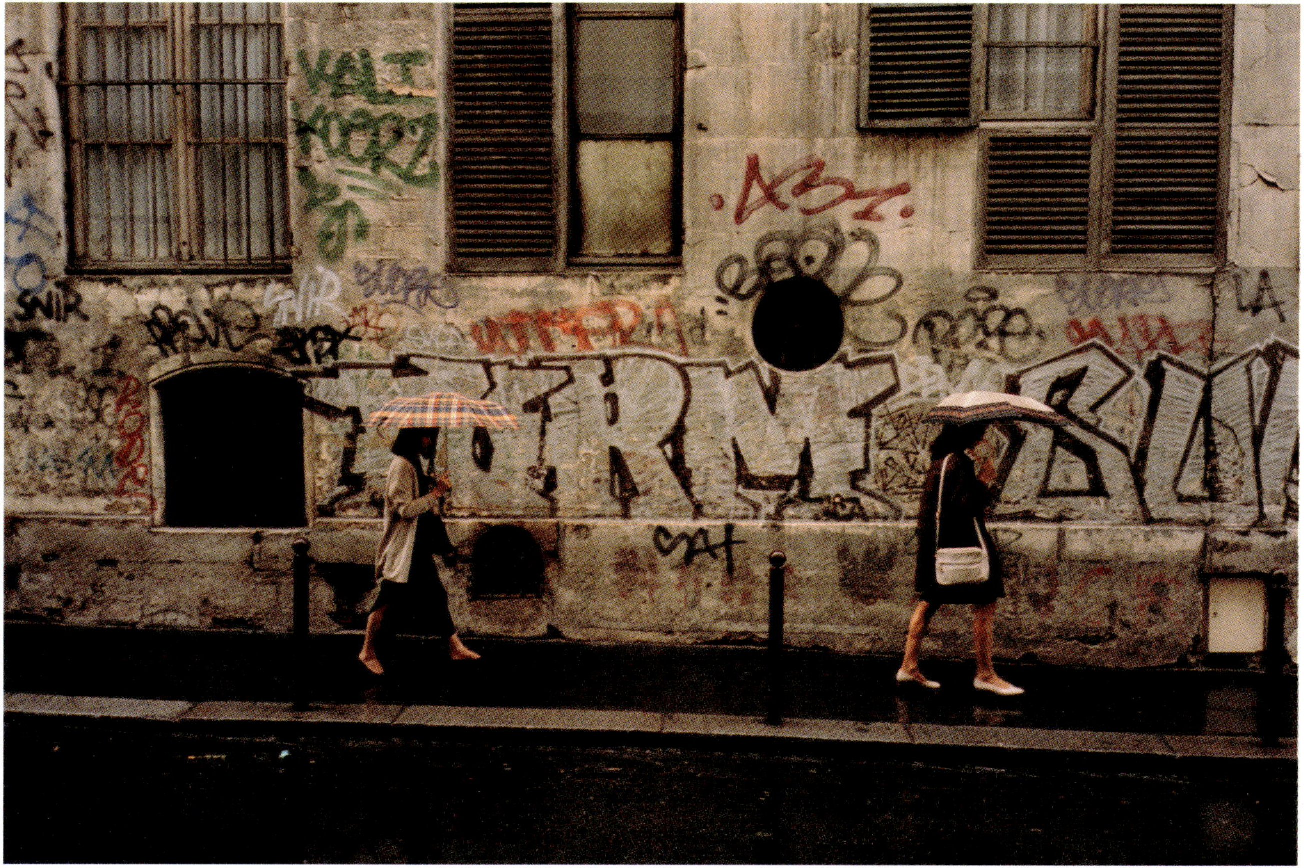

Thursday, October 21. Paris. Rainy day in the Latin Quarter

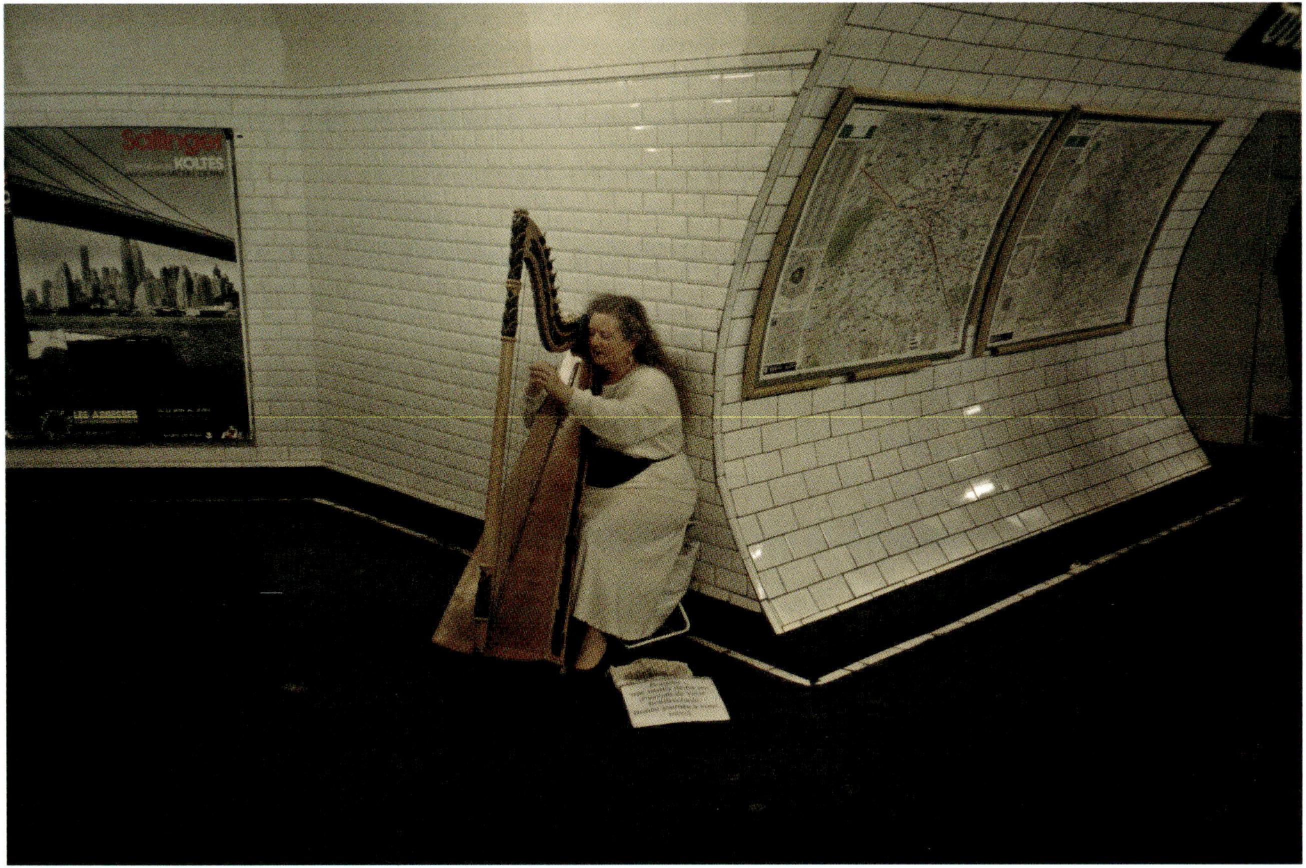

Friday, October 22. Paris. Métro scene

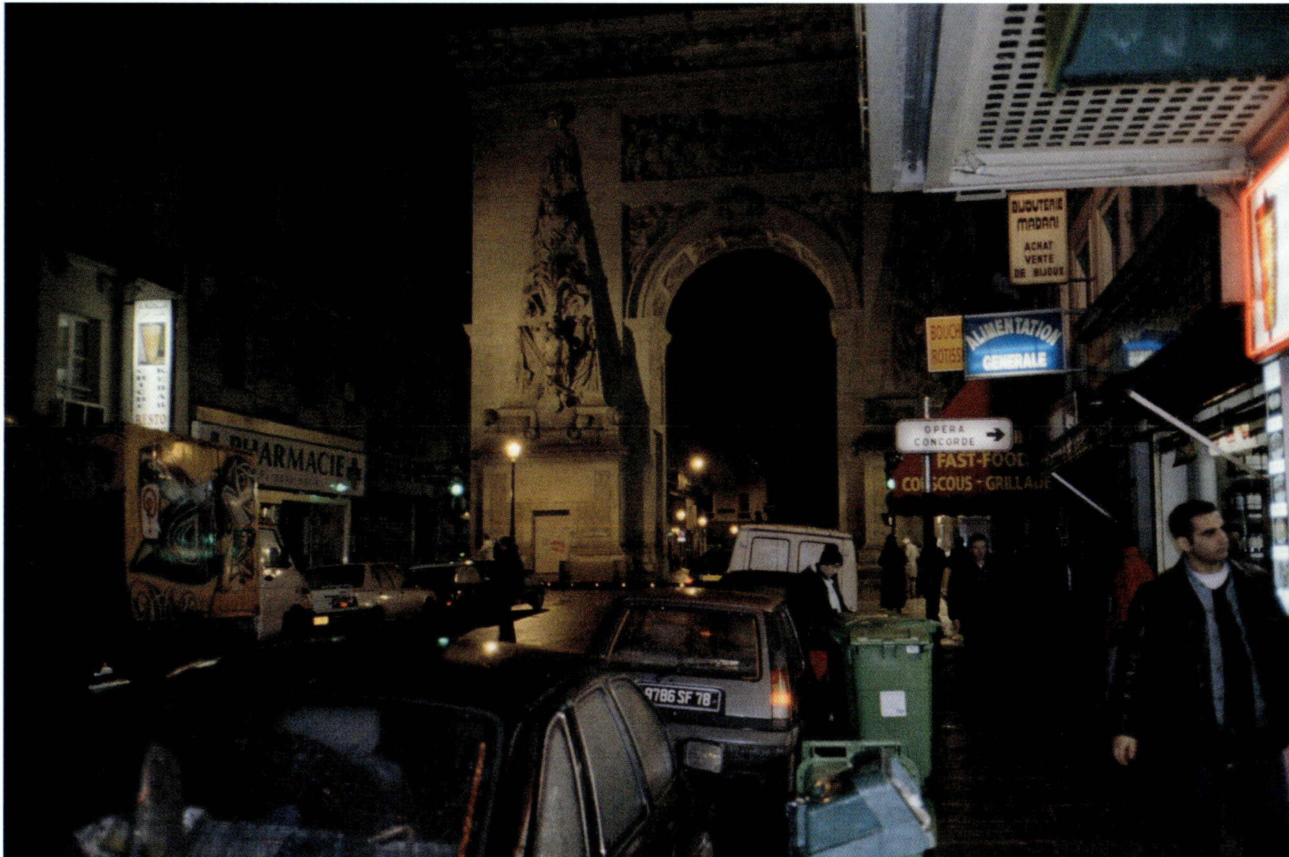

Saturday, October 23. Paris. Street scene, in the Saint-Denis area

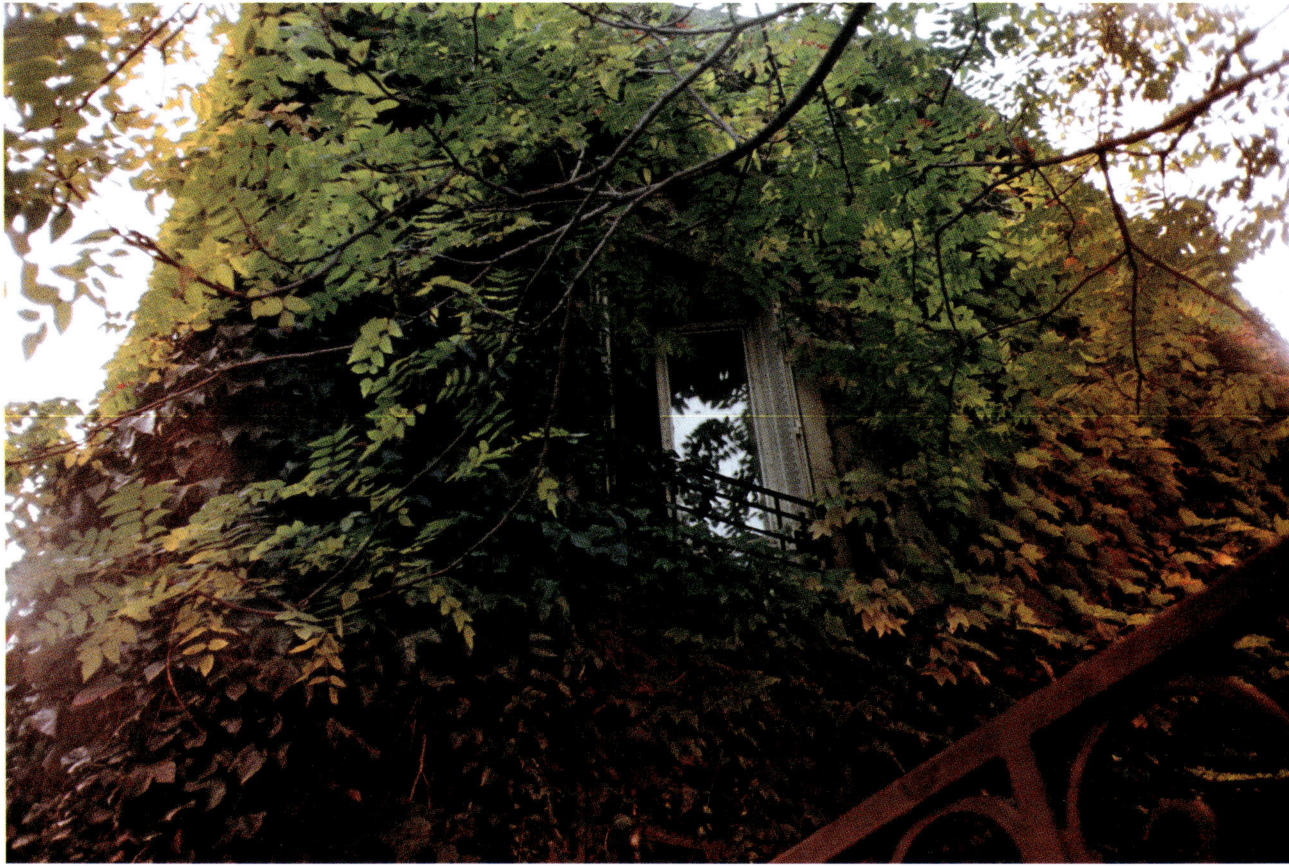

Sunday, October 24. Boulogne, France. My son Marco's home

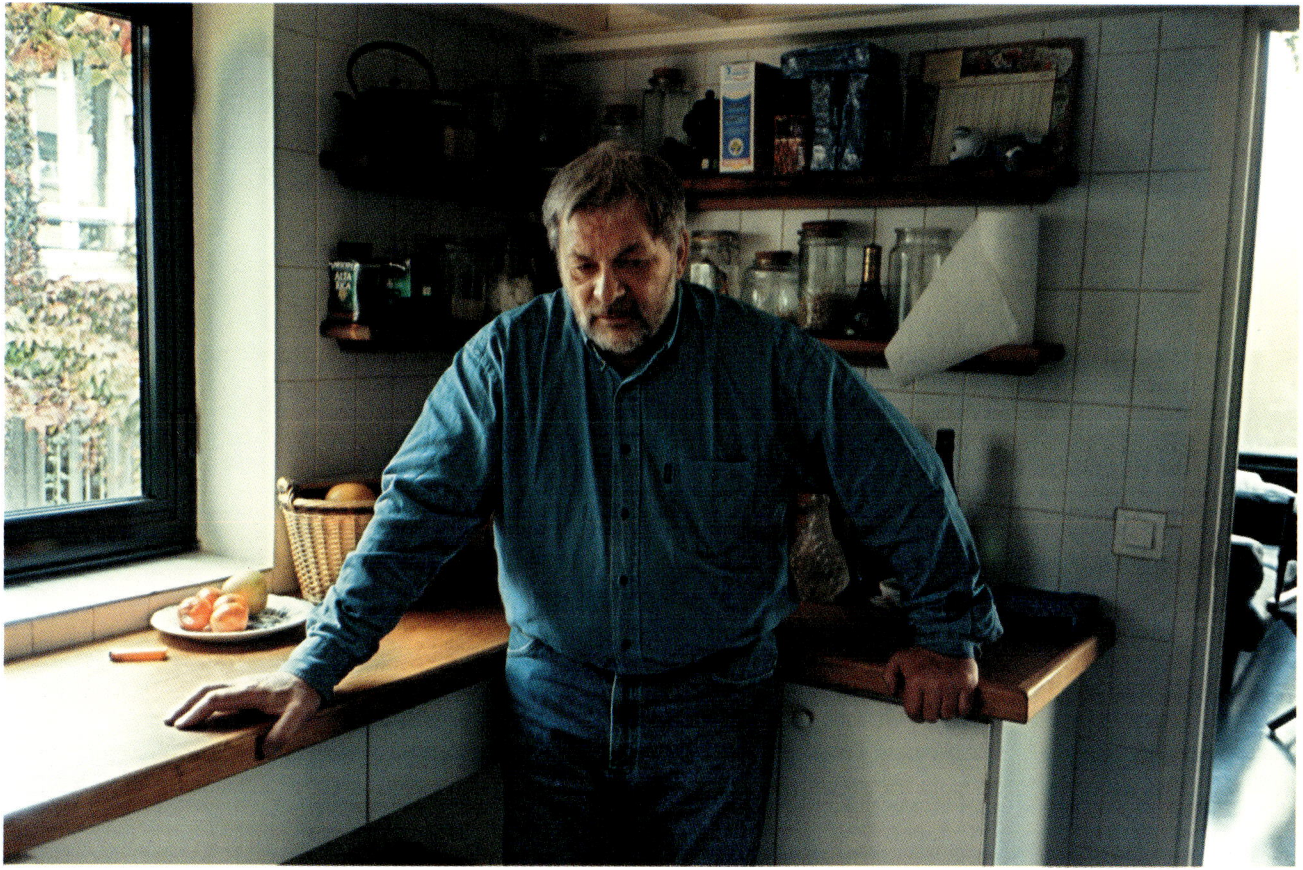

Sunday, October 24. Boulogne, France. Benoît Gillain, graphic designer

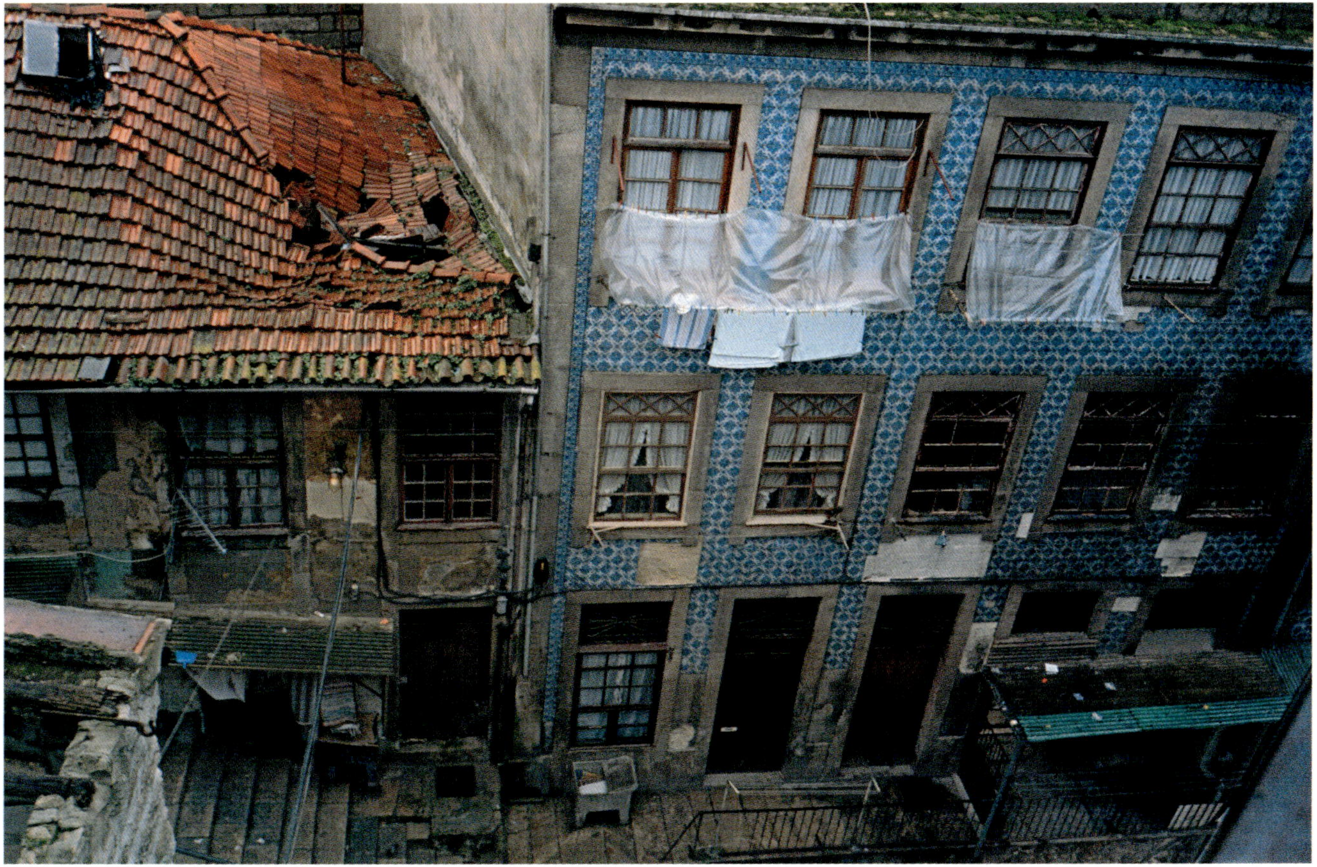

Monday, October 25. Porto, Portugal. In the old town

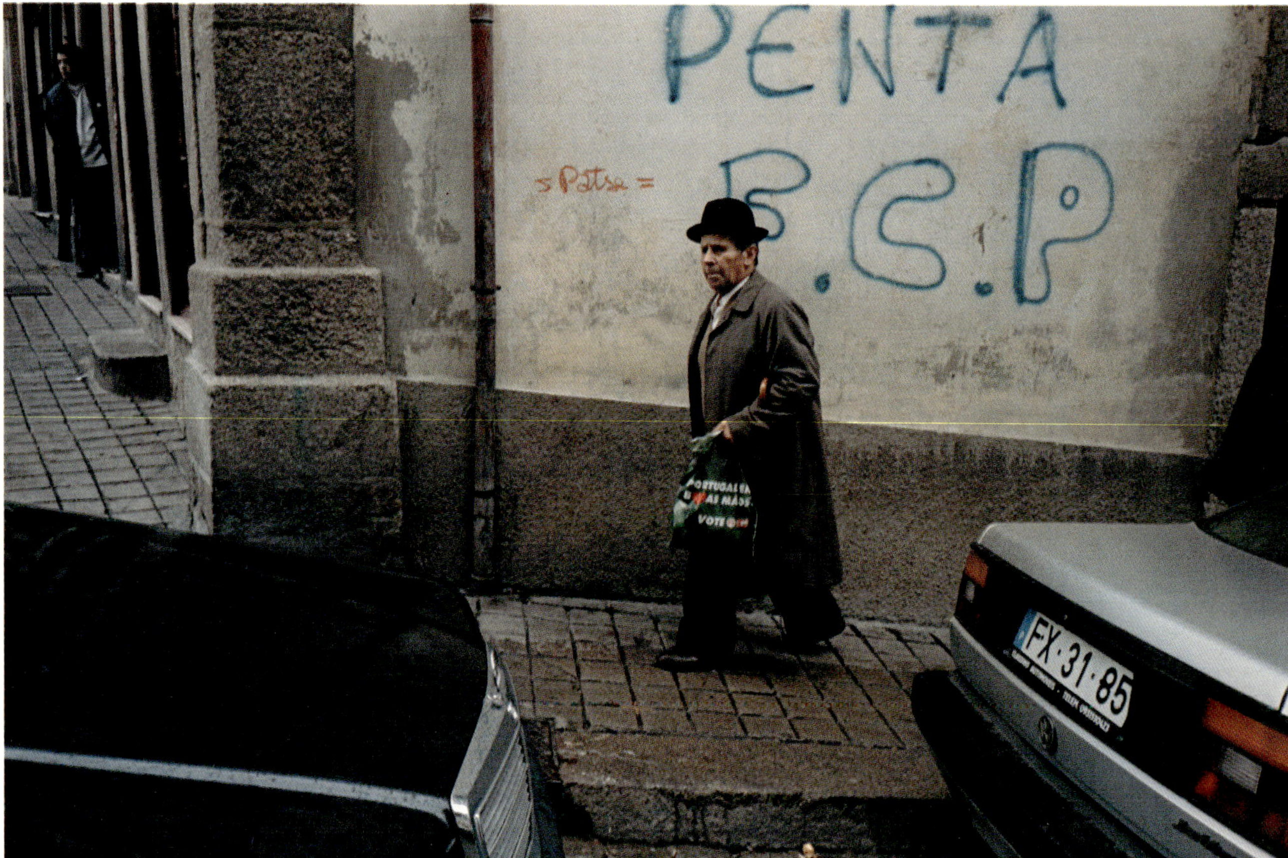

Tuesday, October 26. Porto, Portugal. Street scene

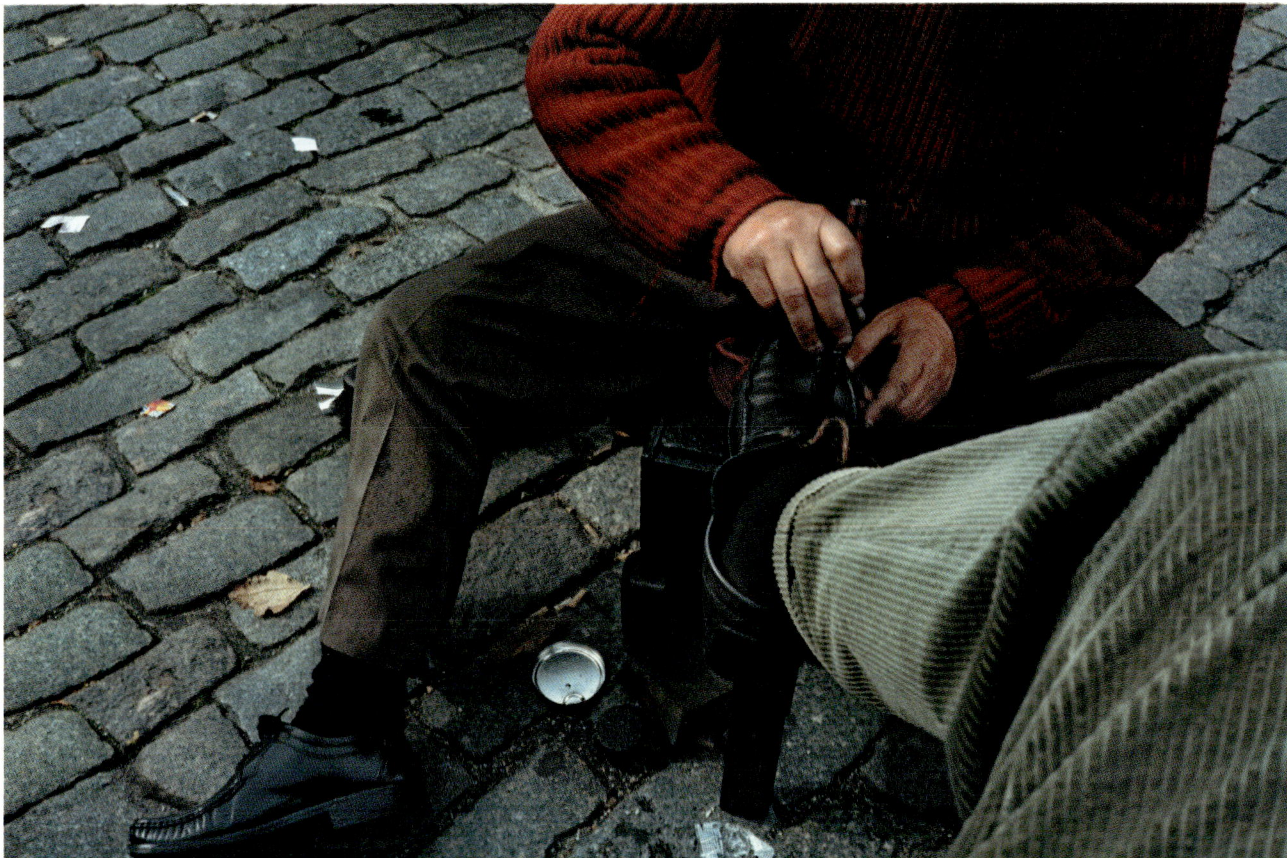

Wednesday, October 27. Porto, Portugal. Shoe-shine

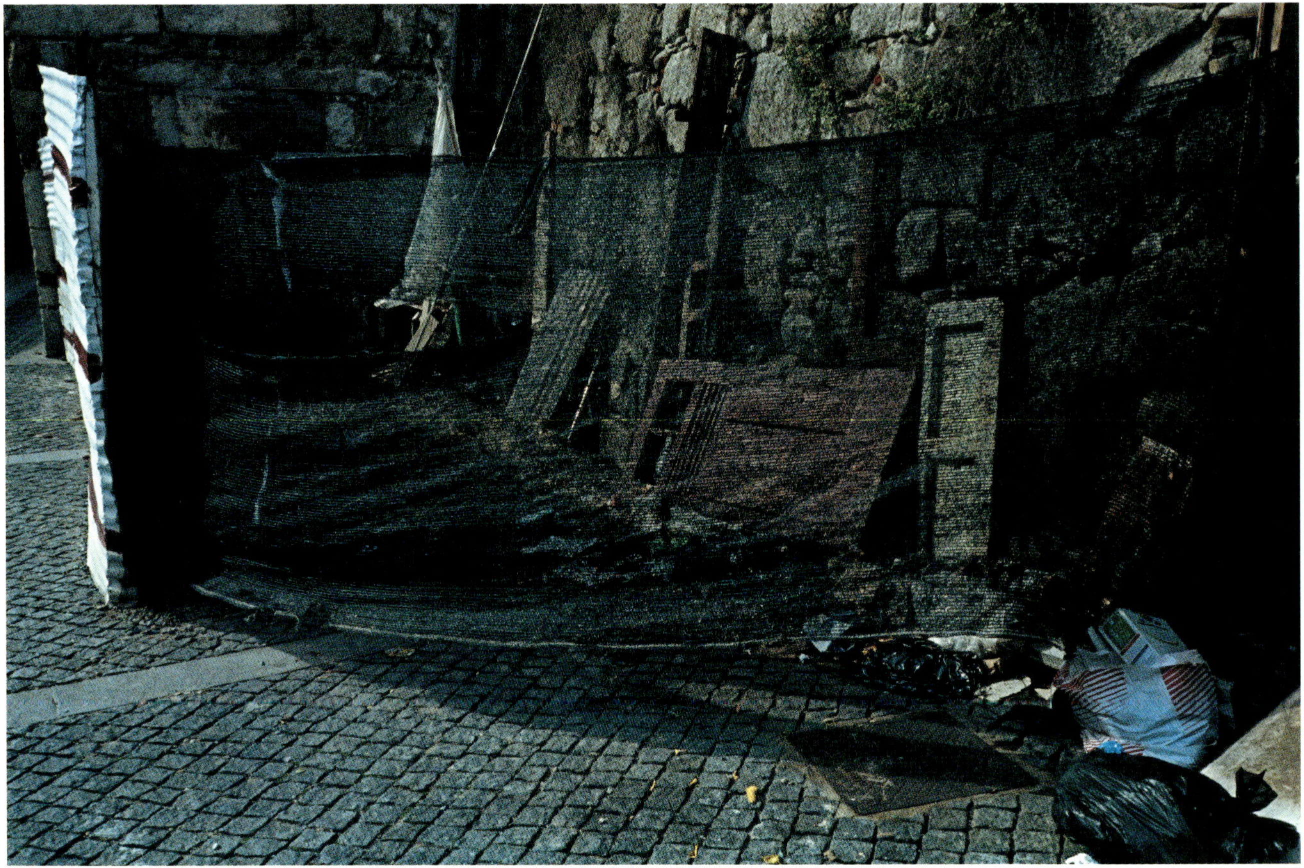

Thursday, October 28. Porto, Portugal. Construction work in the old town

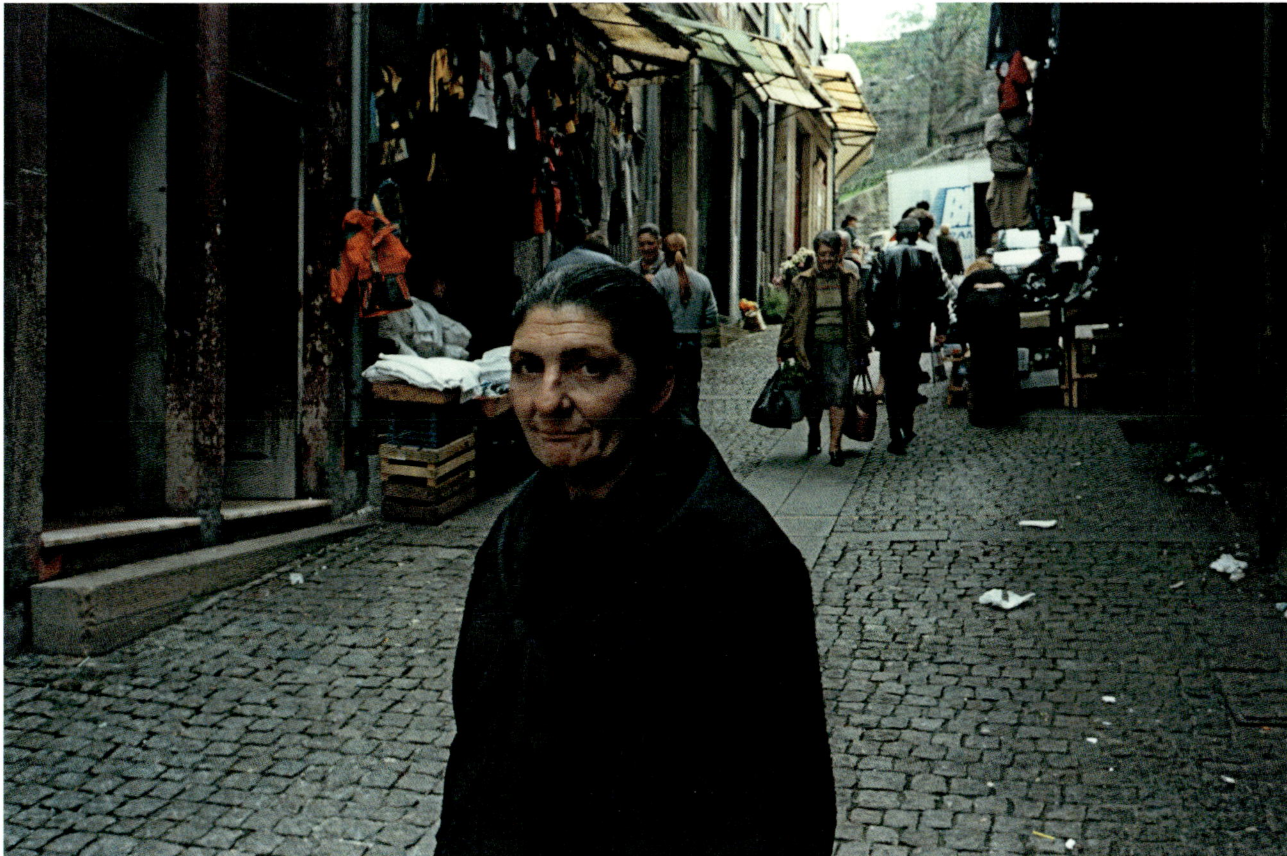

Friday, October 29. Porto, Portugal. Street encounter

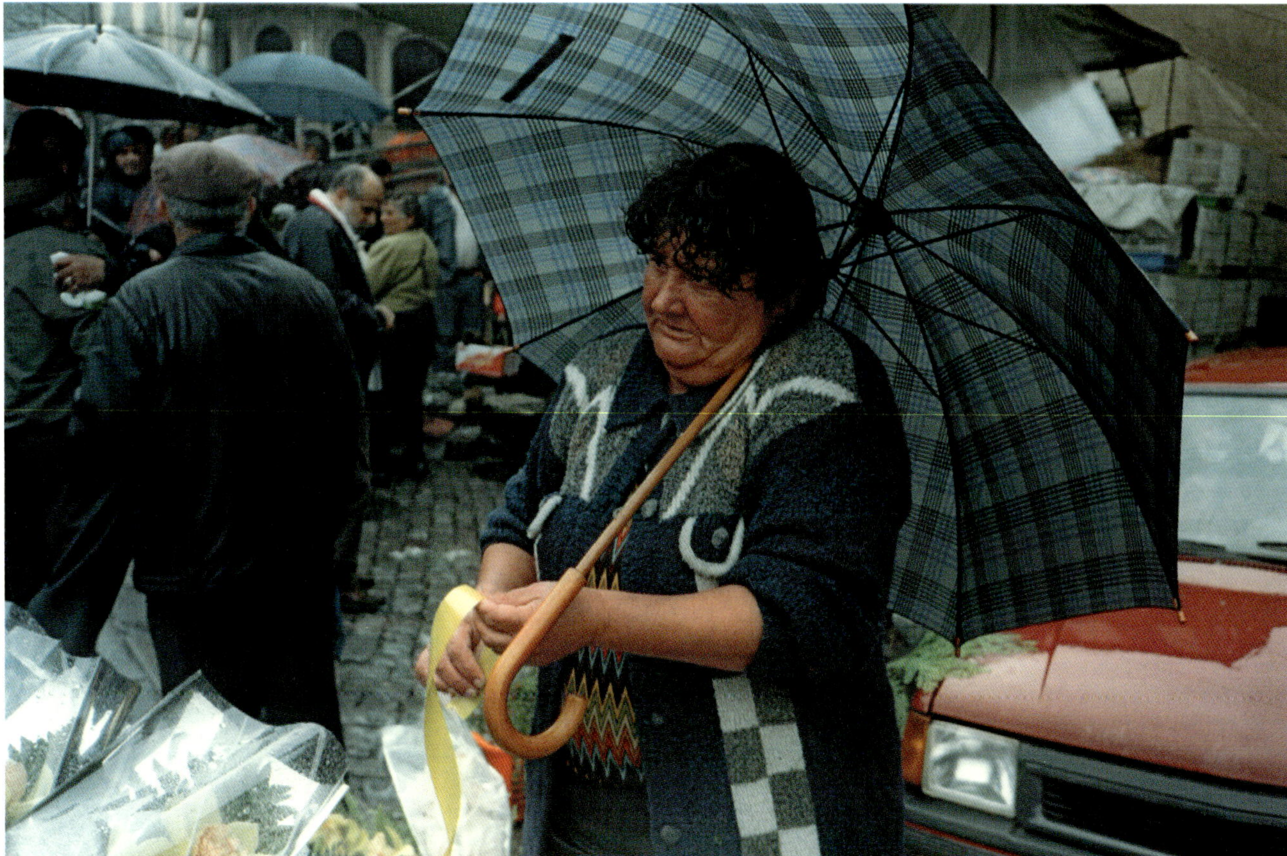

Saturday, October 30. Porto, Portugal. Market scene

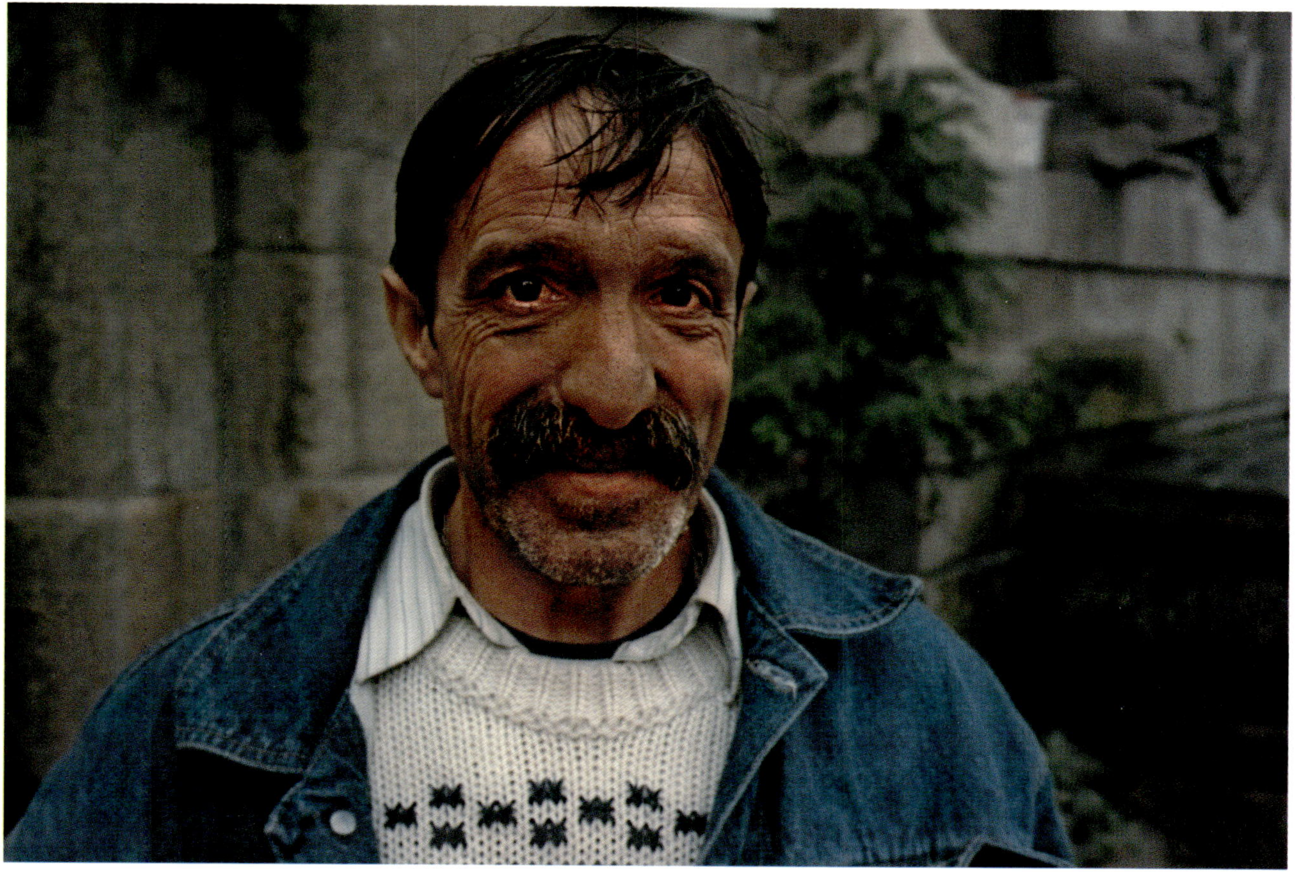

Sunday, October 31. Porto, Portugal. A friendly face

NOVEMBER

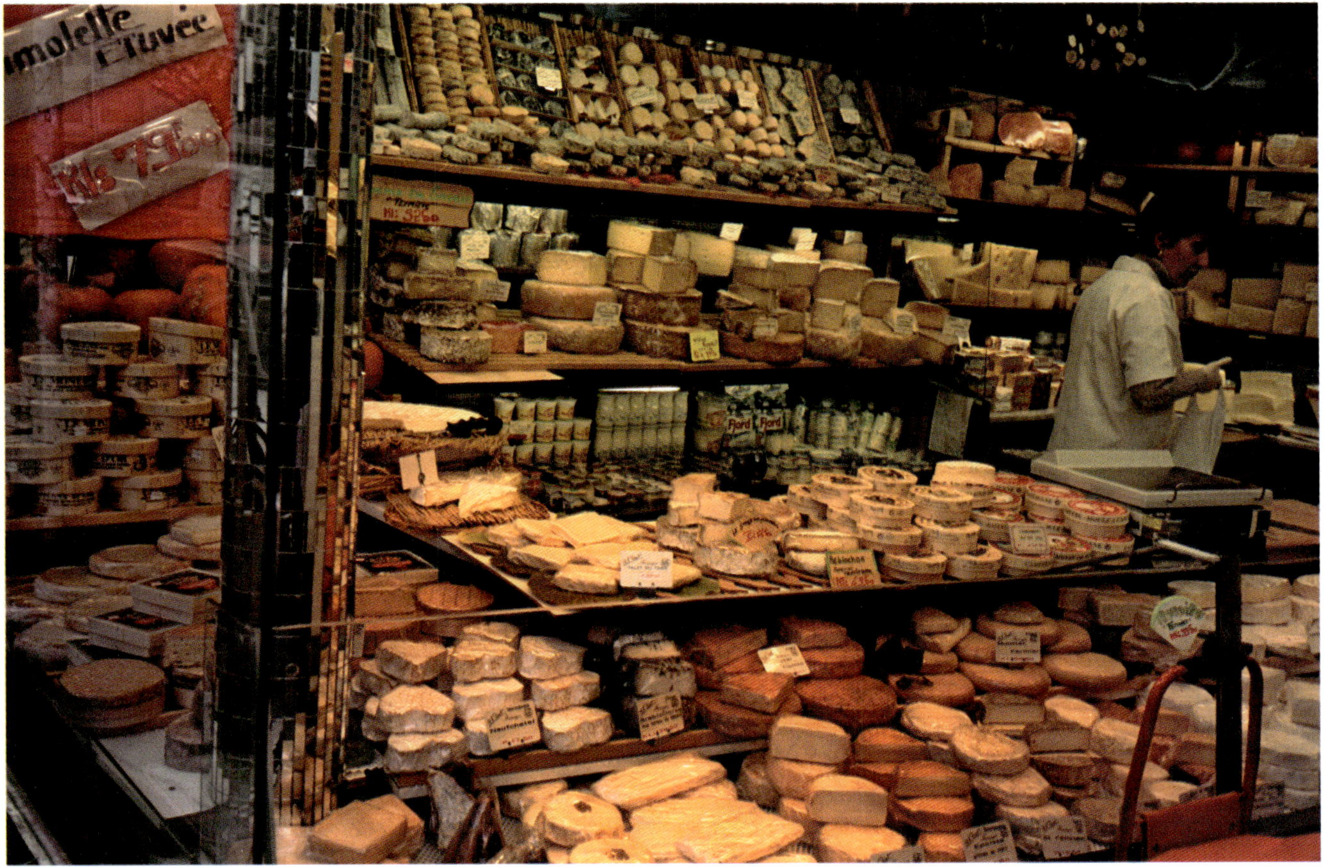

Monday, November 1. Boulogne, France. My favourite cheese shop

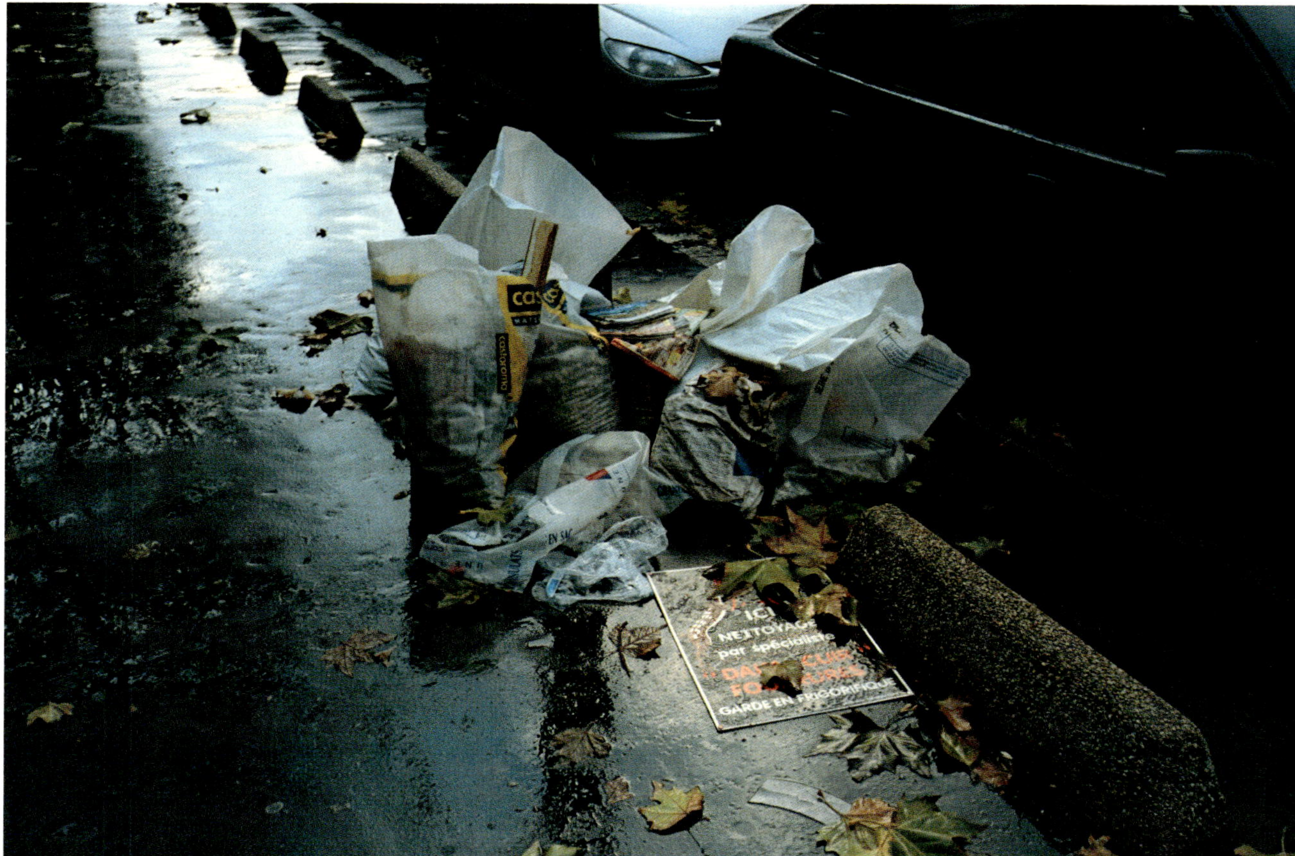

Tuesday, November 2. Near Paris. Still life on the pavement

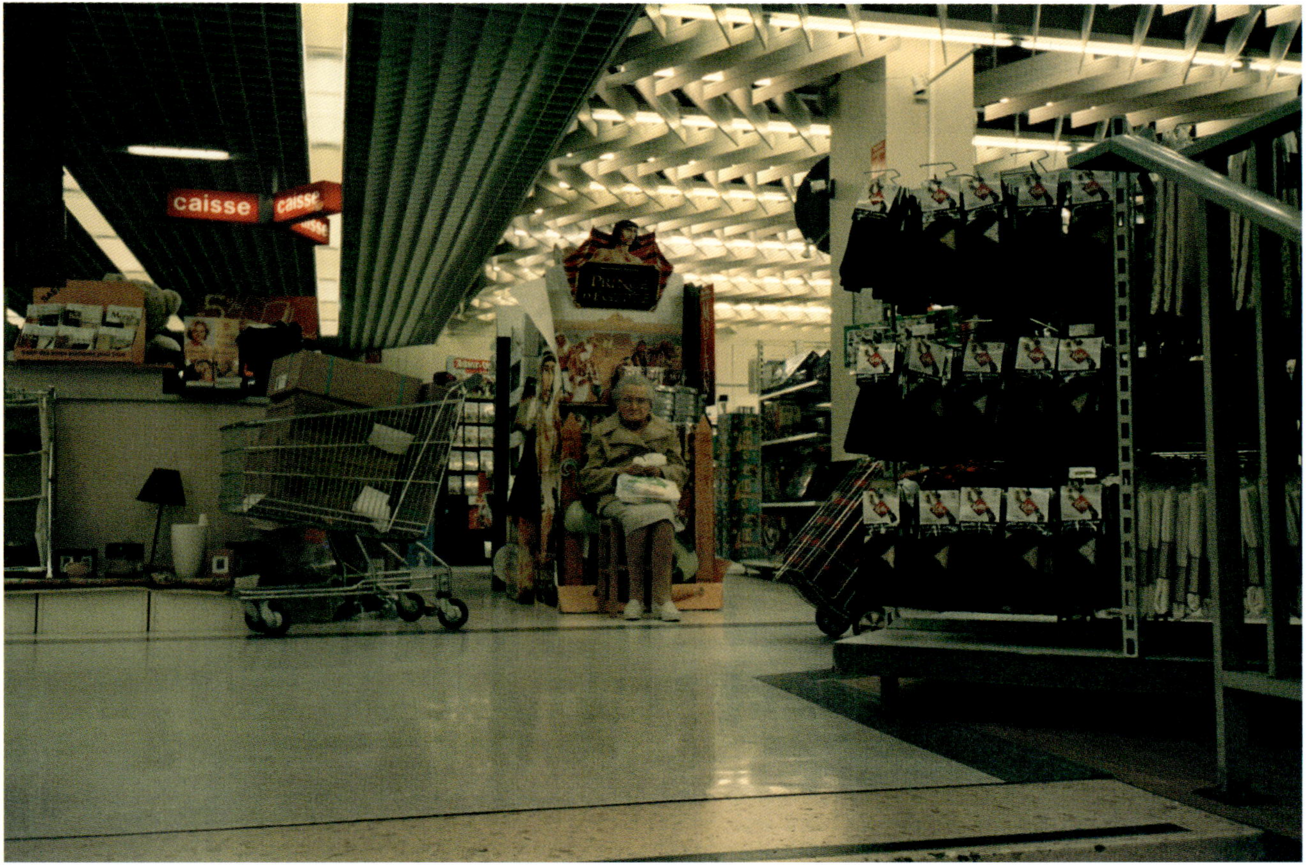

Wednesday, November 3. Near Paris. Shop scene

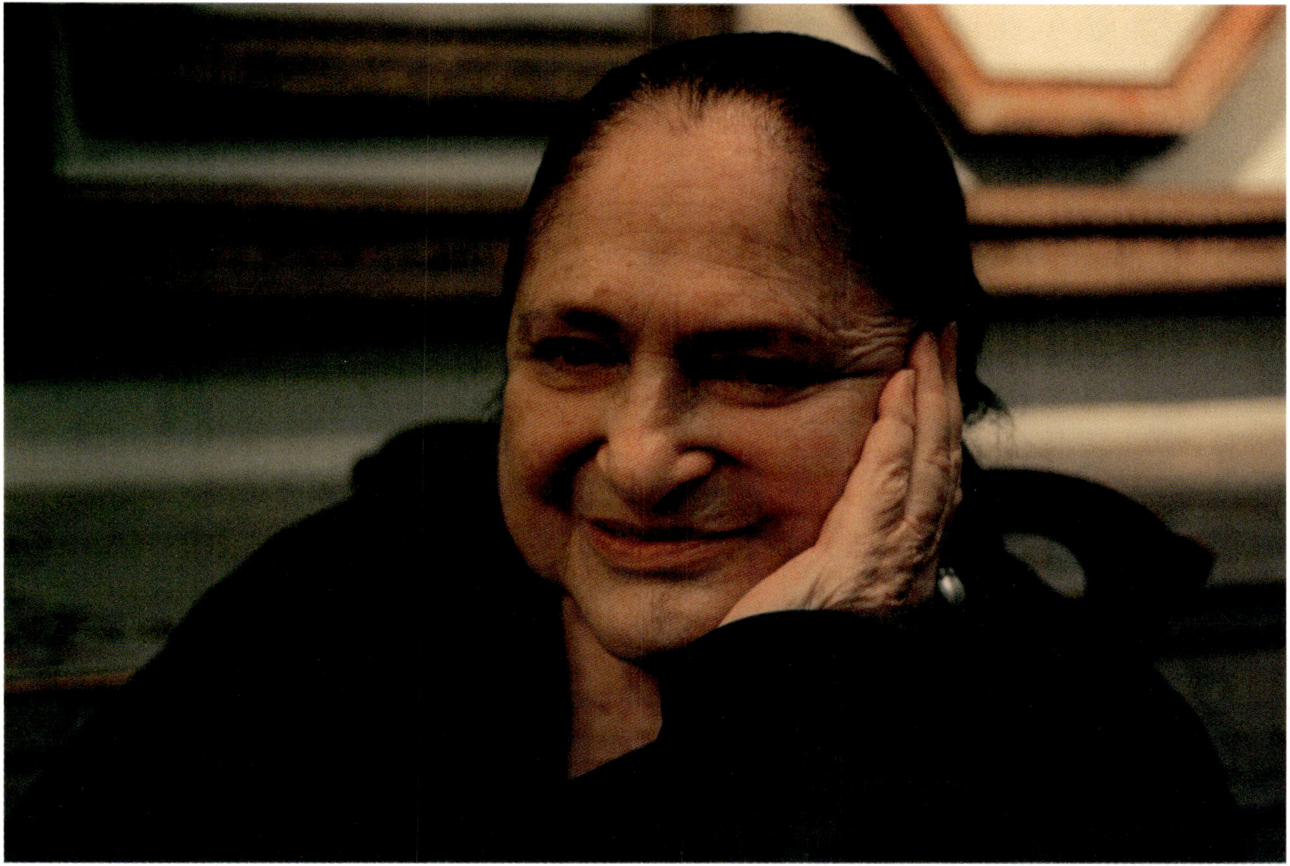

Thursday, November 4. Paris. Dina Vierny, founder of the Musée Maillol

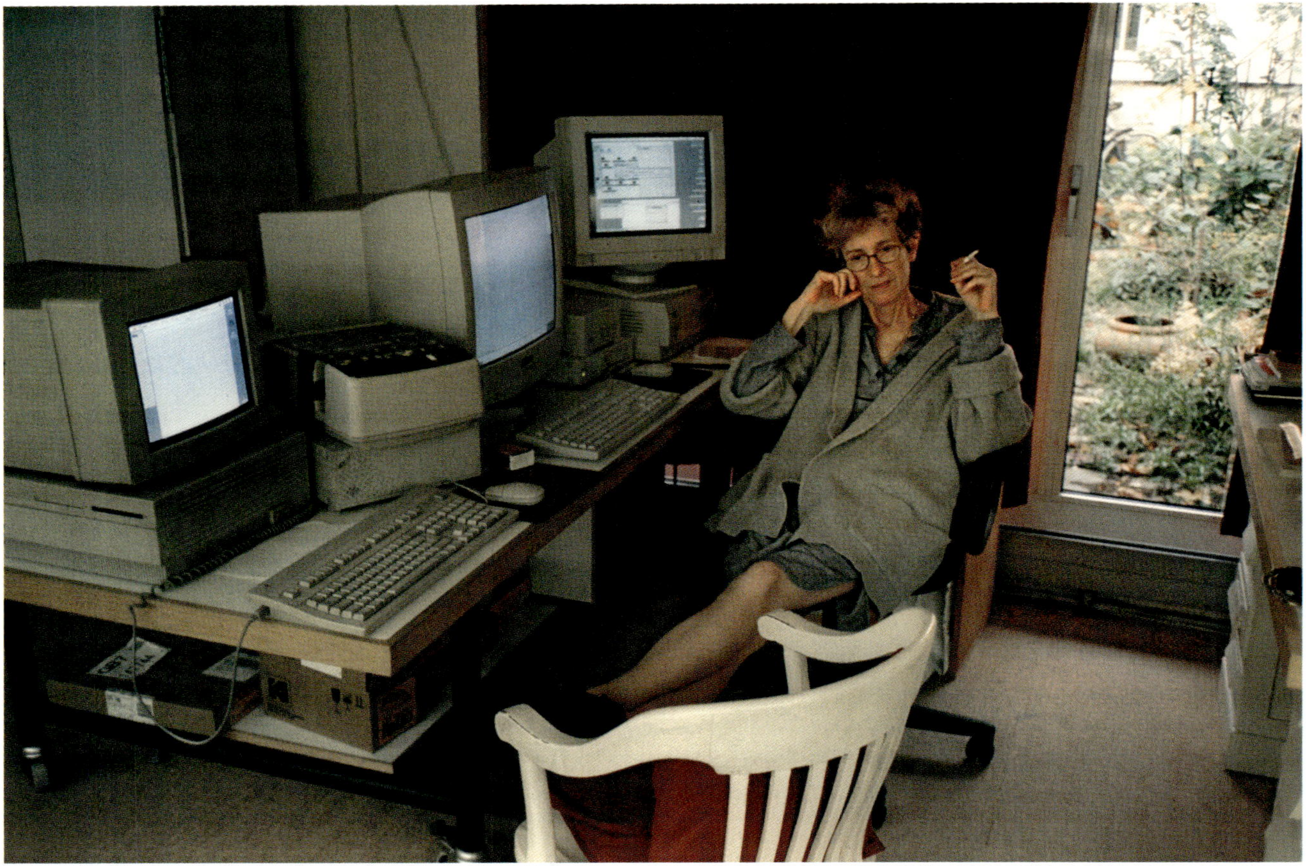

Friday, November 5. Boulogne, France. Véronique Aubry

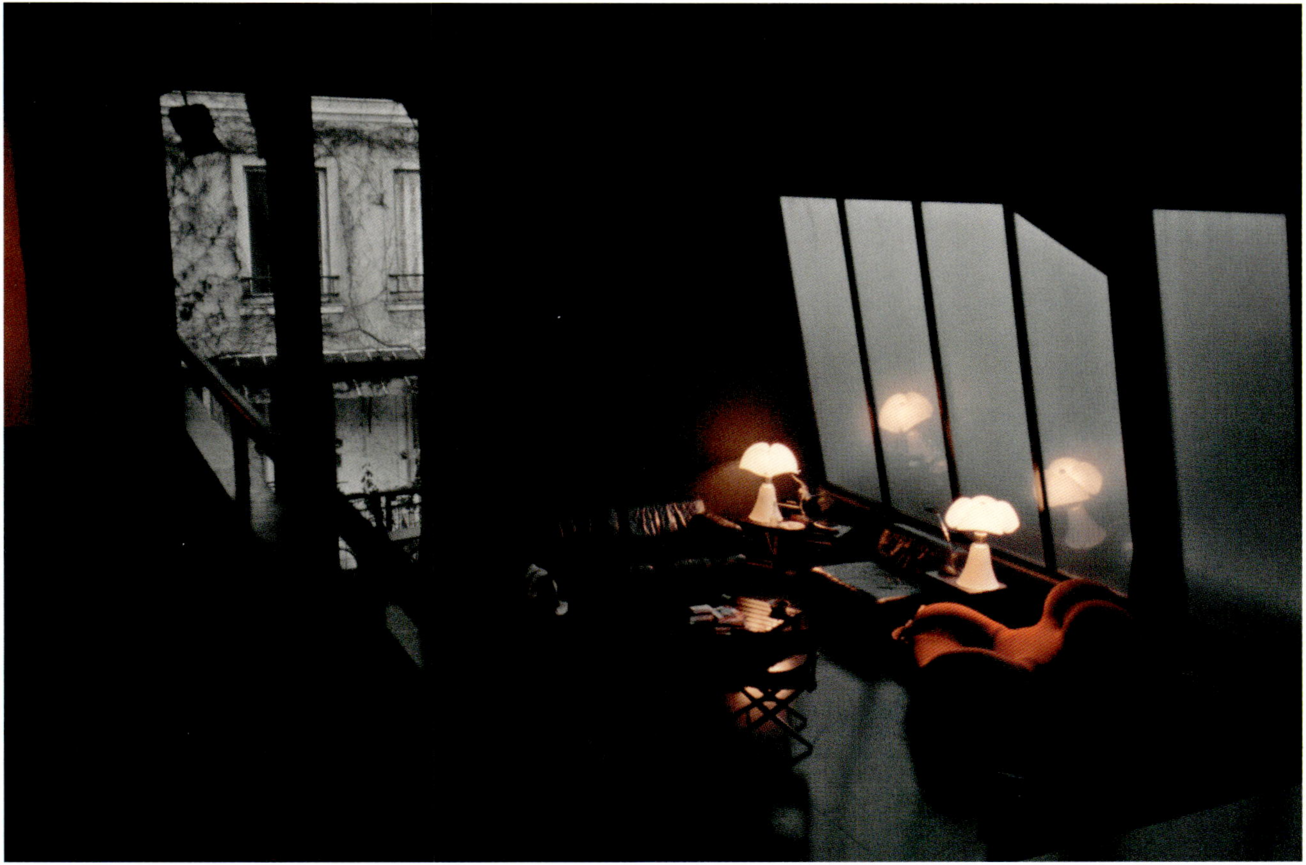

Friday, November 5. Boulogne, France. View of my studio

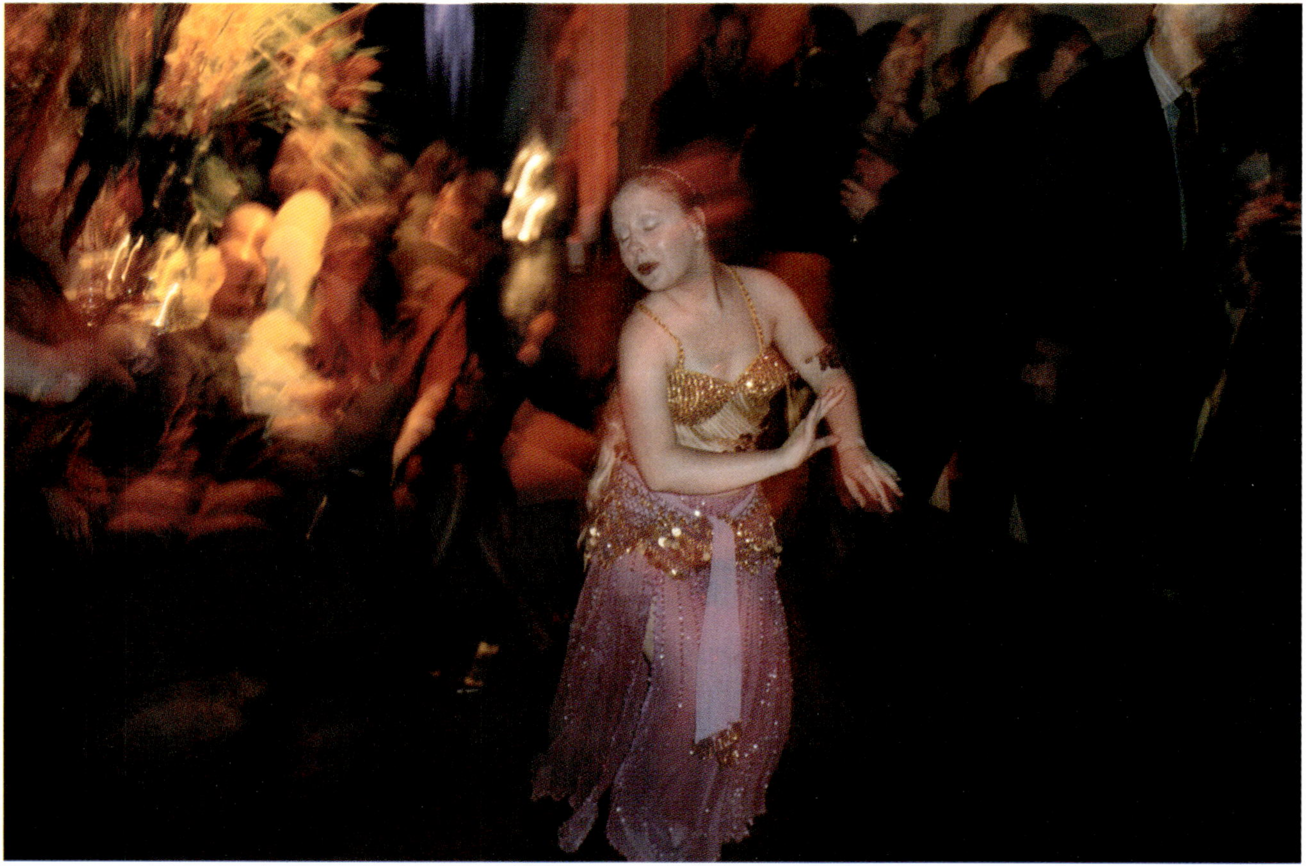

Saturday, November 6. London. Belly dancer, at Marcus Bury's birthday party

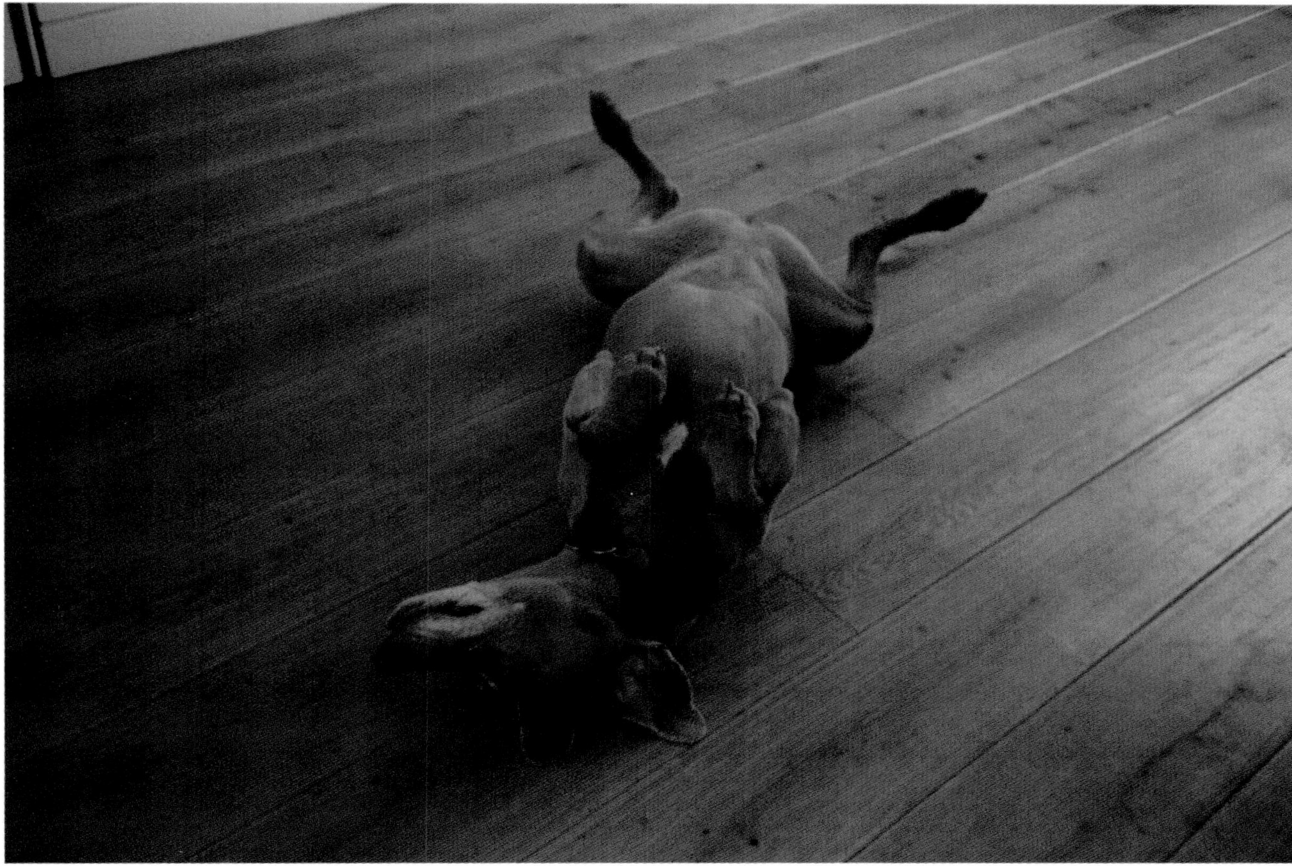

Sunday, November 7. London. Finn, Sascha and Marcus's dog

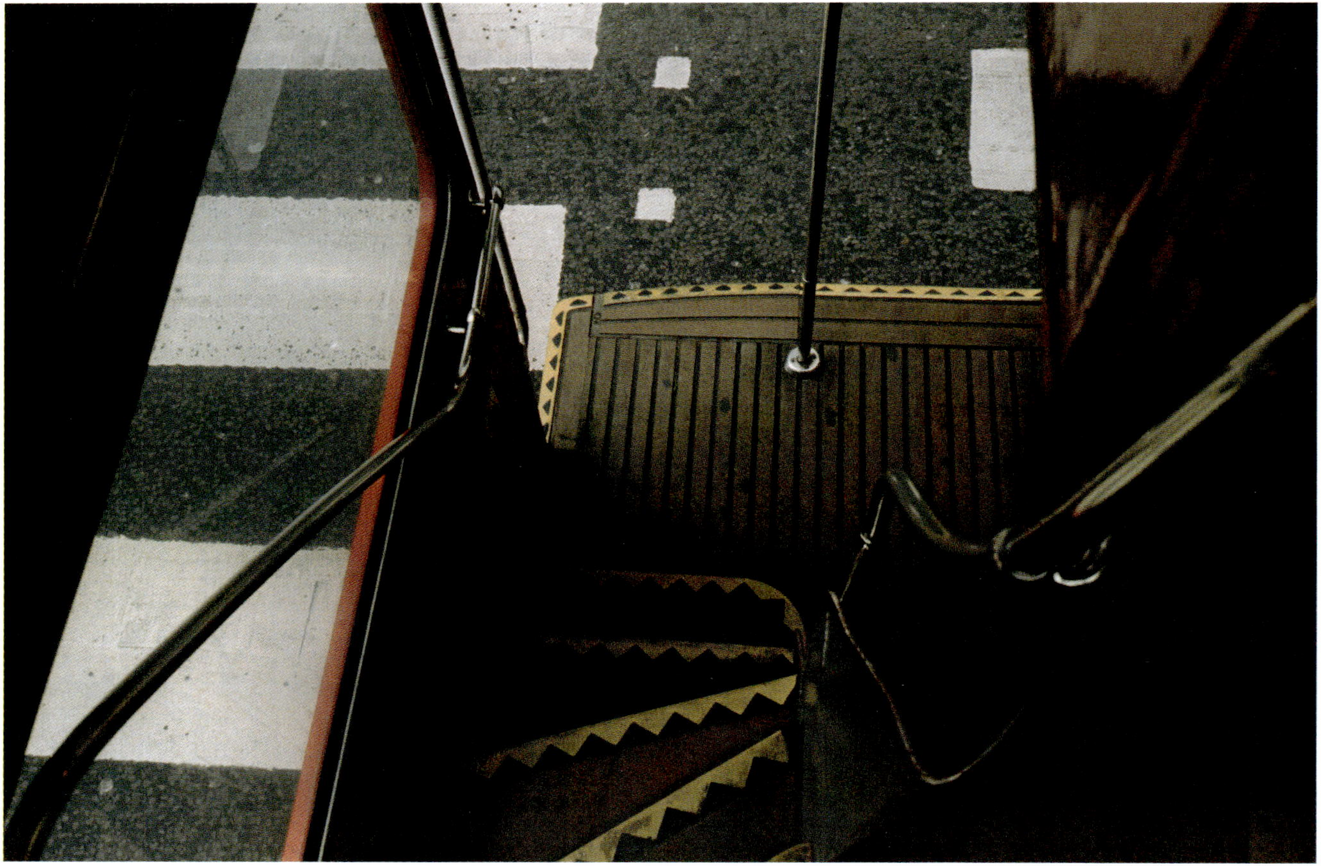

Monday, November 8. London. Steps of a bus

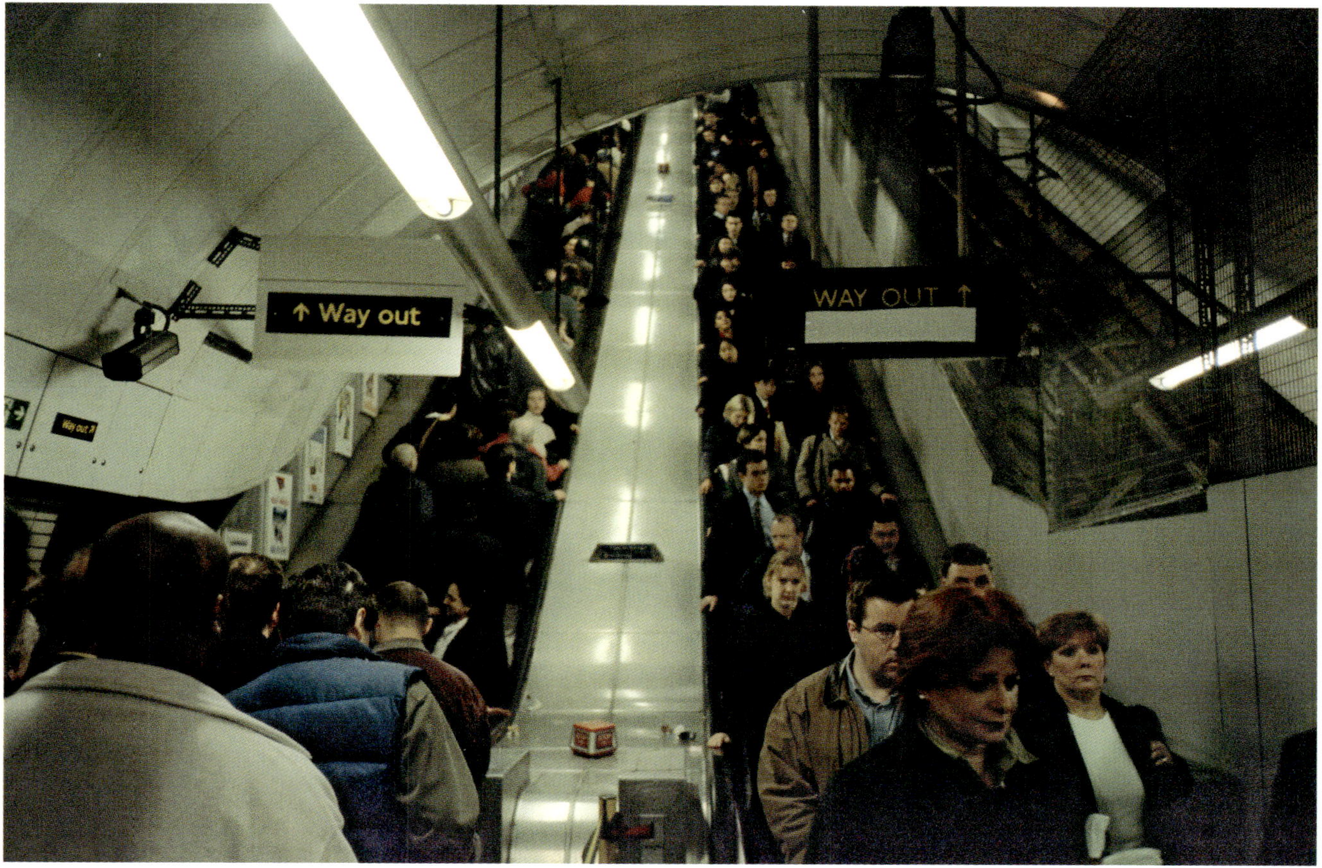

Tuesday, November 9. London. Underground scene

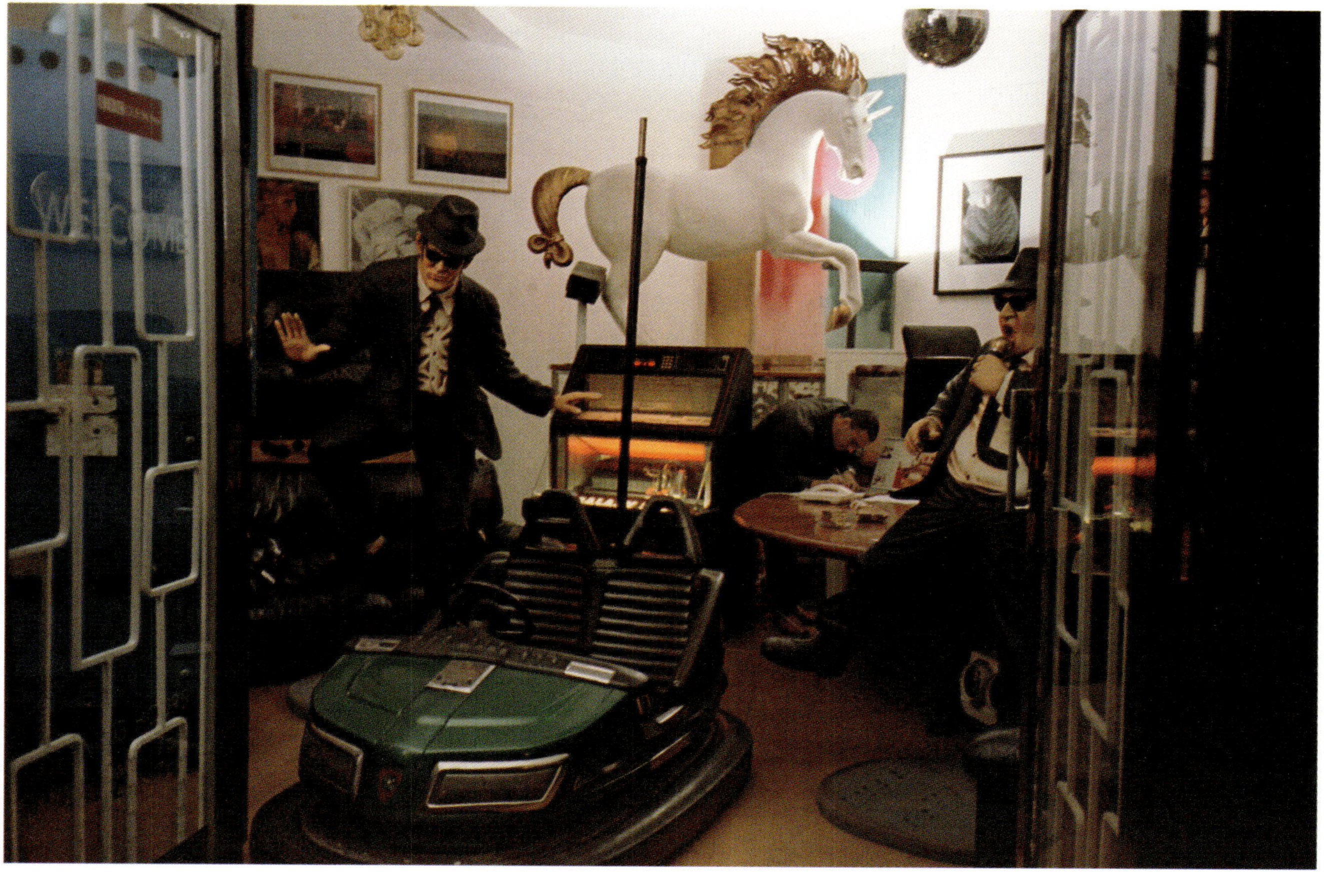

Wednesday, November 10. London. Antique shop

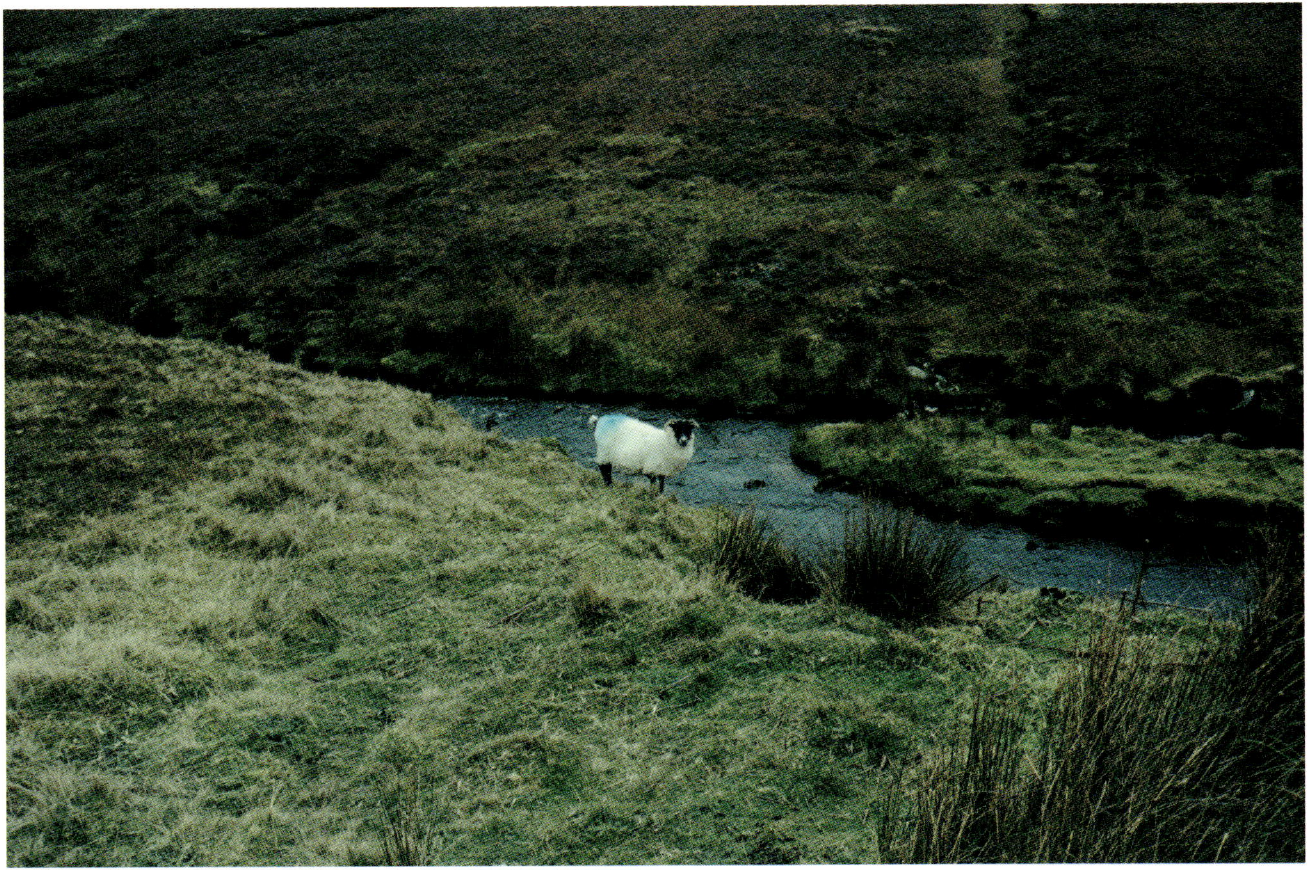

Thursday, November 11. County Donegal, Ireland. On the moors

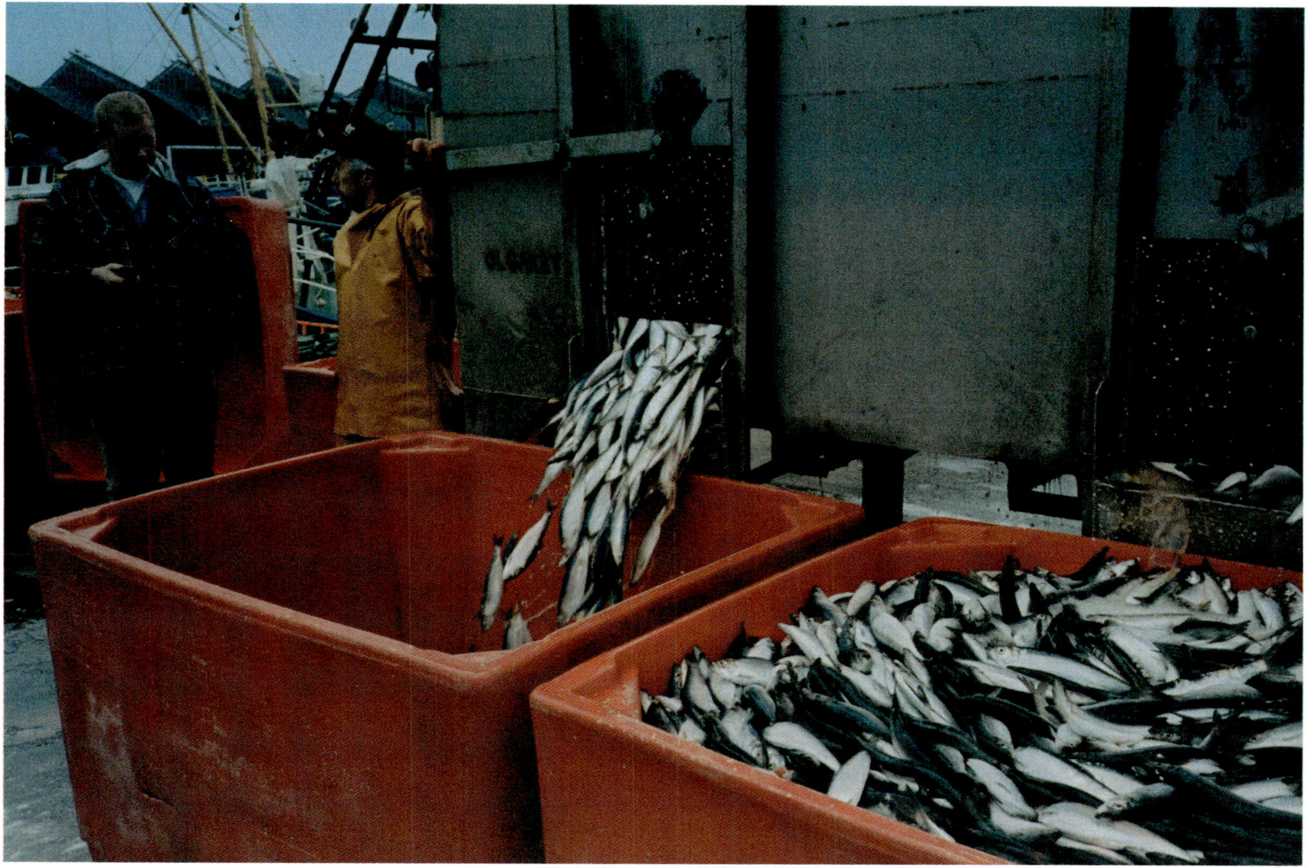

Friday, November 12. Killybegs, Ireland. Fishing catch

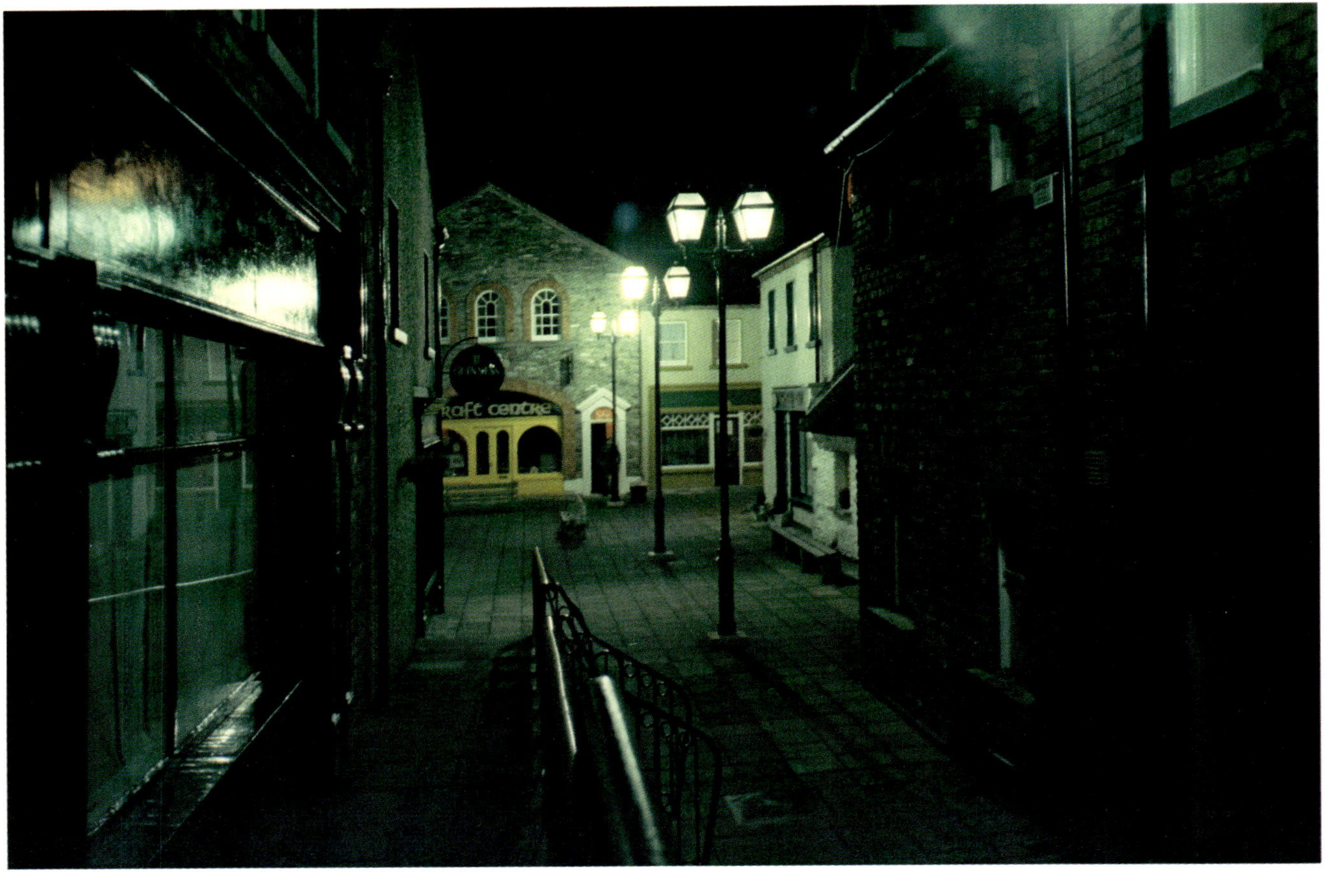

Saturday, November 13. Londonderry, Northern Ireland. Night scene

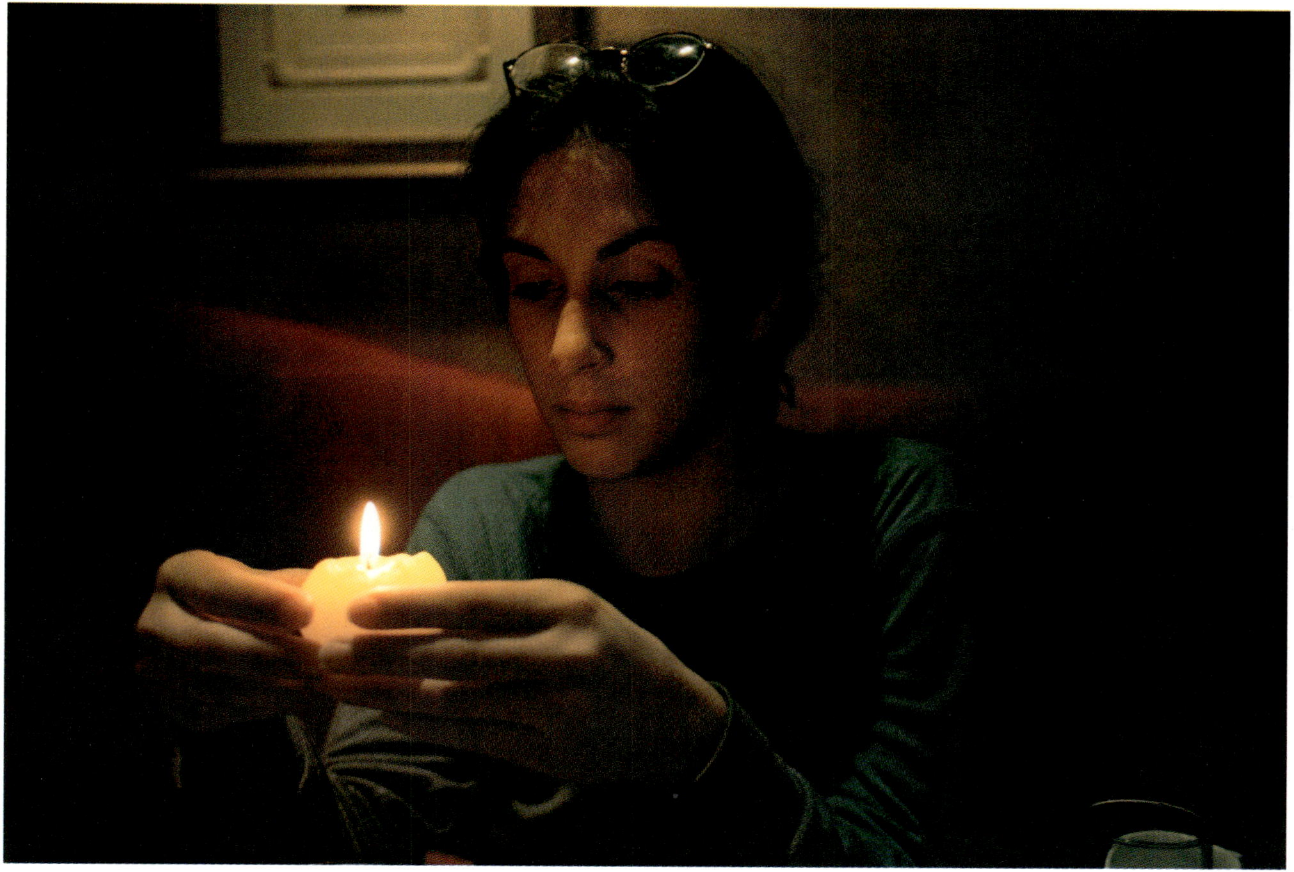

Sunday, November 14. Londonderry, Northern Ireland. My daughter Fiammetta

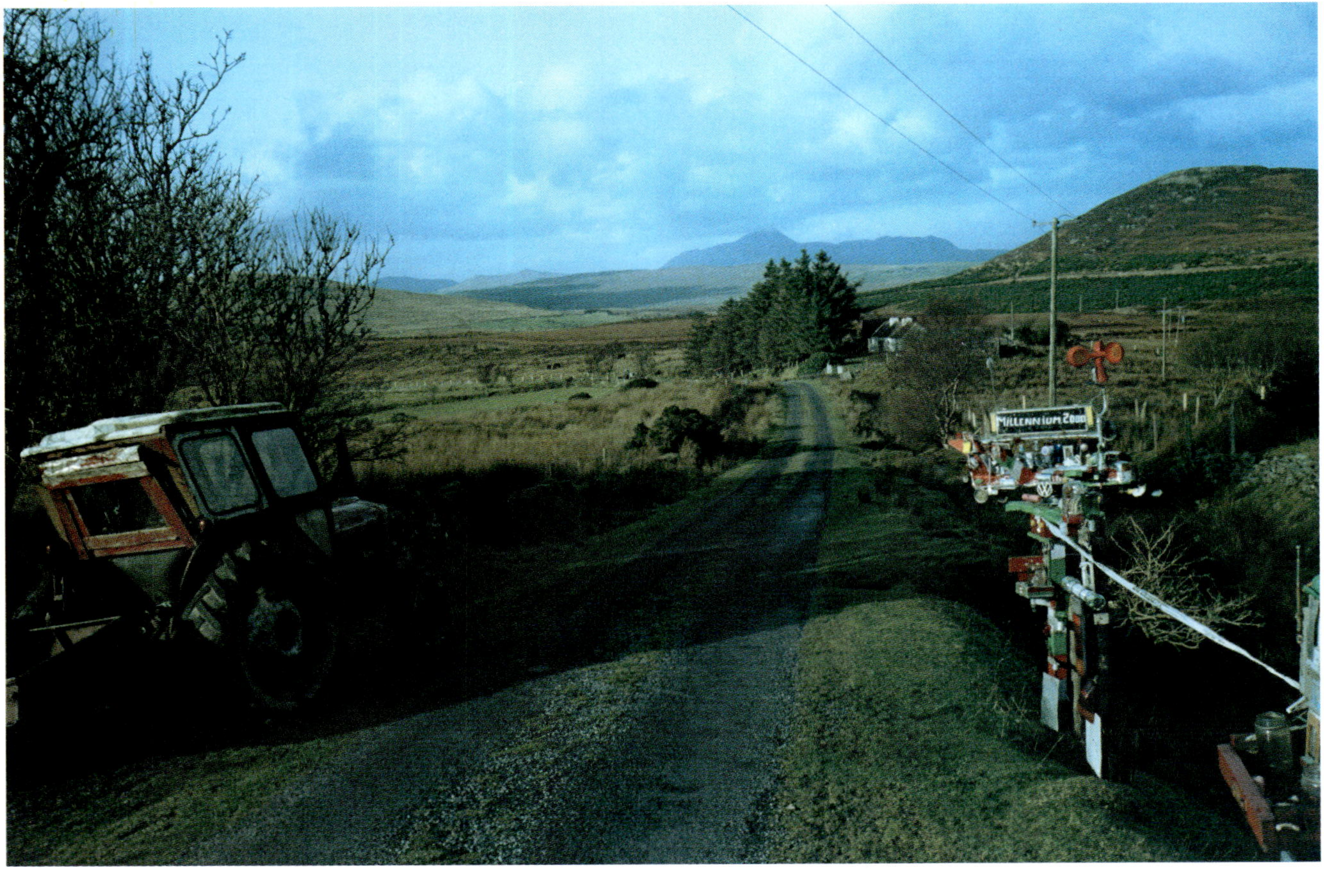

Monday, November 15. Connemara, Ireland. Landscape with naive art

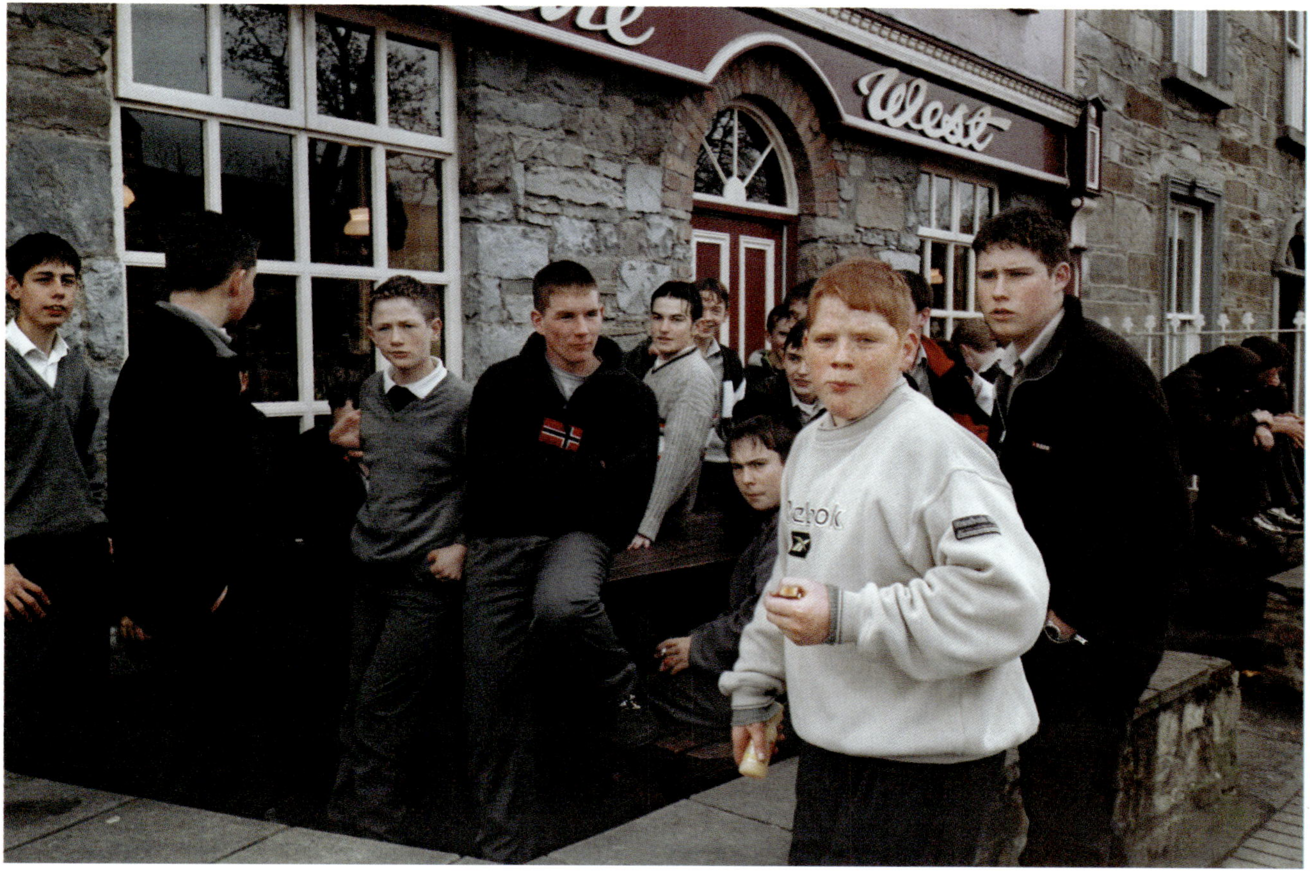

Tuesday, November 16. Westport, Ireland. Schoolboys

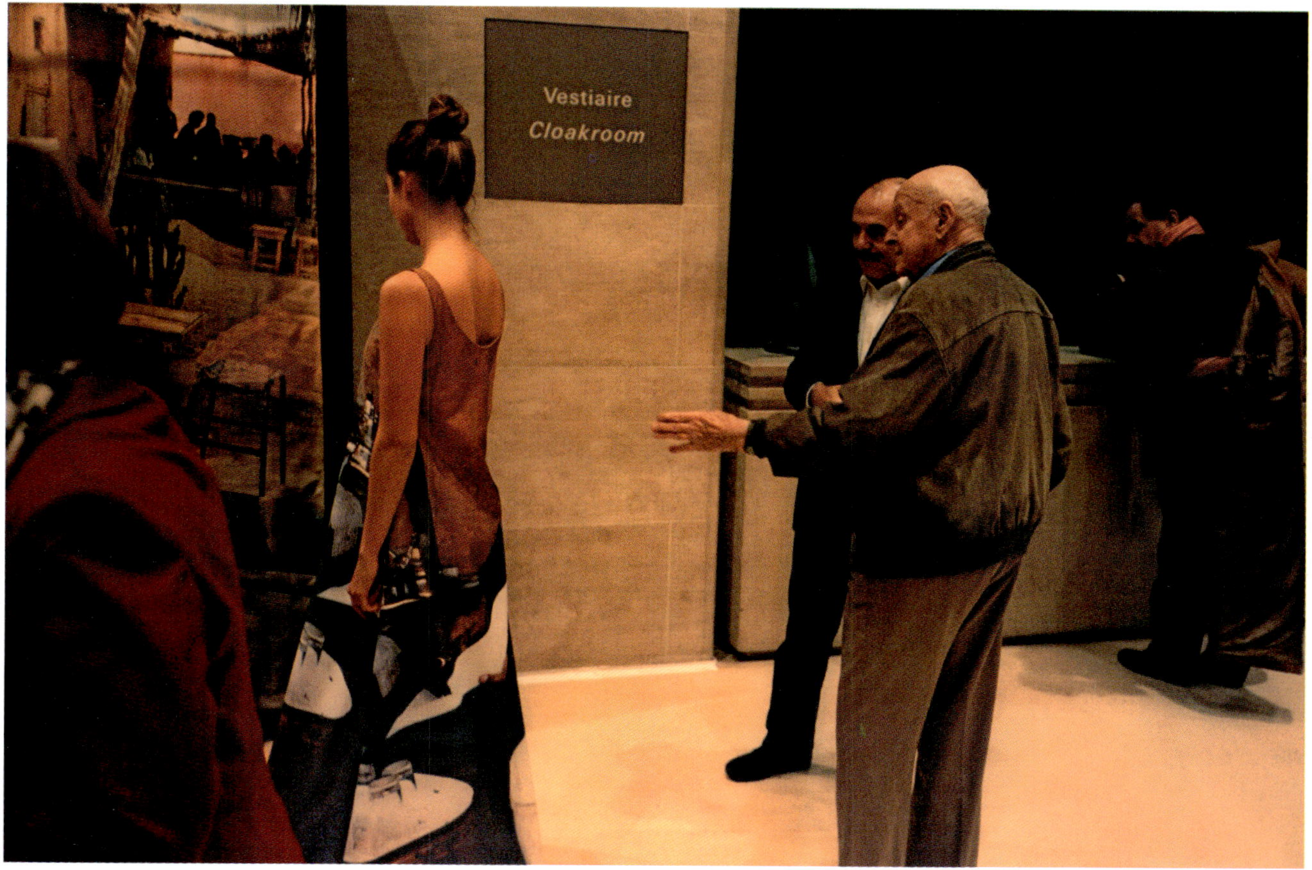

Wednesday, November 17. Paris. Candid shot of Henri Cartier-Bresson, with his biographer Pierre Assouline (see note)

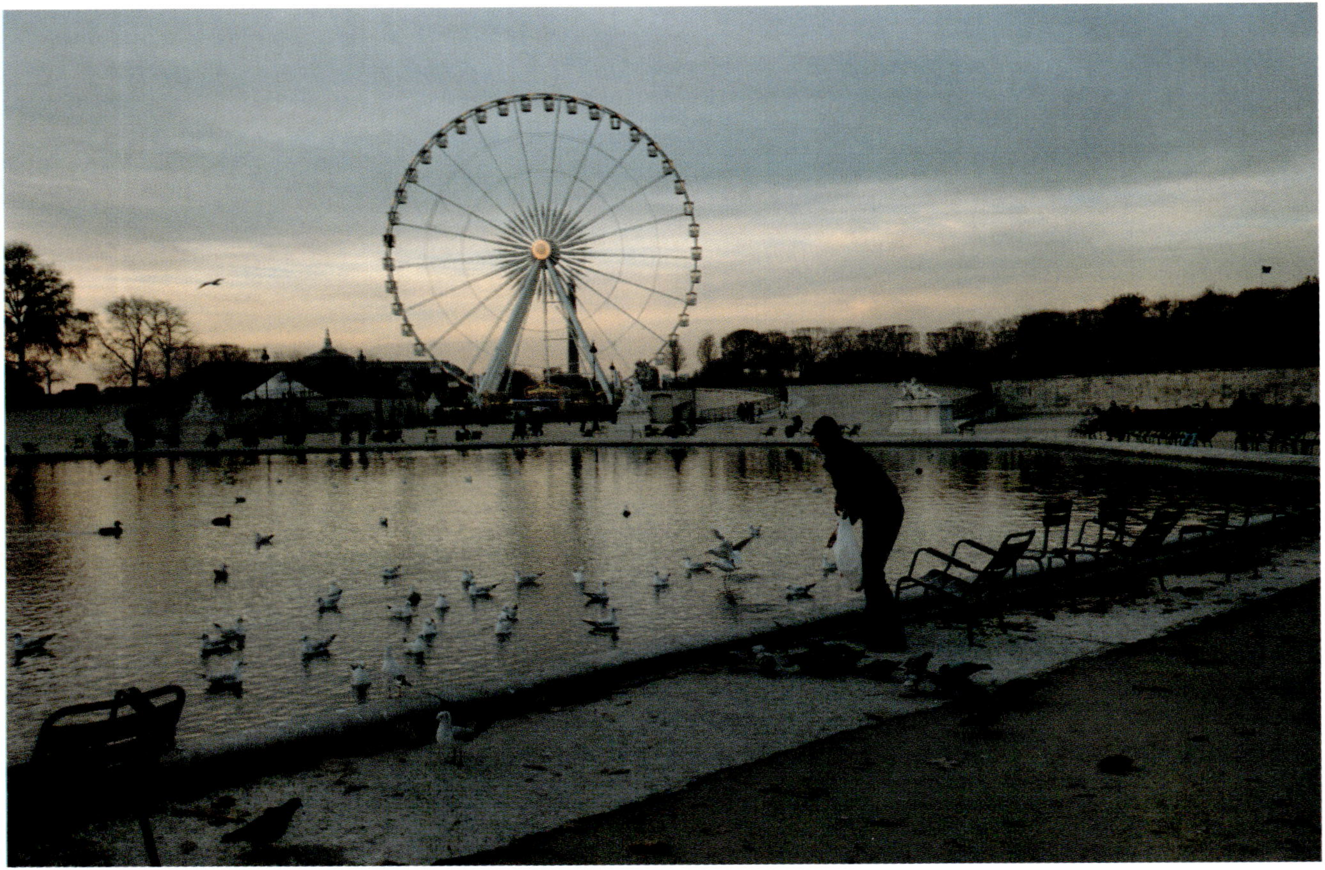

Thursday, November 18. Paris. Jardin des Tuileries, the Millennium Wheel

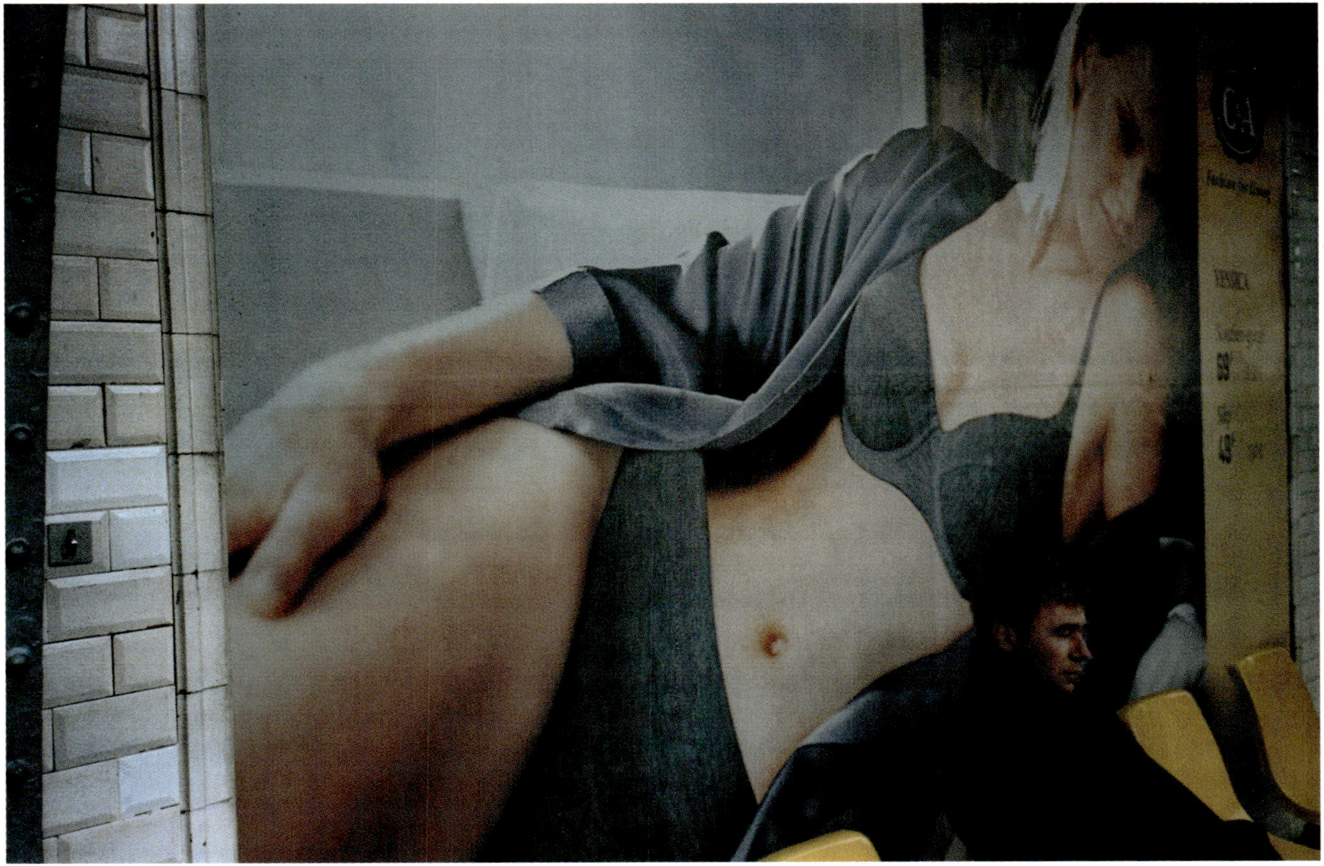

Friday, November 19. Paris. Métro scene

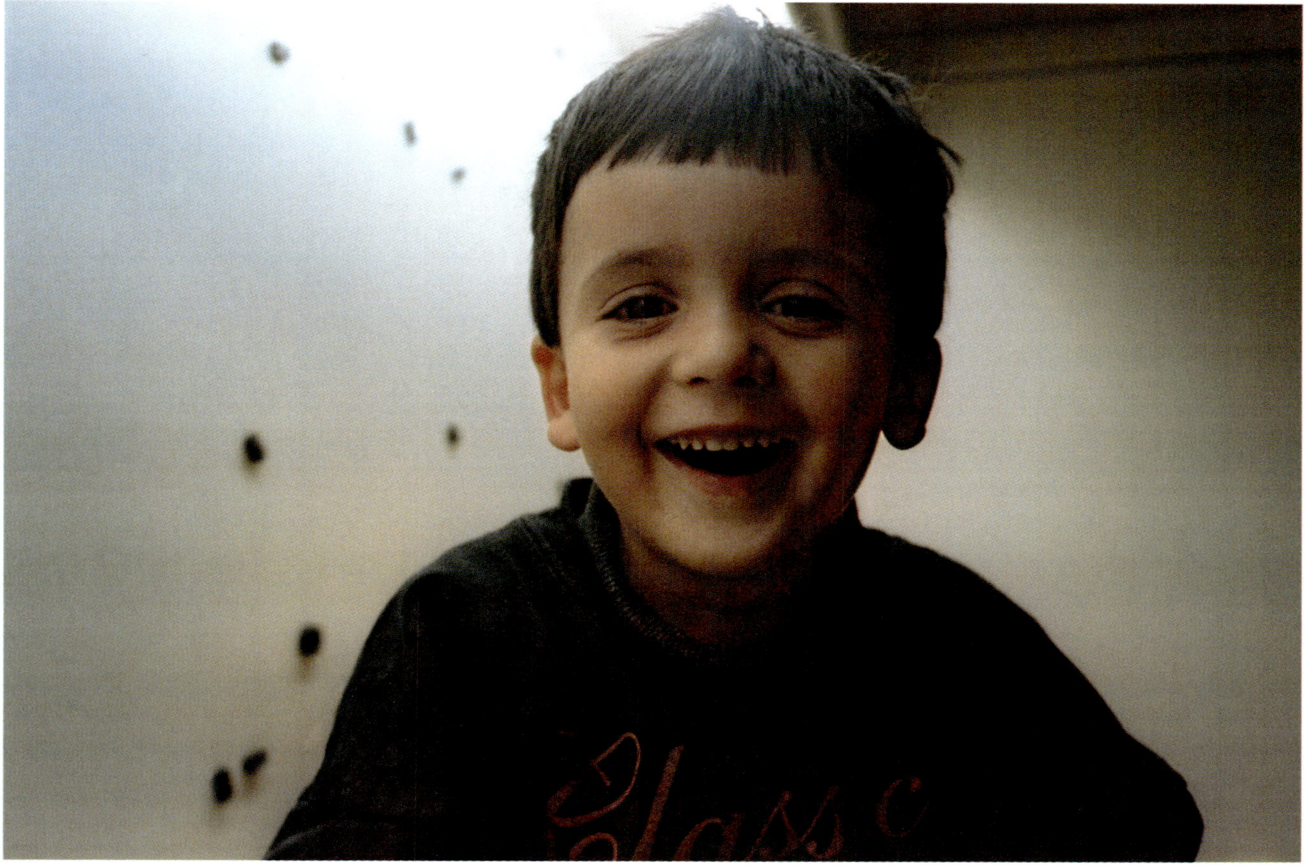

Saturday, November 20. Boulogne, France. My grandson Gabriel

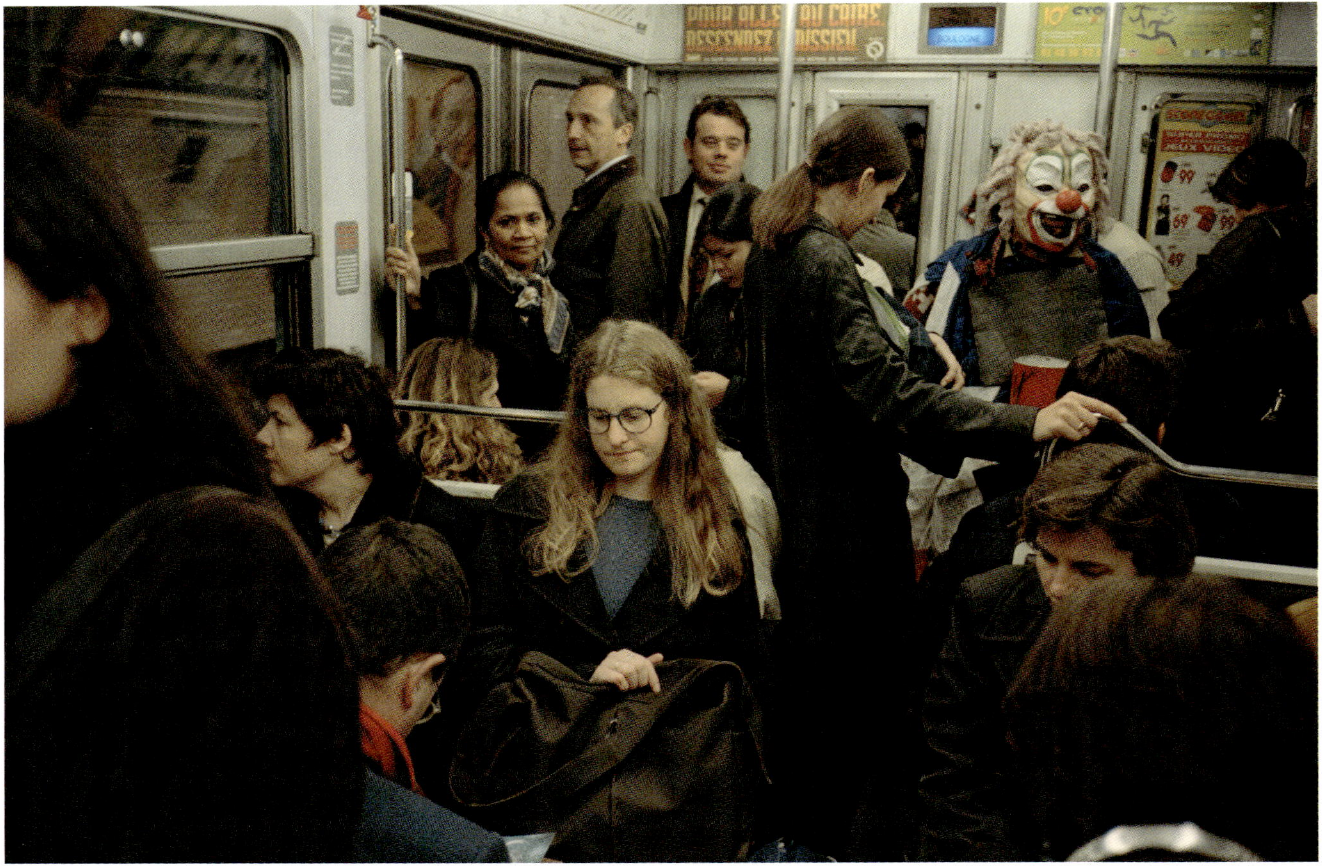

Sunday, November 21. Paris. Métro scene

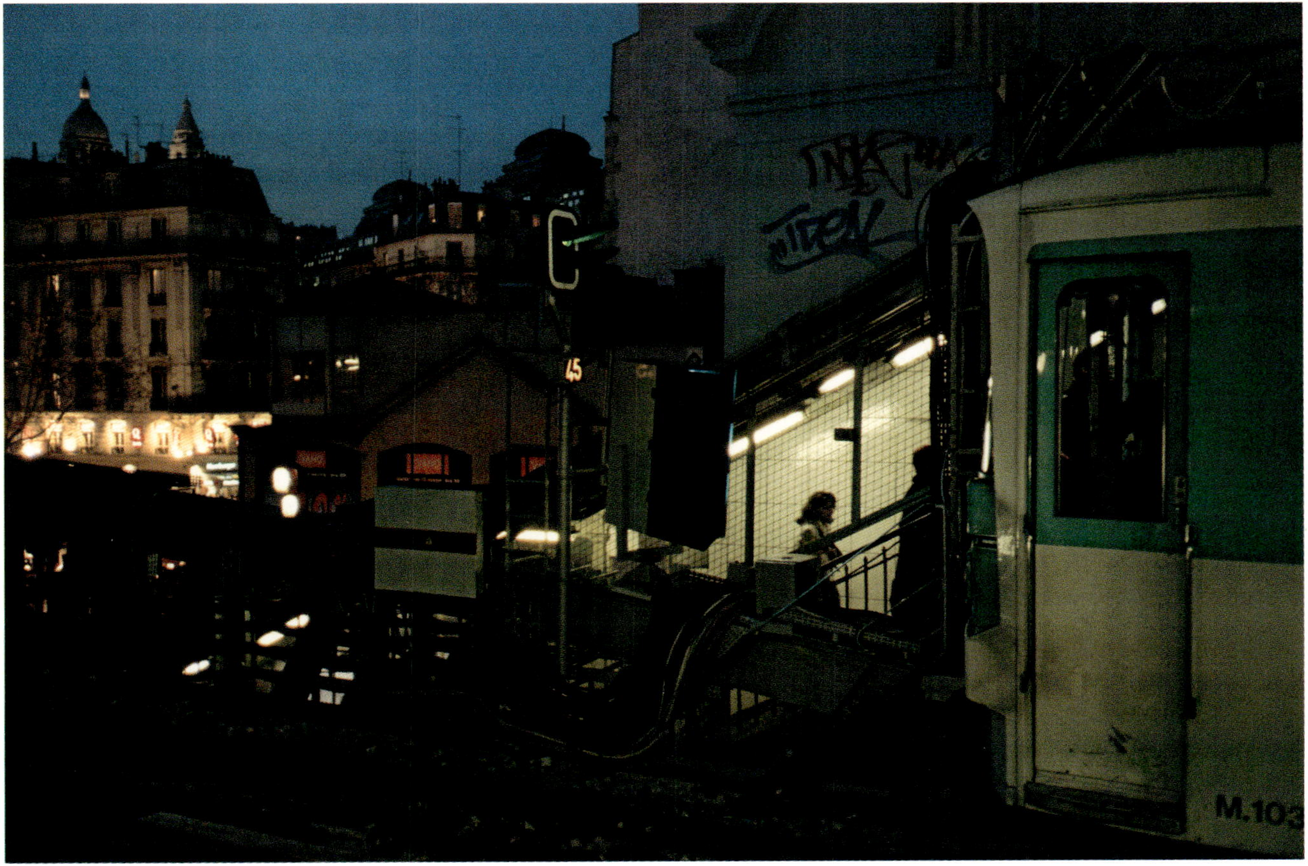

Monday, November 22. Paris. Barbès-Rochechouart métro station

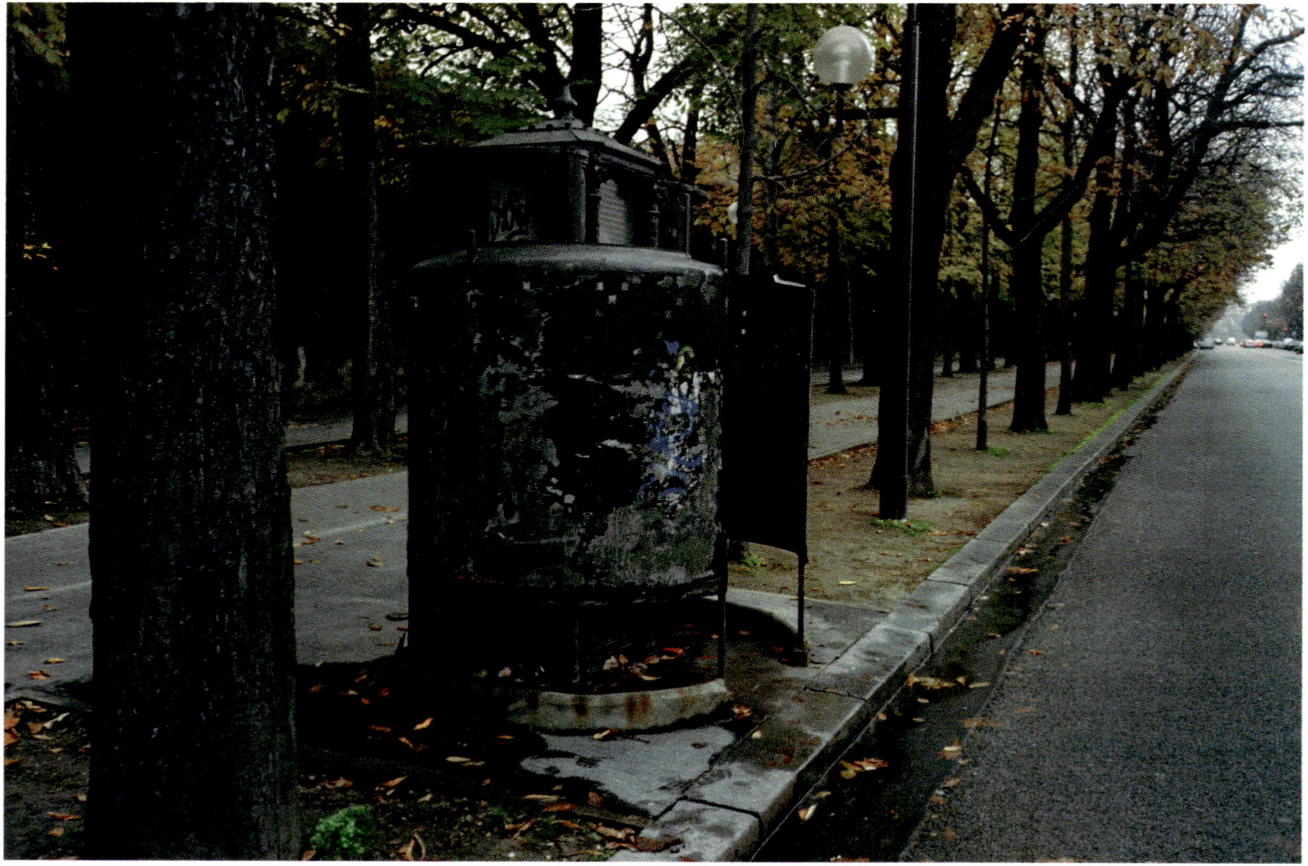

Tuesday, November 23. Paris. Outside Santé prison, the last old style "urinoir"

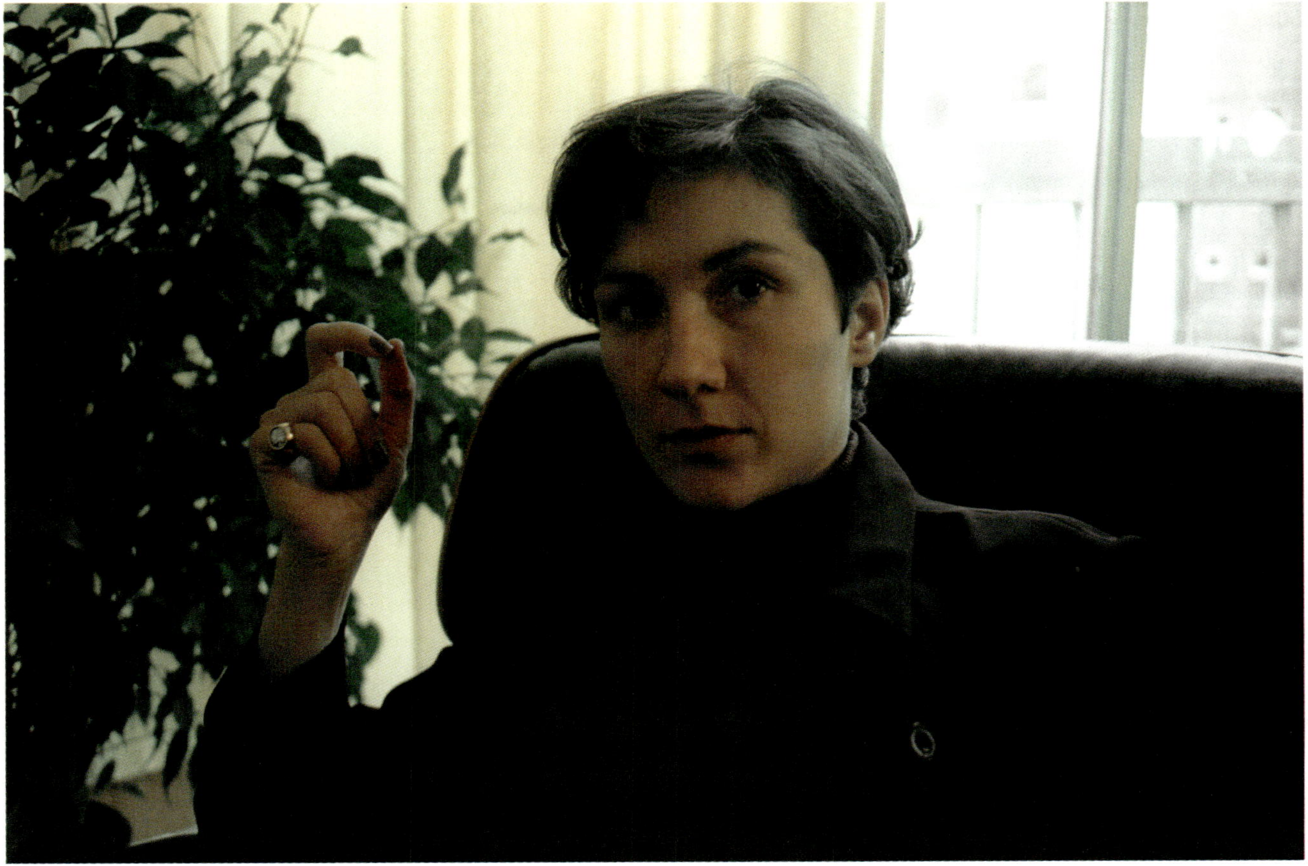

Wednesday, November 24. Paris. Delphine Miermont-Schilton, psychoanalyst

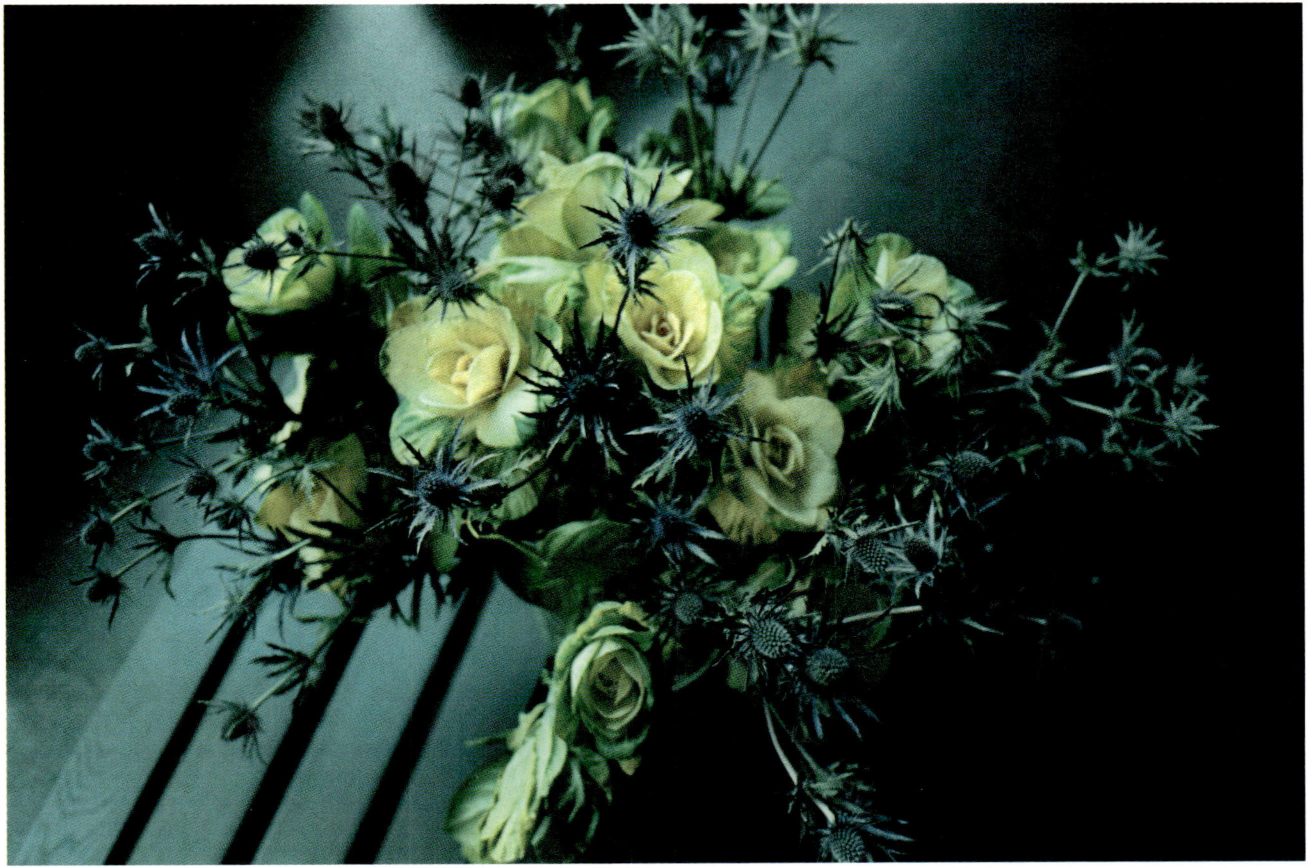

Thursday, November 25. Boulogne, France. Still life

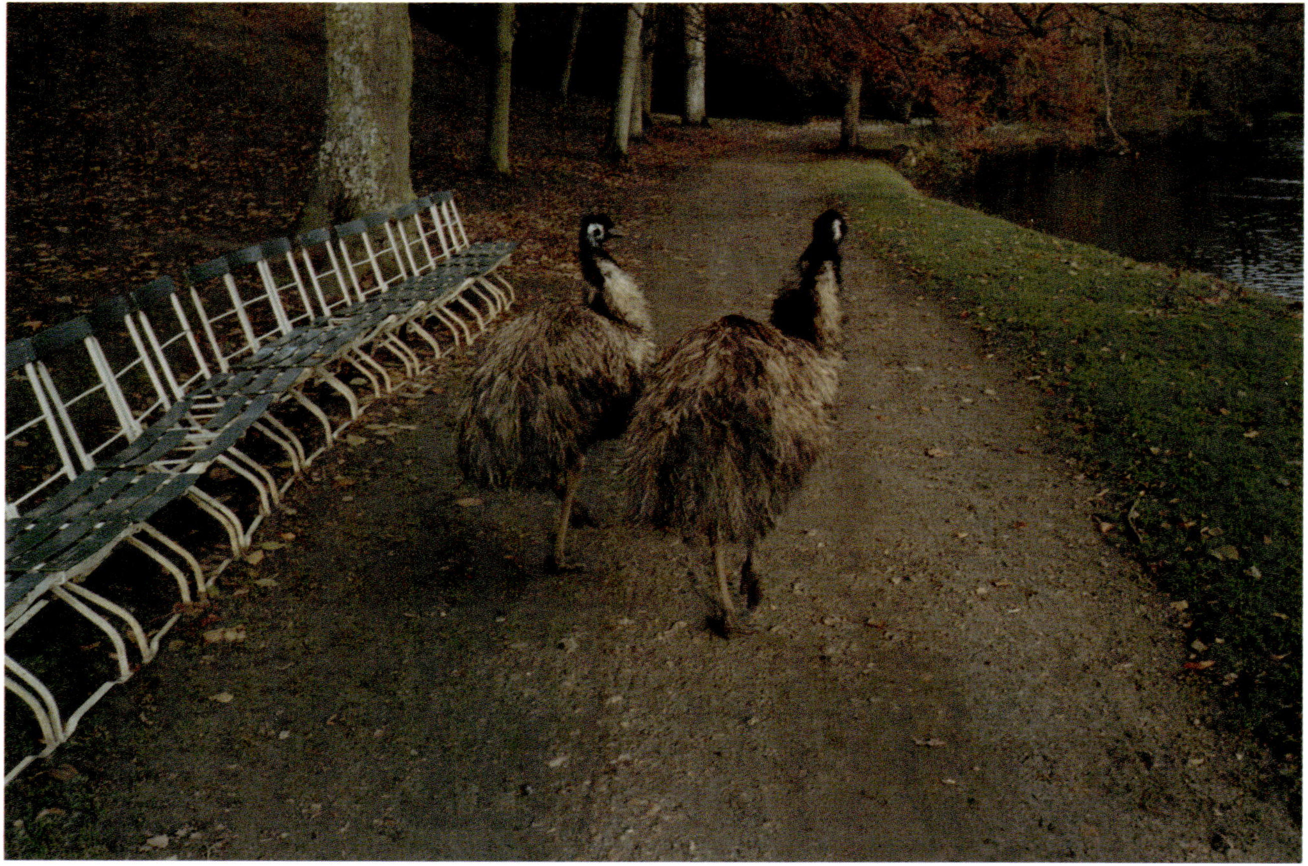

Friday, November 26. Rambouillet, France. In the zoological gardens

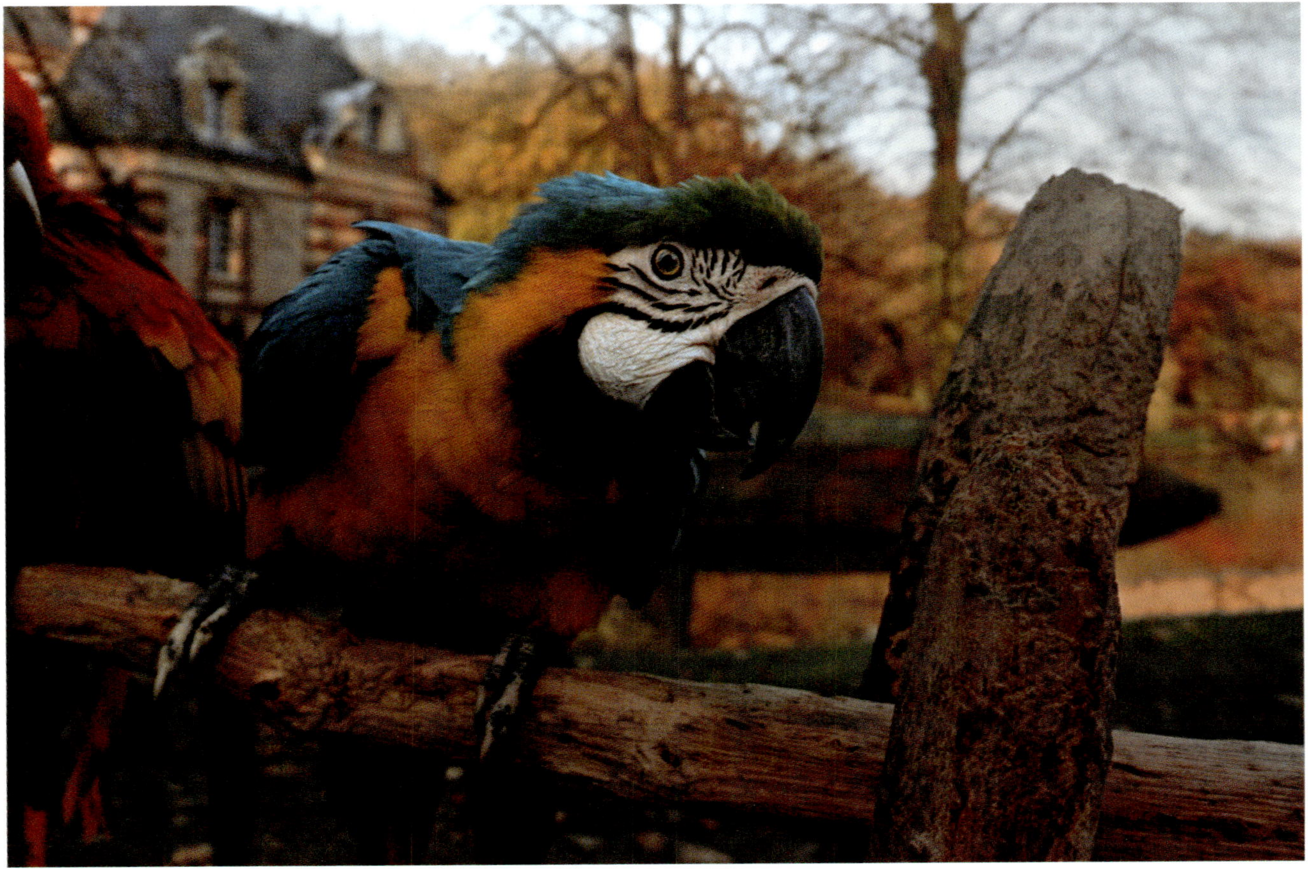

Friday, November 26, Rambouillet, France. In the zoological gardens

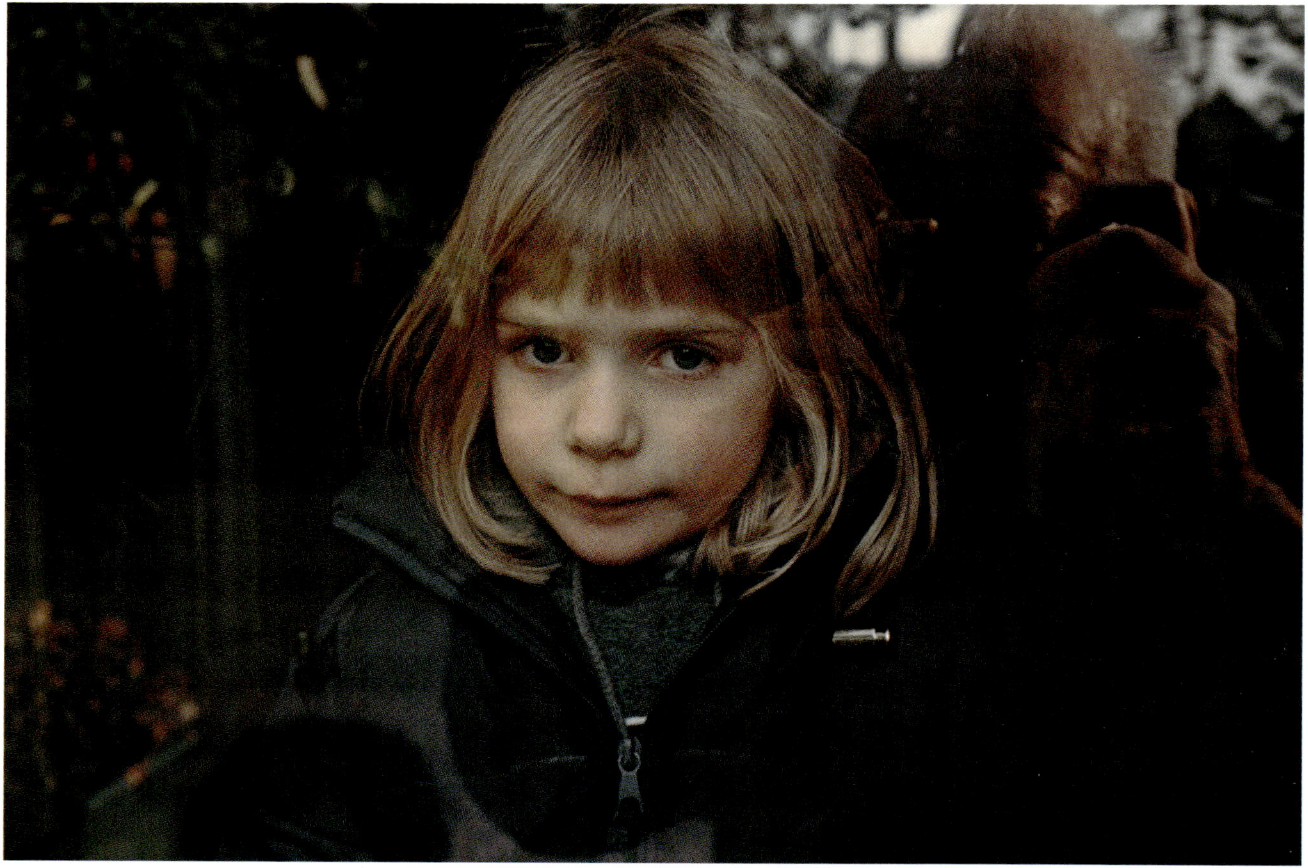

Saturday, November 27. Rambouillet, France. My granddaughter Alba

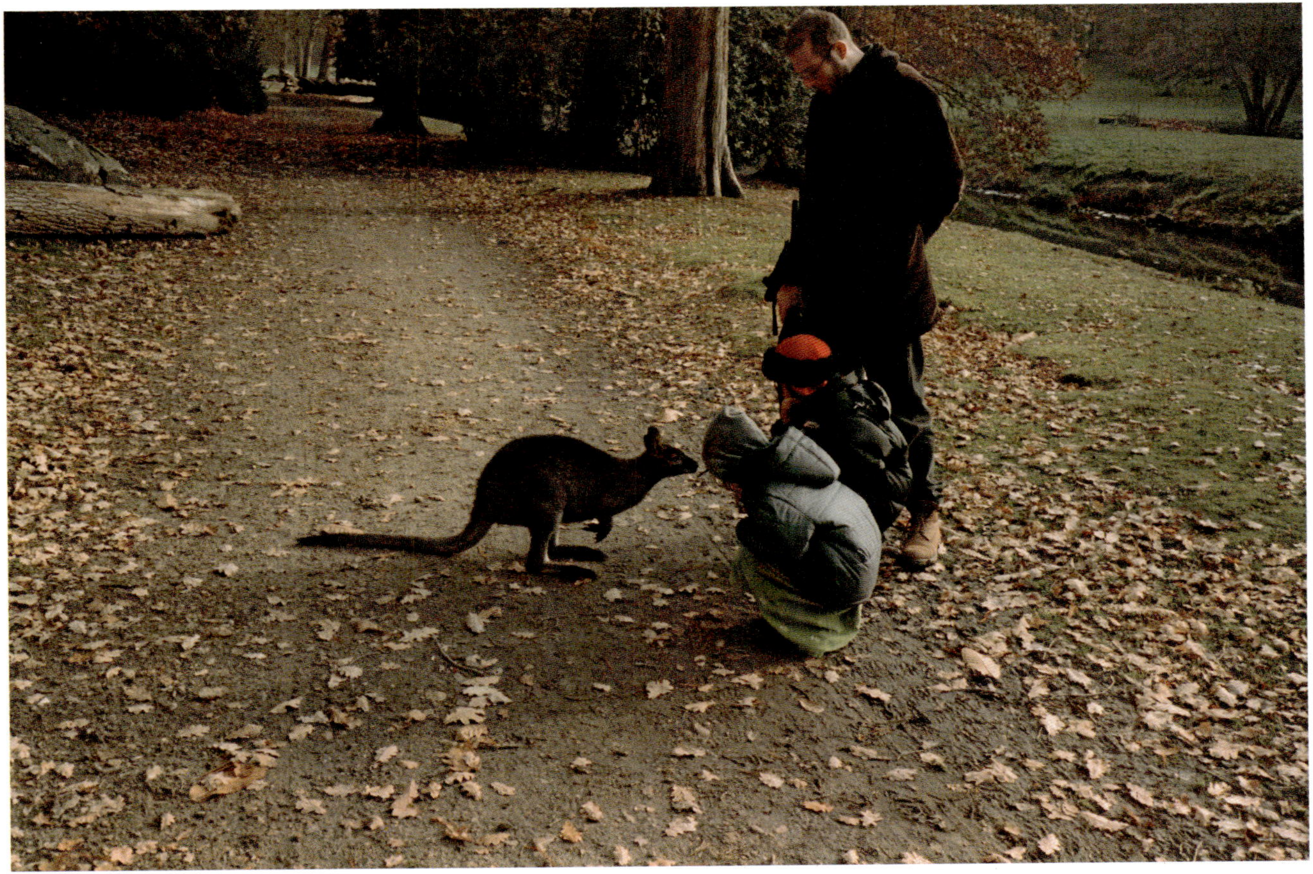

Saturday, November 27. Rambouillet, France. David, Louise and Alba Horvat

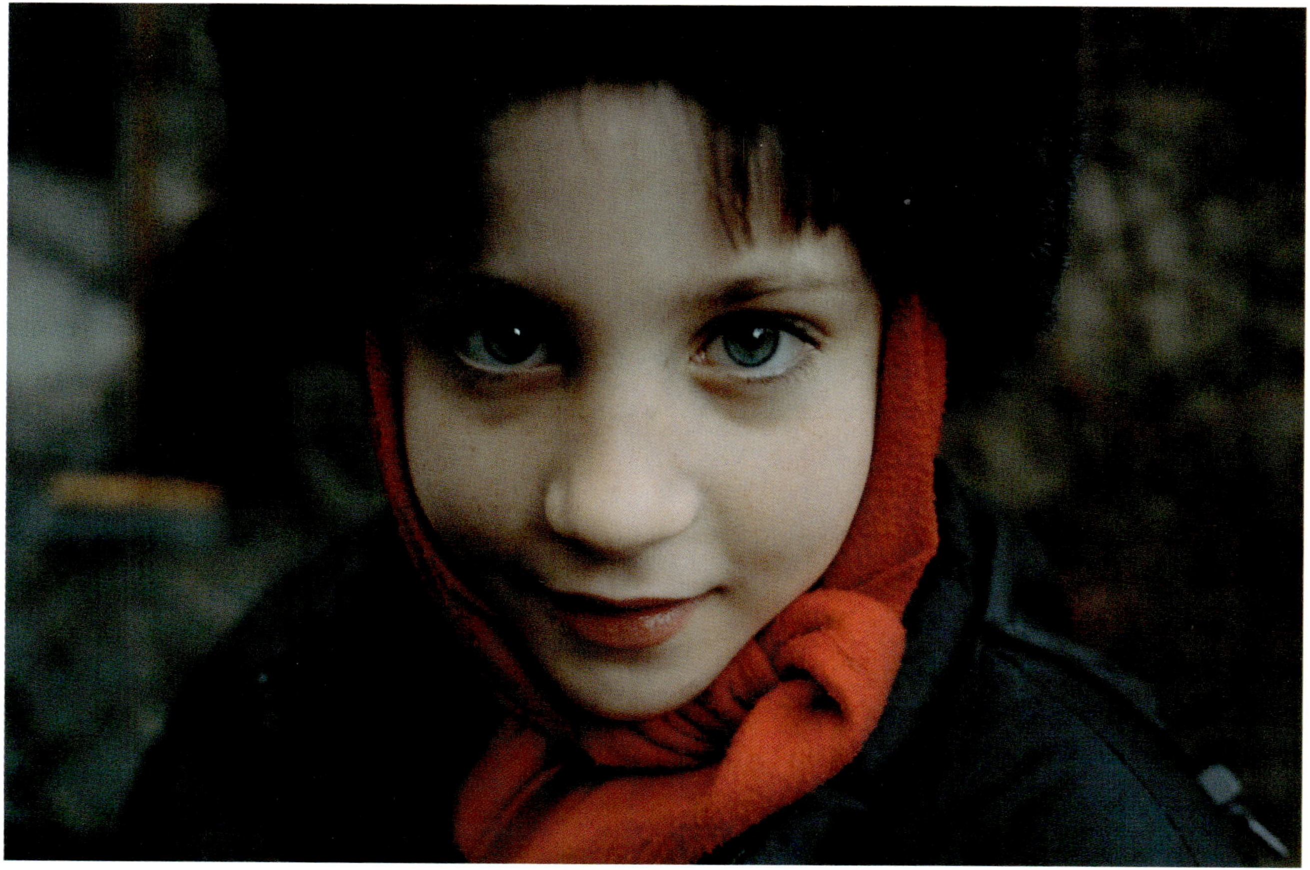

Sunday, November 28. Rambouillet, France. My granddaughter Louise

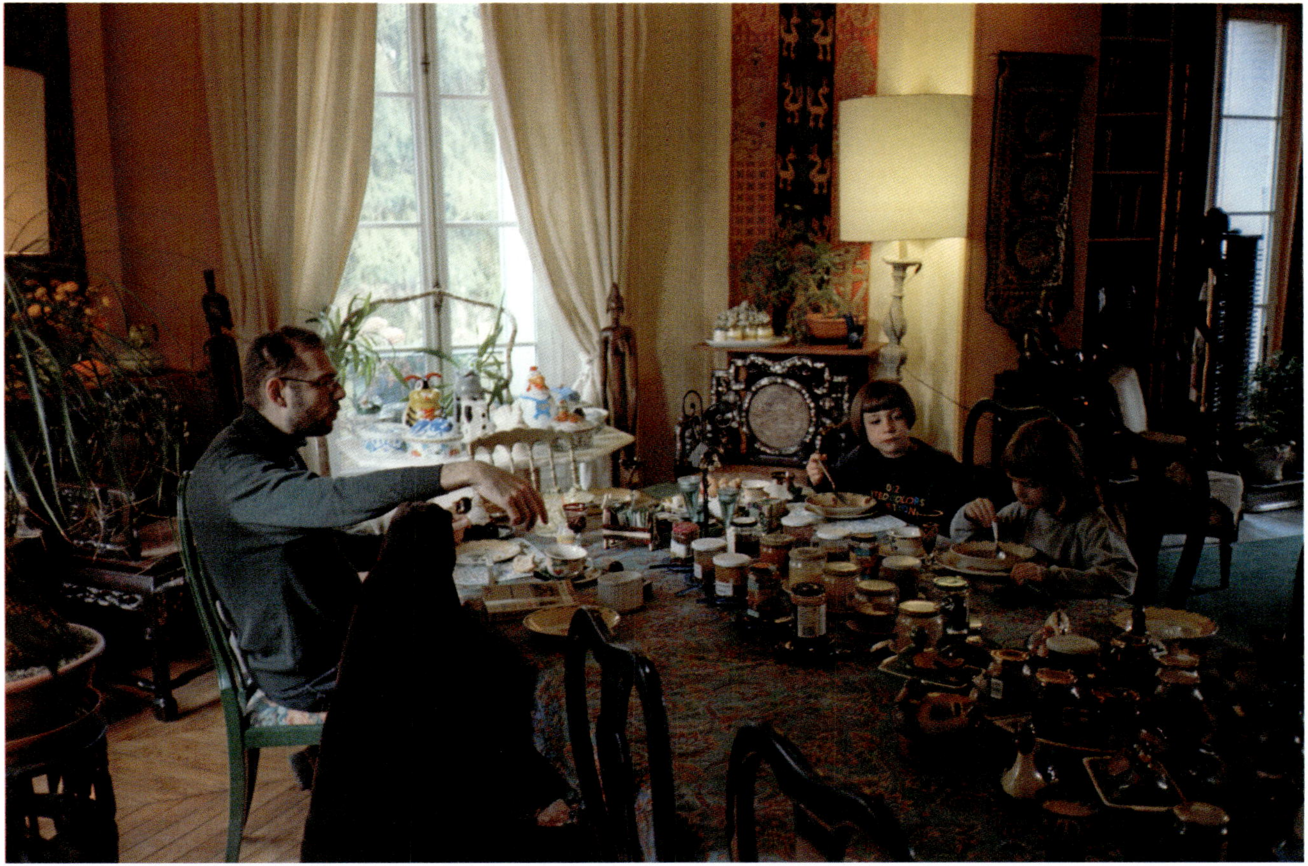

Monday, November 29. Rambouillet, France. David, Louise and Alba Horvat

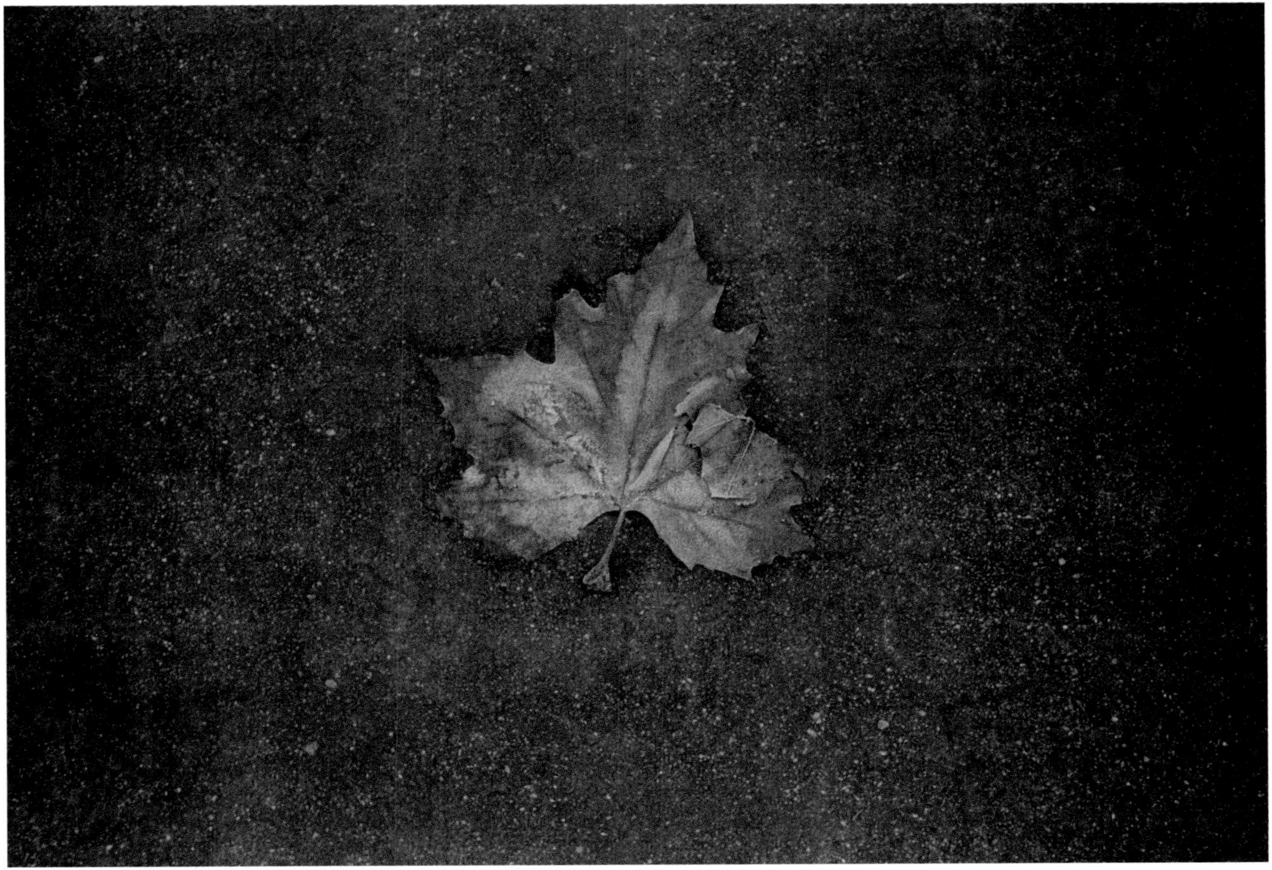

Tuesday, November 30. Paris. Still life on a pavement

DECEMBER

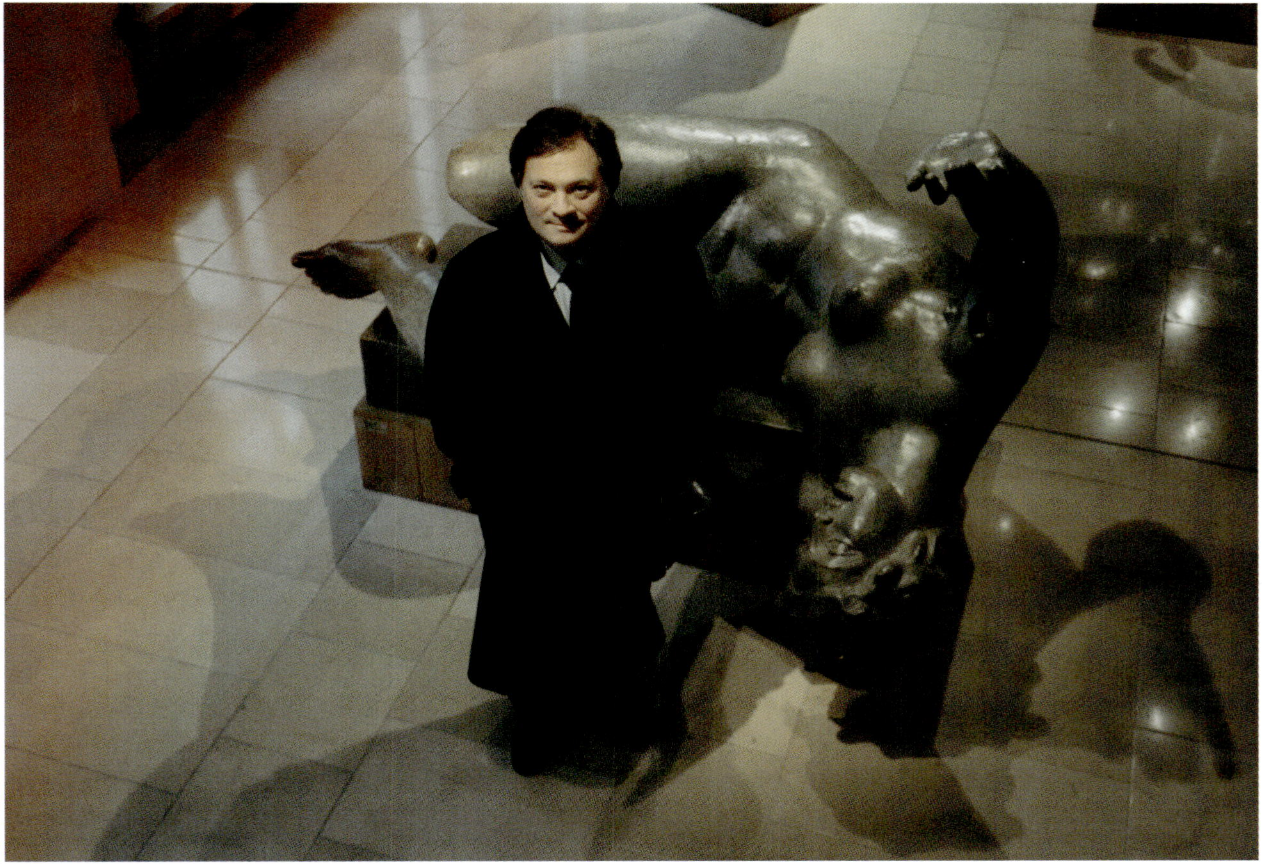

Wednesday, December 1. Paris. Jeffrey Loria, art collector

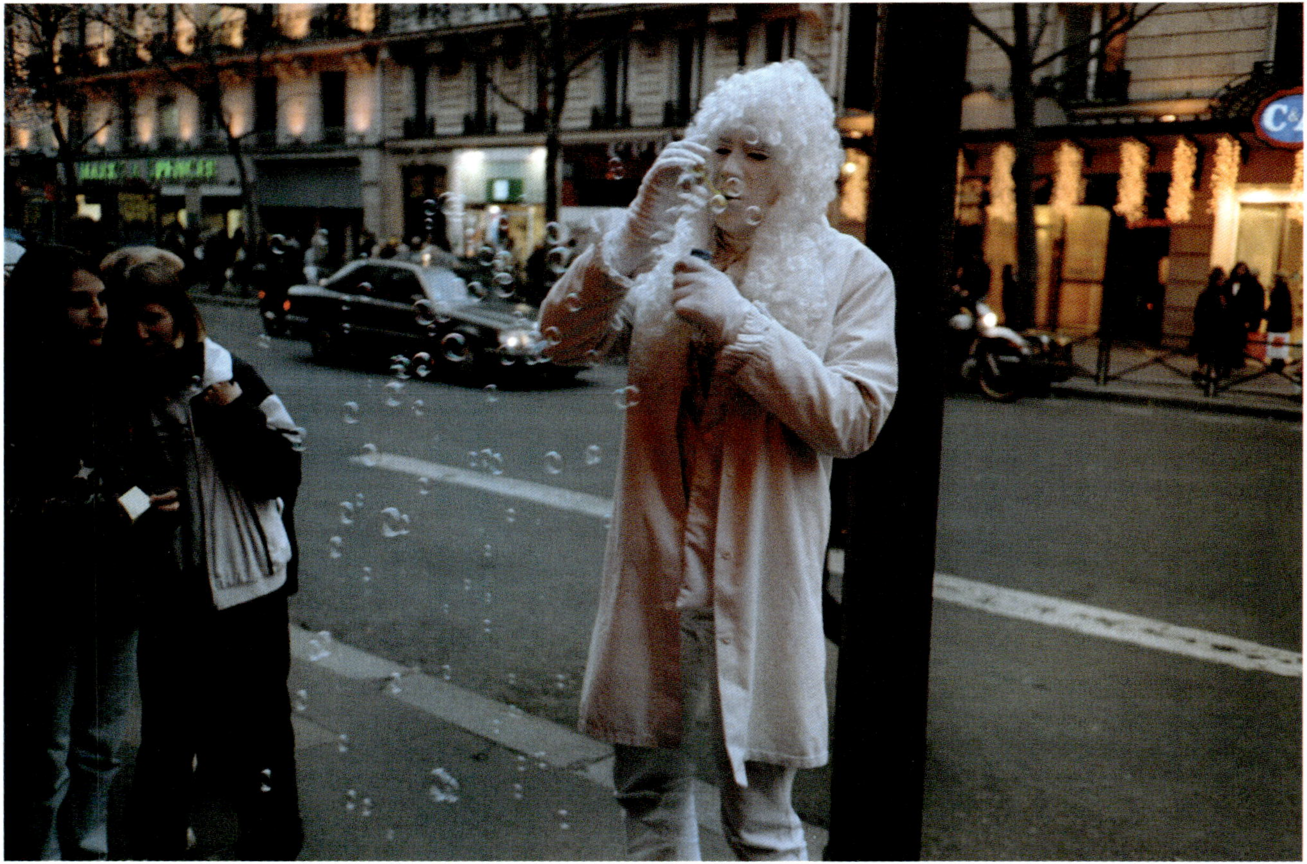

Thursday, December 2. Paris. Street show, in front of the department stores

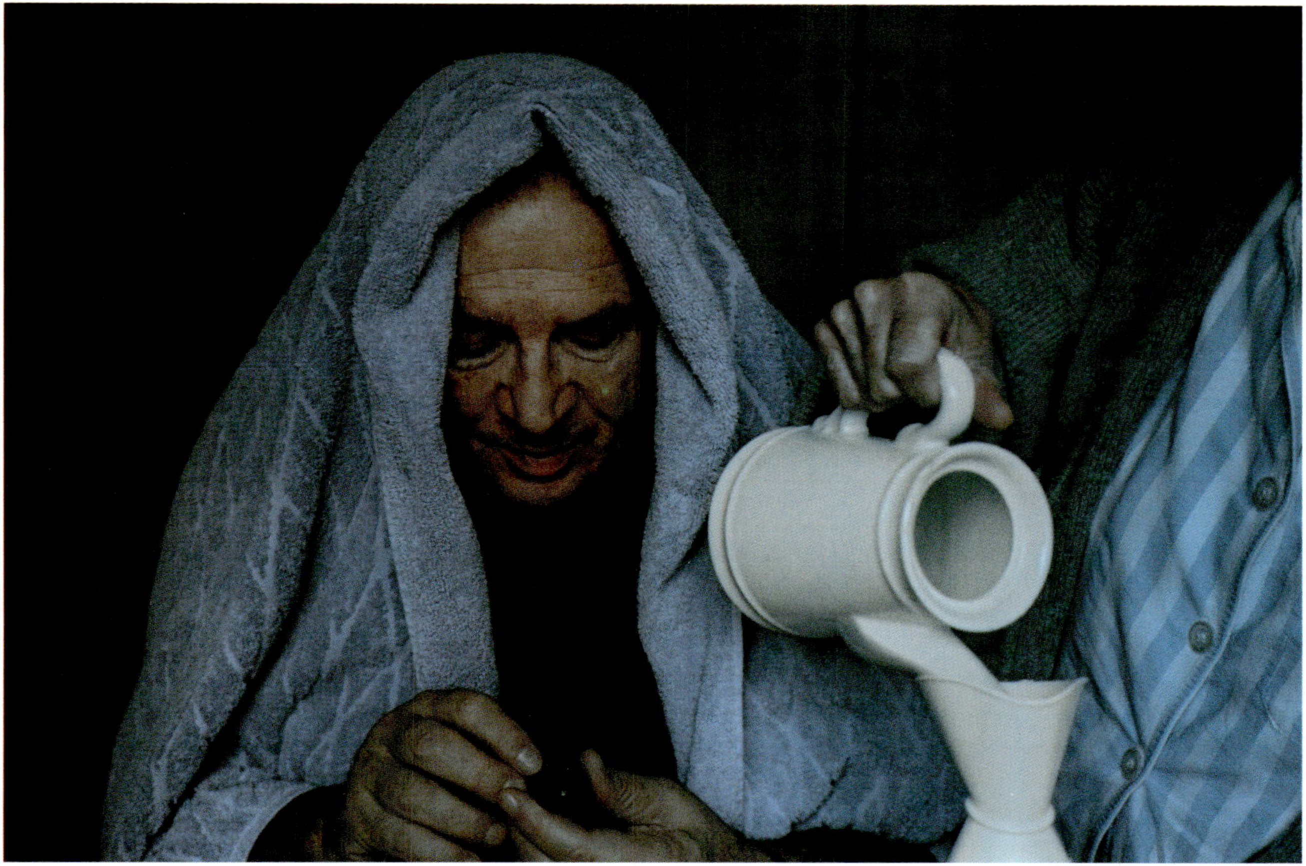

Friday, December 3. Boulogne, France. Self-portrait with a cold

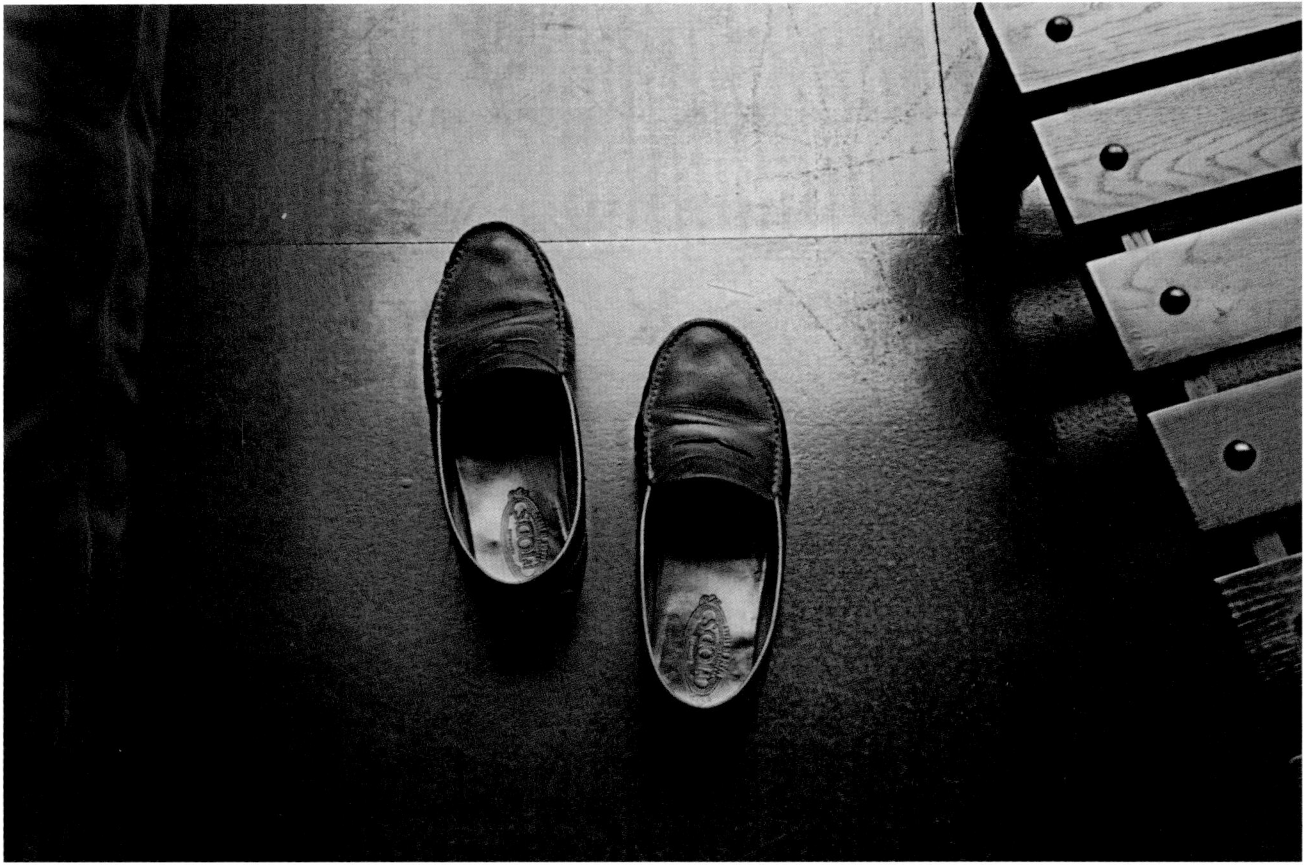

Saturday, December 4. Boulogne, France. I must stay home

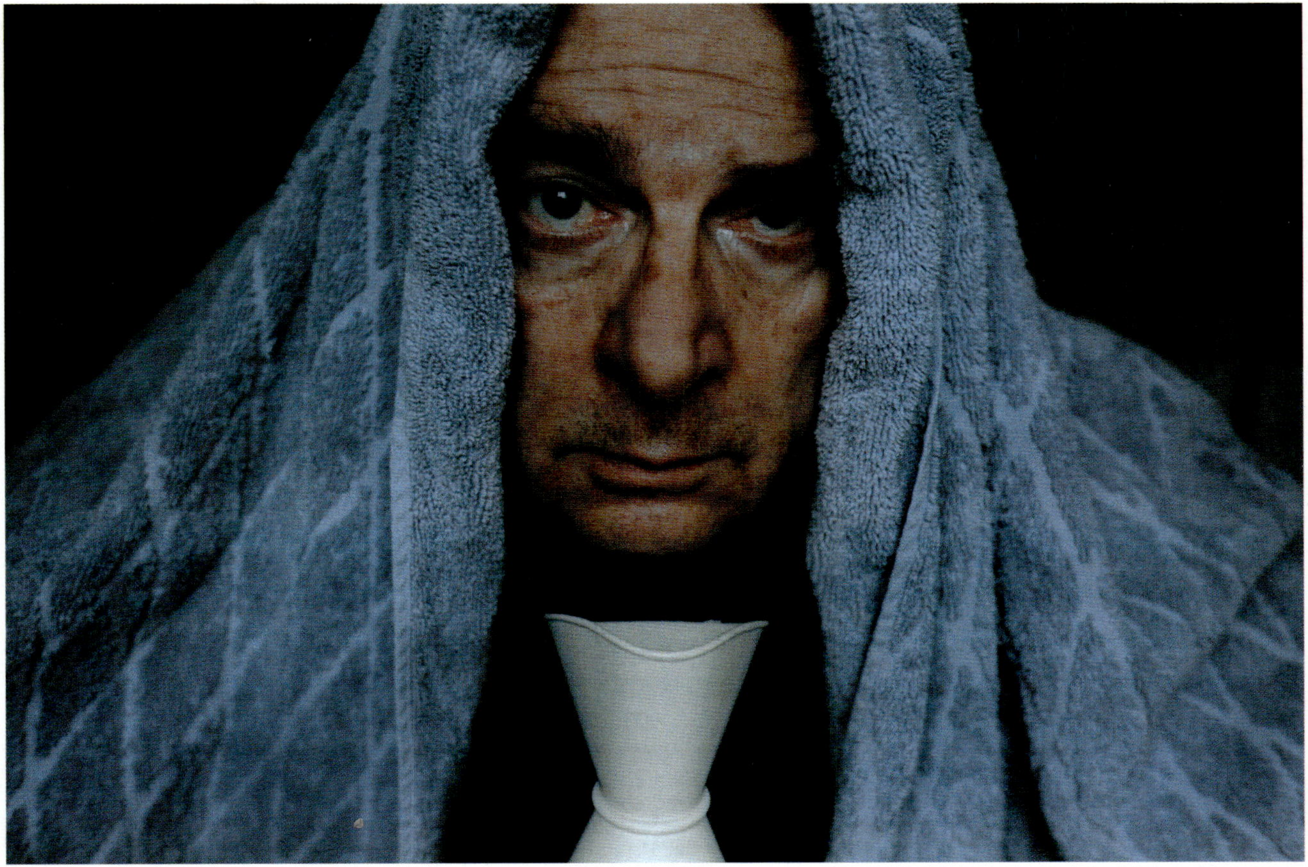

Sunday, December 5. Boulogne, France. Self-portrait with a cold

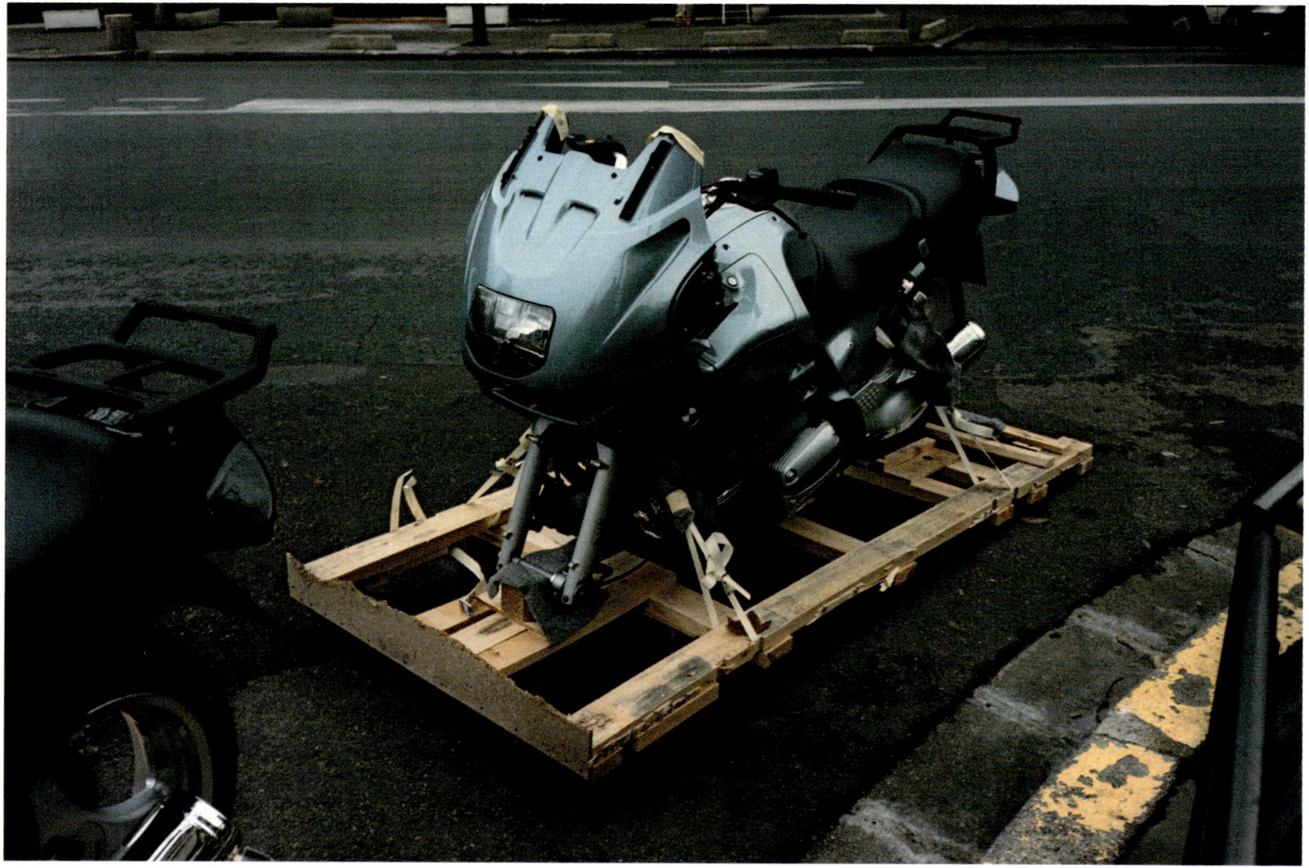

Monday, December 6. Boulogne, France. Street scene

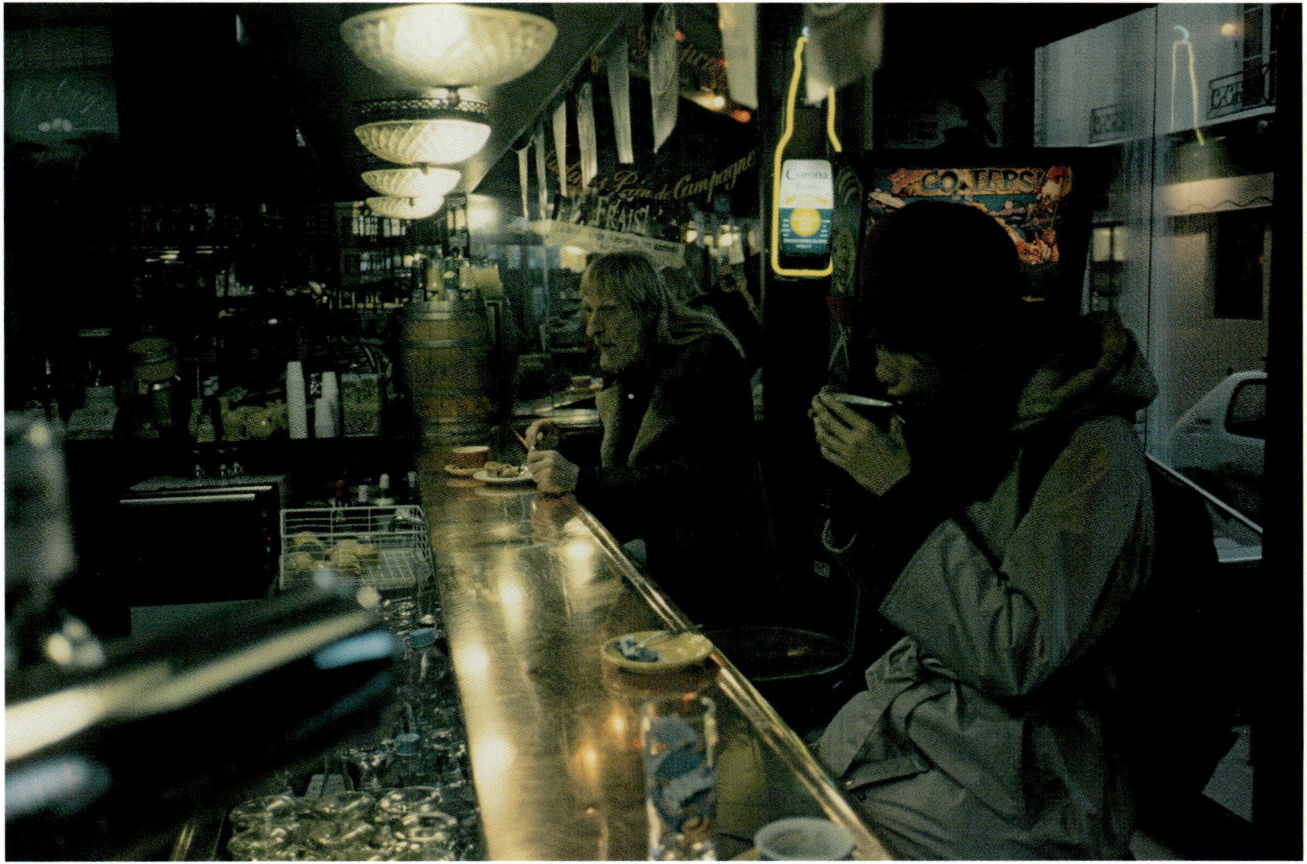

Tuesday, December 7. Paris. Café scene, in the Bastille area

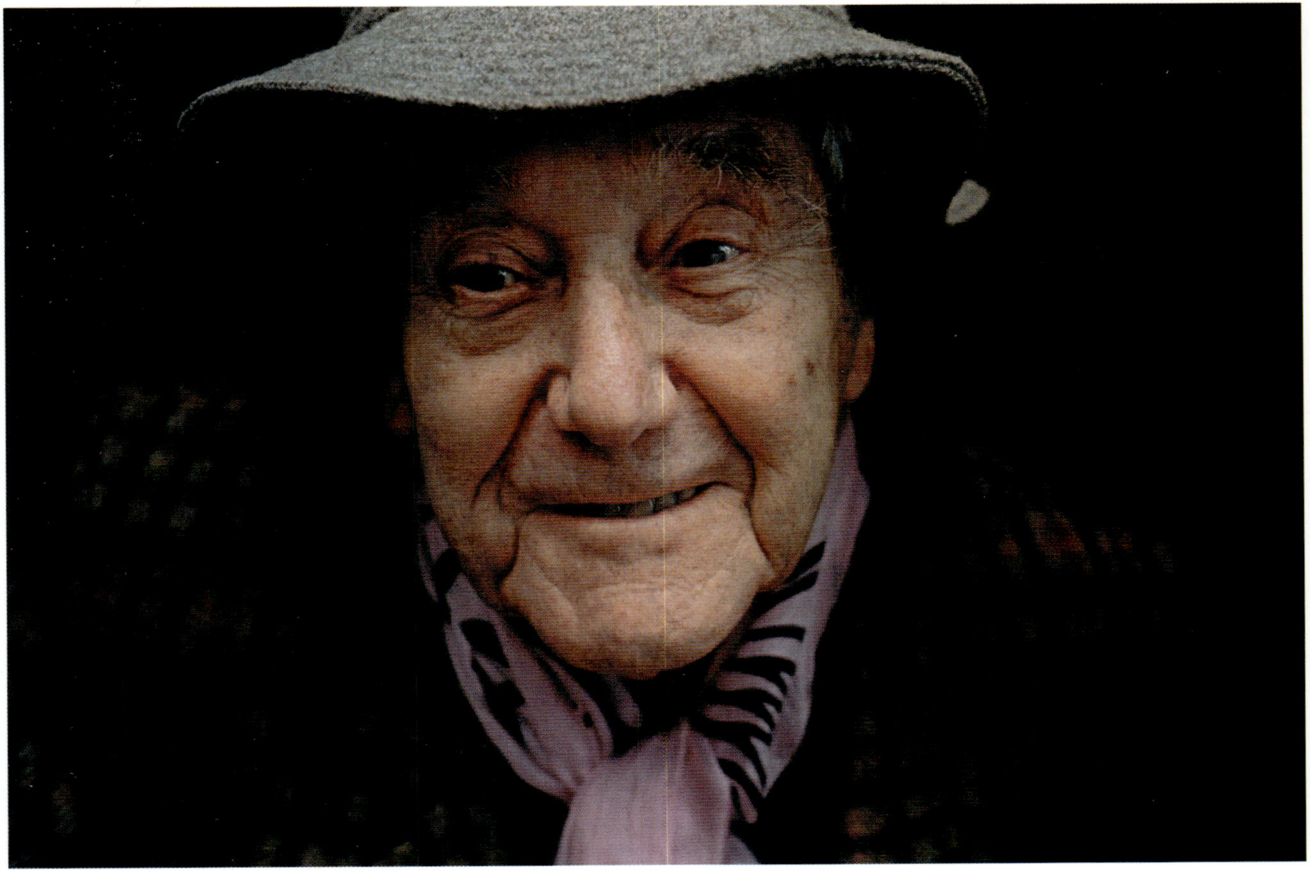

Wednesday, December 8. Paris. Matta, architect and painter

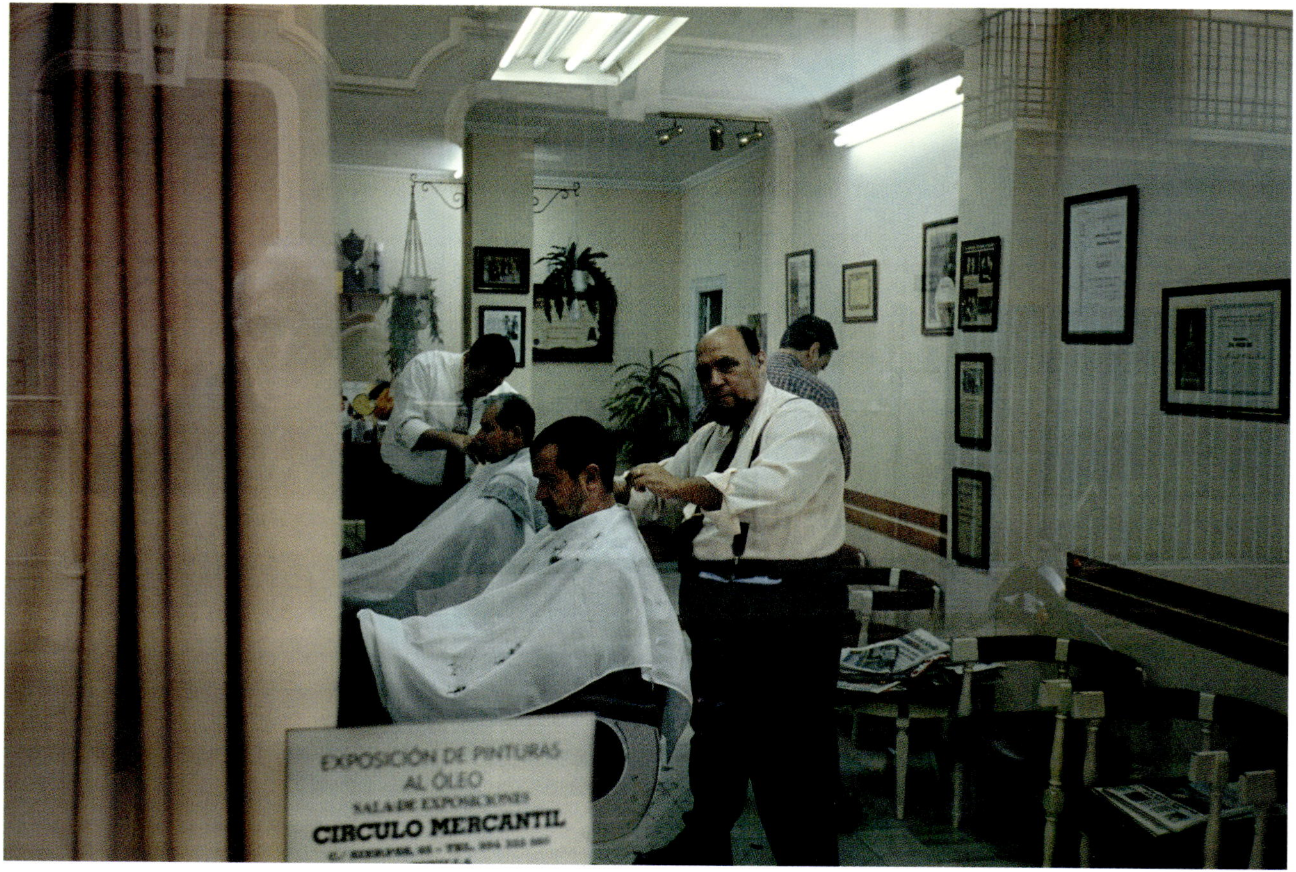

Thursday, December 9. Seville, Spain. A barber of Seville

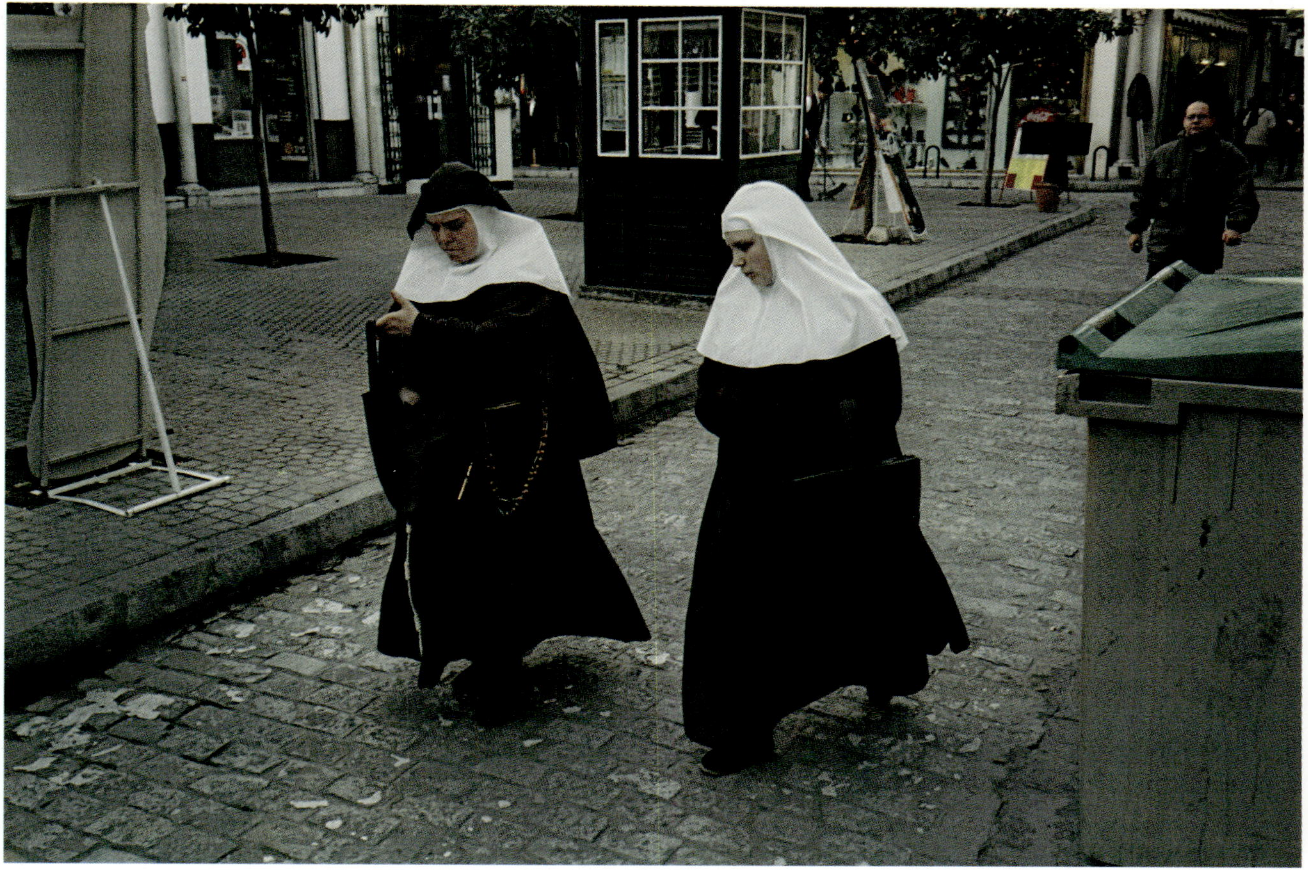

Thursday, December 9. Seville, Spain. Street scene

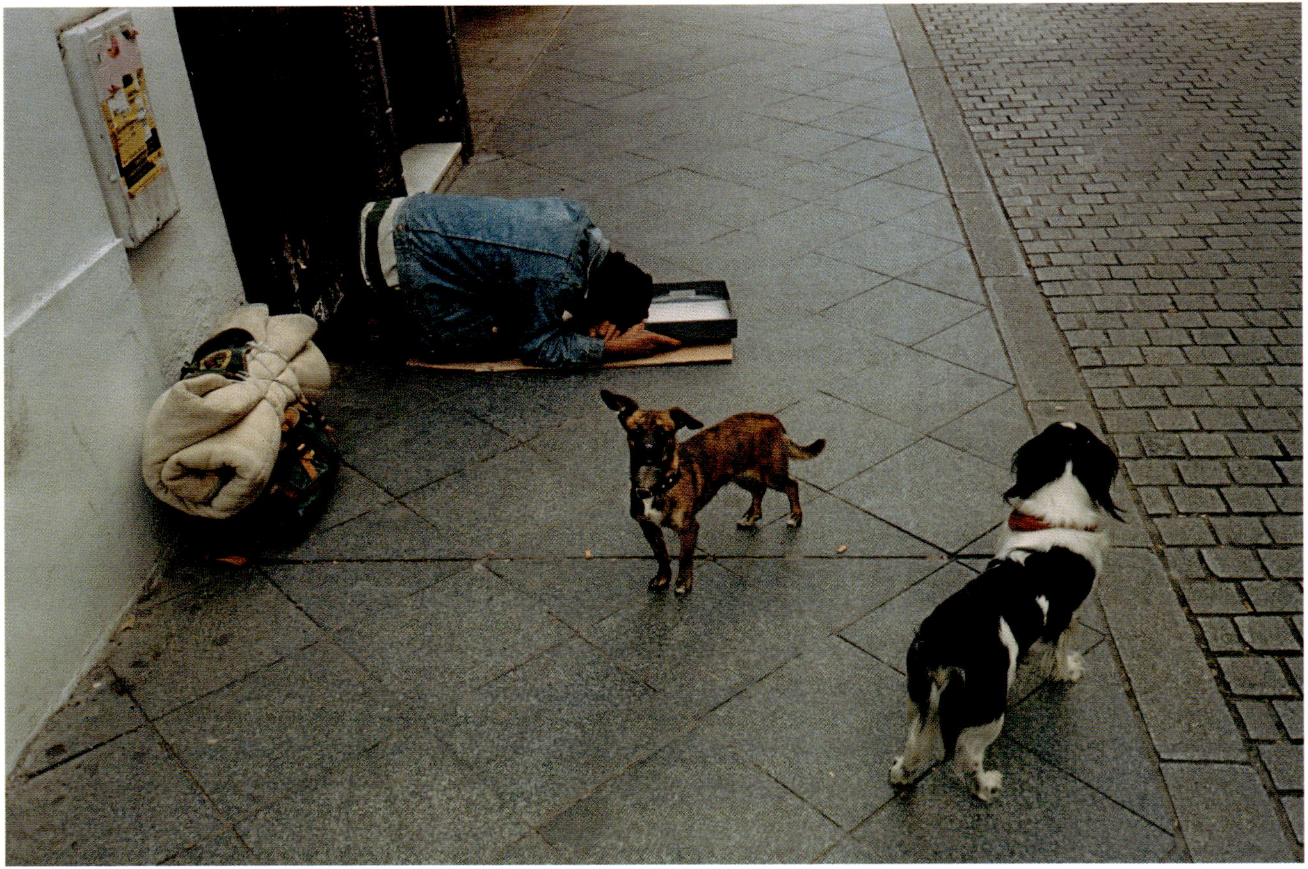

Friday, December 10. Seville, Spain. Street scene

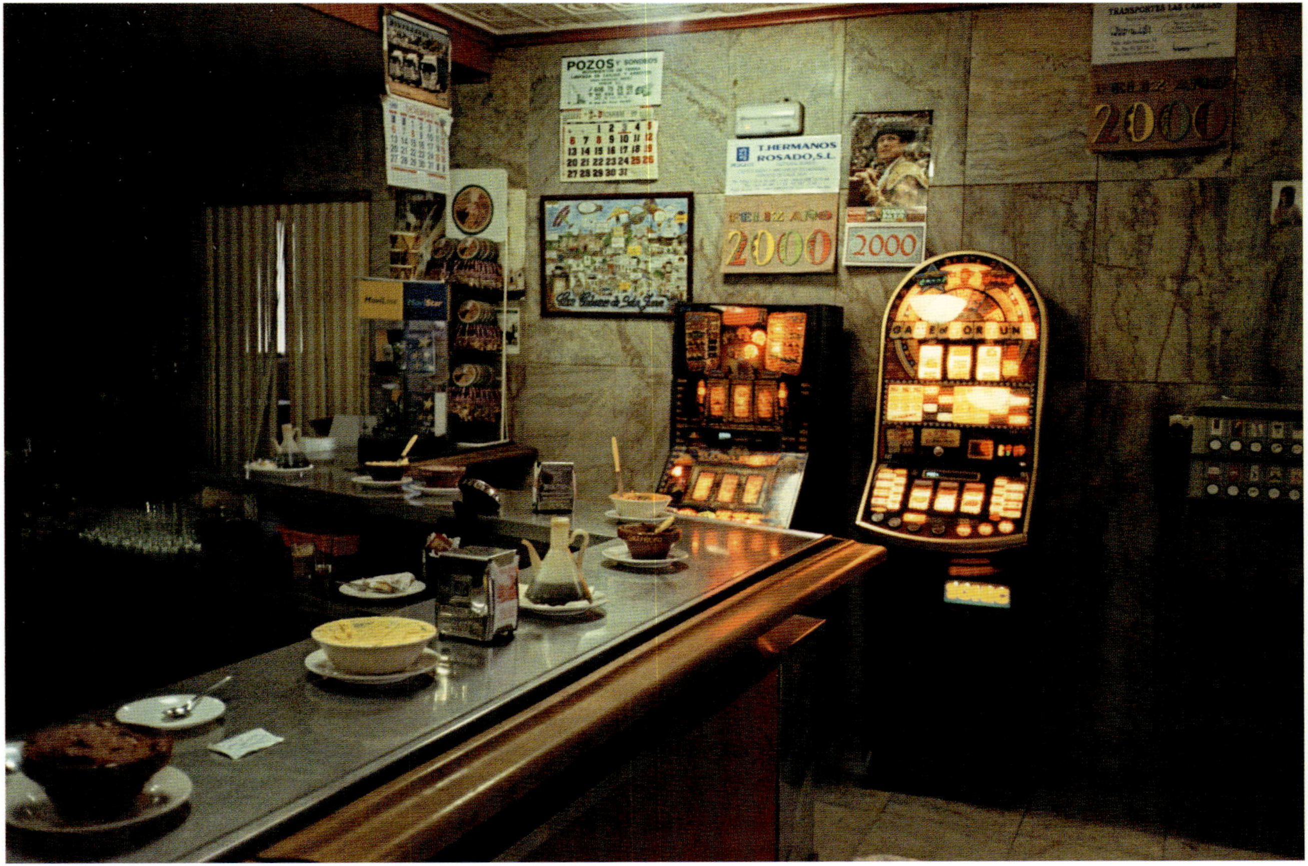

Saturday, December 11. Andalusia, Spain. Motorway restaurant

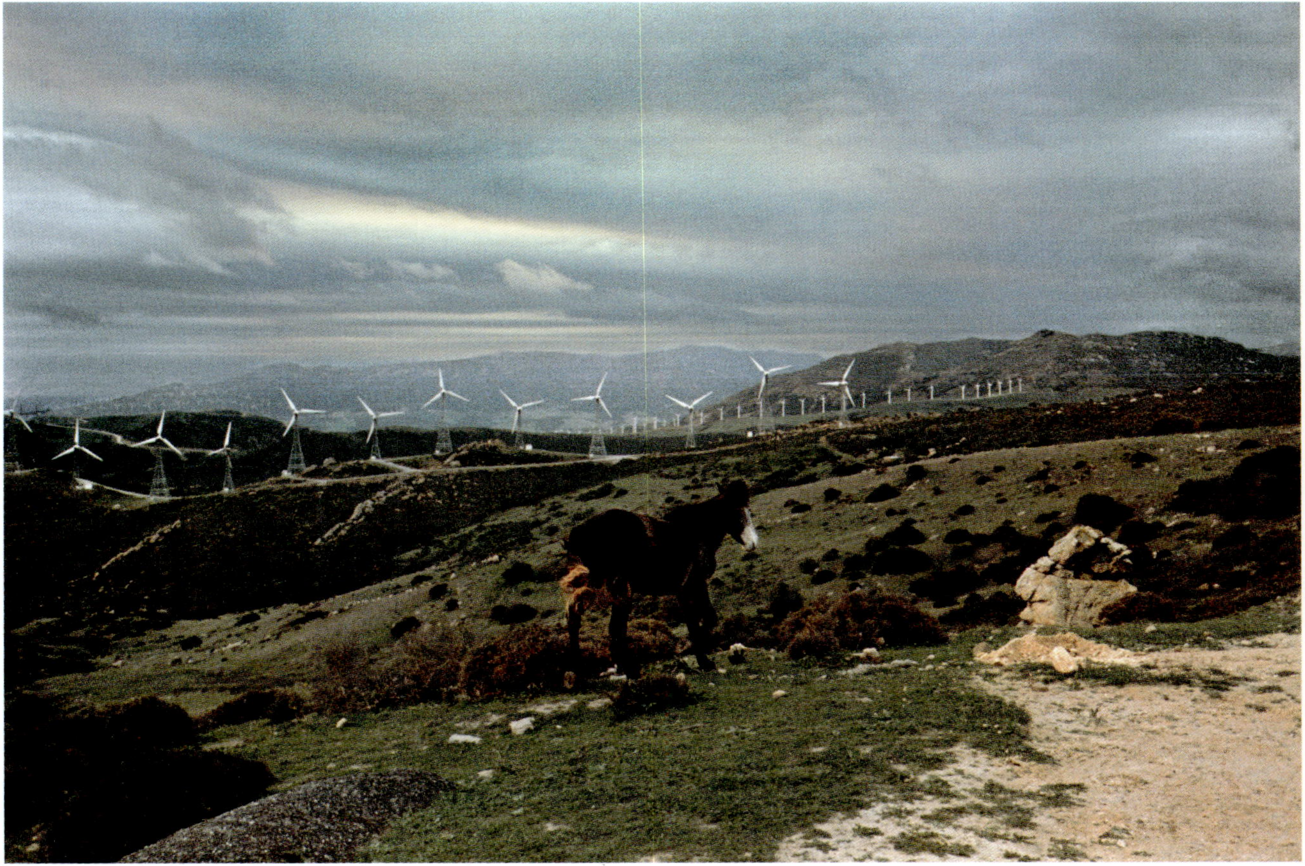

Saturday, December 11. Andalusia, Spain. Homage to Cervantes

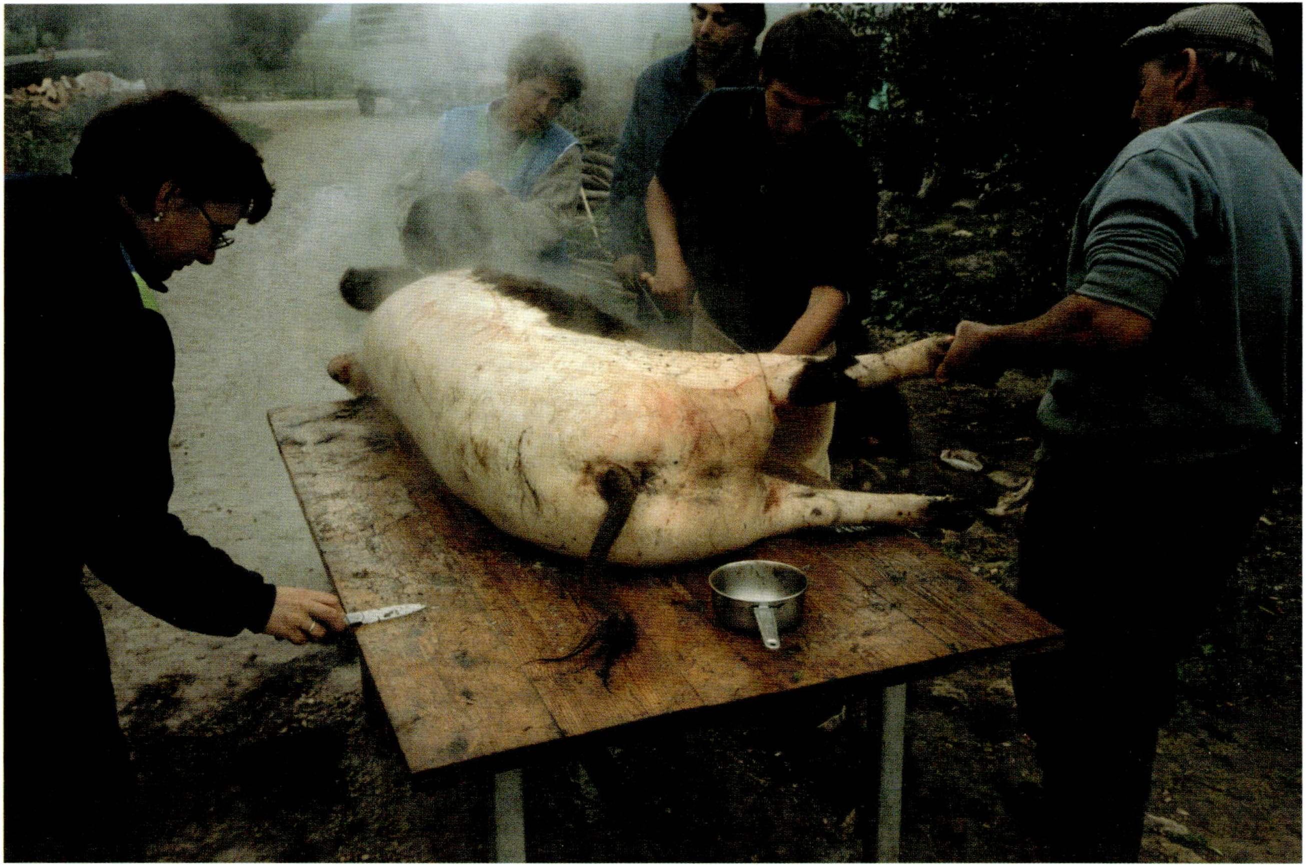

Sunday, December 12. Andalusia, Spain. Slaughtering the pig

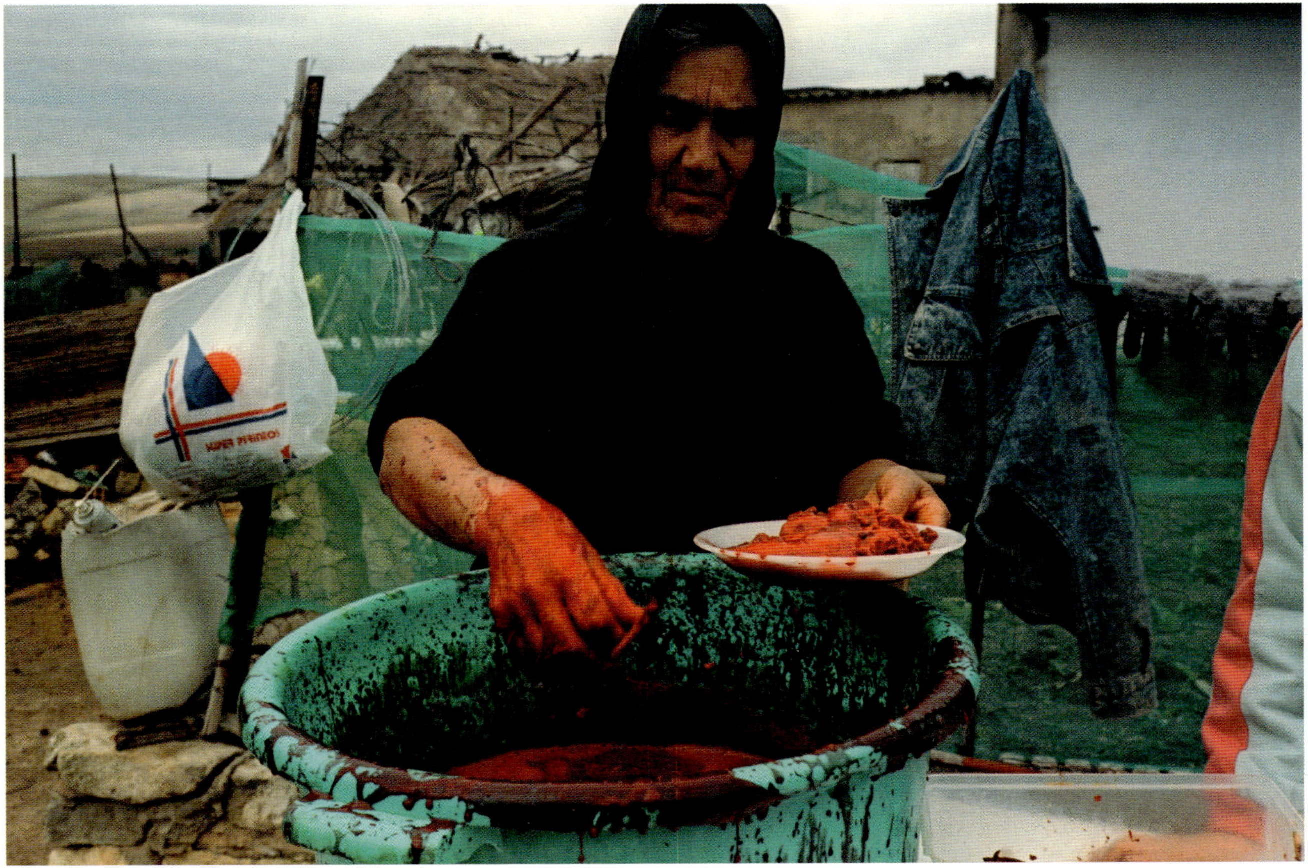

Sunday, December 12. Andalusia, Spain. Slaughtering the pig

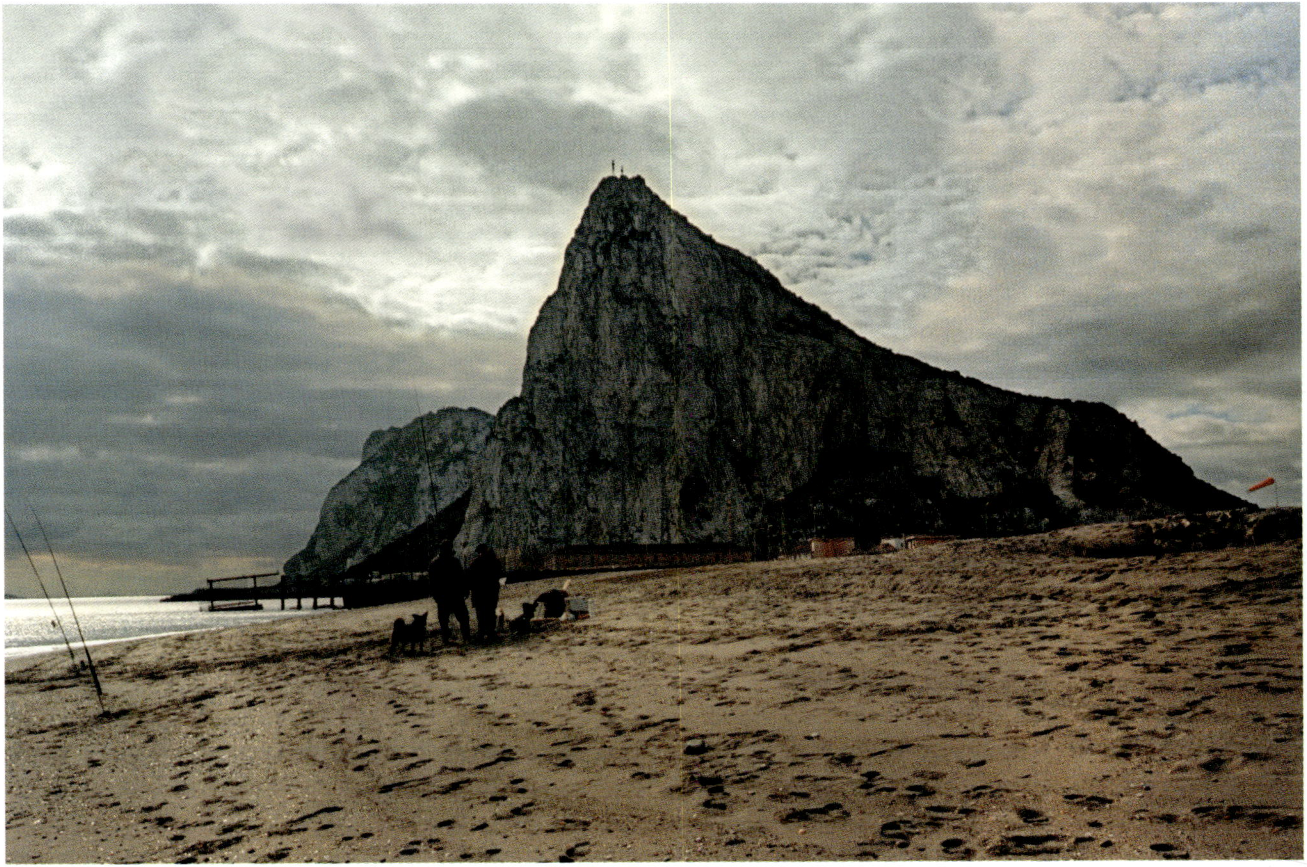

Monday, December 13. Andalusia, Spain. The rock of Gibraltar

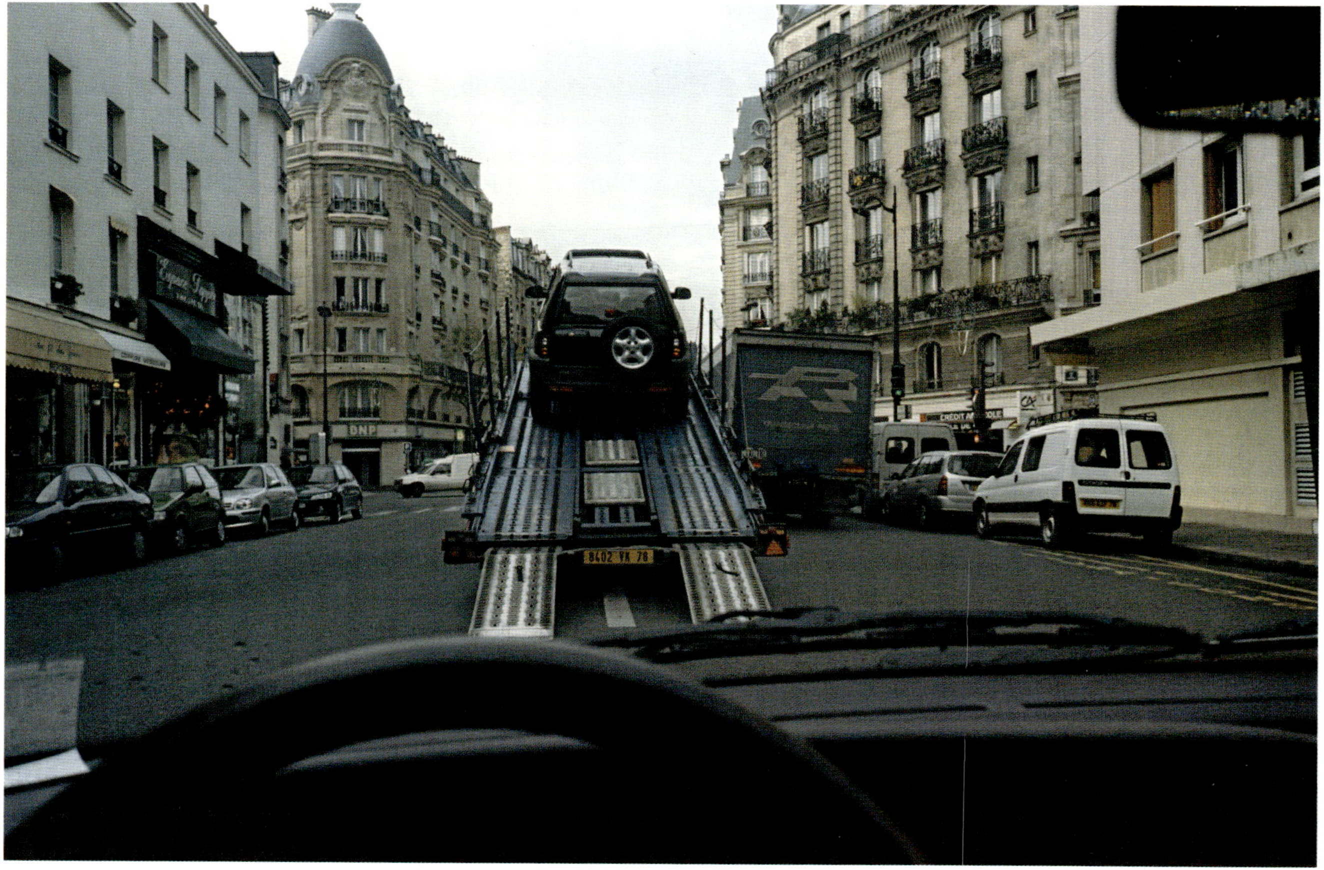

Tuesday, December 14. Paris. Street scene

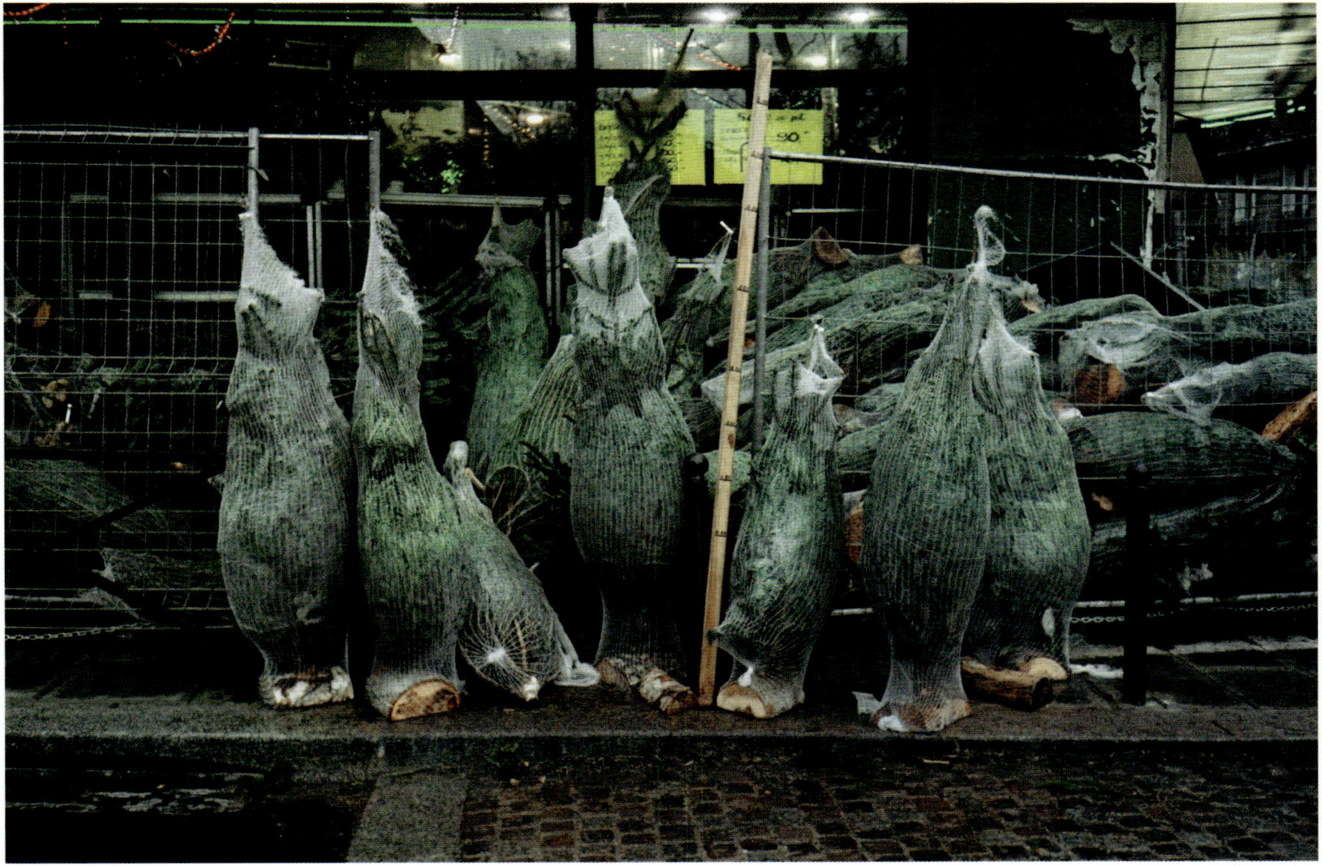

Tuesday, December 14. Paris. Christmas trees

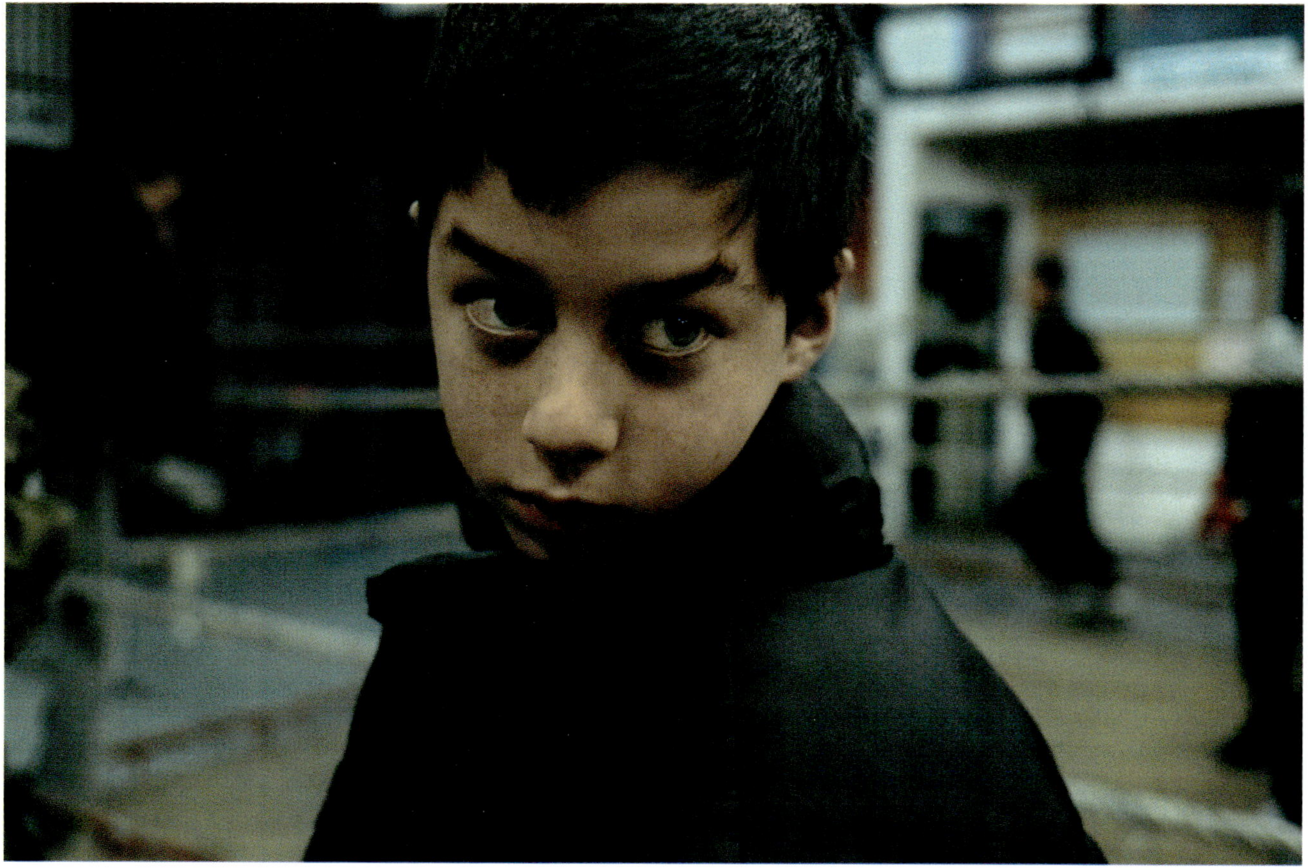

Wednesday, December 15. Aubervilliers, France. My grandson Grégoire

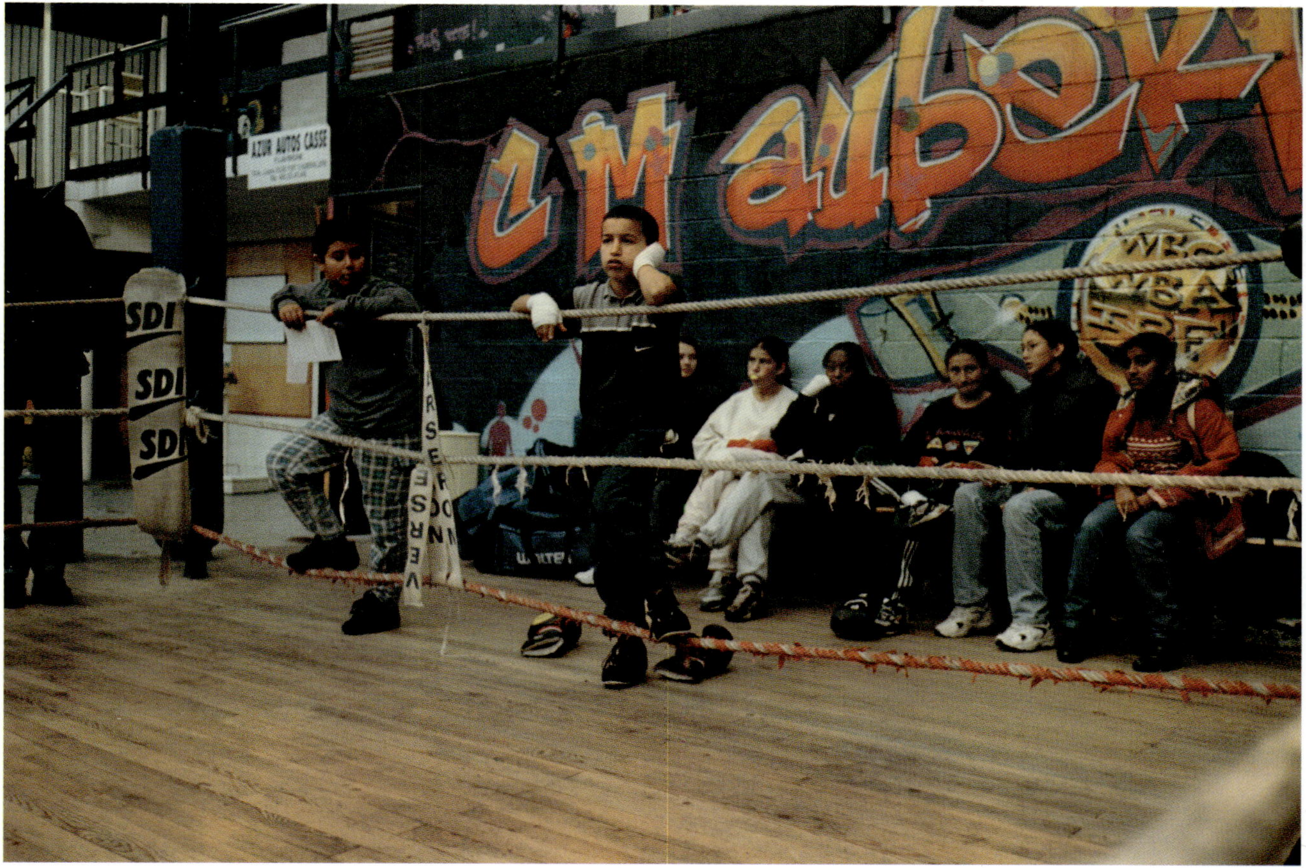

Wednesday, December 15. Aubervilliers, France. In a boxing club

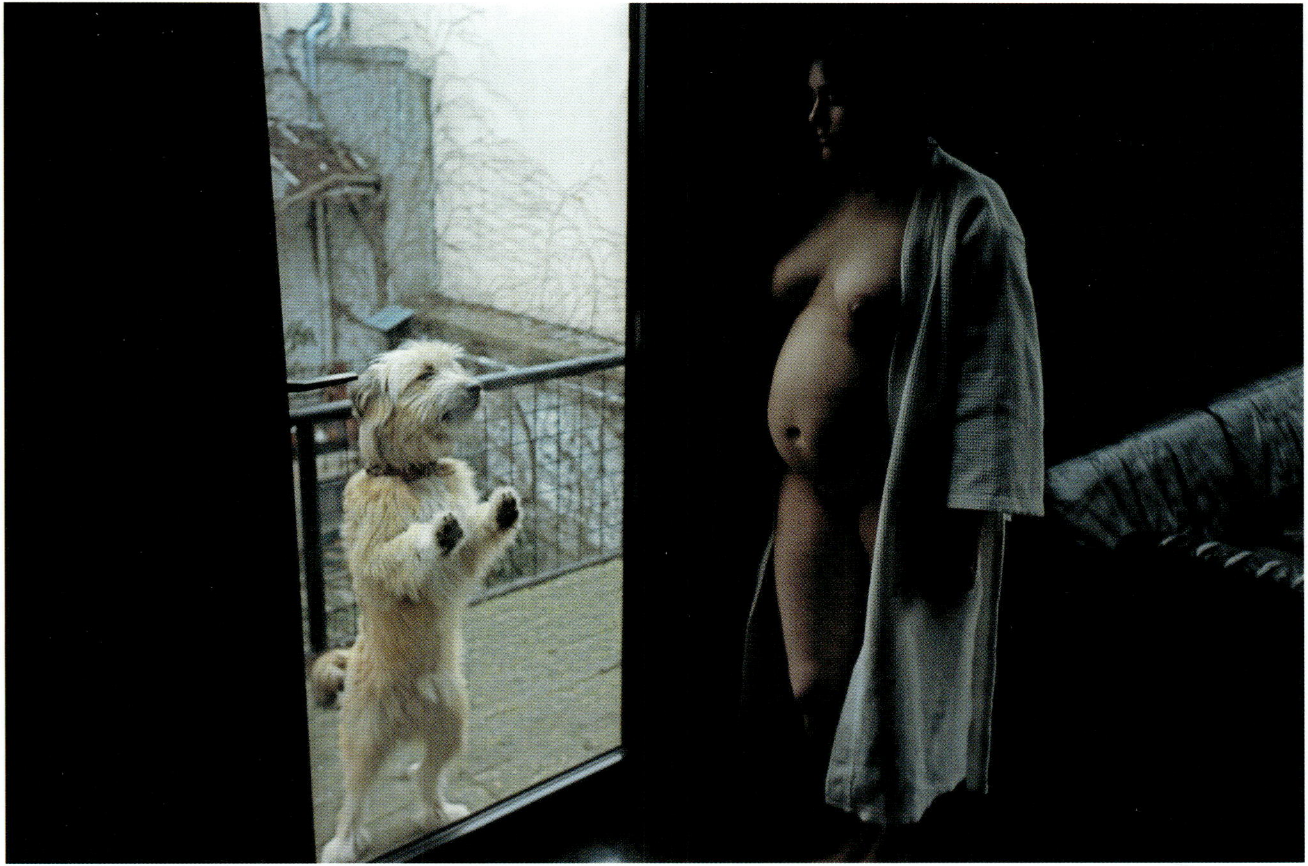

Thursday, December 16. Boulogne, France. Véronique Leyrit, pregnant

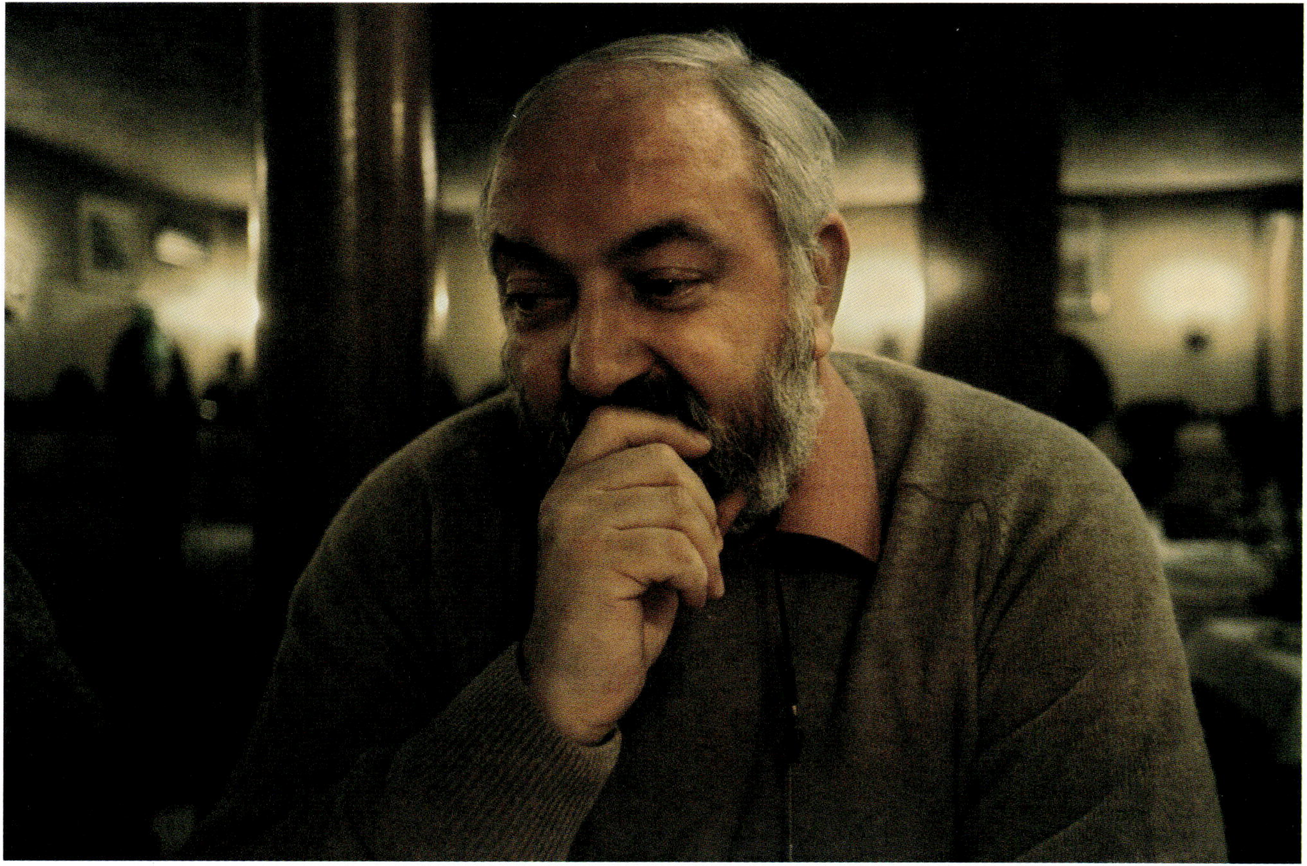

Friday, December 17. Tourcoing, France. Jean Pierre Salomon, teacher

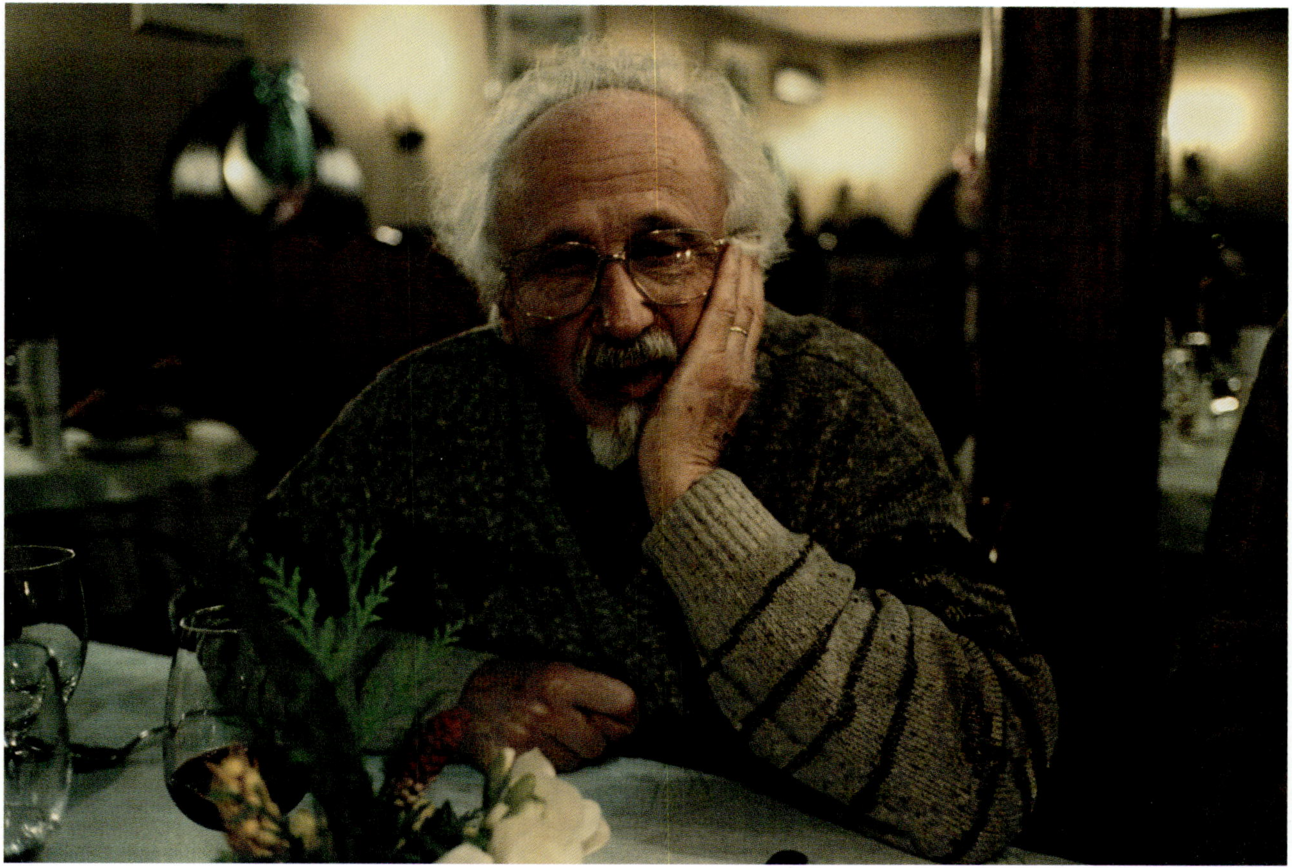

Friday, December 17. Tourcoing, France. Daniel Liénard, retired teacher

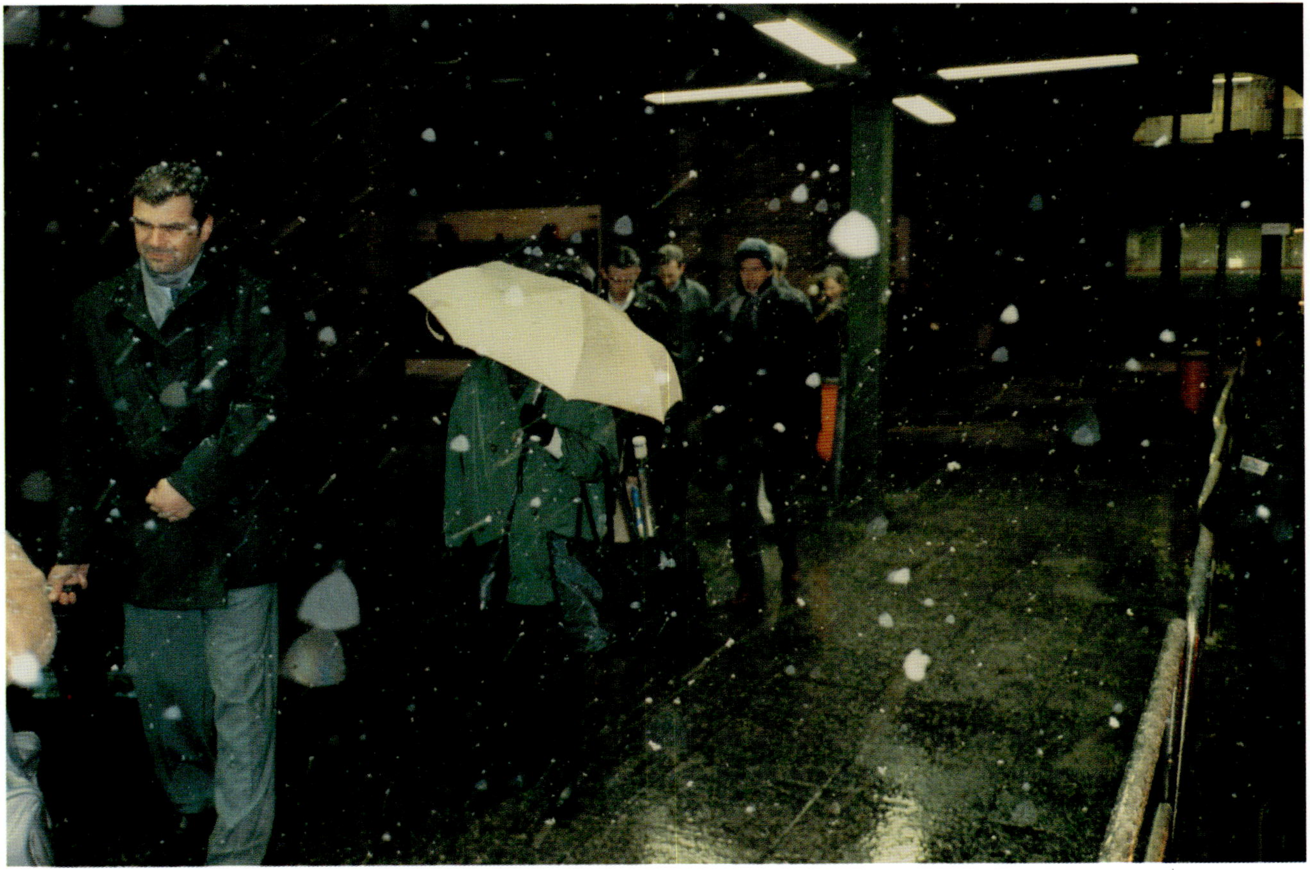

Saturday, December 18. Frankfurt, Germany. Street scene

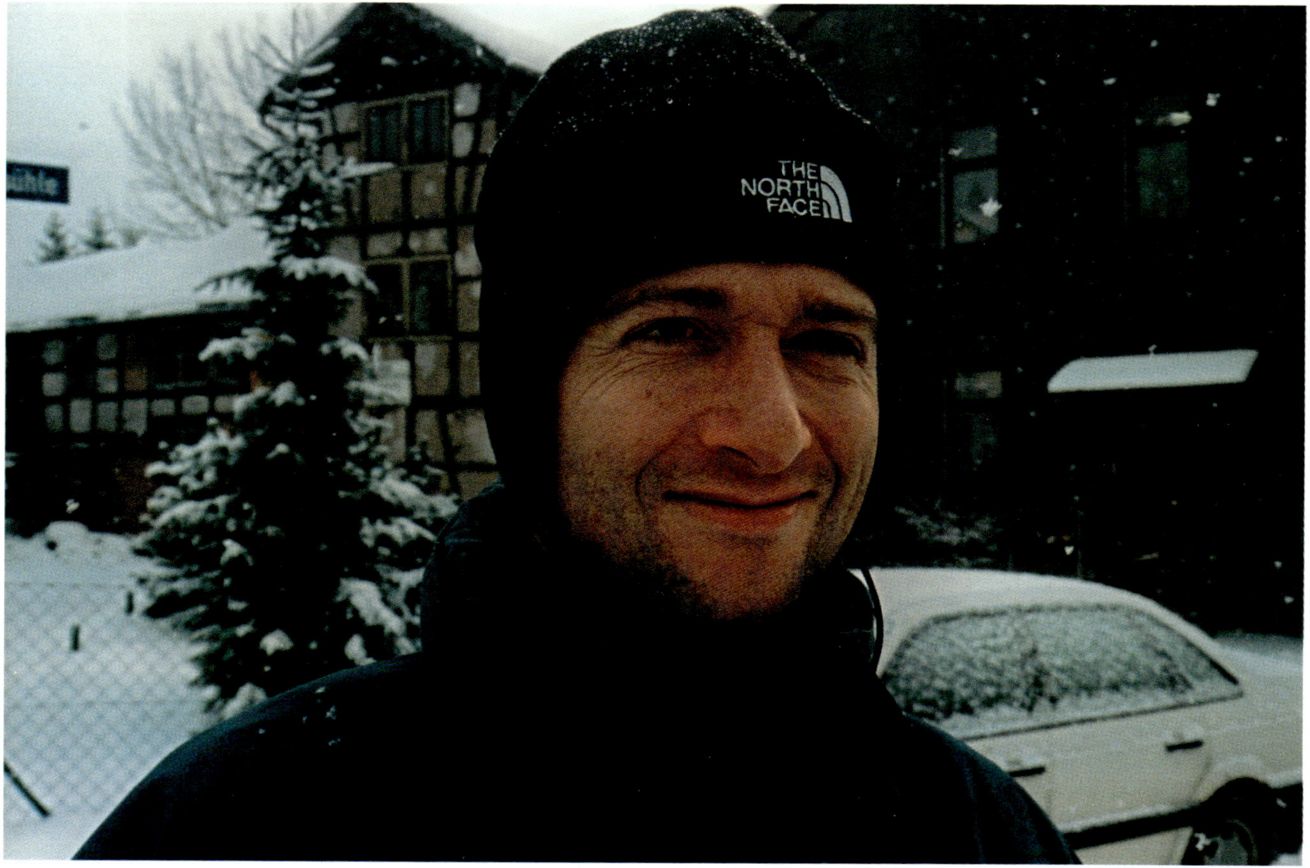

Sunday, December 19. Zella Mehlis, Germany. Lorenzo Horvat

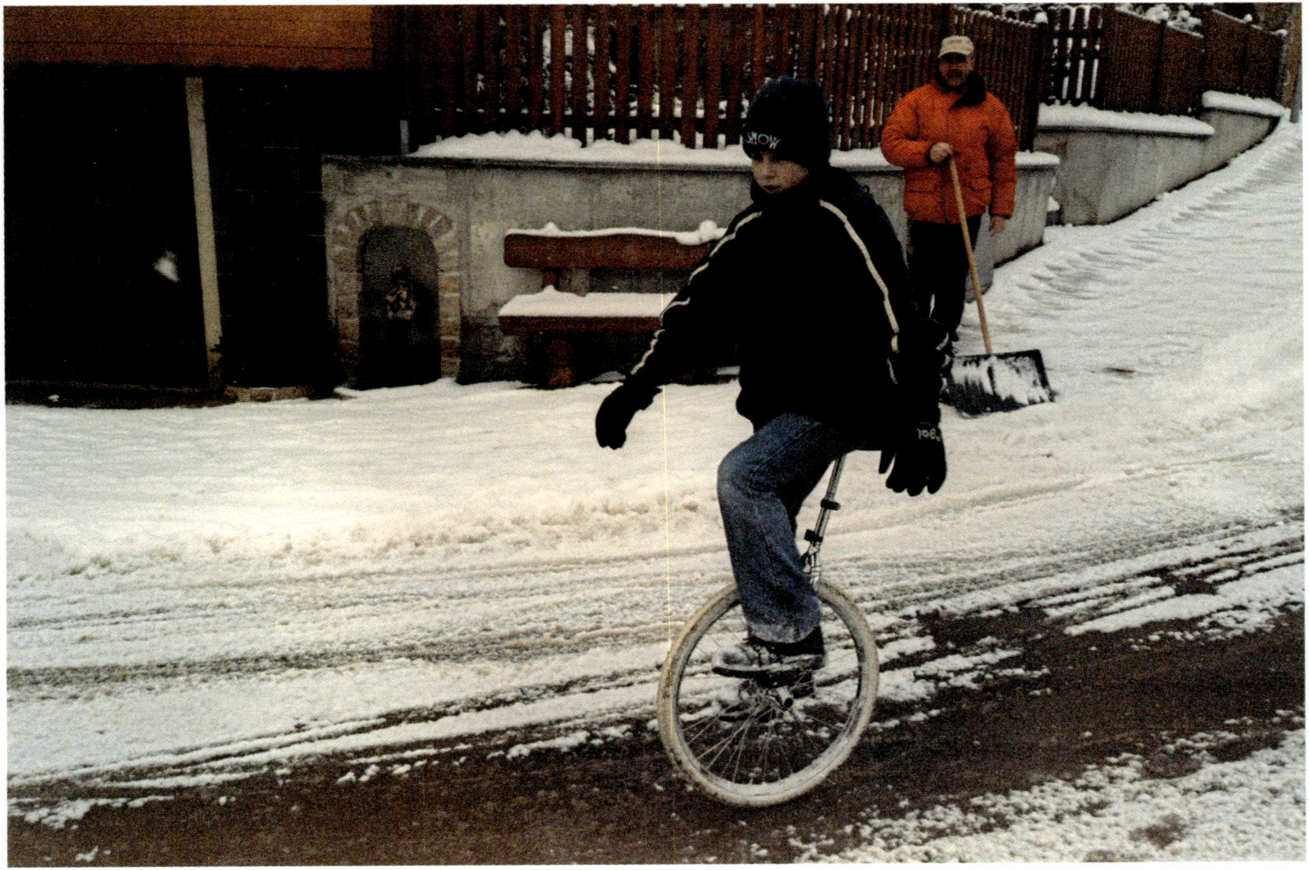

Sunday, December 19. Zella Mehlis, Germany. My grandson Malte

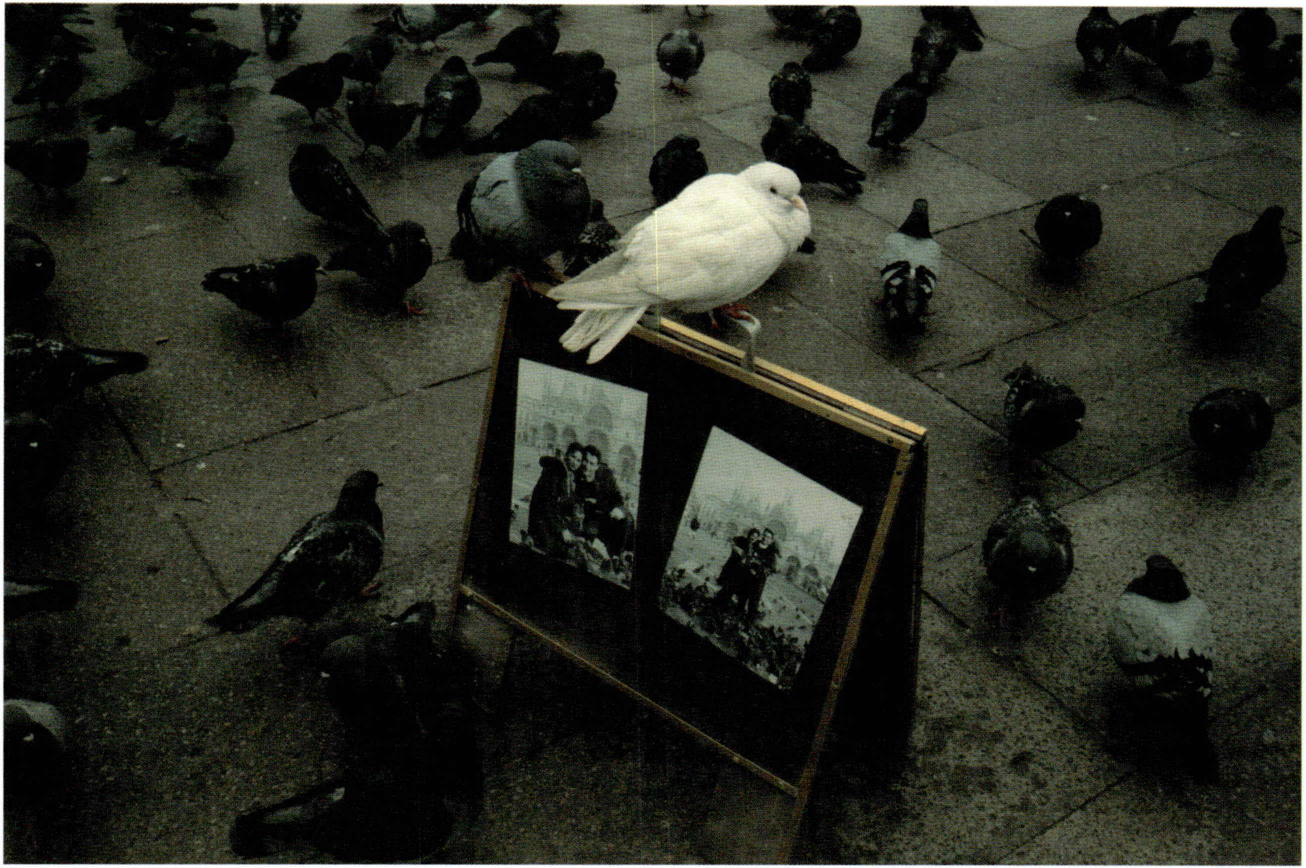

Monday, December 20. Venice, Italy. Piazza San Marco

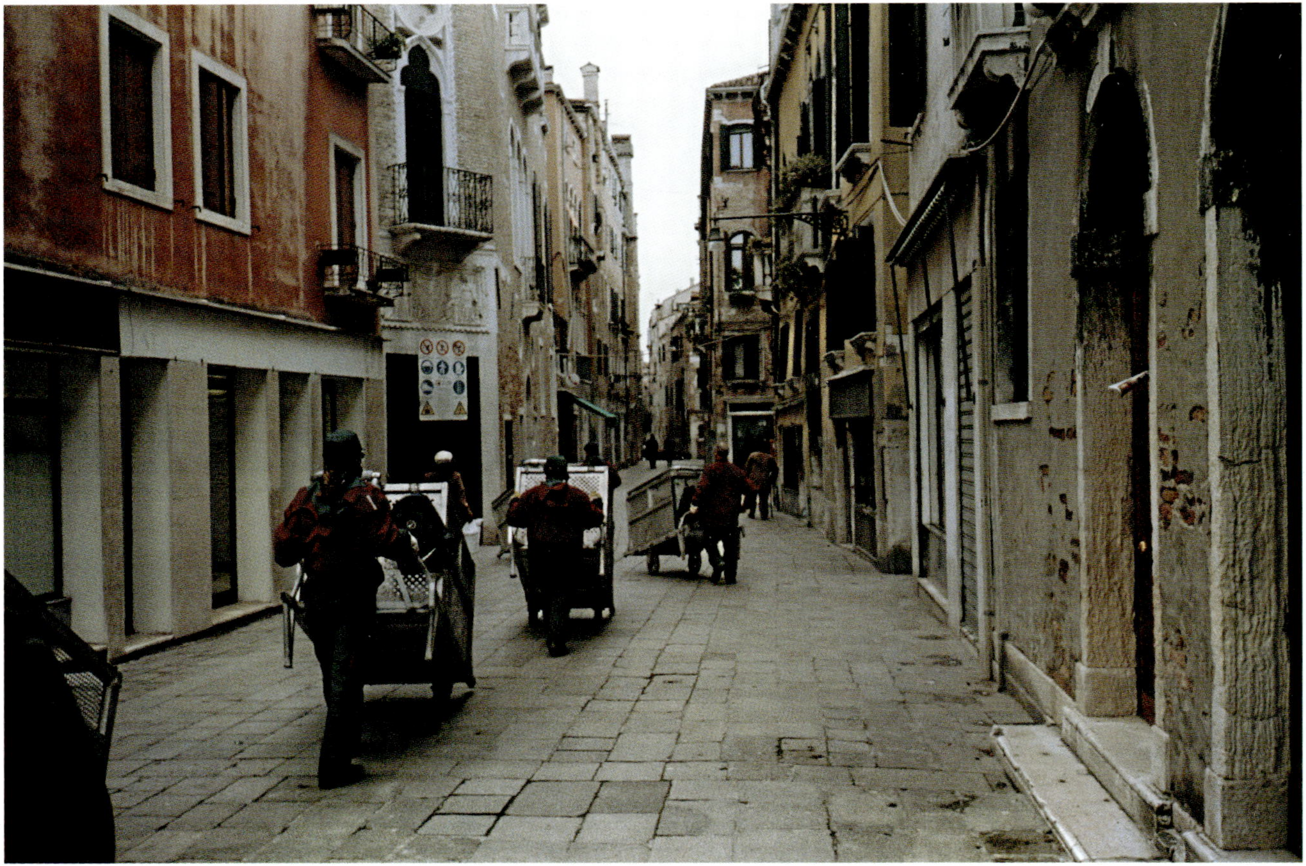

Tuesday, December 21. Venice, Italy. Street scene

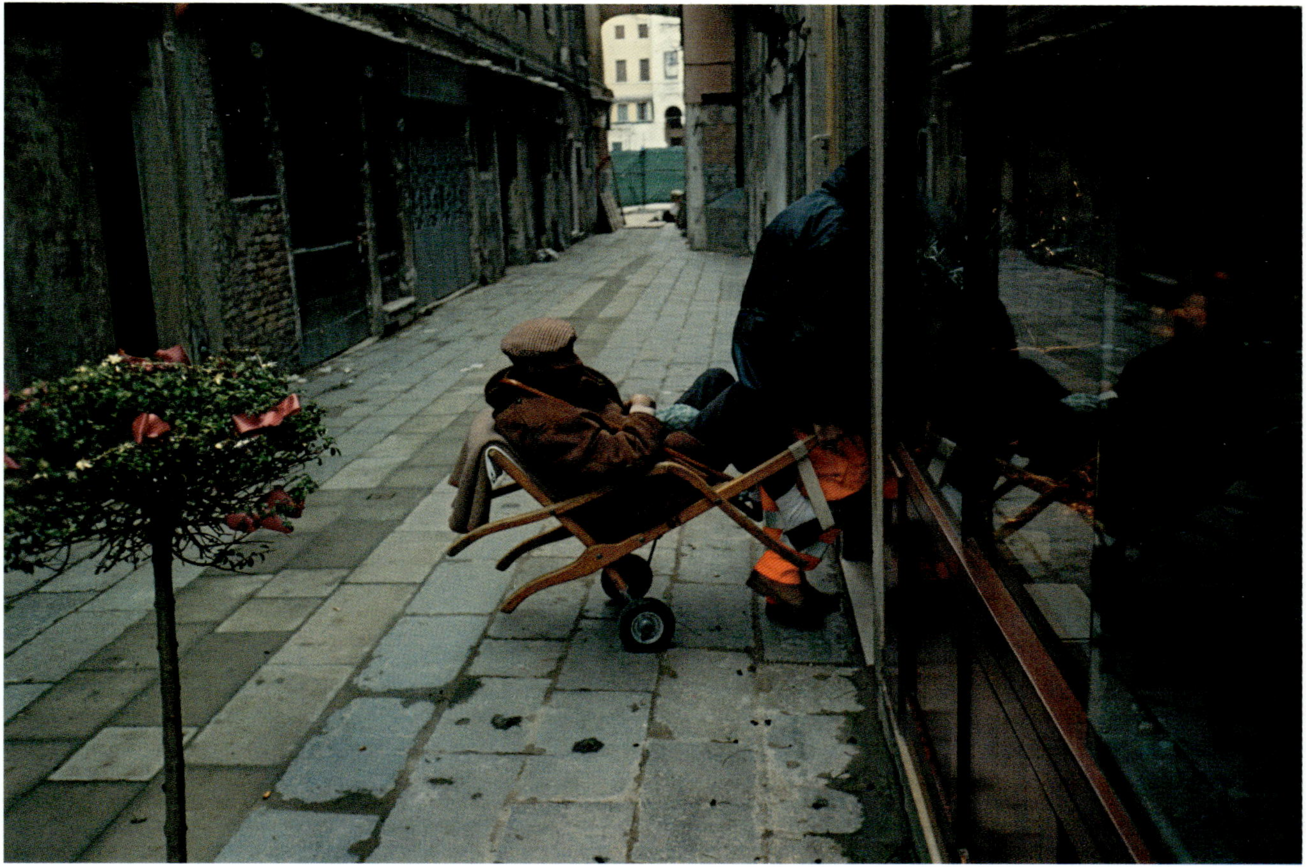

Tuesday, December 21. Venice, Italy. Street scene

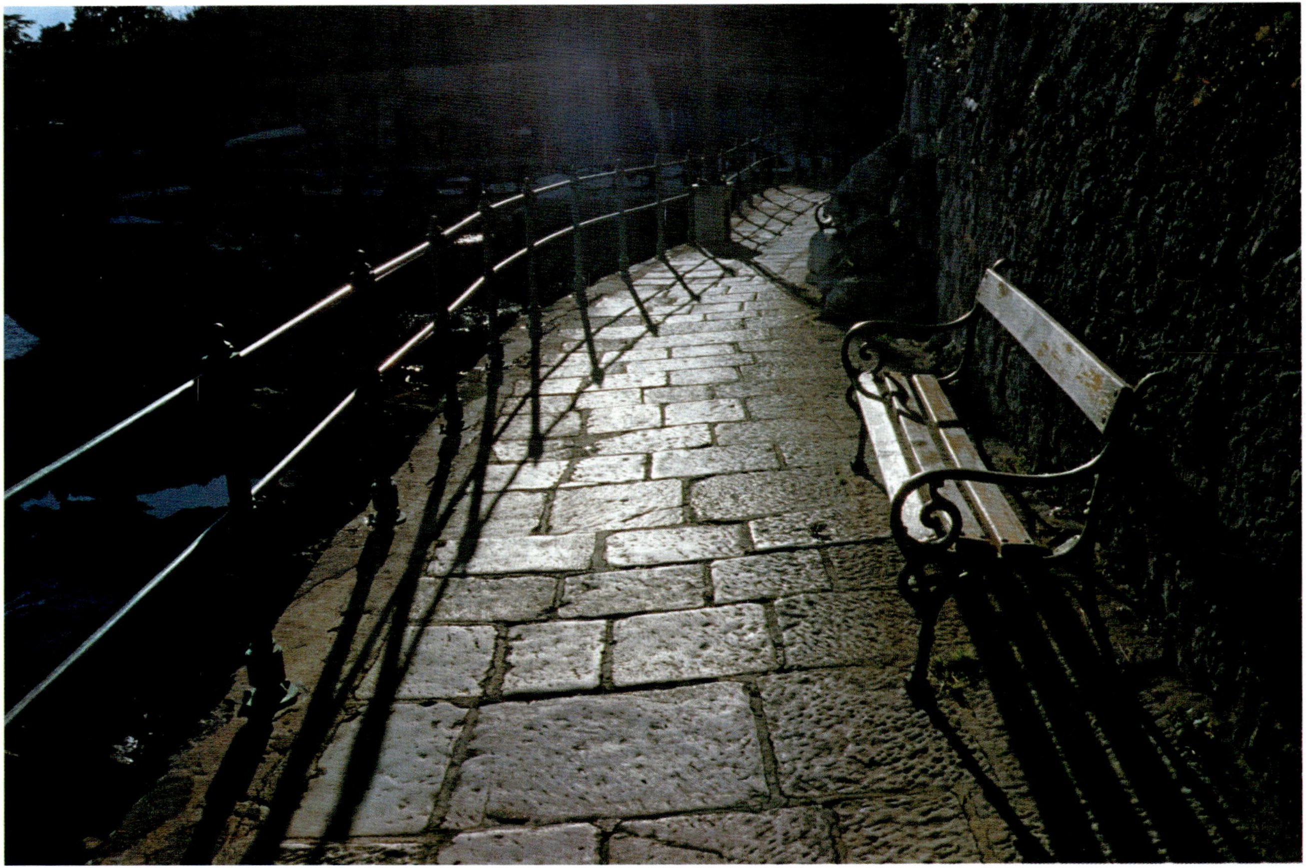

Wednesday, December 22. Opatija, Croatia. My birth place. Footpath by the sea (see note)

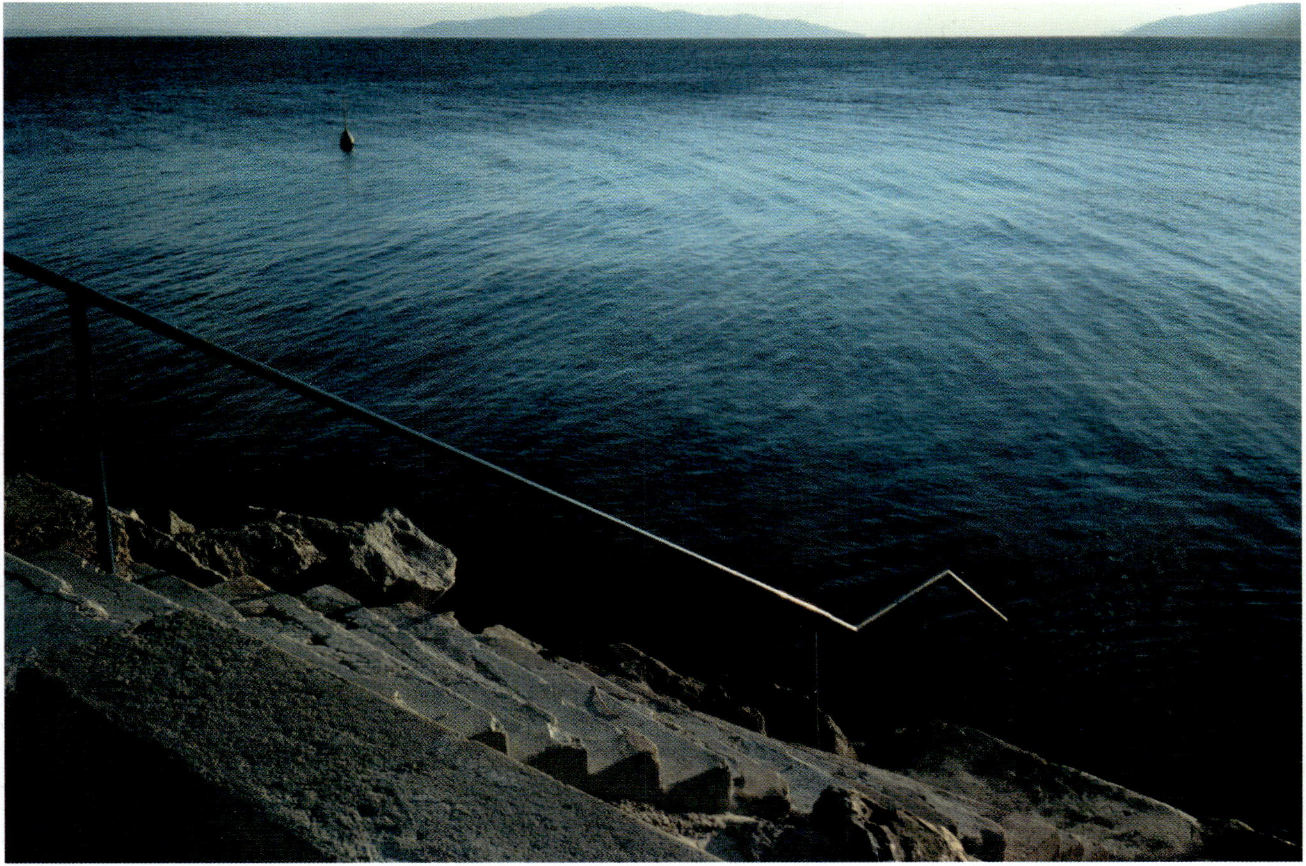

Wednesday, December 22. Opatija, Croatia. My birth place. View of the Carnaro gulf

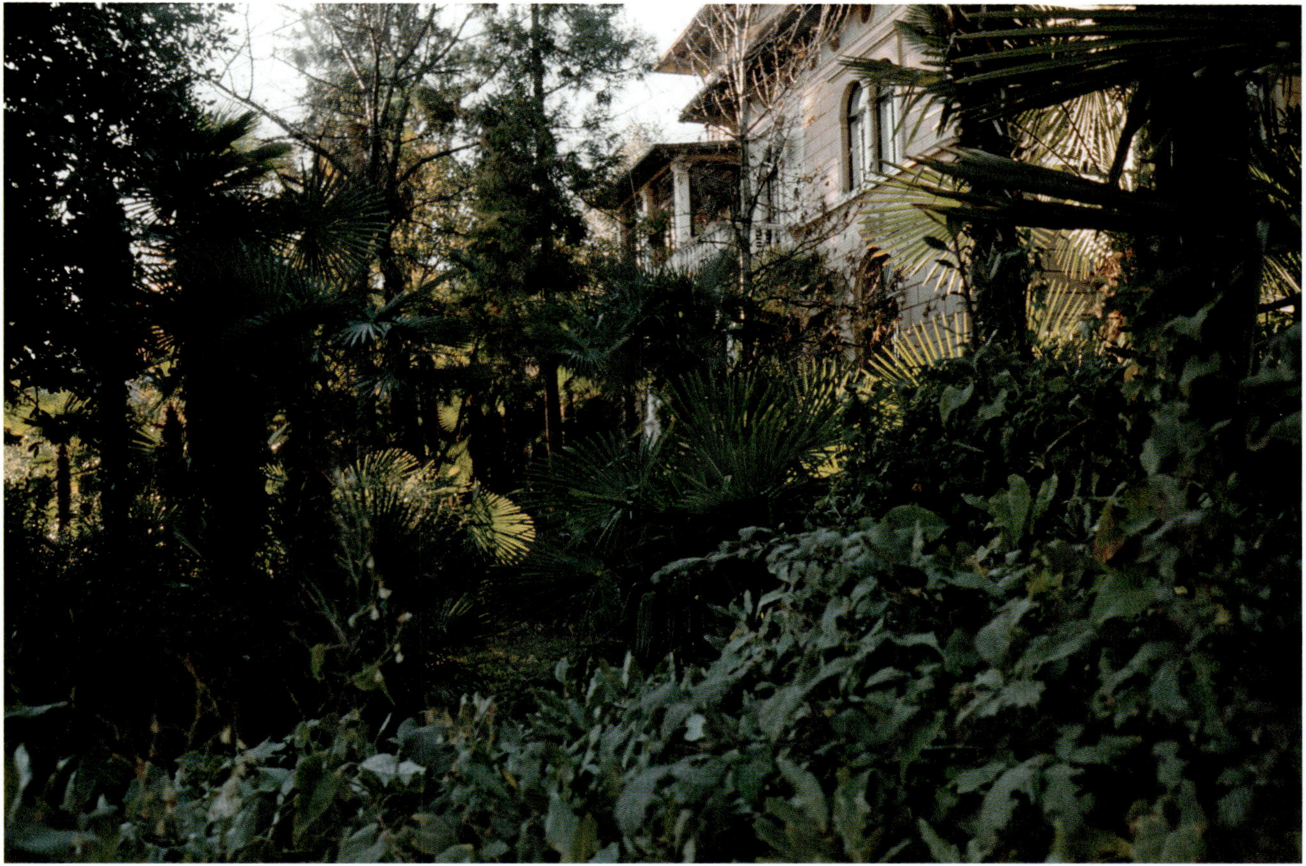

Thursday, December 23. Opatija, Croatia. My childhood home

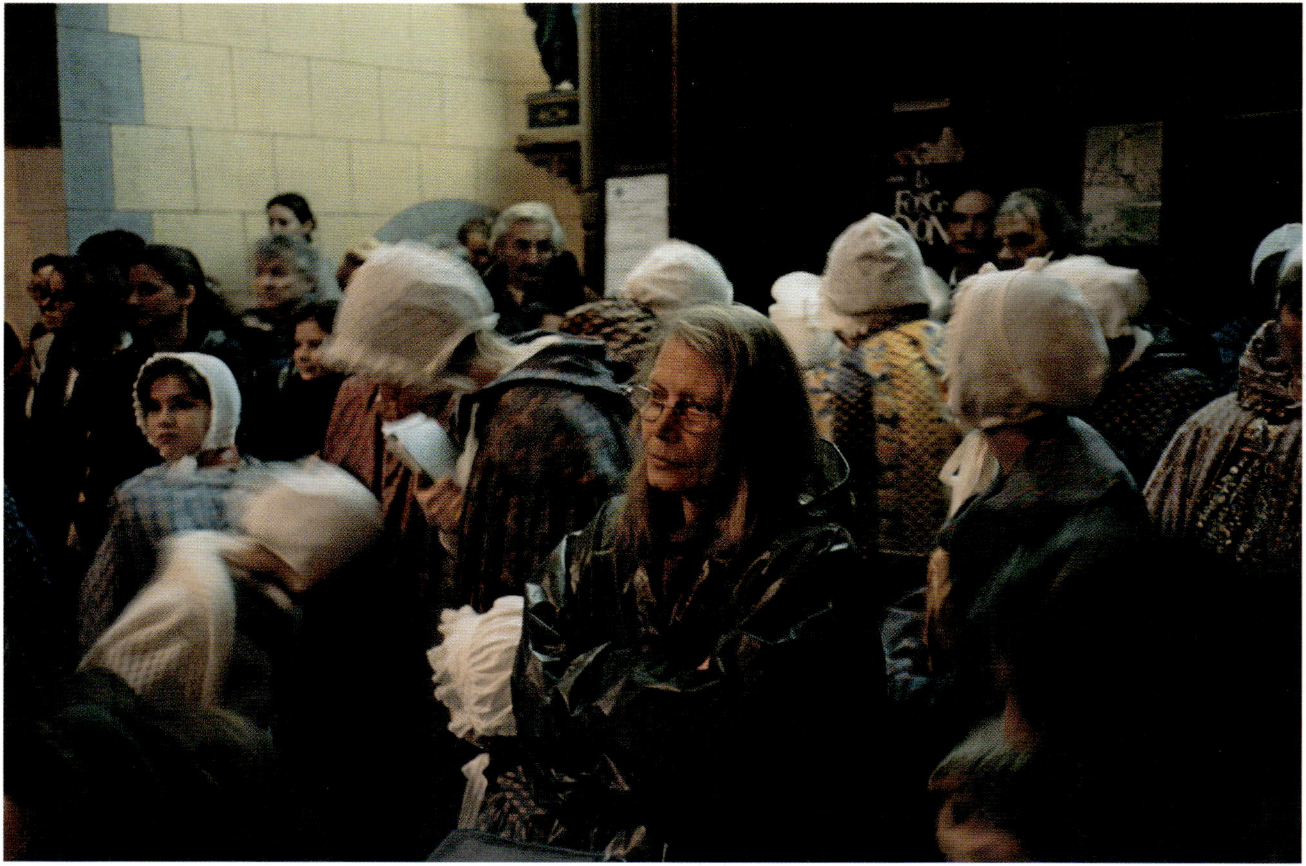

Friday, December 24. Villecroze, France. Midnight mass

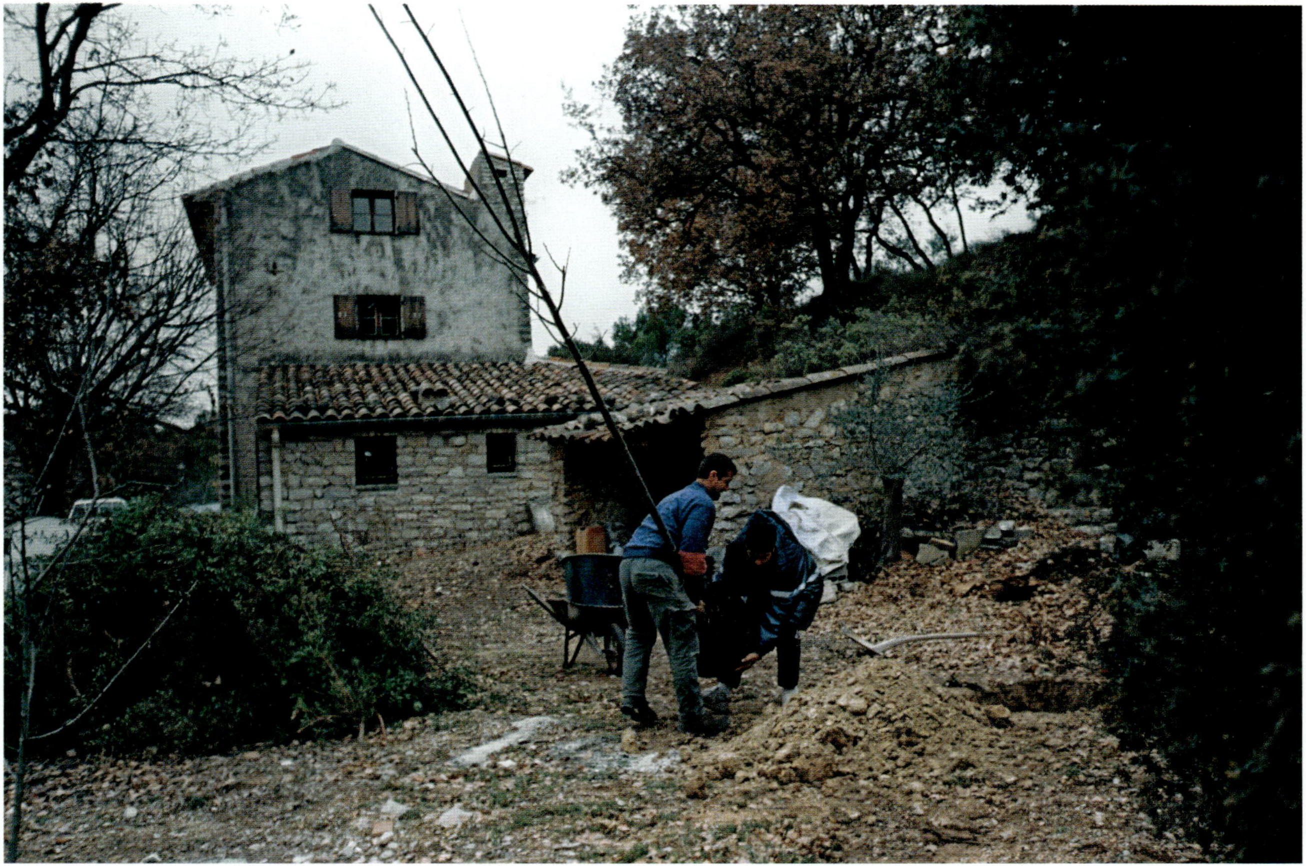

Saturday, December 25. Cotignac, France. At "La Véronique", Joël Gattini plants a lime tree for the third millennium

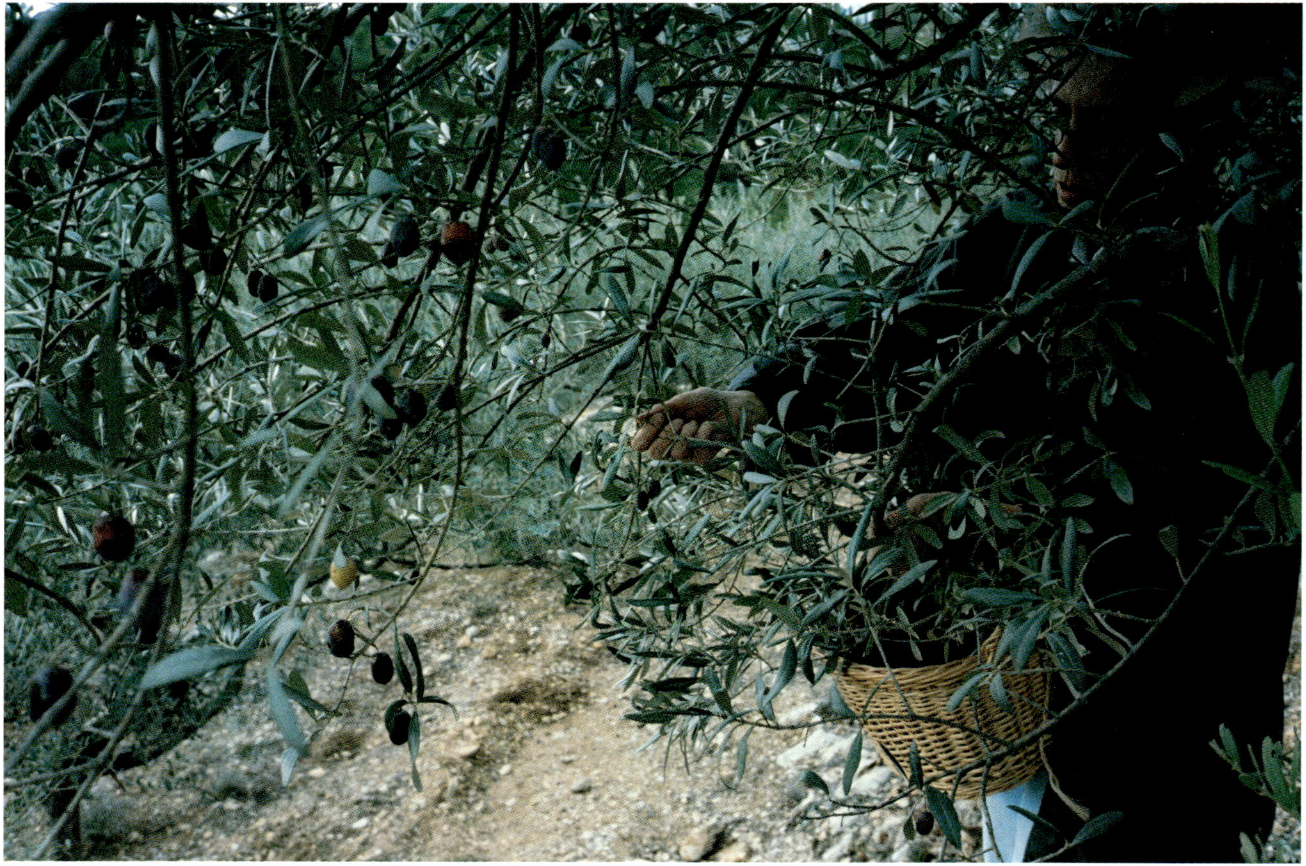

Sunday, December 26. Cotignac, France. At "La Véronique", harvesting our olives

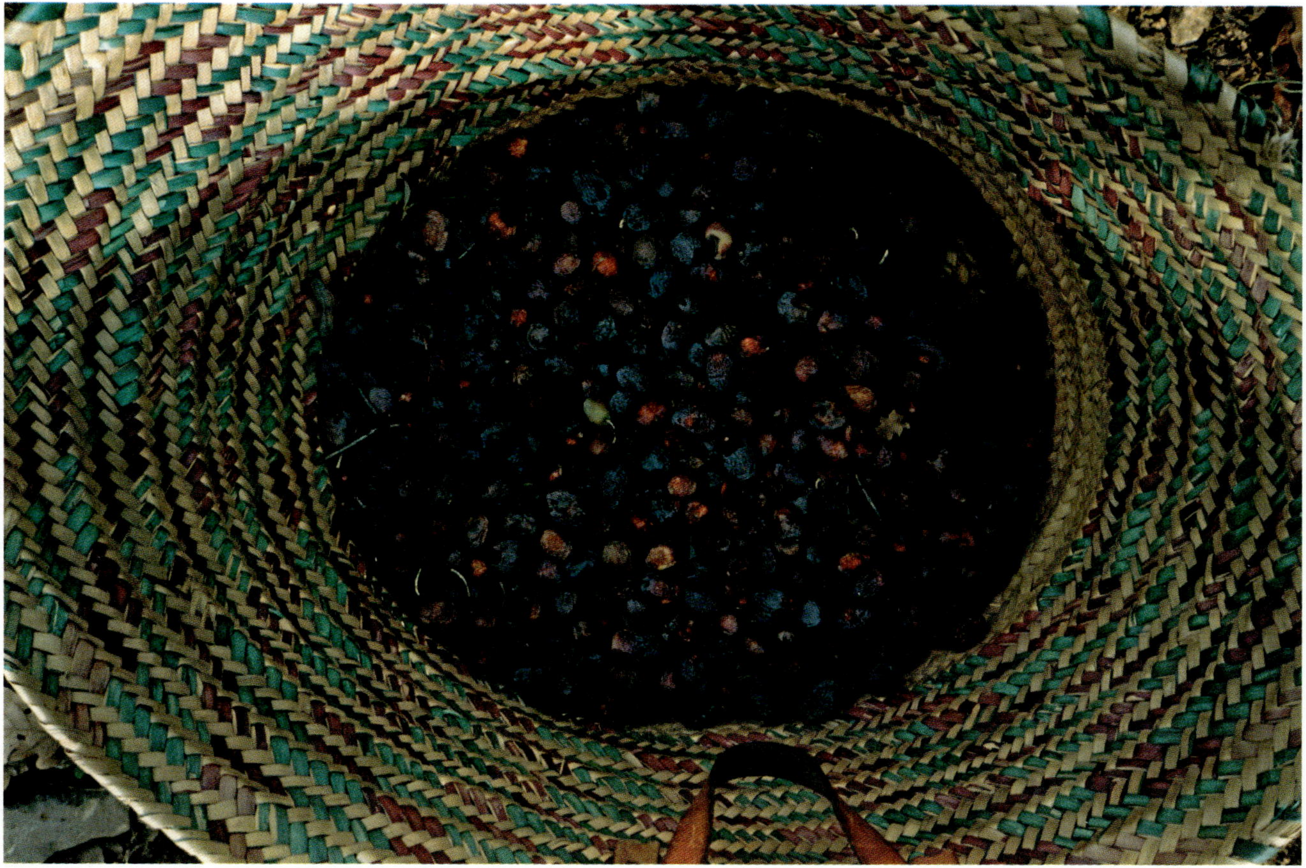

Monday, December 27. Cotignac, France. A basket of olives

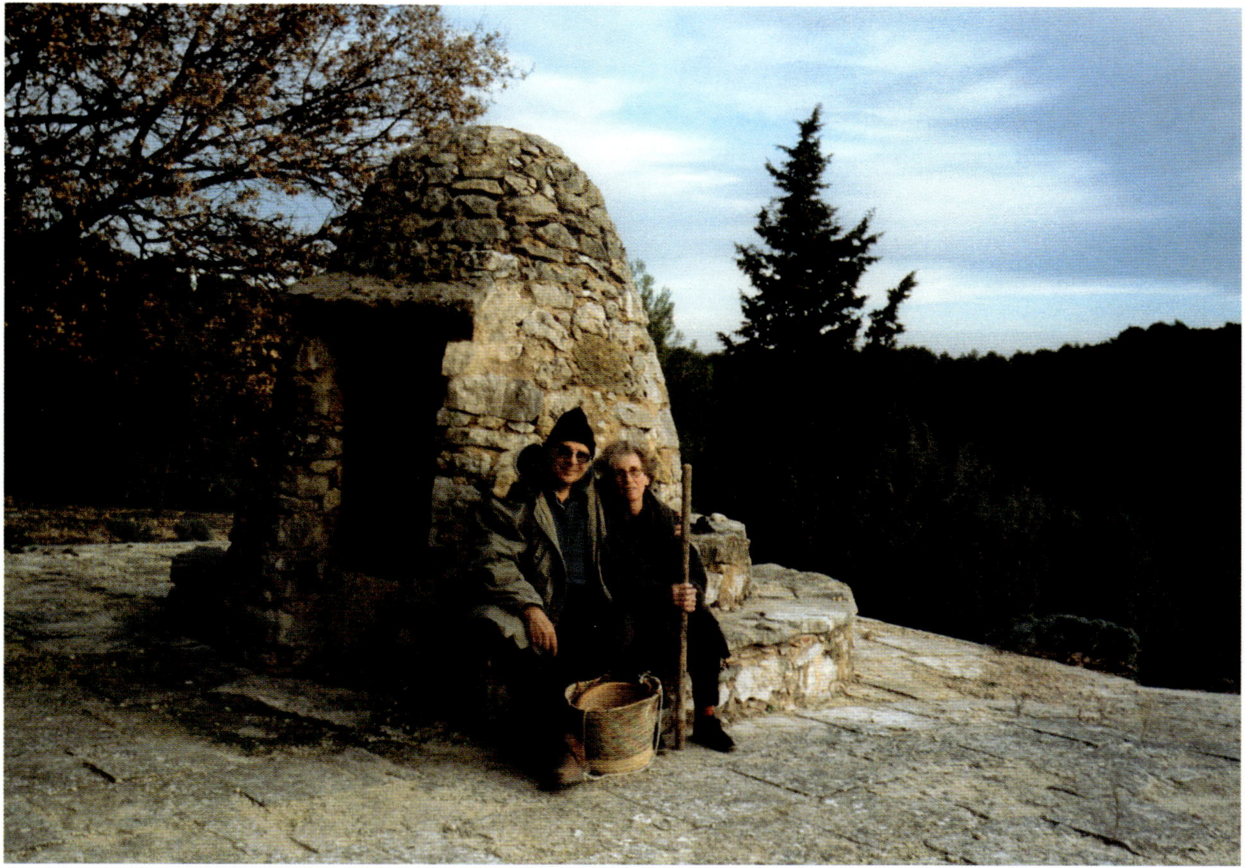

Tuesday, December 28. Cotignac, France. Self-portrait with Véronique Aubry

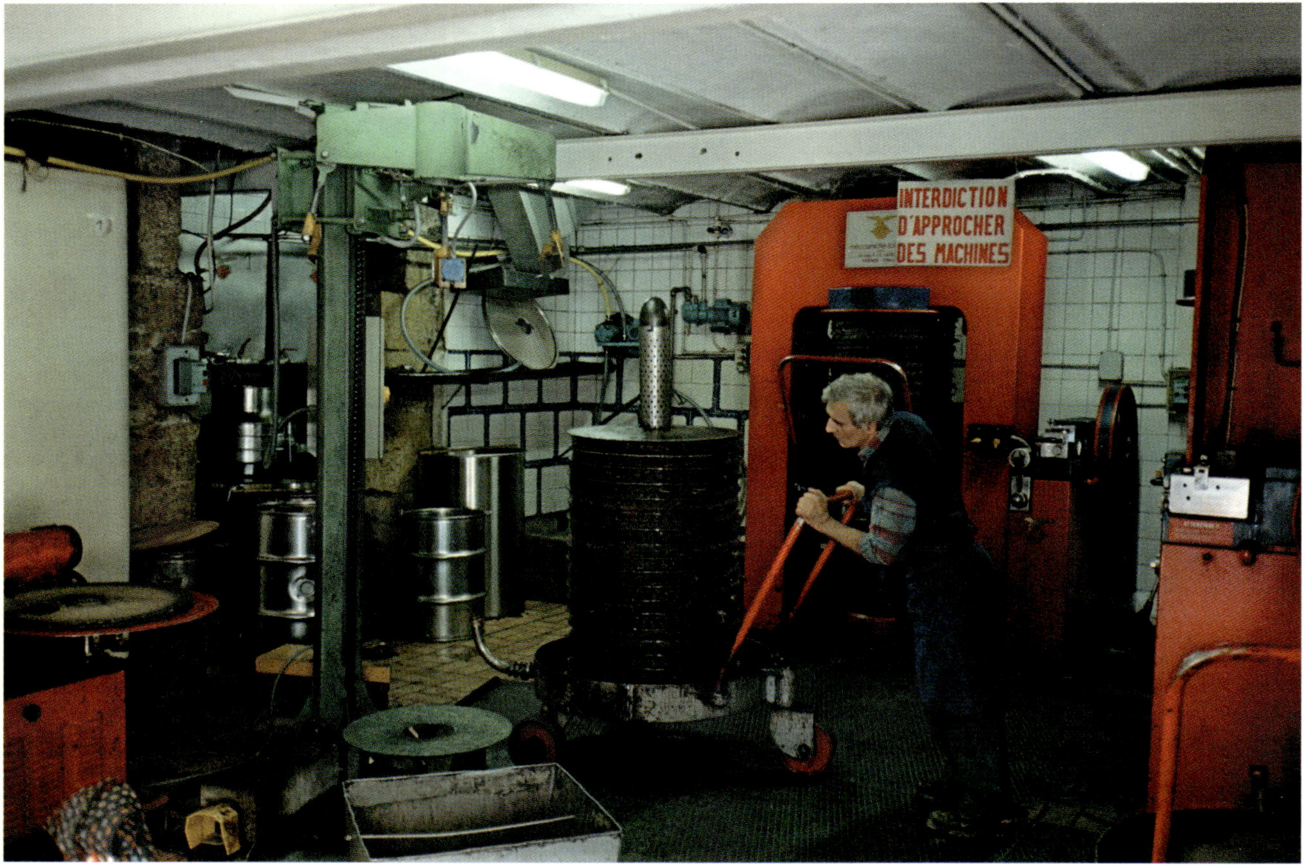

Wednesday, December 29. Aups, France. At the olive press

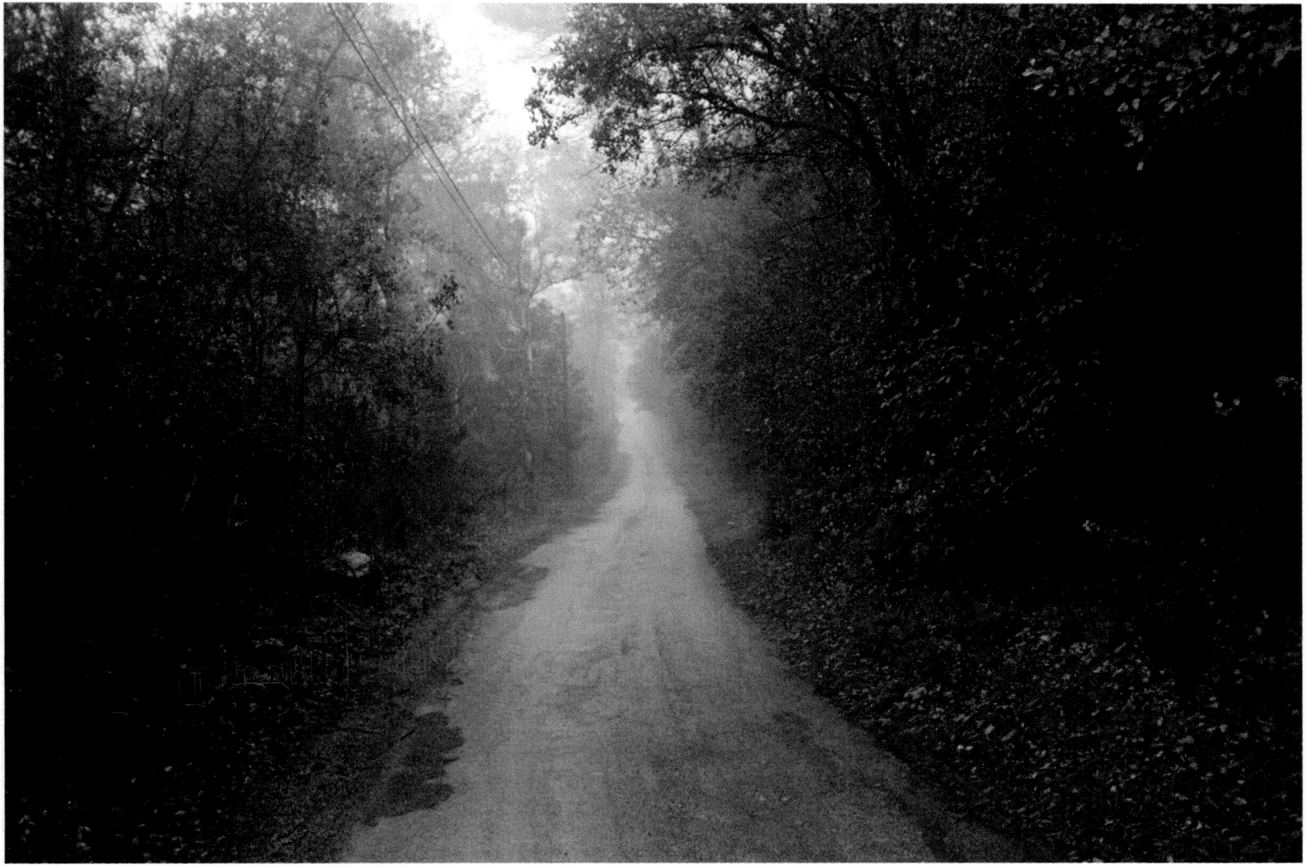

Thursday, December 30. Cotignac, France. On the way to "La Véronique"

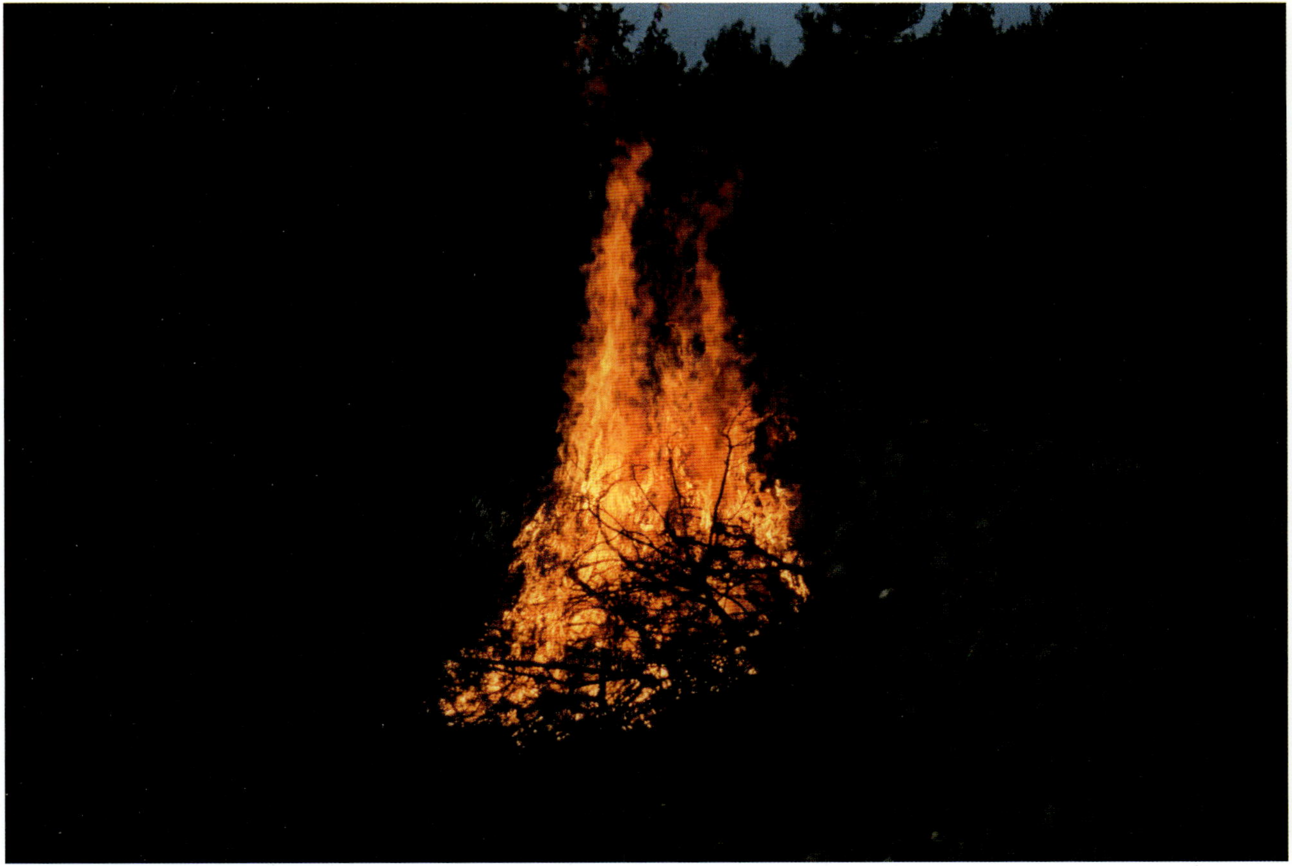

Friday, December 31. Cotignac, France. Burning the year's dead branches

Biography

1928
Born April 28th, in Abbazia, Italy (now Opatija, Croatia). His parents, Karl Horvat and Adele Edelstein, were both doctors, his mother later becoming a psychoanalyst.

1939-45
Lived in Lugano, Switzerland. Aged fifteen, he swapped his stamp collection for a 35 mm Retinamat camera.

1947-50
Moved to Milan, Italy. Studied art at the Accademia di Brera, then worked in advertising. Purchased a Rolleicord camera and freelanced for Italian magazines.

1950
First trip to Paris, met Henri Cartier-Bresson and Robert Capa.

1952-53
Trip to Pakistan and India, as free-lance photographer.

1954-55
Moved to London, working mainly for *Life* and *Picture Post.*

1955
Moved to Paris, where he still lives.

1957-62
Became a fashion photographer, travelling between Paris, London and New York, working for *Jardin des Modes, Elle, Glamour, Vogue, Harper's Bazaar,* etc. Between 1958 and 1961 he was an associate member of Magnum.

1962-63
World trip, for the German magazine *Revue*.

1964-88
Fashion and advertising photography in Europe and the USA.

1976-86
Personal projects in colour: *Portraits of trees*, *Very Similar, New York up and down.*

1986-87
Worked on *Entre-vues*: interviews with famous photographers, published by Nathan, Paris, in 1988.

1989
Began experimenting with digital imaging.

1990-98
Worked mainly on projects for books: *Les Sculptures de Degas, Bestiarium, Chimerae, Ovid's Metamorphoses, Walks around Boulogne-Billancourt; La Mode au Musée Galliera, Figures romanes.*

1999
Worked on *1999: A Daily Report.*

Other books by Frank Horvat

1962
La Télévision,
Editions Rencontre, Lausanne.

1962
Le Strip-tease,
Editions Rencontre, Lausanne.

1979
The Tree,
(with text by John Fowles),
Aurum Press, London,
and Little Brown, New York
and Boston.

1982
Goethe in Sicilia,
Edizioni Novecento, Palermo.

1988
Entre vues,
Editions Nathan, Paris
(also published in Chinese
and Japanese).

1989
Frank Horvat, côté mode,
Editions Paris Audiovisuel,
Paris.

1991
Les Sculptures de Degas,
Imprimerie nationale, Paris.

1992
Le Chat botté,
Editions Gautier Languereau,
Paris (also published in Taiwan).

1994
Arbres,
Imprimerie nationale, Paris.

1994
Le Bestiaire d'Horvat,
published by Centre national de la Photographie, Paris, and Actes Sud, Arles, France (Italian edition published 1995 by Motta, Milan).

1996
Paris-London,
Editions de la Ville de Paris, Paris.

1997
La mode au palais Galliera,
Imprimerie nationale, Paris.

1998
51 Photographs in black and white,
Peliti Associati, Roma (English edition by Dewi Lewis Publishing, Manchester, England).

1999
Very Similar,
Dewi Lewis Publishing, Manchester.
(Also *Vraies Semblances,*
Peliti Associati, Roma,
Vom Wahren Schein,
Umschau Braus, Heidelberg,
Vraies Semblances,
Photovision, Sevilla).

2000
Frank Horvat,
Photopoche N°88, Nathan, Paris.

Website:
http://www.horvatland.com

Notes

Page 19
Friday, January 1. Cotignac, France.
Our house in Provence, "La Véronique".
The new bathroom.

'La Véronique' (named after my wife) is a small house, surrounded by three hectares of olive groves, that had been abandoned by its inhabitants after the great freeze of 1956, and that we purchased and restored in 1971.

The view from the terrace extends over the surrounding hills, which had been cultivated in the past and have now returned to wilderness, up to the Maures mountains, about 30 kilometres to the south. Beyond them is the Mediterranean, which we cannot see.

Page 21
Sunday, January 3. Cotignac, France.
The old public laundry.

I wonder why the graffitist wrote "nie ta mère" (deny your mother) instead of the more common "nique ta mère" (fuck your mother).

One of my psychoanalyst friends believes that denying one's mother is worse than fucking her.

Page 33
Tuesday, January 12. Villecroze, France.
Véronique Aubry, my partner.

Véronique has shared my life for two decades (though at two different periods, with another decade between them). She is also my collaborator, often for the less conspicuous and more boring tasks, like the scanning, spotting and filing of the 1500 and more images, from which we chose the photographs in this book.

In fact, Véronique is my first point of feedback and my main advisor. This is not to say that I always follow her advice: but sometimes I do, and I must admit that I have never regretted it.

Page 41
Tuesday, January 19. Boulogne, France.
At the Ambroise Paré hospital, self-portrait before a check-up.

In 1994, I had to undergo heart surgery. This brought some changes in my way of life, one of which is the necessity of periodical check-ups.

Page 48
Sunday, January 24. Boulogne, France.
Pruned plane trees, rue de Paris.

I have always been amazed by the ruthlessness with which the French cut the trees of their avenues, leaving them no way of expressing their own character.

Page 49
Monday, January 25. Boulogne, France.
At my home. Alba and Saskia Horvat.

a) Here are the names of my children and grandchildren, that the reader will meet in these pages: Michel (or Jean-Michel), born in 1956, father of Grégoire and Louise. Lorenzo, born in 1957, father of Malte. Marco, born in 1961, father of Gabriel. David, born in 1967, father of Alba and Saskia. Fiammetta (or Sara-Fiammetta), born in 1979.

b) My main home, where I have lived since 1968, is in Boulogne-Billancourt, a close suburb of Paris. There are in fact two buildings: a small house, which is now occupied by my son Marco, and a large warehouse, that I had transformed into a daylight studio, and that is both my living and working place. The walls are painted black, for a better light and shadow effect (and also because I happen to like it).

Page 93

Monday, February 22. Cotignac, France.

The old almond tree.

Thirty years ago, when I bought 'La Véronique', this almond tree was already quite ancient. Every year I cut some of the older branches, and tie some young ones with strings, to make them grow in the right direction. I hope the old chap will last a little longer than me.

Page 157

Wednesday, April 7. Paris.

Bois de Boulogne. Policemen.

Not having found anything of more interest, I was photographing a mark on a tree, when these two policemen, who were passing on their bikes and to whom my activity seemed suspect, seized me by the arms and asked for my papers. Having been satisfied by my explanations, they allowed me to photograph them. It made my picture of the day.

Page 197

Tuesday, May 4. Paris.

Édouard Boubat, photographer.

Édouard was my best friend. We have often photographed each other. This image is the last one I took of him.

Page 231

Saturday, May 29. Intragna, Switzerland.

In the house of my adolescence.

Between 1939 and 1945, my family took refuge in Switzerland. Most of this time we lived in an eighteenth century village house, which has now been transformed into a regional museum. This nineteenth century religious fresco is on the landing that led to my room.

Page 269

Saturday, June 26. Cotignac, France. After the fire.

The day before, the radio had reported a forest fire in Cotignac. On the phone, the firemen told us that it had indeed come close to our property. We made the trip to find out for ourselves: the damage, as shown in the photograph, was extensive. But our terraces had been spared.

Page 273
Tuesday, June 29. Paris.
In the Invalides area,
near Édouard Boubat's home.

I had just seen Édouard for the last time (he had already lost consciousness). On avenue de Breteuil, I noticed this detail on the Pasteur monument, that I had often passed without paying it any attention.

Page 319
Wednesday, July 28. Boulogne, France.
A dying pigeon.

I noticed this pigeon, motionless on the railing of my terrace. I came closer and closer with my camera, but forgot to disable the flash. When it went off, the bird did not react. I realised it was sick, and decided to leave it alone. But "Perdu" realized it as well: when I came back, a little later, all I found were some bloodstained feathers.

Page 479
Wednesday, November 17.
Paris. Candid shot of Henri Cartier-Bresson,
with his biographer Pierre Assouline

I know that this is not a great image, but it commemorates my meeting with Henri – the year before, on the same occasion – that had been the starting point of the present project. Here is what I wrote about it, some months later:

"Last November, at an opening at Le Carrousel du Louvre in Paris, I met Henri Cartier-Bresson, whom I hadn't seen for some time, in the company of a common friend, the Italian photographer Ferdinando Scianna.

As we sat in the pretentiously designed and abominably lit cafeteria of the underground shopping centre, I asked: "Henri, if you were a few years younger, and still eager to photograph the world, would you consider taking pictures in such a place?"

"Most certainly not!" was his unhesitating reply "Nothing in here is authentic, nothing is real!" "Or if it is," added Ferdinando with his habitual subtlety "its reality is too complex to be photographed."

"I've tried to photograph similar places," I said "but never got a satisfying image. Maybe the world is moving towards some kind of virtual reality, beyond the reach of photographic representation."

We left it at that, but the question kept bothering me. One morning, while brushing my teeth (which seems to be the time of day when bright ideas flash through my mind), I said to myself that the problem may not lie so much with present reality, as with my own lack of motivation to photograph it: in the Fifties and Sixties, picturing the world had seemed urgent, partly because, after the forced confinement of the war years, I was eager to discover it for my own benefit, partly because magazine editors assigned me to cover it for their readers.

Then, in a second mental flash, it occurred to me that the year 99, that was about to begin, would bring another urgency to show the contemporary world, of a very different kind than in post-war decades, but possibly just as compelling: every image, taken in the course of that year, would necessarily become, on the following first of January, an image of the past century (and even of the past millennium). And, a few decades from now, it may seem as distant and as exotic as Atget's views of Paris seem to us.

Of course concepts such as centuries and millenniums are but mental frameworks: but what they stand for is the flow of change, which at this point of history seems to move faster than ever, and which to someone like myself, who has lived through almost three quarters of the ending century, seems particularly poignant.

Project 1999, as it dawned on me at that instant, would be a daily report on the present, in terms of everyday life and from a personal point of view. I would try to produce at least one image every day: of my surroundings, my family, the places that matter to me, the persons, objects, animals or plants that for whatever reason I may consider meaningful.

And beyond that limited horizon, I would spend some time in each of the fifteen countries of the European Union, which is (hopefully) taking shape with the new millennium and which I like to think of as my homeland.

There may be days, of course, when some illness (or some other impediment) may prevent me from going out: then I would photograph my cat, or the view from the window, or my own feet sticking out from under the blanket... In other words, the urgency to photograph would come not only from my subject – the last glimpses of the century – but also from a self-imposed constraint.

Just as the subjects of my photography, my techniques would have to be typical of the present. I wouldn't yet use digital cameras (which for my purpose are still too low in resolution, too heavy or too expensive), but rather one of those tiny, automatic 35 mm 'super-compacts', with a single wide angle lens, that can be carried in a pocket and that allows to shoot fast and unobtrusively. The inevitable drawbacks of such an instrument – less control over the image and a narrower range of possibilities than a professional reportage camera – could be turned into an advantage, if these very limitations were to create a style. On the other hand, I would use digital techniques to scan and retouch the films, in order to obtain exactly the colours I want.

For I had decided, from the beginning, that this body of work had to be in colour: black and white was fine in the Fifties and Sixties, when this was the habitual way of representing reality – but today it would lead me to a kind of estheticism, which is the very opposite of my intention."

Page 536
Wednesday, December 22. Opatija, Croatia, (my birth place). Footpath along the sea.

At the time of my birth, Opatija was called Abbazia. It has belonged in turn to the Austro-Hungarian Empire, to Italy and to Yugoslavia, and is presently part of the Croatian Republic.

The Quarner Coast, on which it is situated, had been the Austro-Hungarian equivalent of the French Riviera, as witnessed by its charming (though rather decayed) 'Sezession' villas.

My father, who was a physician, used to speak Hungarian to his parents, German to my mother, Croatian to his employees, Italian to the tax collectors, and occasionally French, or English, to visiting tourists.

For similar reasons my first name has been Franz, Francesco, Franco, before I eventually decided to be called Frank.

All this may help to explain why I like to think of Europe as my home country.